It's mightier than the sword.

A signature on a will can go a long way to provide for the ex-Service men and women of Erskine Hospital.

In our Homes across Scotland we care for over 750 Scottish veterans who, for one reason or another, are unable to lead their lives in the outside world.

Every year we need to raise more than £4 million from legacies and donations to provide the care and special facilities they require.

That's why it's so important people remember us, and those who so bravely serve their country, when they make their will.

Legacies or donations should be made payable to Erskine Hospital, and sent to Mr Iain W. Grimmond, Director of Finance, Erskine Hospital, Bishopton, Renfrewshire PA7 5PU. Telephone: 0141 812 1100

ERSKINE HOSPITAL

Scottish Charity No. SC00609

Caring for ex-Service men and women across Scotland

Noticeboards & Signs

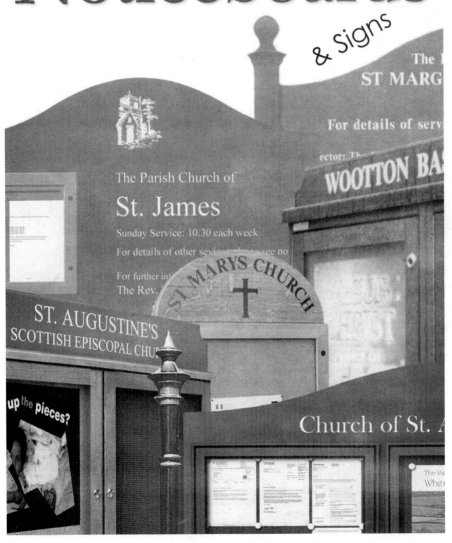

Greenbarnes Ltd.

Unit K1, Lincoln Court, Borough Road, BRACKLEY, Northants., NN13 7BE
T: 01280 701093, F: 01280 702843,
E: sales@greenbarnes.co.uk W: www.greenbarnes.co.uk

SCOTTISH CHRISTIAN PRESS

bringing you quality resources for

Christian education...

visit us at

Scottish
Christian PRESS

www.scottishchristianpress.org.uk
buy ONLINE from October 2003.

Scottish Christian Press

announce the new catalogue

for Autumn 2003/2004. For your free copy
please contact us at 21 Young Street, Edinburgh
EH2 4HU, tel: 0131 260 3110, or email:
enquiries@parished.org.uk.

The Widening Road: from Bethlehem to Emmaus, an
exploration of the Gospel of Luke, by Leith Fisher

101 Ways to Worship for Children, by Doug Swanney

Sexuality and Salvation, Why can't we live together,
by Steve Mallon, creating a new vocabulary for
inclusion.

Two by Two, A Biblical Childrens' Musical by
Margaret Grant and Paul Christie.

Inside Verdict: A Changing Church in a Changing
Scotland by Steve Mallon et al. - the new and
much-acclaimed examination into the future of the
Church of Scotland. AVAILABLE NOW!!

The Right Reverend Prof. Iain R. Torrance TD MA BD DPhil

MODERATOR

The Church of Scotland
YEAR BOOK
2003/2004

Editor
Rev. Ronald S. Blakey
MA BD MTh

Published on behalf of
THE CHURCH OF SCOTLAND
BOARD OF COMMUNICATION
by SAINT ANDREW PRESS
121 George Street, Edinburgh EH2 4YN

THE OFFICES OF THE CHURCH

121 George Street
Edinburgh EH2 4YN

Tel: 0131-225 5722
Fax: 0131-220 3113
Internet: http://www.churchofscotland.org.uk/

Office Hours:
Office Manager:

Monday–Friday 9.00 am–5.00 pm
Mrs Dorothy H. Woodhouse

PARISH EDUCATION
21 Young Street, Edinburgh EH2 4HU

Tel: 0131-260 3110

SOCIAL RESPONSIBILITY
Charis House   47 Milton Road East, Edinburgh EH15 2SR
[E-mail: info@charis.org.uk]

Tel: 0131-657 2000
Fax: 0131-657 5000

NATIONAL MISSION
Glasgow Office   59 Elmbank Street, Glasgow G2 4PQ
Kirkcaldy Office   St Bryce Kirk Centre,
St Brycedale Avenue, Kirkcaldy KY1 1ET

Tel: 0141-333 1948

Tel/Fax: 01592 646406

(Youth Adviser: Presbytery of Glasgow)
110 St James Road, Glasgow G4 0PS

Tel: 0141-400 7788

QUICK DIRECTORY

A.C.T.S. 01786 823588
Badenoch Centre 01540 651373
Board of Communication 0131-240 2236
Bridgeton, St Francis-in-the-East Church House 0141-554 8045
Carberry 0131-665 3135/7604
Christian Aid London 020 7620 4444
Christian Aid Scotland 0131-220 1254
Glasgow Lodging House Mission 0141-552 0285
Kirk Care 0131-225 7246
Netherbow 0131-556 9579/2647
Media Relations Unit (Press Office) 0131-240 2243
Pathway Productions 0131-225 5722
Scottish Churches Parliamentary Office 0131-622 2278
Society, Religion and Technology Project 0131-556 2953

First published in 2003 by SAINT ANDREW PRESS, 121 George Street, Edinburgh EH2 4YN on behalf of the
BOARD of COMMUNICATION of the CHURCH of SCOTLAND

Copyright © The BOARD of COMMUNICATION of the CHURCH of SCOTLAND, 2003

ISBN 0 86153 353 4

British Library Cataloguing in Publication Data
A catalogue record for this book is available from the British Library.

Printed and bound by Bell and Bain Ltd, Glasgow

CONTENTS

All correspondence regarding the *Year Book* should be sent to
The Editor, *Church of Scotland Year Book*,
Saint Andrew Press, 121 George Street, Edinburgh EH2 4YN
Fax: 0131-220 3113
[E-mail: yearbookeditor@cofscotland.org.uk]

GENERAL ASSEMBLY OF 2004
The General Assembly of 2004 will convene on
Saturday, 15th May 2004

FROM THE MODERATOR

The rootlessness produced by globalisation is part of contemporary angst. It has been appropriately noted how important it is, in the vastness of the Internet, to have a homepage. Increasingly, yearbooks, directories, university calendars and many similar publications have been abandoned in paper form. Change is so constant and the desire for instant updating so insistent that to produce a paper copy seems too much like holding back the tide.

Yet, until we have flawless archiving and are genuinely confident of our ability to store electronic data reliably and accessibly over the long term, a paper copy is not a luxury but the only means available of acknowledging the contribution of individuals and ensuring a broad continuity of Church history at the local level. This Year Book is not merely a good place for searching. It is a tangible means of testifying to the faithful work and endurance of the thousands of individuals who provide leadership within the Church. It is detailed and painstaking, constantly improved and so amazingly accurate that it is an eloquent testimony to the dedication of its editor, Ronald Blakey.

I have a copy of the Year Book for every year since I was licensed. I wouldn't be without it, and it is with the greatest pleasure that I commend the 2003/2004 volume to the Church.

Iain Torrance
April 2003

FROM THE EDITOR

Normal changes apart, this edition of the Year Book updates information in two key areas and offers additional facts in a third:

- Relevant parts of the new Acts dealing with Procedure in a Vacancy are included, as are the related Schedules.
- The section dealing with the Minister and Baptism has been revised to reflect important decisions taken by this year's General Assembly.
- The Congregational Statistics now include figures for 'the number of children and young people aged 17 years and under who are involved in the life of the congregation'.

Saint Andrew Press has always said that it listens to any suggestions whereby the contents or appearance of the Year Book might be improved. There is evidence on three fronts this year that this is no idle boast:

- It was suggested that the appearance would be improved if the pages were less obviously filled to overflowing. In particular, the aesthetic appeal of a bottom margin was extolled. We readily concurred.
- The cover design was felt by some to be dated. It first saw the light of day in 1993 when it replaced the style that, with one exception, had been in use since 1966. The odd one out was the cover for 1983, which featured a line drawing of Pencaitland Church. For whatever reason, that experiment was not repeated. In fact, the major 'popular' concern over the years has been that, whatever the design, the colour of the covers should continue to be red: there was even sporadic anxiety when the shade of red underwent change. The Editor looks forward to the promised new cover but has stressed that, for the peace of the Church, the colour is sacrosanct.
- A telephone call to the Editor found fault with the fact that the list of deceased ministers appeared before the list of those ordained for sixty years and upwards. The Editor is suitably chastened. Longevity now precedes eternity.

By its very nature, the Year Book does not lend itself to one-off articles. There is this year an exception, but one which will at once be recognised as fitting. Andrew Herron was Editor from 1962 until 1992. This volume could not pass without tribute to him.

Andrew's successor, the late Jim Black, talked once of awarding a prize to the first person to point out an error in the Year Book. Andrew was quick to assure him that no such incentive was required to elicit a prompt response from those whose day had thus been made. The present Editor can only concur, and so – in fairness to those who indulge in this particular sport – points out that one apparent omission in this volume is in fact the result of deliberate planning. It concerns the number fifteen. There are those who memorise not only their own Presbytery number but everyone else's as well. To such people, the sight of the number twenty-two, for example, does not trigger the thought that here is a palindrome whose square is also palindromic. Nor do they reflect on the fact that twenty-two is the maximum number of pieces into which a pancake can be cut with six slices. Rather, they think 'Falkirk'. When the volume for 1976 was published, there must have been not a few such souls who took immediate study leave or, worse, were admitted to intensive care – for in that year the number of Presbyteries was reduced from sixty to forty-nine.

No similar upheaval is in prospect, but over the next few years there will be a number of mergers. This year, Greenock and Paisley come together; next year, South Argyll, Dunoon, and Lorn and Mull will become one; other mergers are being discussed. For the moment, the Year Book will retain existing numbers. The new Presbytery of Greenock and Paisley will carry the number fourteen, and there will be no fifteen; next year, numbers twenty and twenty-one will be missing. In due course, when the dust has settled, there will be fresh numbering throughout, with all the anguish this will doubtless cause.

Taking leave of a minister whose stay had been fairly brief, the Moderator of his Presbytery remarked that 'where we used to talk of a settled ministry, now they perch'. Be that as it may, the Editor is happy to pay tribute to two ministers so settled that not since Thomas Caldwell and Joseph Easton, respectively, occupied the Editor's chair have their names had to be moved. Charles Armour, who retired earlier this year, had been in Holy Trinity, St Andrews since 1949; Bill Scott was inducted to Durisdeer in 1953 and is still there, albeit now with the added responsibility of Closeburn. No less remarkable is Alan Cowe, whose name has featured in every Year Book since 1965 as Secretary and Clerk of the General Trustees. The Editor could wish that Alan would devote some of his retirement to encouraging fellow Secretaries, Presbytery Clerks and the like to emulate his promptness in responding to the annual request for material for the Year Book. In this Editor's experience, Alan was invariably the first to respond – even when this year, because of his own imminent retiral, he could not at once provide all the information requested, he was first to reply stating why he would not be replying.

There are those who imagine that, for the Editor, time hangs heavy. At different times during the past year, I have been asked what is the greatest number of post-nominal letters (degrees, decorations and the like) which follow a minister's name in the Year Book, and what is the longest e-mail address in the Book. I have not worked out the answer to the latter, but I think the current record for the former stands at forty-two.

As always, I am indebted to those who provide information for these pages. Many provide it on time; some heed the plea to supply e-mail addresses in printed form; a few continue to demonstrate that the art of writing legibly is not one of the gifts that the Spirit confers at ordination. I was several times reminded of the English bishop who said of one of his clergy that he had been blessed with the gift of writing in tongues. Sandy Gemmill is just one of a number of saints who cheerfully go the second mile in providing highly detailed information in legible and coherent form.

Ronald S. Blakey
August 2003

The Very Reverend Andrew Herron MA BD LLB DD LLD

When he learned that I had been appointed Editor of the *Year Book*, Andrew Herron congratulated me, commiserated with me and, as was his wont, offered a number of pithy, pungent and pertinent pieces of advice. High on his list of temptations to resist was any suggestion that carefully selected obituaries might find space in the publication. 'Don't touch them,' he said, 'however venerated the deceased was, might have been or should have been.' That was sound advice; but it would surely be inconceivable that this particular edition of the *Year Book* should make no mention of that same Andrew who was its esteemed Editor from 1962 to 1992 and who died on 27 February 2003.

The first edition of the *Year Book* was published in 1886, and for the first thirty-one years no individual editor's name appeared on its title page. When the Committee on Publications decided to restore editorial anonymity in 1961, the Preface explained that the reversion to that original practice seemed appropriate on account of changes in the method of (the Book's) compilation. Just one year later, however, the *Year Book* for 1962 recorded that the 'experience' of the past year had indicated that 'there was much to be said for having an Editor who would be responsible for the compilation of the book'. It was Andrew Herron who convened that Committee which had such rapid change of heart, and it was Andrew who, with genuine reluctance and no little foreboding, accepted his Committee's invitation to 'have a go' at restoring the fluency of compilation and production which editing by committee had failed to achieve. In his 1985 Preface, Andrew reflected a little wryly on the fact that he had taken on the job 'on the clear understanding that it was for one year, or at most two, until a "proper" Editor could be appointed'. Many a church treasurer, Guild Secretary, stand-in organist and the like knows well that temporary appointments in the Church have a habit of becoming permanent to the point of everlasting. In many cases, this is for the great good, and certainly to the great relief, of the congregation concerned. Only very rarely, however, can a temporary appointment have been so inspired, ideally qualified for the task as Andrew was both by experience and by temperament. It was with a very real sense of loss that the Church accepted Andrew's decision that the 1992 edition would be the last to be produced under his temporary editorship.

The work involved in editing this volume has always been considerable; but Andrew never saw it as a chore. It always claimed his total commitment, to the extent that – even in the journeying of his Moderatorial year – the ever-changing text of the next *Year Book* was a non-negotiable part of his luggage. As Andrew's tenure pre-dated the computer and relied on what he fondly referred to as 'hot metal', it was massive galley proofs and not a floppy disk that went everywhere with him.

He loved the work – and, with only the occasional half-raised eyebrow, the Church greatly appreciated what he did. When occasionally he used his summary of the preceding General Assembly not merely to report decisions but also to air his own distinctive views, some Establishment figures were at times momentarily discomfited; but they could hardly feign surprise, as in everything he did Andrew was an independent mind, his own man, beholden to no party or group.

Deeply respectful of the Assembly, Andrew was nevertheless never slow to point to some of its less glorious moments. For example, he branded the 1981 Assembly as being 'of unprecedented dullness'. When there was anxious debate as to whether or not the Assembly could be reduced in length from ten days to seven, he supported the view that 'the business was likely to occupy as much time as we were prepared to set aside for it, whether that was a week or a month'. He spoke more than once of Assemblies which, 'while they lacked sufficient life or enthusiasm to start a revival, usually had enough to start a fight'.

There were within the Assembly some Committees which Andrew valued more than others – and he did not always disguise that fact. In one *Year Book*, for instance, he wrote: 'I have always maintained that the courts of the church are heard at their best when they are discussing issues that are properly their own business. To that extent, perhaps, it was good that Church and Nation should be delayed by a theological debate.' He was fully in support of local churches working together, but felt little warmth towards the orchestrated manoeuvres of the ecumenical movement: he may not have been the first to coin the disparaging phrase 'ecclesiastical joinery', but he had a fondness for it. He felt a weary disillusionment with the succession of new visionary Committees, Commissions and Councils. They seemed to him consistently to do one of two things – to reinvent yet again that distinctively ecclesiastical wheel which had mastered the art of ever faster rotation without the distraction of any forward movement, or to produce as startlingly new something that an earlier Commission had discarded as irredeemably worn out. The findings of one such body he branded 'a not very magic roundabout'. He did not oppose all change, but did need persuading that what was to replace the known was demonstrably an improvement – a challenge which few relished. The move towards offering early-morning Sunday services which would be briefer and more informal than the norm did not receive his unqualified blessing: they offered 'not so much a diet of worship as a snack'. Only occasionally did he leave the reader to deduce what might be his own stance. Writing of the 1973 General Assembly, at which there had been debate as to the wisdom or otherwise of using instrumental music at the Assembly session designed to introduce the Third Edition of the Church Hymnary, Andrew merely wrote: 'those who have opposed such an innovation doubtless regarded as divine intervention the failure of the Assembly Hall organ to function that Wednesday evening'.

When Andrew became Editor in 1962, the *Year Book* cost ten shillings or, in today's currency, fifty pence. When he retired in 1992, that cost had risen to £9.95. Several times in the course of his thirty-one editorials, he tackled the issue of the frequent increases in price. He regularly demonstrated that in percentage terms the minimum stipend had risen more steeply, so that any ministers investing their total stipend in copies of the *Year Book* would steadily obtain more to fill their shelves. Airing this frankly eccentric possibility merely emphasised his further recurring theme that the *Year Book* represented unfailingly good value for money. His main concern in this area, however, was that ministers should buy a copy every year: 'it neither matures nor improves with age', he told the Assembly, 'and in any event we need the money to keep the accountants happy'. Warming to his theme, he expounded the founding principle of what for a time was known as 'Herron economics': 'it is true that we make a loss on every copy we sell, but if we could sell enough copies at a loss, we would start to make a profit'. Andrew did not always think highly of the Assembly Council of which I was Secretary; but, in the nature of the kindly and gracious man that he was, we never fell out over it. I think he even came to forgive some of our more wayward innovations when the Council urged the Assembly to provide each parish each year with a free copy of the *Year Book*. It was very largely due to Andrew's unremitting labours which had made the book an indispensable tool that the Assembly warmly approved and implemented that recommendation.

Ronald S. Blakey

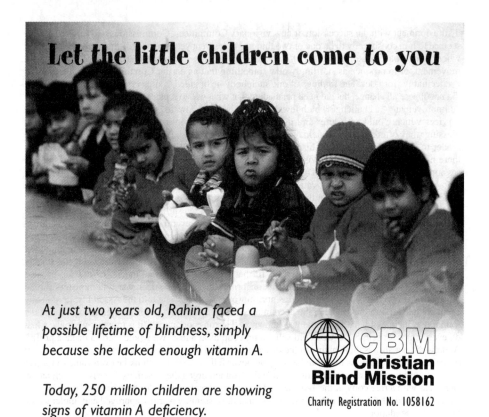

SECTION 1

Assembly Boards
and Committees

MEETINGS OF BOARDS AND COMMITTEES

The following Boards and Committees have indicated that they plan to meet on the dates listed.

ASSEMBLY COUNCIL
2003	23 October, 11 December (provisional)
2004	22 January, 11 March (provisional), 6 May

BOARD OF MINISTRY
2003	30 September to 1 October, 10 December
2004	11 February, 25 February (provisional), 16 June, 28–29 September

BOARD OF PRACTICE AND PROCEDURE
2003	16 September, 18 November
2004	20 January, 17 February, 20 April

BOARD OF STEWARDSHIP AND FINANCE
2003	12–13 November
2004	25 February, 31 March, 30 June

BOARD OF WORLD MISSION
2003	10 September, 26–27 November
2004	4 February, 31 March, 16–17 June

CHURCH OF SCOTLAND TRUST
2003	9 December

COMMITTEE ON ECUMENICAL RELATIONS
2003	25–26 September
2004	22 January, 25 March, 24 June, 23–24 September

COMMITTEE ON EDUCATION
2003	10–12 September, 26 November
2004	11 February, 16 June

GENERAL TRUSTEES

General Trustees
2003	22 September, 21 October, 18 November, 16 December
2004	27 January, 24 February, 23 March, 27 April, 25 May, 6 July, 28 September

Fabric, Glebes and Chairman's Committees
2003	2 September, 7 October, 4 November, 2 December
2004	13 January, 10 February, 9 March, 6 April, 11 May, 15 June, 27 July, 7 September

INDEX OF ASSEMBLY BOARDS AND COMMITTEES

[Note: Years, where given, indicate the year of appointment]

(1) PRACTICE AND PROCEDURE

MEMBERSHIP
BOARD OF PRACTICE AND PROCEDURE
(38 members: 32 appointed by the Assembly, plus Moderator, Moderator Designate, Clerks, Procurator and Law Agent *ex officiis*)

Convener:	Rev. David W. Lacy BA BD (2000)
Vice Convener:	Rev. Alastair H. Symington MA BD (2002)
Secretary:	The Principal Clerk

COMMITTEE TO NOMINATE THE MODERATOR
(54 members: three surviving immediate past Moderators, three elders appointed through the Nomination Committee and one member from each Presbytery)

Convener:	The earliest serving former Moderator present and willing to act
Secretary:	The Principal Clerk

JUDICIAL COMMISSION OF THE GENERAL ASSEMBLY

Chairman:	Rev. Alistair G.C. McGregor QC BD
Vice Chairman:	Mr Noel Glen
Secretaries:	The Clerks of Assembly

STAFF

Principal Clerk:	Very Rev. Finlay A.J. Macdonald MA BD PhD DD
Depute Clerk:	Rev. Marjory A. MacLean LLB BD
Principal Administration Officer:	Mrs Alison Murray MA

REMIT: BOARD OF PRACTICE AND PROCEDURE

1. To advise the General Assembly on questions of Church Law and of Constitutional Law affecting the relationship between Church and State.
2. To advise and assist Committees of the General Assembly in the preparation of proposed legislation and on questions of interpretation, including interpretation of and proposed changes to their remits.
3. To make all necessary arrangements for the General Assembly each year.
4. To advise the Moderator anent his or her official duties, if so required.
5. To be responsible to the General Assembly for the care and maintenance of all Assembly buildings and its other property.
6. To compile the statistics of the Church, except Youth and Finance; and to supervise on behalf of the General Assembly all arrangements for care of Church Records and for Presbytery Visits.
7. To attend to the general interests of the Church in matters which are not covered by the remit of any other Committee; and to perform such other duties as may be assigned to it by Act or Deliverance of the General Assembly.
8. To deal with urgent issues arising between meetings of the General Assembly or the Commission of Assembly which do not fall within the remit of any Board, provided that

(a) it shall not be competent for the Board to take or authorise an action which is
   (i)   of such a nature that it would have been *ultra vires* of the Commission of
         Assembly, or
   (ii) of a legislative or judicial nature, or
   (iii) an order or instruction to any Court or Courts of the Church;
(b) any action taken in terms of this Clause shall be reported by the Board to the next meeting
     of the General Assembly or the Commission of Assembly, whichever is the sooner.

---

(2) CENTRAL CO-ORDINATING COMMITTEE

MEMBERSHIP
(11 members: seven appointed by the General Assembly, and four *ex officiis* and non-voting,
namely the Principal Clerk, the Solicitor of the Church, the General Treasurer and the Personnel
Manager)
Convener: Mr Leon Marshall CA (2001)
Vice Convener: Mr John Neil OBE

STAFF
Administrative Secretary: Mrs Pauline Wilson BA
                             (E-mail: pwilson@cofscotland.org.uk)

REMIT
1. To be responsible for the proper maintenance and insurance of the Church Offices at
    117–123 George Street, Edinburgh ('the George Street Offices').
2. To be responsible for matters relating to Health and Safety within the George Street Offices.
3   To be responsible for matters relating to Data Protection within the George Street Offices
    and with respect to the General Assembly Boards and Committees based elsewhere.
4. To be responsible for the allocation of accommodation within the George Street Offices and
    the annual determination of rental charges to the Boards, Committees and other parties
    accommodated therein.
5. To oversee the delivery of central services to Departments within the George Street Offices
    and to the General Assembly Boards and Committees based elsewhere, namely:
    •   those facilities directly managed by the Office Manager
    •   information technology (including the provision of support services to Presbytery
        Clerks)
    •   insurance
    •   purchasing and travel
    •   personnel services
    •   financial services (as delivered by the General Treasurer's Department)
    •   legal services (as delivered by the Law Department and subject to such oversight not
        infringing principles of 'client/solicitor' confidentiality).
6. To provide an internal audit function to the General Assembly Boards, Statutory Corporations
    and Committees (other than the Board of Social Responsibility).
7. The Committee shall act as one of the five employing agencies of the Church.
8. The Committee shall act as a consultative and advisory body to the General Assembly
    Boards, Statutory Corporations and Committees.

(3) GENERAL TREASURER'S DEPARTMENT

STAFF

General Treasurer:	Mr Donald F. Ross MA CA
Deputy General Treasurers:	Mr Alexander F. Gemmill BAcc CA
	Mr John S. Steven CA
	Mr William J. McKean BAcc CA
Assistant Treasurer:	Mrs Anne Macintosh BA CA
Accountants:	Mr Ross Donaldson
	Mr Derek Cant FCCA

Responsibilities of the General Treasurer's Department include:
- payroll processing for the Board of Ministry, Board of National Mission and Central Co-ordinating Committee
- issuing to congregations their annual requirement figures for Ministry Funds and the Mission and Renewal Fund
- receiving payments from congregations towards their central requirements
- making Deed of Covenant tax recoveries on behalf of congregations
- making Gift Aid and Deed of Covenant tax recoveries on behalf of Boards, Committees and Statutory Corporations
- making VAT returns and tax recoveries on behalf of Boards, Committees and Statutory Corporations and providing VAT information to congregations
- providing support, training and advice on financial matters to congregational treasurers
- receiving and discharging legacies and bequests on behalf of Boards, Committees and Statutory Corporations
- providing banking arrangements and operating a central banking system for Boards, Committees and Statutory Corporations
- providing accountancy systems and services for Boards, Committees, Statutory Corporations and the Trustees of the Church's Pension Schemes
- providing Finance Departments for the Boards of World Mission and Parish Education.

(4) INFORMATION TECHNOLOGY DEPARTMENT

STAFF

Information Technology Manager:	Alastair Chalmers
Depute Information Technology Manager:	Veronica Hay

The Department provides computing facilities for Boards and Departments within 121 George Street, Presbytery Clerks, National Mission personnel outwith George Street, the Scottish Churches Parliamentary Office and Pathway Productions. It is also responsible for the telephone services within the George Street Offices.

The facilities provided include:
- the provision and maintenance of networks for both data and voice

- the purchase and installation of hardware and software
- support for problems and guidance on the use of software
- development of in-house software
- maintenance of data within the central databases and finance systems.

(5) THE LAW DEPARTMENT

STAFF

Solicitor of the Church and of the General Trustees:	Mrs Janette S. Wilson LLB NP
Depute Solicitor:	Miss Mary E. Macleod LLB NP
Assistant Solicitors:	Mr Ian K. Johnstone MA LLB
	Mrs Elizabeth M. Kemp MA LLB
	Mrs Jennifer M. Hamilton BA NP
	Mrs Elspeth Annan LLB NP
	Miss Susan Killean LLB NP

The Law Department of the Church was created in 1937/38. The Department acts in legal matters for the Church and all of its Courts, Boards, Committees, the Church of Scotland General Trustees, the Church of Scotland Trust and the Church of Scotland Investors Trust. It also acts for individual congregations and is available to give advice on any legal matter arising.

The Department is under the charge of the Solicitor of the Church, a post created at the same time as the formation of the Department and a post which is now customarily held along with the traditional posts of Law Agent of the General Assembly and the Custodier of former United Free Church titles (E-mail: lawdept@cofscotland.org.uk).

(6) OFFICE MANAGER'S DEPARTMENT

STAFF

Office Manager:	Mrs Dorothy Woodhouse (E-mail: dwoodhouse@cofscotland.org.uk)

The responsibilities of the Office Manager's Department include:
- management of a maintenance budget for the upkeep of the Church Offices at 121 George Street, Edinburgh
- responsibility for all aspects of health and safety for staff, visitors and contractors working in the building
- managing a team of staff providing the Offices with security, reception, mail room, print room, switchboard, day-to-day maintenance services and Committee room bookings

- overseeing all sub-contracted services to include catering, cleaning, boiler-room maintenance, intruder alarm, fire alarms and lifts
- maintaining building records in accordance with the requirements of statutory legislation
- overseeing all alterations to the building and ensuring, where applicable, that they meet Planning and Building Control regulations.

(7) THE PERSONNEL DEPARTMENT

STAFF
Personnel Manager: Mr George B.B. Eadie BA
Deputy Personnel Manager: Miss Angela Brady MCIPD
Personnel Officer: Miss Maria Carena
Personnel Assistant: Mrs Dorothy Menzies

REMIT
The Personnel Committee was set up in 1978 on the Report of the Advisory Board to determine salaries, length of service and conditions generally for Secretaries and Members of Office Staff. In 1991, and again in 1996, the General Assembly made certain minor adjustments to the remit, including a requirement that the Personnel Committee should conduct an annual salary review of those members of staff for which it is the employing agency.

In recognition of the aim that the Personnel Committee may in time operate as the co-ordinating body for the Church in respect of the salaries and conditions of employment of all persons employed by the five employing agencies, the other four employing agencies are required to provide all information on such matters as requested by the Personnel Committee.

This remit passed to the new Central Co-ordinating Committee as from 1 September 2001.

(8) GENERAL TRUSTEES

MEMBERSHIP
(New Trustees are appointed, as required, by the General Assembly, on the recommendation of the General Trustees)
Chairman: Rev. James H. Simpson BD LLB (2003)
Vice Chairman: Mr W. Findlay Turner CA (2003)
Secretary and Clerk: Mr David D. Robertson LLB NP
Depute Secretary and Clerk: Mr T.R.W. Parker LLB

COMMITTEES:
Fabric Committee
Convener: Rev. Angus T. Stewart MA BD PhD (2003)

Chairman's Committee
Convener: Rev. James H. Simpson BD LLB (2003)

Glebes Committee
Convener: Rev. William Paterson BD (2003)

Finance Committee
Convener: Mr R.G. Burnett BComm CA FCMA (1999)

Law Committee
Convener: Professor J. Alistair M. Inglis CBE MA LLB (1999)

STAFF
Secretary and Clerk: Mr. David D. Robertson LLB NP
Depute Secretary and Clerk: Mr T.R.W. Parker LLB
Assistants: Miss P.M. Burnside LLB NP (Glebes)
Mr Keith S. Mason LLB NP (Ecclesiastical Buildings)
Treasurer: Mr Donald F. Ross MA CA
Deputy Treasurer: Mr W.J. McKean BAcc CA

REMIT

The General Trustees are a Property Corporation created and incorporated under the Church of Scotland (General Trustees) Order Confirmation Act 1921. Their duties, powers and responsibilities were greatly extended by the Church of Scotland (Property & Endowments) Acts and Orders 1925 to 1995, and they are also charged with the administration of the Central Fabric Fund (see below) and the Consolidated Fabric Fund and the Consolidated Stipend Fund in which monies held centrally for the benefit of individual congregations are lodged.

The scope of the work of the Trustees is broad, covering all facets of property administration, but particular reference is made to the following matters:

1. **ECCLESIASTICAL BUILDINGS.** The Trustees' Fabric Committee considers proposals for work at buildings, regardless of how they are vested, and plans of new buildings. Details of all such projects should be submitted to the Committee before work is commenced. The Committee also deals with applications for the release of fabric monies held by the General Trustees for individual congregations, and considers applications for assistance from the Central Fabric Fund from which grants and/or loans may be given to assist congregations faced with expenditure on fabric. Application forms relating to consents for work and possible financial assistance from the Central Fabric Fund are available from the Secretary of the Trustees and require to be submitted through Presbytery with its approval. The Committee normally meets on the first or second Tuesday of each month, apart from July, when it meets on the last Tuesday, and August, when there is no meeting.

2. **SALE, PURCHASE AND LETTING OF PROPERTIES.** All sales or lets of properties vested in the General Trustees fall to be carried out by them in consultation with the Financial Board of the congregation concerned, and no steps should be taken towards any sale or let without prior consultation with the Secretary of the Trustees. Where property to be purchased is to be vested in the General Trustees, it is essential that contact be made at the earliest possible stage with the Solicitor to the Trustees, who is responsible for the lodging of offers for such properties and all subsequent legal procedure.

3.   **GLEBES.** The Trustees are responsible for the administration of Glebes vested in their ownership. All lets fall to be granted by them in consultation with the minister concerned. It should be noted that neither ministers nor Kirk Sessions may grant lets of Glebe land vested in the General Trustees. As part of their Glebe administration, the Trustees review regularly all Glebe rents.

4.   **INSURANCE.** Properties vested in the General Trustees must be insured with the Church of Scotland Insurance Co. Ltd, a company wholly owned by the Church of Scotland whose profits are applied for Church purposes. Insurance enquiries should be sent directly to the Company at 67 George Street, Edinburgh EH2 2JG (Tel: 0131-220 4119; Fax: 0131-220 4120; E-mail: enquiries@cosic.co.uk).

---

(9) NOMINATION

MEMBERSHIP – NOMINATION COMMITTEE
(44 members)

Convener:	Rev. Keith F. Hall BD (2002)
Vice Convener:	Rev. Iain D. Cunningham MA BD (2002)
Secretary:	The Principal Clerk

REMIT
To bring before the General Assembly names of persons to serve on the Boards and Standing Committees of the General Assembly.

---

(10) CHURCH OF SCOTLAND INVESTORS TRUST

MEMBERSHIP
(Trustees are appointed by the General Assembly, on the nomination of the Investors Trust)

Chairman:	Mr J.B.M. Dick ACIB
Vice Chairman:	Mr D.M. Simpson BA FFA
Treasurer:	Mr D.F. Ross MA CA
Secretary:	Mr Fred Marsh MCIBS

REMIT
The Church of Scotland Investors Trust, established in 1994 by Act of Parliament, offers to Boards, Committees and congregations of the Church a simple and economical medium for the investment of their funds. Investors are at liberty to invest in the Church of Scotland Investors Trust to an unlimited extent, and it is felt that the facilities afforded thereby are preferable to the powers of investment offered by the Trustee Investments Act 1961, with all the attendant

restrictions and conditions. The Church of Scotland Investors Trust provides three Funds for Church investors:

1.   **THE DEPOSIT FUND** is intended for short-term investment and aims to provide a high rate of interest. Deposits are repayable on demand. Interest is calculated quarterly in arrears and paid gross on 15 May and 15 November. The Fund is invested mainly in short-term loans to Banks, Building Societies and Licensed Deposit-Taking Institutions. The Deposit Fund is professionally managed by Noble Grossart Limited, Edinburgh.

2.   **THE GROWTH FUND** is very largely equity-based and is intended for long-term investment. The Fund is operated on a unitised basis and aims to provide capital growth. Units can be purchased or sold monthly. Income is distributed gross on 15 May and 15 November. The Growth Fund is professionally managed by Henderson Global Investors Limited, London.

3.   **THE INCOME FUND** is intended for medium-term investment and aims to provide immediate high income. The Fund is invested predominantly in fixed-interest securities and is operated on a unitised basis. Units can be purchased or sold monthly. Income is distributed gross on 15 March and 15 September. The Income Fund is professionally managed by Baillie Gifford & Company, Edinburgh.

Application Forms for investment and further information may be had from the Secretary of the Church of Scotland Investors Trust, 121 George Street, Edinburgh EH2 4YN.

---

(11) THE CHURCH OF SCOTLAND
HOUSING AND LOAN FUND FOR RETIRED MINISTERS AND WIDOWS AND WIDOWERS OF MINISTERS

MEMBERSHIP
(The Board of Trustees has a maximum limit of 11: three appointed by the General Assembly on the nomination of the Board, three appointed by the Baird Trust, four appointed by the Board of Ministry (three ministers and one member) and the General Secretary of the Board of Ministry *ex officio*)

Chairman: Mr William McVicar RD CA
Secretary: Miss Lin J. Macmillan MA

STAFF
Property Administrator: Miss Hilary J. Hardy

REMIT
The Fund, as established by the General Assembly, facilitates the provision of housing accommodation for retired ministers and widow(er)s of ministers. When provided, help may take the form of either a house to rent or a house-purchase loan.

The Trustees may grant tenancy of one of their existing houses or they may agree to purchase for rental occupation an appropriate house of an applicant's choosing. Leases are normally on very advantageous terms as regards rental levels. Alternatively, the Trustees may grant a housing loan of up to 70 per cent of a house-purchase price but with an upper limit. Favourable rates of interest are charged.

The Trustees are also prepared to consider assisting those who have managed to house themselves but are seeking to move to more suitable accommodation. Those with a mortgaged home on retirement may be granted a loan to enable them to repay such a mortgage and thereafter to enjoy the favourable rates of interest charged by the Fund.

Ministers making application within five years of retirement, upon their application being approved, will be given a fairly firm commitment that, in due course, either a house will be made available for renting or a house-purchase loan will be offered. Only within nine months of a minister's intended retiral date will the Trustees initiate steps to find a suitable house; only within one year of that date will a loan be advanced. Preliminary applications submitted about ten years prior to retirement have the benefit of initial review and, if approved, a place on the waiting-list for appropriate decision in due time.

Donations and legacies over the years have been significant in building up this Fund, and the backbone has been provided by congregational contributions.

The Board of Trustees is a completely independent body answerable to the General Assembly, and enquiries and applications are dealt with in the strictest confidence.

Further information can be obtained from the Secretary, Miss Lin J. Macmillan MA, at the Church of Scotland Offices, 121 George Street, Edinburgh EH2 4YN (Tel: 0131-225 5722 ext. 310; Fax: 0131-220 3113; E-mail: lmacmillan@cofscotland.org.uk; Website: www.churchofscotland.org.uk).

---

(12) STEWARDSHIP AND FINANCE

MEMBERSHIP – BOARD OF STEWARDSHIP AND FINANCE
(77 members: 24 appointed by the Assembly, plus Convener and Vice Convener, and 47 Presbytery Representatives who attend three meetings of the Board, at which they have full rights as Board members. The Convener and Secretary of the Co-ordinating Forum, the General Treasurer and the Director of Stewardship are *ex officiis* members of the Board.)

Convener:	Rev. J. Colin Caskie BA BD (2001)
Vice Convener:	Mrs Vivienne A. Dickson CA (2001)

STAFF

General Treasurer:	Mr Donald F. Ross MA CA
Director of Stewardship:	Rev. Gordon D. Jamieson MA BD
Administrative Secretary:	Mr Fred Marsh MCIBS

BOARD REMIT
1.   To promote teaching and understanding of Christian Stewardship throughout the Church.
       To provide programmes and training to assist congregations in visiting members, making

known the work of the Church, promoting Christian giving and administering congregational finances.

2. To be responsible for preparing and submitting to the General Assembly a Co-ordinated Budget for the following financial year and a projected Rolling Budget for the next four years.

3. To be responsible with the Board of Ministry and Presbyteries for allocating among congregations the expenditure contained in the Co-ordinated Budget approved by the General Assembly, and for seeking to ensure that congregations meet their obligations by transmitting contributions towards their allocations regularly throughout the year.

4. To provide financial, administrative and accounting services and standards for Boards, Committees and Statutory Corporations.

STEWARDSHIP DEPARTMENT

The Stewardship Department is responsible for the promotion of Christian Stewardship throughout the Church (part 1 of the Board Remit). This involves the production of material to assist congregations in developing an understanding of Christian Stewardship and encouraging a higher level of giving of time, talents and money from members of the Church. The staff of the Stewardship Department are regularly involved in meetings with congregations and Presbyteries.

STAFF

Director of Stewardship: Rev. Gordon D. Jamieson MA BD
Deputy Director: Mr W. Crawford Conochie
Stewardship Consultants: Mrs Gillian M. Paterson
                              Mr W. John Gray
                              Mrs Edith Scott

GIFT AID

As a result of changes to the Gift Aid Scheme which were introduced in April 2000, the £250 minimum for Gift Aid donations has been abolished, so that the scheme now applies to all donations from taxpayers, whether large or small, regular or one-off.

The separate tax relief for payments made under Deed of Covenant has been withdrawn, and relief for such payments is now given under the Gift Aid Scheme.

Gift Aid Certificates have now been replaced by new, simpler and more flexible Gift Aid Declarations, which can be made in advance of the donation, at the time of the donation, or at any time after the donation (subject to the normal six-year limit), and can cover one or more donations.

Donors no longer must pay basic rate income tax – they simply have to pay an amount of income tax or capital gains tax, whether at the basic rate or some other rate, equal to the tax deducted from their donations.

Donors who pay tax at the higher rate will be able to claim further relief in their Self-Assessment tax return against either income tax or capital gains tax.

Companies will no longer be required to deduct tax from their donations to charities.

The new Gift Aid Scheme offers an opportunity for congregations to increase the tax recovered on both regular offerings and one-off donations from taxpayers. In order to meet Inland Revenue requirements, offerings must be received from the donor by cheque, Banker's

Order, or cash through Offering Envelopes. Cash put into the Open Plate, which cannot be recorded against the name of the particular person, cannot be treated as Gift Aid donations.

Each congregation is responsible for maintaining proper records, for obtaining Gift Aid Declarations from the donors, and for making repayment claims to the Inland Revenue.

Claims should be submitted on Charity Repayment Claim Form R68 (2000), supported by Schedule R68 (New Gift Aid), to IR (Charities) Scotland, Meldrum House, 15 Drumsheugh Gardens, Edinburgh EH3 7UL (Tel: 0131-777 4040).

GIVING WITH A WILL

Making a will is a sensitive but wise decision. It is also an aspect of good stewardship. The provisions of a will can show our love and concern for our families and friends. They can also provide us with an opportunity to continue supporting the work of the Church of Scotland. The Church acknowledges with gratitude the many legacies it has received over the years and the kind and generous thoughts which have been their inspiration. Such giving is encouraged by the government: gifts of money to the Church are exempt from Inheritance Tax without limit.

The General Treasurer or the Solicitor of the Church of Scotland will always be ready to give information about the work of the Church to members (and their solicitors) interested in providing a legacy.

---

(13) THE CHURCH OF SCOTLAND PENSION TRUSTEES

Chairman:	Mr W.D.B. Cameron CA
Vice Chairman:	Mr W.J. McCafferty ACII ASFA CIP
Secretary:	Mrs S. Dennison BA

STAFF

Pensions Manager:	Mrs S. Dennison BA
Assistant Pensions Administrators:	Mrs M. Marshall
	Mr M. Hannam

REMIT

The body acts as Trustees for the Church of Scotland's three Pension Schemes:
1.   The Church of Scotland Pension Scheme for Ministers and Overseas Missionaries
2.   The Church of Scotland Pension Scheme for Staff
3.   The Church of Scotland Pension Scheme for Board of National Mission staff.
The Trustees have wide-ranging duties and powers detailed in the Trust Law, Pension Acts and other regulations, but in short the Trustees are responsible for the administration of the Pension Schemes and for the investment of the Scheme Funds. Six Trustees are appointed by the General Assembly, and members nominate up to three Trustees for each Scheme.

The investment of the Funds is delegated to external Investment Managers under the guidelines and investment principles set by the Trustees: Baillie Gifford & Co., Tilney Fund Management and SVM Asset Management.

The benefits provided by the three Pension Schemes differ in detail, but all provide a pension to the Scheme member and dependants on death of the member, and a lump sum death benefit on death in service. Scheme members also have the option to improve their benefits by paying additional voluntary contributions (AVCs) to arrangements set up by the Trustees with leading Insurance Companies.

Further information on any of the Church of Scotland Pension Schemes or on individual benefits can be obtained from the Pensions Manager, Mrs S. Dennison, at the Church of Scotland Offices, 121 George Street, Edinburgh EH2 4YN (Tel: 0131-225 5722 ext. 206; Fax: 0131-240 2220; E-mail: sdennison@cofscotland.org.uk).

---

(14) THE CHURCH OF SCOTLAND GUILD

NATIONAL OFFICE-BEARERS AND EXECUTIVE STAFF
Convener: Miss Moira Alexander RGN SCM RNT MBA
Vice Convener: Mrs Elspeth Dale
General Secretary: Mrs Alison Twaddle MA JP
                        (E-mail: atwaddle@cofscotland.org.uk)
Information Officer: Mrs Fiona J. Lange MIPR
                        (Tel: 0131-225 5722 ext. 317; 0131-240 2217;
                        E-mail: flange@cofscotland.org.uk)

The Church of Scotland Guild is a movement within the Church of Scotland whose aim is **'to invite and encourage both women and men to commit their lives to Jesus Christ and to enable them to express their faith in worship, prayer and action'**. Membership of the Guild is open to all who subscribe to that aim.

Groups at congregational level are free to organise themselves under the authority of the Kirk Session, as best suits their own local needs and circumstances. Large groups with frequent meetings and activities continue to operate with a committee or leadership team, while other, smaller groups simply share whatever tasks need to be done among the membership as a whole. Similarly, at Presbyterial Council level, frequency and style of meetings vary according to local needs, as do leadership patterns. Each Council may nominate one person to serve at national level, where six committees made up of these representatives take forward the work of the Guild in accordance with the stated Aim. These Committees are:

- Executive
- Finance and General Purposes
- Projects and Topics
- Programmes and Resources
- Marketing and Publicity
- Matters Relating to Younger People

There has always been a close relationship between the Boards and Committees of the Church and the Guild, and members welcome the opportunity to contribute to the wider work of the Church through the Project Partnership Scheme.

This scheme affords groups at congregational level the opportunity to select a project, or projects, from a range of up to six, selected by the Projects and Topics Committee from submissions by a wide range of Church Departments and other Church-related bodies. A project partner in each group seeks ways of promoting the project locally, increasing awareness of the issues raised by it, and encouraging support of a financial and practical nature. Support is offered by the Project Co-ordinator at Council level and by the Information Officer based at the Guild Office.

The Guild is very aware of the importance of good communication in any large organisation, and regularly sends mailings to its groups to pass on information and resources to the members. In addition, the Newsletter, sent to members three times per session, is a useful communication tool. It is a means of sharing both local news and experiences, and of communicating something of the wider interest and influence of the Guild, which is represented on other national bodies such as the Network of Ecumenical Women in Scotland and the Women's National Commission.

Each year, the Guild follows a Theme and produces a resources pack covering worship and study material. In recent years, there has also been a Discussion Topic with supporting material and background information. The theme, topic and projects all relate to a common three-year strategy which, for 2003–6, is **'Dare to Care'**. Each of the six current projects – from National Mission, World Mission (2), Social Responsibility, L'Arche, Tearfund and Prison Fellowships – reflects some aspect of daring to care. The 2003–4 theme is **'Dare to Care with Courage'**, and Guilds are invited to explore this in a variety of ways. The related discussion topic is **'Who Cares?'**, which addresses the issue of support for those who act as carers for family members and others.

---

(15) ASSEMBLY COUNCIL

MEMBERSHIP
(16 members appointed by the Assembly)
Convener: Rev. David W. Denniston BD DipMin (2003)
Vice Convener: Rev. Ian Y. Gilmour BD (2003)

[The Principal Clerk attends in an advisory capacity, but without the right to vote.]

STAFF
Research and Development Officer: Eleanor Todd BA MPhil
                                   (Tel: 0131-225 5722 ext. 311;
                                   E-mail: etodd@cofscotland.org.uk)
Administrative Secretary: Valerie Smith MA
                                   (Tel: 0131-225 5722 ext. 336;
                                   E-mail: vsmith@cofscotland.org.uk)

REMIT
The revised remit of the Assembly Council, as determined by the General Assembly of 1999, is as follows:

> 'In ongoing consultation with *inter alia* Presbyteries, Boards, Committees, congregations, other denominations and appropriate ecumenical bodies, and in collaboration with the Co-ordinating Forum, to assess the changing needs, challenges and responsibilities of the

Church, to identify priority areas and tasks, and to make recommendations to the General Assembly.'

(16) CHURCH AND NATION

MEMBERSHIP – CHURCH AND NATION COMMITTEE
(48 members: 32 appointed by the Assembly; 16 appointed by Presbyteries)
Convener: Rev. Alan D. McDonald LLB BD MTh (2000)
Vice Convener: Mrs Morag Mylne BA LLB (2001)
Secretary: Rev. David I. Sinclair BSc BD PhD DipSW
                    (E-mail: dsinclair@cofscotland.org.uk)

REMIT
The remit of the Church and Nation Committee as defined by the Assembly is:

'to watch over developments of the Nation's life in which moral and spiritual considerations specially arise, and to consider what action the Church from time to time may be advised to take to further the highest interests of the people'.

The committee's work is divided among four groups:
- Holyrood Group
- Westminster Group
- Europe Group
- International Group

(17) PANEL ON DOCTRINE

MEMBERSHIP
(20 members: 16 appointed by the Assembly, and four from the four University Faculties/ Departments of Divinity, with the Principal Clerk, the Procurator and the Convener of the Board of Practice and Procedure *ex officiis*)
Convener: Rev. John McPake BA BD PhD (1999)
Vice Convener: Rev. Norma D. Stewart MA MEd BD (2002)

STAFF
Secretary: Rev. Douglas Galbraith MA BD BMus MPhil ARSCM
                    (E-mail: dgalbraith@cofscotland.org.uk)

REMIT
The responsibilities of the Panel on Doctrine include: the fulfilling of remits from the General Assembly on matters concerning doctrine; drawing the attention of the General Assembly to

matters inside the Church of Scotland or elsewhere which might have significant doctrinal implications, with recommendations for action; being available for consultation by other Committees of the General Assembly on any matter which might be of doctrinal significance; communicating and consulting in an ecumenical context on matters involving doctrine.

(18) PANEL ON WORSHIP

MEMBERSHIP
(28 members: all appointed by the Assembly)
Convener: Rev. M. Leith Fisher MA BD (2003)
Vice Convener: Mr Ian McCrorie BSc (2001)

STAFF
Secretary: Rev. Douglas Galbraith MA BD BMus MPhil ARSCM
                         (E-mail: dgalbraith@cofscotland.org.uk)

REMIT
The Panel on Worship exists to witness to the importance of worship as a primary function of the Church. It has three major committees:

1. The Liturgical Committee is concerned with the provision of worship materials for public use and is responsible, among other things, for the production of *Common Order*.
2. The Prayer and Devotion Committee is responsible for *Pray Now* and for courses and retreats to promote spiritual growth.
3. The Music Committee encourages new developments in church music, the training of musicians and the publication of relevant materials.

The Panel is also engaged in providing materials for worship in Gaelic and is involved in the compilation of new hymn books and supplements. From time to time, it publishes occasional papers on aspects of the practice of Public Worship.

(19) COMMITTEE ON ARTISTIC MATTERS

MEMBERSHIP
(22 members (of whom no fewer than five shall have professional or practical skills and knowledge) appointed by the General Assembly, one appointed from the General Trustees and two appointed from the Committee on New Charge Development, plus up to five co-opted persons with special knowledge)
Convener: Professor John Hume OBE (2003)
Vice Convener: Rev. Richard E. Frazer BA BD DMin (2002)

STAFF

Administrative Secretary: Rev. Douglas Galbraith MA BD BMus MPhil ARSCM
                            (E-mail: dgalbraith@cofscotland.org.uk)
Congregational Liaison: Mrs Alison Robertson MA BMus

REMIT

The Committee advises congregations and Presbyteries regarding the most appropriate way of carrying out renovations, alterations and reordering of interiors, having regard to the architectural quality of Church buildings. It also advises on the installation of stained glass, tapestries, memorials, furniture and furnishings, and keeps a list of accredited artists and craftsworkers.

Any alteration to the exterior or interior of a Church building which affects its appearance must be referred to the Committee for approval, which is given through the General Trustees. Congregations contemplating alterations are urged to consult the Committee at an early stage.

Members of the Committee are prepared, when necessary, to visit churches and meet office-bearers. The Committee's services are given free.

The Committee seeks the conservation of the nation's heritage as expressed in its Church buildings, while at the same time helping to ensure that these buildings continue to serve the worship and witness of the Church in the present day.

In recent years, the General Assembly has conferred these additional duties on the Committee:
1.   preparation of reports on the architectural, historical and aesthetic merit of the buildings of congregations involved in questions of readjustment
2.   verification of the propriety of repair and renovation work forming the basis of grant applications to public bodies
3.   the offering of advice on the maintenance and installation of organs
4.   facilitating the transfer of unwanted furnishings from one church to another through the quarterly *Exchange and Transfer*
5.   the compilation of a Register of Churches
6.   the processing of applications from congregations for permission to dispose of surplus communion plate, and the carrying out of an inventory of sacramental vessels held by congregations.

---

(20) DEPARTMENT OF MINISTRY
Tel: 0131-225 5722;   Fax: 0131-240 2201
E-mail: ministry@cofscotland.org.uk

BOARD OF MINISTRY
MEMBERSHIP
(91 members: 28 appointed by the Assembly, the Convener and four Vice Conveners, 48 Presbytery Representatives, the Chairperson and Secretary of the Housing and Loan Fund, the Convener and Vice Convener of the Committee on Chaplains to Her Majesty's Forces, the President and Vice President of the Diaconate Council and one member each from the Faculties of Divinity in the Universities of Aberdeen, Edinburgh, Glasgow and St Andrews)

Convener:	Rev. R. Douglas Cranston MA BD
Vice Conveners:	Rev. Alan F.M. Downie MA BD
	Rev. Barry W. Dunsmore MA BD
	Rev. E. Lorna Hood (Mrs) MA BD
	Rev. John W. Paterson BSc BD DipEd

REMIT

The Board of Ministry is responsible for all aspects of the recruitment, education, training, in-service training and support of ministers, auxiliary ministers and deacons as well as for making the financial provision for that work. To enable the Board to discharge these responsibilities and fulfil its Remit, the Board shall determine from time to time what Constituent Committees are required. The exceptions to this will be in respect of the Housing and Loan Fund for Retired Ministers and Widows and Widowers of Ministers and the Committee on Chaplains to Her Majesty's Forces, the Trustees and members respectively of which continue to be appointed as at present. They report separately to the General Assembly.

STAFF

Acting General Secretary and Senior Pastoral Adviser:	Rev. John P. Chalmers BD (Tel: ext. 309; E-mail: jchalmers@cofscotland.org.uk)
Director of Educational Services:	Rev. Nigel J. Robb FCP MA BD ThM MTh (Tel: ext. 347; E-mail: nrobb@cofscotland.org.uk)
Senior Vocational Guidance Officer:	Rev. Martin Scott DipMusEd RSAM BD PhD (Tel: ext. 389; E-mail: mscott@cofscotland.org.uk)
Accountant:	Mrs Pauline Willder MA PgDipIS (Tel: ext. 269; E-mail: pwillder@cofscotland.org.uk)
Finance Officer:	Miss Elizabeth Dailly (Tel: ext. 361; E-mail: edailly@cofscotland.org.uk)
Vocational Guidance Officer:	Mrs Elizabeth Chalmers (Tel: ext. 348; E-mail: echalmers@cofscotland.org.uk)
Education and Development Officer:	Rev. Angus R. Mathieson MA BD (Tel: ext. 315; E-mail: amathieson@cofscotland.org.uk)

DEPARTMENT OF MINISTRY

Further information about the Board's work and services is obtainable through the Department of Ministry at the Church Offices. Information is available on a wide range of matters including the Consolidated Stipend Fund, Stipend and Aid, Endowment Grants, Travelling and other Expenses, Pulpit Supply, Study Leave, Ministry Development conferences, pastoral care services including occupational health, Enquiry and Assessment, Education and Training and so on.

COMMITTEES

The policy development and implementation of the work of the Board of Ministry is managed under the following committees:

1.   CO-ORDINATING AND RESOURCING COMMITTEE

Convener: Rev. R. Douglas Cranston MA BD

The Co-ordinating and Resourcing Committee is the Board's executive committee. Its function is to link the Board to the work of its Policy Committees, to ensure the integrated implementation of the Board's strategy and, further, to ensure that the Board's work is contained within agreed budgets. The Co-ordinating and Resourcing Committee also serves as the Board's 'nomination committee'.

2.   **MINISTRY SUPPORT AND DEVELOPMENT POLICY COMMITTEE**
     Convener: Rev. John W. Paterson BSc BD DipEd
     In the light of the *Ministers of the Gospel* report, the Ministry Support and Development Policy Committee is responsible for reviewing and developing policy on all financial, developmental and pastoral matters related to ministry. This includes such matters as Stipend Policy, manses and housing issues, listed expenses, hardship grants, travel expenses, Study Leave provision, Ministerial Review, Child Protection, Ministry Conferences, Manse Family Counselling, Occupational Health, Shetland Arrangements and so on.
     The following Implementation Committees work in conjunction with the Ministry Support and Development Policy Committee:

     2.1   Ministry Finance Implementation Committee
     Convener: Rev. Jeffrey A. McCormick BD
     The Ministry Finance Implementation Committee operates with powers to deal with anomalous Vacancy and Revision Schedules, Maintenance Allowances, Hardship Grants and Bursaries, Stipend Advances, management of investments, writing-off shortfalls and the granting of further endowments.

     2.2   Ministry Development Implementation Committee
     Convener: Rev. Ian Dick MA MSc BD
     The Ministry Development Implementation Committee is responsible for running and evaluating the current programme of conferences, the promotion of ministry development, processing Study Leave applications, continuing to deliver Child Protection training and developing the personal ministerial review process.

     2.3   Pastoral Support Implementation Committee
     Convener: Rev. Catherine E.E. Collins BA BD
     The Pastoral Support Implementation Committee is responsible for the oversight of the Board's concerns in all areas of pastoral care. This includes liaison with the Medical Panel, the integration of Occupational Health with other ministerial support services, the development of the Pastoral Colleague Scheme as well as the telephone and face-to-face counselling services and oversight of the working of Act X 2000 anent the Ill-Health of Ministers.

     2.4   Interim Ministry Implementation Committee
     Convener: Mrs Fiona B. Cameron
     The Interim Ministry Implementation Committee is responsible for maintaining current arrangements, reporting progress on current assignments and reviewing guidelines for the future deployment of interim ministries. It is responsible for the review and investigation of the future development of Interim Ministry within the Church, and, where appropriate, it works in consultation with the Board of National Mission.

3.   **VOCATIONAL GUIDANCE EDUCATION AND TRAINING POLICY COMMITTEE**

Convener: Rev Alan F.M. Downie MA BD

In the light of the *Ministers of the Gospel* report, the Vocational Guidance Education and Training Policy Committee is responsible for reviewing and developing policy on the promotion of vocations in the Church, the enquiry and assessment process, the admission and readmission of ministers and the supervision and training of students and Graduate Candidates.

The following Implementation Committees work in conjunction with the Vocational Guidance Education and Training Policy Committee:

3.1   Assessment Scheme Implementation Committee

Convener: Rev. James Dewar MA BD

The Assessment Scheme Implementation Committee is responsible for overseeing and reviewing the current enquiry and selection process for Ministers, Auxiliaries and Deacons. The Committee has powers to make final recommendations on suitability for training, hearing appeals, recruiting and training Assessors, Director training and feedback, the recruitment of post-selection counsellors, liaison with presbyteries, running the Selection Conference AGM and liaison with external advisers.

3.2   Candidate Supervision Implementation Committee

Convener: Rev. Karen K. Watson BD

The Candidate Supervision Implementation Committee is responsible for the supervision of students and probationers (including deacons), the production of candidates' reports, operating with powers to sustain placements, university liaison, the recruitment and training of Supervisors, arranging placements, delivering the residential and conference programme, liaison with presbyteries, Bible exams and other Church requirements and Auxiliary Ministry training.

4.   **CHAPLAINS TO HM FORCES** (20 members)

Convener: Professor Herbert Kerrigan QC
Vice Convener: Rev. John Shedden CBE BD DipPSS
Secretary: Mr Douglas M. Hunter WS
                    Henderson Boyd Jackson
                    Exchange Tower
                    19 Canning Street
                    Edinburgh EH3 8EH.

Recruitment

The Chaplains' Committee is entrusted with the task of recruitment of Chaplains for the Regular, Reserve and Auxiliary Forces. Vacancies occur periodically, and the Committee is happy to receive enquiries from all interested ministers.

Forces Registers

The Committee maintains a Register of all those who have been baptised and/or admitted to Communicant Membership by Service Chaplains.

At the present time, registers are being meticulously prepared and maintained. Parish Ministers are asked to take advantage of the facilities by applying for Certificates from the Secretary of the Committee.

Full information may be obtained from the Honorary Secretary, Mr Douglas M. Hunter, Henderson Boyd Jackson, Exchange Tower, 19 Canning Street, Edinburgh EH3 8EH (Tel: 0131-228 2400).

A list of Chaplains may be found in List B in Section 6.

---

(21) NATIONAL MISSION

MEMBERSHIP –
BOARD OF NATIONAL MISSION (34 members)
Convener: Rev. James Gibson TD LTh (2000)
Vice Conveners: Rev. John C. Matthews MA BD (2001)
                                        Mrs Fiona M.H. Campbell BA (2000)
PARISH APPRAISAL (52 members)
Convener: Rev. David W. Clark MA BD (2003)
Vice Convener: Mr Andrew M. Blake BSc FRSA (2003)

NEW CHARGE DEVELOPMENT (23 members)
Convener: Rev. Norman A. Smith MA BD (2003)
Vice Convener: Mr William Greenock (2003)

PARISH ASSISTANCE (16 members)
Convener: Rev. Stanley A. Brook BD (2000)
Vice Convener: Mrs Alison Henderson (2000)

MISSION AND EVANGELISM RESOURCES (30 members)
Convener: Rev. Rosemary Frew (Mrs) MA BD (2003)
Vice Convener: Dr John Berkeley (2001)

CHAPLAINCIES (25 members)
Convener: Lady Elinor Arbuthnott (2001)
Vice Conveners:
  Church and Industry: Rev. Colin M. Anderson BA BD STM MPhil (2002)
  Hospitals, Healthcare and
    Universities: Rev. T. David Watson BSc BD (2003)
  Prisons: Rev. David C. Cameron BD CertMin (2003)

IONA COMMUNITY BOARD
Convener: Rev. Tom Gordon MA BD (2000)

JOINT FAITHS ADVISORY BOARD ON CRIMINAL JUSTICE
Father Andrew Mann (2003)

SCOTTISH CHURCHES COMMUNITY TRUST
Church of Scotland representative: Rev. Ian A. Moir MA BD (2000)

STAFF

General Secretary:	Rev. Douglas A.O. Nicol MA BD
Secretary Depute:	Rev. Alex M. Millar MA BD MBA
Accountant:	Miss Elizabeth Orr BSc CA
Property and Safety Manager:	Mr Colin Wallace
Chaplaincies Administrator:	Mr John K. Thomson
Parish Staffing Administrator:	Post vacant
New Developments Administrator:	Mr Garry B.J. Leach BD BSc
Communications Officer:	Mrs Laura Vermeulen

REMIT

1.   THE BOARD OF NATIONAL MISSION

Established on 1 January 1990, the Board, with its Constituent Committees, has the responsibility for planning and co-ordinating the Church's strategy and provision for the fulfilment of its mission as the National Church.

The Board's policy is that the most effective missionary strategy for our time is 'the development of strong congregations, adequately resourced, with a missionary concern for the parishes they are called to serve – and all this work at congregational level backed by an interface with strategic areas of Scottish life'.

Subject to the General Assembly, the Board's remit is as follows:

1. **Development of Policy:**
   Aided by reflecting on regular consultations, the Board will develop its policy which will be communicated to, and pursued by, its five Constituent Committees.

2. **Finance:**
   The agreement of the annual budget and the monitoring of income and expenditure will be the responsibility of the Board.

3. **New Work:**
   Constituent Committees will refer to the Board new work and work which is likely to exceed the budget of the Committee. The Board will consider such referrals and grant permission if agreed.

4. **Property:**
   The Board will have responsibility for the acquisition and disposal of properties and for the proper maintenance of all its properties.

5. **Presbytery Representatives:**
   The Board will have the responsibility of resolving on which Constituent Committees Presbytery representatives would serve.

6. **General Assembly Report:**
   The Board will have the responsibility for the approval of the Report to the General Assembly on the work of the Board and the five Constituent Committees.

Reporting to the General Assembly in association with the Board of National Mission are:

The Iona Community Board
The Joint Faiths Advisory Board on Criminal Justice
The Scottish Churches Community Trust
The Committee on the Parish Development Fund.

In addition, the Board receives reports from the following groups:

1. **Glasgow Lodging House Mission:** This work is based in the Institute in East Campbell Street, Glasgow, and its object is to care for the thousands of homeless in Scotland's industrial capital. Oversight of the work is by a Management Committee appointed by the Presbytery of Glasgow (Tel: 0141-552 0285).

2. **Project Rejoice Group:** This group, which has ecumenical support, produces visual materials for use by congregations in mission related to the key Christian Festivals (E-mail: nmrejoice@uk.uumail.com).

3. **Residential Centres' Executive:** On behalf of the Board, this group manages National Mission's residential centre, the Badenoch Christian Centre. Situated at Kincraig in Strathspey, this Centre offers individuals, families and groups opportunities for enjoying retreats, short breaks and the many outdoor pursuits of the area from a base of Christian fellowship. Opened in 1976, the Centre is mainly self-catering. Full information from the Manager (Tel: 01540 651373; E-mail: badenoch@uk.uumail.com).

4. **Support Group for Ministry among Deaf People:** The Board appoints three community ministers for ministry among deaf people. Currently, they are the Rev. John R. Osbeck in Aberdeen, the Rev. Alistair F. Kelly in Edinburgh and the Rev. Richard C. Durno in Glasgow.

5. **Statistics for Mission:** The Board has information available about parish statistics based on the 2001 census.

6. **World Exchange Scotland:** The Board operates a career gap programme: full information is available from the Board's office in Edinburgh.

7. **Scottish Mission Studies Project:** The Board supports a project to bring lessons from current missiological thinking to the practice of mission in Scotland. The Project Director is the Rev. Dr Eric Stoddart, who can be contacted through the offices of the Board.

2.   COMMITTEE ON CHAPLAINCIES

In accordance with the overall policy of the Board, the Committee on Chaplaincies will be responsible, through its subcommittees on Hospitals, Healthcare and Universities, Church and Industry, and Prisons, for the encouragement, development, support and, where appropriate, review of chaplaincies in hospitals, healthcare, universities, industry and prisons.

Healthcare Chaplaincies: The Committee administers the scheme by which, under the 1947 National Health Act, ministers and others are appointed as chaplains in all hospitals in Scotland. There are currently well over thirty full-time and around 220 part-time chaplains. Appointments of chaplains are made by the General Secretary of the Board as the 'appointing authority' after consultation with, where appropriate, the Presbytery of the bounds and the relevant hospital authority. Presbyteries are responsible for the oversight of part-time chaplains' work. The Committee also employs some full-time and half-time chaplains' assistants.

A List of Hospital Chaplains will be found in List C in Section 6.

Church and Industry: The aim of industrial mission is threefold:

1. to provide pastoral care and witness to the gospel for men and women in all branches of industry in their place of work;

2. to assess in the interest of the gospel the nature of the influence which industry exerts both on individuals and on society;

3.   to promote the desire for just relationships and understanding at all levels of our industrial society. The work, which is fully ecumenical in character, is now involved in most key industrial sectors. There are about eighty part-time industrial chaplains and seven full-time industrial chaplains. The Co-ordinator of Scottish Churches Industrial Mission is the Rev. Erik M. Cramb (Tel: 01382 458764).

A list of Industrial Chaplains will be found in List D in Section 6.

Prison Chaplaincies: The Committee takes an interest in all matters relating to Church of Scotland chaplains appointed by the Scottish Prison Service.

A list of Church of Scotland Prison Chaplains will be found in List E in Section 6.

Universities: The Committee takes an interest in all matters relating to the appointment and support of chaplains to universities.

A list of University Chaplains will be found in List F in Section 6.

3.   COMMITTEE ON CONGREGATIONAL AND MISSION DEVELOPMENT

In accordance with the overall policy of the Board, the Committee on Congregational and Mission Development will be responsible for:
*   encouraging mission and evangelism in parishes through congregations of the Church of Scotland by means of research, development and training;
*   co-operating with other Boards and Committees in strengthening the life of congregations;
*   ensuring that the personnel and centres under the Committee's direction are serving the missionary and evangelistic purposes of the Church to the best advantage;
*   identifying, originating and supporting projects which are advancing mission and evangelism in key areas of life in Scotland.

The Committee will have responsibility for the work of the Advisers in Mission and Evangelism and Area Facilitators and will include the work of the Rural Committee, 'Project Rejoice!', www.trustfunding.com, John Knox House and the Netherbow – the Scottish Storytelling Centre, 'The Well', Badenoch Christian Centre, Society, Religion and Technology Project, Projects in Evangelism (including 'Impact Teams'), World Exchange Scotland, Statistics for Mission and Apologetics.

A full list of Advisers will be found in List J in Section 6.

The Committee is also responsible for the work of a number of component Committees, projects and centres:

1.   **The Apologetics Committee** engages in the work of apologetics with key areas of Scottish thought and culture, and produces resources to equip churches in the task of giving a reason for the Christian faith.

2.   **The Netherbow: Scottish Storytelling Centre:** The integrated facilities of the **Netherbow Theatre** and the **John Knox House Museum**, together with the **Scottish Storytelling Centre**, are an important cultural and visitor centre on the Royal Mile in Edinburgh and provide advice and assistance nationally in the use of the arts in mission,

education and worship. 'Story Source', 'Script Aid' and other resources are available. Contact the Director, The Netherbow, 43–45 High Street, Edinburgh EH1 1SR (Tel: 0131-556 9579/2647; Website: http://www.storytellingcentre.org.uk). (From October 2003, the Netherbow will be undergoing development, but advice and assistance will still be available.)

3. **The Projects in Evangelism Committee** oversees the work of **Mission Projects** and **'Impact' Teams**, whereby teams of volunteers are recruited and trained to assist parish-based and high-school missions. Youth mission is a priority. Details can be obtained from the Missions Co-ordinator's office at 59 Elmbank Street, Glasgow G2 4PQ (Tel: 0141-352 6946). In addition, the Committee's remit is to identify, originate and support projects in mission and evangelism of a short-term, trial or temporary nature and to liaise with and advise on local or national evangelistic campaigns. (Website: http://www.summermission.org.uk).

4. **The Rural Committee** maintains an awareness of developments in rural Scottish life on both regional and topical bases and seeks to share good practice in mission and evangelism in rural Scotland through its publication *The Rural Spirit*, local consultations and the Church of Scotland Stand at the Royal Highland Show. Contact the National Mission Kirkcaldy office (Tel: 01592 646406; E-mail: natmisskdy@dial.pipex.com).

5. **The Society, Religion and Technology Project:** This unique project, initiated in 1970, studies the impact of new technologies on society and helps the Church to form its response in ways which are practical and prophetic. The project is a forum for all who wish to shape the Church's response to some of the most pressing issues of our time. A newsletter, the *SRT Bulletin*, is available. Contact the SRT Director at John Knox House, 45 High Street, Edinburgh EH1 1SR (Tel: 0131-556 2953; E-mail: srtp@srtp.org.uk; Website: http://www.srtp.org.uk).

6. **The Urban Priority Areas Committee** oversees the implementation of relevant strategies within Urban Priority Areas and monitors the work of the Church within these areas at both local and national levels. Consultations are held on an annual basis, and a regular publication, *UPA News*, is circulated. Contact the UPA Adviser's office, 59 Elmbank Street, Glasgow G2 4PQ (Tel: 0141-333 1948; E-mail: nmglasgow@uk.uumail.com).

7. **The Well Asian Information and Advice Centre:** The Committee provides support and funding for the Presbytery of Glasgow's innovative project that serves the south side of Glasgow by assisting with welfare, housing, immigration, asylum and personal problems. The Well has a strong mission basis on the clear principles that sharing the love of Christ has to include accepting people for who they are and respecting the beliefs of others. A regular prayer letter is available. Contact the Well, 48/50 Albert Road, Glasgow G42 8DN (Tel: 0141-424 4523; Fax: 0141-422 1722; E-mail: info@the-well.clara.co.uk).

8. **Church Pastoral Aid Society:** The Board has accredited the work of the Church Pastoral Aid Society; and the CPAS Scotland Consultant, the Rev. Richard Higginbottom, encourages local congregations in mission and evangelism through consultancy, preaching, training and resources. Mr Higginbottom can be contacted at: 2 Highfield Place, Bankfoot, Perth PH1 4AX (Tel: 01738 787429; E-mail: rhigginbottom@cpas.org.uk).

4.   COMMITTEE ON NEW CHARGE DEVELOPMENT

In accordance with the overall policy of the Board of National Mission, the Committee on New Charge Development, without prejudice to any other body such as the General Assembly's Committee on Parish Appraisal which may have prior rights or jurisdiction, will be responsible for the following areas of work.

1.   Following the instructions of the Committee on Parish Appraisal, and in accordance with the provisions of Act XIII 2000 and equivalent subsequent legislation, to facilitate the creation of new charges. The Committee, in co-operation with other bodies, including Boards, Committees and Presbyteries, will enable the new charge to begin their mission in the new parish area, and will be responsible for:
    (a)   the development of the Charge
    (b)   the appointment of the Minister
    (c)   the provision of a suitable building as the place of worship which may be a new church funded and erected by the Committee, or an existing location within a community which would be suitable for the purpose of worship.
2.   In the case of established charges where significant change is being experienced by the construction of new housing, the Committee on New Charge Development will, on the instruction of the Committee on Parish Appraisal, enter into discussion with Presbyteries and appropriate committees to determine the needs of the area with respect to the provision of a place of witness.
3.   Facilitating and supporting the mission of new charges and those not yet in full status in co-operation with other Committees or Boards as deemed necessary.
4.   Church Extension Charges.
5.   (a)   Advising on, and, within the limitations of its budget, assisting with major problems and expenditure associated with ongoing necessary maintenance of buildings, where there are building debts outstanding on the part of the congregations concerned, or where the congregation concerned is not yet in full status.
    (b)   The purchase of land and the purchase or erection, maintenance and disposal of buildings pertaining to the work of the Committee on New Charge Development are the express responsibility of the Committee.
6.   Providing arbiters to make the choice of buildings to be retained in a readjustment situation.

The Committee has responsibility for twelve New Church Developments and nine Church Extension Charges, with a number of other projects at various stages of development.

5.   COMMITTEE ON PARISH APPRAISAL

In accordance with the overall policy of the Board, the Committee on Parish Appraisal
• Will undertake full responsibilities and rights in connection with the implementation of Act IV 1984, Act VII 2003, Act VIII 2003 and equivalent subsequent legislation directly to the General Assembly
• Will be responsible for dealing with all matters coming from Presbyteries regarding planning and vacancies
• Will deal with proposals for the staffing needs of parishes
• Will, in consultation with the Presbyteries concerned, and following detailed discussion with the Committee on New Charge Development, determine where new charges shall be established, or where, as a result of significant change in an existing charge, an

alternative location for the place of worship is deemed desirable
* Will be available, when requested, to assist and advise Presbyteries in regard to their own forward and readjustment planning.

6.   COMMITTEE ON PARISH STAFFING

In accordance with the overall policy of the Board, and to meet the staffing needs of parishes in regard to National Mission appointments as determined by Presbyteries with the approval of the Committee on Parish Appraisal, the Committee will:
* Be responsible for investigating all applications for National Mission appointments
* Be responsible for Departmental matters relating to the selection, recruitment, training, personal development, employment, deployment and support of National Mission appointments
* Be responsible for sharing with others such as the Inter-Board Group on Team Ministry the development of team ministry
* Be responsible for the Departmental matters relating to existing 'New Forms of Parish Ministry' appointments
* Be responsible for summer student appointments.

The Committee has responsibility for over seventy Deacons, Parish Assistants and Project Workers, and also for ministers appointed through National Mission appointments. Posts are advertised, and people are recruited who have the relevant educational standards, expertise and skills and who are called to the work of mission and outreach. Many staff serve in the large housing areas of Scotland's towns and cities where the number of ordained ministers is low in relation to the population.

For more than thirty years, the Board has been providing financial support to **Bridgeton, St Francis-in-the-East Church House**, a centre providing club facilities for young and old who have little or no Church connection. A club leader and assistant are in charge of the work under a Committee of Management whose chair is the minister of the parish (Tel: 0141-554 8045).

7.   COMMITTEE ON PRIORITY AREAS

In accordance with the overall policy of the Board, the Committee on Priority Areas will:
* Develop, encourage, implement and oversee strategy within priority area parishes
* Develop resources to enable other congregations to make appropriate responses to the needs of people living in poverty in their parishes and to raise awareness of the effects of poverty on people's lives in Scotland
* Co-ordinate the strategy of the wider Church in its priority to Scotland's poorest parishes.

8.   BOARDS AND COMMITTEES ASSOCIATED WITH THE BOARD OF NATIONAL MISSION

(a) The Iona Community Board: The Iona Community Board is the body through which the Iona Community reports to the General Assembly. It is made up of members of the Community and members of the Church appointed by the Assembly. It meets twice yearly, to hear reports of the Community's work both on Iona and Mull and on the mainland, and to assist and guide the Community in its task of seeking 'new ways to touch the hearts of all'.

(b) Joint Faiths Advisory Board on Criminal Justice: The General Assembly of 2000 set up this Board with representatives from the Church of Scotland, the Roman Catholic Church, the Scottish Episcopal Church, Action of Churches Together in Scotland (ACTS) and the Scottish Interfaith Council. Its principal remit is to contribute to the development of Criminal Justice philosophy, penal reform, and to the rights of offenders, untried persons and their families, and to stimulate the interest and participation of all faiths in ministry within the Criminal Justice System.

(c) The Scottish Churches Community Trust: The Scottish Churches Community Trust has been fully operational since January 2001. There are currently eight member churches: Baptist Union, Church of Scotland, Congregational Federation, Roman Catholic Church, Scottish Episcopal Church, Methodist Church, Religious Society of Friends, and United Free Church. Each member church has a nominated representative on the Board of Trustees. Awards totalling £247,817.50 have been made to support projects over the period 2001–4. Support has so far gone to out-of-school care, work with ex-offenders, refugees and rehoused homeless people. Grants are also supplemented by additional training allowances which can be requested for specific purposes.

Office-bearers: Rev. Ian Moir: Chair
Miss E. McQuade: Vice Chair
Mr Gordon Armour: Treasurer
Mr John Dornan: Development Co-ordinator

Applications or offers of support should be made to: Scottish Churches Community Trust, 200 Balmore Road, Glasgow G22 6LJ (Tel/Fax: 0141-336 3766; E-mail: admin@scct.org.uk).

(d) The Committee on the Parish Development Fund: A Parish Development Fund was envisaged in the *Report of the Special Commission anent Review and Reform* to the 2001 General Assembly, with the purpose of providing central funding for local mission initiatives. The 2002 Assembly established the Parish Development Fund for a period of five years from 1 January 2003. It was hoped that such central funding by the Church would attract further funding from outside agencies. It was envisaged that projects would primarily be concerned with the employment of people to engage in particular aspects of mission. However, it is also envisaged that the Fund could assist in a minor way with related fabric needs of new projects. Information about the Parish Development Fund can be obtained from Mr Iain Johnston at the offices of the Board of National Mission.

---

(22) SOCIAL RESPONSIBILITY
Charis House, 47 Milton Road East, Edinburgh EH15 2SR
Tel: 0131-657 2000;   Fax: 0131-657 5000
E-mail: info@charis.org.uk

BOARD OF SOCIAL RESPONSIBILITY
The Board of Social Responsibility engages in social care as part of the Christian witness of the Church to the people of Scotland. In addition, the Board offers guidance to the Church and the media about social, moral and ethical issues.

MEMBERSHIP
(96 members: 44 appointed by the Assembly plus Convener and two Vice Conveners; 47 from Presbyteries; a representative of the Church of Scotland Guild; and a representative from the Committee on Church and Nation. They attend three meetings of the Board per year, in February, June and October, and may be asked to serve on one of the five committees.)

Convener: Rev. James M. Cowie (2001)
Vice Conveners: Rev. David L. Court (2001)
                                Mrs Lyn Hair (2003)

STAFF
Director of Social Work: Mr Ian G. Manson
                                                    (E-mail: imanson@charis.org.uk)
Deputy Director (Central Services):   Mr James Maguire
                                                    (E-mail: jmaguire@charis.org.uk)
Deputy Director (Operations):   Mr David J. Kellock
                                                    (E-mail: dkellock@charis.org.uk)
Deputy Director (Planning and Development):   Mrs Joyce M. Buchanan
                                                    (E-mail: jbuchanan@charis.org.uk)

REMIT
The Board of Social Responsibility is one of Scotland's largest social-work agencies in the voluntary sector, employing 2,200 full- and part-time staff. The purpose of the Board of Social Responsibility can be broadly defined as follows:
1.   to offer care and help through the varied establishments and projects it operates, and to encourage and enable caring work at parish level
2.   to offer to the Church informed opinion on contemporary social, moral and ethical issues
3.   to encourage balanced judgements on these issues in the light of the Christian faith, and to put forward these judgements at all levels of influence.

DIVISIONAL STRUCTURE
Operationally, the Board's work is split into five geographical areas which cover Scotland. Each of these areas is administered by a Divisional Manager and Assistant Divisional Managers. They are physically located in their own Division, and manage and develop services at a local level. The general administration of the Board, which includes finance, publicity, training and fund-raising, is carried out by staff based at the Board's offices in Charis House, Edinburgh (Tel: 0131-657 2000).

DIVISION 1   CITY OF GLASGOW, EAST DUNBARTONSHIRE, NORTH LANARKSHIRE

Divisional Office: Tom Allan Centre, 23 Elmbank Street, Glasgow G2 4PD
                         (Tel: 0141-243 2897; Fax: 0141-229 0423;
                         E-mail: division1.cos@uk.uumail.com)
Divisional Manager: Paul Robinson
A.D.M. (Planning and Development):   Flora Mackenzie
A.D.M. (Operations):   Marlene Smith

DIVISION 2   **CENTRAL AND SOUTH-WEST SCOTLAND**

Divisional Office: Adams House, 136 Auchenlodment Road, Elderslie, Johnstone,
Renfrewshire PA5 9NX
(Tel: 01505 337303; Fax: 01505 382022;
E-mail: division2.cos@uk.uumail.com)

Divisional Manager: Archie Henderson
A.D.M. (Planning and Development):   David Clark
A.D.M. (Operations):   George McNeilly

DIVISION 3   **EDINBURGH AND SOUTH-EAST SCOTLAND**

Divisional Office: Gate Lodge, 27 Milton Road East, Edinburgh EH15 2NL
(Tel: 0131-669 9576; Fax: 0131-669 5185;
E-mail: division3.cos@uk.uumail.com)

Divisional Manager: Jeannette S. Deacon
A.D.M. (Planning and Development):   Graham Lumb
A.D.M. (Operations):   Ruby Rawcliffe
                                             Dominic Gray

DIVISION 4   **FORTH VALLEY AND NORTH-EAST SCOTLAND**

Divisional Office: Kandahar House, 71 Meadowside, Dundee DD1 1EN
(Tel: 01382 305920; Fax: 01382 305921
E-mail: division4.cos@uk.uumail.com)

Divisional Manager: Calum Murray
A.D.M.   Brenda Fraser

DIVISION 5   **HIGHLANDS AND ISLANDS**

Divisional Office: Cameron House, Culduthel Road, Inverness IV2 4YG
(Tel: 01463 236136; Fax: 01463 236247;
E-mail: division5.cos@uk.uumail.com)

Divisional Manager: Margaret Wilkinson
A.D.M. (Planning and Development):   Gerald Robson
A.D.M. (Operations):   Donald MacAskill

THE BOARD'S SERVICES
Details of the Board's services can be obtained from either the Divisional Officer or Charis House on 0131-657 2000.

FUNDRAISING
Head of Fundraising: Pam Taylor (E-mail: ptaylor@charis.org.uk)
The Head of Fundraising aims to increase income development within the Board to enable us to ensure the long-term sustainability of our valuable services across Scotland. We want to inform people about our mission and our work with the most needy people in our society. We invite people

to donate money to support our work and to volunteer their time – either to fundraise or to help carry out essential tasks of all kinds. We also ask people to pray with us about the day-to-day running of our services. If you want to know more or would like to help in any way, please contact Pam Taylor (Tel: 0131-657 2000; E-mail: ptaylor@charis.org.uk).

MEDIA AND PUBLIC RELATIONS
Communications Officer (Media): Hugh Brown (E-mail: hbrown@charis.org.uk)
The Board takes every opportunity to publicise the caring work of the Church, through *Life & Work*, newspapers, and articles in the press. The Communications Officer (Media) co-ordinates contact with the various media, and is responsible for press statements (in consultation with the Church's Media Relations Unit).

The *Circle of Care* calendar, which is produced each year, highlights some of the Board's services, and sells 22,000 copies through the channels of the Guild and Church members; 42,000 copies of the *Circle of Care* newspaper are distributed three times a year with the latest news about the Board. Leaflets, brochures and videos are available to explain the Board's work. Some of the Board's reports to the General Assembly (*The Future of the Family*, *Euthanasia*, *Human Genetics*, *Human Fertilisation and Embryology*, *Health and Healing*) have been published as books by Saint Andrew Press. There are 'user-friendly' packs on various topics: HIV/AIDS Resource Material, Marriage PLUS – A Study Pack for Couples, and Social Inclusion – A Study Pack for Churches.

CONGREGATIONAL LIAISON
Communications Officer (Congregations): Maggie Chalmers
(E-mail: mchalmers@charis.org.uk)
The Communications Officer (Congregations) links the social care managed and developed by the Board of Social Responsibility at a national level with the social work of the Church initiated at parish level. The tasks of the Communications Officer (Congregations) fall into three main categories:
1. to encourage and enable local congregations to identify and meet the needs of local people
2. to ensure and enable local congregations to have knowledge and understanding of the Board's work
3. to maintain a database of projects which can be shared with other congregations wishing support and ideas.

CONGREGATIONAL CONTACTS
Congregational Contacts are the link people between the Board and local churches. Each church should have an appointed Contact who receives mailings three times per year. There are currently over 1,000 Congregational Contacts. They undertake work in a variety of ways. They provide current, correct and appropriate information to their Church. They often act as distributors for the *Circle of Care* newspaper and they act as agents for our calendar, Christmas-card and merchandise sales.

Church members are the most important part of the 'Circle of Care' provided by the Church of Scotland. It is the caring work in the communities of Scotland which is our largest area of service provision. Congregational Contacts provide the vital link between the formal services provided by the Board and the community work and prayers of the local churches, and the Board greatly appreciates all the work done by these volunteer champions.

To find out more about how Social Responsibility works with local communities, write, phone or e-mail Maggie Chalmers, Communications Officer (Congregations) with your enquiry.

SOCIAL INTERESTS
Social Interests Officer: Kristine Gibbs (E-mail: kristine@charis.org.uk)
The remit of the Board of Social Responsibility instructs it 'to study and present essential Christian judgements on social and moral issues arising within the area of its concern'. It does this through Study Groups, which present their findings to the Board of Social Responsibility. The Board then reports to the General Assembly. Some of the recent issues reported upon have been: Euthanasia; Human Sexuality; Human Genetics; Human Fertilisation and Embryology; Decriminalisation of Drugs; Prostitution; Human Cloning; Begging.

SPEAKERS FOR GUILDS AND GROUPS
Members of staff and of the Board will gladly visit congregations and other Church organisations to speak about the work of the Board. To request a speaker, please write to the Communications Officer (Congregations) at Charis House, 47 Milton Road East, Edinburgh EH15 2SR.

---

(23) WORLD MISSION
Tel: 0131-225 5722;   Fax: 0131-226 6121
Update: 0131-226 4121;   Answerphone: 0131-240 2231
E-mail: world@cofscotland.org.uk

MEMBERSHIP – BOARD OF WORLD MISSION
(27 members: 12 from Presbyteries, 12 nominated by the General Assembly, Convener and two Vice Conveners)

Convener:	Rev. Alan Greig BSc BD (2002)
Vice Conveners:	Dr Fiona Burnett BSc PhD (2003)
	Rev. Andrew F. Anderson MA BD (2002)

DEPARTMENTAL STAFF

General Secretary:	Rev. Prof. Kenneth R. Ross BA BD PhD
Partnership Team:	
Leader and Overseas Charges:	Mr Walter T. Dunlop ARICS
Sub-Saharan Africa:	Mr Calum J. Strang
Europe, Middle East, Americas:	Rev. Ian W. Alexander BA BD STM
Asia:	Mr Sandy Sneddon
Local Involvement:	Carol Findlay RGN RMN OIPCNE MSc
Finance:	Mrs Anne Macintosh BA CA
	(General Treasurer's Department)
Personnel:	Miss Sheila Ballantyne MA PgDipPM

REMIT
- Give life to the Church of Scotland's understanding that it is part of the Universal Church committed to the advance of the Kingdom of God throughout the world.
- Discern priorities and form policies to guide the Church of Scotland's ongoing worldwide participation in God's transforming mission, through the gospel of Jesus Christ.

- Develop and maintain mutually enriching relationships with partner churches overseas through consultation and the two-way sharing of human and material resources.
- Equip and encourage Church of Scotland members at local, Presbytery and national levels to enjoy being involved in the life of the world church.
- Help the people of Scotland to appreciate the worldwide nature of the Christian faith.

The Board carries on its work through the following constituent committees and groups:

Europe:	Convener: Rev. Gillean Maclean
Israel Centres:	Convener: Rev. Alistair G. Bennett
Overseas Charges:	Convener: Rev. Alastair H. Gray
Local Involvement:	Convener: Rev. Neil Urquhart
Asia:	Convener: Mr John Milne
Americas:	Convener: Rev. Alastair H. Gray
Budget and Finance:	Convener: Rev. Gavin J. Elliott
Middle East and North Africa:	Convener: Rev. Colin Renwick
Personnel:	Convener: Mr Robert Scott
Sub-Saharan Africa:	Convener: Mrs Elizabeth Paterson

STRATEGIC COMMITMENTS: 2001–10
- Working with partner churches on new initiatives in evangelism
- Working for justice, peace and reconciliation in situations of conflict or threat
- Resourcing the Church to set people free from the oppression of poverty
- Contributing meaningfully to the struggle against the HIV/AIDS epidemic
- Increasing the involvement of Scottish Christians in the world Church.

PARTNERSHIP PRIORITIES

Following a consultation with partner Churches held in St Andrews in September 1999, the Board has identified the following priority areas for partnership in mission:

1. **Theological Education:** developing ministerial and lay training at appropriate levels in all our churches.

2. **Evangelism:** helping one another to create new models and launch new initiatives to take the Gospel to all people.

3. **Holistic Mission:** enabling one another to respond with Christian compassion to human needs in our rapidly changing societies.

4. **Mission in Pluralistic Societies:** strengthening Christian identity in our multi-religious and multi-cultural societies by supporting one another and sharing our experiences.

5. **Prophetic Ministry:** inspiring one another to discern and speak God's Word in relation to critical issues which arise in our times.

6. **Human and Material Resources:** finding new and imaginative ways of sharing our resources at all levels of Church life.

WORLD MISSION AND WORLD RESOURCES

Sharing in the mission of God worldwide requires a continuing commitment to sharing the Church of Scotland's resources of people and money for mission in six continents as contemporary evidence that it is 'labouring for the advancement of the Kingdom of God throughout the world' (First Article Declaratory). Such resource-sharing remains an urgent matter because most of our overseas work is in the so-called 'Third World', or 'South', in nations where the effects of the widening gap between rich and poor is *the* major issue for the Church. Our partner Churches in Africa, most of Asia, in the Caribbean, South and Central America are desperately short of financial and technical resources, which we can to some extent meet with personnel and grants. However, they are more than willing to share the resources of their Christian Faith with us, including things which the Church in the West often lacks: enthusiasm in worship, hospitality and evangelism, and a readiness to suffer and struggle for righteousness, and in many areas a readiness to sink denominational differences. Mutual sharing in the World Church witnesses to its international nature, and has much to offer a divided world, not least in Scotland.

VACANCIES OVERSEAS. The Board welcomes enquiries from men and women interested in serving in the Church overseas. This is usually with indigenous denominations and related organisations with which we are in partnership overseas, in Church of Scotland congregations mostly in Europe, or our work in Israel. Those interested in more information are invited to write to the Assistant Secretary (Personnel) in the first instance.

HIV/AIDS PROJECT. The General Assembly of 2002 adopted an HIV/AIDS Project to be run by the Board of World Mission in 2002–7. The Project aims to raise awareness in congregations about the impact of HIV/AIDS and seeks to channel urgently needed support to partner churches. For further information, contact the Co-ordinator, HIV/AIDS Project, Board of World Mission, 121 George Street, Edinburgh EH2 4YN.

JUBILEE SCOTLAND. The Board plays an active role in the coalition which works within Scotland for the cancellation of unpayable international debt. For further information, contact the Co-ordinator, Jubilee Scotland, 41 George IV Bridge, Edinburgh EH1 1EL (Tel: 0131-225 4321; Fax: 0131-225 8861; E-mail: mail@jubileescotland.org.uk).

CHRISTIAN AID SCOTLAND. Christian Aid is an official relief development agency of churches in Britain and Ireland. Christian Aid's mandate is to challenge and enable us to fulfil our responsibilities to the poor of the world. Half a million volunteers and collectors and nearly 200 paid staff make this possible, with money given by millions of supporters. The Church of Scotland marks its commitment as a church to this vital part of its mission through an annual grant from the Mission and Aid Fund, transmitted through World Mission, which keeps in close touch with Christian Aid and its work.

   Up-to-date information about projects and current emergency relief work can be obtained from the National Secretary, Rev. John Wylie, Christian Aid Scotland, 41 George IV Bridge, Edinburgh EH1 1EL (Tel: 0131-220 1254); the three area co-ordinators, Ms Eildon Dyer and Mrs Ailsa Henderson, Glasgow Office, 759a Argyle Street G3 8DS (Tel: 0141-221 7475), Miss Marjorie Clark, Perth Office, 28 Glasgow Road, Perth PH2 0NX (Tel: 01738 643982); or the Director, Dr Daleep Mukarji, Christian Aid Office, PO Box 100, London SE1 7RT (Tel: 020 7620 4444).

ACCOMMODATION IN ISRAEL. The Church of Scotland has two Christian Guest Houses in Israel which provide comfortable accommodation for pilgrims and visitors to the Holy Land. Further information is available from the St Andrew's Guest House, PO Box 8619, Jerusalem (Tel: 00 972 2 6732401; Fax: 00 972 2 6731711; E-mail: standjer@netvision.net.il), and the St Andrew's Galilee Centre, PO Box 104, Tiberias (Tel: 00 972 6 6721165; Fax: 00 972 6 6790145; E-mail: scottie@rannet.com). The St Andrew's Galilee Centre is presently closed for redevelopment and is expected to reopen in 2003.

A list of Overseas Appointments will be found in List K in Section 6.

A *World Mission Year Book* is available with more details of our partner churches and of people currently serving abroad, including those with ecumenical bodies and para-church bodies.

A list of Retired Missionaries will be found in List L in Section 6.

(24) ECUMENICAL RELATIONS

MEMBERSHIP –
COMMITTEE ON ECUMENICAL RELATIONS
(27 members: 12 nominated by the General Assembly, 13 appointed by the main Boards and Committees of the Church, plus five Corresponding Members – the General Secretary of ACTS, one from the Roman Catholic Church in Scotland and three on a rotating basis from the Scottish Episcopal Church, the Synod of the Methodist Church in Scotland, the Salvation Army, the Religious Society of Friends, the United Free Church of Scotland, the United Reformed Church and the Baptist Union of Scotland: Convener and Vice Convener)

Convener: Rev. Erik M. Cramb LTh (2002)
Secretary: Rev. Sheilagh M. Kesting BA BD

REMIT
The purpose of the Committee is to enable the Church of Scotland, at local, Presbytery and national levels, increasingly to maximise opportunities and resources for worship, witness and service together with other churches and related organisations in this country and overseas, working wherever possible through existing Boards and Committees of the Church.

In fulfilment of this remit, the Committee will
1.   be the body within the Church of Scotland through which WCC, ACTS, CTBI and, as appropriate, the other Ecumenical Instruments in Britain and Ireland relate
2.   call together for planning, briefing and the exchanging of information, the Church of Scotland's representatives on WCC, ACTS (Scottish Churches' Forum and Networks), CTBI (the Assembly and the Church Representatives Meetings) and the like
3.   bring to the General Assembly for the approval of the General Assembly the names of those who might serve for the following year (or appropriate term) on ACTS, on CTBI and, as appropriate, on Committees, Commissions and the like of these bodies
4.   following consultation with the Board of World Mission, bring to the General Assembly for the approval of the General Assembly the names of those who might serve for the following year (or appropriate term) on such bodies as the World Alliance of Reformed Churches, the Conference of European Churches and the World Council of Churches
5.   bring to the General Assembly for the approval of the General Assembly the names of those who might be invited to represent the Church of Scotland at the Assemblies or Synods of other Churches in Britain and at Conferences and Gatherings organised on an ecumenical basis at which official Church of Scotland representation is appropriate

6. (a) call for and receive reports from representatives of the Church of Scotland attending the Assemblies or Synods of other Churches and those ecumenical Conferences and Gatherings which are from time to time held
    (b) ensure that appropriate parts of such reports are made available to relevant Boards and Committees
7. (a) be informed of, assist centrally where appropriate, and report to the General Assembly on the Local Ecumenical Partnerships which already exist in Scotland and which may in the future come to exist
    (b) in consultation with the Board of Practice and Procedure (where matters of Church Law and Practice are involved), advise congregations and Presbyteries seeking to establish new Ecumenical Partnerships or to amend existing Partnerships
8. be the Committee through which reports are submitted to the General Assembly from Groups appointed to take part on behalf of the Church of Scotland in formal conversations and doctrinal dialogues with other Church and ecumenical bodies.

INTER-CHURCH ORGANISATIONS

WORLD COUNCIL OF CHURCHES

The Church of Scotland is a founder member of the World Council of Churches, formed in 1948. As its basis declares, it is 'a fellowship of Churches which confess the Lord Jesus Christ as God and Saviour according to the Scriptures, and therefore seek to fulfil their common calling to the Glory of the one God, Father, Son and Holy Spirit'. Its member Churches, which number over 300, are drawn from all continents and include all the major traditions (except the Roman Catholic) – Eastern and Oriental Orthodox, Reformed, Lutheran, Anglican, Baptist, Disciples, Methodist, Moravian, Friends, Pentecostalist and others. Its Eighth Assembly was held in Harare, Zimbabwe, from 3–14 December 1998. This Assembly marked the fiftieth Anniversary of the World Council with an act of recommitment by the member Churches. The theme was: 'Turn to God: Rejoice in Hope'. The Council is once again restructuring to form a more flexible working pattern among the staff.

The General Secretary is Rev. Dr Konrad Raiser, 150 route de Ferney, 1211 Geneva 2, Switzerland (Tel: 00 41 22 791 61 11; Fax: 00 41 22 791 03 61).

WORLD ALLIANCE OF REFORMED CHURCHES

The Church of Scotland is a founder member of the World Alliance of Reformed Churches, which began in 1875 as 'The Alliance of the Reformed Churches Throughout the World Holding the Presbyterian System' and which now includes also Churches of the Congregational tradition. Today it is composed of more than 200 Churches in nearly 100 countries, with an increasing number in Asia. It brings together, for mutual help and common action, large Churches which enjoy majority status and small minority Churches. It engages in theological dialogue with other Christian traditions – Orthodox, Roman Catholic, Lutheran, Methodist, Baptist and so on. It is organised in three main departments – Co-operation with Witness, Theology, and Partnership.

The General Secretary is Rev. Dr Setri Nyomi, 150 route de Ferney, 1211 Geneva 2, Switzerland (Tel: 00 41 22 791 62 38; Fax: 00 41 22 791 65 05).

CONFERENCE OF EUROPEAN CHURCHES

The Church of Scotland is a founder member of the Conference of European Churches, formed in 1959 and until recently the only body which involved in common membership representatives of every European country (except Albania) from the Atlantic to the Urals. More than 100 Churches, Orthodox and Protestant, are members. Although the Roman

Catholic Church is not a member, there is very close co-operation with the Council of European Catholic Bishops' Conferences. With the removal of the long-standing political barriers in Europe, the Conference has now opportunities and responsibilities to assist the Church throughout the continent to offer united witness and service.

Its General Secretary is Rev. Dr Keith Clements, 150 route de Ferney, 1211 Geneva 2, Switzerland (Tel: 00 41 22 791 61 11; Fax: 00 41 22 791 03 61).

CEC: CHURCH AND SOCIETY COMMISSION

The Church of Scotland is a founder member of the European Ecumenical Commission for Church and Society (EECCS). The Commission owes its origins to the Christian concern and vision of a group of ministers and European civil servants about the future of Europe. It was established in 1973 by Churches recognising the importance of this venture. Membership included Churches and ecumenical bodies from the European Union. The process of integration with CEC was completed in 2000, and the name, Church and Society Commission (CSC), established. In Brussels, CSC monitors Community activity, maintains contact with MEPs and promotes dialogue between the Churches and the institutions. It plays an educational role and encourages the Churches' social and ethical responsibility in European affairs. It has a General Secretary, a study secretary and an executive secretary in Brussels and a small office in Strasbourg and Geneva.

The Director is Rev. Rudiger Noll, Ecumenical Centre, 174 rue Joseph II, B-1000 Brussels, Belgium (Tel: 00 32 2 230 17 32; Fax: 00 32 2 231 14 13).

CHURCHES TOGETHER IN BRITAIN AND IRELAND (CTBI)
and ACTION OF CHURCHES TOGETHER IN SCOTLAND (ACTS)

In September 1990, Churches throughout Britain and Ireland solemnly committed themselves to one another, promising to one another to do everything possible together. To provide frameworks for this commitment to joint action, the Churches established CTBI for the United Kingdom and Ireland, and for Scotland, ACTS, with sister organisations for Wales and for England.

CTBI has a large Assembly meeting once every three years, a Church Representatives Meeting held twice a year, and a Steering Committee meeting five times a year. It has commissions on Mission, Racial Justice and Interfaith Relations. It is staffed by a General Secretary and Co-ordinating Secretaries for Church Life, Church and Society, and International Affairs.

The General Secretary of CTBI is Dr David R. Goodbourn, Inter-Church House, 35–41 Lower Marsh, London SE1 7SA (Tel: 020 7523 2121; Fax: 020 7928 0010).

ACTS was restructured at the beginning of 2003. The new structure comprises the Scottish Churches' Forum (replacing the Central Council) composed of church representatives from trustee member churches. There will be four Networks: Church Life, Faith Studies, Mission, and Church and Society. Contributing to the life of the Networks will be associated ecumenical groups. Such groups are expressions of the churches' commitment to work together and to bring together key people in a defined field of interest or expertise. ACTS is an expression of the commitment of the churches to one another.

ACTS is staffed by a General Secretary, two Network Officers, an Administration and Booking Officer and a Bursar. Scottish Churches House has a Warden and a Deputy Warden.

These structures facilitate regular consultation and intensive co-operation among those who frame the policies and deploy the resources of the churches in Scotland and throughout Britain and Ireland. At the same time, they afford greater opportunity for a wide range of members of different churches to meet in common prayer and study.

The General Secretary is Rev. Dr Kevin Franz, Scottish Churches House, Dunblane FK15 0AJ (Tel: 01786 823588; Fax: 01786 825844; E-mail: ecumenical@acts-scotland.org).

The Scottish Churches Parliamentary Office: The Scottish Churches Parliamentary Office supports the churches in their relationships with the Scottish Parliament and Executive, providing briefings and updates on Parliamentary activity and advice on contacting MSPs and so on. The Parliamentary Officer is Rev. Dr Graham K. Blount, and the Office is at 14 Johnston Terrace, Edinburgh   EH1   2PW   (Tel: 0131-622   2278;   Fax: 0131-622   7226;   E-mail: gkblount@dial.pipex.com; Website: www.actsparl.org).

---

(25) PARISH EDUCATION
21 Young Street, Edinburgh EH2 4HU
Tel: 0131-260 3110;   Fax: 0131-260 3120
E-mail: enquiries@parished.org.uk

MEMBERSHIP: BOARD OF PARISH EDUCATION
(Convener, Vice-Convener, 50 members appointed by the General Assembly, one representative from the Church of Scotland Guild)

Convener:	Rev John C. Christie (2001)
Vice-convener:	Mr Ron Lavalette (2003)
Director and General Secretary:	Mr Iain W. Whyte

STAFF

Section Head, Publications:	Ms Gillian Cloke / Ms Janet de Vigne
Section Head, Adult Education:	Mr Stewart Cutler
Regional Development Worker (Tayforth):	Rev. Jane Denniston
Regional Development Worker (Highlands):	Ms Shuna Dicks
Section Head, Youth Ministry:	Mr Steve Mallon
Regional Development Worker (South-west):	Mr Calum Sabey
Secretary for the Readership:	Ms Mary Stobo
National Adviser in Elder Training:	Ms Sheilah Steven
Section Head, Children's Ministry and Regional Services:	Mr Doug Swanney
Cowal Education Field Officer:	Ms Jen Zielinski

Child Protection Unit

National Adviser in Child Protection:	Ms Jennifer McCreanor
Child Protection Trainer:	Ms Caroline McLoughlin
Associate National Adviser in Child Protection:	Post vacant

REMIT
Based at 21 Young Street, Edinburgh, the Board of Parish Education's remit is to oversee the development of an education and leadership training service for the Church of Scotland. The Board's provision covers a wide spectrum of courses and events catering for all ages and abilities. This involves training and resources for children's workers, youth workers, elders and the Readership. Resource material and publications to support this work are also produced through

Scottish Christian Press (formerly Parish Education Publications).

COMMITTEES
The Board itself meets twice annually, in February and September, with its committees meeting four or five times per annum. The committees are organised to reflect the Board's commitment to learning for all, and to developing the concept of the Faith Community.

ADULT MINISTRIES
The remit of the Adult Ministries Section is to support and develop the vast range of adult learning that takes place in the church.

Adult Education
The development of a vibrant and growing congregation rests in two areas – worship and education. For many folk in the church, education has historically been a difficulty, but many congregations have at least some form of adult education programme – including discussion groups, Bible study, prayer groups and Lent groups – which they are keen to expand. The Adult Education Advisor's role is to assist in this development and to help congregations examine new areas of development. In particular, we have developed a congregational renewal programme based on the *Church Without Walls* report, with study material and an evaluation package to help congregations identify where they can develop and how they can go about taking the necessary steps to achieve their goals.

Eldership
Being an elder is a demanding but rewarding role – an important part of the Church of Scotland in its team ministry. The Eldership Working Party supports this crucial leadership role within the Church, working with a network of Elder Trainers – at present forty-five in twenty-five Presbyteries, with six more in training. Elder Trainers are regularly impressed by the commitment of time and talent to the Church shown by the elders with whom they come in contact, and the Eldership Working Party supports this by holding regular conferences and training days for elders and session clerks, and by providing a variety of study material on eldership, including books and videos. Interest in eldership is increasing as elders seek to rediscover their spiritual role. Workshops are available locally: topics include Exploring Eldership, Pastoral Care, Faith Sharing, and Leading Worship. Enquiries are always welcome.

Readership
The Board of Parish Education provides training opportunities and services to maintain this important component of the Church's team ministry. A Reader is a member of the Church set apart by his or her Presbytery for 'duties principally concerned with the Ministry of the Word and the conduct of public worship'. Recently the Reader's role has developed; while still associated primarily with worship and preaching, there are new opportunities for the fully trained Reader. Further information for those interested in Readership is available from the Board on request.

CHILDREN'S, YOUTH AND REGIONAL MINISTRY
Children's and Youth Ministry in the Board is based around the principles of education, empowerment and creating best practice for the whole Church. The Board is involved in training children's and youth leaders through its *Choices* programme – a series of sessions available to local churches in CD format. Both the children's and the youth programmes cover a wide range of subjects and provide a grounding for anyone working with children and youth. Both areas are served by websites offering updates and information for the whole Church. Youth ministry can

be found at www.cosy.net.uk and Children's Ministry through www.chok.org.uk (launching in the autumn of 2003).

Children's Ministry

Chok, the Children's Ministry newsletter, continues to be available to children's workers across the country. Children's Forums also meet locally, with two regional gatherings a year, one focused on enabling the children of the Church to have an input into the General Assembly.

Youth Ministry

The Board is also responsible for both the National Youth Assembly and the Youth Representatives to the General Assembly. The Youth Assembly is an annual event attracting young adults from all over the UK, centring around debate, fellowship, worship and community. As well as events at home, the Board organises and participates in ecumenical events and trips abroad. It also resources youth groups by providing training for youth leaders and by supplying educational material. The Board is also a major contributor to the Crossover Festival, a weekend event of worship, speakers, debates, fun and reflection.

Regional Ministry

The Board believes in working with local churches as closely as it can. Through the work of its three Regional Development Workers (South-west region based in Dumfries, Tayforth region based in Perth and the Highland area based in Inverness) and a Children's and Youth Worker in the Cowal area, the Board builds relationships by providing local education and training. Each member of the Regional Services staff is committed to providing quality educational resources and experiences for local churches.

SCOTTISH CHRISTIAN PRESS

The Scottish Christian Press (formerly Parish Education Publications, or PEP) is the publishing and information unit of the Board of Parish Education. To support parish development, SCP produces a wide variety of resources which derive both from ongoing work in the field by the Board's own staff and from commissions within the Church.

The unit produces an annual catalogue listing SCP's own publications in the field of Christian education. It offers also resources available from other bodies within the Church, some of the best available parish resourcing material from other denominations and material from educational publishers world-wide. Details of SCP's current catalogue can be found through our website on www.scottishchristianpress.org.uk.

SCP also produces a regular online newsletter, *Online Parish Education News* (OPEN), with a circulation of around 7,000; for information, or to receive this, contact SCP through the Edinburgh office or the general enquiry line.

CHILD PROTECTION

It has long been the vision of the Board that integrating the principles of protection and safety with the nurture and education of our young people is essential in the Church. The Child Protection Unit puts this ideal into practice, regularly organising training throughout the country for children's and youth workers, ensuring the highest standards and best practice. This section also has responsibility for implementing the Church's policy on Child Protection through the network of Child Protection Co-ordinators. It has produced a handbook on good practice within this area which will be regularly updated, and a policy statement for the protection of children within the Church. In addition, this Unit has been given by the General Assembly responsibility for administration concerned with criminal-records checks enabled by recent legislation.

(26) EDUCATION COMMITTEE

MEMBERSHIP:
(20 members together with Convener and Vice Convener)
Convener: Mr David Alexander (2003)
Vice Convener: Rev. Professor Duncan B. Forrester MA BD DPhil DD

STAFF
Secretary: Ms Susan Leslie

REMIT
The Education Committee is the oldest continuing Committee of the General Assembly
(formed in 1825) and has a long and historic connection with Scottish Education. The key
aspects of the Committee's remit are:

1. to represent the Church on matters of state education at every level
2. to support the Church Representatives whom it appoints on behalf of the General
    Assembly to deal with education on each of Scotland's thirty-two Local Authorities
3. to co-operate with Presbyteries and Local Authorities in undertaking the support and
    training of chaplains in schools and in Further Education Colleges
4. to promote good learning and teaching in the curriculum and ensure the place of Religious
    and Moral Education
5. to commission and produce resources to ensure that Scottish Christianity and the life and
    work of the Church of Scotland can be properly represented in the curriculum
6. to co-operate with other Churches and faith groups working to enhance Scottish Education.

The Committee responds to consultation documents from the Scottish Executive and seeks to
develop and maintain links with Education Ministers, with Members of the Scottish Parliament
and with the relevant Committees.

It participates in the work of the Scottish Joint Committee on Religious and Moral
Education and is represented on the Religious Education Movement (Scotland) and the
Association for the Teaching of Religious Education in Scotland (ATRES).

It has established useful and practical links with the Roman Catholic Church through its
Education Commission, and it has a good record of liaison with the Educational Institute of
Scotland and other unions in the educational field. It nominates one person to represent the
Church on the General Teaching Council.

(27) COMMUNICATION

MEMBERSHIP
BOARD OF COMMUNICATION
(18 members, appointed by the Assembly)
Convener: Rev. W. Peter Graham (2003)
Vice Convener: Rev. Iain F. Paton (2002)
Secretary: Mr Brian McGlynn

STAFF

Secretary and Director:	Mr Brian McGlynn
Management Accountant:	Post vacant
Media Relations Unit:	Mrs Pat Holdgate, Head of Media Relations
Design Services:	Mr Peter J.F. Forrest, Head of Design Services
Life & Work:	Ms Lynne Robertson, Editor
Saint Andrew Press:	Mrs Ann Crawford, Head of Publishing
Pathway Productions:	Mr Laurence P. Wareing, Director
Ministers' Forum:	Rev. John A. Ferguson, Editor
Year Book:	Rev. Ronald S. Blakey, Editor

REMIT

Under a revised constitution approved by the General Assembly in 1995, the Board is responsible for providing the Church with professional communication services as well as promoting effective communication within the Church and to the outside world. The Board's services are as follows:

DIRECTOR

Mr Brian McGlynn   direct line 0131-240 2236
                          (E-mail: bmcglynn@cofscotland.org.uk)

Marketing and Publicity Officer

Alison Fleming   0131-225 5722 ext. 239
                          (E-mail: afleming@cofscotland.org.uk)

1.   MEDIA RELATIONS UNIT

Head of Media Relations:	Pat Holdgate	0131-240 2243
Senior Media Relations Officer:	Brian McGuire	0131-240 2204
Senior Media Relations Officer:	Catherine Kinghorn	0131-240 2202
Website Editor:	Lynsae Tulloch	0131-225 5722 ext. 244

(E-mail: cofsmedia@dial.pipex.com)

The Media Relations Unit is the link between the media and the Church, and is the first point of contact for journalists seeking information on the work and views of the Church's Boards and Committees. The Unit issues regular press releases on matters of interest and provides an audio release service to independent local radio. The Unit develops and maintains the Church's website (www.churchofscotland.org.uk). Unit staff maintain close links with a large network of media contacts and are happy to facilitate interviews with key personnel within the Church. The Unit also supports parish ministers and Church members by promoting local news and events on their behalf and offering advice on local media work.

2.   DESIGN SERVICES

(Tel: 0131-225 5722/240 2224; Fax: 0131-220 5407; E-mail: design@churchofscotland.co.uk)
This part of the Board's work is concerned with the design and production of a wide range of promotional literature, display materials and exhibitions. Members of staff are pleased to advise congregations and Presbyteries on their particular communications needs.

A mailing list is maintained to provide parish magazine editors with suitable material and resources for their publications. Anyone wishing to be added to this list should provide their name and address to the Department.

3. PATHWAY PRODUCTIONS – the Church's audio-visual production unit
(Tel: 0131-225 5722; Fax: 0131-240 2236; E-mail: pathway@cofscotland.org.uk)
From its premises at 123 George Street, Edinburgh EH2 4YN, the Unit produces and markets videos, tape-slide sets and audio cassettes. One of the Unit's key initiatives is developing webcasting as a new means of communication. Short training courses in television, radio and video are also held here. The Unit has pioneered Church production and use of video as a means of Christian communication. It also produces occasional programmes for broadcast television. In conjunction with the Media Relations Unit, Pathway supports religious output on Independent Local Radio.

Videos and audio cassettes may be hired or bought from Wesley Owen Bookshops in Scotland or bought through Pathway's distributor, Saint Andrew Press.

4. LIFE & WORK
(Tel: 0131-225 5722; Fax: 0131-240 2207; E-mail: magazine@lifeandwork.org)
Life & Work is the Church of Scotland's monthly magazine. Its purpose is to keep the Church informed about events in church life at home and abroad and to provide a forum for Christian opinion and debate on a variety of topics. It has an independent editorial policy. Contributions which are relevant to any aspect of the Christian faith are welcome.

The price of Life & Work this year is £1.20. With a circulation of around 46,000, it also offers advertisers a first-class opportunity to reach a discerning readership in all parts of Scotland.

5. SAINT ANDREW PRESS
(Tel: 0131-240 2253; Fax: 0131-220 3113; E-mail: rallen@cofscotland.org.uk)
Saint Andrew Press is the Church of Scotland's publishing house. Since its creation in 1954, it has published many titles that have made a major contribution to Christian literature. The much-loved series of New Testament commentaries by the late Professor William Barclay is world-renowned. The series is currently being sensitively updated for a twenty-first-century readership and is published as the New Daily Study Bible series in seventeen volumes. Other best-sellers include the Glasgow Gospel by Jamie Stuart, and now Outside Verdict by Harry Reid, a headline-grabbing, Scottish top-ten book that probes the very heart of the Church of Scotland and makes a series of radical, inspiring proposals. Saint Andrew Press has also published on behalf of the Church of Scotland Panel on Worship the critically acclaimed Common Order and the ecumenical songbook Common Ground.

Saint Andrew Press also acts as distributor for Wild Goose Publications, Pathway Productions and Church of Scotland stationery.

All proposals for new publications should be sent to the Head of Publishing in the form of a two-page description of the book and its readership together with one sample chapter. Saint Andrew Press staff are always willing to offer professional help and advice.

LOCAL BROADCASTING
The Board of Communication encourages the work of a number of ecumenical groups assisting local radio stations with their religious broadcasting. Enquiries about local religious broadcasting should be made to the Media Relations Unit (see above).

CHURCHES ADVISORY COUNCIL FOR LOCAL BROADCASTING (CACLB)
CACLB was formed in 1967 to provide an advisory body to the Churches and to the broadcasters. Membership of the Council is drawn from members of ACTS, the Roman Catholic Church and the Evangelical Alliance, with representatives of the BBC and ILR, together with three members co-opted from the Association of Christians in Broadcasting (see over).

Present Officers

President: Baroness Nicholson of Winterbourne MEP

Chairman: Rt Rev. Dr Tom Butler

Director: Peter Blackman, PO Box 6613, South Woodham Ferrers, Essex CM3 5DY
(Tel: 01245 322158; Fax: 01245 321957;
E-mail: office@caclb.org.uk; Website: www.caclb.org.uk)

ASSOCIATION OF CHRISTIANS IN BROADCASTING (ACB)

ACB was formed at a CACLB Conference in 1980 to meet the evident need for an association to provide 'mutual support, help and comfort' for Christians involved in local radio, in whatever role. Membership is also open to those who, though not directly involved in local radio, appreciate its importance and wish to keep in touch with its problems and development.

For further information about membership, contact Peter Blackman, PO Box 6613, South Woodham Ferrers, Essex CM3 5DY (Tel: 01245 322158; Fax: 01245 321957; E-mail: office@caclb.org.uk; Website: www.caclb.org.uk).

---

(28) CHURCH OF SCOTLAND TRUST

MEMBERSHIP

(Members are appointed by the General Assembly, on the Nomination of the Trust)

Chairman: Mr J.M. Hodge WS

Vice Chairman: Mr C.N. Mackay WS

Treasurer: Mr D.F. Ross MA CA

Secretary and Clerk: Mrs J.M. Hamilton BA

REMIT

The Church of Scotland Trust was established by Act of Parliament in 1932. The Trust's function since 1 January 1995 has been to hold properties outwith Scotland and to act as Trustee in a number of third-party trusts.

Further information can be obtained from the Secretary and Clerk of the Church of Scotland Trust, 121 George Street, Edinburgh EH2 4YN (Tel: 0131-240 2222; E-mail: jhamilton@ cofscotland.org.uk).

SECTION 2

General Information

(1) OTHER CHURCHES IN THE UNITED KINGDOM

ASSOCIATED PRESBYTERIAN CHURCHES
Clerk of Presbytery: Rev. A.N. McPhail, APC Manse, Polvimister Road, Oban PA34 5TN
    (Tel: 01631 567076).

THE REFORMED PRESBYTERIAN CHURCH OF SCOTLAND
Stated Clerk: Rev. G.M. Milligan, RP Manse, 1 Albert Terrace, London Road, Stranraer DG9 8AB.

THE FREE CHURCH OF SCOTLAND
Principal Clerk: Rev. James MacIver, The Mound, Edinburgh EH1 2LS (Tel: 0131-226 4978/5286;
    E-mail: freechurch@compuserve.com).

THE FREE PRESBYTERIAN CHURCH OF SCOTLAND
Clerk of Synod: Rev. John Macleod, 16 Matheson Road, Stornoway HS1 2LA (Tel: 01851
    702755).

THE UNITED FREE CHURCH OF SCOTLAND
General Secretary: Rev. John Fulton BSc BD, United Free Church Offices, 11 Newton Place,
    Glasgow G3 7PR (Tel: 0141-332 3435; E-mail: ufcos@charis.co.uk).

THE PRESBYTERIAN CHURCH IN IRELAND
Clerk of the General Assembly and General Secretary: Very Rev. Dr Samuel Hutchinson BA
    BD MTH DD, Church House, Fisherwick Place, Belfast BT1 6DW (Tel: 02890 322284;
    E-mail: clerk@presbyterianireland.org).

THE PRESBYTERIAN CHURCHES OF WALES
General Secretary: Rev. Ifan R.H. Roberts, 53 Richmond Road, Cardiff CF24 3WJ (Tel: 02920
    494913; Fax: 02920 464293; E-mail: ebcpcw@aol.com).

THE UNITED REFORMED CHURCH
General Secretary: Rev. David Cormick, 86 Tavistock Place, London WC1H 9RT (Tel: 020 7916
    2020; Fax: 020 7916 2021).

UNITED REFORMED CHURCH SCOTLAND SYNOD
Synod Clerk: Rev. Kenneth M. Forbes BA BD, Church House, PO Box 189, Glasgow G1 2BX
    (Tel: 0141-332 7667; E-mail: scotland@urc.org.uk).

BAPTIST UNION OF SCOTLAND
General Secretary: Rev. William G. Slack, 14 Aytoun Road, Glasgow G41 5RT (Tel: 0141-423
    6169; E-mail: admin@scottishbaptist.org.uk).

CONGREGATIONAL FEDERATION IN SCOTLAND
Rev. James Smith, Auchanshangan Drive, Saltcoats KA21 6DT.

RELIGIOUS SOCIETY OF FRIENDS (QUAKERS)
Clerk to the General Meeting of Scotland: Margaret Peacock, 16 Drumlin Drive, Milngavie,
    Glasgow G62 6LN (Tel: 0141-956 1183; E-mail: nmjpeacock@yahoo.co.uk).

ROMAN CATHOLIC CHURCH
The Rt Rev. Mgr Henry Docherty, General Secretariat, Bishops' Conference for Scotland, 64 Aitken Street, Airdrie ML6 6LT (Tel: 01236 764061; Fax: 01236 762489; E-mail: gensec@bpsconfscot.com).

THE SALVATION ARMY
Scotland Secretary: Major Robert McIntyre, Scotland Secretariat, 12A Dryden Road, Loanhead EH20 9LZ (Tel: 0131-440 9101; E-mail: scotland@salvationarmy.org.uk).

SCOTTISH EPISCOPAL CHURCH
General Secretary: Mr John F. Stuart, 21 Grosvenor Crescent, Edinburgh EH12 5EL (Tel: 0131-225 6357; E-mail: secgen@scotland.anglican.org).

THE SYNOD OF METHODIST CHURCH IN SCOTLAND
Secretary: Rev. David Cooper, Methodist Central Hall, West Tollcross, Edinburgh EH3 9BP (Tel: 0131-221 9029; E-mail: edinmethodistmission@talk21.com).

GENERAL SYNOD OF THE CHURCH OF ENGLAND
Secretary General: Mr William Fitall, Church House, Great Smith Street, London SW1P 3NZ (Tel: 020 7898 1000).

---

(2) OVERSEAS CHURCHES

PRESBYTERIAN CHURCH IN AMERICA
Stated Clerk: 1700 North Brown Road, Suite 105, Lawrenceville, GA 30043, USA (E-mail: ac@pcanet.org; Website: http://www. pcanet.org).

PRESBYTERIAN CHURCH IN CANADA
Clerk of Assembly: 50 Wynford Drive, North York, Ontario M3C 1J7, Canada (E-mail: pccadmin@presbycan.ca; Website: http://www.presbycan.ca).

UNITED CHURCH OF CANADA
General Secretary: Suite 300, 3250 Bloor Street West, Toronto, Ontario M8X 2Y4, Canada (Website: http://www.united-church.ca).

PRESBYTERIAN CHURCH (USA)
Stated Clerk: 100 Witherspoon Street, Louisville, KY 40202-1396, USA (E-mail: presbytel@pcusa.org; Website: http://www.pcusa.org).

REFORMED PRESBYTERIAN CHURCH IN NORTH AMERICA
Stated Clerk: 7408 Penn Avenue, Pittsburgh, PA15208, USA (Website: http://www.reformedpresbyterian.org).

CUMBERLAND PRESBYTERIAN CHURCH
General Secretary: 1978 Union Avenue, Memphis, TN 38104, USA (E-mail: gac@cumberland.org; Website: http://www.cumberland.org).

REFORMED CHURCH IN AMERICA
General Secretary: 475 Riverside Drive, NY 10115, USA (E-mail: rcamail@rca.org).

UNITED CHURCH OF CHRIST
General Minister: 700 Prospect Avenue, Cleveland, Ohio 44115, USA
Website: (http://www.ucc.org).

UNITING CHURCH IN AUSTRALIA
General Secretary: PO Box A2266, Sydney South, New South Wales 1235, Australia (E-mail:
enquiries@nat.uca.org.au).

PRESBYTERIAN CHURCH OF AUSTRALIA
Clerk of Assembly: PO Box 2196, Strawberry Hills, NSW 2012; 168 Chalmers Street, Surry
Hills, NSW 2010, Australia (E-mail: general@pcnsw.org.au).

PRESBYTERIAN CHURCH OF AOTEAROA, NEW ZEALAND
Executive Secretary: PO Box 9049, 100 Tory Street, Wellington, New Zealand (E-mail:
aes@pccnz.org.nz; Website: http://www.presbyterian.org.nz).

EVANGELICAL PRESBYTERIAN CHURCH, GHANA
Synod Clerk: PO Box 18, Ho, Volta Region, Ghana.

PRESBYTERIAN CHURCH OF GHANA
Synod Clerk: PO Box 1800, Accra, Ghana.

PRESBYTERIAN CHURCH OF EAST AFRICA
Depute Secretary General: PO Box 48268, Nairobi, Kenya.

CHURCH OF CENTRAL AFRICA PRESBYTERIAN
Senior Clerk, General Synod, PO Box 30398, Lilongwe, Malawi.
General Secretary, Blantyre Synod, PO Box 413, Blantyre, Malawi.
General Secretary, Livingstonia Synod, PO Box 112, Mzuzu, Malawi.
General Secretary, Nkhoma Synod, PO Box 45, Nkhoma, Malawi.

**IGREJA EVANGELICA DE CRISTO EM MOÇAMBIQUE (EVANGELICAL CHURCH
OF CHRIST IN MOZAMBIQUE)**
(Nampula) General Secretary: Cx. Postale 284, Nampula 70100, Mozambique.
(Zambezia) General Secretary: Cx. Postale 280, Zambezia, Quelimane, Mozambique.

PRESBYTERIAN CHURCH OF NIGERIA
Principal Clerk: PO Box 2635, Aba, Abia State, Nigeria.

UNITING PRESBYTERIAN CHURCH IN SOUTHERN AFRICA (SOUTH AFRICA)
General Secretary: PO Box 96188, Brixton 2019, South Africa.

UNITING PRESBYTERIAN CHURCH IN SOUTHERN AFRICA (ZIMBABWE)
Presbytery Clerk: PO Box CY224, Causeway, Harare, Zimbabwe.

PRESBYTERIAN CHURCH OF SUDAN (A)
Executive Secretary: PO Box 66168, Nairobi, Kenya.

PRESBYTERIAN CHURCH OF SUDAN (M)
General Secretary: PO Box 3421, Khartoum, Sudan.

UNITED CHURCH OF ZAMBIA
General Secretary: Nationalist Road at Burma Road, PO Box 50122, 15101 Ridgeway, Lusaka, Zambia.

CHURCH OF BANGLADESH
Moderator: Synod Office, 54 Johnson Road, Dhaka 1100, Bangladesh.

CHURCH OF NORTH INDIA
General Secretary: Synod Office, 16 Pandit Pant Marg, New Delhi, 110 001, India.

CHURCH OF SOUTH INDIA
General Secretary: Synod Office, 5 White's Road, Royapettah, Chennai 600 114, India.

PRESBYTERIAN CHURCH OF KOREA
General Secretary: CPO Box 1125, Seoul 110 611, Korea.

PRESBYTERIAN CHURCH IN THE REPUBLIC OF KOREA
General Secretary: 1501 The Korean Ecumenical Building, 136–156 Yunchi-Dong, Chongno-Ku, Seoul, Korea.

THE UNITED MISSION TO NEPAL
Executive Director: PO Box 126, Kathmandu, Nepal.

CHURCH OF PAKISTAN
General Secretary: Mission Compound, Daska, Distr Sialkot, Punjab, Pakistan.

PRESBYTERY OF LANKA
Moderator: 127/1 D S Senanayake Veedyan, Kandy, Sri Lanka.

PRESBYTERIAN CHURCH IN TAIWAN
General Secretary: 3 Lane 269 Roosevelt Road, Sec. 3, Taipei, Taiwan 10763, ROC.

CHURCH OF CHRIST IN THAILAND
General Secretary: 109 CCT (13th Floor), Surawong Road, Khet Bangrak, Bangkok 10500, Thailand.

PRESBYTERY OF GUYANA
Moderator: 81 Croal Street, PO Box 10151, Georgetown, Guyana.

NATIONAL PRESBYTERIAN CHURCH OF GUATEMALA
Executive Secretary: Av. Simeon Canas 7–13, Zona 2, Aptdo 655, Guatemala City, Guatemala (E-mail: ienpg@terra.com.gt).

UNITED CHURCH IN JAMAICA AND THE CAYMAN ISLANDS
General Secretary: 12 Carlton Crescent, PO Box 359, Kingston 10, Jamaica (E-mail: unitedchurch@colis.com).

PRESBYTERIAN CHURCH IN TRINIDAD AND TOBAGO
General Secretary: Box 92, Paradise Hill, San Fernando, Trinidad (E-mail: pctt@tstt.net.tt).

BELGIAN PROTESTANT CHURCH
Rue de Champ de Mars 5, B-1050 Bruxelles, Belgium (E-mail: epub@epub.be; Website: http://www.protestanet.be/epub).

REFORMED CHRISTIAN CHURCH IN CROATIA
Bishop's Office: Vladimira Nazora 31, HR-32100 Vinkovci, Croatia (E-mail: reformed.church.rcc@vk.tel.hr; Website: http://www.geocities.com/langh.geo/).

EVANGELICAL CHURCH OF THE CZECH BRETHREN
Moderator: Jungmannova 9, PO Box 466, CZ-11121 Praha 1, Czech Republic (E-mail: exumena@srcce.cz; Website: http://www.srcce.cz).

EGLISE REFORMEE DE FRANCE
General Secretary: 47 rue de Clichy, F-75311 Paris, France (E-mail: erf@unacerf.org; Website: http://www.eglise-reformee-fr.org).

HUNGARIAN REFORMED CHURCH
General Secretary: H-1440 Budapest, PO 5, Hungary (E-mail: zsinatko@axelero.hu; Website: http://www.reformatus.hu).

WALDENSIAN CHURCH
Moderator: Via Firenze 38, 00184, Rome, Italy (E-mail: tvmode@tin.it; Website: http://www.chiesavaldese.org).

NETHERLANDS REFORMED CHURCH
Landelijk Dienstcentrum Samen op Weg-Kerken, Postbus 8504, NL-3503 RM Utrecht (E-mail: ccs@ngk.nl; Website: http://www.ngk.nl).

REFORMED CHURCH IN ROMANIA
Bishop's Office: Str. IC Bratianu No. 51, R-3400, Cluj-Napoca, Romania (E-mail: office@reformatus.ro).

REFORMED CHRISTIAN CHURCH IN YUGOSLAVIA
Bishop's Office: Bratstva 26, YU-24323 Feketic, Yugoslavia.

SYNOD OF THE NILE OF THE EVANGELICAL CHURCH
General Secretary: Synod of the Nile of the Evangelical Church, PO Box 1248, Cairo, Egypt (E-mail: pcegypt@link.net).

DIOCESE OF THE EPISCOPAL CHURCH IN JERUSALEM AND THE MIDDLE EAST
Bishop's Office: PO Box 19122, Jerusalem 91191, via Israel (E-mail: ediosces@netvision.net.il; Website: http://www.jerusalem.anglican.org).

NATIONAL EVANGELICAL SYNOD OF SYRIA AND LEBANON
General Secretary: PO Box 70890, Antelias, Lebanon (E-mail: nessl@minero.net).

[Full information on Churches overseas may be obtained from the Board of World Mission.]

(3) SCOTTISH DIVINITY FACULTIES
[*denotes a Minister of the Church of Scotland]
[(R) Reader   (SL) Senior Lecturer   (L) Lecturer]

ABERDEEN
(University Faculty of Arts and Divinity and Christ's College)
King's College, Old Aberdeen AB24 3UB
(Tel: 01224 272380;   Fax: 01224 273750;
E-mail: divinity@abdn.ac.uk)

Master of Christ's College:	Right Rev. Prof. I.R. Torrance* TD MA BD DPhil
Head of School	
of Divinity and	
Religious Studies:	S. Kunin BA PhD

Professors:
Right Rev. I.R. Torrance* TD MA BD DPhil
(Patristics and Christian Ethics)
F.B. Watson BA DPhil (New Testament)
Rev. J. Swinton* BD PhD RNM (Practical Theology and Pastoral Care)

Lecturers:
K.T. Aitken BD PhD (Hebrew)
A.D. Clarke BA MA PhD (SL) (New Testament)
Rev. J.W. Drane MA PhD (SL) (Practical Theology)
S. Gathercole BA MA PhD (New Testament)
S. Kunin BA PhD (SL) (Anthropology of Religion)
Ian A. McFarland BA MDiv ThM MPhil PhD (Systematic Theology)
M.A. Mills MA PhD (Anthropology of Religion)
F.A. Murphy BA MA PhD (R) (Systematic Theology)
N.J. Thompson BA MA MTh PhD   (Church History)
Rev. Karla Wubbenhorst BA MDiv (Doctrine and Ethics)

ST ANDREWS
(University College of St Mary)
St Mary's College, St Andrews, Fife KY16 9JU
(Tel: 01334 462850/1;   Fax: 01334 462852)

Head of School and Principal: T.A. Hart BA PhD
Dean of Faculty: M.I. Aguilar BA MA STB PhD

Chairs:
R.J. Bauckham BA MA PhD FBA (New Testament Studies)
P.F. Esler BA LLB LLM DPhil (Biblical Criticism)

T.A. Hart BA PhD (Divinity)
R.A. Piper BA BD PhD (Christian Origins)
C.R. Seitz AB MTS MA MPhil PhD
  (Old Testament and Theological Studies)
A.J. Torrance* MA BD DrTheol (Systematic Theology)

Readerships, Senior Lectureships, Lectureships:

M.I. Aguilar BA MA STB PhD (SL) (Religion and Contextual Theology)
I.C. Bradley* BA MA BD DPhil (SL) (Practical Theology)
J.R. Davila BA MA PhD (Early Jewish Studies)
B.W. Longenecker BA MRel PhD (New Testament)
E.D. Reed BA PhD (Theology and Ethics)
N. MacDonald MA MPhil (Old Testament and Hebrew)

Teaching Fellows and Research Fellows:

S.R. Guthrie BMus BD PhD (RF) (Institute of Theology, Imagination and the Arts)
O. Crisp BD MTh PhD (TF) (Theology)

EDINBURGH
(School of Divinity and New College)
New College, Mound Place, Edinburgh EH1 2LX
(Tel: 0131-650 8900; Fax: 0131-650 1952; E-mail: divinity.faculty@ed.ac.uk)

Head of School: Prof. Stewart J. Brown BA MA PhD FRHistS
Principal of New College: Rev. A. Graeme Auld* MA BD PhD DLitt FSAScot

Chairs: Rev. A. Graeme Auld* MA BD PhD DLitt FSAScot
                              (Hebrew Bible)
                             Stewart J. Brown BA MA PhD FRHistS
                              (Ecclesiastical History)
                             Rev. David A.S. Fergusson* MA BD DPhil (Divinity)
                             Larry W. Hurtado BA MA PhD
                              (New Testament Language, Literature and Theology)
                             David Kerr MA BA DPhil
                              (Christianity in the Non-Western World)
                             Rev. William F. Storrar* MA BD PhD
                              (Christian Ethics and Practical Theology)
                             Nicolas Wyatt BA BD MTh PhD
                              (Ancient Near Eastern Religions)

Readers, Senior Lecturers and Lecturers:

Hebrew and Old Testament: A. Peter Hayman BA PhD (SL)
Timothy Lim BA MPhil DPhil (R)
David J. Reimer BTh BA MA MA (SL)

New Testament Language, Literature and Theology:
Helen K. Bond MTheol PhD (L)

Christian Ethics and Practical Theology:
Marcella Althaus Reid BTh PhD (SL)
Jolyon Mitchell BA MA (SL)
Michael S. Northcott MA PhD (R)
Murray Chalmers* MA (Part-time) (L)
Ewan Kelly* MB ChB BD (L)

Ecclesiastical History: Jane E.A. Dawson BA PhD DipEd (SL)
Jack Thompson BA PhD (SL)
Susan Hardman Moore MA PhD (L)

Systematic Theology: Nicholas S. Adams BA PhD (L)
John C. McDowell BD PhD (L)
Michael Purcell MA PhD PhL PhB (L)

Religious Studies: James L. Cox BA MDiv PhD (R)
Jeanne Openshaw BA MA PhD (L)

World Christianity: Elizabeth Kopping MA PhD DipSocSci MTh (L)

Fulton Lecturer in Speech and Communication:
Richard Ellis BSc MEd LGSM

GLASGOW
(School of Divinity and Trinity College)
4 The Square, University of Glasgow, Glasgow G12 8QQ
(Tel: 0141-330 6526; Fax: 0141-330 4943; E-mail: m.macmillan@arts.gla.ac.uk)

Head of School: Professor John M.G. Barclay
Head of Department: Dr Mona Siddiqui
Principal of Trinity College: Rev. Prof. George M. Newlands*

Chairs: John M.G. Barclay MA PhD (New Testament and Christian Origins)
Joseph Houston MA BD DPhil (Philosophical Theology)
Rev. David Jasper MA PhD BD DD (Literature and Theology)
Rev. Donald Macleod MA (Visiting Hon. Professor)

Rev. George M. Newlands* MA BD PhD (Divinity)
Rev. John K. Riches MA (Hon. Professor)
Perry Schmidt-Leukel Dipl theol MA Dr theol Dr theol habil (Munich)
 (Systematic Theology and Religious Studies)
Reader: W. Ian P. Hazlett BA BD Dr theol DLitt (Ecclesiastical History)

Senior Lecturers and Lecturers: Theology and Religious Studies:
Julie P. Clague BSc PGCE PGDip MTh (L)
Rev. Alastair G. Hunter* MSc BD PhD (SL)
Rev. Jeffrey F. Keuss BA MDiv PhD (L)
Sarah Nicholson MTheol PhD (L)
Lesley Orr MA BD PhD (L)
Lloyd V.J. Ridgeon BA MA PhD (L)
Yvonne M. Sherwood BA PhD DipJS (SL)
Mona Siddiqui MA MLL PhD DLitt (SL)
Kyoshi Tsuchiya MA PhD (L)
Heather E. Walton BA MA(Econ) PhD (L)

Centre for Study of Literature, Theology and the Arts:
Director: Rev. Dr Jeffrey F. Keuss
Assistant Director: Dr Kyoshi Tsuchiya

---

(4) SOCIETIES AND ASSOCIATIONS

The undernoted list shows the name of the Association, along with the name and address of the Secretary.

INTER-CHURCH ASSOCIATIONS

THE FELLOWSHIP OF ST ANDREW: The fellowship promotes dialogue between churches of the east and the west in Scotland. Further information available from Mr Peter Desmond, 4 Ballengeich Road, Stirling FK8 1TN (Tel: 01786 479875).

THE FELLOWSHIP OF ST THOMAS: An ecumenical association formed to promote informed interest in and learn from the experience of Churches in South Asia (India, Pakistan, Bangladesh, Nepal, Sri Lanka). Secretary: Dr R.L. Robinson, 43 Underwood Road, Burnside, Rutherglen, Glasgow G73 3TE (Tel: 0141-643 0612).

THE SCOTTISH ORDER OF CHRISTIAN UNITY: Secretary: Rev. William D. Brown MA, 121 Dalkeith Road, Edinburgh EH16 5AJ (Tel/Fax: 0131-667 1124; E-mail: wdbrown@woolsackbc.fsnet.co.uk; Website: www.socu.org.uk).

CHURCH PASTORAL AID SOCIETY (CPAS): Consultant for Scotland: Rev. Richard W. Higginbottom, 2 Highfield Place, Bankfoot, Perth PH1 4AX (Tel: 01738 787429). A home mission agency working cross-denominationally through consultancy training and resources to encourage churches in local evangelism: accredited officially to the Board of National Mission.

FRONTIER YOUTH TRUST: Encourages and resources those engaged in youth work, particularly with disadvantaged young people. Co-ordinator: Feri Salvesen, c/o Anderson/ Kelvingrove Church, 759b Argyle Street, Glasgow G3 8DS (Tel: 0141-204 4800).

IONA COMMUNITY: Leader: Rev. Kathy Galloway, Fourth Floor, Savoy House, 140 Sauchiehall Street, Glasgow G2 3DH (Tel: 0141-332 6343; Fax: 0141-332 1090); Warden: Ms Jan Sutch Pickard, Iona Abbey, Isle of Iona, Argyll PA76 6SN (Tel: 01681 700404; E-mail: ionacomm@gla.iona.org.uk; Website: http://www.iona.org.uk).

SCOTTISH CHRISTIAN YOUTH ASSEMBLY: Chairperson: Mr Eric Whitten, 41 Kingston Avenue, Glasgow G14 0EB.

SCOTTISH CHURCHES HOUSING AGENCY: Provides the Churches with information, education, advice and support concerning homelessness. Co-ordinator: Alastair Cameron, 28 Albany Street, Edinburgh EH1 3QH (Tel: 0131-477 4500; Fax: 0131-477 2710; E-mail: scotchho@ednet.co.uk; Website: www.churches-housing.org).

SCOTTISH CHURCHES WORLD EXCHANGE: Arranges overseas placements for forty to fifty volunteers annually. Placements are for periods of up to two years, mainly in Africa, Asia, Latin America and the Middle East. Chief Executive: Rev. Robert S. Anderson, St Colm's International House, 23 Inverleith Terrace, Edinburgh EH3 5NS (Tel: 0131-315 4444; Website: www.worldexchange.org.uk).

ST COLM'S INTERNATIONAL HOUSE: English-language and Capacity Building Courses for community leaders from the developing world. A place to meet in the heart of the Capital on the perimeter of the Royal Botanic Gardens (Tel: 0131-315 4444).

SCOTTISH JOINT COMMITTEE ON RELIGIOUS AND MORAL EDUCATION: Ms Susan Leslie, 121 George Street, Edinburgh EH2 4YN (Tel: 0131-225 5722), and Mr Lachlan Bradley, 6 Clairmont Gardens, Glasgow G3 7LW (Tel: 0141-353 3595).

SCOTTISH NATIONAL COUNCIL OF YMCAs: National General Secretary: Mr Peter Crory, 11 Rutland Street, Edinburgh EH1 2AE (Tel: 0131-228 1464; E-mail: info@ymcascotland.org; Website: www.ymcascotland.org).

INTERSERVE SCOTLAND: Interserve is an evangelical and interdenominational mission agency with roots stretching back over 150 years to India. Currently, the International Fellowship of Interserve is active in twenty-six countries in the Middle East and Asia, where nearly 600 missionary partners serve, twenty-four of whom are from Scotland. Director: Mr John M. Jackson, 12 Elm Avenue, Lenzie, Glasgow G66 4HJ (Tel: 0141-578 0207; Fax: 0141-578 0208; E-mail: info@isscott.org; Website: www.interservescotland.org.uk).

SCRIPTURE UNION SCOTLAND: 9 Canal Street, Glasgow G4 0AB (Tel: 0141-332 1162; Fax: 0141-352 7600; E-mail: postmaster@scriptureunionscotland.org.uk; Website: http://www.suscotland.org.uk).

STUDENT CHRISTIAN MOVEMENT: Mr Nick Davies, 1 Bristo Square, Edinburgh EH8 9AL (Tel: 0131-667 4321).

UNIVERSITIES AND COLLEGES CHRISTIAN FELLOWSHIP: Alan Hewerdine, 38 De Montfort Street, Leicester LE1 7GP (Tel: 0116-255 1700; E-mail: agh@uccf.org.uk).

WORLD DAY OF PRAYER: SCOTTISH COMMITTEE: Convener: Col. Ruth Flett; Secretary: Mrs Margaret Broster, St Columba's Manse, Dipple Road, Kilbirnie, Ayrshire KA25 7JU (Tel: 01505 682098; Fax 01505 684024; E-mail: sec@wdpscotland.org.uk; Website: http://www.wdpscotland.org.uk).

CHURCH OF SCOTLAND SOCIETIES

ASSOCIATION OF GENERAL ASSEMBLY AND PRESBYTERY CLERKS: Rev. R.A. Baigrie MA, 32 Inchcolm Terrace, South Queensferry EH30 9NA (Tel: 0131-331 4311).

AROS (Association of Returned Overseas Staff of the Church of Scotland Board of World Mission): Hon. Secretary: Miss Mary S. Ritchie, 1 Afton Bridgend, New Cumnock KA18 4AX (Tel: 01290 338218).

SCOTTISH CHURCH SOCIETY: Secretary: Rev. Matthew Z. Ross LLB BD FSAScot, 89/62 Holyrood Road, Edinburgh EH8 8BA (Tel: 0131-557 5626).

SCOTTISH CHURCH THEOLOGY SOCIETY: Rev. William D. Brown MA, 121 Dalkeith Road, Edinburgh EH16 5AJ (Tel: 0131-667 1124).

SOCIETY OF FRIENDS OF ST ANDREW'S JERUSALEM: Hon. Secretary: Major D.J. McMicking LVO, Board of World Mission, 121 George Street, Edinburgh EH2 4YN. Hon. Treasurer: Mr Donald Ross, General Treasurer, The Church of Scotland, 121 George Street, Edinburgh EH2 4YN (Tel: 0131-225 5722).

THE CHURCH OF SCOTLAND CHAPLAINS' ASSOCIATION: Hon. Secretary: Rev. Donald M. Stephen TD MA BD ThM, 10 Hawkhead Crescent, Edinburgh EH16 6LR (Tel: 0131-658 1216).

THE CHURCH OF SCOTLAND RETIRED MINISTERS' ASSOCIATION: Hon. Secretary: Rev. Elspeth G. Dougall MA BD, 60B Craigmillar Park, Edinburgh EH16 5PU (Tel: 0131-668 1342).

THE CHURCH SERVICE SOCIETY: Secretary: Rev. Neil N. Gardner MA BD, Cambridge Street, Alyth, Blairgowrie PH11 8AW (Tel: 01828 632104).

THE IRISH MINISTERS' FRATERNAL: Secretary: Rev. Colin R. Williamson LLB BD, Manse of Aberdalgie, Perth PH2 0QD (Tel: 01738 625854).

THE NATIONAL CHURCH ASSOCIATION: Membership Secretary: Miss Margaret P. Milne, 10 Balfron Crescent, Hamilton ML3 9UH.

BIBLE SOCIETIES

THE SCOTTISH BIBLE SOCIETY: Executive Director: Rev. M. Douglas Campbell BA MDiv, 7 Hampton Terrace, Edinburgh EH12 5XU (Tel: 0131-337 9701).

WEST OF SCOTLAND BIBLE SOCIETY: Rev. Alexander Macdonald MA BD, Manse of Neilston, Glasgow G78 3NP (Tel: 0141-881 1958).

GENERAL

THE BOYS' BRIGADE: Scottish Headquarters, Carronvale House, Carronvale Road, Larbert FK5 3LH (Tel: 01324 562008; Fax: 01324 552323; E-mail: carronvale@boys-brigade.org.uk).

THE GIRLS' BRIGADE: Scottish Headquarters, Paxton House, 11A Woodside Crescent, Charing Cross, Glasgow G3 7UL (Tel: 0141-332 1765).

GIRLGUIDING SCOTLAND: 16 Coates Crescent, Edinburgh EH3 7AH (Tel: 0131-226 4511; Fax: 0131-220 4828; E-mail: administrator@girlguiding-scot.org.uk).

THE SCOUT ASSOCIATION: Scottish Headquarters, Fordell Firs, Hillend, Dunfermline KY11 7HQ (Tel: 01383 419073; E-mail: shq@scouts-scotland.org.uk).

BOYS' AND GIRLS' CLUBS OF SCOTLAND: 88 Giles Street, Edinburgh EH6 6BZ (Tel: 0131-555 1729; E-mail: bgcs@freezone.co.uk).

YOUTH SCOTLAND: Balfour House, 19 Bonnington Grove, Edinburgh EH6 4BL (Tel: 0131-554 2561; fax: 0131-454 3438; E-mail: office@youthscotland.org.uk).

CHRISTIAN AID SCOTLAND: National Secretary: Rev. John Wylie, 41 George IV Bridge, Edinburgh EH1 1EL (Tel: 0131-220 1254; Fax: 0131-225 8861).

FEED THE MINDS: Scottish Secretary, Mr Stanley Bonthron, 41 George IV Bridge, Edinburgh EH1 1EL (Tel: 0131-226 5254; Fax: 0131-225 8861; E-mail: ftm@churchuk.net).

LADIES' GAELIC SCHOOLS AND HIGHLAND BURSARY ASSOCIATION: Mr Donald J. Macdonald, 9 Hatton Place, Edinburgh EH9 1UD (Tel: 0131-667 1740).

COUPLE COUNSELLING SCOTLAND: Chief Executive: Mrs Hilary Campbell, 18 York Place, Edinburgh EH1 3EP (Tel: 0131-558 9669; Fax: 0131-556 6596; E-mail: enquiries@couplecounselling.org.uk; Website: www.couplecounselling.org).

RUTHERFORD HOUSE: Warden: Rev. Robert Fyall MA BD PhD, 17 Claremont Park, Edinburgh EH6 7PJ (Tel: 0131-554 1206; Fax: 0131-555 1002).

SCOTTISH CHURCH HISTORY SOCIETY: Rev. Peter H. Donald MA PhD BD, 39 Southside Road, Inverness IV2 4XA (Tel: 01463 231140; Fax: 01463 230537).

SCOTTISH EVANGELICAL THEOLOGY SOCIETY: Secretary: Rev. Canon Peter Cook, Bel Abri, Leadgate, Alston, Cumbria CA9 3EL (Tel: 01434 381873).

CHRISTIAN ENDEAVOUR IN SCOTLAND: Winning, Teaching and Training Youngsters for Christ and the Church: The Murray Library, 8 Shore Street, Anstruther, Fife KY10 3EA (Tel: 01333 310345).

TEARFUND: 100 Church Road, Teddington TW11 8QE (Tel: 020 8977 9144). Manager: Peter Chirnside, Tearfund Scotland, Challenge House, Canal Street, Glasgow G4 0AD (Tel: 0141-332 3621).

THE LEPROSY MISSION: 89 Barnton Street, Stirling FK8 1HJ (Tel: 01786 449266; Fax 01786 449766). Executive Director: Miss Linda Todd. Scottish Meetings Co-ordinator: Rev. J.G. McConnell, 7 Henderson Court, East Calder EH53 0RQ (Tel: 01506 881125).

THE LORD'S DAY OBSERVANCE SOCIETY: Rev. A. Hanna, 2 The Gallolee, Edinburgh EH13 9QJ (Tel: 0131-441 3116).

THE MONTHLY VISITOR TRACT SOCIETY: 122 Thirlestane Road, Edinburgh EH9 1AN.

THE SCOTTISH REFORMATION SOCIETY: The Society, The Magdalene Chapel, 41 Cowgate, Edinburgh EH1 1JR (Tel: 0131-220 1450).

THE SOCIETY IN SCOTLAND FOR PROPAGATING CHRISTIAN KNOWLEDGE: David McLetchie Esq., Tods Murray WS, 66 Queen Street, Edinburgh EH2 4NE (Tel: 0131-226 4771).

THE WALDENSIAN MISSIONS AID SOCIETY FOR WORK IN ITALY: David A. Lamb SSC, 36 Liberton Drive, Edinburgh EH16 6NN (Tel: 0131-664 3059; E-mail: dlamb@dial.pipex.com.uk).

YWCA SCOTLAND: Chief Executive: Elaine Samson, 7B Randolph Crescent, Edinburgh EH3 7TH (Tel: 0131-225 7592; Website: info@ywcascotland.org).

---

(5) TRUSTS AND FUNDS

THE SOCIETY FOR THE BENEFIT OF THE SONS AND DAUGHTERS
OF THE CLERGY OF THE CHURCH OF SCOTLAND

Chairman: Dr Douglas Grant
Secretary and Treasurer: R. Graeme Thom FCA
                                17 Melville Street
                                Edinburgh EH3 7PH (Tel: 0131-473 3500)

Annual grants are made to assist in the education of the children (normally between the ages of 12 and 25 years) of ministers of the Church of Scotland. The Society also gives grants to aged and infirm daughters of ministers and ministers' unmarried daughters and sisters who are in need. Applications are to be lodged by 31 May in each year.

THE GLASGOW SOCIETY OF THE SONS AND DAUGHTERS OF MINISTERS
OF THE CHURCH OF SCOTLAND

President: Rev. John P. Cubie
Secretary and Treasurer: R. Graeme Thom FCA
                                17 Melville Street
                                Edinburgh EH3 7PH (Tel: 0131-473 3500)

The Society's primary purpose is to grant financial assistance to children (no matter what age) of deceased ministers of the Church of Scotland. Applications are to be submitted by 1 February in each year. To the extent that funds are available, grants are also given for the children of ministers or retired ministers, although such grants are normally restricted to students. These latter grants are considered in conjunction with the Edinburgh-based Society. Limited funds are also available for individual application for special needs or projects. Applications are to be submitted by 31 May in each year. Emergency applications can be dealt with at any time when need arises. Application forms may be obtained from the Secretary.

HOLIDAYS FOR MINISTERS

The undernoted hotels provide special terms for ministers and their families. Fuller information may be obtained from the establishments:

CRIEFF HYDRO HOTEL and MURRAYPARK HOTEL: The William Meikle Trust Fund and Paton Fund make provision whereby active ministers and their spouses, members of the Diaconate and other full-time Church workers may enjoy the accommodation and leisure facilities. Facilities available are Leisure Centre, Lagoon, Cinema and many others both indoor and out. Self-catering Chalets are also available. Enquiries to the Accommodation Sales Team, Crieff Hydro Hotel, Crieff PH7 3LQ (Tel: 01764 651670; E-mail enquiries@crieffhydro.com).

THE CINTRA BEQUEST: The Trust provides financial assistance towards the cost of accommodation in Scotland for missionaries on leave, or for ministers on temporary holiday, or on rest. Applications should be made to Mrs J.S. Wilson, Solicitor, 121 George Street, Edinburgh EH2 4YN.

THE LYALL BEQUEST: Makes available the following benefits to ministers of the Church of Scotland:
1. A payment towards the cost of holiday accommodation at any hotel or guest house or self-catering accommodation in St Andrews will be paid to any minister and to his or her spouse at the rate of £10 per day each for a minimum stay of three days and a maximum stay of one week. Due to the number of applications which the Trustees now receive, an applicant will not be considered to be eligible if he or she has received a grant from the Bequest during the three years prior to the holiday for which application is made. Applications should be made prior to the holiday to the Secretaries.
2. Grants towards costs of sickness and convalescence so far as not covered by the National Health Service or otherwise may be available to applicants, who should apply to the Secretaries giving relevant details.
All communications should be addressed to Pagan Osborne, Solicitors, Secretaries to the Lyall Bequest, 106 South Street, St Andrews KY16 9QD (Tel: 01334 475001; E-mail: elcalderwood@pagan.co.uk).

MARGARET AND JOHN ROSS TRAVELLING FUND: Offers grants to ministers and their spouses for travelling and other expenses for trips to the Holy Land where the purpose is recuperation or relaxation. Applications should be made to the Secretary and Clerk, Church of Scotland Trust, 121 George Street, Edinburgh EH2 4YN (Tel: 0131-240 2222; E-mail: jhamilton@cofscotland.org.uk).

The undernoted represents a list of the more important trusts available for ministers, students and congregations. A brief indication is given of the trust purposes, but application should be made in each case to the person named for full particulars and forms of application.

THE ABERNETHY TRUST: Offers residential accommodation and outdoor activities for Youth Fellowships, Church family weekends, Bible Classes and so on at four outdoor centres in Scotland.

Further details from the Executive Director, Abernethy Trust, Nethybridge PH25 3ED (Tel/Fax: 01479 821279; Website: www.abernethytrust.org.uk).

THE ARROL TRUST: The object of the Trust is 'to promote the benefit and advance the education of young people between the ages of 16 and 25 years who are physically or mentally disadvantaged or are in necessitous circumstances by assisting such persons to gain experience through education and training for their future careers through travel within or without the United Kingdom'. Further details and forms of application can be obtained from C.S. Kennedy WS, Lindsays WS, 11 Atholl Crescent, Edinburgh EH3 8HE (Tel: 0131-229 1212).

THE BAIRD TRUST: Assists in the building and repair of churches and halls, endows Parishes and generally assists the work of the Church of Scotland. Apply to Ronald D. Oakes CA ACMA, 182 Bath Street, Glasgow G2 4HG (Tel: 0141-332 0476; Fax: 0141-331 0874).

THE REV. ALEXANDER BARCLAY BEQUEST: Assists mother, daughter, sister or niece of deceased minister of the Church of Scotland who at the time of his death was acting as his housekeeper and who is in needy circumstances. Apply to Robert Hugh Allan LLB DipLP NP, Pomphreys, 79 Quarry Street, Hamilton ML3 7AG (Tel: 01698 891616).

BELLAHOUSTON BEQUEST FUND: Gives grants to Protestant evangelical denominations in the City of Glasgow and certain areas within five miles of the city boundary for building and repairing churches and halls and the promotion of religion. Apply to Mr John A.M. Cuthbert, Mitchells Roberton, 36 North Hanover Street, Glasgow G1 2AD.

BEQUEST FUND FOR MINISTERS: Assists ministers in outlying districts with manse furnishings, pastoral efficiency aids, educational or medical costs. Apply to A. Linda Parkhill CA, 60 Wellington Street, Glasgow G2 6HJ.

CARNEGIE TRUST: In cases of hardship, the Carnegie Trust is prepared to consider applications by students of Scottish birth or extraction (at least one parent born in Scotland), or who have had at least two years' education at a secondary school in Scotland, for financial assistance with the payment of their fees for a first degree. For further details, students should apply to the Secretary, Carnegie Trust for the Universities of Scotland, Cameron House, Abbey Park Place, Dunfermline, Fife KY12 7PZ (Tel: 01383 622148; E-mail: jgray@carnegie-trust.org; Website: www.carnegie-trust.org).

CHURCH OF SCOTLAND INSURANCE CO. LTD: Undertakes insurance of Church property and pays surplus profits to Church schemes. The company can also arrange household insurance for members and adherents of the Church of Scotland. At 67 George Street, Edinburgh EH2 2JG (Tel: 0131-220 4119; Fax: 0131-220 4120; E-mail: enquiries@cosic.co.uk).

CHURCH OF SCOTLAND MINISTRY BENEVOLENT FUND: Makes grants to retired men and women who have been ordained or commissioned for the ministry of the Church of Scotland and to widows, widowers, orphans, spouses or children of such, who are in need. Apply to the General Secretary, Board of Ministry, 121 George Street, Edinburgh EH2 4YN (Tel: 0131-225 5722).

CLARK BURSARY: Awarded to accepted candidate(s) for the ministry of the Church of Scotland whose studies for the ministry are pursued at the University of Aberdeen. Applications or recommendations for the Bursary to the Clerk to the Presbytery of Aberdeen, Mastrick Church, Greenfern Road, Aberdeen AB16 6TR by 16 October annually.

THE REV. JOHN CLARK FUND: Provides annuities (1) for blind persons and (2) for orphan or fatherless children of ministers or missionaries of the Church of Scotland. Apply to Fyfe Ireland WS, Orchard Brae House, 30 Queensferry Road, Edinburgh EH4 2HG.

CRAIGCROOK MORTIFICATION:
Chairman: G.A. Henry WS
Clerk and Factor: R. Graeme Thom FCA
                                   17 Melville Street
                                   Edinburgh EH3 7PH (Tel: 0131-473 3500)
Pensions are paid to poor men and women over 60 years old, born in Scotland or who have resided in Scotland for not less than ten years. At present, pensions amount to £600 p.a.
   Ministers are invited to notify the Clerk and Factor of deserving persons and should be prepared to act as a referee on the application form.

THE ALASTAIR CRERAR TRUST FOR SINGLE POOR: Provides churches, Christian organisations and individual Christians with grants to help single adults and groups of single people, who live on low incomes and have little capital, to improve their quality of life. Apply to the Secretary, Michael I.D. Sturrock, Garden Flat, 34 Mayfield Terrace, Edinburgh EH9 1RZ (Tel: 0131-668 3524).

CROMBIE SCHOLARSHIP: Provides grants annually on the nomination of the Deans of Faculty of Divinity of the Universities of St Andrews, Glasgow, Aberdeen and Edinburgh, who each nominate one matriculated student who has taken a University course in Greek (Classical or Hellenistic) and Hebrew. Award by recommendation only.

THE DRUMMOND TRUST: Makes grants towards the cost of publication of books of 'sound Christian doctrine and outreach'. The Trustees are willing to receive grant requests towards the cost of audio-visual programme material, but not equipment. Requests for application forms should be made to the Secretaries, Hill and Robb, 3 Pitt Terrace, Stirling FK8 2EY (Tel: 01786 450985; E-mail: douglaswhyte@hillandrobb.co.uk). Manuscripts should *not* be sent.

THE DUNCAN TRUST: Makes grants annually to students for the ministry in the Faculties of Arts and Divinity. Preference is given to those born or educated within the bounds of the former Presbytery of Arbroath. Applications not later than 31 October to G.J.M. Dunlop, Brothockbank House, Arbroath DD11 1NJ (Tel: 01241 872683).

ESDAILE TRUST:
Chairman: Dr Douglas Grant
Clerk and Treasurer: R. Graeme Thom FCA
                                   17 Melville Street
                                   Edinburgh EH3 7PH (Tel: 0131-473 3500)
Assists education and advancement of daughters of ministers, missionaries and widowed deaconesses of the Church of Scotland between 12 and 25 years of age. Applications are to be lodged by 31 May in each year.

FERGUSON BEQUEST FUND: For the maintenance and promotion of religious ordinances and education and missionary operations in the first instance in the Counties of Ayr, Kirkcudbright,

Wigtown, Lanark, Renfrew and Dunbarton. Apply to Ronald D. Oakes CA ACMA, 182 Bath Street, Glasgow G2 4HG (Tel: 0141-332 0476; Fax: 0141-331 0874).

GEIKIE BEQUEST: Makes small grants to students for the ministry, including students studying for entry to the University, preference being given to those not eligible for SAAS awards. Apply to the Accountant, Board of Ministry, 121 George Street, Edinburgh EH2 4YN.

JAMES GILLAN'S BURSARY FUND: Bursaries are available for students for the ministry who were born or whose parents or parent have resided and had their home for not less than three years continually in the old counties (not Districts) of Moray or Nairn. Apply to R. and R. Urquhart, 121 High Street, Forres IV36 0AB.

HALDANE TRUST FUND: Provides grants to ministers of the Church of Scotland on their first induction, towards the purchase of theological books. Apply to Bennett and Robertson LLP Solicitors, 25 George IV Bridge, Edinburgh EH1 1EP (Tel: 0131-226 2011).

HAMILTON BURSARY TRUST: Awarded, subject to the intention to serve overseas under the Church of Scotland Board of World Mission or to serve with some other Overseas Mission Agency approved by the Committee, to a student at the University of Aberdeen. Preference given to a student born or residing in (1) Parish of Skene, (2) Parish of Echt, (3) the Presbytery of Aberdeen, Kincardine and Deeside, or Gordon; failing which to Accepted Candidate(s) for the Ministry of the Church of Scotland whose studies for the Minstry are pursued at Aberdeen University. Applications or recommendations for the Bursary to the Clerk to the Presbytery of Aberdeen by 16 October annually.

MARTIN HARCUS BEQUEST: Makes annual grants to candidates for the ministry resident within the City of Edinburgh. Applications to the Clerk to the Presbytery of Edinburgh, 10 Palmerston Place, Edinburgh EH12 5AA by 15 October.

THE HOGARTH FUND: Provides annuities to orphan or fatherless children of ministers and missionaries of the Church of Scotland. Apply to Fyfe Ireland WS, Orchard Brae House, 30 Queensferry Road, Edinburgh EH4 2HG.

THE HOPE TRUST: Gives some support to organisations involved in combating drink and drugs, and has as its main purpose the promotion of the Reformed Faith throughout the world. There is also a Scholarship programme for Postgraduate Theology Study in Scotland. Apply to Robert P. Miller SSC LLB, 31 Moray Place, Edinburgh EH3 6BY (Tel: 0131-226 5151).

GILLIAN MACLAINE BURSARY FUND: Open to candidates for the ministry of the Church of Scotland of Scottish or Canadian nationality. Preference is given to Gaelic-speakers. Bursaries are awarded after an examination which is held annually in November. Information and application forms from Rev. Jeffrey A. McCormick BD, The Manse, Ardchattan, Connel, Argyll PA37 1QZ (Tel: 01631 710364; E-mail: akph64@uk.uumail.com).

THE MISSES ANN AND MARGARET McMILLAN'S BEQUEST: Makes grants to ministers of the Free and United Free Churches, and of the Church of Scotland, in charges within the Synod of Argyll, with income not exceeding the minimum stipend of the Church of Scotland. Apply by 30 June in each year to Business Manager, Royal Bank of Scotland, 37 Victoria Street, Rothesay, Isle of Bute PA20 0AP.

THE MANSE AUXILIARY: Convener: Mrs Jean Baigrie, 32 Inchcolm Terrace, South Queensferry EH30 9NA (Tel: 0131-331 4311). Assists with clothing and household linen to parish ministers, missionaries, ministers' widows and others, especially those in remote areas. Enquiries to the Convener or to the Secretary, Miss Joan McNeel-Caird, 2/26 Goldenacre Terrace, Edinburgh EH3 5RD (Tel: 0131-551 2720).

MORGAN BURSARY FUND: Makes grants to students for the ministry in Arts and Divinity at the University of Glasgow. Apply to Rev. David W. Lunan MA BD, 260 Bath Street, Glasgow G2 4JP (Tel/Fax: 0141-332 6606).

NOVUM TRUST: Provides small short-term grants to initiate projects in Christian research and action which cannot readily be financed from other sources. Special consideration is given to proposals aimed at the welfare of young people, the training of lay people, and new ways of communicating the faith. Applications to Rev. Alex M. Millar, 121 George Street, Edinburgh EH2 4YN (E-mail: amillar@cofscotland.org.uk).

PARK MEMORIAL BURSARY FUND: Provides grants for the benefit of Divinity students from the Presbytery of Glasgow who are nominated candidates under full-time training for the Ministry of the Church of Scotland. Apply to Rev. David W. Lunan MA BD, Presbytery of Glasgow, 260 Bath Street, Glasgow G2 4JP (Tel: 0141-332 6606).

PATON TRUST: Assists ministers in ill health to have a recuperative holiday outwith, and free from the cares of, their parishes. Apply to Iain A.T. Mowat CA, Alexander Sloan, Chartered Accountants, 144 West George Street, Glasgow G2 2HG (Tel: 0141-354 0354; Fax: 0141-354 0355; E-mail iatm@alexandersloan.co.uk).

RENFIELD STREET TRUST: Assists in the building and repair of churches and halls. Apply to Ronald D. Oakes CA ACMA, 182 Bath Street, Glasgow G2 4HG (Tel: 0141-332 0476; Fax 0141-331 0874).

SCOTTISH CHURCHES ARCHITECTURAL HERITAGE TRUST: Assists congregations of any denomination in the preservation of churches regularly used for public worship and of architectural value and historic interest. Apply to the Secretary, 15 North Bank Street, The Mound, Edinburgh EH1 2LP (Tel/Fax: 0131-225 8644).

SMIETON FUND: Makes small holiday grants to ministers on the minimum stipend. Applications to the General Secretary, Board of Ministry, 121 George Street, Edinburgh EH2 4YN.

MARY DAVIDSON SMITH CLERICAL AND EDUCATIONAL FUND FOR ABERDEENSHIRE: Assists ministers who have been ordained for five years or over and are in full charge of a congregation in Aberdeen, Aberdeenshire and the north, to purchase books, or to travel for educational purposes, and assists their children with scholarships for further education or vocational training. Apply to Alan J. Innes MA LLB, 100 Union Street, Aberdeen AB10 1QR.

THE NAN STEVENSON CHARITABLE TRUST FOR RETIRED MINISTERS: Provides houses, or loans to purchase houses, for retired ministers or missionaries on similar terms to the Housing and Loan Fund, with preference given to those with a North Ayrshire connection. Secretary: Rev. David Broster, Manse of St Columba's, Kilbirnie KA25 7JU.

SYNOD OF ARGYLL BURSARY FUND: Provides book grants for candidates for the ministry of the Church of Scotland who are native to or have strong connections within the bounds of the former Synod of Argyll (i.e. the Presbyteries of Dunoon, Lorn and Mull and South Argyll). Applications should be made by 31 October to Rev. Jeffrey A. McCormick BD, The Manse, Ardchattan, Connel, Argyll PA37 1QZ (Tel: 01631 710364; E-mail: akph64@uk.uumail.com).

SYNOD OF GRAMPIAN CHILDREN OF THE CLERGY FUND: Makes annual grants to children of deceased ministers. Apply to Rev. Iain U. Thomson, Clerk and Treasurer, The Manse, Skene, Westhill AB32 6LX.

SYNOD OF GRAMPIAN WIDOWS FUND: Makes annual grants (currently £225 p.a.) to widows of deceased ministers who have served in a charge in the former Synod. Apply to Rev. Iain U. Thomson, Clerk and Treasurer, The Manse, Skene, Westhill AB32 6LX.

YOUNG MINISTERS' FURNISHING LOAN FUND: Makes loans (of £1,000) to ministers in their first charge to assist with furnishing the manse. Apply to the Accountant, Board of Ministry, 121 George Street, Edinburgh EH2 4YN.

---

(6) RECENT LORD HIGH COMMISSIONERS
TO THE GENERAL ASSEMBLY

1965/66	The Hon. Lord Birsay CBE QC TD
1967/68	The Rt Hon. Lord Reith of Stonehaven GCVO GBE CB TD
1969	Her Majesty the Queen attended in person
1970	The Rt Hon. Margaret Herbison PC
1971/72	The Rt Hon. Lord Clydesmuir of Braidwood CB MBE TD
1973/74	The Rt Hon. Lord Ballantrae of Auchairne and the Bay of Islands GCMG GCVO DSO OBE
1975/76	Sir Hector MacLennan KT FRCPGLAS FRCOG
1977	Francis David Charteris, Earl of Wemyss and March KT LLD
1978/79	The Rt Hon. William Ross MBE LLD
1980/81	Andrew Douglas Alexander Thomas Bruce, Earl of Elgin and Kincardine KT DL JP
1982/83	Colonel Sir John Edward Gilmour BT DSO TD
1984/85	Charles Hector Fitzroy Maclean, Baron Maclean of Duart and Morvern KT GCVO KBE
1986/87	John Campbell Arbuthnott, Viscount of Arbuthnott CBE DSC FRSE FRSA
1988/89	Sir Iain Mark Tennant KT FRSA
1990/91	The Rt Hon. Donald MacArthur Ross FRSE
1992/93	The Rt Hon. Lord Macfarlane of Bearsden
1994/95	Lady Marion Fraser
1996	Her Royal Highness the Princess Royal LG GCVO
1997	The Rt Hon. Lord Macfarlane of Bearsden
1998/99	The Rt Hon. Lord Hogg of Cumbernauld
2000	His Royal Highness the Prince Charles, Duke of Rothesay
2001/02	The Rt Hon. Viscount Younger of Leckie
2003	The Rt Hon. Lord Steel of Aikwood

(7) RECENT MODERATORS
OF THE GENERAL ASSEMBLY

1965	Archibald Watt STM DD, Edzell and Lethnot
1966	R. Leonard Small OBE DD, Edinburgh St Cuthbert's
1967	W. Roy Sanderson DD, Stenton with Whittingehame
1968	J.B. Longmuir TD DD, Principal Clerk of Assembly
1969	T.M. Murchison MA DD, Glasgow St Columba Summertown
1970	Hugh O. Douglas CBE DD LLD, Dundee St Mary's
1971	Andrew Herron MA BD LLB, Clerk to the Presbytery of Glasgow
1972	R.W.V. Selby Wright JP CVO TD DD FRSE, Edinburgh Canongate
1973	George T.H. Reid MC MA BD DD, Aberdeen Langstane
1974	David Steel MA BD DD, Linlithgow St Michael's
1975	James G. Matheson MA BD DD, Portree
1976	Thomas F. Torrance MBE DLitt DD FRSE, University of Edinburgh
1977	John R. Gray VRD MA BD ThM, Dunblane Cathedral
1978	Peter P. Brodie MA BD LLB DD, Alloa St Mungo's
1979	Robert A.S. Barbour MA BD STM DD, University of Aberdeen
1980	William B. Johnston MA BD DD, Edinburgh Colinton
1981	Andrew B. Doig BD STM DD, National Bible Society of Scotland
1982	John McIntyre CVO DD DLitt FRSE, University of Edinburgh
1983	J. Fraser McLuskey MC DD, London St Columba's
1984	John M.K. Paterson MA ACII BD, Milngavie St Paul's
1985	David M.B.A. Smith MA BD DUniv, Logie
1986	Robert Craig CBE DLitt LLD DD, Emeritus of Jerusalem
1987	Duncan Shaw *Bundesverdienstkreuz* PhD ThDr JP, Edinburgh Craigentinny St Christopher's
1988	James A. Whyte MA LLD, University of St Andrews
1989	William J.G. McDonald MA BD DD, Edinburgh Mayfield
1990	Robert Davidson MA BD DD FRSE, University of Glasgow
1991	William B.R. Macmillan MA BD LLD DD, Dundee St Mary's
1992	Hugh R. Wyllie MA MCIBS DD, Hamilton Old Parish Church
1993	James L. Weatherhead CBE MA LLB DD, Principal Clerk of Assembly
1994	James A. Simpson BSc BD STM DD, Dornoch Cathedral
1995	James Harkness CB OBE MA DD, Chaplain General (Emeritus)
1996	John H. McIndoe MA BD STM DD, London: St Columba's linked with Newcastle: St Andrew's
1997	Alexander McDonald BA CMIWSc DUniv, General Secretary, Department of Ministry
1998	Alan Main TD MA BD STM PhD, Professor of Practical Theology at Christ's College, University of Aberdeen
1999	John B. Cairns LTh LLB, Dumbarton Riverside
2000	Andrew R.C. McLellan MA BD STM DD, Edinburgh St Andrew's and St George's
2001	John D. Miller BA BD DD, Glasgow Castlemilk East
2002	Finlay A.J. Macdonald MA BD PhD DD, Principal Clerk of Assembly
2003	Iain R. Torrance TD MA BD DPhil, Professor of Patristics and Christian Ethics at the University of Aberdeen and Master of Christ's College

MATTER OF PRECEDENCE
The Lord High Commissioner to the General Assembly of the Church of Scotland (while the Assembly is sitting) ranks next to the Sovereign and the Duke of Edinburgh and before the rest of the Royal Family.

The Moderator of the General Assembly of the Church of Scotland ranks next to the Lord Chancellor of Great Britain and before the Prime Minister and the Dukes.

---

(8) HER MAJESTY'S HOUSEHOLD IN SCOTLAND
ECCLESIASTICAL

Dean of the Chapel Royal:	Very Rev. James Harkness CB OBE MA DD
Dean of the Order of the Thistle:	Very Rev. Gilleasbuig Macmillan CVO MA BD Drhc DD
Domestic Chaplain:	Rev. Robert P. Sloan MA BD

Chaplains in Ordinary:

Very Rev. Gilleasbuig Macmillan
    CVO MA BD Drhc DD
Rev. Charles Robertson MA JP
Very Rev. James A. Simpson BSc STM DD
Rev. Norman W. Drummond MA BD
Rev. John L. Paterson MA BD STM
Rev. Alastair H. Symington MA BD
Very Rev. John B. Cairns LTh LLB DD
Right Rev. Prof. Iain R. Torrance TD MA BD DPhil
Very Rev. Finlay A.J. Macdonald
    MA BD PhD DD

Extra Chaplains:

Very Rev. W. Roy Sanderson DD
Very Rev. Prof. John McIntyre
    CVO DD DLitt Drhc FRSE
Rev. H.W.M. Cant MA BD STM
Rev. Kenneth MacVicar MBE DFC TD MA
Very Rev. Prof. Robert A.S. Barbour
    KCVO MC BD STM DD
Rev. Alwyn Macfarlane MA
Very Rev. William B. Johnston
    MA BD DD DLitt
Rev. Colin Forrester-Paton MA BD
Rev. Mary I. Levison BA BD DD
Very Rev. William J. Morris KCVO PhD LLD DD JP
Rev. John MacLeod MA
Rev. A. Stewart Todd MA BD DD
Very Rev. James L. Weatherhead CBE MA LLB DD
Rev. Maxwell D. Craig MA BD ThM

(9) LONG SERVICE CERTIFICATES

Long Service Certificates, signed by the Moderator, are available for presentation to elders and others in respect of not less than thirty years of service. It should be noted that the period is years of *service*, not (for example) years of ordination in the case of an elder.

In the case of Sunday School teachers and Bible Class leaders, the qualifying period is twenty-one years of service.

Certificates are not issued posthumously, nor is it possible to make exceptions to the rules, for example by recognising quality of service in order to reduce the qualifying period, or by reducing the qualifying period on compassionate grounds, such as serious illness.

A Certificate will be issued only once to any particular individual.

Applications for Long Service Certificates should be made in writing to the Principal Clerk at 121 George Street, Edinburgh EH2 4YN by the parish minister, or by the session clerk on behalf of the Kirk Session. Certificates are not issued from this office to the individual recipients, nor should individuals make application themselves.

(10) LIBRARIES OF THE CHURCH

GENERAL ASSEMBLY LIBRARY AND RECORD ROOM
Most of the books contained in the General Assembly Library have been transferred to the New College Library. Records of the General Assembly, Synods, Presbyteries and Kirk Sessions are now in HM Register House, Edinburgh. All records more than fifty years old and not in current use should be sent to the Principal Clerk.

CHURCH MUSIC
The Library of New College contains a selection of works on Church music.

(11) RECORDS OF THE CHURCH OF SCOTLAND

Church records more than fifty years old, unless still in use, should be sent or delivered to the Principal Clerk for onward transmission to the Scottish Record Office. Where ministers or session clerks are approached by a local repository seeking a transfer of their records, they should inform the Principal Clerk, who will take the matter up with the National Archives of Scotland.

Where a temporary retransmission of records is sought, it is extremely helpful if notice can be given three months in advance so that appropriate procedures can be carried out satisfactorily.

SECTION 3

Church Procedure

(1) THE MINISTER AND BAPTISM

The administration of Baptism to infants is governed by Act V 2000 as amended by Act IX 2003. A Statement and Exposition of the Doctrine of Baptism may be found at page 13/8 in the published volume of Reports to the General Assembly of 2003.

The Act itself is as follows:

3.   Baptism signifies the action and love of God in Christ, through the Holy Spirit, and is a seal upon the gift of grace and the response of faith.
    (a)   Baptism shall be administered in the name of the Father and of the Son and of the Holy Spirit, with water, by sprinkling, pouring, or immersion.
    (b)   Baptism shall be administered to a person only once.
4.   Baptism may be administered to a person upon profession of faith.
    (a)   The minister and Kirk Session shall judge whether the person is of sufficient maturity to make personal profession of faith, where necessary in consultation with the parent(s) or legal guardian(s).
    (b)   Baptism may be administered only after the person has received such instruction in its meaning as the minister and Kirk Session consider necessary, according to such basis of instruction as may be authorised by the General Assembly.
    (c)   In cases of uncertainty as to whether a person has been baptised or validly baptised, baptism shall be administered conditionally.
5.   Baptism may be administered to a person with learning difficulties who makes an appropriate profession of faith, where the minister and Kirk Session are satisfied that the person shall be nurtured within the life and worship of the Church.
6.   Baptism may be administered to a child:
    (a)   where at least one parent, or other family member (with parental consent), having been baptised and being on the communion roll of the congregation, will undertake the Christian upbringing of the child;
    (b)   where at least one parent, or other family member (with parental consent), having been baptised but not on the communion roll of the congregation, satisfies the minister and Kirk Session that he or she is an adherent of the congregation and will undertake the Christian upbringing of the child;
    (c)   where at least one parent, or other family member (with parental consent), having been baptised, professes the Christian faith, undertakes to ensure that the child grows up in the life and worship of the Church and expresses the desire to seek admission to the communion roll of the congregation;
    (d)   where the child is under legal guardianship, and the minister and Kirk Session are satisfied that the child shall be nurtured within the life and worship of the congregation;
and, in each of the above cases, only after the parent(s), or other family member, has received such instruction in its meaning as the minister and Kirk Session consider necessary, according to such basis of instruction as may be authorised by the General Assembly.
7.   Baptism shall normally be administered during the public worship of the congregation in which the person makes profession of faith, or of which the parent or other family member is on the communion roll, or is an adherent. In exceptional circumstances, baptism may be administered elsewhere (e.g. at home or in hospital). Further, a minister may administer baptism to a person resident outwith the minister's parish, and who is not otherwise connected with the congregation, only with the consent of the minister of the parish in

which the person would normally reside, or of the Presbytery.

8. In all cases, an entry shall be made in the Kirk Session's Baptismal Register and a Certificate of Baptism given by the minister. Where baptism is administered in a chaplaincy context, it shall be recorded in the Baptismal Register there, and, where possible, reported to the minister of the parish in which the person resides.

9. Baptism shall normally be administered by an ordained minister. In situations of emergency,

   (a)   a minister may, exceptionally, notwithstanding the preceding provisions of the Act, respond to a request for baptism in accordance with his or her pastoral judgement, and

   (b)   baptism may be validly administered by a person who is not ordained, always providing that it is administered in the name of the Father and of the Son and of the Holy Spirit, with water.

   In every occurrence of the latter case, of which a minister or chaplain becomes aware, an entry shall be made in the appropriate Baptismal Register and where possible reported to the Clerk of the Presbytery within which the baptism was administered.

10. Each Presbytery shall form, or designate, a committee to which reference may be made in cases where there is a dispute as to the interpretation of this Act. Without the consent of the Presbytery, no minister may administer baptism in a case where to his or her knowledge another minister has declined to do so.

11. The Church of Scotland, as part of the Universal Church, affirms the validity of the sacrament of baptism administered in the name of the Father and of the Son and of the Holy Spirit, with water, in accordance with the discipline of other members of the Universal Church.

---

(2) THE MINISTER AND MARRIAGE

1. BACKGROUND

Prior to 1939, every marriage in Scotland fell into one or other of two classes: regular or irregular. The former was marriage by a minister of religion after due notice of intention had been given; the latter could be effected in one of three ways: (1) declaration *de presenti*, (2) by promise *subsequente copula*, or (3) by habit and repute.

The Marriage (Scotland) Act of 1939 put an end to (1) and (2) and provided for a new classification of marriage as either religious or civil.

The law of marriage as it was thus established in 1939 had two important limitations to the celebration of marriage: (1) certain preliminaries had to be observed; and (2) in respect of religious marriage, the service had to be conducted according to the forms of either the Christian or the Jewish faith.

2. THE MARRIAGE (SCOTLAND) ACT 1977

These two conditions were radically altered by the Marriage (Scotland) Act 1977.

Since 1 January 1978, in conformity with the demands of a multi-racial society, the benefits of religious marriage have been extended to adherents of other faiths, the only requirements being the observance of monogamy and the satisfaction of the authorities with the forms of the vows imposed.

Since 1978, the calling of banns has also been discontinued. The couple themselves must each complete a Marriage Notice form and return this to the District Registrar for the area in which they are to be married, irrespective of where they live, at least fifteen days before the ceremony is due to take place. The form details the documents which require to be produced with it.

If everything is in order, the District Registrar will issue, not more than seven days before the date of the ceremony, a Marriage Schedule. This must be in the hands of the minister officiating at the marriage ceremony before the service begins. Under no circumstances must the minister deviate from this rule. To do so is an offence under the Act.

Ministers should note the advice given by the Procurator of the Church in 1962, that they should not officiate at any marriage until at least one day after the 16th birthday of the younger party.

3. THE MARRIAGE (SCOTLAND) ACT 2002

Although there have never been any limitations as to the place where a religious marriage can be celebrated, civil marriage can take place only in the Office of a Registrar. The Marriage (Scotland) Act 2002, when it comes into effect, will, however, permit the solemnisation of civil marriages at places approved by Local Authorities. Regulations are to be made to specify the kinds of place which may be 'approved' with a view to ensuring that the places approved will not compromise the solemnity and dignity of civil marriage and will have no recent or continuing connection with any religion so as to undermine the distinction between religious and civil ceremonies.

4. PROCLAMATION OF BANNS

Proclamation of banns is no longer required in Scotland; but, in the Church of England, marriage is governed by the provisions of the Marriage Act 1949, which requires that the parties' intention to marry has to have been proclaimed and which provides that in the case of a party residing in Scotland a Certificate of Proclamation given according to the law or custom prevailing in Scotland shall be sufficient for the purpose. In the event that a minister is asked to call banns for a person resident within the registration district where his or her church is situated, the proclamation needs only to be made on one Sunday if the parties are known to the minister. If they are not, it should be made on two Sundays. In all cases, the Minister should, of course, have no reason to believe that there is any impediment to the marriage.

Proclamation should be made at the principal service of worship in this form:

> There is a purpose of marriage between AB (Bachelor/Widower/Divorced), residing at .... in this Registration District, and CD (Spinster/Widow/Divorced), residing at .... in the Registration District of ...., of which proclamation is hereby made for the first and only (second and last) time.

Immediately after the second reading, or not less than forty-eight hours after the first and only reading, a Certificate of Proclamation signed by either the minister or the Session Clerk should be issued in the following terms:

> At .... the ...... day of ...... 20 ....
> It is hereby certified that AB, residing at ...., and CD, residing at ...., have been duly proclaimed in order to marriage in the Church of .... according to the custom of the Church of Scotland, and that no objections have been offered.
> Signed .... minister or
> Signed .... Session Clerk

5. MARRIAGE OF FOREIGNERS

Marriages in Scotland of foreigners, or of foreigners with British subjects, are, if they satisfy the requirements of Scots Law, valid within the United Kingdom and the various British overseas territories; but they will not necessarily be valid in the country to which the foreigner belongs. This will be so only if the requirements of the law of his or her country have also been complied with. It is therefore most important that, before the marriage, steps should be taken to obtain from the Consul, or other diplomatic representative of the country concerned, a satisfactory assurance that the marriage will be accepted as valid in the country concerned.

6. REMARRIAGE OF DIVORCED PERSONS

By virtue of Act XXVI 1959, a minister of the Church of Scotland may lawfully solemnise the marriage of a person whose former marriage has been dissolved by divorce and whose former spouse is still alive. The minister, however, must carefully adhere to the requirements of the Act which, as slightly altered in 1985, are briefly as follows:

1.   The minister should not accede as a matter of routine to a request to solemnise such a marriage. To enable a decision to be made, he or she should take all reasonable steps to obtain relevant information, which should normally include the following:
     (a)   Adequate information concerning the life and character of the parties. The Act enjoins the greatest caution in cases where no pastoral relationship exists between the minister and either or both of the parties concerned.
     (b)   The grounds and circumstances of the divorce case.
     (c)   Facts bearing upon the future well-being of any children concerned.
     (d)   Whether any other minister has declined to solemnise the proposed marriage.
     (e)   The denomination to which the parties belong. The Act enjoins that special care should be taken where one or more parties belong to a denomination whose discipline in this matter may differ from that of the Church of Scotland.
2.   The minister should consider whether there is danger of scandal arising if he or she should solemnise the remarriage, at the same time taking into careful consideration before refusing to do so the moral and spiritual effect of a refusal on the parties concerned.
3.   As a determinative factor, the minister should do all he or she can to be assured that there has been sincere repentance where guilt has existed on the part of any divorced person seeking remarriage. He or she should also give instruction, where needed, in the nature and requirements of a Christian marriage.
4.   A minister is not required to solemnise a remarriage against his or her conscience. Every Presbytery is required to appoint certain individuals with one of whom ministers in doubt as to the correct course of action may consult if they so desire. The final decision, however, rests with the minister who has been asked to officiate.

---

(3) CONDUCT OF MARRIAGE SERVICES
(CODE OF GOOD PRACTICE)

The code which follows was submitted to the General Assembly in 1997. It appears, on page 1/10, in the Volume of Assembly Reports for that year within the Report of the Board of Practice and Procedure.

1. *Marriage in the Church of Scotland is solemnised by an ordained minister in a religious ceremony wherein, before God, and in the presence of the minister and at least two competent witnesses, the parties covenant together to take each other as husband and wife as long as they both shall live, and the minister declares the parties to be husband and wife. Before solemnising a marriage, a minister must be assured that the necessary legal requirements are being complied with and that the parties know of no legal impediment to their marriage, and he or she must afterwards ensure that the Marriage Schedule is duly completed.* (Act I 1977)

2. Any ordained minister of the Church of Scotland who is a member of Presbytery or who holds a current Ministerial Certificate may officiate at a marriage service (see Act II 1987).

3. While the marriage service should normally take place in church, a minister may, at his or her discretion, officiate at a marriage service outwith church premises. Wherever conducted, the ceremony will be such as to reflect appropriately both the joy and the solemnity of the occasion. In particular, a minister shall ensure that nothing is done which would bring the Church and its teaching into disrepute.

4. A minister agreeing to conduct a wedding should endeavour to establish a pastoral relationship with the couple within which adequate pre-marriage preparation and subsequent pastoral care may be given.

5. 'A minister should not refuse to perform ministerial functions for a person who is resident in his or her parish without sufficient reason' (Cox, *Practice and Procedure in the Church of Scotland*, sixth edition, page 55). Where either party to the proposed marriage has been divorced and the former spouse is still alive, the minister invited to officiate may solemnise such a marriage, having regard to the guidelines in the Act anent the Remarriage of Divorced Persons (Act XXVI 1959 as amended by Act II 1985).

6. A minister is acting as an agent of the National Church which is committed to bringing the ordinances of religion to the people of Scotland through a territorial ministry. As such, he or she shall not be entitled to charge a fee or allow a fee to be charged for conducting a marriage service. When a gift is spontaneously offered to a minister as a token of appreciation, the above consideration should not be taken to mean that he or she should not accept such an unsolicited gift. The Financial Board of a congregation is at liberty to set fees to cover such costs as heat and light, and in addition Organists and Church Officers are entitled to a fee in respect of their services at weddings.

7. A minister should not allow his or her name to be associated with any commercial enterprise that provides facilities for weddings.

8. A minister is not at liberty to enter the bounds of another minister's parish to perform ministerial functions without the previous consent of the minister of that parish. In terms of Act VIII 1933, a minister may 'officiate at a marriage or funeral by private invitation', but, for the avoidance of doubt, an invitation conveyed through a commercial enterprise shall not be regarded as a 'private invitation' within the meaning of that Act.

9. A minister invited to officiate at a Marriage Service where neither party is a member of his or her congregation or is resident within his or her own parish or has any connection with the parish within which the service is to take place should observe the following courtesies:
   (a) he or she should ascertain from the parties whether either of them has a Church of Scotland connection or has approached the appropriate parish minister(s);
   (b) if it transpires that a ministerial colleague has declined to officiate, then he or she (the invited minister) should ascertain the reasons therefor and shall take these and all other relevant factors into account in deciding whether or not to officiate.

(4) THE MINISTER AND WILLS

The Requirements of Writing (Scotland) Act 1995, which came into force on 1 August 1995, has removed the power of a minister to execute wills notarially. Further clarification, if required, may be obtained from the Solicitor of the Church.

---

(5) PROCEDURE IN A VACANCY

Procedure in a vacancy is regulated by Acts VII and VIII 2003. The text of the most immediately relevant sections is given here for general information. Schedules of Intimation referred to are also included. The full text of both Acts can be obtained from the Principal Clerk.

1. Vacancy Procedure Committee

(1)   Each Presbytery shall appoint a number of its members to be available to serve on Vacancy Procedure Committees and shall provide information and training as required for those so appointed.

(2)   As soon as the Presbytery Clerk is aware that a vacancy has arisen or is anticipated, he or she shall consult the Moderator of the Presbytery and they shall appoint a Vacancy Procedure Committee of five persons from among those appointed in terms of subsection (1), which Committee shall (a) include at least one minister and at least one elder and (b) exclude any communicant member or former minister of the vacant charge or of any constituent congregation thereof. The Vacancy Procedure Committee shall include a Convener and Clerk, the latter of whom need not be a member of the Committee but may be the Presbytery Clerk. The same Vacancy Procedure Committee may serve for more than one vacancy at a time.

(3)   The Vacancy Procedure Committee shall have a quorum of three for its meetings.

(4)   The Convener of the Vacancy Procedure Committee may, where he or she reasonably believes a matter to be non-contentious, consult members individually, provided that reasonable efforts are made to consult all members of the Committee. A meeting shall be held at the request of any member of the Committee.

(5)   Every decision made by the Vacancy Procedure Committee shall be reported to the next meeting of Presbytery, but may not be recalled by Presbytery where the decision was subject to the provisions of section 2 below.

2. Request for Consideration by Presbytery

Where in this Act any decision by the Vacancy Procedure Committee is subject to the provisions of this section, the following rules shall apply:

(1)   The Presbytery Clerk shall intimate to all members of the Presbytery by mailing or at a Presbytery meeting the course of action or permission proposed, and shall arrange for one Sunday's pulpit intimation of the same to be made to the congregation or congregations concerned, in terms of Schedule A. The intimation having been made, it shall be displayed as prominently as possible at the church building for seven days.

(2)   Any four individuals, being communicant members of the congregation or full members of

the Presbytery, may give written notice requesting that action be taken in terms of subsection (3) below, giving reasons for the request, within seven days after the pulpit intimation.

(3) Upon receiving notice in terms of subsection (2), the Presbytery Clerk shall sist the process or permission referred to in subsection (1), which shall then require the approval of the Presbytery.

(4) The Moderator of the Presbytery shall in such circumstances consider whether a meeting *pro re nata* of the Presbytery should be called in order to avoid prejudicial delay in the vacancy process.

(5) The Presbytery Clerk shall cause to have served upon the congregation or congregations an edict in terms of Schedule B citing them to attend the meeting of Presbytery for their interest.

(6) The consideration by Presbytery of any matter under this section shall not constitute an appeal or a Petition, and the decision of Presbytery shall be deemed to be a decision at first instance subject to the normal rights of appeal or dissent-and-complaint.

3. Causes of Vacancy

The causes of vacancy shall normally include:

(a) the death of the minister of the charge;

(b) the removal of status of the minister of the charge or the suspension of the minister in terms of section 20(2) of Act III 2001;

(c) the dissolution of the pastoral tie in terms of Act I 1988 or Act XV 2002;

(d) the demission of the charge and/or status of the minister of the charge;

(e) the translation of the minister of the charge to another charge;

(f) the termination of the tenure of the minister of the charge in terms of Act VI 1984.

4. Release of Departing Minister

The Presbytery Clerk shall be informed as soon as circumstances have occurred that cause a vacancy to arise or make it likely that a vacancy shall arise. Where the circumstances pertain to section 3(d) or (e) above, the Vacancy Procedure Committee shall

(1) except in cases governed by subsection (2) below, decide whether to release the minister from his or her charge and, in any case involving translation to another charge or introduction to an appointment, instruct him or her to await the instructions of the Presbytery or another Presbytery;

(2) in the case of a minister in the first five years of his or her first charge, decide whether there are exceptional circumstances to justify releasing him or her from his or her charge and proceeding in terms of subsection (1) above;

(3) determine whether a vacancy has arisen or is anticipated and, as soon as possible, determine the date upon which the charge becomes actually vacant, and

(4) inform the congregation or congregations by one Sunday's pulpit intimation as soon as convenient;

(5) The provisions of section 2 above shall apply to the decisions of the Vacancy Procedure Committee in terms of subsections (1) and (2) above.

5. Demission of Charge

(1) Subject to the provisions of subsection (2) below, when a vacancy has occurred in terms of section 3(c), (d) or (f) above, the Presbytery shall determine whether the minister is, in the circumstances, entitled to a seat in the Presbytery in terms of section 16 of Act III 2000 (as amended).

(2) In the case where it is a condition of any basis of adjustment that a minister shall demit his

or her charge to facilitate union or linking, and the minister has agreed in writing in terms of the appropriate regulations governing adjustments, formal application shall not be made to the Presbytery for permission to demit. The minister concerned shall be regarded as retiring in the interest of adjustment, and he or she shall retain a seat in Presbytery unless in terms of Act III 2000 (as amended) he or she elects to resign it.

(3) A minister who demits his or her charge without retaining a seat in the Presbytery shall, if he or she retains status as a minister, be subject to the provisions of sections 5 to 15 of Act II 2000 (as amended).

6. Appointment of Interim Moderator

At the same time as the Vacancy Procedure Committee makes a decision in terms of section 4 above, or where circumstances pertain to section 3(a), (b), (c) or (f) above, the Vacancy Procedure Committee shall appoint an Interim Moderator for the charge and make intimation thereof to the congregation subject to the provisions of section 2 above. The Interim Moderator shall be either a ministerial member of the Presbytery in terms of Act III 2000 or Act V 2001 or a member of the Presbytery selected from a list of those who have received such preparation for the task as the Board of Ministry shall from time to time recommend or provide, and he or she shall not be a member in the vacant charge nor a member of the Vacancy Procedure Committee. The name of the Interim Moderator shall be forwarded to the Board of Ministry.

7. Duties of Interim Moderator

(1) It shall be the duty of the Interim Moderator to preside at all meetings of the Kirk Session (or of the Kirk Sessions in the case of a linked charge) and to preside at all congregational meetings in connection with the vacancy, or at which the minister would have presided had the charge been full. In the case of a congregational meeting called by the Presbytery in connection with adjustment, the Interim Moderator, having constituted the meeting, shall relinquish the chair in favour of the representative of the Presbytery, but he or she shall be at liberty to speak at such a meeting. In consultation with the Kirk Session and the Financial Court, he or she shall make arrangements for the supply of the vacant pulpit.

(2) The Interim Moderator appointed in a prospective vacancy may call and preside at meetings of the Kirk Session and of the congregation for the transaction of business relating to the said prospective vacancy. He or she shall be associated with the minister until the date of the actual vacancy; after that date, he or she shall take full charge.

(3) The Interim Moderator shall act as an assessor to the Nominating Committee, being available to offer guidance and advice. If the Committee so desire, he or she may act as their Convener, but in no case shall he or she have a vote.

(4) In the event of the absence of the Interim Moderator, the Vacancy Procedure Committee shall appoint a member of the Presbytery who is not a member of the vacant congregation to fulfil any of the rights and duties of the Interim Moderator in terms of this section.

(5) The Interim Moderator shall have the same duties and responsibilities towards all members of ministry teams referred to in section 16 of Act VII 2003 anent Appraisal and Adjustment as if he or she were the parish minister, both in terms of this Act and in respect of the terms and conditions of such individuals.

8. Permission to Call

When the decision to release the minister from the charge has been made and the Interim Moderator appointed, the Vacancy Procedure Committee shall consider whether it may give permission to call a minister in terms of Act VII 2003, and may proceed subject to the provisions of section 2 above. The Vacancy Procedure Committee must refer the question of permission to call to the Presbytery if:

(a)   shortfalls exist which in the opinion of the Committee require consideration in terms of section 9 hereunder;

(b)   the Committee has reason to believe that the vacancy schedule referred to in section 10 below will not be approved;

(c)   the Committee has reason to believe that the Presbytery will, in terms of section 11 below, instruct work to be carried out on the manse before a call can be sustained, and judges that the likely extent of such work warrants a delay in the granting of permission to call, or

(d)   the Committee has reason to believe that the Presbytery may wish to delay or refuse the granting of permission for any reason.

Any decision by Presbytery to refuse permission to call shall be subject to appeal or dissent-and-complaint.

9. Shortfalls

(1)   As soon as possible after intimation of a vacancy or anticipated vacancy reaches the Presbytery Clerk, the Presbytery shall ascertain whether the charge has current or accumulated shortfalls in contributions to central funds, and shall determine whether and to what extent any shortfalls that exist are justified.

(2)   If the vacancy is in a charge in which the Presbytery has determined that shortfalls are to any extent unjustified, it shall not resolve to allow a call of any kind until:

(a)   the shortfalls have been met to the extent to which the Presbytery determined that they were unjustified, or

(b)   a scheme for the payment of the unjustified shortfall has been agreed between the congregation and the Presbytery and receives the concurrence of the Board of Ministry and/or the Board of Stewardship and Finance for their respective interests, or

(c)   a fresh appraisal of the charge in terms of Act VII 2003 has been carried out, regardless of the status of the charge in the current Presbytery plan:

(i)   During such appraisal, no further steps may be taken in respect of filling the vacancy, and the Presbytery shall make final determination of what constitutes such steps.

(ii)   Following such appraisal and any consequent adjustment or deferred adjustment, the shortfalls shall be met or declared justifiable or a scheme shall be agreed in terms of subsection (b) above; the Presbytery shall inform the Board of Ministry and the Board of Stewardship and Finance of its decisions in terms of this section; and the Presbytery shall remove the suspension-of-vacancy process referred to in sub-paragraph (i).

10. Vacancy Schedule

(1)   When in terms of sections 4 and 6 above the decision to release the minister from the charge has been made and the Interim Moderator appointed, there shall be issued by the Board of Ministry a Schedule or Schedules for completion by the responsible Financial Board(s) of the vacant congregation(s) in consultation with representatives of the Presbytery, setting forth the proposed arrangements for stipend and payment of ministerial expenses and for provision of a manse, and showing the amount of aid, if any, to be given to, or to be received from, the Minimum Stipend Fund, with details of any endowment income. The Schedule, along with an extract minute from each relevant Kirk Session containing a commitment fully and adequately to support a new ministry, shall be forwarded to the Presbytery Clerk.

(2) The Schedule shall be considered by the Vacancy Procedure Committee and, if approved, transmitted to the Board of Ministry by the Presbytery Clerk. The Vacancy Procedure Committee or Presbytery must not sustain an appointment and call until the Schedule has been approved by them and by the Board of Ministry, which shall intimate its decision within six weeks of receiving the schedule from the Presbytery.

(3) The accuracy of the Vacancy Schedule shall be kept under review by the Vacancy Procedure Committee.

(4) The provisions of section 2 above shall apply to the decisions of the Vacancy Procedure Committee.

11. Manse

As soon as possible after the Manse becomes vacant, the Presbytery Property Committee shall inspect the Manse and come to a view on what work, if any, must be carried out to render it suitable for a new incumbent. The views of the Property Committee should then be communicated to the Presbytery which should, subject to any modifications which might be agreed by that Court, instruct the Financial Board of the congregation to have the work carried out. No induction date shall be fixed until the Presbytery Property Committee has again inspected the Manse and confirmed that the work has been undertaken satisfactorily.

12. Advisory Committee

(1) As soon as possible after intimation of a vacancy or anticipated vacancy reaches the Presbytery Clerk, the Vacancy Procedure Committee shall appoint an Advisory Committee of three, subject to the following conditions:

    (a) at least one member shall be an elder and at least one shall be a minister;

    (b) the Advisory Committee shall contain no more than two members of the Vacancy Procedure Committee;

    (c) the Advisory Committee may contain individuals who are not members of the Presbytery;

    (d) the appointment shall be subject to section 2 above.

(2) The Advisory Committee shall meet:

    (a) before the election of the Nominating Committee, with the Kirk Session, or Kirk Sessions both separately and together, of the vacant charge to consider together in the light of the whole circumstances of the parish or parishes, what kind of ministry would be best suited to their needs;

    (b) with the Nominating Committee before it has taken any steps to fill the vacancy, to consider how it should proceed;

    (c) with the Nominating Committee before it reports to the Kirk Session and Presbytery the identity of the nominee, to review the process followed and give any further advice it deems necessary;

    (d) with the Nominating Committee at any other time by request of either the Nominating Committee or the Advisory Committee.

    In the case of charges which are in the opinion of the Presbytery remote, it will be adequate if the Interim Moderator (accompanied if possible by a member of the Nominating Committee) meets with the Advisory Committee for the purposes listed in paragraphs (a) to (c) above.

13. Electoral Register

(1) It shall be the duty of the Kirk Session of a vacant congregation to proceed to make up the Electoral Register of the congregation. This shall contain (1) as communicants the names of those persons (a) whose names are on the communion roll of the congregation as at the date on which it is made up and who are not under Church discipline, (b) whose names have been added or restored to the communion roll on revision by the Kirk Session subsequently to the occurrence of the vacancy, and (c) who have given in valid Certificates of Transference by the date specified in terms of Schedule C hereto; and (2) as adherents the names of those persons who, being parishioners or regular worshippers in the congregation at the date when the vacancy occurred, being at least 18 years of age, and not being members of any other congregation, have claimed (in writing in the form prescribed in Schedule D and within the time specified in Schedule C) to be placed on the Electoral Register, the Kirk Session being satisfied that they desire to be permanently connected with the congregation and knowing of no adequate reasons why they should not be admitted as communicants should they so apply.

(2) At a meeting to be held not later than fourteen days after intimation has been made in terms of Schedule C hereto, the Kirk Session shall decide on the claims of persons to be placed on the Electoral Register, such claims to be sent to the Session Clerk before the meeting. At this meeting, the Kirk Session may hear parties claiming to have an interest. The Kirk Session shall thereupon prepare the lists of names and addresses of communicants and of adherents which it is proposed shall be the Electoral Register of the congregation, the names being arranged in alphabetical order and numbered consecutively throughout. The decision of the Kirk Session in respect of any matter affecting the preparation of the Electoral Register shall be final.

(3) The proposed Electoral Register having been prepared, the Interim Moderator shall cause intimation to be made on the first convenient Sunday in terms of Schedule E hereto that on that day an opportunity will be given for inspecting the Register after service, and that it will lie for inspection at such times and such places as the Kirk Session shall have determined; and further shall specify a day when the Kirk Session will meet to hear parties claiming an interest and will finally revise and adjust the Register. At this meeting, the list, having been revised, numbered and adjusted, shall on the authority of the court be attested by the Interim Moderator and the Clerk as the Electoral Register of the congregation.

(4) This Register, along with a duplicate copy, shall without delay be transmitted to the Presbytery Clerk, who, in name of the Presbytery, shall attest and return the principal copy, retaining the duplicate copy in his or her own possession. For all purposes connected with this Act, the congregation shall be deemed to be those persons whose names are on the Electoral Register, and no other.

(5) If after the attestation of the Register any communicant is given a Certificate of Transference, the Session Clerk shall delete that person's name from the Register and initial the deletion. Such a Certificate shall be granted only when application for it has been made in writing, and the said written application shall be retained until the vacancy is ended.

(6) When a period of more than six months has elapsed between the Electoral Register being attested and the congregation being given permission to call, the Kirk Session shall have power, if it so desires, to revise and update the Electoral Register. Intimation of this intention shall be given in terms of Schedule F hereto. Additional names shall be added to the Register in the form of an Addendum which shall also contain authority for the deletions which have been made; two copies of this Addendum, duly attested, shall be lodged with the Presbytery Clerk who, in name of the Presbytery, shall attest and return the principal copy, retaining the duplicate copy in his or her own possession.

14. Appointment of Nominating Committee

(1)   When permission to call has been given and the Electoral Register has been attested, intimation in terms of Schedule G shall be made that a meeting of the congregation is to be held to appoint a Committee of its own number for the purpose of nominating one person to the congregation with a view to the appointment of a minister.

(2)   (a)   The Interim Moderator shall preside at this meeting, and the Session Clerk, or in his or her absence a person appointed by the meeting, shall act as Clerk.

(b)   The Interim Moderator shall remind the congregation of the number of members it is required to appoint in terms of this section and shall call for Nominations. To constitute a valid Nomination, the name of a person on the Electoral Register has to be proposed and seconded, and assurance given by the proposer that the person is prepared to act on the Committee. The Clerk shall take a note of all Nominations in the order in which they are made.

(c)   When it appears to the Interim Moderator that the Nominations are complete, they shall be read to the congregation and an opportunity given for any withdrawals. If the number of persons nominated does not exceed the maximum fixed in terms of subsection (4) below, there is no need for a vote, and the Interim Moderator shall declare that these persons constitute a Nominating Committee. If the number exceeds the maximum, the Interim Moderator shall submit the names one by one as they appear on the list to the vote of the congregation, each member having the right to vote for up to the maximum number fixed for the Committee, and voting being by standing up. In the event of a tie for the last place, a vote shall be taken between those tying.

(d)   The Interim Moderator shall announce the names of those thus elected to serve on the Nominating Committee, and intimate to them the time and place of their first meeting, which may be immediately after the congregational meeting provided that has been intimated along with the intimation of the congregational meeting.

(3)   Where there is an agreement between the Presbytery and the congregation or congregations that the minister to be inducted shall serve either in a team ministry involving another congregation or congregations, or in a designated post such as a chaplaincy, it shall be competent for the agreement to specify that the Presbytery shall appoint up to two representatives to serve on the Nominating Committee.

(4)   The Vacancy Procedure Committee shall, subject to the provisions of section 2 above, determine the number who will act on the Nominating Committee, being an odd number up to a maximum of thirteen.

(5)   When the vacancy is in a linked charge, or when a union or linking of congregations has been agreed but not yet effected, or when there is agreement to a deferred union or a deferred linking, or where the appointment is to more than one post, the Vacancy Procedure Committee shall, subject to the provisions of section 2 above, determine how the number who will act on the Nominating Committee will be allocated among the congregations involved, unless provision for this has already been made in the Basis of Union or Basis of Linking as the case may be.

(6)   The Nominating Committee shall not have power to co-opt additional members, but the relevant Kirk Session shall have power when necessary to appoint a replacement for any of its appointees who ceases, by death or resignation, to be a member of the Nominating Committee, or who, by falling ill or by moving away from the area, is unable to serve as a member of it.

15. Constitution of the Nominating Committee

It shall be the duty of the Interim Moderator to summon and preside at the first meeting of the Nominating Committee, which may be held at the close of the congregational meeting at which it is appointed and at which the Committee shall appoint a Convener and a Clerk. The Clerk, who need not be a member of the Committee, shall keep regular minutes of all proceedings. The Convener shall have a deliberative vote (if he or she is not the Interim Moderator) but shall in no case have a casting vote. If the Clerk is not a member of the Committee, he or she shall have no vote. At all meetings of the Committee, only those present shall be entitled to vote.

16. Task of the Nominating Committee

(1)   The Nominating Committee shall have the duty of nominating one person to the congregation with a view to the election and appointment of a minister. It shall proceed by a process of announcement in a monthly vacancy list, application and interview, and may also advertise, receive recommendations and pursue enquiries in other ways.

(2)   The Committee shall give due weight to any guidelines which may from time to time be issued by the Board of Ministry or the General Assembly.

(3)   The Committee shall make themselves aware of the roles of the other members of any ministry team as described in section 16 of Act VII 2003 anent Appraisal and Adjustment and may meet with them for this purpose, but shall not acquire responsibility or authority for the negotiation or alteration of their terms and conditions.

17. Eligibility for Election

The following categories of persons, and no others, are eligible to be nominated, elected and called as ministers of parishes in the Church of Scotland, but always subject, where appropriate, to the provisions of Act IX 2002 anent Admission and Readmission of Ministers and Others:

(1)   A minister of a parish of the Church, a minister holding some other appointment that entitles him or her to a seat in Presbytery or a minister holding a current Practising Certificate in terms of section 5 of Act II 2000.

(2)   A minister of the Church of Scotland who has retired from a parish or appointment as above, provided he or she has not reached his or her 65th birthday.

(3)   (a)   A licentiate of the Church of Scotland who has satisfactorily completed, or has been granted exemption from, his or her period of probationary service.

       (b)   A graduate candidate in terms of sections 26 and 27 of Act V 1998 (as amended).

(4)   A minister, licentiate or graduate candidate of the Church of Scotland who with the approval of the Board of World Mission, has entered the courts of an overseas Church as a full member, provided he or she has ceased to be such a member.

(5)   A minister, licentiate or graduate candidate of the Church of Scotland, who has neither relinquished nor been judicially deprived of the status he or she possessed and who has served, or is serving, furth of Scotland in any Church which is a member of the World Alliance of Reformed Churches.

(6)   The holder of a Certificate of Eligibility in terms of Act IX 2002 anent Admission and Readmission of Ministers and Others.

18. Ministers of a Team

Ministers occupying positions within a team ministry in the charge, or larger area including the charge, and former holders of such positions, shall be eligible to apply and shall not by virtue of office be deemed to have exercised undue influence in securing the call. A *locum tenens* in the vacant charge shall not by virtue of office be deemed to have exercised undue influence in securing the call. Any Interim Moderator in the current vacancy shall not be eligible to apply.

19. Ministers of Other Churches

(1) Where a minister of a church furth of Scotland, who holds a certificate of eligibility in terms of Act IX 2002 anent Admission and Readmission of Ministers and Others, is nominated, the nominee, Kirk Session and Presbytery may agree that he or she shall be inducted for a period of three years only and shall retain status as a minister of his or her denomination of origin.

(2) Upon induction, such a minister shall be accountable to the Presbytery for the exercise of his or her ministry and to his or her own church for matters of life and doctrine. He or she shall be awarded corresponding membership of the Presbytery.

(3) With the concurrence of the Presbytery and the Board of Ministry, and at the request of the congregation, the period may be extended for one further period of not more than three years.

20. Nomination

(1) Before the candidate is asked to accept Nomination, the Interim Moderator shall ensure that the candidate is given an adequate opportunity to see the whole ecclesiastical buildings (including the manse) pertaining to the congregation, and to meet privately with all members of staff of the charge or of any wider ministry team, and shall be provided with a copy of the constitution of the congregation, a copy of the current Presbytery Plan and of any current Basis of Adjustment or Basis of Reviewable Tenure, and the most recent audited accounts and statement of funds, and the candidate shall acknowledge receipt in writing to the Interim Moderator.

(2) Before any Nomination is intimated to the Kirk Session and Presbytery Clerk, the Clerk to the Nominating Committee shall secure the written consent thereto of the nominee.

(3) Before reporting the Nomination to the Vacancy Procedure Committee, the Presbytery Clerk shall obtain from the nominee or Interim Moderator evidence of the eligibility of the nominee to be appointed to the charge.

    (a) In the case of a minister not being a member of any Presbytery of the Church of Scotland, this shall normally constitute an Exit Certificate in terms of Act V 1998 as amended, or evidence of status from the Board of Ministry, or a current practising certificate, or certification from the Board of Ministry of eligibility in terms of Act IX 2002.

    (b) In the case of a minister in the first five years of his or her first charge, this shall consist of an extract minute either from the Vacancy Procedure Committee of his or her current Presbytery, or from that Presbytery, exceptionally releasing the minister.

21. Preaching by Nominee

(1) The Interim Moderator, on receiving notice of the Committee's Nomination, shall arrange that the nominee conduct public worship in the vacant church or churches, normally within four Sundays, and that the ballot take place immediately after each such service.

(2) The Interim Moderator shall thereupon cause intimation to be made on two Sundays regarding the arrangements made in connection with the preaching by the nominee and the ballot thereafter – all in terms of Schedule H hereto.

22. Election of Minister

(1) The Interim Moderator shall normally preside at all congregational meetings connected with the election, which shall be in all cases by ballot. The Interim Moderator shall be in charge of the ballot.

(2) The Interim Moderator may invite one or more persons (not being persons whose names are on the Electoral Register of the vacant congregation) to assist him or her in the conduct of a ballot vote when he or she judges this desirable.

(3)   When a linking or a deferred union or deferred linking is involved, the Interim Moderator shall consult and reach agreement with the minister or Interim Moderator of the other congregation regarding the arrangements for the conduct of public worship in these congregations by the nominee as in section 21(1) above. The Interim Moderator shall in writing appoint a member of Presbytery to take full charge of the ballot vote for the other congregation. In the case of a deferred union or deferred linking, the minister already inducted shall not be so appointed, nor shall he or she be in any way involved in the conduct of the election.

23. Ballot Procedure
(1)   The Kirk Session shall arrange to have available at the time of election a sufficient supply of voting-papers printed in the form of Schedule I hereto, and these shall be put into the custody of the Interim Moderator who shall preside at the election, assisted as in section 22 above. He or she shall issue on request to any person whose name is on the Electoral Register a voting-paper, noting on the Register that this has been done. Facilities shall be provided whereby the voter may mark the paper in secrecy, and a ballot-box shall be available wherein the paper is to be deposited when marked. The Interim Moderator may assist any person who asks for help in respect of completing the voting-paper, but no other person whatever shall communicate with the voter at this stage. The Interim Moderator, or the deputy appointed by him or her, shall be responsible for the safe custody of ballot-box, papers and Electoral Register.
(2)   As soon as practicable, and at latest within twenty-four hours after the close of the voting, the Interim Moderator shall constitute the Kirk Session, or the joint Kirk Sessions when more than one congregation is involved, and in presence of the Kirk Session shall proceed with the counting of the votes, in which he or she may be assisted as provided in section 22 above. When more than one ballot-box has been used and when the votes of more than one congregation are involved, all ballot-boxes shall be emptied and the voting-papers shall be mixed together before counting begins so that the preponderance of votes in one area or in one congregation shall not be disclosed.
(3)   If the number voting For exceeds the number voting Against, the nominee shall be declared elected and the Nominating Committee shall be deemed to be discharged.
(4)   If the number voting For is equal to or less than the number voting Against, the Interim Moderator shall declare that there has been failure to elect and that the Nominating Committee is deemed to have been discharged. He or she shall proceed in terms of section 26(b) without further reference to the Presbytery.
(5)   After the counting has been completed, the Interim Moderator shall sign a declaration in one of the forms of Schedule J hereto, and this shall be recorded in the minute of the Kirk Session or of the Kirk Sessions. An extract shall be affixed to the notice-board of the church, or of each of the churches, concerned. In the presence of the Kirk Session, the Interim Moderator shall then seal up the voting-papers along with the marked copy of the Electoral Register, and these shall be transmitted to the Presbytery Clerk in due course along with the other documents specified in section 27 below.

24. Withdrawal of Nominee
(1)   Should a nominee intimate withdrawal before he or she has preached as nominee, the Nominating Committee shall continue its task and seek to nominate another nominee.
(2)   Should a nominee intimate withdrawal after he or she has been elected, the Interim Moderator shall proceed in terms of sections 23(4) above and 26(b) below without further reference to the Presbytery.

25. The Call

(1) The Interim Moderator shall, along with the intimation regarding the result of the voting, intimate the arrangements made for members of the congregation over a period of not less than eight days to subscribe the Call (Schedule K). Intimation shall be in the form of Schedule L hereto.

(2) The Call may be subscribed on behalf of a member not present to sign in person, provided a mandate authorising such subscription is produced as in Schedule M. All such entries shall be initialled by the Interim Moderator or by the member of the Kirk Session appending them.

(3) Those eligible to sign the call shall be all those whose names appear on the Electoral Roll. A paper of concurrence in the Call may be signed by regular worshippers in the congregation over 14 years of age and by adherents whose names have not been entered on the Electoral Register.

26. Failure to Nominate

The exercise by a congregation of its right to call a minister shall be subject to a time-limit of one year; this period shall be calculated from the date when intimation is given of the agreement to grant leave to call. If it appears that an appointment is not to be made within the allotted time (allowing one further calendar month for intimation to the Presbytery), the congregation may make application to the Presbytery for an extension, which will normally be for a further three months. In exceptional circumstances, and for clear cause shown, a further extension of three months may be granted. If no election has been made and intimated to the Presbytery by the expiry of that time, the permission to call shall be regarded as having lapsed. The Presbytery may thereupon look afresh at the question of adjustment. If the Presbytery is still satisfied that a minister should be appointed, it shall itself take steps to make such an appointment, proceeding in one of the following ways:

(1) (a) The Presbytery may discharge the Nominating Committee, strengthen the Advisory Committee which had been involved in the case by the appointment of an additional minister and elder, instruct that Committee to bring forward to a subsequent meeting the name of an eligible individual for appointment to the charge and intimate this instruction to the congregation. If satisfied with the recommendation brought by the Advisory Committee, the Presbytery shall thereupon make the appointment.

(b) The Presbytery Clerk shall thereupon intimate to the person concerned the fact of his or her appointment, shall request him or her to forward a letter of acceptance along with appropriate Certificates if these are required in terms of section 27 below, and shall arrange with him or her to conduct public worship in the vacant church or churches on an early Sunday.

(c) The Presbytery Clerk shall cause intimation to be made in the form of Schedule N that the person appointed will conduct public worship on the day specified and that a Call in the usual form will lie with the Session Clerk or other suitable person for not less than eight free days to receive the signatures of the congregation. The conditions governing the signing of the Call shall be as in section 25 above.

(d) At the expiry of the time allowed, the Call shall be transmitted by the Session Clerk to the Presbytery Clerk, who shall lay it, along with the documents referred to in sub-paragraph (b) above, before the Presbytery at its first ordinary meeting or at a meeting *in hunc effectum*.

(2) Otherwise, the Presbytery shall instruct that a fresh Nominating Committee be elected in terms of section 14 above. The process shall then be followed in terms of this Act from the point of the election of the Nominating Committee.

27. Transmission of Documents

(1) After an election has been made, the Interim Moderator shall secure from the person appointed a letter of acceptance of the appointment.

(2) The Interim Moderator shall then without delay transmit the relevant documents to the Presbytery Clerk. These are: the minute of Nomination by the Nominating Committee, all intimations made to the congregation thereafter, the declaration of the election and appointment, the voting-papers, the marked copy of the Register and the letter of acceptance. He or she shall also inform the Clerk of the steps taken in connection with the signing of the Call, and shall arrange that, at the expiry of the period allowed for subscription, the Call shall be transmitted by the Session Clerk to the Presbytery Clerk.

(3) After the person elected has been inducted to the charge, the Presbytery Clerk shall:
   (a) deliver to him or her the approved copy of the Vacancy Schedule referred to in section 10(2) above, and
   (b) destroy the intimations and voting-papers lodged with him or her in terms of subsection (2) above and ensure that confidential documents and correspondence held locally are destroyed.

28. Sustaining the Call

(1) All of the documents listed in section 27 above shall be laid before the Vacancy Procedure Committee, which may resolve to sustain the call and determine arrangements for the induction of the new minister, subject to (a) the release, if appropriate, of the minister from his or her current charge in terms of this Act and (b) the provisions of section 2 above. The Moderator of the Presbytery shall, if no ordinary meeting of the Presbytery falls before the proposed induction date, call a meeting *pro re nata* for the induction.

(2) In the event that the matter comes before the Presbytery in terms of section 2 above, the procedure shall be as follows:
   (a) The Call and other relevant documents having been laid on the table, the Presbytery shall hear any person whom it considers to have an interest. In particular, the Advisory Committee shall be entitled to be heard if it so desires, or the Presbytery may ask for a report from it. The Presbytery shall then decide whether to sustain the appointment in terms of subsection (1) above, and in doing so shall give consideration to the number of signatures on the Call. It may delay reaching a decision and return the Call to the Kirk Session to give further opportunity for it to be subscribed.
   (b) If the Presbytery sustain an appointment and Call to a Graduate Candidate, and there be no appeal tendered in due form against its judgement, it shall appoint the day and hour and place at which the ordination and induction will take place.
   (c) If the Presbytery sustain an appointment and Call to a minister of the Church of Scotland not being a minister of a parish, or to a minister of another denomination, and there be no ecclesiastical impediment, the Presbytery shall appoint the day and hour and place at which the induction will take place.

(3) In the event that the Call is not sustained, the Presbytery shall determine either (1) to give more time for it to be signed in terms of section 25 above or (2) to proceed in terms of subsection (a) or (b) of section 26 above.

29. Admission to a Charge

(1) When the Presbytery has appointed a day for the ordination and induction of a Graduate Candidate, or for the induction of a minister already ordained, the Clerk shall arrange for an edict in the form of Schedule O to be read to the congregation on the two Sundays preceding the day appointed.

(2) At the time and place named in the edict, the Presbytery having been constituted, the Moderator shall call for the return of the edict attested as having been duly served. If the minister is being translated from another Presbytery, the relevant minute of that Presbytery or of its Vacancy Procedure Committee agreeing to translation shall also be laid on the table. Any objection, to be valid at this stage, must have been intimated to the Presbytery Clerk at the objector's earliest opportunity, must be strictly directed to life or doctrine and must be substantiated immediately to the satisfaction of the Presbytery, in which case procedure shall be sisted and the Presbytery shall take appropriate steps to deal with the situation that has arisen. Otherwise the Presbytery shall proceed with the ordination and induction, or with the induction, as hereunder.

(3) The Presbytery shall proceed to the church where public worship shall be conducted by those appointed for the purpose. The Clerk shall read a brief narrative of the cause of the vacancy and of the steps taken for the settlement. The Moderator, having read the Preamble, shall, addressing him or her by name, put to the person to be inducted the questions prescribed (*see the Ordinal of the Church as authorised from time to time by the General Assembly*). Satisfactory answers having been given, the person to be inducted shall sign the Formula. If he or she has not already been ordained, the person to be inducted shall then kneel, and the Moderator by prayer and the imposition of hands, in which members of the Presbytery, appointed by the Presbytery for the purpose, and other ordained persons associated with it, if invited to share in such imposition of hands, shall join, shall ordain him or her to the office of the Holy Ministry. Prayer being ended, the Moderator shall say: 'I now declare you to have been ordained to the office of the Holy Ministry, and in the name of the Lord Jesus Christ, the King and Head of the Church, and by authority of this Presbytery, I induct you to this charge, and in token thereof we give you the right hand of fellowship'. The Moderator with all other members of Presbytery present and those associated with it shall then give the right hand of fellowship. The Moderator shall then put the prescribed question to the members of the congregation. Suitable charges to the new minister and to the congregation shall then be given by the Moderator or by a minister appointed for the purpose.

(4) When an ordained minister is being inducted to a charge, the act of ordination shall not be repeated and the relevant words shall be omitted from the declaration. In other respects, the procedure shall be as in subsection (3) above.

(5) When the appointment is for a limited or potentially limited period (including Reviewable Tenure, or an appointment in terms of section 19 above), the service shall proceed as in subsections (3) or (4) above, except that in the declaration the Moderator shall say: 'I induct you to this charge on the Basis of [specific Act and Section] and in terms of Minute of Presbytery of date …'.

(6) After the service, the Presbytery shall resume its session, when the name of the new minister shall be added to the Roll of Presbytery, and the Clerk shall be instructed to send certified intimation of the induction to the Session Clerk to be engrossed in the minutes of the first meeting of Kirk Session thereafter, and, in the case of a translation from another Presbytery or where the minister was prior to the induction subject to the supervision of another Presbytery, to the Clerk of that Presbytery.

30. Service of Introduction

(1) When a minister has been appointed to a linked charge, the Presbytery shall determine in which of the churches of the linking the induction is to take place. This shall be a service of induction to the charge, in consequence of which the person inducted shall become minister of each of the congregations embraced in the linking. The edict regarding the induction, which shall be in terms of Schedule P, shall be read in all of the churches

concerned. There shall be no other service of induction; but, if the churches are far distant from one another, or for other good reason, the Presbytery may appoint a service of introduction to be held in the other church or churches. Intimation shall be given of such service, but not in edictal form.

(2)   In any case of deferred union or deferred linking, the minister elected and appointed shall be inducted 'to the vacant congregation of A in deferred union (or linking) with the congregation of B' and there shall be no need for any further act to establish his or her position as minister of the united congregation or of the linked congregation as the case may be. The Presbytery, however, shall in such a case arrange a service of introduction to the newly united congregation of AB or the newly linked congregation of B. Intimation shall be given of such service, but not in edictal form.

(3)   When an appointment has been made to an extra-parochial office wholly or mainly under control of the Church (community ministry, full-time chaplaincy in hospital, industry, prison or university, full-time clerkship and so on), the Presbytery may deem it appropriate to arrange a service of introduction to take place in a church or chapel suitable to the occasion.

(4)   When an appointment has been made to a parochial appointment other than that of an inducted minister, the Presbytery may arrange a service of introduction to take place within the parish. If ordination is involved, suitable arrangements shall be made and edictal intimation shall be given in terms of Schedule P.

(5)   A service of introduction not involving ordination shall follow the lines of an induction except that instead of putting the normal questions to the minister the Moderator shall ask him or her to affirm the vows taken at his or her ordination. Where the service, in terms of subsection (3) or (4) above, includes the ordination of the minister, the vows shall be put in full. In either case, in the declaration, the Moderator in place of 'I induct you to ...' shall say: 'I welcome you as ...'.

31. Demission of Status
If a minister seeks to demit his or her status as a minister of the Church of Scotland, any accompanying demission of a charge will be dealt with by the Vacancy Procedure Committee in terms of section 4 of this Act without further delay, but the question of demission of status shall be considered by the Presbytery itself. The Moderator of Presbytery, or a deputy appointed by him or her, shall first confer with the minister regarding his or her reasons and shall report to the Presbytery if there appears to be any reason not to grant permission to demit status. Any decision to grant permission to demit status shall be immediately reported to the Board of Ministry.

32. Miscellaneous
For the purposes of this Act, intimations to congregations may be made (a) verbally during every act of worship or (b) in written intimations distributed to the whole congregation provided that the congregation's attention is specifically drawn to the presence of an intimation there in terms of this Act.

For the purposes of this Act, attestation of all intimations to congregations shall consist of certification thereof by the Session Clerk as follows:

(1)   Certification that all intimations received have been duly made on the correct number of Sundays shall be sent to the Presbytery Clerk before the service of induction or introduction.

(2)   Certification that any particular intimation received has been duly made on the correct number of Sundays shall be furnished on demand to the Vacancy Procedure Committee or the Presbytery Clerk.

(3)   Intimation shall be made immediately to the Presbytery Clerk in the event that intimation has not been duly made on the appropriate Sunday.

SCHEDULES

A   INTIMATION OF ACTION OR DECISION OF VACANCY PROCEDURE COMMITTEE – Section 2(1)

To be read on one Sunday

The Vacancy Procedure Committee of the Presbytery of .... proposes [here insert action or permission proposed] .... Any communicant member of the congregation(s) of A [and B] may submit to the Presbytery Clerk a request for this proposal to be considered at the next meeting of the Presbytery: where such requests are received from four individuals, being communicant members of the congregation(s) or full members of the Presbytery, the request shall be met. Such request should be submitted in writing to [name and postal address of Presbytery Clerk] by [date seven days after intimation].

A .... B ....   Presbytery Clerk

B   EDICT CITING A CONGREGATION TO ATTEND – Section 2(5)

To be read on one Sunday

Intimation is hereby given that in connection with the [anticipated] vacancy in this congregation a valid request has been made for the matter of [here insert action or permission which had been proposed] to be considered by the Presbytery. [The proposed course of action] is in the mean time sisted.

Intimation is hereby further given that the Presbytery will meet to consider this matter at .... on .... the .... day of .... at .... o'clock and that the congregation are hereby cited to attend for their interests.

A .... B ....   Presbytery Clerk

C   PREPARATION OF ELECTORAL REGISTER – Section 13(1) and (2)

To be read on two Sundays

Intimation is hereby given that in view of the [1]anticipated vacancy, the Kirk Session is about to make up an Electoral Register of this congregation. Any communicant whose name is not already on the Communion Roll as a member should hand in to the Session Clerk a Certificate of Transference, and anyone wishing his or her name added to the Register as an adherent should obtain from the Session Clerk, and complete and return to him or her, a Form of Adherent's Claim. All such papers should be in the hands of the Session Clerk not later than .... The Kirk Session will meet in .... on .... at .... to make up the Electoral Register when anyone wishing to support his or her claim in person should attend.

C .... D ....   Interim Moderator

[1] This word to be included where appropriate – otherwise to be deleted

D FORM OF ADHERENT'S CLAIM – Section 13(1)

I, [1]......... of [2]........., being not under 18 years of age, being a parishioner or regular worshipper in the Church of .... and not being a member of any other congregation in Scotland, claim to have my name put on the Electoral Register of the parish of .... as an adherent.

Date ....   (Signed) ....

[1] Here enter full name in block capitals
[2] Here enter address in full

E INSPECTION OF ELECTORAL REGISTER – Section 13(3)

To be read on one Sunday

Intimation is hereby given that the proposed Electoral Register of this congregation has now been prepared and that an opportunity of inspecting it will be given today in .... at the close of this service, and that it will be open for inspection at .... on .... between the hours of .... and .... each day. Any questions regarding entries in the Register should be brought to the notice of the Kirk Session which is to meet in .... on .... at .... o'clock when it will finally make up the Electoral Register.

C .... D ....   Interim Moderator

F REVISION OF ELECTORAL REGISTER – Section 13(6)

To be read on two Sundays

Intimation is hereby given that more than six months having elapsed since the Electoral Register of this congregation was finally made up, it is now proposed that it should be revised. An opportunity of inspecting the Register will be given in .... at the close of this service, and also at .... on .... between the hours of .... and .... each day. Anyone wishing his or her name added to the Electoral Register as a member should give in a Transference Certificate, or as an adherent should give in a Form of Adherent's Claim (copies of which may be had from the Session Clerk) not later than .... The Kirk Session will meet in .... on .... at .... o'clock when it will finally make up the Revised Register.

C .... D ....   Interim Moderator

G INTIMATION OF ELECTION OF NOMINATING COMMITTEE – Section 14(1)

To be read on two Sundays

Intimation is hereby given that a meeting of this congregation will be held in the Church [or other arrangement may be given here] on Sunday .... at the close of morning worship for the purpose of appointing a Nominating Committee which will nominate one person to the congregation with a view to the appointment of a minister.

C .... D ....   Interim Moderator

H   MINUTE OF NOMINATION BY NOMINATING COMMITTEE – Section 21

To be read on two Sundays

(1)   The Committee chosen by this congregation to nominate a person with a view to the election and appointment of a minister, at a meeting held at .... on .... resolved to name and propose [1]......... and they accordingly do name and propose the said ....

Date ....

E .... F ....   Convener of Committee

[1] The name and designation of the person should at this point be entered in full

(2)   Intimation is therefore hereby given that the Nominating Committee having, as by minute now read, named and proposed [Name], arrangements have been made whereby public worship will be conducted in this Church by him or her on Sunday the .... day of .... at .... o'clock; and that a vote will be taken by voting-papers immediately thereafter; and that electors may vote For or Against electing and appointing the said [Name] as minister of this vacant charge.

C .... D ....   Interim Moderator

I VOTING-PAPER – Section 23

FOR Electing [Name]
AGAINST Electing [Name]

Directions to Voters: If you are in favour of electing [Name], put a cross (x) on the upper space. If you are not in favour of electing [Name], put a cross (x) in the lower space. Do not put a tick or any other mark upon the paper; if you do, it will be regarded as spoilt and will not be counted.

Note: The Directions to Voters must be printed prominently on the face of the voting-paper

J DECLARATION OF ELECTION RESULT – Section 23(5)

First Form (Successful Election)

I hereby declare that the following are the results of the voting for the election and appointment of a minister to the vacant charge of [1]......... and that the said [Name] has accordingly been elected and appointed subject to the judgement of the courts of the Church.

Date ....   C .... D ....   Interim Moderator

[1] Here enter details

FOR Electing [*Name*]
AGAINST Electing [*Name*]

Second Form (Failure to Elect)

I hereby declare that the following are the results of the voting for the election and appointment of a minister to the vacant charge of [1]........ and that in consequence of this vote there has been a failure to elect, and the Nominating Committee is deemed to have been discharged. [Continue in terms of Schedule G if appropriate.]

Date ....   C .... D ....   Interim Moderator

[1] Here enter details

FOR Electing [*Name*]
AGAINST Electing [*Name*]

K THE CALL – Section 25(1)

Form of Call

We, members of the Church of Scotland and of the congregation known as .... , being without a minister, address this Call to be our minister to you, ..., of whose gifts and qualities we have been assured, and we warmly invite you to accept this Call, promising that we shall devote ourselves with you to worship, witness, mission and service in this parish, and also to the furtherance of these in the world, to the glory of God and for the advancement of His Kingdom.

Paper of Concurrence

We, regular worshippers in the congregation of the Church of Scotland known as ......, concur in the Call addressed by that congregation to .... to be their minister.
N.B. The Call and Paper of Concurrence should be dated and attested by the Interim Moderator before they are transmitted to the Clerk of the Presbytery

L SUBSCRIBING THE CALL – Section 25(1)

To be read on at least one Sunday

Intimation is hereby given that this congregation, having elected [*Name*] to be their minister, a Call to the said [*Name*] has been prepared and will lie in .... on .... the .... day of .... between the hours of .... and .... when those whose names are on the Communion Roll of the congregation may sign in person or by means of mandates. Forms of mandate may be obtained from the Session Clerk.

A paper of Concurrence will also be available for signature by persons of 14 years of age or over who are connected with the congregation but whose names are not on the Communion Roll of the congregation.

C .... D ....   Interim Moderator

M MANDATE TO SIGN CALL – Section 25(2)

I, ... of ...., being a person whose name is on the Electoral Register of the congregation, hereby authorise the Session Clerk, or other member of Session, to add my name to the Call addressed to [Name] to be our minister.

(Signed) ....

N CITATION IN CASE OF NOMINATION BY PRESBYTERY – Section 26(a)(iii)
To be read on one Sunday

Intimation is hereby given that [Name] whom the Presbytery has appointed to be minister of this congregation will conduct public worship in the Church on Sunday the .... day of .... at .... o'clock.

Intimation is hereby further given that a Call addressed to the said [Name] will lie in .... on .... the .... day of .... between the hours of .... and .... during the day and between the hours of .... and .... in the evening, when members may sign in person or by means of mandates, forms of which may be had from the Session Clerk.

Intimation is hereby further given that the Presbytery will meet to deal with the appointment and Call at .... on .... the .... day of .... at .... o'clock and that the congregation are hereby cited to attend for their interests.

A .... B ....   Presbytery Clerk

O EDICTAL INTIMATION OF ADMISSION – Section 29(1)
To be read on two Sundays

Whereas the Presbytery of .... has received a Call from this congregation addressed to [Name] to be their minister, and the said Call has been sustained as a regular Call, and has been accepted by him/her[1]:
And whereas the said Presbytery, having judged the said [Name] qualified[2] for the ministry of the Gospel and for this charge, has resolved to proceed to his or her[3] ordination and induction on .... the .... day of .... at .... o'clock unless something occurs which may reasonably impede it:
Notice is hereby given to all concerned that if they, or any of them, have anything to object to in the life or doctrine of the said [Name] they may appear at the Presbytery which is to meet at .... on .... the .... day of .... at .... o'clock; with certification that if no relevant objection be then made and immediately substantiated, the Presbytery will proceed without further delay.

By order of the Presbytery

A .... B ....   Presbytery Clerk

[1] add, where appropriate, 'and his or her translation has been agreed to by the Presbytery of ....'
[2] omit 'for the ministry of the Gospel and' if the minister to be inducted has been ordained previously
[3] omit, where appropriate, 'ordination and'

P EDICTAL INTIMATION OF ORDINATION IN CASE OF INTRODUCTION –
Section 30(1)

To be read on two Sundays

Whereas [narrate circumstances requiring service of introduction]

And whereas the Presbytery, having found the said [*Name*] to have been regularly appointed and to be qualified for the ministry of the Gospel and for the said appointment, has resolved to proceed to his or her ordination to the Holy Ministry and to his or her introduction as [specify appointment] on .... the .... day of .... at .... o'clock unless something occur which may reasonably impede it;

Notice is hereby given to all concerned that if they, or any of them, have anything to object to in the life or doctrine of the said [Name] they may appear at the Presbytery which is to meet at .... on .... the .... day of .... at .... o'clock; with certification that if no relevant objection be then made and immediately substantiated, the Presbytery will proceed without further delay.

By order of the Presbytery

A .... B ....   Presbytery Clerk

SECTION 4

The
General Assembly
of 2003

(1) OFFICIALS OF THE GENERAL ASSEMBLY

The Lord High Commissioner:	The Rt Hon. Lord Steel of Aikwood
Moderator:	Right Rev. Prof. Iain R. Torrance TD MA BD DPhil
Chaplains to the Moderator:	Rev. Iain C. Barclay MBE TD MA BD MTh MPhil PhD
	Rev. Jane L. Barron BA DipEd BD MTh
Acting Principal Clerk:	Rev. Marjory A. MacLean LLB BD
Acting Depute Clerk:	Rev. Matthew Z. Ross LLB BD FSAScot
Procurator:	Mr Patrick S. Hodge QC
Law Agent:	Mrs Janette S. Wilson LLB NP
Convener of the Business Committee:	Rev. David W. Lacy BA BD
Vice-Convener of the Business Committee:	Rev. William C. Hewitt BD DipPS
Precentor:	Rev. Douglas Galbraith MA BD BMus MPhil ARSCM
Assembly Officer:	Mr David McColl
Assistant Assembly Officer:	Mr Craig Marshall

(2) THE MODERATOR

The Right Reverend Professor Iain R. Torrance TD MA BD DPhil

Professor Torrance is Dean of the Faculty of Arts and Divinity at the University of Aberdeen and Master of Christ's College, Aberdeen. He holds a personal Chair in Patristics and Christian Ethics and is Senate Assessor to the University Court. He is a Chaplain to Her Majesty the Queen in Scotland.

Born in Aberdeen on 13 January 1949, Professor Torrance was educated at Edinburgh Academy and Monkton Combe School, Bath. He studied at the Universities of Edinburgh (MA Mental Philosophy) and St Andrews (BD New Testament Language and Literature) and at Oriel College in the University of Oxford, where he was awarded a DPhil in Syriac Patristics. He is the son of the Very Reverend Professor Thomas Torrance, who was Moderator of the 1976 General Assembly of the Church of Scotland.

From 1982, Professor Torrance was Minister of Northmavine, Shetland, leaving in 1985 to become Lecturer in New Testament and Christian Ethics at Queen's Theological College,

Birmingham. Queen's is an ecumenical college, training ministers and lay workers for the Church of England, the Methodist Church and the United Reformed Church. After a period as Lecturer in New Testament and Patristics at the University of Birmingham, Professor Torrance moved to the University of Aberdeen, where he became Professor in Patristics and Christian Ethics and, since 2001, Dean of the Faculty of Arts and Divinity.

Professor Torrance was a TA Chaplain from 1982 until 1997 and ACF Chaplain from 1996 until 2000. As Convener of the Church of Scotland Committee on Chaplains to Her Majesty's Forces (1998–2002), Professor Torrance led the Forces' Chaplaincy Services through a time of change, interfacing the needs of the military with the realities of parish ministry. He was twice invited by General Sir Michael Rose to address Adjutants General of the NATO nations. He also served as a member of the Ministry of Defence Committee that produced the McGill report on *Spiritual Values in Today's Army*.

Professor Torrance has been co-editor of the *Scottish Journal of Theology* since 1982. His publications include *Christology after Chalcedon* (1988) and *Ethics and the Military Community* (1998). He was co-editor and part author of *Human Genetics: A Christian Perspective* (1995), co-editor and part author of *To Glorify God: Essays on Modern Reformed Liturgy* (1999) and editor of *Bioethics for the New Millennium* (2001).

Married to Morag, who is manager of the IT Training Unit at the University of Aberdeen, Professor Torrance has a son and a daughter, both students.

His hobbies are Scottish art since 1860, literature and history.

(From information supplied through the Media Relations Unit)

---

(3) DIGEST OF ASSEMBLY DECISIONS

The full text of the Reports, Acts and Deliverances of each General Assembly can be obtained from the Principal Clerk. What has traditionally been included in this section of the *Year Book* is nothing more significant than the Editor's personal selection of those decisions of the most recent Assembly which, in his view at the time of writing, seemed likely to be of most immediate interest not only to the committed Church member but also to the more casual observer of the Assembly. The Assembly of 2003 took many decisions which may well turn out to have far-reaching implications for the future life, work and structures of our Church. As events unfold and as the various Boards and Committees develop further some of their quite radical proposals, it may be all too clear that the Editor was in this selection – and that to a greater extent even than normal – guilty of a number of serious sins of omission. As things stand, however, the following seemed to him likely to catch the interest of those who, for whatever reason, chance upon and read these pages.

ASSEMBLY COUNCIL

The Council and the Co-ordinating Forum were instructed to formulate proposals for strategic planning, including the determination of priorities, and structural change. A report is to be given to the Assembly of 2004.

BOARD OF COMMUNICATION

The National Youth Assembly was invited to consider the relationship between the Church of Scotland and the media, and the Church's use of the media. Their findings are to be reported to the Principal Clerk.

The Assembly reaffirmed the editorial independence of *Life & Work*.
(See also under the Board of Parish Education.)

BOARD OF MINISTRY

The Assembly encouraged the Board in its provision of study leave for ministers and expressed satisfaction that the ongoing professional development of ministers was being provided through this means. The Board was instructed to prepare recommendations for the Assembly of 2004 regarding the continuing funding of the scheme.

The Assembly approved proposals allowing flexibility in respect of the retirement age for ministers and noted the intention of the Board to bring to the Assembly of 2004 working regulations and a suitable amendment of the relevant Act. The Board was meantime instructed to devise and implement by 1 June 2003 a pilot scheme, with appointments commencing no later than the Assembly of 2004 and lasting up to twelve months.

With Deacons, Readers, worship leaders and elders being, of increasing necessity, used by the Church in worship and pastoral roles, the Board was instructed to provide practical definition of the particular Ministry of Word and Sacrament and to express this in terms of collaborative, reflective and team working. A Report is to be presented to the Assembly in either 2004 or 2005.

BOARD OF NATIONAL MISSION

The Assembly endorsed Team Ministry as a principal way of developing ministry within the Church of Scotland. Presbyteries were instructed to undertake the promotion of Team Ministry within groups of congregations through conference, consultation and other appropriate means. The Board of Ministry was instructed to include, in pre- and post-ordination training programmes, courses about working in Team Ministry.

The Assembly Council, through the Co-ordinating Forum, was instructed to bring to the Assembly of 2004 proposals for a unified Parish Staffing budget, including, *inter alia*, the cost of parish ministers. The Board of National Mission was instructed to draw on reserve funds to maintain the present establishment of parish field staff over the years 2004–6 or until a new scheme of funding Parish Staffing had been agreed, whichever was the sooner.

The Royal Mail was encouraged to make available to the people of the United Kingdom at Christmas time, as an option, a stamp or stamps with a specifically Christian theme.

BOARD OF PARISH EDUCATION

The Assembly noted with regret the dissolution of the Scottish Churches' Open College with effect from December 2003.

The Assembly encouraged Boards, Committees and Courts of the Church to keep before them issues of gender attitude in their work.

The Board of Parish Education, the Board of Communication and the Assembly Council were instructed to investigate the possibility of amalgamating the Scottish Christian Press and Saint Andrew Press.

BOARD OF PRACTICE AND PROCEDURE

The Assembly determined that, except where the sensitive or confidential nature of the business to be discussed made openness inappropriate, meetings of Boards and Committees of the Assembly shall be deemed to be open to members of the Church and to the public generally.

The Solicitor of the Church was instructed to produce a written version of the Unitary (quoad omnia) Constitution and to distribute a sample copy to all Presbyteries by 31 October 2003. The Board was instructed to produce guidelines relating to the operation of Unitary congregations and to issue these to Presbyteries by 31 October 2003. Presbyteries were empowered to authorise the adoption of a Unitary Constitution from 1 November 2003.

BOARD OF SOCIAL RESPONSIBILITY

The Assembly commended the Board for setting up a Review Group on Older People's Residential Care and encouraged the Board to continue to monitor changes in service needs and provision, using a variety of methodologies to tailor its needs to the twenty-first century. The Board was instructed to put into practice lessons learned from past experience – especially the closure programme of 2002. The Assembly agreed a sequential process to be followed in deciding to close a care home.

The Assembly reaffirmed its opposition to euthanasia and urged Her Majesty's Government to oppose any attempts to introduce euthanasia to the United Kingdom.

BOARD OF STEWARDSHIP AND FINANCE

The Assembly adopted 'The Mission and Renewal Fund' as the new name for 'The Mission and Aid Fund' from 1 January 2004.

Having heard that budget cuts of around £2,320,000 would be required over the next five years, the Assembly granted powers to the Board of Stewardship and Finance to ensure, by such management action as it deemed necessary, that these cuts were effected by 2008.

BOARD OF WORLD MISSION

The Assembly instructed the Board of World Mission to continue to respond to the threat posed by HIV/AIDS. Presbyteries, congregations and members were urged to support the HIV/AIDS Project through learning, prayer, giving and action.

The Board of World Mission was instructed to enter into discussion with the Assembly Council, the Board of Stewardship and Finance and the Co-ordinating Forum on ways in which, at a time of emphasis on congregational resourcing and parish staffing, due consideration could be given to the expression of meaningful solidarity with partner churches in needy and strife-torn countries. There is to be a report to the Assembly of 2004.

CENTRAL CO-ORDINATING COMMITTEE

The General Assembly instructed the Central Co-ordinating Committee to establish an Advisory, Negotiating and Consultative Group comprising management and employee-elected representatives to advise the Committee on matters of pay, conditions of service and other relevant matters such as the management of structural change. The arrangements made are to be reported to the Assembly of 2004.

CHURCH OF SCOTLAND GUILD

The Assembly approved a Revised Constitution for the Guild: though relatively minor, the changes represented 'a spirit of welcome and inclusion and a desire for clarity and flexibility'. The Constitution sets out the Aim of the Guild in the following terms: 'The Church of Scotland Guild is a movement within the Church of Scotland which invites and encourages both women and men to commit their lives to Jesus Christ and enables them to express their faith in worship, prayer and action'.

COMMITTEE ON ARTISTIC MATTERS

The Committee on Artistic Matters was encouraged to produce an illustrated publication with the aim of furthering the imaginative use and development of church buildings, bearing in mind also the special conditions of charges using non-ecclesiastical buildings.

COMMITTEE ON CHURCH AND NATION

The Assembly called on Her Majesty's Government to recognise the continuing value of Post Offices to rural and urban communities.

The Assembly affirmed that, in a representative democracy, direct election is the basis on which those promoting and revising legislation should be chosen.

The Assembly commended those communities which had received and supported refugees and asylum-seekers, expressed regret at the politicisation of this area and encouraged MPs, MSPs and the Church to continue to look for creative solutions to address the issue on humanitarian grounds.

The Assembly encouraged Church members, where possible, to promote the use of Fair Trade Products.

COMMITTEE ON ECUMENICAL RELATIONS

The Assembly welcomed the development of friendly and creative discussion with sister Presbyterian churches in Scotland.

The Assembly instructed the Committee on Ecumenical Relations to appoint five people to serve on a Committee with a similar number from the United Free Church to explore issues detailed in the Committee's report. The report made it clear that this was not an initiative for union but for closer co-operation.

The Assembly noted the valuable work that had been carried out by all involved over the past seven years in the Scottish Churches Initiative for Union (SCIFU) but acknowledged that the growing spirit of unity among Christians in Scotland was unlikely to be advanced by implementing the SCIFU proposals. The Assembly accordingly instructed the Committee on Ecumenical Relations to withdraw from further involvement with SCIFU. In view of this, the Committee was asked to review the ecumenical strategy of the Church of Scotland in Scotland and to report to a future General Assembly.

COMMITTEE ON EDUCATION

The Committee on Education was instructed to work in conjunction with the Board of Parish Education to draw up for those working with young people in the Church advice on dealing with incidents of drug misuse.

COMMITTEE TO REVISE THE HYMNARY

The Assembly authorised *The Church Hymnary: Fourth Edition* for use throughout the Church. (See also under the Panel on Worship.)

GENERAL TRUSTEES

Congregations were reminded of the availability of the Better Heating Scheme under which skilled advice could be obtained in the matters of saving money on heating bills and improving the standard of comfort in buildings.

The General Trustees were instructed to pursue their investigations into how the Church might reduce its liabilities in the matter of the maintenance of buildings.

The General Trustees were urged to develop strategies for funding in order to support congregations who have difficulty altering the fabric of their buildings to meet the requirements of the Disability Discrimination Act 1995.

IONA COMMUNITY BOARD

The General Assembly noted with pleasure the constructive and cordial relationships being developed on Iona with Historic Scotland and through the Iona Liaison Group.

JOINT COMMITTEE ON THE PROTECTION OF CHILDREN
AND YOUNG PEOPLE IN THE CHURCH

Kirk Sessions were reminded of the need to comply with the systems relating to the selection and appointment of volunteers and paid staff working with children as contained in the Child Protection Handbook. Presbyteries were instructed to monitor congregations in regard to this.

Kirk Sessions were instructed to insist that all Child Protection Co-ordinators attend appropriate Church of Scotland-approved training when appointed to their position.

PANEL ON DOCTRINE

Act V 2000 (Consolidating Act anent the Sacraments) was amended. The amended Act, *inter alia*, makes provision for another family member to act, in place of the parent but with the parent's consent, in the baptism of a child. In making this change, the Church recognised that in a number of cases it is in reality a grandparent or other family member, rather than one of the parents, who seeks the child's baptism. (For fuller information, see section 3, subsection 1, of the *Year Book*.) The Panel on Doctrine and the Board of Parish Education were instructed to prepare a basis of instruction on baptism consonant with the amended Act.

PANEL ON WORSHIP

The Panel was instructed to proceed with the production of *Prayers for the Christian Year* as a companion to *Common Order* (1994).

On the Report of the Church Hymnary Trustees, the General Assembly approved the proposal of the Trustees to apply funds surplus after the payment of the production costs of *The Church Hymnary: Fourth Edition* towards discounting the purchase price of that Hymnary.

RETURNS TO OVERTURES

The Board of Ministry was instructed by the Assembly to recommend or provide training for those who, preparing for the task of acting as Interim Moderators, are not ministers.

The Assembly instructed the Board of Practice and Procedure to review the working of the Barrier Act and to report to the Assembly of 2005.

The Church of Scotland

HOUSING & LOAN FUND FOR MINISTERS AND WIDOWS AND WIDOWERS OF MINISTERS

Many Ministers and their widow(er)s need help to secure a home for their retirement. They live in manses during their years of service, but as these are tied houses, the manse families must move and put down new roots. The Church of Scotland Housing and Loan Fund owns and acquires houses for renting, or gives loans, which make it possible for the manse family to secure retirement housing.

The Fund can also assist Retired Ministers and their widow(er)s by helping them move to more suitable accommodation.

Over the years, these services on favourable terms have been greatly valued. Ministers and others remember our fund in their wills and gifts enable our work to continue into the future and are welcome at any time.

Donations, Legacies and Gift Aid Contributions will be welcomed with gratitude. Applications for assistance should be directed to The Secretary, Miss Lin J Macmillan, MA, The Church of Scotland Housing and Loan Fund for Retired Ministers and Widows and Widowers of Ministers, 121 George Street, Edinburgh, EH2 4YN. Tel: 0131 225 5722   Direct Fax: 0131 240 2264 [e] lmacmillan@cofscotland.org.uk

THE CHURCH OF SCOTLAND

CHARITY No. Sc 015273

SECTION 5

Presbytery Lists

SECTION 5 – PRESBYTERY LISTS

In each Presbytery list, the congregations are listed in alphabetical order. In a linked charge, the names appear under the first named congregation. Under the name of the congregation will be found the name of the minister and, where applicable, that of an associate minister, auxiliary minister and member of the Diaconate. The years indicated after a minister's name in the congregational section of each Presbytery list are the year of ordination (column 1) and the year of current appointment (column 2). Where only one date is given, it is both the year of ordination and the year of appointment.

In the second part of each Presbytery list, those named are listed alphabetically. The first date is the year of ordination, and the following date is the year of appointment or retirement. If the person concerned is retired, then the appointment last held will be shown in brackets.

KEY TO ABBREVIATIONS

(E) Indicates a Church Extension charge. New Charge Developments are separately indicated.

(GD) Indicates a charge where it is desirable that the minister should have a knowledge of Gaelic.

(GE) Indicates a charge where public worship must be regularly conducted in Gaelic.

(H) Indicates that a Hearing Aid Loop system has been installed. In Linked charges, the (H) is placed beside the appropriate building as far as possible.

(L) Indicates that a Chair Lift has been installed.

(T) Indicates that the minister has been appointed on the basis of Terminable Tenure.

PRESBYTERY NUMBERS

1	Edinburgh	18	Dumbarton
2	West Lothian	19	South Argyll
3	Lothian	20	Dunoon
4	Melrose and Peebles	21	Lorn and Mull
5	Duns	22	Falkirk
6	Jedburgh	23	Stirling
7	Annandale and Eskdale	24	Dunfermline
8	Dumfries and Kirkcudbright	25	Kirkcaldy
9	Wigtown and Stranraer	26	St Andrews
10	Ayr	27	Dunkeld and Meigle
11	Irvine and Kilmarnock	28	Perth
12	Ardrossan	29	Dundee
13	Lanark	30	Angus
14	Greenock and Paisley	31	Aberdeen
15		32	Kincardine and Deeside
16	Glasgow	33	Gordon
17	Hamilton	34	Buchan

35	Moray
36	Abernethy
37	Inverness
38	Lochaber
39	Ross
40	Sutherland
41	Caithness
42	Lochcarron–Skye
43	Uist
44	Lewis
45	Orkney
46	Shetland
47	England
48	Europe
49	Jerusalem

(1) EDINBURGH

Meets at Palmerston Place Church, Edinburgh, on the first Tuesday of October, November, December, February, March, April and May and on the second Tuesday in September and on the last Tuesday of June. When the first Tuesday of April falls in Holy Week, the meeting is on the second Tuesday.

Clerk: REV. W. PETER GRAHAM MA BD | 10 Palmerston Place, Edinburgh EH12 5AA [E-mail: akph50@uk.uumail.com] | 0131-225 9137

1 **Edinburgh: Albany Deaf Church of Edinburgh (H)**
Alistair F. Kelly BL (Locum) — 1961
19 Avon Place, Edinburgh EH4 6RE | 0131-317 9877

2 **Edinburgh: Balerno (H)**
Jared W. Hay BA MTh DipMin — 1987 — 2001
3 Johnsburn Road, Balerno EH14 7DN [E-mail: jared.hay@blueyonder.co.uk] | 0131-449 3830
Charles W.H. Barrington MA BD (Assoc) — 1997
502 Lanark Road, Edinburgh EH14 5DH [E-mail: charles.barrington@classicfm.net] | 0131-453 4826

3 **Edinburgh: Barclay (0131-229 6810)**
Vacant
38 Cluny Gardens, Edinburgh EH10 6BN | 0131-447 8702

4 **Edinburgh: Blackhall St Columba (0131-332 4431)**
Alexander B. Douglas BD — 1979 — 1991
5 Blinkbonny Crescent, Edinburgh EH4 3NB [E-mail: alexandjill@btopenworld.com] | 0131-343 3708

5 **Edinburgh: Bristo Memorial Craigmillar**
Angus L. Bayne LTh BEd MTh — 1969 — 1994
72 Blackchapel Close, Edinburgh EH15 3SL [E-mail: baynez@aol.com] | 0131-657 3266
Agnes M. Rennie (Miss) DCS
3/1 Craigmillar Court, Edinburgh EH16 4AD | 0131-661 8475

6 **Edinburgh: Broughton St Mary's (H) (0131-556 4786)**
Vacant
103 East Claremont Street, Edinburgh EH7 4JA | 0131-556 7313

7 **Edinburgh: Canongate (H)**
Charles Robertson MA — 1965 — 1978
Manse of Canongate, Edinburgh EH8 8BR [E-mail: canongate1@aol.com] | 0131-556 3515

8 **Edinburgh: Carrick Knowe (H) (0131-334 1505)**
Fiona M. Mathieson (Mrs) BEd BD — 1988 — 2001
21 Traquair Park West, Edinburgh EH12 7AN [E-mail: fiona.mathieson@ukgateway.net] | 0131-334 9774

9 **Edinburgh: Colinton (H) (0131-441 2232)**
George J. Whyte BSc BD — 1981 — 1992
The Manse, Colinton, Edinburgh EH13 0JR [E-mail: georgewhyte@vestry.fsnet.co.uk] | 0131-441 2315
Mark Evans DCS
13 East Drylaw Drive, Edinburgh EH4 2QA | 0131-343 3089

No.	Congregation / Minister	Ord.	Ind.	Address / E-mail	Telephone
10	**Edinburgh: Colinton Mains (H)**				
	Ian A. McQuarrie BD	1993		17 Swanston Green, Edinburgh EH10 7EW [E-mail: ian.mcquarrie@talk21.com]	0131-445 3451
11	**Edinburgh: Corstorphine Craigsbank (H) (0131-334 6365)**				
	Stewart M. McPherson BD CertMin	1991	2003	22 Belgrave Road, Edinburgh EH12 6NF	0131-334 3557 / 07814 901429 (Mbl)
12	**Edinburgh: Corstorphine Old (H) (0131-334 7864)**				
	James Bain BD DipMin	1996	2002	23 Manse Road, Edinburgh EH12 7SW	0131-334 5425
13	**Edinburgh: Corstorphine St Anne's (0131-316 4740)**				
	Maryann M. Rennie BD MTh	1998	2002	23 Belgrave Road, Edinburgh EH12 6NG [E-mail: maryann.rennie@btinternet.com]	0131-334 3188
14	**Edinburgh: Corstorphine St Ninian's (H)**				
	Alexander T. Stewart MA BD FSAScot	1975	1995	17 Templeland Road, Edinburgh EH12 8RZ [E-mail: alextstewart@blueyonder.co.uk]	0131-334 2978
	Margaret Gordon (Mrs) DCS			92 Lanark Road West, Currie EH14 5LA	0131-449 2554
15	**Edinburgh: Craigentinny St Christopher's**				
	Lilly C. Easton (Mrs)	1999		61 Milton Crescent, Edinburgh EH15 3PQ	0131-669 2429
16	**Edinburgh: Craiglockhart (H)**				
	Andrew Ritchie BD DipMin DMin	1984	1991	202 Colinton Road, Edinburgh EH14 1BP [E-mail: arit202@aol.com]	0131-443 2020
17	**Edinburgh: Craigmillar Park (T) (H) (0131-667 5862)**				
	Sarah E.C. Nicol (Mrs) BSc BD	1985	1994	14 Hallhead Road, Edinburgh EH16 5QJ [E-mail: sneditions@easynet.co.uk]	0131-667 1623
18	**Edinburgh: Cramond (H)**				
	G. Russell Barr BA BD MTh DMin	1979	1993	Manse of Cramond, Edinburgh EH4 6NS [E-mail: rev.r.barr@blueyonder.co.uk]	0131-336 2036
19	**Edinburgh: Currie (H) (0131-451 5141) (E-mail: currie.kirk@btinternet.com)**				
	Keith W. Ross MA BD	1984	2000	43 Lanark Road West, Currie EH14 5JX	0131-449 4719 / 07779 909801 (Mbl)
	Paul Middleton BMus BD	2000	2001	7/1 Atholl Crescent Lane, Edinburgh EH3 8ET	
20	**Edinburgh: Dalmeny**				
	To be linked with Kirkliston				

21   Edinburgh: Davidson's Mains (H) (0131-312 6282) (E-mail: dmains_parish_church@talk21.com)
Jeremy R.H. Middleton LLB BD   1981   1988   1 Hillpark Terrace, Edinburgh EH4 7SX   0131-336 3078

22   Edinburgh: Dean (H)
Mark M. Foster BSc BD   1998   1 Ravelston Terrace, Edinburgh EH4 3EF   0131-332 5736
                                                      [E-mail: markmfoster@mac.com]

23   Edinburgh: Drylaw (0131-343 6643)
I. Maxwell Homewood MSc BD   1997   2001   5 Essex Brae, Edinburgh EH4 6LN   0131-339 3554
                                                      [E-mail: max.homewood@btinternet.com]

24   Edinburgh: Duddingston
James A.P. Jack DMin BSc BArch BD   1989   2001   Manse of Duddingston, Old Church Lane, Edinburgh EH15 3PX   0131-661 4240
                                                      [E-mail: jamesapjack@aol.com]

25   Edinburgh: Fairmilehead (H) (0131-445 2374)
John R. Munro BD   1976   1992   6 Braid Crescent, Edinburgh EH10 6AU   0131-446 9363

26   Edinburgh: Gilmerton (New Charge Development)
Paul H. Beautyman MA BD   1993   2002   43 Ravenscroft Street, Edinburgh EH17 8QJ   0131-664 2147

27   Edinburgh: Gorgie (H) (0131-337 7936)
Peter I. Barber MA BD   1984   1995   90 Myreside Road, Edinburgh EH10 5BZ   0131-337 2284
                                                      [E-mail: pibarber@supanet.com]

28   Edinburgh: Granton (H) (0131-552 3033)
Vacant   8 Wardie Crescent, Edinburgh EH5 1AG   0131-551 2159
Marilynn Steele (Mrs) DCS   2 Northfield Gardens, Prestonpans EH32 9LQ   01875 811497

29   Edinburgh: Greenbank (H) (0131-447 9969)
Ian G. Scott BSc BD STM   1965   1983   112 Greenbank Crescent, Edinburgh EH10 5SZ   0131-447 4032
                                                      [E-mail: igscott@blueyonder.co.uk]

30   Edinburgh: Greenside (H) (0131-556 5588)
Andrew F. Anderson MA BD   1981   80 Pilrig Street, Edinburgh EH6 5AS   0131-554 3277 (Tel/Fax)
                                                      [E-mail: andrew@pilrig.fsnet.co.uk]

31   Edinburgh: Greyfriars Tolbooth and Highland Kirk (GE) (H) (0131-225 1900)
Richard E. Frazer BA BD DMin   1986   2003   12 Tantallon Place, Edinburgh EH9 1NZ   0131-667 6610

32   Edinburgh: High (St Giles') (0131-225 4363)
Gilleasbuig Macmillan
CVO MA BD Drhc DD   1969   1973   St Giles' Cathedral, Edinburgh EH1 1RE   0131-225 4363
                                                      [E-mail: minister.stgiles@btconnect.com]

No.	Name / Church			Address	Tel
33	**Edinburgh: Holyrood Abbey (H) (0131-661 4883)**		1980		
	Philip R. Hair BD		1998	100 Willowbrae Avenue, Edinburgh EH8 7HU [E-mail: hairmail@compuserve.com]	0131-652 0640
34	**Edinburgh: Holy Trinity (H) (0131-442 3304)**		1977		
	Stanley A. Brook BD MTh		1988	16 Thorburn Road, Edinburgh EH13 0BQ [E-mail: stan_brook@hotmail.com]	0131-441 7167
	Michael S. Dawson BTech BD (Assoc)	1979	1992	12 Sighthill Crescent, Edinburgh EH11 4QE	0131-453 6279
	Joyce Mitchell (Mrs) DCS			16/4 Murrayburn Place, Edinburgh EH14 2RR	0131-453 6548
	Linda Black (Miss) DCS			378 Alwyn Green, Glenrothes KY7 6TS	01592 742346
35	**Edinburgh: Inverleith (H)**		1965		
	D. Hugh Davidson MA		1975	43 Inverleith Gardens, Edinburgh EH3 5PR [E-mail: hdavidson@freeuk.com]	0131-552 3874
36	**Edinburgh: Juniper Green (H)**		1983		
	James S. Dewar MA BD		2000	476 Lanark Road, Juniper Green, Edinburgh EH14 5BQ [E-mail: jsdewar@supanet.com]	0131-453 3494
37	**Edinburgh: Kaimes Lockhart Memorial**		1977		
	Iain D. Penman BD		1995	76 Lasswade Road, Edinburgh EH16 6SF [E-mail: iainpenmanklm@aol.com]	0131-664 2287
38	**Edinburgh: Kirkliston**		1996		
	Glenda J. Keating (Mrs) MTh			43 Main Street, Kirkliston EH29 9AF [E-mail: kirkglen@aol.com]	0131-333 3298
39	**Edinburgh: Kirk o' Field (T) (H)**		1977		
	Ian D. Maxwell MA BD PhD		1996	31 Hatton Place, Edinburgh EH9 1UA [E-mail: i.d.maxwell@quista.net]	0131-667 7954
40	**Edinburgh: Leith North (H) (0131-553 7378)**		1998		
	Kenneth S. Baird MSc PhD BD CEng MIMarE		2003	6 Craighall Gardens, Edinburgh EH6 4RJ	0131-552 4411
41	**Edinburgh: Leith St Andrew's (H)**		1967		
	John Cook MA BD		1984	13 Claremont Park, Edinburgh EH6 7PJ	0131-554 7695
42	**Edinburgh: Leith St Serf's (T) (H)**		1977		
	Sara R. Embleton (Mrs) BA BD		1999	20 Wilton Road, Edinburgh EH16 5NX [E-mail: sara.embleton@which.net]	0131-478 1624
43	**Edinburgh: Leith St Thomas' Junction Road (T)**		1981		
	George C. Shand MA BD		2003	107 Easter Warriston, Edinburgh EH7 4QZ	0131-467 7789

44 Edinburgh: Leith South (H) (0131-554 2578) (E-mail: slpc@dial.pipex.com)
Ian Y. Gilmour BD   1985   1995   37 Claremont Road, Edinburgh EH6 7NN   0131-554 3062
[E-mail: ianyg@aol.com]
Jennifer Booth (Mrs) BD (Assoc)   1996   39 Lilyhill Terrace, Edinburgh EH8 7DR   0131-661 3813

45 Edinburgh: Leith Wardie (H) (0131-551 3847)
Brian C. Hilsley LLB BD   1990   35 Lomond Road, Edinburgh EH5 3JN   0131-552 3328
[E-mail: brian@wardie10.freeserve.co.uk]

46 Edinburgh: Liberton (H)
John N. Young MA BD PhD   1996   7 Kirk Park, Edinburgh EH16 6HZ   0131-664 3067
[E-mail: john@nicolyoung.freeserve.co.uk]

47 Edinburgh: Liberton Northfield (H) (0131-551 3847)
John M. McPake LTh   2000   9 Claverhouse Drive, Edinburgh EH16 6BR   0131-658 1754

48 Edinburgh: London Road (H) (0131-661 1149)
William L. Armitage BSc BD   1976   1991   26 Inchview Terrace, Edinburgh EH7 6TQ   0131-669 5311
[E-mail: billarm@blueyonder.co.uk]

49 Edinburgh: Marchmont St Giles' (H) (0131-447 4359)
Karen K. Watson (Mrs) BD   1997   2002   19 Hope Terrace, Edinburgh EH9 2AP   0131-447 2834
[E-mail: karen@marchmontstgiles.org.uk]

50 Edinburgh: Mayfield Salisbury (0131-667 1522)
Scott S. McKenna BA BD   1994   26 Seton Place, Edinburgh EH9 2JT   0131-667 1286
[E-mail: scottsmckenna@aol.com]
John R. Wells BD DipMin (Assoc)   1991   18 West Mayfield, Edinburgh EH9 1TQ   0131-662 0367

51 Edinburgh: Morningside (H) (0131-447 6745)
Derek Browning MA BD DMin   1987   2003   20 Braidburn Crescent, Edinburgh EH10 6EN   0131-447 1617 (Tel/Fax)
[E-mail: derek.browning@btinternet.com]   07050 133876 (Mbl)

52 Edinburgh: Morningside United (H) (0131-447 3152)
John R. Smith MA BD   1973   1998   1 Midmar Avenue, Edinburgh EH10 6BS   0131-447 8724
[E-mail: ministermuc@aol.com]

53 Edinburgh: Muirhouse St Andrew's (E)
Frederick D.F. Shewan MA BD   1970   1980   35 Silverknowes Road, Edinburgh EH4 5LL   0131-336 4546

54 Edinburgh: Murrayfield (H) (0131-337 1091) (E-mail: murrayfield@parish-church.fsnet.co.uk)
William D. Brown BD CQSW   1987   2001   45 Murrayfield Gardens, Edinburgh EH12 6DH   0131-337 5431
[E-mail: wdb@fish.co.uk]

55 Edinburgh: Newhaven (H)
Grant MacLaughlan BA BD   1998   158 Granton Road, Edinburgh EH5 3RF   0131-552 8906

No.	Church / Minister		Address	Tel
56	**Edinburgh: New Restalrig (H) (0131-661 5676)** David L. Court BSc BD	1989 2000	19 Abercorn Road, Edinburgh EH8 7DP [E-mail: david@lamont-court.freeserve.co.uk]	0131-661 4045
57	**Edinburgh: Old Kirk (H)** Vacant		24 Pennywell Road, Edinburgh EH4 4HD	0131-332 4354
58	**Edinburgh: Palmerston Place (H) (0131-220 1690)** Colin A.M. Sinclair BA BD	1981 1996	30B Cluny Gardens, Edinburgh EH10 6BJ [E-mail: colins@globalnet.co.uk]	0131-447 9598 0131-225 3312 (Fax)
59	**Edinburgh: Pilrig St Paul's (0131-553 1876)** John M. Tait BSc BD	1985 1999	78 Pilrig Street, Edinburgh EH6 5AS [E-mail: john.m.tait@btinternet.com]	0131-554 1842
60	**Edinburgh: Polwarth (H) (0131-346 2711)** John K.S. McMahon MA BD	1998	6 Trotter Haugh, The Grange, Edinburgh EH9 2GZ [E-mail: j.k.s.mcmahon@virgin.net]	0131-667 4055
61	**Edinburgh: Portobello Old (H)** Neil Buchanan BD	1991	6 Hamilton Terrace, Edinburgh EH15 1NB	0131-669 5312
62	**Edinburgh: Portobello St James' (H)** Peter Webster BD	1977 2002	34 Brighton Place, Edinburgh EH15 1LT	0131-669 1767
63	**Edinburgh: Portobello St Philip's Joppa (H) (0131-669 3641)** Stewart G. Weaver BA BD PhD	2003	6 St Mary's Place, Edinburgh EH15 2QF [E-mail: stewartweaver@beeb.net]	0131-669 2410
64	**Edinburgh: Priestfield (H) (0131-667 5644)** Thomas N. Johnston LTh	1972 1990	13 Lady Road, Edinburgh EH16 5PA [E-mail: tomjohnston@blueyonder.co.uk]	0131-668 1620
65	**Edinburgh: Queensferry (H)** John G. Carrie BSc BD	1971	1 Station Road, South Queensferry EH30 9HY [E-mail: john.carrie@virgin.net]	0131-331 1100
66	**Edinburgh: Ratho** Ian J. Wells BD	1999	Ratho, Newbridge EH28 8NP [E-mail: ian@rathomanse.fsnet.co.uk]	0131-333 1346

67 **Edinburgh: Reid Memorial (H) (0131-662 1203)**
Brian M. Embleton BD   1985
20 Wilton Road, Edinburgh EH16 5NX
[E-mail: brian.embleton@which.net]   0131-667 3981

68 **Edinburgh: Richmond Craigmillar (H) (0131-661 6561)**
Elizabeth M. Henderson (Miss)   1985 1997
MA BD MTh
13 Wisp Green, Edinburgh EH15 3QX
[E-mail: lizhende@aol.com]   0131-669 1133

69 **Edinburgh: St Andrew's and St George's (H) (0131-225 3847)**
Vacant
James Aitken BD (Assistant)   2002
25 Comely Bank, Edinburgh EH4 1AJ   0131-332 5324
85 Henderson Row, Edinburgh EH3 5BE   0131-556 2688

70 **Edinburgh: St Andrew's Clermiston**
Alistair H. Keil BD DipMin   1989
87 Drum Brae South, Edinburgh EH12 8TD
[E-mail: alistair.h.keil@talk21.com]   0131-339 4149

71 **Edinburgh: St Catherine's Argyle (H) (0131-667 7220)**
Victor W.N. Laidlaw BD   1975
5 Palmerston Road, Edinburgh EH9 1TL
[E-mail: vandslaidlaw@supanet.com]   0131-667 9344

72 **Edinburgh: St Colm's (T) (H)**
Vacant
1 Merchiston Gardens, Edinburgh EH10 5DD   0131-337 1107

73 **Edinburgh: St Cuthbert's (H) (0131-229 1142)**
Tom C. Cuthell MA BD MTh   1965 1976
34A Murrayfield Road, Edinburgh EH12 6ER   0131-337 6637

74 **Edinburgh: St David's Broomhouse (H) (0131-443 9851)**
Vacant
33 Traquair Park West, Edinburgh EH12 7AN   0131-334 1730

75 **Edinburgh: St George's West (H) (0131-225 7001)**
Peter J. Macdonald BD DipMin   1986 1998
6 Wardie Avenue, Edinburgh EH5 2AB
[E-mail: pjmacdon@aol.com]   0131-552 4333

76 **Edinburgh: St John's Oxgangs**
Vacant
2 Caiystane Terrace, Edinburgh EH10 6SR   0131-445 1688

77 **Edinburgh: St Margaret's (H) (0131-554 7400)**
Carol H.M. Ford DSD RSAMD BD   2003
43 Moira Terrace, Edinburgh EH7 6TD
[E-mail: fordcaro@fish.co.uk]   0131-669 7329
Marion Buchanan (Mrs) DCS
6 Hamilton Terrace, Edinburgh EH15 1NB   0131-669 5312

78 **Edinburgh: St Martin's**
Elizabeth J.B. Ross (Ms) BD   1996 1999
5 Duddingston Crescent, Edinburgh EH15 3AS
[E-mail: elizabethross@ugenie.co.uk]   0131-657 9894
Liz Crocker (Mrs) DCS
77C Craigcrook Road, Edinburgh EH4 3PH   0131-332 0227

79 Edinburgh: St Michael's (H)
Vacant

80 Edinburgh: St Nicholas' Sighthill
Kenneth J. Mackay MA BD   1971 1976   122 Sighthill Loan, Edinburgh EH11 4NT   0131-453 6921

81 Edinburgh: St Stephen's Comely Bank (0131-315 4616)
Graham T. Dickson MA BD   1985 1996   8 Blinkbonny Crescent, Edinburgh EH4 3NB   0131-332 3364 (Tel/Fax)
[E-mail: mail@dickson22.fsnet.co.uk]

82 Edinburgh: Slateford Longstone
Vacant   50 Kingsknowe Road South, Edinburgh EH14 2JW   0131-443 2960
Mary Gargrave (Mrs) DCS   229/3 Calder Road, Edinburgh EH11 4RG   0131-476 3493

83 Edinburgh: Stenhouse St Aidan's
Colin A. Strong BSc BD   1989 2001   65 Balgreen Road, Edinburgh EH12 5UA   0131-337 7711
[E-mail: cstrong@bigfoot.com]
Mary Gargrave (Mrs) DCS   229/3 Calder Road, Edinburgh EH11 4RG   0131-476 3493

84 Edinburgh: Stockbridge (H) (0131-332 0122)
Anne T. Logan (Mrs) MA BD MTh   1981 1993   19 Eildon Street, Edinburgh EH3 5JU   0131-557 6052
[E-mail: anne@logan68.freeserve.co.uk]

85 Edinburgh: Tron Moredun
Stephen Manners MA BD   1989   467 Gilmerton Road, Edinburgh EH17 7JG   0131-666 2584
[E-mail: sk.manners@btinternet.com]

86 Edinburgh: Viewforth (T) (H) (0131-229 1917)
Anthony P. Thornthwaite MTh   1995   91 Morningside Drive, Edinburgh EH10 5NN   0131-447 6684
[E-mail: tony.thornthwaite@blueyonder.co.uk]

Aitken, Alexander R. MA   1965 1997   (Newhaven)   36 King's Meadow, Edinburgh EH16 5JW   0131-667 1404

Alexander, Ian W. BA BD STM   1990 1995   Board of World Mission   c/o 121 George Street, Edinburgh EH2 4YN   0131-225 5722

Anderson, Robert S. BD   1988 1997   Scottish Churches World Exchange   St Colm's International House, 23 Inverleith Terrace, Edinburgh EH3 5NS   0131-315 4444

Auld, A. Graeme MA BD PhD DLitt FSAScot   1973 1973   University of Edinburgh   Nether Swanshiel, Hobkirk, Bonchester Bridge, Hawick TD9 8JU

Baigrie, R.A. MA   1945 1985   (Kirkurd with Newlands)   32 Inchcolm Terrace, South Queensferry EH30 9NA   0131-331 4311

Baxter, Richard F. OBE MA BD   1954 1990   (Assistant at St Andrew's and St George's)   138 Braid Road, Edinburgh EH10 6JB   0131-447 7735

Beckett, David M. BA BD   1964 2002   (Greyfriars, Tolbooth and Highland Kirk)   1F1, 31 Sciennes Road, Edinburgh EH9 1NT   0131-667 2672
[E-mail: davidbeckett3@aol.com]

Blakey, Ronald S. MA BD MTh   1962 2000   Editor: The Year Book   61 Orchard Brae Avenue, Edinburgh EH4 2UR   0131-343 6039
(Mbl) 07752 450642

Brady, Ian D. BSc ARCST BD	1967	2001	(Edinburgh: Corstorphine Old)	28 Frankfield Crescent, Dalgety Bay, Dunfermline KY11 9LW [E-mail: pidb@dbay28.fsnet.co.uk]	01383 825104
Brown, William D. MA	1963	1989	(Wishaw Thornlie)	121 Dalkeith Road, Edinburgh EH16 5AJ	0131-667 1124
Bruce, Lilian M. (Miss) BD MTh	1971	2001	(Daviot and Dunlichity with Moy, Dalarossie and Tomatin)	33 Falcon Avenue, Edinburgh EH10 4AF	
Cameron, G. Gordon MA BD STM	1957	1997	(Juniper Green)	4 Ladywell Grove, Clackmannan FK10 4JQ	01259 723769
Cameron, John W.M. MA BD	1957	1996	(Liberton)	10 Plewlands Gardens, Edinburgh EH10 5JP	0131-447 1277
Cattanach, William D. DD	1951	1990	(Geneva)	145 Craigleith Road, Edinburgh EH4 2ED	0131-332 4503
Chalmers, John P. BD	1979	1995	Department of Ministry	10 Liggars Place, Dunfermline KY12 7XZ	01383 739130
Chalmers, Murray MA	1965	1991	Hospital Chaplain	25 Greenbank Road, Edinburgh EH10 5RX	0131-447 3387
Cheyne, Alexander C. MA BD BLitt DLitt	1958	1986	(University of Edinburgh)	12 Crossland Crescent, Peebles EH45 8LF	01721 722288
Clinkenbeard, William W. BSc BD STM	1966	2000	(Edinburgh: Carrick Knowe)	4 Aline Court, Dalgety Bay, Dunfermline KY11 5GP [E-mail: bjclinks@compuserve.com]	01383 824011
Cobain, Alan R. BD	2000		Army Chaplain	13 Wellington Road, Bulford Camp, Salisbury SP4 9BQ	01980 632331
Cook, John Weir MA BD	1962	2002	(Edinburgh: Portobello St Philip's Joppa)	74 Pinkie Road, Musselburgh EH21 7QT [E-mail: jwc@freeuk.com]	0131-653 0992
Cross, Brian F. MA	1961	1998	(Coalburn)	23 Broomlee Court, Broomlee Crescent, West Linton EH46 7EY	01968 660705
Currie, David E.P. BSc BD	1983	2000	Adviser in Evangelism	21 Rosa Burn Avenue, Lindsayfield, East Kilbride G75 9DE	01355 248510
Davidson, Ian M.P. MBE MA BD	1957	1994	(Stirling: Allan Park South with Church of the Holy Rude)	13/8 Craigend Park, Edinburgh EH16 5XX	0131-664 0074
Dilbey, Mary D. (Miss) BD	1997	2002	(West Kirk of Calder)	41 Bonaly Rise, Edinburgh EH13 0QU	0131-441 9092
Dougall, Elspeth G. (Mrs) MA BD	1989	2001	(Edinburgh: Marchmont St Giles')	60B Craigmillar Park, Edinburgh EH16 5PU	0131-668 1342
Doyle, Ian B. MA BD PhD	1946	1991	(Department of National Mission)	21 Lygon Road, Edinburgh EH16 5QD	0131-667 2697
Drummond, R. Hugh	1953	1991	(Balmaclellan with Kells)	19 Winton Park, Edinburgh EH10 7EX	0131-445 3634
Drummond, Rhoda (Miss) DCS			(Deaconess)	Flat K, 23 Grange Loan, Edinburgh EH9 2ER	0131-668 3631
Dunn, W. Iain C. DA LTh	1983	1998	(Pilrig and Dalmeny Street)	10 Fox Covert Avenue, Edinburgh EH12 6UQ	0131-334 1665
Elders, I. Alasdair MA BD	1964	2002	(Edinburgh: Broughton St Mary's)	The Limes, Ancaster Lane, Comrie, Crieff PH6 2DT	01764 679588
Faulds, Norman L. MA BD FSAScot	1968	2000	(Aberlady with Gullane)	Wellwood, 8 Juniper Place, Juniper Green, Edinburgh EH14 5TX	0131-453 4984
Ferguson, David A.S. MA BD DPhil	1984	2000	University of Edinburgh	23 Riselaw Crescent, Edinburgh EH10 6HN	0131-447 4022
Finlayson, J. Clarence MA	1930	1972	(Grange)	52 Falcon Avenue, Edinburgh EH10 4AW	0131-447 6550
Forrester, Duncan B. MA BD DPhil DD	1962	1978	(University of Edinburgh)	25 Kingsburgh Road, Edinburgh EH12 6DZ	0131-337 5646
Forrester, Margaret R. (Mrs) MA BD	1974	2003	(Edinburgh: St Michael's)	25 Kingsburgh Road, Edinburgh EH12 6DZ [E-mail: margaret@theforresters.fsnet.co.uk]	0131-337 5646
Fraser, Shirley A. (Miss) MA BD	1992	2001	Edinburgh Team Leader: Friends International	30 Parkhead Avenue, Edinburgh EH11 4SG	0131-443 7268
Galbraith, Douglas MA BD BMus MPhil ARSCM	1965	1995	Office for Worship, Doctrine and Artistic Matters	c/o 121 George Street, Edinburgh EH2 4YN [E-mail: dgalbraith@cofscotland.org.uk]	0131-240 2233
Gibson, John C.L. MA BD DPhil	1959	1994	(University of Edinburgh)	Cairnbank, Morton Street South, Edinburgh EH15 2NB	0131-669 3635
Gillon, J. Blair MA	1935	1980	(Borthwick with Heriot)	12A Craigmillar Park, Edinburgh EH16 5PS	0131-667 0004
Glass, Irene (Miss) DCS			(Deaconess)	3E Falcon Road West, Edinburgh EH10 4AA	0131-447 6554
Gordon, Tom MA BD	1974	1994	Chaplain: Fairmile Marie Curie Centre	22 Gosford Road, Port Seton, Prestonpans EH32 0HF	01875 812262
Graham, W. Peter MA BD	1967	1993	Presbytery Clerk	23/6 East Comiston, Edinburgh EH10 6RZ [E-mail: akph50@uk.uumail.com]	0131-445 5763

Harkness, James CB OBE QHC MA DD	(Chaplain General: Army)	1961	1995	13 Saxe Coburg Place, Edinburgh, EH3 5BR	0131-343 1297
Harvey, W. John BA BD	(Edinburgh: Corstorphine Craigsbank)	1965	2002	501 Shields Road, Glasgow G41 2RF	0141-429 3774
Hepburn, James L. MA BD	(Ardoch with Blackford)	1950	1991	16 Marchmont Road, Edinburgh EH9 1HZ	0131-229 6170
Hill, J. William BA BD	(Corstorphine St Anne's)	1967	2001	33/9 Murrayfield Road, Edinburgh EH12 6EP	
Hutchison, Maureen (Mrs) DCS	(Deaconess)			23 Drylaw Crescent, Edinburgh EH4 2AU	0131-332 8020
Jamieson, Gordon D. MA BD	Director of Stewardship	1974	2000	41 Goldpark Place, Livingston EH54 6LW	01506 412020
Jeffrey, Eric W.S. JP MA	(Edinburgh Bristo Memorial)	1954	1994	18 Gillespie Crescent, Edinburgh EH10 4HT	0131-229 7815
Johnston, William B. MA BD DD DLitt	(Colinton)	1945	1991	15 Elliot Road, Edinburgh EH14 1DU	0131-441 3387
Kant, Everard FVCM MTh	(Kinghorn)	1953	1988	38 Redford Loan, Edinburgh EH13 0AX	0131-441 3853
Kelly, Ewan R. MB ChB BD	Edinburgh University	1994	1998	29 Buckstone Crescent, Edinburgh EH10 6RJ	
Kesting, Sheilagh M. (Miss) BA BD	Ecumenical Relations	1980	1993	12 Glenview Drive, Falkirk FK1 5JU	01324 671489
Lamont, A. Donald BSc BD	(Nakuru)	1941	1975	36 St Clair Terrace, Edinburgh EH10 5PS	0131-447 4267
Lawson, Kenneth C. MA BD	(Adviser in Adult Education)	1963	1999	56 Easter Drylaw View, Edinburgh EH4 2QP	0131-539 3311
Lyall, David BSc BD STM PhD	(University of Edinburgh)	1965	2002	1 North Meggetland, Edinburgh EH14 1XG	0131-443 7640
Lyon, D.H.S. MA BD STM	(Board of World Mission and Unity)	1952	1986	30 Mansfield Road, Balerno EH14 7JZ	0131-449 5031
Macdonald, Finlay A.J. MA BD PhD	Principal Clerk	1971	1996	c/o 121 George Street, Edinburgh EH2 4YN	0131-225 5722
McDonald, James I.H. MA BD MTh PhD	(University of Edinburgh)	1958	1998	23 Ravelston House Road, Edinburgh EH4 3LP	0131-332 2172
Macdonald, William J. BD	(Board of National Mission: New Charge Development)	1976	1999	1/13 North Werber Park, Edinburgh EH4 1SY	0131-332 0254
McDonald, Brian	(Mayfield)	1953	1992	7 Blacket Place, Edinburgh EH9 1RN	0131-667 2100
McDowell, Brian	Chaplain: Fettes College		1999	6 West Woods, Fettes College, Edinburgh EH4 1RA	0131-332 9510
McGillivray, A. Gordon MA BD STM	(Presbytery Clerk)	1951	1993	7 Greenfield Crescent, Balerno EH14 7HD	0131-449 4747
MacGregor, Margaret S. (Miss) MA BD DipEd	(Calcutta)	1985	1994	16 Learmonth Court, Edinburgh EH4 1PB	0131-332 1089
McGregor, Alistair G.C. QC BD	(Edinburgh: Leith North)	1987	2002	22 Primrose Bank Road, Edinburgh EH5 3JG	0131-551 2802
McGregor, T. Stewart MBE MA BD	(Chaplain: Edinburgh Royal Infirmary)	1957	1998	19 Lonsdale Terrace, Edinburgh EH3 9HL [E-mail: cetsm@dircon.uk]	0131-229 5332
McIntyre, John CVO DLitt DD Drhc FRSE	(University of Edinburgh)	1941	1986	27/317 West Savile Terrace, Edinburgh EH9 3DT	0131-667 1203
Maclean, Ailsa G. (Mrs) BD DipCE	Chaplain: George Heriot's School	1979	1988	28 Swan Spring Avenue, Edinburgh EH10 6NJ	0131-445 1320
MacLean, Marjory A. (Miss) LLB BD	Board of Practice and Procedure	1991	1998	c/o 121 George Street, Edinburgh EH2 4YN	0131-225 5722
McLeod, Roderick MA BD	(Lochwinnoch)	1951	1990	2 East Savile Road, Edinburgh EH16 5ND	0131-667 1475
MacMurchie, F. Lynne LLB BD	Health Care Chaplain	1998	2003	Edinburgh Community Mental Health Chaplaincy, 41 George IV Bridge, Edinburgh EH1 1EL	0131-220 5150
McPheat, Elspeth DCS	Deaconess: Social Responsibility			11/5 New Orchardfield, Edinburgh EH6 5ET	
McPhee, Duncan C. MA BD	(Department of National Mission)	1953	1993	8 Belvedere Park, Edinburgh EH6 4LR	0131-554 4143
Macpherson, Allan S. MA	Chaplain: Merchiston Castle School	1967	1993	The Fairway, Merchiston Castle School, Edinburgh EH13 0PU	0131-552 6784
Macpherson, Colin C.R. MA BD	(Dunfermline St Margaret's)	1958	1996	7 Eva Place, Edinburgh EH9 3ET	0131-667 1456

Name	Ord.	Ind.	Position	Address	Telephone
Mathieson, Angus R. MA BD	1988	1998	Department of Ministry	21 Traquair Park West, Edinburgh EH12 7AN [E-mail: angus.mathieson@which.net]	0131-334 9774
Moir, Ian A MA BD	1962	2000	(Adviser for Urban Priority Areas)	28/6 Comely Bank Avenue, Edinburgh EH4 1EL	0131-332 2748
Morrice, William G. MA BD STM PhD	1957	1991	(St John's College Durham)	Flat 37, The Cedars, 2 Manse Road, Edinburgh EH12 7SN [E-mail: w.g.morrice@btinternet.com]	0131-316 4845
Morrison, Mary B. (Mrs) MA BD DipEd	1978	2000	(Edinburgh: Stenhouse St Aidan's)	14 Eildon Terrace, Edinburgh EH3 5LU	0131-556 1962
Morton, Andrew R. MA BD DD	1956	1994	(Board of World Mission and Unity)	11 Oxford Terrace, Edinburgh EH4 1PX	0131-332 6592
Morton, R. Colin BA BD	1960	1998	(Jerusalem)	313 Lanark Road West, Currie EH14 5RS	0131-449 7359
Moyes, Sheila A. (Miss) DCS			(Deaconess)	158 Pilton Avenue, Edinburgh EH5 2JZ	0131-551 1731
Mulligan, Anne (Miss) DCS			Deaconess: Hospital Chaplain's Assistant	27A Craigour Avenue, Edinburgh EH17 1NH	0131-664 3426
Munro, George A.M.	1968	2000	(Edinburgh: Cluny)	108 Caiyside, Edinburgh EH10 7HR	0131-445 5829
Murison, William G.	1951	1990	(Department of World Mission and Unity)	21 Hailes Gardens, Edinburgh EH13 0JL	0131-441 2460
Murrie, John BD	1953	1996	(Kirkliston)	31 Nicol Road, The Whins, Broxburn EH52 6JJ	01506 852464
Neilson, Peter MA BD MTh	1975	2003	Board of National Mission: Mission Developments Facilitator	12 Strathalmond Court, Edinburgh EH4 8AE	0131-339 4536
Nicol, Douglas A.O. MA BD	1974	1991	National Mission Secretary	24 Corbiehill Avenue, Edinburgh EH4 5DR	0131-336 1965
Page, Ruth MA BD DPhil	1976	2000	(University of Edinburgh)	22/5 West Mill Bank, West Mill Road, Edinburgh EH13 0QT	0131-441 3740
Paterson, Ian M. MA	1947	1985	(Eccles with Greenlaw)	45/15 Maidencraig Crescent, Edinburgh EH4 2UU	0131-332 9735
Paterson, J.M.K. MA ACII BD DD	1964	1987	(Mingavie St Paul's)	58 Orchard Drive, Edinburgh EH4 2DZ	0131-332 5876
Paterson, John M.	1976	1987	(Blackbraes and Shieldhill)	28/21 Roseburn Place, Edinburgh EH12 5NX	0131-337 0095
Philip, James MA	1948	1997	(Holyrood Abbey)	3 Ferguson Gardens, Musselburgh EH21 6XF	0131-653 2310
Philip, Connie (Miss) BD	1980	1995	(Arbuthnott with Bervie)	22/5 South Elixa Place, Baronscourt View, Edinburgh EH8 7PG	0131-661 3124
Plate, Maria A.G. (Miss) LTh BA	1983	2000	(South Ronaldsay and Burray)	Flat 29, 77 Barnton Park View, Edinburgh EH4 6EL	0131-339 8539
Porteous, Norman W. DD	1929	1968	(University of Edinburgh)	3 Hermitage Gardens, Edinburgh EH10 6DL	0131-447 4632
Potts, Jean (Miss) DCS			(Deaconess)	28B East Claremont Street, Edinburgh EH7 4JP	0131-557 2144
Rae, David L.	1955	1990	(Kolhapur)	29 Falcon Avenue, Edinburgh EH10 4AL	0131-447 3158
Reid, W. Scott BD MA DipPS PhD	1950	1990	(London Road)	14/37 Ethel Terrace, Edinburgh EH10 5NA	0131-447 7642
Renton, Ian P.	1958	1990	(St Colm's)	98 Homeross House, Stratheam Road, Edinburgh EH9 2QY	0131-447 0601
Ridland, Alistair K. MA BD	1982	2000	Chaplain: Western General Hospital	13 Stewart Place, Kirkliston EH29 0BQ	0131-333 2711
Rodland, Norma A. (Miss) MBE DCS			(Deaconess)	43/26 Gillespie Crescent, Edinburgh EH10 4HY	0131-228 1008
Ross, Andrew C. MA BD STM PhD	1958	1998	(University of Edinburgh)	27 Colinton Road, Edinburgh EH10 5DR	0131-447 5987
Ross, Kenneth R. BA BD PhD	1982	1999	General Secretary, Board of World Mission	c/o 121 George Street, Edinburgh EH2 4YN	0131-225 5722
Sandilands, Ian S.	1986	1999	(Black Mount)	51 Little Road, Edinburgh EH16 6SH	0131-664 6924
Schofield, Melville F. MA	1960	2000	(Chaplain: Western General Hospitals)	25 Rowantree Grove, Currie EH14 5AT	0131-449 4745
Scott, Jayne E. BA MEd		2003	Principal: SCOC	7/4 Blandfield, Edinburgh EH7 4QJ	0131-477 9584
Scott, Martin DipMus RSAM BD PhD	1986	2000	Department of Ministry	7/4 Blandfield, Edinburgh EH7 4QJ	0131-477 9584
Sim, John G. MA	1946	1987	(Kirkcaldy Old)	7 Grosvenor Crescent, Edinburgh EH12 5EP	0131-226 3190
Skinner, Donald M. MBE JP FIES	1962	2000	(Edinburgh: Gilmerton)	12 Straid a Cnoc, Clynder, Helensburgh G84 0QX	
Sloan, Elma C. (Miss) DCS			(Deaconess)		
Stephen, Donald M. TD MA BD ThM	1962	2001	(Edinburgh: Marchmont St Giles')	10 Hawkhead Crescent, Edinburgh EH16 6LR	0131-658 1216
Stevenson, John MA BD	1963	2001	(Department of Education)	12 Swanston Gardens, Edinburgh EH10 7DL	0131-445 3960
Stiven, Iain K. MA BD	1960	1997	(Strachur and Strathlachlan)	3 Gloucester Place, Edinburgh EH3 6EE	0131-225 8177
Storrar, William F. MA BD PhD	1984	2000	University of Edinburgh	35 Strathalmond Park, Edinburgh EH4 8AH	
Taylor, Howard G. BSc BD MTh	1971	1998	Chaplain: Heriot Watt University	The Chaplaincy, Heriot Watt University, Riccarton, Currie EH14 4AS	0131-449 5111 (ext 4508)

Teague, Yvonne (Mrs) DCS	1978	2001	(Board of Ministry)	46 Craigcrook Avenue, Edinburgh EH4 3PX	0131-336 3113
Telfer, Iain J. BD DPS			Chaplain: Royal Infirmary	32 Alnwickhill Park, Edinburgh EH16 6UH	0131-536 3084
Thom, Helen (Miss) DCS			(Deaconess)	84 Great King Street, Edinburgh EH3 6QU	0131-556 5687
Thomson, J.G.S.S. MA BD BA PhD	1951	1981	(Wigtown)	4 Drum Brae South, Edinburgh EH12 8SJ	0131-334 6035
Torrance, James B. MA BD	1954	1989	(University of Aberdeen)	3 Greenbank Crescent, Edinburgh EH10 5TE	0131-447 3230
Torrance, Thomas F. MBE DLitt DD DSc DrTheol DrTeol FBA FRSE	1940	1979	(University of Edinburgh)	37 Braid Farm Road, Edinburgh EH10 6LE	0131-667 0578
Walker, R.W. MB ChB	1941	1981	(Lesmahagow Abbeygreen)	39/22 Blackford Avenue, Edinburgh EH9 3HN	0131-220 5150
Whyte, Iain A. BA BD STM	1968	2001	Community Mental Health Chaplain	41 George IV Bridge, Edinburgh EH1 1EL	
Wigglesworth, J. Christopher MBE BSc PhD BD	1967	1999	(St Andrew's College, Selly Oak)	12 Leven Terrace, Edinburgh EH3 9LW	0131-228 6335
Wilkie, James L. MA BD	1959	1998	(Board of World Mission)	7 Comely Bank Avenue, Edinburgh EH4 1EW [E-mail: jl.wilkie@btinternet.com]	0131-343 1552
Wilkinson, John BD MD FRCP DTM&H	1946	1975	(Kikuyu)	70 Craigleith Hill Gardens, Edinburgh EH4 2JH	0131-332 2994
Williams, Jenny M. (Miss) BSc CQSW BD	1996	1997	Christian Fellowship of Healing	16 Blantyre Terrace, Edinburgh EH10 5AE	0131-447 0050
Wilson, John M. MA	1964	1995	(Adviser in Religious Education)	27 Bellfield Street, Edinburgh EH15 2BR	0131-669 5257
Young, Alexander W. BD DipMin	1988	1999	Chaplain: Western General Hospitals	19B Craigour Drive, Edinburgh EH17 7NY	0131-664 0388

EDINBURGH ADDRESSES

Albany	At Greenside
Balerno	Johnsburn Road, Balerno
Barclay	Barclay Place
Blackhall St Columba	Queensferry Road
Bristo Memorial	Peffermill Road, Craigmillar
Broughton St Mary's	Bellevue Crescent
Canongate	Canongate
Carrick Knowe	North Saughton Road
Colinton	Dell Road
Colinton Mains	Oxgangs Road North
Corstorphine	
Craigsbank	Craig's Crescent
Old	Kirk Loan
St Anne's	Kaimes Road
St Ninian's	St John's Road
Craigentinny	
St Christopher's	Craigentinny Road
Craiglockhart	Craiglockhart Avenue
Craigmillar Park	Craigmillar Park
Cramond	Cramond Glebe Road
Currie	Kirkgate, Currie
Davidson's Mains	Quality Street
Dean	Dean Path
Drylaw	Groathill Road North
Duddingston	Old Church Lane, Duddingston
Fairmilehead	Frogston Road West, Fairmilehead
Gilmerton	Ravenscroft Street
Gorgie	Gorgie Road
Granton	Boswall Parkway
Greenbank	Braidburn Terrace
Greenside	Royal Terrace
Greyfriars Tolbooth and Highland Kirk	Greyfriars Place
High (St Giles')	High Street
Holyrood Abbey	Dalziel Place x London Road
Holy Trinity	Hailesland Place, Wester Hailes
Inverleith	Inverleith Gardens
Juniper Green	Lanark Road, Juniper Green
Kaimes Lockhart Memorial	Gracemount Drive
Kirkliston	The Square, Kirkliston
Kirk o' Field	Pleasance
Leith	
North	Madeira Street off Ferry Road
St Andrew's	Easter Road
St Serf's	Ferry Road
St Thomas' Junction Road	Great Junction Street
South	Kirkgate, Leith
Wardie	Primrosebank Road
Liberton	Kirkgate, Liberton
Northfield	Gilmerton Road, Liberton
London Road	London Road
Marchmont St Giles'	Kilgraston Road
Mayfield Salisbury	Mayfield Road x West Mayfield
Morningside	Cluny Gardens
Morningside United	Bruntsfield Place x Chamberlain Road
Muirhouse St Andrew's	Pennywell Gardens
Murrayfield	Abinger Gardens
Newhaven	Craighall Road
New Restalrig	Willowbrae Road
Old Kirk	Pennywell Road
Palmerston Place	Palmerston Place
Pilrig St Paul's	Pilrig Street
Polwarth	Polwarth Terrace x Harrison Road
Portobello	
Old	Bellfield Street
St James'	Rosefield Place
St Philip's, Joppa	Abercorn Terrace
Priestfield	Dalkeith Road x Marchhall Place
Queensferry	The Loan, South Queensferry
Ratho	Baird Road, Ratho
Reid Memorial	West Savile Terrace
Richmond Craigmillar	Niddrie Mains Road
St Andrew's and St George's	George Street
St Andrew's Clermiston	Clermiston View
St Catherine's Argyle	Grange Road x Chalmers Crescent

St Colm's	Dalry Road x Cathcart Place	St Margaret's	Restalrig Road South	Slateford Longstone	Kingsknowe Road North
St Cuthbert's	Lothian Road	St Martin's	Magdalene Drive	Stenhouse St Aidan's	Chesser Avenue
St David's Broomhouse	Broomhouse Crescent	St Michael's	Slateford Road	Stockbridge	Saxe Coburg Street
St George's West	Shandwick Place	St Nicholas' Sighthill	Calder Road	Tron Kirk Moredun	Fernieside Drive
St John's Oxgangs	Oxgangs Road	St Stephen's Comely Bank	Comely Bank	Viewforth	Gilmore Place

(2) WEST LOTHIAN

Meets in the church of the incoming Moderator on the first Tuesday of September and in St John's Church Hall, Bathgate, on the first Tuesday of every other month, except December, when the meeting is on the second Tuesday, and January, July and August, when there is no meeting.

Clerk: REV. DUNCAN SHAW BD MTh   St John's Manse, Mid Street, Bathgate EH48 1QD   **01506 653146**
[E-mail: akph78@uk.uumail.com]

Abercorn linked with Pardovan, Kingscavil and Winchburgh
A. Scott Marshall DipComm BD   1984 1998   The Manse, Winchburgh, Broxburn EH52 6TT   01506 890919
[E-mail: pkwla@aol.com]

Armadale (H)
Vacant   2000   70 Mount Pleasant, Armadale EH48 3HB   01501 730358
Glenda Wilson (Mrs) DCS   118 Old Rows, Seafield, West Lothian EH47 7AW   01506 655298

Avonbridge linked with Torphichen
Clifford R. Acklam BD MTh   1997 2000   Manse Road, Torphichen, Bathgate EH48 4LT   01506 652794
[E-mail: cracklam@waitrose.com]

Bathgate: Boghall (H)
John McLean MA BD   1967 1970   1 Manse Place, Ash Grove, Bathgate EH48 1NJ   01506 652940

Bathgate: High (H)
Ronald G. Greig MA BD   1987 1998   19 Hunter Grove, Bathgate EH48 1NN   01506 652654
[E-mail: ron.greig@care4free.net]

Bathgate: St David's
Elliot G.S. Wardlaw BA BD DipMin   1984   70 Marjoribanks Street, Bathgate EH48 1AH   01506 653177
[E-mail: elliot@stdavidschurch.fsnet.co.uk]

Bathgate: St John's (H)
Duncan Shaw BD MTh   1975 1978   St John's Manse, Mid Street, Bathgate EH48 1QD   01506 653146
[E-mail: duncanshaw@uk.uumail.com]

Blackburn and Seafield
Robert A. Anderson MA BD DPhil	1980	1998	Blackburn, Bathgate EH47 7QR [E-mail: robertaland@supanet.com]	01506 652825

Blackridge linked with Harthill St Andrew's
H. Warner Hardie BD	1979	East Main Street, Harthill, Shotts ML7 5QW [E-mail: warner@hardies55.freeserve.co.uk]	01501 751239

Breich Valley
Thomas Preston BD	1978	2001	Stoneyburn, Bathgate EH47 8AU	01501 762018

Broxburn (H)
Richard T. Corbett BSc MSc PhD BD	1992	2 Church Street, Broxburn EH52 5EL [E-mail: revcorbett@pgen.net]	01506 852825

Fauldhouse: St Andrew's
Elizabeth Smith (Mrs) BD	1996	2000	7 Glebe Court, Fauldhouse, Bathgate EH47 9DX [E-mail: smithrevb@btinternet.com]	01501 771190

Harthill St Andrew's See Blackridge

Kirknewton and East Calder
Ann M. Ballentine (Miss) MA BD	1981	1993	8 Manse Court, East Calder EH53 0HF [E-mail: annballentine@hotmail.com]	01506 880802

Kirk of Calder (H)
John M. Povey MA BD	1981	19 Maryfield Park, Mid Calder EH53 0SB [E-mail: revjpovey@aol.com]	01506 882495

Linlithgow: St Michael's (H) (E-mail: info@stmichaels-parish.org.uk)
Vacant		St Michael's Manse, Kirkgate, Linlithgow EH49 7AL	
James Francis BD PhD (Assoc)	2002	Cross House, Linlithgow EH49 7AL [E-mail: jim.francis@lineone.net]	01506 842195 / 01506 842665
Thomas S. Riddell BSc (Aux)	1993	1994	4 The Maltings, Linlithgow EH49 6DS [E-mail: tsriddell@blueyonder.co.uk]	01506 843251

Linlithgow: St Ninian's Craigmailen (H)
Iain C. Morrison BA BD	1990	29 Philip Avenue, Linlithgow EH49 7BH [E-mail: cmo2@dial.pipex.com]	01506 845535

Livingston Ecumenical Parish
Incorporating the Worship Centres at:
Carmondean and Craigshill (St Columba's)
Gillean P. Maclean (Mrs) BD	1994	2000	53 Garry Walk, Craigshill, Livingston EH54 5AS [E-mail: gmaclean@fish.co.uk]	01506 434536

Knightsridge and Ladywell (St Paul's)
Colin R. Douglas MA BD STM 1969 1987 27 Heatherbank, Ladywell, Livingston EH54 6EE [E-mail: colin-douglas@tiscali.co.uk] 01506 432326

Dedridge (The Lanthorn)
Marion Keston MB ChB MTh (*Scottish Episcopal Church*) 12B Carrick Gardens, Murieston, Livingston EH54 9ET [E-mail: mkeston@fish.co.uk] 01506 410668

Livingston: Old (H)
Graham W. Smith BA BD FSAScot 1995 Manse of Livingston, Charlesfield Lane, Livingston EH54 7AJ [E-mail: gws@livoldpar.org.uk] 01506 420227

Pardovan, Kingscavil and Winchburgh See Abercorn

Polbeth Harwood linked with West Kirk of Calder (H)
Vacant 27 Learmonth Crescent, West Calder EH55 8AF 01506 870460

Strathbrock
David W. Black BSc BD 1968 1984 1 Manse Park, Uphall, Broxburn EH52 6NX 01506 852550

Torphichen See Avonbridge

Uphall South (H)
Margaret Steele (Miss) BSc BD 2000 8 Fernlea, Uphall, Broxburn EH52 6DF [E-mail: msteele@beeb.net] 01506 852788

West Kirk of Calder (H) See Polbeth Harwood

Whitburn: Brucefield (H)
Vacant Brucefield Drive, Whitburn, Bathgate EH47 8NU 01501 740263

Whitburn: South (H)
Vacant 5 Mansewood Crescent, Whitburn EH47 8HA 01501 740333

Cameron, Ian MA BD	1953	1981	(Kilbrandon and Kilchattan)	37 Burghmuir Court, Linlithgow EH49 7LJ	01506 847987
Crichton, Thomas JP ChStJ MA	1965	1989	Hospital Chaplain	18 Carlton Terrace, Edinburgh EH7 5DD	0131-557 0009
Dickson, A. Stuart	1963	1995	(Glasgow: Govan Old – Assoc)	74 Netherwood Park, Deans, Livingston EH54 8RW	01506 420167
Dundas, Thomas B.S. LTh	1969	1996	(West Kirk of Calder)	35 Coolkill, Sandyford, Dublin 18, Republic of Ireland	00353 12953061
Manson, Robert L. MA DPS	1956	1991	(Chaplain: Royal Edinburgh Hospital)	4 Murieston Drive, Livingston EH54 9AU	01506 434746
Moore, J.W. MA	1950	1983	(Daviot with Rayne)	31 Lennox Gardens, Linlithgow EH49 7PZ	01506 842534

Morrice, Charles S. MA BD PhD	1959	1997	(Kenya)	104 Baron's Hill Avenue, Linlithgow EH49 7JG	01506 847167
Moyes, Andrew	1959	1992	(Broxburn)	5 Grange Road, Broxburn EH52 5HL	01506 858203
Murray, Ronald N.G. MA	1946	1986	(Pardovan and Kingscavil with Winchburgh)	42 Lennox Gardens, Linlithgow EH49 7QA	01506 845680
Nelson, Georgina (Mrs) MA BD PhD DipEd	1990	1995	Hospital Chaplain	6 Pentland Park, Craigshill, Livingston EH54 5NR	01506 434874
Robertson, Emmanuel ThM ThD	1953	1993	(Armadale)	39 Drumcross Road, Bathgate EH48 4HF	01506 654766
Russell, Archibald MA	1949	1991	(Duror with Glencoe)	4 Bonnytoun Avenue, Linlithgow EH49 7JS	01506 842530
Smith, W. Ewing BSc	1962	1994	(Livingston: Old)	8 Hardy Gardens, Bathgate EH48 1NH [E-mail: wesmith@hardygdns.freeserve.co.uk]	01506 652028
Stirling, A. Douglas BSc	1956	1994	(Rhu and Shandon)	162 Avontoun Park, Linlithgow EH49 6QH [E-mail: douglas@stirling162.fsnet.co.uk]	01506 845021
Trimble, Robert DCS	1959	1999	(Deacon)	5 Temple Rise, Dedridge, Livingston EH54 6PJ	01506 412504
Whitson, William S. MA			(Cumbernauld: St Mungo's)	2 Chapman's Brae, Bathgate EH48 4LH [E-mail: williambarbara@amserve.net]	01506 650027

(3) LOTHIAN

Meets at Musselburgh: St Andrew's High Parish Church on the last Thursday of January and June and the first Thursday of March, April, May, September, October, November and December. (Alternative arrangements are made to avoid meeting on Maundy Thursday.)

| **Clerk:** | **MR JOHN D. McCULLOCH DL** | | | **Auchindinny House, Penicuik EH26 8PE [E-mail: akph65@uk.uumail.com]** | **01968 676300 (Tel/Fax)** |

Aberlady (H) linked with Gullane (H)

| John B. Cairns LTh LLB DD | 1974 | 2001 | The Manse, Hummel Road, Gullane EH31 2BG [E-mail: john@cairns3018.freeserve.co.uk] | 01620 843192 |

Athelstaneford linked with Whitekirk and Tyninghame

| Kenneth D.F. Walker MA BD PhD | 1976 | | The Manse, Athelstaneford, North Berwick EH39 5BE [E-mail: kandv-walker@connectfree.co.uk] | 01620 880378 |

Belhaven (H) linked with Spott

| Laurence H. Twaddle MA BD MTh | 1977 | 1978 | The Manse, Belhaven Road, Dunbar EH42 1NH [E-mail: revtwaddle@aol.com] | 01368 863098 |

Bolton and Saltoun linked with Humbie linked with Yester (H)

| Donald Pirie LTh | 1975 | 1999 | The Manse, Tweeddale Avenue, Gifford, Haddington EH41 4QN | 01620 810515 |

Bonnyrigg (H)
John Mitchell LTh CMin   1991
9 Viewbank View, Bonnyrigg EH19 2HU
[E-mail: rev.jmitchell@tiscali.co.uk]
0131-663 8287 (Tel/Fax)

Borthwick (H) linked with Cranstoun, Crichton and Ford (H) linked with Fala and Soutra (H)
D. Graham Leitch MA BD   1974   2003
Cranstoun Cottage, Ford, Pathhead EH37 5RE
01875 320314

Cockenzie and Port Seton: Chalmers Memorial (H)
Robert L. Glover BMus BD ARCO   1971   1997
Braemar Villa, 2 Links Road, Port Seton, Prestonpans EH32 0HA
[E-mail: rlglover@btinternet.com]
01875 812481

Cockenzie and Port Seton: Old (H)
Continued Vacancy
1 Links Road, Port Seton, Prestonpans EH32 0HA
01875 812310

Cockpen and Carrington (H) linked with Lasswade (H) linked with Rosewell (H)
Wendy F. Drake (Mrs) BD   1978   1992
11 Pendreich Terrace, Bonnyrigg EH19 2DT
[E-mail: drake@pendreich.fsnet.co.uk]
0131-663 6884

Cranstoun, Crichton and Ford (H)   See Borthwick

Dalkeith: St John's and King's Park (H)
Keith L. Mack BD MTh DPS   2002
13 Weir Crescent, Dalkeith EH22 3JN
[E-mail: kthmacker@aol.com]
0131-454 0206

Dalkeith: St Nicholas' Buccleuch (H)
Vacant
116 Bonnyrigg Road, Dalkeith EH22 3HZ
0131-663 3036

Dirleton (H) linked with North Berwick: Abbey (H) (01620 890110)
David J. Graham BSc BD PhD   1982   1998
20 Westgate, North Berwick EH39 4AF
[E-mail: davidjohn@grahams.fsbusiness.co.uk]
01620 892410

Dunbar (H)
Eric W. Foggitt MA BSc BD   1991   2000
The Manse, Bayswell Road, Dunbar EH42 1AB
[E-mail: ericleric3@btopenworld.com]
01368 863749 (Tel/Fax)

Dunglass
Anne R. Lithgow (Mrs) MA BD   1992   1994
The Manse, Cockburnspath TD13 5XZ
[E-mail: anne.lithgow@btinternet.com]
01368 830713

Fala and Soutra   See Borthwick

Garvald and Morham linked with Haddington: West (H)
Cameron Mackenzie BD   1997
15 West Road, Haddington EH41 3RD
01620 822213

Gladsmuir linked with Longniddry (H)
Vacant — The Manse, Elcho Road, Longniddry EH32 0LB — 01875 853195

Glencorse (H) linked with Roslin (H)
James A. Manson LTh — 1981 — 38 Penicuik Road, Roslin EH25 9LH [E-mail: jamanson@supanet.com] — 0131-440 2012

Gorebridge (H)
Mark S. Nicholas MA BD — 1999 — 100 Hunterfield Road, Gorebridge EH23 4TT [E-mail: mark.nicholas@fish.co.uk] — 01875 820387

Gullane See Aberlady

Haddington: St Mary's (H)
James M. Cowie BD — 1977 2002 — 21 Sidegate, Haddington EH41 4BZ [E-mail: jim@jimcowie.demon.co.uk] — 01620 823109

Haddington: West See Garvald and Morham

Howgate (H) linked with Penicuik: South (H)
Frank Ribbons MA BD DipEd — 1985 — 18 Broomhill Avenue, Penicuik EH26 9EG — 01968 674692

Humbie See Bolton and Saltoun
Lasswade See Cockpen and Carrington

Loanhead
Graham L. Duffin BSc BD DipEd — 1989 2001 — 120 The Loan, Loanhead EH20 9AJ [E-mail: gduffin@fish.co.uk] — 0131-448 2459

Longniddry See Gladsmuir

Musselburgh: Northesk (H)
Alison P. Matheson MA BD — 1991 1998 — 16 New Street, Musselburgh EH21 6JP [E-mail: alison.matheson@btinternet.com] — 0131-665 2128

Musselburgh: St Andrew's High (H) (0131-665 7239)
Vacant — 8 Ferguson Drive, Musselburgh EH21 6XA — 0131-665 5583

Musselburgh: St Clement's and St Ninian's
Moira McDonald MA BD — 1997 — The Manse, Wallyford Loan Road, Wallyford, Musselburgh EH21 8BU [E-mail: moira.mc@tesco.net] — 0131-653 6588

Gordon R. Steven BD DCS — 51 Nantwich Drive, Edinburgh EH7 6RB — 0131-669 2054

Musselburgh: St Michael's Inveresk
Andrew B. Dick BD DipMin — 1986 — 1999 — 8 Hope Place, Musselburgh EH21 7QE [E-mail: dixbit@aol.com] — 0131-665 0545

Newbattle (H) (http://freespace.virgin.net/newbattle.focus)
Vacant — 70 Newbattle Abbey Crescent, Dalkeith EH22 3LW — 0131-663 3245
(Charge formed by the union of Newbattle and Newtongrange)

Newton
Jan E. Gillies (Mrs) BD — 1998 — 2001 — The Manse, Newton, Dalkeith EH22 1SR [E-mail: jgillies@fish.co.uk] — 0131-663 3845

North Berwick: Abbey See Dirleton

North Berwick: St Andrew Blackadder (H)
Neil J. Dougall BD — 1991 — 2003 — 7 Marine Parade, North Berwick EH39 4LD — 01620 892132

Ormiston linked with Pencaitland
Mark Malcolm MA BD — 1999 — The Manse, Pencaitland, Tranent EH34 5DL [E-mail: mark.minister@virgin.net] — 01875 340208

Pencaitland See Ormiston

Penicuik: North (H)
John W. Fraser MA BD — 1974 — 1982 — 93 John Street, Penicuik EH26 8AG [E-mail: john1946@fish.co.uk] — 01968 672213

Penicuik: St Mungo's (H)
Vacant — 31a Kirkhill Road, Penicuik EH26 8JB — 01968 672916

Penicuik: South See Howgate

Prestonpans: Prestongrange
Robert R. Simpson BA BD — 1994 — The Manse, East Loan, Prestonpans EH32 9ED [E-mail: robert@pansmanse.co.uk] — 01875 810308

Christine A. Y. Ritchie (Mrs) BD DipMin (Aux) — 2002 — Through-Gate, 78 High Street, Dunbar EH42 1JH [E-mail: critchie@fish.co.uk] — 01368 863141

Rosewell See Cockpen and Carrington
Roslin See Glencorse
Spott See Belhaven

Tranent
Thomas M. Hogg BD — 1986 — 244 Church Street, Tranent EH33 1BW [E-mail: tom@hoggtran.freeserve.co.uk] — 01875 610210

Traprain
Howard J. Haslett BA BD   1972 2000   Preston Road, East Linton EH40 3DS   01620 860227 (Tel/Fax)
[E-mail: howard.haslett@btopenworld.com]

Whitekirk and Tyninghame See Athelstaneford
Yester See Bolton and Saltoun

Name	Dates	Role	Address	Tel
Black, A. Graham MA	1964 2003	(Gladsmuir with Longniddry)	26 Hamilton Crescent, Gullane EH31 2HR [E-mail: grablack@aol.com]	01620 843899
Brown, Ronald H.	1974 1998	(Musselburgh: Northesk)	6 Monktonhall Farm Cottages, Musselburgh EH21 6RZ	0131-653 2531
Brown, William BD	1972 1997	(Edinburgh: Polwarth)	13 Thornyhall, Dalkeith EH22 2ND	(Tel/Fax) 0131-654 0929
Chalmers, William R. MA BD STM	1953 1992	(Dunbar)	18 Forest Road, Burghead, Elgin IV30 5XL	01343 835674
Donaldson, Colin V.	1982 1998	(Ormiston with Pencaitland)	3A Playfair Terrace, St Andrews KY16 9HX	01334 472889
Fraser, John W. BEM MA BD PhD	1950 1983	(Farnell)	12 Quarryfoot Green, Bonnyrigg EH19 2EJ	0131-663 8037
Gilfillan, James LTh	1968 1997	(East Kilbride: Old)	15 Long Cram, Haddington EH41 4NS	01620 824843
Hill, Arthur T.	1940 1981	(Ormiston with Prestonpans: Grange)	8A Hamilton Road, North Berwick EH39 4NA	01620 893961
Hutchison, Alan E.W.		(Deacon)	132 Lochbridge Road, North Berwick EH39 4DR	01620 894077
Jones, Anne M. (Mrs) BD	1998 2002	Hospital Chaplain	7 North Elphinstone Farm, Tranent EH33 2ND [E-mail: revamjones@aol.com]	01875 614442
Levison, L. David MA BD	1943 1982	(Ormiston with Pencaitland)	Westdene Conservatory Flat, 506 Perth Road, Dundee DD2 1LS	01382 630460
Macdonell, Alasdair W. MA BD	1955 1992	(Haddington: St Mary's)	St Andrews Cottage, Duns Road, Gifford, Haddington EH41 4QW	01620 810341
Macrae, Norman C. MA DipEd	1942 1985	(Loanhead)	49 Lixmount Avenue, Edinburgh EH5 3EW [E-mail: nandc.macrae@btopenworld.com]	0131-552 2428
Maule-Brown, Robert MA	1949 1985	(Strathy and Halladale)	5 Acredales Walk, Haddington EH41 4RR	01620 824959
Ritchie, James McL. MA BD MPhil	1950 1985	(Coalsnaughton)	46 St James's Gardens, Penicuik EH26 9DU [E-mail: ritchjm@aol.com]	01968 676123
Robertson, James LTh	1970 2000	(Newton)	11 Southfield Square, Edinburgh EH15 1QS	
Sanderson, W. Roy DD	1933 1973	(Stenton with Whittingehame)	20 Craigleith View, Station Road, North Berwick EH39 4BF	01620 892780
Sawers, E.A.H. VRD	1950 1989	(Cranstoun Crichton and Ford with Fala and Soutra)		
Swan, Andrew F. BD	1983 2000	(Loanhead)	18 Lydgait Gardens, Haddington EH41 3DB	01620 825830
Thomson, William H.	1964 1999	(Edinburgh: Liberton Northfield)	3 Mackenzie Gardens, Dolphinton, West Linton EH46 7HS	01968 682247
			3 Baird's Way, Bonnyrigg EH19 3NS [E-mail: w.h.thomson@tesco.net]	0131-654 9799
Torrance, David W. MA BD	1955 1991	(Earlston)	38 Forth Street, North Berwick EH39 4JQ [E-mail:dwtmet@connectfree.co.uk]	(Tel/Fax) 01620 895109
Underwood, Florence A. (Mrs) BD	1992 2003	(Assistant at Gladsmuir with Longniddry)	The Shieling, Main Street, Stenton, Dunbar EH42 1TE	01368 850629
Underwood, Geoffrey H. BD DipTh FPhS	1964 1992	(Cockenzie and Port Seton: Chalmers Memorial)	The Shieling, Main Street, Stenton, Dunbar EH42 1TE	01368 850629
Whiteford, David H. CBE MA BD PhD	1943 1985	(Gullane)	3 Old Dean Road, Longniddry EH32 0QY	01875 852980

(4) MELROSE AND PEEBLES

Meets at Innerleithen on the first Tuesday of February, March, May, October, November and December, and on the fourth Tuesday of June, and in places to be appointed on the first Tuesday of September.

Clerk: MR JACK STEWART   3 St Cuthbert's Drive, St Boswells, Melrose TD6 0DF   01835 822600
[E-mail: akph66@uk.uumail.com]

Ashkirk linked with Selkirk (H)
James W. Campbell BD   1995   1 Loanside, Selkirk TD7 4DJ   01750 22833
[E-mail: revjimashkirk@aol.com]

Bowden (H) linked with Newtown
Joseph F. Crawford BA   1970   2000   The Manse, Newtown St Boswells, Melrose TD6 0PL   01835 822106
[E-mail: joe@crawforda86.fsnet.co.uk]

Broughton, Glenholm and Kilbucho (H) linked with Skirling linked with Stobo and Drumelzier linked with Tweedsmuir (H)
Rachel J.W. Dobie (Mrs) LTh   1991   1996   The Manse, Broughton, Biggar ML12 6HQ   01899 830331
[E-mail: revracheldobie@aol.com]

Caddonfoot (H) linked with Galashiels St Ninian's (H)
Hilary W. Smith (Miss) BD DipMin MTh PhD   1999   Mossilee Road, Galashiels TD1 1NF   01896 752058
[E-mail: heloise.smith@virgin.net]

Carlops linked with Kirkurd and Newlands (H) linked with West Linton St Andrew's (H)
Thomas W. Burt BD   1982   1985   The Manse, West Linton EH46 7EN   01968 660221
[E-mail: tomburt@westlinton.com]

Channelkirk linked with Lauder: Old
John M. Shields MBE LTh   1972   1997   Brownsmuir Park, Lauder TD2 6QD   01578 722320

Earlston
Michael D. Scouler MBE BSc BD   1988   1992   The Manse, High Street, Earlston TD4 6DE   01896 849236

Eddleston (H) linked with Peebles Old (H)
Malcolm M. Macdougall BD   1981   2001   The Old Manse, Innerleithen Road, Peebles EH45 8BD   01721 720568
[E-mail: calum.macdougall@lineone.net]

Ettrick and Yarrow
Samuel Siroky BA MTh   2003   Yarrow Manse, Yarrow, Selkirk TD7 5LA   01750 82336
[E-mail: sesiroky@onetel.net.uk]

Galashiels: Old and St Paul's (H)
Leslie M. Steele MA BD — 1973 1988
Barr Road, Galashiels TD1 3HX
[E-mail: lms@stpauls.worldonline.co.uk]
01896 752320

Galashiels: St Aidan's (H)
Vacant
High Road, Galashiels TD1 2BD
01896 752420

Galashiels: St John's (H)
Stephen F. Clipston MA BD — 1982
Hawthorn Road, Galashiels TD1 2JZ
[E-mail: steve.clipston@btinternet.com]
01896 752573 (Tel)
01896 758561 (Fax)

Galashiels: St Ninian's See Caddonfoot

Innerleithen (H), Traquair and Walkerburn
Janice M. Faris (Mrs) BSc BD — 1991 2001
The Manse, 1 Millwell Park, Innerleithen, Peebles EH44 6JF
[E-mail: revjfaris@hotmail.com]
01896 830309

Kirkurd and Newlands See Carlops
Lauder: Old See Channelkirk

Lyne and Manor
Nancy M. Norman (Miss) BA MDiv MTh — 1988 1998
25 March Street, Peebles EH45 8EP
[E-mail: nancy.norman@btopenworld.com]
01721 721699

Maxton and Mertoun linked with St Boswells
Bruce F. Neill MA BD — 1966 1996
St Modans Manse, Main Street, St Boswells, Melrose TD6 0BB
[E-mail: bneill@fish.co.uk]
01835 822255

Melrose (H)
Alistair G. Bennett BSc BD — 1978 1984
Tweedmount Road, Melrose TD6 9ST
[E-mail: agbennettmelrose@aol.com]
01896 822217

Newtown See Bowden
Peebles: Old See Eddleston

Peebles: St Andrew's Leckie (H) (01721 723121)
James H. Wallace MA BD — 1973 1983
Mansefield, Innerleithen Road, Peebles EH45 8BE
[E-mail: jimwallace10@freeuk.com]
01721 721749 (Tel/Fax)

St Boswells See Maxton and Mertoun
Selkirk See Ashkirk
Skirling See Broughton, Glenholm and Kilbucho
Stobo and Drumelzier See Broughton, Glenholm and Kilbucho

Stow: St Mary of Wedale and Heriot

Catherine A. Buchan (Mrs) MA MDiv	2002		The Manse, 209 Galashiels Road, Stow, Galashiels TD1 2RE [E-mail: buchan@alan-cath.freeserve.co.uk]	01578 730237

Tweedsmuir See Broughton, Glenholm and Kilbucho
West Linton St Andrew's See Carlops

Name	Years	Role	Address	Telephone
Brown, Robert BSc	1962 1997	(Kilbrandon and Kilchattan)	11 Thornfield Terrace, Selkirk TD7 4DU [E-mail: thornfield@ukgateway.net]	01750 20311
Cashman, P. Hamilton BSc	1985 1998	(Dirleton with North Berwick: Abbey)	38 Abbotsford Road, Galashiels TD1 3HR [E-mail: mcashman@tiscali.co.uk]	01896 752711
Devenny, Robert P.	2002	Borders Health Board	Blakeburn Cottage, Wester Housebyres, Melrose TD6 9BW	01896 822350
Dick, J. Ronald BD	1973 1996	Hospital Chaplain	5 Georgefield Farm Cottages, Earlston TD4 6BH	01896 848956
Donald, Thomas W. LTh CA	1977 1987	(Bowden with Lilliesleaf)	The Quest, Huntly Road, Melrose TD6 9SB	01896 822345
Duncan, Charles A. MA	1956 1992	(Heriot with Stow St Mary of Wedale)	10 Elm Grove, Galashiels TD1 3JA	01896 753261
Kellet, John M. MA	1962 1995	(Leith: South)	4 High Cottages, Walkerburn EH43 6AZ	01896 870351
Kennon, Stanley BA BD	1992 2000	Chaplain: Navy	1 Anson Way, Helston, Cornwall TR13 8BS	
Laing, William F. DSC VRD MA	1952 1986	(Selkirk: St Mary's West)	10 The Glebe, Selkirk TD7 5AB	01750 21210
McCann, George McD. BSc ATI	1994	Auxiliary Minister	Rosbeg, Parsonage Road, Galashiels TD1 3HS	01896 752055
MacFarlane, David C. MA	1957 1997	(Eddleston with Peebles Old)	11 Station Bank, Peebles EH45 8EJ	01721 720639
Moore, W. Haisley BSc	1966 1996	(Secretary: The Boys' Brigade)	26 Tweedbank Avenue, Tweedbank, Galashiels TD1 3SP	01896 668577
Morton, Alasdair J. MA BD DipEd FEIS	1960 2000	(Bowden with Newtown)	8 Ormiston Grove, Melrose TD6 9SR [E-mail: alasgilmor@compuserve.com]	01896 822033
Morton, Gillian M. (Mrs) MA BD PGCE	1983 1996	(Hospital Chaplain)	8 Ormiston Grove, Melrose TD6 9SR	01896 822033
Rae, Andrew W.	1951 1987	(Annan: St Andrew's Greenknowe Erskine)	Roseneuk, Tweedside Road, Newtown St Boswells TD6 0PQ	01835 823783
Slack, J.W.	1968 1985	(Ashkirk with Selkirk Lawson Memorial)	17 Grenville Avenue, St Anne's-on-Sea, Fylde FY8 2RR	01253 728863
Taverner, Glyn R. MA BD	1957 1995	(Maxton and Mertoun with St Boswells)	Woodcot Cottage, Waverley Road, Innerleithen EH44 6QW	01896 830156
Thomson, George F.M. MA	1956 1988	(Dollar Associate)	6 Abbotsford Terrace, Darnick, Melrose TD6 9AD	01896 823112

(5) DUNS

Meets at Duns, in the Old Parish Church Hall, normally on the first Tuesday of February, March, April, May, October, November, December, on the last Tuesday in June, and in places to be appointed on the first Tuesday of September.

Clerk:	REV. JAMES S.H. CUTLER BD CEng MIStructE	The Manse, Duns Road, Coldstream TD12 4DP [E-mail: akph49@uk.uumail.com]	01890 882537

Ayton (H) and Burnmouth linked with Grantshouse and Houndwood and Reston

J. Christopher Ledgard BA	1969	2002	The Manse, Beanburn, Ayton, Eyemouth TD14 5QY	01890 781333

Berwick-upon-Tweed: St Andrew's Wallace Green (H) and Lowick
Vacant   1999   3 Meadow Grange, Berwick-upon-Tweed TD15 1NW   01289 303304

Bonkyl and Preston linked with Chirnside (H) linked with Edrom Allanton (H)
Celia G. Kenny (Mrs) BA MTh   1995 2002   Parish Church Manse, Chirnside, Duns TD11 3XL   01890 818911

Chirnside See Bonkyl and Preston

Coldingham and St Abb's linked with Eyemouth
Daniel G. Lindsay BD   1978 1979   Victoria Road, Eyemouth TD14 5JD   01890 750327

Coldstream (H) linked with Eccles
James S.H. Cutler BD CEng MIStructE   1986 1995   Duns Road, Coldstream TD12 4DP
[E-mail: akph49@uk.uumail.com]   01890 882537

Duns (H)
Andrew A. Morrice MA BD   1999   The Manse, Duns TD11 3DP
[E-mail: andrew.morrice@ntlworld.com]   01361 883755

Eccles See Coldstream
Edrom Allanton See Bonkyl and Preston
Eyemouth See Coldingham and St Abb's

Fogo and Swinton linked with Ladykirk linked with Leitholm linked with Whitsome (H)
Alan C.D. Cartwright BSc BD   1976   Swinton, Duns TD11 3JJ   01890 860228

Foulden and Mordington linked with Hutton and Fishwick and Paxton
Geraldine H. Hope (Mrs) MA BD   1986   Hutton, Berwick-upon-Tweed TD15 1TS
[E-mail: geraldine.hope@virgin.net]   01289 386396

Gordon: St Michael's linked with Greenlaw (H) linked with Legerwood linked with Westruther
Thomas S. Nicholson BD DPS   1982 1995   The Manse, Todholes, Greenlaw, Duns TD10 6XD   01361 810316

Grantshouse and Houndwood and Reston See Ayton and Burnmouth
Greenlaw See Gordon St Michael's
Hutton and Fishwick and Paxton See Foulden and Mordington

Kirk of Lammermuir linked with Langton and Polwarth
Ann Inglis (Mrs) LLB BD   1986 2003   The Manse, Cranshaws, Duns TD11 3SJ   01361 890289

Ladykirk See Fogo and Swinton
Langton and Polwarth See Kirk of Lammermuir
Legerwood See Gordon St Michael's
Leitholm See Fogo and Swinton
Westruther See Gordon St Michael's
Whitsome See Fogo and Swinton

Name	Years		(Charge)	Address	Telephone
Gaddes, Donald R.	1961	1994	(Kelso North and Ednam)	35 Winterfield Gardens, Duns TD11 3EZ [E-mail: doruga@winterfield.fslife.co.uk]	01361 883172
Gale, Ronald A.A. LTh	1982	1995	(Dunoon Old and St Cuthbert's)	55 Lennel Mount, Coldstream TD12 4NS	01890 883699
Hay, Bruce J.L.	1957	1997	(Makerstoun and Smailholm with Stichill, Hume and Nenthorn)	Tweed House, Tweed Street, Berwick-upon-Tweed TD15 1NG	01289 303171
Higham, Robert D. BD	1985	2002	(Tiree)	36 Low Greens, Berwick-upon-Tweed TD15 1LZ	01289 302329
Jackson, John MA	1958	1990	(Bonnybridge)	2 Milne Graden West, Coldstream TD12 4HE	01890 883435
Kerr, Andrew MA BLitt	1948	1991	(Kilbarchan West)	Meikle Harelaw, Westruther, Gordon TD10 6XT	01578 740263
Macleod, Allan M. MA	1945	1985	(Gordon St Michael's with Legerwood with Westruther)	Silverlea, Machrihanish, Argyll PA28 6PZ	
Paterson, William BD	1977	2001	(Bonkyl and Preston with Chirnside with Edrom Allanton)	Benachie, Gavinton, Duns TD11 3QT	01361 882727
Slorach, Alexander CA BD	1970	2002	(Kirk of Lammermuir with Langton and Polwarth)	61 Inverleith Row, Edinburgh EH3 5PX	

(6) JEDBURGH

Meets at Jedburgh on the first Wednesday of February, March, May, October, November and December and on the last Wednesday of June. Meets in the Moderator's church on the first Wednesday of September.

Clerk   REV. NEIL R. COMBE BSc MSc BD   Teviot Manse, Buccleuch Road, Hawick TD9 0EL   **01450 372150**
[E-mail: akph56@uk.uumail.com]
[E-mail: jedburghpresbytery@uk.uumail.com]

Ancrum linked with Crailing and Eckford with Lilliesleaf (T)   1989 1991
W. Frank Campbell BA BD   22 The Glebe, Ancrum, Jedburgh TD8 6UX   01835 830318

Cavers and Kirkton linked with Hawick St Mary's and Old   1983 1998
William R. Taylor MA BD   Braid Road, Hawick TD9 9LZ   01450 377865
[E-mail: revwrt@aol.com]

Crailing and Eckford See Ancrum

Hawick: Burnfoot
Charles J. Finnie LTh DPS   1991 1997   29 Wilton Hill, Hawick TD9 8BA   01450 373181
[E-mail: charles@finnierev.freeserve.co.uk]
Ronald M. Mackinnon DCS   70 Eildon Road, Hawick TD9 8ES   01450 374816 (Tel)
07808 117538 (Mbl)

Hawick: Teviot (H) and Roberton
Neil R. Combe BSc MSc BD   1984   Teviot Manse, Buccleuch Road, Hawick TD9 0EL   01450 372150
[E-mail: neil.combe@btinternet.com]

Hawick: St Mary's and Old (H) See Cavers and Kirkton

Hawick: Trinity (H)
E.P. Lindsay Thomson MA | 1964 | 1972 | Fenwick Park, Hawick TD9 9PA | 01450 372705

Hawick: Wilton linked with Teviothead
Vacant | 4 Wilton Hill Terrace, Hawick TD9 8BE | 01450 370744

Hobkirk and Southdean linked with Ruberslaw
Vacant | The Manse, Denholm, Hawick TD9 8NB | 01450 870268

Jedburgh: Old and Edgerston
Bruce McNicol JP BL BD | 1967 | 1992 | Honeyfield Drive, Jedburgh TD8 6LQ | 01835 863417

Jedburgh: Trinity
John A. Riddell MA BD | 1967 | 42 High Street, Jedburgh TD8 6DQ | 01835 863223

Kelso: North (H) and Ednam (H) (01573 224154)
Tom McDonald BD | 1994 | 20 Forestfield, Kelso TD5 7BX | 01573 224677
[E-mail: revtom@20thepearlygates.fsnet.co.uk]

Kelso: Old (H) and Sprouston
Marion E. Dodd MA BD LRAM | 1988 | 1989 | Glebe Lane, Kelso TD5 7AU | 01573 226254
[E-mail: mariondodd@macunlimited.net]

Lilliesleaf See Ancrum

Linton linked with Morebattle and Hownam linked with Yetholm (H)
Robin D. McHaffie BD | 1979 | 1991 | The Manse, Main Street, Kirk Yetholm, Kelso TD5 8PF | 01573 420308
[E-mail: robin.mchaffie@virgin.net]

Makerstoun and Smailholm linked with Roxburgh linked with Stichill, Hume and Nenthorn
Valerie G.C. Watson (Ms) MA BD STM | 1987 | 2001 | The Manse, 1 The Meadow, Stichill, Kelso TD5 7TG | 01573 470607
[E-mail: vwatson@tiscali.co.uk]

Morebattle and Hownam See Linton

Oxnam
Continued Vacancy

Roxburgh See Makerstoun and Smailholm
Ruberslaw See Hobkirk and Southdean

Stichill, Hume and Nenthorn See Makerstoun and Smailholm   **(Charge formed by the union of Bedrule, Denholm and Minto)**
Teviothead See Hawick: Wilton
Yetholm See Linton

Bowie, Adam McC.	(Cavers and Kirkton with Hobkirk and Southdean)	Glenbield, Redpath, Earlston TD4 6AD	1976 1996	01896 848173
Brown, Joseph MA	(Linton with Hownam and Morebattle with Yetholm)	The Orchard, Hermitage Lane, Shedden Park Road, Kelso TD5 7AN	1954 1991	01573 223481
Fox, G. Dudley A.	(Kelso Old)	14 Pinnacle Hill Farm, Kelso TD5 8HD	1972 1988	01573 223335
Hamilton, Robert MA BD	(Kelso Old)	Ridge Cottage, 391 Totnes Road, Collaton St Mary, Paignton TQ4 7PW	1938 1979	01803 526440
Longmuir, William LTh	(Bedrule with Denholm with Minto)	112 Weensland Road, Hawick TD9 9PH	1984 2001	01450 379460
McConnell, Robert	(Hawick St Margaret's and Wilton South with Roberton)	Flat 31, Strathclyde House, 31–33 Shore Road, Skelmorlie PA17 5AN	1959 1983	01475 522532
Ritchie, Garden W.M.	(Ardersier with Petty)	23 Croft Road, Kelso TD5 7EP	1961 1995	01573 224419
Thompson, W.M.D. MA	(Crailing and Eckford with Oxnam with Roxburgh)	Beech House, Cornhill-on-Tweed TD12 4RE	1950 1997	01890 820621

HAWICK ADDRESSES

Burnfoot	Fraser Avenue		
St Mary's and Old	Kirk Wynd	Wilton	Princes Street
Teviot	off Buccleuch Road		
Trinity	Central Square		

(7) ANNANDALE AND ESKDALE

Meets on the first Tuesday of February, May, September and December; and the third Tuesday of March, June and October, in a venue to be determined by Presbytery.

Clerk:	REV. C. BRYAN HASTON LTh	The Manse, Gretna Green DG16 5DU [E-mail: cbhaston@cofs.demon.co.uk] [E-mail: cbhaston@uk.uumail.com]	01461 338313 (Tel) 08701 640119 (Fax)

Annan: Old (H)

Vacant		12 Plumdon Park Avenue, Annan DG12 6EY	01461 201405

Annan: St Andrew's (H)

George K. Lind BD MCIBS	1998	1 Annerley Road, Annan DG12 6HE [E-mail: gklind@bosinternet.com]	01461 202626

Applegarth and Sibbaldbie (H) linked with Johnstone linked with Lochmaben (H)

Jack M. Brown BSc BD	1977 2002	Lochmaben, Lockerbie DG11 1QF [E-mail: jackmbrown@tiscali.co.uk]	01387 810066

Brydekirk linked with Hoddam

S. Edwin P. Beveridge BA	1959 1993	Ecclefechan, Lockerbie DG11 3BU	01576 300357

Canonbie (H) linked with Liddesdale (H) 1989 2003
Alan D. Reid MA BD
23 Langholm Street, Newcastleton TD9 0QX
[E-mail: canonbie.liddesdale@btopenworld.com]
01387 375242

Carlisle: Chapel Street linked with Longtown: St Andrew's 2000 2002
David J. Thom BD
30 Dunmail Drive, Carlisle CA2 6DF
[E-mail: david@kirkscotland.org.uk]
01228 819832

Dalton linked with Hightae linked with St Mungo 2001
Alexander C. Stoddart BD
Hightae, Lockerbie DG11 1JL
[E-mail: sandystoddart@supanet.com]
01387 811499

Dornock 1967
Ronald S. Seaman MA
Dornock, Annan DG12 6NR
01461 40268

Eskdalemuir linked with Hutton and Corrie linked with Tundergarth 1988 2003
Alan C. Ross CA BD
Hutton Manse, Boreland, Lockerbie DG11 2PB
[E-mail: alkaross@aol.com]
01576 610213

Gretna: Old (H), Gretna: St Andrew's and Half Morton and Kirkpatrick Fleming 1975
C. Bryan Haston LTh
The Manse, Gretna Green DG16 5DU
[E-mail: cbhaston@cofs.demon.co.uk]
01461 338313 (Tel)
08701 640119 (Fax)

Hightae See Dalton
Hoddam See Brydekirk
Hutton and Corrie See Eskdalemuir
Johnstone See Applegarth and Sibbaldbie

Kirkpatrick Juxta linked with Moffat St Andrew's (H) linked with Wamphray 1979 2001
David M. McKay MA BD
The Manse, 1 Meadowbank, Moffat DG10 9LR
[E-mail: demacmin@ukgateway.net]
01683 220128

Kirtle-Eaglesfield linked with Middlebie linked with Waterbeck 1990 1999
Trevor C. Williams LTh
Kirtlebridge, Lockerbie DG11 3LY
[E-mail: revwill@btopenworld.com]
01461 500378

Langholm, Ewes and Westerkirk 1999 1999
Robert B. Milne BTh
The Manse, Thomas Telford Road, Langholm DG13 0BL
[E-mail: rbmilne@aol.com]
01387 380252 (Tel)
01387 381399 (Fax)

Liddesdale (H) See Canonbie
Lochmaben See Applegarth and Sibbaldbie

Lockerbie: Dryfesdale
David M. Almond BD   1996   The Manse, 5 Carlisle Road, Lockerbie DG11 2DW   01576 202361
[E-mail: rev.almond@btinternet.com]

Longtown: St Andrew's See Carlisle: Chapel Street
Middlebie See Kirtle-Eaglesfield
Moffat St Andrew's (H) See Kirkpatrick Juxta
St Mungo See Dalton
Tundergarth See Eskdalemuir
Wamphray See Kirkpatrick Juxta
Waterbeck See Kirtle-Eaglesfield

Name	Dates	Charge	Address	Phone
Annand, James M. MA BD	1955 1995	(Lockerbie Dryfesdale)	48 Main Street, Newstead, Melrose TD6 9DX	01576 201486
Baillie, David R.	1979 1990	(Crawford with Lowther)	1 Preston Court, Annan DG12 5HS [E-mail: aman@baillie.abel.co.uk]	
Byers, Alan J.	1959 1992	(Gamrie with King Edward)	Meadowbank, Plumdon Road, Annan DG12 6SJ	01461 206512
Byers, Mairi (Mrs) BTh CPS	1992 1998	(Jura)	Meadowbank, Plumdon Road, Annan DG12 6SJ	01461 206512
Fisher, D. Noel MA BD	1939 1979	(Glasgow: Sherbrooke St Gilbert's)	Sheraig Cottage, Killochries Fold, Kilmacolm PA13 4TE	
Kirk, W. Logan MA BD MTh	1988 2000	(Dalton with Hightae with St Mungo)	2 Firpark Cottages, Lockerbie DG11 1BL	01576 204653
McLean, Margaret G. BD	1978 1991	(Community Minister: Annandale and Eskdale)	84 Union Road, Gretna DG16 5JT	01461 338491
MacMillan, William M. LTh	1980 1998	(Kilmory with Lamlash)	Balskia, 61 Queen Street, Lochmaben DG11 1PP	01387 811528
Macpherson, Duncan J. BSc BD	1993 2002	Chaplain: Army	1BW, Fallingbostel, St Barbara's Barracks, Fallingbostel, BFPO 38	
Rennie, John D. MA	1962 1996	(Broughton, Glenholm and Kilbucho with Skirling with Stobo and Drumelzier with Tweedsmuir)	Dundoran, Ballplay Road, Moffat DG10 9JX [E-mail: rennies@dundoran96.freeserve.co.uk]	01683 220223
Swinburne, Norman BA	1960 1993	(Sauchie)	Dameroschay, Birch Hill Lane, Kirkbride, Wigton CA7 5HZ	01697 351497

(8) DUMFRIES AND KIRKCUDBRIGHT

Meets at Dumfries, on the first Wednesday of February, March, April, May, September, October, November and December, and the last Wednesday of June.

Clerk: REV. GORDON M.A. SAVAGE MA BD   11 Laurieknowe, Dumfries DG2 7AH   01387 252929
[E-mail: akph44@uk.uumail.com]
Depute Clerk: REV. WILLIAM T. HOGG MA BD   The Manse, Glasgow Road, Sanquhar DG4 6BS   01659 50247
[E-mail: tervit@btopenworld.com]

Anwoth and Girthon linked with Borgue
Valerie J. Ott (Mrs) BA BD   2002   Gatehouse of Fleet, Castle Douglas DG7 2EQ   01557 814233
[E-mail: dandvott@aol.com]

Auchencairn and Rerrick linked with Buittle and Kelton
James H. Sinclair MA BD   1966 1992   Auchencairn, Castle Douglas DG7 1QS   01556 640288

Balmaclellan and Kells (H) linked with Carsphairn (H) linked with Dalry (H)
David S. Bartholomew BSc MSc PhD BD   1994   Dalry, Castle Douglas DG7 3PJ   01644 430380
[E-mail: dhbart@care4free.net]

Balmaghie linked with Tarff and Twynholm (H)
Christopher Wallace BD DipMin   1988   Twynholm, Kirkcudbright DG6 4NY   01557 860381
[E-mail: c.wallace3@ntlworld.com]

Borgue   See Anwoth and Girthon
Buittle and Kelton   See Auchencairn and Rerrick

Caerlaverock
Continued Vacancy

Carsphairn   See Balmaclellan and Kells

Castle Douglas (H)
Robert J. Malloch BD   1987 2001   1 Castle View, Castle Douglas DG7 1BG   01556 502171
[E-mail: robert@scotnish.freeserve.co.uk]

Closeburn linked with Durisdeer
James W. Scott MA CDA   1952 1953   Durisdeer, Thornhill, Dumfriesshire DG3 5BJ   01848 500231

Colvend, Southwick and Kirkbean
Vacant   Colvend, Dalbeattie DG5 4QN   01556 630255

Corsock and Kirkpatrick Durham linked with Crossmichael and Parton
James A. Guthrie   1969 1999   Knockdrocket, Clarebrand, Castle Douglas DG7 3AH   01556 503645

Crossmichael and Parton   See Corsock and Kirkpatrick Durham

Cummertrees linked with Mouswald linked with Ruthwell (H)
James Williamson BA BD   1986 1991   Ruthwell, Dumfries DG1 4NP   01387 870217
[E-mail: jimwill@rcmkirk.freeserve.co.uk]

Dalbeattie (H) linked with Urr (H)
Norman M. Hutcheson MA BD   1973 1988   36 Mill Street, Dalbeattie DG5 4HE   01556 610029
[E-mail: norman.hutcheson@virgin.net]

Dalry See Balmaclellan

Dumfries: Greyfriars (T) (H)
Vacant — 4 Georgetown Crescent, Dumfries DG1 4EQ — 01387 257045

Dumfries: Lincluden linked with Holywood (T)
Vacant — 96 Glasgow Road, Dumfries DG2 9DE — 01387 264298

Dumfries: Lochside
Vacant — 27 St Anne's Road, Dumfries DG2 9HZ — 01387 252912

Dumfries: Maxwelltown West (H)
Gordon M.A. Savage MA BD — 1977 1984 — Maxwelltown West Manse, 11 Laurieknowe, Dumfries DG2 7AH [E-mail: gordonsavage@uk.uumail.com] — 01387 252929

Dumfries: St George's (H)
Donald Campbell BD — 1997 — 9 Nunholm Park, Dumfries DG1 1JP [E-mail: donald@campbell3.freeserve.co.uk] — 01387 252965

Dumfries: St Mary's (H)
Vacant — 47 Moffat Road, Dumfries DG1 1NN — 01387 254873
Elizabeth A. Mack (Miss) DipPEd (Aux) — 1994 2003 — 24 Roberts Crescent, Dumfries DG2 7RS — 01387 264847

Dumfries: St Michael's and South
Maurice S. Bond MTh BA DipEd PhD — 1981 1999 — 39 Cardoness Street, Dumfries DG1 3AL — 01387 253849

Dumfries: Troqueer (H)
William W. Kelly BSc BD — 1994 — Troqueer Road, Dumfries DG2 7DF [E-mail: wwkelly@ntlworld.com] — 01387 253043

Dunscore linked with Glencairn and Moniaive
Christine Sime (Miss) BSc BD — 1994 — Wallaceton, Auldgirth, Dumfries DG2 0TJ [E-mail: revsime@aol.com] — 01387 820245

Durisdeer See Closeburn
Glencairn and Moniaive See Dunscore
Holywood See Dumfries: Lincluden

Irongray, Lochrutton and Terregles
David J. Taylor MA BD — 1982 2002 — Shawhead Road, Dumfries DG2 9SJ [E-mail: david@bunessan.f9.co.uk] — 01387 730287

Kirkconnel (H)
David Deas Melville BD — 1989 1999 — The Manse, 31 Kingsway, Kirkconnel, Sanquhar DG4 6PN [E-mail: ddm@kirkconn.freeserve.co.uk] — 01659 67241

Kirkcudbright (H)
Douglas R. Irving LLB BD WS   1984   1998
6 Bourtree Avenue, Kirkcudbright DG6 4AU   01557 330489
[E-mail: douglasirving@kirkcudbright99.freeserve.co.uk]

Kirkgunzeon
Continued Vacancy

Kirkmahoe
Dennis S. Rose LTh   1996
Kirkmahoe, Dumfries DG1 1ST   01387 710572
[E-mail: dennros@aol.com]

Kirkmichael, Tinwald and Torthorwald
Louis C. Bezuidenhout MA DD   1978   2000
Manse of Tinwald, Tinwald, Dumfries DG1 3PL   01387 710246
[E-mail: macbez@btinternet.com]

Lochend linked with New Abbey
William Holland MA   1967   1971
New Abbey, Dumfries DG2 8BY   01387 850232
[E-mail: bilholland@aol.com]

Mouswald See Cummertrees
New Abbey See Lochend

Penpont, Keir and Tynron linked with Thornhill (H)
Donald Keith MA BD   1971   2002
Beechhill, Manse Park, Thornhill DG3 5ER   01848 331191

Ruthwell (H) See Cummertrees

Sanquhar: St Bride's (H)
William T. Hogg MA BD   1979   2000
Glasgow Road, Sanquhar DG4 6BS   01659 50247
[E-mail: tervit@btopenworld.com]

Tarff and Twynholm See Balmaghie

Thornhill (H) See Penpont, Keir and Tynron

Urr See Dalbeattie

Bennett, David K.P. BA	1974	2000	53 Anne Arundel Court, Heathhall, Dumfries DG1 3SL	01387 257755
(Kirkpatrick Irongray with Lochrutton with Terregles)				
Calderwood, Walter M. MA BD	1934	1974	Flat 10, Daar Lodge, 6 St Mary Street, Kirkcudbright DG6 4AQ	01557 330330
(Leven Forman)				
Craig, N. Douglas MA BD	1947	1987	33 Albert Road, Dumfries DG2 9DN	01387 252187
(Dalbeattie Craignair with Urr)				
Elder, Albert B. MA	1960	1998	87 Glasgow Street, Dumfries DG2 9AG	01387 249778
(Dumfries: St Michael's & South)				
Geddes, Alexander J. MA BD	1960	1998	166 Georgetown Road, Dumfries DG1 4DT	01387 252287
(Stewarton: St Columba's)				

Name	(Charge)	Ord	App	Address	Tel
Gillespie, Ann M. (Miss) DCS	(Deaconess)	1961	1987	Barlochan House, Palnackie, Castle Douglas DG7 1PF	01556 600378
Grant, James BA	(Penpont Keir and Tynron)	1956	1996	147A Drumlanrig Street, Thornhill DG3 5LJ	01848 330829
Greer, A. David C. LLB DMin DipAdultEd	(Barra)			10 Watling Street, Dumfries DG1 1HF	01387 256113
Hamill, Robert BA	(Castle Douglas St Ringan's)	1956	1989	11 St Andrew Drive, Castle Douglas DG7 1EW	01556 502962
Hutchison, Mary L. (Mrs) BD	(Dumfries Lincluden with Holywood)	1982	1995	Monzie, 25 Twiname Way, Heathhall, Dumfries DG1 3ST	01387 250610
Johnston, John MA BD	(Hospital Chaplain)	1963	1999	Near Bye, Amisfield, Dumfries DG1 3LN	01387 710254
Leishman, James S. LTh BD MA(Div)	(Kirkmichael with Tinwald with Torthorwald)	1969	1999	11 Hunter Avenue, Heathhall, Dumfries DG1 3UX	01387 249241
Mackay, Donald MBE FCP FSAScot	(Ardrossan: St John's)	1951	1986	8 Urquhart Crescent, Dumfries DG1 8XF	01387 259132
McKenzie, William M. DA	(Dumfries: Troqueer)	1958	1993	41 Kingholm Road, Dumfries DG1 4SR [E-mail: mckenzie.dumfries@virgin.net]	01387 253688
Miller, John R. MA BD	(Carsphairn with Dalry)	1958	1992	4 Fairgreen Court, Rhonehouse, Castle Douglas DG7 1SA	01556 680428
Morrison, James G. MBE MA	(Rotterdam)	1942	1980	Auchenshiel, Rhonehouse, Castle Douglas DG7 1SA	01556 680526
Owen, John J.C. LTh	(Applegarth and Sibbaldbie with Lochmaben)	1967	2001	5 Galla Avenue, Dalbeattie DG5 4JZ [E-mail: jjowen@macunlimited.net]	01556 612125
Robertson, Ian W. MA BD	(Colvend, Southwick and Kirkbean)	1956	1995	10 Marjoriebanks, Lochmaben, Lockerbie DG11 1QH	01387 810541
Robertson, Thomas R. MA BD	(Broughton, Glenholm and Kilbucho with Skirling)	1934	1976	1 Church Row, Kirkcudbright DG6 4AP	01557 330795
Smith, Richmond OBE MA BD	(World Alliance of Reformed Churches)	1952	1983	Aignish, Merse Way, Kippford, Dalbeattie DG5 4LH	01556 620624
Strachan, Alexander E. MA BD	(Dumfries Health Care Chaplain)	1974	1999	2 Leafield Road, Dumfries DG1 2DS [E-mail: aestrachan@aol.com]	01387 279460
Vincent, C. Raymond MA FSAScot	(Stonehouse)	1952	1992	Rosebank, Newton Stewart Road, New Galloway, Castle Douglas DG7 3RT	01644 420451
Wilkie, James R. MA MTh	(Penpont, Keir and Tynron)	1957	1993	31 West Morton Street, Thornhill DG3 5NF	01848 331028
Wotherspoon, Robert C. LTh	(Corsock and Kirkpatrick Durham with Crossmichael and Parton)	1976	1998	7 Hillowton Drive, Castle Douglas DG7 1LL	01556 502267
Young, John MTh DipMin	(Airdrie: Broomknoll)	1963	1999	Craigview, North Street, Moniaive, Thornhill DG3 4HR	01848 200318

DUMFRIES ADDRESSES

Church	Address	Church	Address	Church	Address
Greyfriars	Church Crescent	Maxwelltown West	Laurieknowe	St Michael's and South	St Michael's Street
Lincluden	Stewartry Road	St George's	George Street	Troqueer	Troqueer Road
Lochside	Lochside Road	St Mary's	St Mary's Street		

(9) WIGTOWN AND STRANRAER

Meets at Glenluce, in the church hall, on the first Tuesday of March, October and December for ordinary business; on the first Tuesday of September for formal business followed by meetings of committees; on the first Tuesday of November, February and May for worship followed by meetings of committees; and at a church designated by the Moderator on the first Tuesday of June for Holy Communion followed by ordinary business.

Clerk: REV. D.W. DUTTON BA   High Kirk Manse, Leswalt High Road, Stranraer DG9 0AA
[E-mail: akph79@uk.uumail.com]   **01776 703268**

Ervie Kirkcolm linked with Leswalt
Michael J. Sheppard BD   1997   Ervie Manse, Stranraer DG9 0QZ
[E-mail: michael@erviecos.freeserve.co.uk]   01776 854225

Glasserton and Isle of Whithorn linked with Whithorn: St Ninian's Priory
Alexander I. Currie BD CPS   1990   Whithorn, Newton Stewart DG8 8PY   01988 500267

Inch linked with Stranraer: St Andrew's (H)
John H. Burns BSc BD   1985   1988   Bay View Road, Stranraer DG9 8BE   01776 702383

Kirkcowan (H) linked with Wigtown (H)
Martin Thomson BSc DipEd BD   1988   Harbour Road, Wigtown, Newton Stewart DG8 9AL
[E-mail: martin@thomsonm40.freeserve.co.uk]   01988 402242

Kirkinner linked with Sorbie (H)
Jeffrey M. Mead BD   1978   1986   Kirkinner, Newton Stewart DG8 9AL   01988 840643

Kirkmabreck linked with Monigaff (H)
Hugh D. Steele LTh DipMin   1994   Cree Bridge, Newton Stewart DG8 6NR   01671 403361

Kirkmaiden (H) linked with Stoneykirk
Ian McIlroy BSS BD   1996   Church Street, Sandhead, Stranraer DG9 9JJ   01776 830337
Mary Munro (Mrs) BA (Aux)   1993   High Barbeth, Leswalt, Stranraer DG9 0QS   01776 870250

Leswalt See Ervie Kirkcolm

Mochrum (H)
Roger A.F. Dean LTh   1983   1995   Port William, Newton Stewart DG8 9QP   01988 700257

Monigaff (H) See Kirkmabreck

New Luce (H) linked with Old Luce (H)
Thomas M. McWhirter MA MSc BD   1992 1997   Glenluce, Newton Stewart DG8 0PU   01581 300319

Old Luce See New Luce

Penninghame (H)
Neil G. Campbell BA BD   1988 1989   The Manse, Newton Stewart DG8 6HH   01671 402259
[E-mail: neilcampbell@yahoo.com]

Portpatrick linked with Stranraer: St Ninian's (H)
Gordon Kennedy BSc BD   1993 2000   London Road, Stranraer DG9 9AB   01776 702443
[E-mail: gordon.kennedy1@btinternet.com]

Sorbie See Kirkinner
Stoneykirk See Kirkmaiden

Stranraer: High Kirk (H)
David W. Dutton BA   1973 1986   Leswalt High Road, Stranraer DG9 0AA   01776 703268
[E-mail: akph79@uk.uumail.com]

Stranraer: Old (H)
Samuel McC. Harris BA BD   1974 1990   Linden, Leswalt High Road, Stranraer DG9 0AA   01776 706387

Stranraer St Andrew's See Inch
Stranraer St Ninian's See Portpatrick
Whithorn: St Ninian's Priory See Glasserton and Isle of Whithorn
Wigtown See Kirkcowan

Cairns, Alexander B. MA	1957	1997	(Ervie Kirkcolm with Leswalt)	Beechwood, Main Street, Sandhead, Stranraer DG9 9JG	01776 830389
Cordiner, John	1950	1986	(Portpatrick)	Tara, Fellview Road, Stranraer DG9 8BK	01776 704720
Harkes, George	1962	1988	(Cumbernauld Old)	11 Main Street, Sorbie, Newton Stewart DG8 8EG	01988 850255
McCreadie, David W.	1961	1995	(Kirkmabreck)	77 St John Street, Creetown, Newton Stewart DG8 7JB	01671 820390
McGill, David W.	1972	1990	(Portpatrick with Stranraer St Ninian's)	Ravenstone Moor, Dramrae, Whithorn, Newton Stewart DG8 8DS	01988 700449
Ogilvy, Oliver M.	1959	1985	(Leswalt)	8 Dale Crescent, Stranraer DG9 0HG	01776 706285

(10) AYR

Meets on the first Tuesday of every month from September to May, excluding January, and on the fourth Tuesday of June. The June meeting will be held in the Moderator's Church. One meeting will be held in a venue to be determined by the Business Committee. Other meetings will be held in Alloway Church Hall.

Clerk:	REV. JAMES CRICHTON MA BD MTh		Presbytery Office	30 Garden Street, Dalrymple KA6 6DG [E-mail: akph39@uk.uumail.com] [E-mail: akph40@uk.uumail.com]	01292 560263 (Fax) 01292 560574 (Fax) 01292 262184 (Tel/Fax)

Alloway (H) Neil A. McNaught BD MA	1987	1999	1A Parkview, Alloway, Ayr KA7 4QG [E-mail: neilmcnaught3427.freeserve.co.uk]	01292 441252
Annbank (H) linked with Tarbolton Vacant			1 Kirkport, Tarbolton, Mauchline KA5 5QJ	01292 541236
Arnsheen Barrhill linked with Colmonell John S. Lochrie BSc BD MTh PhD	1967	1999	Manse Road, Colmonell, Girvan KA26 0SA	01465 881224
Auchinleck (H) linked with Catrine James Sloan BA MD	1987	2002	28 Mauchline Road, Auchinleck KA18 2BN	01290 421108
Ayr: Auld Kirk of Ayr (St John the Baptist) (H) David R. Gemmell MA BD	1991	1999	58 Monument Road, Ayr KA7 2UB [E-mail: DRGemmell@aol.com]	01292 262580 (Tel/Fax)
Ayr: Castlehill (H) Peter B. Park BD MCIBS	1997	2003	3 Old Hillfoot Road, Ayr KA7 3LF [E-mail: peter.park1@virgin.net]	01292 267332
Ayr: Newton on Ayr (H) G. Stewart Birse CA BD BSc	1980	1989	9 Nursery Grove, Ayr KA7 3PH [E-mail: gstewart@birse21.freeserve.co.uk]	01292 264251
Ayr: St Andrew's (H) Harry B. Mealyea BArch BD	1984	2000	31 Bellevue Crescent, Ayr KA7 2DP [E-mail: harrybellmealyea@netscapeonline.co.uk]	01292 261126

Ayr: St Columba (H)
Fraser R. Aitken MA BD — 1978 — 1991 — 2 Hazelwood Road, Ayr KA7 2PY
[E-mail: fraser.aitken@columba92.fsnet.co.uk] — 01292 284177

Ayr: St James'
Gillian Weighton (Mrs) BD STM — 1992 — 1 Prestwick Road, Ayr KA8 8LD
[E-mail: gillweighton@aol.com] — 01292 262420

Ayr: St Leonard's (H)
Robert Lynn MA BD — 1984 — 1989 — 7 Shawfield Avenue, Ayr KA7 4RE
[E-mail: robert@shawfield200.fsnet.co.uk] — 01292 442109

Ayr: St Quivox (H)
David T. Ness LTh — 1972 — 1988 — 11 Springfield Avenue, Prestwick KA9 2HA
[E-mail: dness@fish.co.uk] — 01292 478306

Ayr: Wallacetown (H)
Mary C. McLauchlan (Mrs) LTh — 1997 — 2003 — 87 Forehill Road, Ayr KA7 3JR
[E-mail: mcmclauchlan@ntlworld.com] — 01292 263878

Ballantrae (H)
Robert P. Bell BSc — 1968 — 1998 — Ballantrae, Girvan KA26 0NH
[E-mail: revbobbell@aol.com] — 01465 831252 (Tel) 01465 831260 (Fax)

Barr linked with Dailly linked with Girvan South
Ian K. McLachlan MA BD — 1999 — 30 Henrietta Street, Girvan KA26 9AL
[E-mail: iankmclachlan@yetiville.freeserve.co.uk] — 01465 713370

Catrine See Auchinleck
Colmonell See Arnsheen Barrhill

Coylton linked with Drongan: The Schaw Kirk
Paul R. Russell MA BD — 1984 — 1991 — 4 Hamilton Place, Coylton, Ayr KA6 6JQ
[E-mail: russellpr@btinternet.com] — 01292 570272

Craigie linked with Symington
Alastair M. Sanderson BA LTh — 1971 — 2000 — 16 Kerrix Road, Symington, Kilmarnock KA1 5QD
[E-mail: alel@sanderson29.fsnet.co.uk] — 01563 830205

Crosshill linked with Dalrymple
James Crichton MA BD MTh — 1969 — 30 Galrymple Street, Dalrymple KA6 6DG
[E-mail: akph39@uk.uumail.com] — 01292 560263 (Tel) 01292 560574 (Fax)

Dailly See Barr

Dalmellington
Kenneth B. Yorke BD DipEd   1982 1999   4 Carsphairn Road, Dalmellington, Ayr KA6 7RE   01292 550353
[E-mail: k.yorke@zoom.co.uk]

Dalrymple See Crosshill
Drongan: The Schaw Kirk See Coylton

Dundonald (H)
Robert Mayes BD   1982 1988   64 Main Street, Dundonald, Kilmarnock KA2 9HG   01563 850243

Fisherton (H) linked with Kirkoswald
Arrick D. Wilkinson BSc BD   2000 2003   The Manse, Kirkoswald, Maybole KA19 8HZ   01655 760210

Girvan: North (Old and St Andrew's) (H)
Douglas G. McNab BA BD   1999   38 The Avenue, Girvan KA26 9DS   01465 713203
[E-mail: dougmcnab@aol.com]

Girvan: South See Barr linked with Dailly

Kirkmichael linked with Straiton: St Cuthbert's
W. Gerald Jones MA BD MTh   1984 1985   Patna Road, Kirkmichael, Maybole KA19 7PJ   01655 750286
[E-mail: revgerald@jonesg99.freeserve.co.uk]

Kirkoswald (H) See Fisherton

Lugar linked with Old Cumnock: Old (H)
John W. Paterson BSc BD DipEd   1994   33 Barrhill Road, Cumnock KA18 1PJ   01290 420769
[E-mail: ocochurchwow@hotmail.com]

Mauchline (H)
Alan B. Telfer BA BD   1983 1991   4 Westside Gardens, Mauchline KA5 5DJ   01290 550386
[E-mail: abtelfer@btinternet.com]

Maybole
David Whiteman BD   1998   64 Culzean Road, Maybole KA19 8AH   01655 889456
[E-mail: davesoo@aol.com]

Monkton and Prestwick: North (H)
Arthur A. Christie BD   1997 2000   40 Monkton Road, Prestwick KA9 1AR   01292 477499
[E-mail: revaac@compuserve.com]

Muirkirk (H) linked with Sorn
Alex M. Welsh BD — 1979 2003 — 2 Smallburn Road, Muirkirk, Cumnock KA18 3RF — 01290 661157

New Cumnock (H)
Rona M. Young (Mrs) BD DipEd — 1991 2001 — 37 Castle, New Cumnock, Cumnock KA18 4AG
[E-mail: revronyoung@hotmail.com] — 01290 338296

Ochiltree linked with Stair
Carolyn M. Baker (Mrs) BD — 1997 — 10 Mauchline Road, Ochiltree, Cumnock KA18 2PZ
[E-mail: carolynmbaker2001@yahoo.co.uk] — 01290 700365

Old Cumnock: Crichton West and St Ninian's
J. Edward Andrews MA BD DipCG — 1985 2002 — 46 Ayr Road, Cumnock KA18 1DW
[E-mail: edward.andrews@btinternet.com] — 01290 422145

Old Cumnock: Old See Lugar

Patna Waterside
Vacant
Muriel Wilson (Ms) DCS — 23 Jellieston Terrace, Patna, Ayr KA6 7JZ
[E-mail: murielw@fish.co.uk] — 01292 532492

Prestwick: Kingcase (H) (E-mail: office@kingcase.freeserve.co.uk)
T. David Watson BSc BD — 1988 1997 — 15 Bellrock Avenue, Prestwick KA9 1SQ
[E-mail: tdwatson@tesco.net] — 01292 479571

Prestwick: St Nicholas' (H)
George R. Fiddes BD — 1979 1985 — 3 Bellevue Road, Prestwick KA9 1NW
[E-mail: george@gfiddes.freeserve.co.uk] — 01292 477613

Prestwick: South (H)
Kenneth C. Elliott BD CertMin — 1989 — 68 St Quivox Road, Prestwick KA9 1JF
[E-mail: kenneth@revelliott.freeserve.co.uk] — 01292 478788

Sorn See Muirkirk
Stair See Ochiltree
Straiton St Cuthbert's See Kirkmichael
Symington See Craigie
Tarbolton See Annbank

Troon: Old (H)
Alastair H. Symington MA BD — 1972 1998 — 85 Bentinck Drive, Troon KA10 6HZ
[E-mail: revahs@care4free.net] — 01292 313644

Troon: Portland (H)
Ronald M.H. Boyd BD DipTh   1995   1999   89 South Beach, Troon KA10 6EQ   01292 313285
[E-mail: rmhboyd@btopenworld.com]

Troon: St Meddan's (H) (E-mail: st.meddan@virgin.net)
David L. Harper BSc BD   1972   1979   27 Bentinck Drive, Troon KA10 6HX   01292 311784
[E-mail: d.l.harper@btinternet.com]

Andrew, R.J.M. MA	1955	1994	(Uddingston Old)	6A Ronaldshaw Park, Ayr KA7 2TS	01292 263430
Banks, John BD	1968	2001	(Hospital Chaplain)	19 Victoria Drive, Troon KA10 6JF	01292 317758
Barr, John BSc PhD BD	1958	1979	(Kilmacolm Old)	7 Kilbrandon Way, Doonfoot, Ayr KA7 4JY	01292 445631
Bird, John W.	1965	1997	(Bathgate High)	14 Springfield Avenue, Prestwick KA9 2HA	01292 476037
Blyth, James G.S. BSc BD	1963	1986	(Glenmuick)	40 Robsland Avenue, Ayr KA7 2RW	01292 261276
Bogle, Thomas C. BD	1983	2003	(Fisherton with Maybole West)	38 McEwan Crescent, Mossblown, Ayr KA6 5DR	01292 521215
Campbell, Effie C. (Mrs) BD	1981	1991	(Old Cumnock Crichton West with St Ninian's)		
Cranston, George BD	1976	2001	(Rutherglen: Wardlawhill)	7 Lansdowne Road, Ayr KA8 8LS	01292 264282
Dickie, Michael M. BSc	1955	1994	(Ayr Castlehill)	20 Capperview, Prestwick KA9 1BH	01292 476627
Garrity, T. Alan W. BSc BD MTh	1969	1999	Christ Church, Warwick, Bermuda	8 Noltmire Road, Ayr KA8 9ES PO Box PG88, Paget PG BX, Bermuda [E-mail: revtawg@logic.bm]	
Glencross, William M. LTh	1968	1999	(Bellshill: Macdonald Memorial)	1 Lochay Place, Troon KA10 7HH	01292 317097
Grant, J. Gordon MA BD	1957	1997	(Edinburgh: Dean)	33 Fullarton Drive, Troon KA10 6LE	01292 311852
Hannah, William BD MCAM MIPR	1987	2001	(Muirkirk)	8 Dovecot View, Kirkintilloch, Glasgow G66 3HY	0141-776 1337
Helon, George G. BA BD	1984	2000	(Barr linked with Dailly)	9 Park Road, Maxwelltown, Dumfries DG2 7PW	01387 259255
Johnston, Kenneth L. BA LTh	1969	2001	(Annbank)	2 Rylands, Prestwick KA9 2DX	01292 471980
Kent, Arthur F.S.	1966	1999	(Monkton and Prestwick: North)	17 St David's Drive, Evesham, Worcs WR11 6AS	01386 421562
Macdonald, Ian U.	1960	1997	(Tarbolton)	18 Belmont Road, Ayr KA7 2PF	01292 283085
McNidder, Roderick H. BD	1987	1997	Chaplain, South Ayrshire Hospitals Trust	6 Hollow Park, Alloway, Ayr KA7 4SR	01292 442554
McPhail, Andrew M. BA	1968	2002	(Ayr: Wallacetown)	25 Maybole Road, Ayr KA7 2QA	01292 282108
Mitchell, Sheila M. (Miss) BD MTh	1995	2002	Chaplain: Ayrshire and Arran Primary Care Trust	Ailsa Hospital, Ayr	01292 610556
Robertson, Daniel M. MA	1960	2000	(Auchinleck)	14 Corrie Place, Drongan, Ayr KA6 7DU	01292 590150
Saunders, Campbell M. MA BD	1952	1989	(Ayr St Leonard's)	42 Marle Park, Ayr KA7 4RN	01292 441673
Stirling, Ian R. BSc BD	1990	2002	Chaplain: The Ayrshire Hospice	Ayrshire Hospice, 35–37 Racecourse Road, Ayr KA7 2TG	01292 269200
Sutherland, Alexander S.	1952	1987	(Symington with Craigie)	8 Phillips Avenue, Largs KA30 9EP	01475 674846

AYR ADDRESSES

Ayr
Auld Kirk — Kirkport (116 High Street)
Castlehill — Castlehill Road x Hillfoot Road
Lochside — Lochside Road x Murray Street
Newton-on-Ayr — Main Street
St Andrew's — Park Circus
St Columba — Midton Road x Carrick Park
St James' — Prestwick Road x
         Falkland Park Road
St Leonard's — St Leonard's Road x
         Monument Road
Wallacetown — John Street x Church Street

Girvan
North — Montgomerie Street
South — Stair Park

Maybole (both buildings still in use)
Old — Centre of Cassillis Road
West — Foot of Coral Glen

Prestwick
Kingcase — Waterloo Road
Monkton and
   Prestwick North — Monkton Road
St Nicholas — Main Street
South — Main Street

Troon
Old — Ayr Street
Portland — St Meddan's Street
St Meddan's — St Meddan's Street

(11) IRVINE AND KILMARNOCK

The Presbytery meets ordinarily at 6:30 pm in the Hall of Howard St Andrew's Church, Kilmarnock, on the first Tuesday of each month from September to May, (except January when it meets on the second Tuesday for the celebration of Holy Communion and in conference or socially) and on the fourth Tuesday in June.

Clerk:	REV. COLIN G.F. BROCKIE BSc(Eng) BD	51 Portland Road, Kilmarnock KA1 2EQ [E-mail: akph57@uk.uumail.comm]	01563 525311
Depute Clerk:	I. STEUART DEY LLB NP	72 Dundonald Road, Kilmarnock KA1 1RZ [E-mail: steuart@dey5929.freeserve.co.uk]	01563 521686
Treasurer:	JAMES McINTOSH BA CA	15 Dundonald Road, Kilmarnock KA1 1RU	01563 523552

Crosshouse
S. Ian Dennis BD   1992   2002   27 Kilmarnock Road, Crosshouse, Kilmarnock KA2 0EZ   01563 521035

Darvel
Charles M. Cameron BA BD PhD   1980   2001   46 West Main Street, Darvel KA17 0AQ   01560 322924

Dreghorn and Springside
Gary E. Horsburgh BA   1976   1983   96A Townfoot, Dreghorn, Irvine KA11 4EZ   01294 217770

Dunlop
Maureen M. Duncan (Mrs) BD   1996   4 Dampark, Dunlop, Kilmarnock KA3 4BZ   01560 484083

Fenwick (H)
Geoffrey Redmayne BSc BD MPhil — 2000 — 2 Kirkton Place, Fenwick, Kilmarnock KA3 6DW [E-mail: geoff@gredmayne.fsnet.co.uk] — 01560 600217

Galston (H)
T.J. Loudon Blair MA BD — 1965 — 60 Brewland Street, Galston KA4 8DX [E-mail: loudon.blair@virgin.net] — 01563 820246
John H.B. Taylor MA BD DipEd FEIS (Assoc) — 1952 1990 — 62 Woodlands Grove, Kilmarnock KA3 1TZ — 01563 526698

Hurlford (H)
James D. McCulloch BD MIOP — 1996 — 12 Main Road, Crookedholm, Kilmarnock KA3 6JT — 01563 535673

Irvine: Fullarton (H)
Neil Urquhart BD DipMin — 1989 — 48 Waterside, Irvine KA12 8QJ [E-mail: neilurquhart@beeb.net] — 01294 279909

Irvine: Girdle Toll (E) (H)
Clare B. Sutcliffe BSc BD — 2000 — 2 Littlestane Rise, Irvine KA11 2BJ — 01294 213565

Irvine: Mure (H)
Hugh M. Adamson BD — 1976 — West Road, Irvine KA12 8RE — 01294 279916

Irvine: Old (H) (01294 273503)
Robert Travers BA BD — 1993 1999 — 22 Kirk Vennel, Irvine, Ayrshire KA12 0DQ [E-mail: robert@travers46.freeserve.co.uk] — 01294 279265

Irvine: Relief Bourtreehill (H)
Vacant — 4 Kames Court, Irvine KA11 1RT — 01294 216939

Irvine: St Andrew's (H) (01294 276051)
Morag A. Dawson BD — 1999 — 206 Bank Street, Irvine KA12 0YD — 01294 211403

Kilmarnock: Grange (H) (01563 534490)
Colin G.F. Brockie BSc(Eng) BD — 1967 1978 — 51 Portland Road, Kilmarnock KA1 2EQ [E-mail: revcol@revcol.demon.co.uk] — 01563 525311

Kilmarnock: Henderson (H) (01563 541302)
David W. Lacy BA BD — 1976 1989 — 52 London Road, Kilmarnock KA3 7AJ [E-mail: thelacys@tinyworld.co.uk] — 01563 523113 (Tel/Fax)

Kilmarnock: Howard St Andrew's (H)
Malcolm MacLeod BA BD — 1979 1989 — 1 Evelyn Villas, Holehouse Road, Kilmarnock KA3 7AX [E-mail: cal.macleod@ntlworld.com] — 01563 522278

Kilmarnock: Laigh West High (H) David S. Cameron BD	2001	1 Holmes Farm Road, Kilmarnock KA1 1TP [E-mail: david@cmron05.freeserve.co.uk]	01563 525416
Kilmarnock: Old High Kirk (H) William M. Hall BD	1972 1979	107 Dundonald Road, Kilmarnock KA1 1UP	01563 525608
Kilmarnock: Riccarton (H) Thomas W. Jarvie BD	1953 1968	2 Jasmine Road, Kilmarnock KA1 2HD	01563 525694
Kilmarnock: St John's Onthank (H) Susan M. Anderson (Mrs)	1997	84 Wardneuk Drive, Kilmarnock KA3 2EX [E-mail: stjohnthank@yahoo.co.uk]	01563 521815
Catherine A.M. Shaw MA (Aux)	1998	40 Merrygreen Place, Stewarton, Kilmarnock KA3 5EP [E-mail: catherine.shaw@tesco.net]	01560 483352
Kilmarnock: St Kentigern's S. Grant Barclay LLB BD	1995	1 Thirdpart Place, Kilmarnock KA1 1UL [E-mail: grant.barclay@bigfoot.com]	01563 571280
Kilmarnock: St Marnock's (H) (01563 541337) James McNaughtan BD DipMin	1983 1989	35 South Gargieston Drive, Kilmarnock KA1 1TB [E-mail: jmcnaughtan@cwcom.net]	01563 521665
Kilmarnock: St Ninian's Bellfield (01563 524705) linked with Kilmarnock: Shortlees H. Taylor Brown BD CertMin	1997 2002	14 McLelland Drive, Kilmarnock KA1 1SF	01563 529920
Kilmarnock: Shortlees See Kilmarnock: St Ninian's Bellfield			
Kilmaurs: St Maur's Glencairn (H) John A. Urquhart BD	1993	9 Standalane, Kilmaurs, Kilmarnock KA3 2NB	01563 538289
Newmilns: Loudoun (H) John Macleod MA BD	2000	116A Loudoun Road, Newmilns KA16 9HH	01560 320174
Stewarton: John Knox Samuel Hosain BD MTh PhD	1979 1993	27 Avenue Street, Stewarton, Kilmarnock KA3 5AP	01560 482418
Stewarton: St Columba's (H) Elizabeth A. Waddell (Mrs) BD	1999	1 Kirk Glebe, Stewarton, Kilmarnock KA3 5BJ	01560 482453
Ayrshire Mission to the Deaf S. Grant Barclay LLB BD (Chaplain)	1991 1998	89 Mure Avenue, Kilmarnock KA3 1TT [E-mail: grant.barclay@bigfoot.com]	01563 571280

Campbell, George H.	1957	1992	(Stewarton: John Knox)	20 Woodlands Grove, Kilmarnock KA3 1TZ	01563 536365
Campbell, John A. JP FIEM	1984	1998	(Irvine St Andrew's)	Flowerdale, Balmoral Lane, Blairgowrie PH10 7AF	01250 872795
Christie, Robert S. MA BD ThM	1964	2001	(Kilmarnock: West High)	69 Dundonald Road, Kilmarnock KA1 1TJ	01563 525302
Crawford, Robert MA	1933	1972	(Annan Erskine)	Torrance Lodge Nursing Home, Riccarton Road, Hurlford, Kilmarnock KA1 5LQ	
Davidson, James BD DipAFH	1989	2002	(Wishaw Old)	13 Redburn Place, Irvine KA12 9BQ	01294 312515
Downie, Andrew A. BD BSc DipEd DipMin ThB	1994	1999	Prison Chaplain	HMP Bowhouse, Mauchline Road, Kilmarnock KA1 5AA	01563 548928
Goudie, Stuart M. MA BD	1951	1988	(Perceton and Dreghorn)	6 Charles Drive, Troon KA10 7AG	01292 311610
Hare, Malcolm M.W. BA BD	1956	1994	(Kilmarnock St Kentigern's)	21 Raith Road, Fenwick, Kilmarnock KA3 6DB	01560 600388
Hay, W.J.R. MA BD	1959	1995	(Buchanan with Drymen)	18 Jamieson Place, Stewarton, Kilmarnock KA3 3AY	01560 482799
Huggett, Judith A. (Miss) BA BD	1990	1998	Hospital Chaplain	4 Westmoor Crescent, Kilmarnock KA1 1TX	
Jamieson, Robert C. MA	1943	1980	(Galston Old)	20 Brewland Street, Galston KA4 8DR	
Kelly, Thomas A. Davidson MA BD FSAScot	1975	2002	(Glasgow: Govan Old)	2 Springhill Stables, Portland Road, Kilmarnock KA1 2EJ	01563 820304
McAlpine, Richard H.M. BA FSAScot	1968	2000	(Lochgoilhead and Kilmorich)	7 Kingsford Place, Kilmarnock KA3 6FG	01563 572075
MacDonald, James M.	1964	1987	(Kilmarnock St John's Onthank)	29 Carmel Place, Kilmaurs, Kilmarnock KA3 2QU	01563 525254
McGarva, Sarah (Miss) DCS			(Deaconess)	87 Hunter Drive, Irvine KA12 9BS	01294 271257
Martin, Robert A.K. MA	1957	2002	(Kilmarnock: St Andrew's Glencairn)	11 Wellpark Avenue, Kilmarnock KA3 7DH	01563 525023
Patience, Donald MA	1954	1993	(Kilmaurs)	Kirkhill, 42 Fenwick Road, Kilmaurs, Kilmarnock KA3 2TD	01560 482185
Roy, James BA	1967	1982	(Irvine Girdle Toll)	23 Bowes Rigg, Stewarton, Kilmarnock KA3 5EL [E-mail: jroy@dougyr-globalnet.co.uk]	
Scott, Thomas T.	1968	1989	(Kilmarnock St Marnock's)	6 North Hamilton Place, Kilmarnock KA1 2QN [E-mail: 101725.216@compuserve.com]	01563 531415
Urquhart, Barbara (Mrs) DCS			Deaconess, Part-time Hospital Chaplain and Presbytery S.S. Adviser	9 Standalane, Kilmaurs, Kilmarnock KA3 2NB	01563 538289

IRVINE and KILMARNOCK ADDRESSES

Irvine

Dreghorn and Springside	Townfoot x Station Brae
Fullarton	Marress Road x Church Street
Girdle Toll	Bryce Knox Court
Mure	West Road
Old Parish	Kirkgate
Relief	Crofthead, Bourtreehill
St Andrew's	Caldon Road x Oaklands Ave

Kilmarnock

Ayrshire Mission to the Deaf	10 Clark Street	Riccarton	Old Street
Grange	Woodstock Street	St Andrew's	St Andrew's Street
Henderson	London Road	Glencairn	84 Wardneuk Street
Howard	5 Portland Road	St John's Onthank	St Marnock's Street
Laigh	John Dickie Street	St Marnock's	Whatriggs Road
Old High	Church Street x Soulis Street	St Ninian's Bellfield	Central Avenue
		Shortlees	Portland Street
		West High	

(12) ARDROSSAN

Meets at Saltcoats, New Trinity, on the first Tuesday of February, March, April, May, September, October, November and December, and on the second Tuesday of June.

Clerk: REV. DAVID BROSTER BA DipTh CPS — Manse of St Columba's, Kilbirnie KA25 7JU [E-mail: akph38@uk.uumail.com]

01505 683342 (Tel)
01505 684024 (Fax)
07836 380383 (Mbl)

Ardrossan: Barony St John's (H) (01294 465009)
Vacant — 10 Seafield Drive, Ardrossan KA22 8NU — 01294 463868

Ardrossan: Park (01294 463711)

William R. Johnston BD	1998		35 Ardneil Court, Ardrossan KA22 7NQ	01294 471808
Marion L.K. Howie (Mrs) MA ACRS (Aux)	1992		51 High Road, Stevenston KA20 3DY [E-mail: marion.howie@ndirect.co.uk]	01294 466571

Beith: High (H) (01505 502686) linked with Beith: Trinity (H)

Andrew R. Black BD	1987	1998	2 Glebe Court, Beith KA15 1ET [E-mail: rev_black@lineone.net]	01505 503858
Fiona C. Ross (Miss) BD DipMin (Assoc)	1996		16 Spiers Avenue, Beith KA15 1JD [E-mail: fionaross@calvin78.freeserve.co.uk]	01505 502131

Beith: Trinity (H) See Beith: High

Brodick linked with Corrie
Ian MacLeod LTh BA MTh PhD | 1969 | 1974 | 4 Manse Crescent, Brodick, Isle of Arran KA27 8AS | 01770 302334

Corrie See Brodick

Cumbrae
Marjory H. Mackay (Mrs) BD DipEd CCE | 1998 | Marine Parade, Millport, Isle of Cumbrae KA28 0ED | 01475 530416

Dalry: St Margaret's
James A.S. Boag BD | 1992 | 2002 | Bridgend, Dalry KA24 4DA [E-mail: james@boag4458.fsnet.co.uk] | 01294 832234

Dalry: Trinity (H)
David I.M. Grant MA BD | 1969 | West Kilbride Road, Dalry KA24 5DX | 01294 832363

Fairlie (H)
Robert J. Thorburn BD | 1978 | 1980 | 14 Fairlieburne Gardens, Fairlie, Largs KA29 0ER [E-mail: rjthorburn@aol.com] | 01475 568342

Fergushill linked with Kilwinning Erskine
Vacant
14 McLuckie Drive, Kilwinning KA13 6DL
01294 551565

Kilbirnie: Auld Kirk (H)
Ian W. Benzie BD   1999
49 Holmhead, Kilbirnie KA25 6BS
[E-mail: revian@btopenworld.com]
01505 682348

Kilbirnie: St Columba's (H) (01505 685239)
David Broster BA DipTh CPS   1969   1983
Manse of St Columba's, Kilbirnie KA25 7JU
[E-mail: pres@broster.org]
01505 683342 (Tel)
01505 684024 (Fax)
07836 380383 (Mbl)

Kilmory
Vacant

Kilwinning: Abbey (H)
Gordon A. McCracken BD CertMin   1988   2002
54 Dalry Road, Kilwinning KA13 7HE
[E-mail: gordonangus@btopenworld.com]
01294 552606

Kilwinning: Erskine (01294 552188) See Fergushill

Kilwinning: Mansefield Trinity (E) (01294 550746)
Douglas S. Paterson MA BD   1976   1999
27 Treesbank, Kilwinning KA13 6LY
[E-mail: dostpa@aol.com]
01294 552453

Lamlash linked with Lochranza and Pirnmill linked with Shiskine (H)
Barry Knight BD   1991   2002
Shiskine, Brodick, Isle of Arran KA27 8EP
[E-mail: pakurdnga@aol.com]
01770 860380

Largs: Clark Memorial (H) (01475 675186)
Stephen J. Smith BSc BD   1993   1998
31 Douglas Street, Largs KA30 8PT
[E-mail: stephenrevsteve@aol.com]
01475 672370

Largs: St Columba's (01475 686212)
Roderick J. Grahame BD CPS   1991   2002
17 Beachway, Largs KA30 8QH
[E-mail: rjgrahame@supanet.com]
01475 673107

Largs: St John's (H) (01475 674468)
Andrew F. McGurk BD   1983   1993
1 Newhaven Grove, Largs KA30 8NS
[E-mail: afmcg.largs@talk21.com]
01475 676123

Lochranza and Pirnmill See Lamlash

Saltcoats: New Trinity (H) (01294 472001)
Alexander D. McCallum BD   1987   1994   1 Montgomerie Crescent, Saltcoats KA21 5BX   01294 461143
[E-mail: sandy@newtrinity.co.uk]

Saltcoats: North (01294 464679)
Alexander B. Noble MA BD ThM   1982   2003   25 Longfield Avenue, Saltcoats KA21 6DR   01294 604923
[E-mail: alexbnoble@themanse38.freeserve.co.uk]

Saltcoats: St Cuthbert's (H)
Brian H. Oxburgh BSc BD   1980   1988   10 Kennedy Road, Saltcoats KA21 5SF   01294 602674
[E-mail: boxburgh@aol.com]

Shiskine See Lamlash

Stevenston: Ardeer linked with Stevenston: Livingstone (H)
John M.M. Lafferty BD   1999   32 High Road, Stevenston KA20 3DR   01294 464180

Stevenston: High (H)
M. Scott Cameron MA BD   2002   Glencairn Street, Stevenston KA20 3DL   01294 463356
[E-mail: scottie.cameron@ukonline.co.uk]

Stevenston: Livingstone (H) See Stevenston: Ardeer

West Kilbride: Overton (H)
Norman Cruickshank BA BD   1983   Goldenberry Avenue, West Kilbride KA23 9LJ   01294 823186

West Kilbride: St Andrew's (H) (01294 829902)
D. Ross Mitchell BA BD   1972   1980   7 Overton Drive, West Kilbride KA23 9LQ   01294 823142
[E-mail: ross.mitchell@virgin.net]

Whiting Bay and Kildonan
Elizabeth R.L. Watson (Miss) BA BD   1981   1982   Whiting Bay, Brodick, Isle of Arran KA27 8RE   01770 700289
[E-mail: elizabeth@rlwatson.freeserve.co.uk]

Dailly, J.R. BD DipPS	1979	1979	Staff Chaplain: Army	DACG, HQ 42 (NW) Bde, Fulwood Barracks, Preston PR2 8AA	
Downie, Alexander S.	1975	1997	(Ardrossan: Park)	14 Korsankel Wynd, Saltcoats KA21 6HY	01294 464097
Ewing, James MA BD	1948	1987	(Ardrossan Barony)	8 Semple Crescent, Fairlie, Largs KA29 0EN	01475 568115
Fisher, Kenneth H.	1969	1994	(Stronsay with Eday)	33 Halfway Street, West Kilbride KA23 9EQ	01294 829973
Gordon, David C.	1953	1988	(Gigha and Cara)	16 Braeside Avenue, Largs KA30 8HD	
Harbison, David J.H.	1958	1998	(Beith: High with Beith: Trinity)	42 Mill Park, Dalry KA24 5BB	01294 834092
				[E-mail: djh@harbi.fsnet.co.uk]	

Hebenton, David J. MA BD	1958 2002	(Ayton and Burnmouth linked with Grantshouse and Houndwood and Reston)	22B Faulds Wynd, Seamill, West Kilbride KA23 9FA	
McCance, Andrew M. BSc	1986 1995	(Coatbridge: Middle)	15 The Crescent, Skelmorlie PA17 5DX	01475 672960
McKay, Johnston R. MA BA	1969 1987	(Religious Broadcasting: BBC)	27 Stanlane Place, Largs KA30 8DD [E-mail: johnston.mckay@btopenworld.com]	
Maclagan, David W. MA ThD	1965 1991	(Largs: St John's)	Flat C, 1 Greenock Road, Largs KA30 8PQ	01475 673258
Paterson, John H. BD	1977 2000	(Kirkintilloch: St David's Memorial Park)	Creag Bhan, Golf Course Road, Whiting Bay, Arran KA27 8QT	01770 700569
Roy, Iain M. MA BD	1960 1997	(Stevenston: Livingstone)	2 The Fieldings, Dunlop, Kilmarnock KA3 4AU	01560 483072
Selfridge, John BTh BREd	1969 1991	(Eddrachillis)	Strathclyde House, Apt 1, Shore Road, Skelmorlie PA17 5AN	01475 529514
Taylor, Andrew S. BTh FPhS	1959 1992	(Greenock Union)	9 Raillies Avenue, Largs KA30 8QY	01475 674709
Thomson, Margaret (Mrs)	1988 1993	(Saltcoats: Erskine)	72 Knockrivoch Place, Ardrossan KA22 7PZ	01294 468685
Walker, David S. MA	1939 1978	(Markerstoun with Smailholm with Stichill, Hume and Nenthorn)	6 Stairlie Crescent, West Kilbride KA23 9BT	01294 823061

(13) LANARK

Meets at Lanark on the first Tuesday of February, March, April, May, September, October, November and December, and on the third Tuesday of June.

Clerk:	REV. GAVIN J. ELLIOTT MA BD		The Manse, 61 High Street, Biggar ML12 6DA [E-mail: akph60@uk.uumail.com] [E-mail: lanarkpresbytery@uk.uumail.com]	01899 221249 (Tel/Fax)

Biggar (H)

Gavin J. Elliott MA BD	1976	1995	61 High Street, Biggar ML12 6DA [E-mail: biggarkirk@biggar-net.co.uk]	01899 220227

Black Mount linked with Culter linked with Libberton and Quothquan

Vacant			17 Mercat Loan, Biggar ML12 6DG	01899 220625

Cairngryffe linked with Symington

Graham R. Houston BSc BD MTh PhD	1978	2001	16 Abington Road, Symington, Biggar ML12 6JX [E-mail: gandihouston@aol.com]	01899 308838

Carluke: Kirkton (H) (01555 750778)

Iain D. Cunningham MA BD	1979	1987	9 Station Road, Carluke ML8 5AA [E-mail: iaindc@fish.co.uk]	01555 771262 (Tel/Fax)

Charge / Minister	Year(s)	Address / E-mail	Telephone
Carluke: St Andrew's (H) Helen E. Jamieson (Mrs) BD DipED	1989	120 Clyde Street, Carluke ML8 5BG [E-mail: revhelenj@aol.com]	01555 771218
Carluke: St John's (H) Michael W. Frew BSc BD	1978 1991	18 Old Bridgend, Carluke ML8 4HN [E-mail: mwfrew@aol.com]	01555 772259 (Tel/Fax)
Carnwath (H) Beverly G.D.D. Gauld MA BD	1972 1978	The Manse, Carnwath, Lanark ML11 8JY	01555 840259
Carstairs linked with Carstairs Junction J. Melvyn Coogan LTh	1992 1996	80 Lanark Road, Carstairs, Lanark ML11 8QH	01555 870250
Carstairs Junction See Carstairs			
Coalburn linked with Lesmahagow: Old Aileen Robson BD	2003	9 Elm Bank, Lesmahagow, Lanark ML11 0EA [E-mail: amrob65@aol.com]	01555 895325
Crossford linked with Kirkfieldbank Steven Reid BAcc CA BD	1989 1997	74 Lanark Road, Crossford, Carluke ML8 5RE [E-mail: stevenreid@v21mail.co.uk]	01555 860415
Culter See Black Mount			
Douglas: St Bride's linked with Douglas Water and Rigside Bryan Kerr BA BD	2002	The Manse, Douglas, Lanark ML11 0RB [E-mail: bryan@fish.co.uk]	01555 851213 (Tel/Fax)
Forth: St Paul's (H) Vacant		22 Lea-Rig, Forth, Lanark ML11 8EA	01555 811748
Glencaple linked with Lowther Margaret A. Muir (Miss) MA LLB BD	1989 2001	66 Carlisle Road, Crawford, Biggar ML12 6TW	01864 502625
Kirkfieldbank See Crossford			
Kirkmuirhill (H) Ian M. Watson LLB DipLP BD	1998 2003	The Manse, 2 Lanark Road, Kirkmuirhill, Lanark ML11 9RB [E-mail: ian.watson21@btopenworld.com]	01555 892409 (Tel/Fax)
Lanark: Greyfriars Catherine E.E. Collins (Mrs) MA BD David A. Collins BSc BD	1993 1993	2 Friarsdene, Lanark ML11 9EJ [E-mail: greyfriars@webartz.com]	01555 663363

Lanark: St Nicholas'

Alison A. Meikle (Mrs) BD	1999	2002	32 Braxfield Road, Lanark ML11 9BS [E-mail: lanarkstnichs@fsnet.co.uk]	01555 662600 (Tel) 01555 665905 (Fax)

Law

Anne McIvor (Miss) SRD BD	1996	2003	The Manse, 53 Lawhill Road, Law, Carluke ML8 5EZ	01693 373180

Lesmahagow: Abbeygreen

David S. Carmichael	1982	Abbeygreen Manse, Lesmahagow, Lanark ML11 0DB [E-mail: david@6abbeygreen.freeserve.co.uk]	01555 893384

Lesmahagow: Old (H) See Coalburn
Libberton and Quothquan See Black Mount
Lowther See Glencaple
Symington See Cairngryffe

Cowell, Susan G. (Miss) BA BD	1986	1998	(Budapest)	39 Main Street, Symington, Biggar ML12 6LL	01899 308257
Craig, William BA LTh	1974	1997	(Cambusbarron: The Bruce Memorial)	31 Heathfield Drive, Blackwood, Lanark ML11 9SR	01555 893710
Fox, George H.	1959	1977	(Coalsnaughton)	Braehead House, Crossford, Carluke ML8 5NQ	01555 860716
Jones, Philip H.	1968	1987	(Bishopbriggs Kenmure)	39 Bankhouse, 62 Abbeygreen, Lesmahagow, Lanark ML11 0IS	
McCormick, W. Cadzow MA BD	1943	1983	(Glasgow Maryhill Old)	82 Main Street, Symington, Biggar ML12 6LJ	01899 308221
McMahon, Robert J. BD	1959	1997	(Crossford with Kirkfieldbank)	7 Ridgepark Drive, Lanark ML11 9PG	01555 663844
Pacitti, Stephen A. MA	1963	2003	(Black Mount with Culter with Libberton and Quothquan)	157 Nithsdale Road, Glasgow G41 5RD	0141-423 5792
Seath, Thomas J.G.	1980	1992	(Motherwell: Manse Road)	1 Allan Avenue, Carluke ML8 5UA	01555 771644
Stewart, John M. MA BD	1964	2001	(Johnstone with Kirkpatrick Juxta)	5 Rathmor Road, Biggar ML12 6QG	01899 220398
Young, David A.	1972	2003	(Kirkmuirhill)	15 Mannachie Rise, Forres IV36 2US [E-mail: youngdavid@aol.com]	01309 672849

(14) GREENOCK AND PAISLEY

Meets on the second Tuesday of each month, except January, July and August. The meeting place will vary.

Clerk:	REV. DAVID KAY BA BD MTh	6 Southfield Avenue, Paisley PA2 8BY [E-mail: akph69@uk.uumail.com]	0141-884 3600 (Tel/Fax)
Associate Clerk:	REV. DAVID MILL KGSJ MA BD	105 Newark Street, Greenock PA16 7TW	01475 639602

Barrhead: Arthurlie (H) (0141-881 8442)
James S.A. Cowan BD DipMin — 1986 1998
10 Arthurlie Avenue, Barrhead, Glasgow G78 2BU
[E-mail: jim_cowan@ntlworld.com]
0141-881 3457

Barrhead: Bourock (H) (0141-881 9813)
Maureen Leitch (Mrs) BA BD — 1995
14 Maxton Avenue, Barrhead, Glasgow G78 1DY
[E-mail: bourockmanse@compuserve.com]
0141-881 1462

Barrhead: South and Levern (H) (0141-881 7825)
Morris M. Dutch BD — 1998 2002
3 Colinbar Circle, Barrhead, Glasgow G78 2BE
0141-571 4059

Bishopton (H)
Gayle J.A. Taylor (Mrs) MA BD — 1999
The Manse, Newton Road, Bishopton PA7 5JP
01505 862161

Bridge of Weir: Freeland (H) (01505 612610)
Kenneth N. Gray BA BD — 1988
15 Lawmarnock Crescent, Bridge of Weir PA11 3AS
01505 690918

Bridge of Weir: St Machar's Ranfurly (01505 614364)
Suzanne Dunleavy (Miss) BD DipEd — 1990 1992
9 Glen Brae, Bridge of Weir PA11 3BH
01505 612975

Caldwell
John Campbell MA BA BSc — 1973 2000
The Manse of Caldwell, Uplawmoor, Glasgow G78 4AL
[E-mail: johncampbell@minister.com]
01505 850215

Elderslie Kirk (H) (01505 323348)
David N. McLachlan BD — 1985 1994
282 Main Road, Elderslie, Johnstone PA5 9EF
01505 321767

Erskine (0141-812 4620)
Ian W. Bell LTh — 1990 1998
Morag Erskine (Miss) DCS
The Manse, 7 Leven Place, Linburn, Erskine PA8 6AS
111 Main Drive, Erskine PA8 7JJ
0141-581 0955
0141-812 6096

Gourock: Old Gourock and Ashton (H)
Frank J. Gardner MA — 1966 1979
90 Albert Road, Gourock PA19 1NN
[E-mail: frankgardner@oldgourockashton.freeserve.co.uk]
01475 631516

Gourock: St John's (H)
P. Jill Clancy (Mrs) BD — 2000
6 Barrhill Road, Gourock PA19 1JX
[E-mail: jgibson@totalise.co.uk]
01475 632143

Greenock: Ardgowan
Alan H. Ward MA BD — 1978 2002
72 Forsyth Street, Greenock PA16 8SX
[E-mail: alanhward@ntlworld.com]
01475 790849

Greenock: Cartsdyke
Vacant
84 Forsyth Street, Greenock PA16 8QY
01475 721439

Greenock: Finnart St Paul's (H)
David Mill KGSJ MA BD
1978 1979
105 Newark Street, Greenock PA16 7TW
01475 639602

Greenock: Mount Kirk
James H. Simpson BD LLB
1964 1965
76 Finnart Street, Greenock PA16 8HJ
[E-mail: jameshsimpson@ntlworld.com]
01475 790775

Greenock: Old West Kirk
C. Ian W. Johnson MA BD
1997
39 Fox Street, Greenock PA16 8PD
[E-mail: ian_ciw_johnson@tesco.net]
01475 888277

Eileen Manson (Mrs) DipCE (Aux)
1994
1 Cambridge Avenue, Gourock PA19 1XT
[E-mail: jrmanson@ntlworld.com]
01475 632401

Greenock: St George's North
W. Douglas Hamilton BD
1975 1986
67 Forsyth Street, Greenock PA16 8SX
01475 724003

Greenock: St Luke's (H)
William C. Hewitt BD DipPS
1977 1994
50 Ardgowan Street, Greenock PA16 8EP
[E-mail: william.hewitt@ntlworld.com]
01475 721048

Greenock: St Margaret's (01475 781953)
Isobel J.M. Kelly (Miss) MA BD DipEd
1974 1998
105 Finnart Street, Greenock PA16 8HN
01475 786590

Greenock: St Ninian's
Allan G. McIntyre BD
1985
5 Auchmead Road, Greenock PA16 0PY
[E-mail: agmcintyre@lineone.net]
01475 631878

Greenock: Wellpark Mid Kirk
Alan K. Sorensen BD MTh DipMin FSAScot
1983 2000
101 Brisbane Street, Greenock PA16 8PA
[E-mail: alansorensen@beeb.net]
01475 721741

Houston and Killellan (H)
Georgina M. Baxendale (Mrs) BD
1981 1989
The Manse of Houston, Main Street, Houston, Johnstone PA6 7EL
01505 612569

Howwood
David Stewart MA DipEd BD MTh
1977 2001
The Manse, Beith Road, Howwood, Johnstone PA9 1AS
[E-mail: revdavidst@aol.com]
01505 703678

Inchinnan (H) (0141-812 1263)
Marilyn MacLaine (Mrs) LTh
1995
The Manse, Inchinnan, Renfrew PA4 9PH
0141-812 1688

Inverkip (H)
Elizabeth A. Crumlish (Mrs) BD 1995 2002 The Manse, Longhouse Road, Inverkip, Greenock PA16 0BJ 01475 521207
[E-mail: lizcrumlish@aol.com]

Johnstone: High (H) (01505 336303)
Ann C. McCool (Mrs) BD DSD IPA ALCM 1989 2001 76 North Road, Johnstone PA5 8NF 01505 320006

Johnstone: St Andrew's Trinity
May Bell (Mrs) LTh 1998 2002 The Manse, 7 Leven Place, Linburn, Erskine PA8 6AS 0141-581 7352

Johnstone: St Paul's (H) (01505 321632)
Alistair N. Shaw MA BD 1982 2003 9 Stanley Drive, Brookfield, Johnstone PA5 8UF 01505 320060

Kilbarchan: East
John Owain Jones MA BD FSAScot 1981 2002 Church Street, Kilbarchan, Johnstone PA10 2JQ 01505 702621

Kilbarchan: West
Arthur Sherratt BD 1994 West Manse, Shuttle Street, Kilbarchan, Johnstone PA10 2JR 01505 342930
[E-mail: arthur.sherratt@ntlworld.com]

Kilmacolm: Old (H)
Gordon D. Irving BD 1994 1998 Glencairn Road, Kilmacolm PA13 4NJ 01505 873174
[E-mail: g.irving@oldkirkmanse3.freeserve.co.uk]

Kilmacolm: St Columba (H)
R. Douglas Cranston MA BD 1986 1992 6 Churchill Road, Kilmacolm PA13 4LH 01505 873271
[E-mail: robert.cranston@lineone.net]

Langbank (T)
Anna S. Rodwell (Mrs) BD DipMin 1998 Langbank, Port Glasgow PA14 6XB 01475 540252

Linwood (H) (01505 328802)
T. Edward Marshall BD 1987 The Manse, Bridge Street, Linwood, Paisley PA3 3DL 01505 325131
[E-mail: marshall@manse.fslife.co.uk]

Lochwinnoch (T)
Robin N. Allison BD DipMin 1994 1999 1 Station Rise, Lochwinnoch PA12 4NA 01505 843484
[E-mail: robin@mansemob.org]

Neilston (0141-881 9445)
Alexander Macdonald MA BD 1966 1984 The Manse, Neilston Road, Neilston, Glasgow G78 3NP 0141-881 1958
[E-mail: macdonaldal@supanet.com]

Paisley: Abbey (H) (Tel: 0141-889 7654; Fax: 0141-887 3929)
Alan D. Birss MA BD   1979   1988   15 Main Road, Castlehead, Paisley PA2 6AJ   0141-889 3587
                                                        [E-mail: alan.birss@virgin.net]

Paisley: Castlehead
Esther J. Ninian MA BD   1993   1998   28 Fulbar Crescent, Paisley PA2 9AS   01505 812304

Paisley: Glenburn (0141-884 2602)
George C. MacKay BD CertMin   1994   10 Hawick Avenue, Paisley PA2 9LD   0141-884 4903

Paisley: Laigh Kirk (H) (0141-889 7700)
Thomas M. Cant MA BD   1964   1972   18 Oldhall Road, Paisley PA1 3HL   0141-882 2277

Paisley: Lylesland (H) (0141-561 7139)
Andrew W. Bradley BD   1975   1998   36 Potterhill Avenue, Paisley PA2 8BA   0141-884 2882
Greta Gray (Miss) DCS   67 Crags Avenue, Paisley PA3 6SG   0141-884 6178

Paisley: Martyrs' (0141-889 6603)
Alison Davidge (Mrs) MA BD   1990   1997   12 Low Road, Paisley PA2 6AG   0141-889 2182

Paisley: Oakshaw Trinity (H) (Tel: 0141-887 4647; Fax: 0141-848 5139; E-mail: iancurrie@ntlworld.com)
Ian S. Currie MBE BD   1975   1980   9 Hawkhead Road, Paisley PA1 3ND   0141-887 0884
Janette M.K. Black (Mrs) BD (Assist) 1993   2003   5 Craigiehall Avenue, Erskine PA8 7DB   0141-812 0794

Paisley: St Columba Foxbar (H) (01505 812377)
Anthony J.R. Fowler BSc BD   1982   1985   13 Corsebar Drive, Paisley PA2 9QD   0141-889 9988
                                                        [E-mail: ajr.fowler@virgin.net]

Paisley: St James' (0141-889 2422)
Eleanor J. McMahon (Miss) BEd BD   1994   38 Woodland Avenue, Paisley PA2 8BH   0141-884 3246
                                                        [E-mail: eleanor.mcmahon@ukgateway.net]

Paisley: St Luke's (H)
D. Ritchie M. Gillon BD DipMin   1994   31 Southfield Avenue, Paisley PA2 8BX   0141-884 6215
                                                        [E-mail: revgillon@hotmail.com]

Paisley: St Mark's Oldhall (H) (0141-882 2755)
Alistair H. Morrison BTh DipYCS   1985   1989   36 Newtyle Road, Paisley PA1 3JX   0141-889 4279
                                                        [E-mail: alistairmorrison@supanet.com]

Paisley: St Ninian's Ferguslie (E) (0141-887 9436) (New Charge Development)
Vacant   10 Stanely Drive, Paisley PA2 6HE   0141-884 4177

Paisley: Sandyford (Thread Street) (0141-889 5078)
David Kay BA BD MTh — 1974 — 1980 — 6 Southfield Avenue, Paisley PA2 8BY [E-mail: revdkay@hotmail.com] — 0141-884 3600

Paisley: Sherwood Greenlaw (H) (0141-889 7060)
Alasdair F. Cameron BD CA — 1986 — 1993 — 5 Greenlaw Drive, Paisley PA1 3RX [E-mail: alcamron@lineone.net] — 0141-889 3057

Paisley: Wallneuk North (Tel: 0141-889 9265; Fax: 0141-887 6670)
Thomas Macintyre MA BD — 1972 — 1988 — 27 Mansionhouse Road, Paisley PA1 3RG — 0141-581 1505

Port Glasgow: Hamilton Bardrainney
James A. Munro BD DMS — 1979 — 2002 — 80 Bardrainney Avenue, Port Glasgow PA14 6HD [E-mail: james.munro7@btopenworld.com] — 01475 701213

Port Glasgow: St Andrew's (H)
Andrew T. MacLean BA BD — 1980 — 1993 — Barr's Brae, Port Glasgow PA14 5QA [E-mail: standrews.pg@btopenworld.com] — 01475 741486

Port Glasgow: St Martin's
John G. Miller BEd BD MTh — 1983 — 1998 — Clunebraehead, Clune Brae, Port Glasgow PA14 5SL — 01475 704115

Renfrew: North (0141-885 2154)
E. Lorna Hood (Mrs) MA BD — 1978 — 1979 — 1 Alexandra Drive, Renfrew PA4 8UB [E-mail: lorna.hood@ntlworld.com] — 0141-886 2074

Renfrew: Old
Alexander C. Wark MA BD STM — 1982 — 1998 — 31 Gibson Road, Renfrew PA4 0RH [E-mail: alecwark@yahoo.co.uk] — 0141-886 2005

Renfrew: Trinity (H) (0141-885 2129)
Stuart C. Steell BD CertMin — 1992 — 25 Paisley Road, Renfrew PA4 8JH [E-mail: scsren@tinyonline.co.uk] — 0141-886 2131

Skelmorlie and Wemyss Bay
William R. Armstrong BD — 1979 — 3A Montgomerie Terrace, Skelmorlie PA17 5TD [E-mail: william@warmst.freeserve.co.uk] — 01475 520703

Abeledo, Benjamin J.A. BTh DipTh PTh — 1991 2000 — Army Chaplain (Bishopton) — 4 Redford Place, Edinburgh EH13 0AL — 0131-441 5199

Alexander, Douglas N. MA BD — 1961 1999 — West Morningside, Main Road, Langbank, Port Glasgow PA4 6XP — 01475 540249

Bruce, A. William MA — 1942 1981 — (Fortingall and Glenlyon) — 75 Union Street, Greenock PA16 8BG — 01475 787534

Cameron, Margaret (Miss) DCS	1948	1987	(Deaconess)	2 Rowans Gate, Paisley PA2 6RD	0141-840 2479
Chestnut, Alexander MBE BA			(Greenock St Mark's Greenbank)	5 Douglas Street, Largs KA30 8PS	01475 674168
Copland, Agnes M. (Mrs) MBE DCS			(Deacon)	3 Craigmuschat Road, Gourock PA19 1SE	01475 631870
Cubie, John P. MA BD	1961	1999	(Caldwell)	36 Winram Place, St Andrews KY16 8XH	01334 474708
Hetherington, Robert M. MA BD	1966	2002	(Barrhead South and Levern)	31 Brodie Park Crescent, Paisley PA2 6EU	0141-848 6560
				[E-mail: r.hetherington@ntlworld.com]	
Johnston, Mary (Miss) DCS	1950	1988	(Deaconess)	19 Lounsdale Drive, Paisley PA2 9ED	0141-849 1615
Lowe, Edwin MA BD			(Caldwell)	45 Duncarnock Crescent, Neilston, Glasgow G78 3HH	0141-580 5726
McBain, Margaret (Miss) DCS				33 Quarry Road, Paisley PA2 7RD	0141-884 2920
MacColl, James C. BSc BD	1966	2002	(Johnstone: St Andrew's Trinity)	Greenways, Winton, Kirkby Stephen, Cumbria CA17 4HL	01768 372290
MacColl, John BD DipMin	1989	2001	(Teacher: Religious Education)	1 Birch Avenue, Johnstone PA5 0DD	01505 326506
McCully, M. Isobel (Miss) DCS			(Deacon)	10 Broadstone Avenue, Port Glasgow PA14 5BB	01475 742240
				[E-mail: i.mccully@tesco.net]	
McDonald, Alexander BA CMIWSC DUniv	1968	1988	Department of Ministry	36 Alloway Grove, Paisley PA2 7DQ	0141-560 1937
McLachlan, Duncan MA BD ThM	1955	1992	(Paisley: Sherwood)	27 Penilee Road, Paisley PA1 3EU	0141-882 6353
McLachlan, Fergus C. BD	1982	2002	Hospital Chaplain: Inverclyde Royal	46 Queen Square, Glasgow G41 2AZ	0141-423 3830
MacQuien, Duncan DCS			(Deacon)	2 Manor Crescent, Gourock PA19 1UY	01475 633407
Marr, E.R. MA	1933	1977	(Buittle)	41 Stirling Drive, Bearsden, Glasgow G61 4NT	
Marshall, Fred J. BA	1946	1992	(Bermuda)	Flat 4, Varrich House, 7 Church Hill, Edinburgh EH10 4BG	0131-446 0205
Mathers, J. Allan C.	1950	1989	(Inchinnan)	19 Braemar Road, Inchinnan PA4 9QB	0141-561 2870
Moffet, James R. BA	1942	1979	(Paisley: St Matthew's)	Flat 49, Strathclyde House, 31 Shore Road, Skelmorlie PA17 5AN	
Montgomery, Robert A. MA	1955	1992	(Quarrier's Village: Mount Zion)	11 Myreton Avenue, Kilmacolm PA13 4LJ	01505 872028
Nicol, Joyce M. (Mrs) DCS			(Deacon)	93 Brisbane Street, Greenock PA16 8NY	01475 723235
O'Leary, Thomas BD	1983	1998	(Lochwinnoch)	1 Carters Place, Irvine KA12 0BU	
Palmer, S.W. BD	1980	1991	(Kilbarchan: East)	4 Bream Place, Houston PA6 7ZJ	01505 615280
Prentice, George BA BTh	1964	1997	(Paisley: Martyrs)	46 Victoria Gardens, Corsebar Road, Paisley PA2 9AQ	0141-842 1585
Pyper, J. Stewart BA	1951	1986	(Greenock: St George's North)	39 Brisbane Street, Greenock PA16 8NR	01475 793234
Rule, James A.	1952	1991	(Renfrew: Moorpark)	6 St Andrew's Road, Renfrew PA4 0SN	0141-886 2896
Scott, Ernest M. MA	1959	1992	(Port Glasgow: St Andrew's)	17 Brueacre Road, Wemyss Bay PA18 6ER	01475 522267
				[E-mail: ernie.scott@ernest70.fsnet.co.uk]	
Steele, Jean (Miss) DCS	1949	1985	(Deaconess)	93 George Street, Paisley PA1 2JX	0141-889 9512
Stone, W. Vernon MA BD	1946	1986	(Langbank)	36 Woodrow Court, Port Glasgow Road, Kilmacolm KA13 4QA	01505 872644
Whyte, John H. MA			(Gourock: Ashton)	6 Castle Levan Manor, Cloch Road, Gourock PA19 1AY	01475 636788

GREENOCK ADDRESSES

Gourock
Old Gourock and Ashton — 41 Royal Street
St John's — Bath Street x St John's Road

Greenock
Ardgowan — 31 Union Street
Finnart St Paul's — Newark Street x Bentinck Street
Mount Kirk — Dempster Street at Murdieston Park
Old West Kirk — Esplanade x Campbell Street
St George's North — George Square
St Luke's — 9 Nelson Street
St Margaret's — Finch Road x Kestrel Crescent
St Ninian's — Warwick Road, Larkfield
Wellpark Mid Kirk — Cathcart Square

Port Glasgow
Hamilton
Bardrainney — Bardrainney Avenue x Auchenbothie Road
St Andrew's — Princes Street
St Martin's — Mansion Avenue

PAISLEY ADDRESSES

Abbey	Town Centre	Oakshaw: Trinity	Sandyford (Thread St)
Castlehead	Canal Street	St Columba Foxbar	Sherwood Greenlaw
Glenburn	Nethercraigs Drive off Glenburn Road	St James'	Wallneuk North
Laigh	Causeyside Street	St Luke's	
Lylesland	Rowan Street off Neilston Road	St Mark's Oldhall	Gallowhill
Martyrs'	Broomlands	St Ninian's Ferguslie	Glasgow Road
		Churchill	off Renfrew Road
		Amochrie Road, Foxbar	
		Underwood Road	
		Neilston Road	
		Glasgow Road, Ralston	
		Blackstoun Road	

(16) GLASGOW

Meets at New Govan Church, Govan Cross, Glasgow, on the second Tuesday of each month, except June when the meeting takes place on the third Tuesday. In January, July and August there is no meeting.

Clerk: REV. DAVID W. LUNAN MA BD   **260 Bath Street, Glasgow G2 4JP**   **0141-332 6606 (Tel/Fax)**
[E-mail: akph84@uk.uumail.com]
[E-mail: cofs-glasgow.presbytery@uk.uumail.com]

Hon. Treasurer: **COPELAND KNIGHT Esq**   [E-mail: glasgowpres@yahoo.co.uk]

1 **Banton linked with Twechar**
Alexandra Farrington   2003   Manse of Banton, Kilsyth, Glasgow G65 0QL   01236 826129

2 **Bishopbriggs: Kenmure**
Iain A. Laing MA BD   1971 1992   5 Marchfield, Bishopbriggs, Glasgow G64 3PP   0141-772 1468

3 **Bishopbriggs: Springfield**
William Ewart BSc BD   1972 1978   39 Springfield Road, Bishopbriggs, Glasgow G64 1PL   0141-772 1540
[E-mail: wmewart@ukonline.co.uk]

4 **Broom (0141-639 3528)**
James Whyte BD   1981 1987   3 Laigh Road, Newton Mearns, Glasgow G77 5EX   0141-639 2916
                                                                                                      0141-639 3528 (Fax)

Margaret McLellan (Mrs) DCS   18 Broom Road East, Newton Mearns, Glasgow G77 5SD   0141-639 6853

5 **Burnside–Blairbeth (0141-634 4130)**
David J.C. Easton MA BD   1965 1977   59 Blairbeth Road, Burnside, Glasgow G73 4JD   0141-634 1233 (Tel)
[E-mail: david.easton3@ntlworld.com]   0141-634 7383 (Fax)
(Charge formed by the union of Blairbeth Rodger Memorial and Burnside)

6 Busby (0141-644 2073)
Jeremy C. Eve BSc BD — 1998 — 17A Carmunnock Road, Busby, Glasgow G76 8SZ [E-mail: jerry.eve@btinternet.com] — 0141-644 3670

7 Cadder (0141-772 7436)
Graham S. Finch MA BD — 1977 1999 — 6 Balmuildy Road, Bishopbriggs, Glasgow G64 3BS [E-mail: graham@gsf57.plus.com] — 0141-772 1363

8 Cambuslang: Flemington Hallside
R. David Currie BSc BD — 1984 — 103 Overton Road, Cambuslang, Glasgow G72 7XA [E-mail: david@rdcurrie.freeserve.co.uk] — 0141-641 2097

9 Cambuslang: Old
Lee Messeder — 2003 — 74 Stewarton Drive, Cambuslang, Glasgow G72 8DG — 0141-641 3261

10 Cambuslang: St Andrew's
John Stevenson LTh — 1998 — 37 Brownside Road, Cambuslang, Glasgow G72 8NH [E-mail: j.stevenson83@ntlworld.com] — 0141-641 3847 (Tel) 0141-641 0773 (Fax)
James Birch PGDip FRSA FIOC (Aux) — 2001 — 1 Kirkhill Grove, Cambuslang, Glasgow G72 8EH — 0141-583 1722

11 Cambuslang: Trinity St Paul's
William Jackson BD CertMin — 1994 2002 — 4 Glasgow Road, Cambuslang, Glasgow G72 7BW [E-mail: wiljcksn4@aol.com] — 0141-641 3414

12 Campsie (01360 310939)
David J. Torrance BD DipMin — 1993 — 19 Redhills View, Lennoxtown, Glasgow G66 7BL — 01360 312527

13 Chryston (H)
Martin A.W. Allen MA BD ThM — 1977 — Main Street, Chryston, Glasgow G69 9LA [E-mail: allensall@hotmail.com] — 0141-779 1436
David J. McAdam BSc BD (Assoc) — 1990 2000 — 12 Dunellan Crescent, Moodiesburn, Glasgow G69 0GA [E-mail: dmca29@aol.com] — 01236 870472

14 Eaglesham (01355 302047)
W. Douglas Lindsay BD CPS — 1978 — The Manse, Cheapside Street, Eaglesham, Glasgow G76 0NS — 01355 303495

15 Fernhill and Cathkin
Margaret McArthur BD DipMin — 1995 — 82 Blairbeth Road, Rutherglen, Glasgow G73 4JA — 0141-634 1508

16 Gartcosh (H) (01236 873770) linked with Glenboig (01236 875625)
Alexander M. Fraser BD DipMin — 1985 — 26 Inchknock Avenue, Gartcosh, Glasgow G69 8EA [E-mail: sandy@revfraser.freeserve.co.uk] — 01236 872274

17	**Giffnock: Orchardhill (0141-638 3604)** John M. Spiers LTh MTh	1972	1977	58 Woodlands Road, Thornliebank, Glasgow G46 7JQ [E-mail: js@spiers.fslife.co.uk]	0141-638 0632 (Tel/Fax)
18	**Giffnock: South (0141-638 2599)** Edward V. Simpson BSc BD	1972	1983	5 Langtree Avenue, Whitecraigs, Glasgow G46 7LN	0141-638 8767 (Tel) 0141-620 0605 (Fax)
19	**Giffnock: The Park** Calum D. Macdonald BD	1993	2001	41 Rouken Glen Road, Thornliebank, Glasgow G46 7JD [E-mail: calummcd@parkhoose.fsnet.co.uk]	0141-638 3023
20	**Glenboig** See Gartcosh				
21	**Greenbank (H) (0141-644 1891)** Vacant			Greenbank Manse, 38 Eaglesham Road, Clarkston, Glasgow G76 7DJ	0141-644 1395 (Tel) 0141-644 4804 (Fax)
22	**Kilsyth: Anderson** Charles M. MacKinnon BD	1989	1999	Anderson Manse, Kingston Road, Kilsyth, Glasgow G65 0HR [E-mail: cmmack@ukonline.co.uk]	01236 822345
23	**Kilsyth: Burns and Old** Thomas A. McLachlan BSc	1972	1983	The Grange, Glasgow Road, Kilsyth, Glasgow G65 9AE	01236 823116
24	**Kirkintilloch: Hillhead** Vacant	1993	2000	64 Waverley Park, Kensington Gate, Kirkintilloch, Glasgow G66 2BP	0141-776 6270
25	**Kirkintilloch: St Columba's (H)** David M. White BA BD	1988	1992	14 Crossdykes, Kirkintilloch, Glasgow G66 3EU [E-mail: david.m.white@ntlworld.com]	0141-578 4357
26	**Kirkintilloch: St David's Memorial Park (H)** Bryce Calder MA BD	1995	2001	2 Roman Road, Kirkintilloch, Glasgow G66 1EA [E-mail: ministry100@aol.com]	0141-776 1434
27	**Kirkintilloch: St Mary's** Mark E. Johnstone MA BD	1993	2001	St Mary's Manse, 60 Union Street, Kirkintilloch, Glasgow G66 1DH [E-mail: mark.johnstone2@ntlworld.com]	0141-776 1252
28	**Lenzie: Old (H)** Douglas W. Clark LTh	1993	2000	41 Kirkintilloch Road, Lenzie, Glasgow G66 4LB [E-mail: douglaswclark@hotmail.com]	0141-776 2184

No.	Charge / Minister	Ord.	Ind.	Address	Telephone
29	**Lenzie: Union (H)** Vacant			1 Larch Avenue, Lenzie, Glasgow G66 4HX	0141-776 3831
30	**Maxwell Mearns Castle (Tel/Fax: 0141-639 5169)** David C. Cameron BD CertMin	1993		122 Broomfield Avenue, Newton Mearns, Glasgow G77 5JR [E-mail: maxwellmearns@hotmail.com]	0141-616 0642
31	**Mearns (H) (0141-639 6555)** Joseph A. Kavanagh BD DipPTh MTh	1992	1998	Manse of Mearns, Newton Mearns, Glasgow G77 5BU [E-mail: mearnskirk@hotmail.com]	0141-616 2410 (Tel/Fax)
32	**Milton of Campsie (H)** Diane E. Stewart BD	1988		33 Birdstone Road, Milton of Campsie, Glasgow G66 8BX [E-mail: diane.e.stewart@care4free.net]	01360 310548 (Tel/Fax)
33	**Netherlee (H)** Thomas Nelson BSc BD	1992	2002	25 Ormonde Avenue, Glasgow G44 3QY [E-mail: tomnelson@ntlworld.com]	0141-585 7502 (Tel/Fax)
	Daniel Frank (Assoc)	2003		35 Ormonde Avenue, Glasgow G44 3QY	0141-586 0875
34	**Newton Mearns (H) (0141-639 7373)** Angus Kerr BD CertMin ThM	1983	1994	28 Waterside Avenue, Newton Mearns, Glasgow G77 6TJ [E-mail: anguskerr@newtonmearns.ndo.co.uk]	0141-616 2079
35	**Rutherglen: Old (H)** Alexander Thomson BSc BD MPhil PhD	1973	1985	31 Highburgh Drive, Rutherglen, Glasgow G73 3RR [E-mail: alexander.thomson@btopenworld.com]	0141-647 6178
36	**Rutherglen: Stonelaw (0141-647 5113)** Alastair S. May	2002		80 Blairbeth Road, Rutherglen, Glasgow G73 4JA [E-mail: alistair.may@ntlworld.com]	0141-583 0157
37	**Rutherglen: Wardlawhill** Ian Walker BD MEd DipMS	1973		26 Parkhill Drive, Rutherglen, Glasgow G73 2PW	0141-563 9590
38	**Rutherglen: West** John W. Drummond MA BD	1971	1986	12 Albert Drive, Rutherglen, Glasgow G73 3RT	0141-569 8547
39	**Stamperland (0141-637 4999) (H)** Vacant			109 Ormonde Avenue, Glasgow G44 3SN	0141-637 4976 (Tel/Fax)

40 Stepps (H)
Vacant
2 Lenzie Road, Stepps, Glasgow G33 6DX
0141-779 9556

41 Thornliebank (H)
Robert M. Silver BA BD   1995
19 Arthurlie Drive, Giffnock, Glasgow G46 6UR
0141-620 2133

42 Torrance (T) (01360 620970)
Nigel L. Barge BSc BD   1991
27 Campbell Place, Meadow Rise, Torrance, Glasgow G64 4HR
[E-mail: nigel@nbarge.freeserve.co.uk]
01360 622379

43 Twechar See Banton

44 Williamwood
G. Hutton B. Steel MA BD   1982   1990
125 Greenwood Road, Clarkston, Glasgow G76 7LL
[E-mail: hutton@zetnet.co.uk]
0141-571 7949

45 Glasgow: Anderston Kelvingrove (0141-221 9408)
Vacant
16 Royal Terrace, Glasgow G3 7NY
0141-332 3136

46 Glasgow: Baillieston Mure Memorial (0141-773 1216)
Allan S. Vint BSc BD   1989   1996
28 Beech Avenue, Baillieston, Glasgow G69 6LF
[E-mail: allan@vint.co.uk]
0141-771 1217

47 Glasgow: Baillieston St Andrew's (0141-771 6629)
Robert Gehrke BSc BD CEng MIEE   1994   2001
55 Station Park, Baillieston, Glasgow G69 7XY
0141-771 1791

48 Glasgow: Balshagray Victoria Park
Campbell Mackinnon BSc BD   1982   2001
20 St Kilda Drive, Glasgow G14 9JN
0141-954 9780

49 Glasgow: Barlanark Greyfriars
David I.W. Locke MA MSc BD   2000
4 Rhindmuir Grove, Glasgow G69 6NE
[E-mail: revdavidlocke@ntlworld.com]
0141-771 1240

50 Glasgow: Battlefield East (H) (0141-632 4206)
Alan C. Raeburn MA BD   1971   1977
110 Mount Annan Drive, Glasgow G44 4RZ
0141-632 1514

51 Glasgow: Blawarthill
Ian M.S. McInnes BD DipMin   1995   1997
46 Earlbank Avenue, Glasgow G14 9HL
0141-579 6521

52 Glasgow: Bridgeton St Francis in the East (H) (L) (Church House: Tel: 0141-554 8045)
Howard R. Hudson MA BD   1982   1984
10 Albany Drive, Rutherglen, Glasgow G73 3QN
[E-mail: howard.hudson@ntlworld.com]
0141-587 8667

Margaret S. Beaton (Miss) DCS
64 Gardenside Grove, Fernlee Meadows, Carmyle, Glasgow G32 8EZ
0141-646 2297

53 Glasgow: Broomhill (0141-334 2540)
William B. Ferguson BA BD 1971 1987
27 St Kilda Drive, Glasgow G14 9LN
[E-mail: revferg@aol.com]
0141-959 3204

54 Glasgow: Calton Parkhead (0141-554 3866)
Ronald Anderson BD DipTh 1992
98 Drumover Drive, Glasgow G31 5RP
[E-mail: ron@anderson296.freeserve.co.uk]
0141-556 2520

Karen Hamilton (Miss) DCS
6 Beckfield Gate, Glasgow G33 1SW
0141-558 3195

55 Glasgow: Cardonald (0141-882 6264)
Eric McLachlan BD MTh 1978 1983
133 Newtyle Road, Paisley PA1 3LB
[E-mail: eric.mclachlan@ntlworld.com]
0141-561 1891

56 Glasgow: Carmunnock
G. Gray Fletcher BSc BD 1989 2001
The Manse, 161 Waterside Road, Carmunnock, Glasgow G76 9AJ
0141-644 1578 (Tel/Fax)

57 Glasgow: Carmyle linked with Kenmuir Mount Vernon
Murdo Maclean BD CertMin 1997 1999
3 Meryon Road, Glasgow G32 9NW
[E-mail: murdo.maclean@ntlworld.com]
0141-778 2625

58 Glasgow: Carntyne Old linked with Eastbank
Ronald A.S. Craig BACC BD 1983
211 Sandyhills Road, Glasgow G32 9NB
0141-778 1286

59 Glasgow: Carnwadric (E)
Graeme K. Bell BA BD 1983
62 Loganswell Road, Glasgow G46 8AX
0141-638 5884

60 Glasgow: Castlemilk: East (H) (0141-634 2444)
John D. Miller BA BD 1971
15 Castlemilk Drive, Glasgow G45 9TL
[E-mail: mary@millerg45.freeserve.co.uk]
0141-631 1244

61 Glasgow: Castlemilk: West (H) (0141-634 1480)
Janet P.H. MacMahon (Mrs) MSc BD 1992 2002
156 Old Castle Road, Glasgow G44 5TW
0141-637 5451

62 Glasgow: Cathcart Old
Neil W. Galbraith BD CertMin 1987 1996
21 Courthill Avenue, Cathcart, Glasgow G44 5AA
[E-mail: revneilgalbraith@hotmail.com]
0141-633 5248 (Tel/Fax)

63 Glasgow: Cathcart Trinity (H) (0141-637 6658)
Vacant
82 Merrylee Road, Glasgow G43 2QZ
0141-633 3744
(Charge formed by the union of Cathcart South and New Cathcart)

64 **Glasgow: Cathedral (High or St Mungo's)**
William Morris KCVO DD PhD LLD JP   1951   1 Whitehill Grove, Newton Mearns, Glasgow G77 5DH   0141-639 6327

65 **Glasgow: Colston Milton (0141-772 1922)**
Christopher D. Park BSc BD   1977   118 Birsay Road, Glasgow G22 7QP
[E-mail: chrispark.8649@hotmail.com]   0141-772 1958

66 **Glasgow: Colston Wellpark (H)**
Christine M. Goldie (Miss) LLB BD MTh   1984   16 Bishop's Gate Gardens, Colston, Glasgow G21 1XS
[E-mail: christine.goldie@ntlworld.com]   0141-589 8866

67 **Glasgow: Cranhill (H) (0141-774 5593)**
Vacant   31 Lethamhill Crescent, Glasgow G33 2SH   0141-770 6873

68 **Glasgow: Croftfoot (H) (0141-637 3913)**
John M. Lloyd BD CertMin   1986   20 Victoria Road, Burnside, Rutherglen, Glasgow G73 3QG
[E-mail: john.lloyd@croftfootparish.co.uk]   0141-647 5524

69 **Glasgow: Dennistoun Blackfriars (H)**
Vacant   41 Broompark Drive, Glasgow G31 2JB   0141-554 8667

70 **Glasgow: Dennistoun Central (H) (0141-554 1350)**
Adah Younger (Mrs) BD   1996   1978   45 Broompark Drive, Glasgow G31 2JB
[E-mail: adah@youngerg31.prestel.co.uk]   0141-550 4487

71 **Glasgow: Drumchapel Drumry St Mary's (0141-944 1998)**
Brian S. Sheret MA BD DPhil   1982   2002   8 Fruin Road, Glasgow G15 6SQ   0141-944 4493

72 **Glasgow: Drumchapel St Andrew's (0141-944 3758)**
John S. Purves LLB BD   1983   1984   6 Firdon Crescent, Glasgow G15 6QQ
[E-mail: john.s.purves@talk21.com]   0141-944 4566

73 **Glasgow: Drumchapel St Mark's**
Alistair J. MacKichan MA BD   1984   2001   146 Garscadden Road, Glasgow G15 6PR   0141-944 5440

74 **Glasgow: Eastbank** See Carntyne Old

75 **Glasgow: Easterhouse St George's and St Peter's (E) (0141-781 0800)**
Malcolm Cuthbertson BA BD   1984   3 Barony Gardens, Baillieston, Glasgow G69 6TS
[E-mail: malcuth@aol.com]   0141-573 8200 (Tel)
0141-773 4878 (Fax)

No.	Charge / Minister	Year	Year	Address	Tel
76	**Glasgow: Eastwood** Moyna McGlynn (Mrs) BD PhD	1999		54 Mansewood Road, Glasgow G43 1TL	0141-632 0724
77	**Glasgow: Gairbraid (H)** Ian C. MacKenzie MA BD	1970	1971	1515 Maryhill Road, Glasgow G20 9AB [E-mail: ian@revmac.freeserve.co.uk]	0141-946 1568
78	**Glasgow: Gardner Street (GE)** Roderick Morrison MA BD	1974	1994	148 Beechwood Drive, Glasgow G11 7DX	0141-563 2638
79	**Glasgow: Garthamlock and Craigend East (E)** Valerie J. Duff (Miss) DMin	1993	1996	175 Tillycairn Drive, Garthamlock, Glasgow G33 5HS [E-mail: valduff@fish.co.uk]	0141-774 6364
80	**Glasgow: Gorbals** Ian F. Galloway BA BD	1976	1996	44 Riverside Road, Glasgow G43 2EF	0141-649 5250
81	**Glasgow: Govan Old (Tel/Fax: 0141-440 2466)** Norman J. Shanks MA BD Michael S. Edwards BD (Assoc)	1983 1982		1 Marchmont Terrace, Glasgow G12 9LT 108 Cleveden Road, Glasgow G12 0JT [E-mail: michaeledwards@net.ntl.com]	0141-339 4421 0141-579 7115
82	**Glasgow: Govanhill Trinity** Bernard P. Lodge BD	1967	2002	6 Darluith Park, Brookfield, Johnstone PA5 8DD [E-mail: brnlodge@onetel.net.uk]	01505 320378
83	**Glasgow: High Carntyne (0141-778 4186)** Peter W. Nimmo BD ThM	1996	1998	165 Smithycroft Road, Glasgow G33 2RD [E-mail: peternimmo@minister.com]	0141-770 6464
84	**Glasgow: Hillington Park (H)** Ian Morrison BD	1991	1997	61 Ralston Avenue, Glasgow G52 3NB [E-mail: iain@morr.freeserve.co.uk]	0141-882 7000
85	**Glasgow: Househillwood St Christopher's** May M. Allison (Mrs) BD	1988	2001	12 Levendale Court, Crookston, Glasgow G53 7SJ	0141-810 5953
86	**Glasgow: Hyndland (H) (0141-339 1804)** John C. Christie BSc BD	1990		24 Hughenden Gardens, Glasgow G12 9YH	0141-334 1002

87 **Glasgow: Ibrox (H) (0141-427 0896)**
C. Blair Gillon BD   1975   1980
3 Dargarvel Avenue, Glasgow G41 5LD
[E-mail: cb@gillon3.freeserve.co.uk]
0141-427 1282 (Tel/Fax)
07786 326905 (Mbl)

88 **Glasgow John Ross Memorial Church for Deaf People**
(Voice Text: 0141-420 1759; Text Only: 0141-429 6682; Fax: 0141-429 6860; ISDN Video Phone: 0141-418 0579)
Richard C. Durno DSW CQSW   1989   1998
31 Springfield Road, Bishopbriggs, Glasgow G64 1PJ
[E-mail: richard@durnada.freeserve.co.uk]
[www.deafconnections.co.uk]
(Voice/Text) 0141-772 1052

89 **Glasgow: Jordanhill (Tel/Fax: 0141-959 2496)**
Colin C. Renwick BMus BD   1989   1996
96 Southbrae Drive, Glasgow G13 1TZ
[E-mail: jordchurch@aol.com]
0141-959 1310 (Tel)
0141-959 2496 (Fax)

90 **Glasgow: Kelvin Stevenson Memorial (0141-339 1750)**
Gordon Kirkwood BSc BD   1987   2003
94 Hyndland Road, Glasgow G12 9PZ
0141-334 5352

91 **Glasgow: Kelvinside Hillhead**
Jennifer Macrae (Mrs) MA BD   1998   2000
39 Athole Gardens, Glasgow G12 9BQ
[E-mail: jmacrae@supanet.com]
0141-339 2865

92 **Glasgow: Kenmuir Mount Vernon** See Carmyle

93 **Glasgow: King's Park (H) (0141-632 1131)**
G. Stewart Smith MA BD STM   1966   1979
1101 Aikenhead Road, Glasgow G44 5SL
[E-mail: stewart.smith@tinyworld.co.uk]
0141-637 2803 (Tel/Fax)

94 **Glasgow: Kinning Park (0141-427 3063)**
Margaret H. Johnston (Miss) BD   1988   2000
168 Arbroath Avenue, Cardonald, Glasgow G52 3HH
0141-810 3782

95 **Glasgow: Knightswood St Margaret's (H)**
Vacant
26 Airthrey Avenue, Glasgow G14 9LJ
0141-959 1094

96 **Glasgow: Langside (0141-632 7520)**
Vacant
36 Madison Avenue, Glasgow G44 5AQ
0141-637 0797

97 **Glasgow: Lansdowne**
Roy J.M. Henderson MA BD DipMin   1987   1992
18 Woodlands Drive, Glasgow G4 9EH
[E-mail: roy.henderson7@ntlworld.com]
0141-339 2794

98 **Glasgow: Linthouse St Kenneth's**
David A. Keddie MA BD   1966   2001
21 Ilay Road, Bearsden, Glasgow G61 1QG
[E-mail: revked@hotmail.com]
0141-577 1408

No.	Charge	Minister		Address	Tel
99	**Glasgow: Lochwood (H) (0141-771 2649)**	Stuart M. Duff BA	1997	42 Rhindmuir Road, Swinton, Glasgow G69 6AZ [E-mail: stuart@duff58.freeserve.co.uk]	0141-773 2756
100	**Glasgow: Martyrs', The**	Ewen MacLean BA BD	1995	30 Louden Hill Road, Robroyston, Glasgow G33 1GA [E-mail: ewenmaclean@beeb.net]	0141-558 7451
101	**Glasgow: Maryhill (H) (0141-946 3512)**	Anthony J.D. Craig BD	1987	111 Maxwell Avenue, Glasgow G61 1HT [E-mail: craig.glasgow@ntlworld.com]	0141-570 0642
		James Hamilton DCS		6 Beckfield Gate, Robroyston, Glasgow G33 1SW	0141-558 3195
102	**Glasgow: Merrylea (0141-637 2009)**	David P. Hood BD CertMin DipIOB(Scot)	1997 2001	4 Pilmuir Avenue, Glasgow G44 3HY [E-mail: dphood@ntlworld.com]	0141-637 6700
103	**Glasgow: Mosspark (H) (0141-882 2240)**	Alan H. MacKay BD	1974 2002	396 Kilmarnock Road, Glasgow G43 2DJ [E-mail: alanhmackay@aol.com]	0141-632 1247
104	**Glasgow: Mount Florida (H) (0141-561 0307)**	Hugh M. Wallace MA BD	1981 1987	90 Mount Annan Drive, Glasgow G44 4RZ	0141-589 5381
105	**Glasgow: New Govan (H)**	Robert G. McFarlane BD	2001	19 Dumbreck Road, Glasgow G41 5LJ [E-mail: robertmcf@hotmail.com]	0141-427 3197
106	**Glasgow: Newlands South (H) (0141-632 3055)**	John D. Whiteford MA BD	1989 1997	24 Monreith Road, Glasgow G43 2NY [E-mail: jwhiteford@hotmail.com]	0141-632 2588
107	**Glasgow: North Kelvinside**	William G. Alston	1961 1971	41 Mitre Road, Glasgow G14 9LE	0141-954 8250
108	**Glasgow: Partick South**	Alan L. Dunnett LLB BD	1994 1997	17 Munro Road, Glasgow G13 1SQ [E-mail: dustydunnett@prtck.freeserve.co.uk]	0141-959 3732
109	**Glasgow: Partick Trinity (H)**	Stuart J. Smith BEng BD	1994	99 Balshagray Avenue, Glasgow G11 7EQ [E-mail: stuartandelspeth.freeserve.co.uk]	0141-576 7149

No.	Charge / Minister		Address	Phone
110	**Glasgow: Penilee St Andrew (H) (0141-882 2691)**			
	Alastair J. Cherry BA BD	1982 2003	80 Tweedsmuir Road, Glasgow G52 2RX	0141-882 2460
111	**Glasgow: Pollokshaws**			
	Margaret Whyte (Mrs) BA BD	1988 2000	33 Mannering Road, Glasgow G41 3SW	0141-649 0458
112	**Glasgow: Pollokshields (H)**			
	David R. Black MA BD	1986 1997	36 Glencairn Drive, Glasgow G41 4PW	0141-423 4000
113	**Glasgow: Possilpark**			
	W.C. Campbell-Jack BD MTh PhD	1979 2003	108 Erradale Street, Lambhill, Glasgow G22 6PT	0141-336 6909
114	**Glasgow: Priesthill and Nitshill**			
	Douglas M. Nicol BD CA	1987 1996	36 Springkell Drive, Glasgow G41 4EZ	0141-427 7877
	Thomas C. Houston BA (Assoc)	1975 2000	1/1 31 Barrachnie Drive, Glasgow G69 6SH	0141-588 2442
115	**Glasgow: Queen's Park (0141-423 3654)**			
	T. Malcolm F. Duff MA BD	1985 2000	5 Alder Road, Glasgow G43 2UY	0141-637 5491
			[E-mail: malcolm@dufftmf.freeserve.co.uk]	
116	**Glasgow: Renfield St Stephen's (0141-332 4293; Fax: 0141-332 8482)**			
	Peter M. Gardner MA BD	1988 2002	101 Hill Street, Glasgow G3 6TY	0141-353 3395
117	**Glasgow: Robroyston (New Charge Development)**			
	Vacant		7 Beckfield Drive, Robroyston, Glasgow G33 1SR	0141-558 1847
118	**Glasgow: Ruchazie (0141-774 2759)**			
	William F. Hunter MA BD	1986 1999	18 Borthwick Street, Glasgow G33 3UU	0141-774 6860
			[E-mail: bhunter@fish.co.uk]	
	Janet Anderson (Miss) DCS		338 Gartcraig Road, Glasgow G33 2TE	0141-774 5329
119	**Glasgow: Ruchill (0141-946 0466)**			
	John C. Matthews MA BD	1992	9 Kirklee Road, Glasgow G12 0RQ	0141-357 3249
			[E-mail: jmatthews@kirklee9.fsnet.co.uk]	
	Paul McKeown BSc PhD BD (Community Minister)	2000	G/R, 10 Jedburgh Gardens, Glasgow G20 6BP	0141-946 6409
120	**Glasgow: St Andrew's East (0141-554 1485)**			
	Janette G. Reid (Miss) BD	1991	43 Broompark Drive, Glasgow G31 2JB	0141-554 3620
121	**Glasgow: St Columba (GE) (0141-221 3305)**			
	Donald Michael MacInnes	2002	1 Reelick Avenue, Peterson Park, Glasgow G13 4NF	0141-952 0948

122 Glasgow: St David's Knightswood (0141-959 1024; E-mail: dringlis@stdavidschurch.freeserve.co.uk)
W. Graham M. Thain LLB BD   1988   1999   60 Southbrae Drive, Glasgow G13 1QD   0141-959 2904
[E-mail: graham-thain@btopenworld.com]

123 Glasgow: St Enoch's Hogganfield (H) (0141-770 5694; Fax: 0870 284 0084; E-mail: church@st-enoch.org.uk; Website: www.st-enoch.org.uk)
Andrew J. Philip BSc BD   1996   43 Smithycroft Road, Glasgow G33 2RH   0141-770 7593
[E-mail: andrewphilip@minister.com]   0870 284 0085 (Fax)

124 Glasgow: St George's Tron (0141-221 2141)
Vacant   12 Dargarvel Avenue, Glasgow G41 5LU   0141-427 1402
John Rushton BVMS BD (Assoc)   1983   2000   29 Brent Avenue, Thornliebank, Glasgow G46 8JU   0141-638 0837
[E-mail: johnsusanrushton@bigfoot.com]

125 Glasgow: St James' (Pollok) (0141-882 4984)
Vacant   30 Ralston Avenue, Glasgow G52 3NA   0141-883 7405
Ann Merrilees (Miss) DCS   0/1, 15 Crookston Grove, Glasgow G52 3PN   0141-883 2488

126 Glasgow: St John's Renfield (0141-339 7021; Website: www.stjohns-renfield.org.uk)
Dugald J.R. Cameron BD DipMin MTh   1990   1999   26 Leicester Avenue, Glasgow G12 0LU   0141-339 4637
[E-mail: dugald@stjohns-renfield.org.uk]

127 Glasgow: St Luke's and St Andrew's
Ian C. Fraser BA BD   1983   1995   10 Chalmers Street, Glasgow G40 2HA   0141-556 3883
[E-mail: stluke@cqm.co.uk]

128 Glasgow: St Margaret's Tollcross Park
George M. Murray LTh   1995   31 Kenmuir Avenue, Sandyhills, Glasgow G32 9LE   0141-778 5060
[E-mail: george.murray@ntlworld.com]

129 Glasgow: St Nicholas' Cardonald
Roderick I.T. MacDonald BD   1992   104 Lamington Road, Glasgow G52 2SE   0141-882 2065

130 Glasgow: St Paul's (0141-770 8559)
R. Russell McLarty MA BD   1985   38 Lochview Drive, Glasgow G33 1QF   0141-770 9611

131 Glasgow: St Rollox
Vacant   42 Melville Gardens, Bishopbriggs, Glasgow G64 3DE   0141-772 2848

132 Glasgow: St Thomas' Gallowgate
Vacant   8 Helenvale Court, Glasgow G31 4LH   0141-554 0997

133 Glasgow: Sandyford Henderson Memorial (H) 1974 C. Peter White BVMS BD MRCVS	66 Woodend Drive, Glasgow G13 1TG [E-mail: revcpw@ntlworld.com]	1997	0141-954 9013
134 Glasgow: Sandyhills John P.F. Martindale BD	60 Wester Road, Glasgow G32 9JJ	1994	0141-778 2174
135 Glasgow: Scotstoun (T) Richard Cameron BD DipMin	15 Northland Drive, Glasgow G14 9BE [E-mail: rev.rickycam@virgin.net]	2000	0141-959 4637
136 Glasgow: Shawlands (0141-649 2012) Alastair D. McLay BSc BD	29 St Ronan's Drive, Glasgow G41 3SQ [E-mail: alastair@mclay79.freeserve.co.uk]7	1989 2001	0141-649 2034
137 Glasgow: Sherbrooke St Gilbert's (H) (0141-427 1968) Thomas L. Pollock JP BA BD MTh FSAScot	9 Springkell Gate, Glasgow G41 4BY	1982 2003	0141-423 3912
138 Glasgow: Shettleston Old (T) (H) (0141-778 2484) David K. Speed LTh	57 Mansionhouse Road, Mount Vernon, Glasgow G32 0RP	1969 1999	0141-778 8904
139 Glasgow: South Carntyne (H) (0141-778 1343) Gavin W. Forrest MA BD	47 Broompark Drive, Glasgow G31 2JB [E-mail: gavinesque@bbm7.fsnet.co.uk]	1984 2002	0141-554 5930
140 Glasgow: South Shawlands (T) (0141-649 4656) Fiona Gardner (Mrs) BD MA MLitt	391 Kilmarnock Road, Glasgow G43 2NU [E-mail: fionandcolin@hotmail.com]	1997 2000	0141-632 0013
141 Glasgow: Springburn (H) (0141-557 2345) Alan A. Ford BD Helen Hughes (Miss) DCS	3 Tofthill Avenue, Bishopbriggs, Glasgow G64 3PA [E-mail: alan@springburnchurch.freeserve.co.uk]	1977 2000	0141-762 1844 0771 045 5737 (Mbl)
142 Glasgow: Temple Anniesland (0141-959 1814) John Wilson BD	76 Victoria Park Drive North, Glasgow G14 9PJ [E-mail: jwilson@crowroad0.freeserve.co.uk]	1985 2000	0141-959 5835
143 Glasgow: Toryglen (H) Sandra Black (Mrs) BSc BD	36 Glencairn Drive, Glasgow G41 4PW	1988 2003	0141-423 0867
144 Glasgow: Trinity Possil and Henry Drummond Richard G. Buckley BD MTh	50 Highfield Drive, Glasgow G12 0HL	1990 1995	0141-339 2870

145 Glasgow: Tron St Mary's
William T.S. Wilson BSc BD — 1999 — 3 Hurly Hawkin', Bishopbriggs, Glasgow G64 1YL — 0141-772 8555
[E-mail: william.mair@ntlworld.com]

146 Glasgow: Victoria Tollcross
Richard Coley LTh — 1971 — 228 Hamilton Road, Glasgow G32 9QU — 0141-778 2413

147 Glasgow: Wallacewell
John B. MacGregor BD — 1999 — 54 Etive Crescent, Bishopbriggs, Glasgow G64 1ES — 0141-772 1453
[E-mail: john.macgregor2@ntlworld.com]
Joanna Love (Mrs) DCS — 92 Everard Drive, Colston, Glasgow G21 1XQ — 0141-563 5859

148 Glasgow: Wellington (H) (0141-339 0454)
M. Leith Fisher MA BD — 1967 1990 — 27 Kingsborough Gardens, Glasgow G12 9NH — 0141-339 3627
[E-mail: leith@minister22.freeserve.co.uk]

149 Glasgow: Whiteinch (New Charge Development)
Alan McWilliam BD — 1993 2000 — 65 Victoria Park Drive South, Glasgow G14 9NX — 0141-587 4010
[E-mail: alan@whiteinchcofs.co.uk]

150 Glasgow: Yoker (T)
Vacant — 15 Coldingham Avenue, Glasgow G14 0PX — 0141-952 3620
Kenneth MacDonald MA BA (Aux) — 2001 — 5 Henderland Road, Bearsden, Glasgow G61 1AH — 0141-943 1103

Aitken, Andrew J. BD APhS MTh PhD	1951	1981	(Tollcross Central with Park)	18 Dorchester Avenue, Glasgow G12 0EE	0141-357 1617
Alexander, Eric J. MA BD	1958	1997	(St George's Tron)	PO Box 14725, St Andrews KY16 8WB	ex-directory
Allan, A.G.	1959	1989	(Candlish Polmadie)	30 Dalrymple Drive, East Mains, East Kilbride, Glasgow G74 4LF	01355 226190
Barr, Alexander C. MA BD	1950	1992	(St Nicholas' Cardonald)	25 Fisher Drive, Phoenix Park, Paisley PA1 2TP	0141-848 5941
Beattie, John A.	1951	1984	(Dalmuir Overtoun)	0/1, 15 Kelvindale Gardens, Kelvindale Road, Glasgow G20 8DW	0141-946 5928
Bell, John L. MA BD FRSCM DUniv	1978	1988	(Iona Community)	Flat 2/1, 31 Lansdowne Crescent, Glasgow G20 6NH	0141-334 0688
Brain, Ernest J.	1955	1985	(Liverpool St Andrew's)	14 Chesterfield Court, 1240 Great Western Road, Glasgow G12 0BJ	0141-357 2249
Brain, Isobel J. (Mrs) MA	1987	1997	(Ballantrae)	14 Chesterfield Court, 1240 Great Western Road, Glasgow G12 0BJ	0141-357 2249
Brice, Dennis G. BSc BD	1981		(Taiwan)	8 Parkwood Close, Broxbourne, Herts EN10 7PF	
Brough, Robin BA	1968	2002	(Whitburn: Brucefield)	'Kildavanan', 10 Printers Lea, Lennoxtown, Glasgow G66 7GF	01360 310223
Bryden, William A. BD	1977	1984	(Yoker Old with St Matthew's)	145 Bearsden Road, Glasgow G13 1BS	0141-959 52:3
Bull, Alister W. BD DipMin	1994	2001	Chaplain: Royal Hospital for Sick Children	Yorkhill NHS Trust, Yorkhill, Glasgow G3 8SJ	0141-201 0595
Campbell, A. Iain MA DipEd	1961	1997	(Busby)	430 Clarkston Road, Glasgow G44 3QF	0141-637 7460
Campbell, Colin MA BD	1940	1989	(Williamwood)	4 Golf Road, Clarkston, Glasgow G76 7LZ	0141-638 12.5
Campbell, Roderick D.M. TD BD FSAScot	1975	2003	(Board of World Mission)	22 Greenlaw Road, Newton Mearns, Glasgow G77 6ND	0141-639 7338
Cartledge, G.R.G. MA BD STM	1977	1993	Religious Education	5 Briar Grove, Newlands, Glasgow G43 2TD	0141-637 3228

Chester, Stephen J. BA BD	1999		RE Teacher, International Christian College	42 Drumlochy Road, Ruchazie, Glasgow G33 3RE	0141-774 4666
Collard, John K. MA BD	1986	2003	Presbytery Congregational Facilitator	1 Nelson Terrace, East Kilbride, Glasgow G74 2EY	01355 520093
Cullen, William T. BA LTh	1984	1996	(Kilmarnock: St John's Onthank)	71 Fenwick Road, Giffnock, Glasgow G46 6AX	0141-637 8244
Cunningham, Alexander MA BD	1961	2002	(Presbytery Clerk)	The Glen, 103 Glenmavis Road, Airdrie ML6 0PQ	01236 763012
Cunningham, James S.A. MA BD BLitt PhD				'Kirkland', 5 Inveresk Place, Coatbridge ML5 2DA	01236 421541
Currie, Robert MA	1992	2000	(Glasgow: Barlanark Greyfriars) / (Community Minister)	Flat 3/2, 13 Redlands Road, Glasgow G12 0SJ / 759B Argyle Street, Glasgow G3 8DS	0141-334 5111 / 0141-204 4800 (Office)
Dunnett, Linda (Mrs) DCS	1955	1990	Frontier Youth Trust, West of Scotland Development Officer	17 Munro Road, Glasgow G13 1SQ	0141-959 3732
Ferguson, James B. LTh	1972	2002	(Lenzie: Union)	3 Bridgeway Place, Kirkintilloch, Glasgow G66 3HW	
Finlay, William P. MA BD	1969	2000	(Glasgow: Townhead Blochairn)	High Corrie, Brodick, Isle of Arran KA27 8JB	01770 810689
Forbes, George A.R. BD	1971	2000	(Kirkintilloch: Hillhead)	28 Murrayfield, Bishopbriggs, Glasgow G64 3DS	0141-762 0272
Galloway, Allan D. MA BD STM PhD FRSE	1948	1982	(University of Glasgow)	5 Sraid Bheag, Barremman, Clynder, Helensburgh G84 0QX	01436 831432
Galloway, Kathy (Mrs) BD	1977	2002	Leader: Iona Community	20 Hamilton Park Avenue, Glasgow G12 8UU	0141-357 4079
Gibson, H. Marshall MA BD	1957	1996	(St Thomas' Gallowgate)	39 Burntbroom Drive, Glasgow G69 7XG	0141-771 0749
Gibson, Michael BD STM	1974	2001	(Glasgow: Giffnock: The Park)	12 Mile End Park, Pocklington, York YO42 2TH	
Goss, Alister BD	1975	1998	Industrial Mission Organiser	79 Weymouth Crescent, Gourock PA19 1HR	01475 638944
Gregson, Elizabeth M. (Mrs) BD	1996	2001	(Drumchapel: St Andrew's)	17 Westfields, Bishopbriggs, Glasgow G64 3PL	0141-563 1918
Grimstone, A. Frank MA	1949	1986	(Calton Parkhead)	144C Howth Drive, Parkview Estate, Anniesland, Glasgow G13 1RL	0141-954 1009
Haley, Derek BD DPS	1960	1999	(Chaplain: Gartnavel Royal)	9 Kinnaird Crescent, Bearsden, Glasgow G61 2BN	0141-942 9281
Harper, Anne J.M. (Miss) BD STM MTh CertSocPsych	1979	1990	Hospital Chaplain	122 Greenock Road, Bishopton PA7 5AS	01505 862466
Haughton, Frank MA BD	1942	2000	(Kirkintilloch: St Mary's)	64 Regent Street, Kirkintilloch, Glasgow G66 1JF	0141-777 6802
Hope, Evelyn P. (Miss) BA BD	1990	1998	(Wishaw: Thornlie)	Flat 0/1, 48 Moss-side Road, Glasgow G41 3UA	0141-649 1522
Hunter, Alastair G. MSc BD	1976	1980	University of Glasgow	487 Shields Road, Glasgow G41 2RG	0141-429 1687
Hutcheson, J. Murray MA	1943	1987	(Possilpark)	88 Ainslie Road, Kildrum, Cumbernauld, Glasgow G67 2ED	01236 631168
Hutchison, Henry MA BEd BD MLitt PhD LLCM	1948	1993	(Carmunnock)	4A Briar Grove, Newlands, Glasgow G43 2TG	0141-637 2766
Irvine, Euphemia H.C. (Mrs) BD	1972	1988	(Milton of Campsie)	32 Baird Drive, Bargarran, Erskine PA8 6BB	0141-812 2777
Johnston, Robert W.M. MA BD STM	1964	1999	(Temple Anniesland)	13 Kilmardinny Crescent, Bearsden, Glasgow G61 3NP	0141-931 5862
Johnstone, H. Martin J. MA BD MTh	1989	2000	Urban Priority Areas Adviser	3 Herries Road, Glasgow G41 4DE	0141-423 3760
Jolly, John BA	1950	1990	(Old Partick)	10 Kensington Court, 20 Kensington Road, Glasgow G12 9NX	0141-339 8815
Jones, E. Gwynfai BA	1964	2002	(Glasgow: St Rollox)	50 Melville Gardens, Bishopbriggs, Glasgow G64 3DD	0141-563 1770
Langlands, Cameron H. BD MTh ThM	1995	1999	Hospital Chaplain	Flat 3/2, 59 Nursery Street, Glasgow G41 2PL	0141-424 1530
Leask, Rebecca M. (Mrs)	1977	1985	(Callander: St Bride's)	1 Woodrow Court, 17 Woodrow Road, Glasgow G41 5TN	0141-427 2260
Levison, C.L. MA BD	1972	1998	Health Care Chaplaincy Training and Development Officer	5 Deaconsbank Avenue, Stewarton Road, Glasgow G46 7UN	0141-620 3492
Lewis, E.M.H. MA	1962	1993	(Drumchapel St Andrew's)	7 Cleveden Place, Glasgow G12 0HG	0141-334 5411

Name	Charge / Appointment	Ord	Ind	Address	Tel
Liddell, Matthew MA BD	(St Paul's (Outer High) and St David's (Ramshorn))	1943	1982	17 Traquair Drive, Glasgow G52 2TB	0141-810 3775
Lunan, David W. MA BD	Presbytery Clerk	1970	2002	142 Hill Street, Glasgow G3 6UA	0141-353 3687
McAreavey, William BA	(Kelvin Stevenson Memorial)	1950	2001	12B East Donington Street, Darvel KA17 0JW	01560 320073
Macaskill, Marjory (Mrs) LLB BD	Chaplain: University of Strathclyde	1990	1998	44 Forfar Avenue, Cardonald, Glasgow G52 3JQ	0141-883 5955
MacBain, Iain W.	(Coatbridge: Coatdyke)	1971	1993	24 Thornyburn Drive, Baillieston, Glasgow G69 7ER	0141-771 7030
MacDonald, Anne (Miss) BA DCS	Hospital Chaplain			62 Berwick Drive, Glasgow G52 3JA	0141-883 5613
Macdonald, Murdo Ewen DD	(University of Glasgow)	1939	1984	Eastwoodhill, 238 Fenwick Road, Glasgow G46 6UU	0141-638 5127
MacFadyen, Anne M. (Mrs) BSc BD	(Auxiliary Minister)	1995		295 Mearns Road, Glasgow G77 5LT	0141-639 3605
Macfarlane, Thomas G. BSc PhD BD	(South Shawlands)	1956	1992	Flat 0/2, 19 Corrour Road, Glasgow G43 2DY	0141-632 7965
McKenzie, Mary O. (Miss)	(Edinburgh Richmond Craigmillar)	1976	1996	4 Dunellan Avenue, Moodiesburn, Glasgow G69 0GB	01236 870180
McLaren, D. Muir MA BD MTh PhD	(Mosspark)	1971	2001	Flat 24, 28 Lethington Avenue, Glasgow G41 3HB	
MacLeod, William J. DipTh	(Kirkintilloch St David's Memorial)	1963	1988	42 Hawthorn Drive, Banknock, Bonnybridge FK4 1LF	01324 840667
Macnaughton, J.A. MA BD	(Hyndland)	1949	1989	62 Lauderdale Gardens, Glasgow G12 9QW	0141-339 1294
MacPherson, James B. DCS	(Deacon)			0/1, 104 Cartside Street, Glasgow G42 9TQ	0141-616 6463
MacQuarrie, Stuart BD BSc JP	Chaplain: Glasgow University	1984	2001	The Chaplaincy Centre, University of Glasgow, Glasgow G12 8QQ	0141-330 5419
Millar, David A.R. MA	(University of Glasgow)	1956	1989	310A Albert Drive, Glasgow G41 5RS	0141-429 2249
Millar, James	(Shawlands Old)	1949	1989	9 Glenbank Court, Glasgow G46 7EJ	0141-638 625)
Mitchell, David BD MSc DipPTheol	Chaplain: Marie Curie Hospice, Glasgow	1988	1998	48 Leglin Wood Drive, Wallacewell Park, Glasgow G21 3PL [E-mail: davidmitchell@chaplain48.freeserve.co.uk]	0141-558 4679
Morton, Thomas MA BD LGSM	(Rutherglen Stonelaw)	1945	1986	54 Greystone Avenue, Burnside, Rutherglen, Glasgow G73 3SW	0141-647 2682
Muir, Fred C. MA BD ThM ARCM	(Stepps)	1961	1997	20 Alexandra Avenue, Stepps, Glasgow G33 6BP	0141-779 2504
Myers, Frank BA	(Springburn)	1952	1978	18 Birmingham Close, Grantham NG31 8SD	01476 594430
Newlands, George M. MA BD PhD	University of Glasgow	1970	1986	12 Jamaica Street North Lane, Edinburgh EH3 6HQ	0131-339 8855
Philip, George M. MA	(Sandyford Henderson Memorial)	1953	1996	44 Beech Avenue, Bearsden, Glasgow G61 3EX	0141-942 1327
Philip, Robert A. BA BD	(Stepps St Andrew's)	1937	1981	2 Hockley Court, Weston Park West, Bath BA1 4AR	01225 333041
Porter, Richard MA	(Govanhill)	1953	1988	58 Hillend Road, Glasgow G76 7XT	0141-639 4169
Ramsay, W.G.	(Springburn)	1967	1999	53 Kelvinvale, Kirkintilloch, Glasgow G66 1RD	0141-776 2915
Reid, Ian M.A. BD	Hospital Chaplain	1990	2001	Chaplains Office, Victoria Infirmary, Langside Road, Glasgow G42 9TT	
Robertson, Archibald MA BD	(Eastwood)	1957	1999	19 Canberra Court, Braidpark Drive, Glasgow G46 6NS	0141-637 7572
Robertson, Blair MA BD ThM	Chaplain: Southern General Hospital	1990	1998	c/o Chaplain's Office, Southern General Hospital, 1345 Govan Road, Glasgow G51 4TF	
Ross, Donald M. MA	(Industrial Mission Organiser)	1953	1994	14 Cartsbridge Road, Busby, Glasgow G76 8DH	0141-201 2155
Ross, James MA BD	(Kilsyth: Anderson)	1968	1998	53 Turnberry Gardens, Westerwood, Cumbernauld, Glasgow G68 0AY	0141-644 2220)
Saunders, Keith BD	Hospital Chaplain	1983	1999	Western Infirmary, Dumbarton Road, Glasgow G11 6NT	01236 73050)
Scrimgeour, Alice M. (Miss) DCS	(Deaconess)	1960	1996	265 Golfhill Drive, Glasgow G31 2PB	0141-211 2000
Shackleton, William	(Greenock: Wellpark West)				0141-564 9602
Simpson, Neil A. BA BD PhD	(Glasgow: Yoker Old with Yoker St Matthew's)	1992	2001	3 Tynwald Avenue, Burnside, Glasgow G73 4RN	0141-569 9407
Smillie, Andrew M. LTh	(Cathcart South)	1990	2001	7 Turnbull Avenue, West Freeland, Erskine PA8 7DL	0141-812 703)

Smith, A. McLaren	1971 1997	(Cumbrae)	27 Fenwick Road, Glasgow G46 6AU	0141-954 6497
Smith, Hilda C. (Miss) MA BD	1992 2001	Hospital Chaplain	107 Athelstane Road, Glasgow G13 3QY	0141-776 0870
Smith, J. Rankine MA BD	1945 1982	(Barmulloch)	44 Middlemuir Road, Lenzie, Glasgow G66 4ND	0141-883 9666
Smith, James S.A.	1956 1991	(Drongan, The Schaw Kirk)	146 Aros Drive, Glasgow G52 1TJ	0141-883 8973
Spence, Elisabeth G.B. (Miss) BD DipEd	1995 2000	Industrial Missioner: Glasgow Area	45 Selvieland Road, Glasgow G52 4AS	0141-637 6956
Stewart, Norma D. (Miss) MA MEd BD	1977 2000	(Glasgow: Strathbungo Queens Park)	127 Nether Auldhouse Road, Glasgow G43 2YS	01236 731723
Sutherland, Denis I.	1963 1995	(Hutchesontown)	56 Lime Crescent, Cumbernauld, Glasgow G67 3PQ	01360 770154
Sutherland, Elizabeth W. (Miss) BD	1972 1996	(Balornock North with Barmulloch)	20 Kirkland Avenue, Blanefield, Glasgow G63 9BZ	0141-770 6027
Tait, Alexander	1967 1995	(St Enoch's Hogganfield)	129 Lochview Drive, Hogganfield, Glasgow G33 1LN	0141-424 0493
Turner, Angus BD	1976 1998	(Industrial Chaplain)	46 Keir Street, Pollokshields, Glasgow G41 2LA	01698 321108
Tuton, Robert M. MA	1957 1995	(Shettleston: Old)	6 Holmwood Gardens, Uddingston, Glasgow G71 7BH	01360 622281
Walker, A.L.	1955 1988	(Trinity Possil and Henry Drummond)	11 Dundas Avenue, Torrance, Glasgow G64 4BD	
White, Elizabeth (Miss) DCS		(Deaconess)	Woodside House, Rodger Avenue, Rutherglen, Glasgow G73 3QZ	

GLASGOW ADDRESSES

Banton		Kelvinhead Road, Banton
Bishopbriggs		
	Kenmure	Viewfield Road, Bishopbriggs
	Springfield	Springfield Road
Broom		Mearns Road, Newton Mearns
Burnside–Blairbeth		Church Avenue, Burnside
Busby		Church Road, Busby
Cadder		Cadder Road, Glasgow
Cambuslang		
Flemington Hallside		265 Hamilton Road
Old		Cairns Road
St Andrew's		Main Street x Clydeford Road
Trinity St Paul's		Main Street
Campsie		Main Street, Lennoxtown
Chryston		Main Street, Chryston
Eaglesham		Montgomery Street, Eaglesham
Gartcosh		113 Lochend Road, Gartcosh
Giffnock		
Orchardhill		Church Road
South		Eastwood Toll
The Park		Ravenscliffe Drive
Glenboig		138 Main Street, Glenboig
Greenbank		Eaglesham Road, Clarkston
Kilsyth		
Anderson		Kingston Road
Burns and Old		Church Street
Kirkintilloch		
Hillhead		Newdyke Road
St Columba's		Waterside Road nr Old Aisle Road
St David's Mem Pk		Alexander Street
St Mary's		Cowgate
Lenzie		
Old		Kirkintilloch Road x Garngaber Ave
Union		Moncrieff Ave x Kirkintilloch Road
Maxwell		
Mearns Castle		Waterfoot Road
Mearns		Mearns Road, Newton Mearns
Netherlee		Ormonde Drive x Ormonde Avenue
Newton Mearns		Ayr Road, Newton Mearns
Rutherglen		
Old		Main Street at Queen Street
Stonelaw		Stonelaw Road x Dryburgh Avenue
Wardlawhill		Hamilton Road
West		Glasgow Road nr Main Street
Stamperland		Stamperland Gardens, Clarkston
Stepps		Whitehill Avenue
Thornliebank		61 Spiersbridge Road
Torrance		School Road, Torrance
Twechar		Main Street, Twechar
Williamwood		Vardar Avenue x Seres Ave, Clarkston

Glasgow

Anderston Kelvingrove	Argyle Street x Elderslie Street
Baillieston	
St Andrew's	Beech Avenue, Garrowhill
	Church Street
Balshagray Victoria Pk	Broomhill Cross
Barlanark Greyfriars	Edinburgh Road x Hallhill Road
Battlefield East	1216 Cathcart Road
Blawarthill	Millbrix Avenue
Bridgeton St Francis in the East	26 Queen Mary Street
Broomhill	Randolph Rd x Marlborough Ave
Calton Parkhead	122 Helenvale Street
Cardonald	2155 Paisley Road West
Carmunnock	Kirk Road, Carmunnock
Carmyle	South Carmyle Avenue
Carmyne Old	862 Shettleston Road
Carnwadric	556 Boydstone Road, Thornliebank
Castlemilk	
East	Barlia Terrace
West	Carmunnock Road
Cathcart	
Old	119 Carmunnock Road
Trinity	92 Clarkston Road
Cathedral	Cathedral Square
Colston Milton	Egilsay Crescent
Colston Wellpark	1378 Springburn Road
Cranhill	Bellrock Crescent x Bellrock Street
Croftfoot	Croftpark Ave x Crofthill Road
Dennistoun	
Blackfriars	Whitehill Street
Central	Armadale Street
Drumchapel	
Drumry St Mary's	Drumry Road East
St Andrew's	Garscadden Road
St Mark's	Kinfauns Drive
Eastbank	679 Old Shettleston Road
Easterhouse St George's and St Peter's	
Eastwood	Boyndie Street
	Mansewood Road
Fernhill and Cathkin	Neilvaig Drive
Gairbraid	1517 Maryhill Road
Gardner Street	Gardner Street x Muirpark Street
Garthamlock and Craigend East	Porchester Street x Balveny Street
	Eglinton Street x Cumberland Street
Gorbals	866 Govan Road
Govan Old	
Govanhill Trinity	Daisy Street nr Allison Street
High Carntyne	358 Carntynehall Road
Hillington Park	24 Berryknowes Road
Househillwood St Christopher's	Meikle Road
Hyndland	Hyndland Road, opp Novar Drive
Ibrox	Carillon Road x Clifford Street
John Ross Memorial	100 Norfolk Street
Jordanhill	Woodend Drive x Munro Road
Kelvin Stevenson Mem	Belmont Street at Belmont Bridge
Kelvinside Hillhead	Huntly Gardens
Kenmuir Mount Vernon	London Road, Mount Vernon
King's Park	242 Castlemilk Road
Kinning Park	Eaglesham Place
Knightswood St Margaret's	Knightswood Cross
Langside	Ledard Road x Lochleven Road
Lansdowne	Gt Western Road at Kelvin Bridge
Linthouse St Kenneth's	9 Skipness Drive
Lochwood	Lochend Road x Liff Place
Martyrs', The	St Mungo Avenue
Maryhill	1990 Maryhill Road
Merrylea	78 Merrylee Road
Mosspark	149 Ashkirk Drive
Mount Florida	1123 Cathcart Road
New Govan	Govan Cross
Newlands South	Riverside Road x Langside Drive
North Kelvinside	153 Queen Margaret Drive
Partick South Trinity	Dumbarton Road
	20 Lawrence Street
Penilee St Andrew	Bowfield Cres x Bowfield Avenue
Pollokshaws	223 Shawbridge Street
Pollokshields	Albert Drive x Shields Road
Possilpark	124 Saracen Street
Priesthill and Nitshill	Freeland Drive x Muirshiel Cres
Queen's Park	170 Queen's Drive
Renfield St Stephen's	260 Bath Street
Robroyston	
Ruchazie	Elibank Street x Milncroft Road
Ruchill	Shakespeare Street nr Maryhill Rd
St Andrew's East	681 Alexandra Parade
St Columba	300 St Vincent Street
St David's Knightswood	
St Enoch's Hogganfield	Boreland Drive nr Lincoln Avenue
St George's Tron	860 Cumbernauld Road
St James' (Pollok)	163 Buchanan Street
St John's Renfield	Lyoncross Road x Byrebush Road
St Luke's and St Andrew's	22 Beaconsfield Road
St Margaret's Tollcross Pk	Well Street at Bain Square
St Nicholas' Cardonald	
St Paul's Provanmill	179 Braidfauld Street
St Rollox	Hartlaw Crescent nr Gladsmuir Road
St Thomas Gallowgate	Langdale Street x Greenig Street
Sandyford-Henderson Memorial	Fountainwell Road
Sandyhills	Gallowgate opp Bluevale Street
Scotstoun	Kelvinhaugh Street at Argyle Street
Shawlands	28 Baillieston Rd nr Sandyhills Rd
Sherbrooke St Gilbert's	Earlbank Avenue x Ormiston Avenue
Shettleston Old	Shawlands Cross
South Carntyne	Nithsdale Rd x Sherbrooke Avenue
South Shawlands	99–111 Killin Street
Springburn	538 Carntyne Road
	Regwood Street x Deanston Drve
	Springburn Road x Atlas Street
Temple Anniesland	869 Crow Road
Toryglen	Glenmore Ave nr Prospecthill Road
Trinity Possil and Henry Drummond	Crowhill Street x Broadholm Street
Tron St Mary's	128 Red Road
Victoria Tollcross	1134 Tollcross Road
Wallacewell	57 Northgate Road
	Ryehill Road x Quarrywood Road
Wellington	University Ave x Southpark Avenue
Whiteinch	Whiteinch Neighbourhood Centre, Dumbarton Road
Yoker	Dumbarton Road at Hawick Street

(17) HAMILTON

Meets at Motherwell: Dalziel St Andrew's Parish Church Halls, on the first Tuesday of February, March, May, September, October, November, December, and on the third Tuesday of June.

		(Tel)
		(Fax)
Presbytery Office:	18 Haddow Street, Hamilton ML3 7HX [E-mail: akph54@uk.uumail.com]	01698 286837 01698 457258
Clerk:	REV. SHAW J. PATERSON BSc BD	15 Lethame Road, Strathaven ML10 6AD	01357 520019
Treasurer:	MR DAVID FORRESTER CA	Belmont, Lefroy Street, Coatbridge ML5 1PN	01236 421892

1 **Airdrie Broomknoll (H) (Tel: 01236 762101; E-mail: airdrie-broomknoll@presbyteryofhamilton.co.uk)**
   linked with Calderbank (E-mail: calderbank@presbyteryofhamilton.co.uk)
   Andrew Thomson BA   1976   2000   38 Commonhead Street, Airdrie ML6 6NS   01236 602538

2 **Airdrie Clarkston (E-mail: airdrie-clarkston@presbyteryofhamilton.co.uk)**
   Vacant   Forrest Street, Airdrie ML6 7BE   01236 769676

3 **Airdrie: Flowerhill (H) (E-mail: airdrie-flowerhill@presbyteryofhamilton.co.uk)**
   Andrew Gardner BSc BD PhD   1997   31 Victoria Place, Airdrie ML6 9BX   01236 763025
                                         [E-mail: andrewgar@supanet.com]

4 **Airdrie: High (E-mail: airdrie-high@presbyteryofhamilton.co.uk)**
   W. Richard Houston BSc BD   1998   17 Etive Drive, Airdrie ML6 9QL   01236 762010
                                         [E-mail: wrhouston@blueyonder.co.uk]

5 **Airdrie: Jackson (Tel: 01236 733508; E-mail: airdrie-jackson@presbyteryofhamilton.co.uk)**
   Sharon E.F. Colvin (Mrs)   1985   1998   48 Dunrobin Road, Airdrie ML6 8LR   01236 763154
   BD LRAM LTCL

6 **Airdrie: New Monkland (H) (E-mail: airdrie-newmonkland@presbyteryofhamilton.co.uk)**
   linked with Greengairs (E-mail: greengairs@presbyteryofhamilton.co.uk)
   Randolph Scott MA BD   1991   2001   3 Dykehead Crescent, Airdrie ML6 6PU   01236 763554
                                         [E-mail: rev.rs@tinyworld.co.uk]

7 **Airdrie: St Columba's (E-mail: airdrie-stcolumbas@presbyteryofhamilton.co.uk)**
   Margaret F. Currie BEd BD   1980   1987   52 Kennedy Drive, Airdrie ML6 9AW   01236 763173
                                         [E-mail: mfcstcol@surfaid.org]

8 **Airdrie: The New Wellwynd (H) (E-mail: airdrie-newwellwynd@presbyteryofhamilton.co.uk)**
Robert A. Hamilton BA BD   1995   2001   20 Arthur Avenue, Airdrie ML6 9EZ   01236 763022
[E-mail: revrob13@blueyonder.co.uk]

9 **Bargeddie (H) (E-mail: bargeddie@presbyteryofhamilton.co.uk)**
John Fairful BD   1994   2001   Bargeddie, Baillieston, Glasgow G69 6UB   0141-771 1322

10 **Bellshill: Macdonald Memorial (E-mail: bellshill-macdonald@presbyteryofhamilton.co.uk) linked with Bellshill: Orbiston**
Alan McKenzie BSc BD   1988   2001   32 Adamson Street, Bellshill ML4 1DT   01698 849114
[E-mail: rev.a.mckenzie@btopenworld.com]

11 **Bellshill: Orbiston (E-mail: bellshill-orbiston@presbyteryofhamilton.co.uk)** See Bellshill: Macdonald Memorial

12 **Bellshill: West (H) (01698 747581) (E-mail: bellshill-west@presbyteryofhamilton.co.uk)**
Agnes A. Moore (Miss) BD   1987   2001   16 Croftpark Street, Bellshill ML4 1EY   01698 842877

13 **Blantyre: Livingstone Memorial (E-mail: blantyre-livingstone@presbyteryofhamilton.co.uk)**
Colin A. Sutherland LTh   1995   2003   286 Glasgow Road, Blantyre, Glasgow G72 9DB   01698 823794
[E-mail: colin@sutherland.fsnet.co.uk]

14 **Blantyre: Old (H) (E-mail: blantyre-old@presbyteryofhamilton.co.uk)**
Rosemary A. Smith (Ms) BD   1997   The Manse, Craigmuir Road, High Blantyre, Glasgow G72 9UA   01698 823130

15 **Blantyre: St Andrew's (E-mail: blantyre-standrews@presbyteryofhamilton.co.uk)**
J. Peter N. Johnston BSc BD   2001   332 Glasgow Road, Blantyre, Glasgow G72 9LQ   01698 828653
[E-mail: peter.johnston@standrewsblantyre.com]

16 **Bothwell (H) (E-mail: bothwell@presbyteryofhamilton.co.uk)**
James M. Gibson TD LTh LRAM   1978   1989   Manse Avenue, Bothwell, Glasgow G71 8PQ   01698 853189 (Tel)
[E-mail: jamesmgibson@msn.com]   01698 853229 (Fax)

17 **Calderbank** See Airdrie Broomknoll

18 **Caldercruix and Longriggend (H) (E-mail: caldercruix@presbyteryofhamilton.co.uk)**
Vacant   Main Street, Caldercruix, Airdrie ML6 7RF   01236 842279

19 **Carfin (E-mail: carfin@presbyteryofhamilton.co.uk) linked with Newarthill (E-mail: newarthill@presbyteryofhamilton.co.uk)**
Vacant   Church Street, Newarthill, Motherwell ML1 5HS   01698 860316

20 **Chapelhall (H) (E-mail: chapelhall@presbyteryofhamilton.co.uk)**
Vacant   Chapelhall, Airdrie ML6 8SG   01236 763439

21 **Chapelton (E-mail: chapelton@presbyteryofhamilton.co.uk)**
linked with Strathaven: Rankin (H) (E-mail: strathaven-rankin@presbyteryofhamilton.co.uk)
Shaw J. Paterson BSc BD   1991   15 Lethame Road, Strathaven ML10 6AD   01357 520019 (Tel)
[E-mail: shaw@patersonj.freeserve.co.uk]   01357 529316 (Fax)

22 **Cleland (H) (E-mail: cleland@presbyteryofhamilton.co.uk)**
John A. Jackson BD   1997   Bellside Road, Cleland, Motherwell ML1 5NP   01698 860260

23 **Coatbridge: Blairhill Dundyvan (H) (E-mail: coatbridge-blairhill@presbyteryofhamilton.co.uk)**
Vacant   18 Blairhill Street, Coatbridge ML5 1PG   01236 432304

24 **Coatbridge: Calder (H) (E-mail: coatbridge-calder@presbyteryofhamilton.co.uk)**
Vacant   26 Bute Street, Coatbridge ML5 4HF   01236 421516

25 **Coatbridge: Clifton (H) (E-mail: coatbridge-clifton@presbyteryofhamilton.co.uk)**
William G. McKaig BD   1979 2003   132 Muiryhall Street, Coatbridge ML5 3NH   01236 421181

26 **Coatbridge: Middle (E-mail: coatbridge-middle@presbyteryofhamilton.co.uk)**
James Grier BD   1991 1996   47 Blair Road, Coatbridge ML5 1JQ   01236 432427

27 **Coatbridge: Old Monkland (E-mail: coatbridge-oldmonkland@presbyteryofhamilton.co.uk)**
Scott Raby LTh   1991 2003   Old Monkland Manse, Coatbridge ML5 5QT   01236 423788

28 **Coatbridge: St Andrew's (E-mail: coatbridge-standrews@presbyteryofhamilton.co.uk)**
Ian G. Wotherspoon BA LTh   1967 1994   77 Eglinton Street, Coatbridge ML5 3JF   01236 437271
[E-mail: wotherspoonrig@aol.com]

29 **Coatbridge: Townhead (H) (E-mail: coatbridge-townhead@presbyteryofhamilton.co.uk)**
Vacant   Crinan Crescent, Coatbridge ML5 2LH   01236 423150

30 **Dalserf (E-mail: dalserf@presbyteryofhamilton.co.uk)**
D. Cameron McPherson BSc BD   1982   Manse Brae, Dalserf, Larkhall ML9 3BN   01698 882195
[E-mail: dcameronmc@aol.com]

31 **East Kilbride: Claremont (H) (Tel: 01355 238088; E-mail: ek-claremont@presbyteryofhamilton.co.uk)**
Gordon R. Palmer MA BD STM   1986 2003   17 Deveron Road, East Kilbride, Glasgow G74 2HR   01355 248526
Paul Cathcart DCS   5A Atholl Gardens, Rutherglen, Glasgow G73 5HF   0141-569 6865

32 **East Kilbride: Greenhills (E) (Tel: 01355 221746; E-mail: ek-greenhills@presbyteryofhamilton.co.uk)**
John Brewster MA BD DipEd   1988   21 Turnberry Place, East Kilbride, Glasgow G75 8TB   01355 242564
[E-mail: johnbrewster1@activemail.co.uk]

33 **East Kilbride: Moncreiff (H) (Tel: 01355 223328; E-mail: ek-moncreiff@presbyteryofhamilton.co.uk)**
Alastair S. Lusk BD   1974 1983   16 Almond Drive, East Kilbride, Glasgow G74 2HX   01355 238639

34 **East Kilbride: Mossneuk (E) (Tel: 01355 260954; E-mail: ek-mossneuk@presbyteryofhamilton.co.uk)**
    John L. McPake BA BD PhD   1986   2000   30 Eden Grove, Mossneuk, East Kilbride, Glasgow G75 8XU
                                                                                                                            01355 234196

35 **East Kilbride: Old (H) (E-mail: ek-old@presbyteryofhamilton.co.uk)**
    Anne S. Paton BA BD   2001   40 Maxwell Drive, East Kilbride, Glasgow G74 4NG
                                                                                                                            01355 220732

36 **East Kilbride: South (H) (E-mail: ek-south@presbyteryofhamilton.co.uk)**
    John C. Sharp BSc BD PhD   1980   7 Clamps Wood, East Kilbride, Glasgow G74 2HB
                                                                  [E-mail: johncsharp@btinternet.com]
                                                                                                                            01355 247993

37 **East Kilbride: Stewartfield (New Charge Development)**
    Douglas W. Wallace MA BD   1981   2001   8 Thistle Place, Stewartfield, East Kilbride, Glasgow G74 4RH
                                                                                                                            01355 260879

38 **East Kilbride: West (H) (E-mail: ek-west@presbyteryofhamilton.co.uk)**
    Kenneth A.L. Mayne BA MSc CertEd   1976   2001   1 Barr Terrace, East Kilbride, Glasgow G74 1AP
                                                                                                                            01355 239891

39 **East Kilbride: Westwood (H) (Tel: 01355 245657; E-mail: ek-westwood@presbyteryofhamilton.co.uk)**
    Kevin Mackenzie BD DPS   1989   1996   16 Inglewood Crescent, East Kilbride, Glasgow G75 8QD
                                                                  [E-mail: kevin@westwood-church.org.uk]
                                                                                                                            01355 223992

40 **Glasford (E-mail: glassford@presbyteryofhamilton.co.uk) linked with Strathaven: East (E-mail: strathaven-east@presbyteryofhamilton.co.uk)**
    William T. Stewart BD   1980   68 Townhead Street, Strathaven ML10 6BA
                                                                                                                            01357 521138

41 **Greengairs** See Airdrie: New Monkland

42 **Hamilton: Burnbank (E-mail: hamilton-burnbank@presbyteryofhamilton.co.uk)
    linked with Hamilton: North (H) (E-mail: hamilton-north@presbyteryofhamilton.co.uk)**
    Raymond D. McKenzie BD   1978   1987   9 South Park Road, Hamilton ML3 6PJ
                                                                                                                            01698 424609

43 **Hamilton: Cadzow (H) (Tel: 01698 428695; E-mail: hamilton-cadzow@presbyteryofhamilton.co.uk)**
    Arthur P. Barrie LTh   1973   1979   3 Carlisle Road, Hamilton ML3 7BZ
                                                                                                                            01698 421664   (Tel)
                                                                                                                            01698 891126   (Fax)

44 **Hamilton: Gilmour and Whitehill (H) (E-mail: hamilton-gilmourwhitehill@presbyteryofhamilton.co.uk)**
    Ronald J. Maxwell Stitt   1977   2000   86 Burnbank Centre, Burnbank, Hamilton ML3 0NA
    LTh BA ThM BREd DMin FSAScot
                                                                                                                            01698 284201

45 **Hamilton: Hillhouse (E-mail: hamilton-hillhouse@presbyteryofhamilton.co.uk)**
    David W.G. Burt BD DipMin   1989   1998   66 Wellhall Road, Hamilton ML3 9BY
                                                                  [E-mail: dwgburt@blueyonder.co.uk]
                                                                                                                            01698 422300
    William Wishart DCS   17 Swift Bank, Earrock, Hamilton ML3 8PX
                                                                  [E-mail: bill@hillhousechurch.co.uk]
                                                                                                                            01698 429371

46   **Hamilton: North**   See Hamilton: Burnbank

47   **Hamilton: Old (H) (Tel: 01698 281905; E-mail: hamilton-old@presbyteryofhamilton.co.uk)**
John M.A. Thomson TD JP BD ThM   1978   2001   1 Chateau Grove, Hamilton ML3 7DS   01698 422511
[E-mail: johnt@hopc.demon.co.uk]

48   **Hamilton: St Andrew's (T) (E-mail: hamilton-standrews@presbyteryofhamilton.co.uk)**
Norma Moore (Ms) MA BD   1995   15 Bent Road, Hamilton ML3 6QB   01698 891361
[E-mail: norma.moore@blueyonder.co.uk]

49   **Hamilton: St John's (H) (Tel: 01698 283492; E-mail: hamilton-stjohns@presbyteryofhamilton.co.uk)**
Robert M. Kent MA BD   1973   1981   12 Castlehill Crescent, Hamilton ML3 7DG   01698 425002
[E-mail: robert@bobkent.fsnet.co.uk]

50   **Hamilton: South (H) (Tel: 01698 281014; E-mail: hamilton-south@presbyteryofhamilton.co.uk)**
linked with Quarter (E-mail: quarter@presbyteryofhamilton.co.uk)
Vacant   The Manse, Limekilnburn Road, Quarter, Hamilton ML3 7XA   01698 424511

51   **Hamilton: Trinity (Tel: 01698 284254; E-mail: hamilton-trinity@presbyteryofhamilton.co.uk)**
Karen E. Harbison (Mrs) MA BD   1991   69 Buchan Street, Hamilton ML3 8JY   01698 425326

52   **Hamilton: West (H) (Tel: 01698 284670; E-mail: hamilton-west@presbyteryofhamilton.co.uk)**
William M. Murdoch BSc PhD BD STM   1980   2001   43 Bothwell Road, Hamilton ML3 0BB   01698 458770

53   **Holytown (E-mail: holytown@presbyteryofhamilton.co.uk)**
James S. Salmond BA BD MTh ThD   1979   Holytown, Motherwell ML1 5RU   01698 832622

54   **Kirk o' Shotts (H) (E-mail: kirk-o-shotts@presbyteryofhamilton.co.uk)**
Sheila M. Spence (Mrs) MA BD   1979   The Manse, Kirk o' Shotts, Salsburgh, Shotts ML7 4NS   01698 870208
[E-mail: sm-spence@hotmail.com]

55   **Larkhall: Chalmers (H) (E-mail: larkhall-chalmers@presbyteryofhamilton.co.uk)**
James S.G. Hastie CA BD   1990   Quarry Road, Larkhall ML9 1HH   01698 882238
[E-mail: jhastie@chalmers0.demon.co.uk]   0870 056 2133 (Fax)

56   **Larkhall: St Machan's (H) (E-mail: larkhall-stmachans@presbyteryofhamilton.co.uk)**
Vacant   2 Orchard Gate, Larkhall ML9 1HG   01698 882457

57   **Larkhall: Trinity (E-mail: larkhall-trinity@presbyteryofhamilton.co.uk)**
Lindsay Schluter (Miss) ThE CertMin   1995   13 Machan Avenue, Larkhall ML9 2HE   01698 881401

58   **Motherwell: Crosshill (H) (E-mail: mwell-crosshill@presbyteryofhamilton.co.uk)**
W. Stuart Dunn LTh   1970   1982   15 Orchard Street, Motherwell ML1 3JE   01698 263410

59   **Motherwell: Dalziel St Andrew's (H) (Tel: 01698 264097; E-mail: mwell-dalzielstandrews@presbyteryofhamilton.co.uk)**
Derek W. Hughes BSc BD DipEd   1990   1996   4 Pollock Street, Motherwell ML1 1LP   01698 263414
[E-mail: derek@hughes04.freeserve.co.uk]

60 **Motherwell: Manse Road (E-mail: mwell-manseroad@presbyteryofhamilton.co.uk)**
   Vacant   10 Hamilton Drive, Motherwell ML1 2QA   01698 267345

61 **Motherwell: North (E-mail: mwell-north@presbyteryofhamilton.co.uk)**
   Derek H.N. Pope BD   1987   1995   Kirkland Street, Motherwell ML1 3JW   01698 266716

62 **Motherwell: St Margaret's (E-mail: mwell-stmargarets@presbyteryofhamilton.co.uk)**
   Andrew M. Campbell BD   1984   70 Baron's Road, Motherwell ML1 2NB   01698 263803
   [E-mail: drewdorca@hotmail.com]

63 **Motherwell: St Mary's (H) (E-mail: mwell-stmarys@presbyteryofhamilton.co.uk)**
   David W. Doyle MA BD   1977   1987   19 Orchard Street, Motherwell ML1 3JE   01698 263472

64 **Motherwell: South Dalziel (H) (E-mail: mwell-southdalziel@presbyteryofhamilton.co.uk)**
   Phyllis M. Wilson (Mrs) DipCom DipRE   1985   1994   62 Manse Road, Motherwell ML1 2PT   01698 263054
   [E-mail: phylandtomwilson@ukonline.co.uk]

65 **Newarthill** See Carfin

66 **Newmains: Bonkle (H) (E-mail: bonkle@presbyteryofhamilton.co.uk)**
   linked with Newmains: Coltness Memorial (H) (E-mail: coltness@presbyteryofhamilton.co.uk)
   Vacant   5 Kirkgate, Newmains, Wishaw ML2 9BT   01698 383858
   John McAlpine BSc (Aux)   1998   201 Bonkle Road, Newmains, Wishaw ML2 9AA   01698 384610

67 **Newmains: Coltness Memorial** See Newmains: Bonkle

68 **New Stevenston: Wrangholm Kirk (E-mail: wrangholm@presbyteryofhamilton.co.uk)**
   George M. Donaldson MA BD   1984   2003   222 Clydesdale Street, New Stevenston, Motherwell ML1 4JQ   01698 832533

69 **Overtown (E-mail: overtown@presbyteryofhamilton.co.uk)**
   Nan Low (Mrs) BD   2002   The Manse, Main Street, Overtown, Wishaw ML2 0QP   01698 372330
   [E-mail: nanlow@supanet.com]

70 **Quarter** See Hamilton: South

71 **Shotts: Calderhead Erskine (E-mail: calderhead-erskine@presbyteryofhamilton.co.uk)**
   Ian G. Thom BSc PhD BD   1990   2000   The Manse, Kirk Road, Shotts ML7 5ET   01501 820042
   [E-mail: the.thoms@btinternet.com]

72 **Stonehouse: St Ninian's (H) (E-mail: stonehouse@presbyteryofhamilton.co.uk)**
   Paul G.R. Grant BD MTh   2003   4 Hamilton Way, Stonehouse, Larkhall ML9 3PU   01698 792947

73 **Strathaven: Avendale Old and Drumclog (H) (Tel: 01357 529748; E-mail: strathaven-avendaleold@presbyteryofhamilton.co.uk and**
   E-mail: drumclog@presbyteryofhamilton.co.uk)
   Alan W. Gibson BA BD   2001   Kirk Street, Strathaven ML10 6BA   01357 520077
   [E-mail: awgibson82@hotmail.com]

74 **Strathaven: East** See Glasford
75 **Strathaven: Rankin** See Chapelton

76 **Strathaven: West (E-mail: strathaven-west@presbyteryofhamilton.co.uk)**
Una B. Stewart (Ms) BD DipEd   1995   2002   6 Avenel Crescent, Strathaven ML10 6JF   01357 529086
[E-mail: rev.ubs@virgin.net]

77 **Uddingston: Burnhead (H) (E-mail: uddingston-burnhead@presbyteryofhamilton.co.uk)**
Sandi Blackwood (Ms) BD   2002   90 Laburnum Road, Uddingston, Glasgow G71 5DB   01698 813716
[E-mail: rev.sandi@btopenworld.com]
Raymond Deans DCS   22 Garrowhill Drive, Garrowhill, Glasgow G69 6HL   0141-771 6847

78 **Uddingston: Old (H) (Tel: 01698 814015; E-mail: uddingston-old@presbyteryofhamilton.co.uk)**
Norman B. McKee BD   1987   1994   1 Belmont Avenue, Uddingston, Glasgow G71 7AX   01698 814757
[E-mail: normanb.mckee@belmont89.freeserve.co.uk]

79 **Uddingston: Park (T) (H) (E-mail: uddingston-park@presbyteryofhamilton.co.uk)**
W. Bruce McDowall BA BD   1989   1999   25 Douglas Gardens, Uddingston, Glasgow G71 7HB   01698 817256

80 **Uddingston: Viewpark (H) (E-mail: uddingston-viewpark@presbyteryofhamilton.co.uk)**
Michael G. Lyall BD   1993   2001   14 Holmbrae Road, Uddingston, Glasgow G71 6AP   01698 813113

81 **Wishaw: Cambusnethan North (H) (E-mail: wishaw-cambusnethannorth@presbyteryofhamilton.co.uk)**
Mhorag Macdonald (Ms) MA BD   1989   350 Kirk Road, Wishaw ML2 8LH   01698 381305
[E-mail: mhorag@mhorag.force9.co.uk]

82 **Wishaw: Cambusnethan Old (E-mail: wishaw-cambusnethanold@presbyteryofhamilton.co.uk)**
and Morningside (E-mail: wishaw-morningside@presbyteryofhamilton.co.uk)
Iain C. Murdoch MA LLB DipEd BD   1995   22 Coronation Street, Wishaw ML2 8LF   01698 384235
[E-mail: iaincmurdoch@btopenworld.com]

83 **Wishaw: Chalmers (H) (Tel: 01698 375306; E-mail: wishaw-chalmers@presbyteryofhamilton.co.uk)**
Ian O. Coltart CA BD   1988   161 Kirk Road, Wishaw ML2 7BZ   01698 372464

84 **Wishaw: Craigneuk and Belhaven (H) (E-mail: wishaw-craigneukbelhaven@presbyteryofhamilton.co.uk)**
Vacant   100 Glen Road, Wishaw ML2 7NP   01698 372495

85 **Wishaw: Old (H) (Tel: 01698 376080; E-mail: wishaw-old@presbyteryofhamilton.co.uk)**
Vacant   130 Glen Road, Wishaw ML2 7NP   01698 375134

86 **Wishaw: St Mark's (E-mail: wishaw-stmarks@presbyteryofhamilton.co.uk)**
Henry J.W. Findlay MA BD   1965   1967   Coltness Road, Wishaw ML2 7EX   01698 384596 (Tel)
01698 386025 (Fax)

87 Wishaw: Thornlie (H) (E-mail: wishaw-thornlie@presbyteryofhamilton.co.uk)
Klaus O.F. Buwert LLB BD   1984 1999   West Thornlie Street, Wishaw ML2 7AR   01698 372356
                                           [E-mail: revklausb@aol.com]   07801 533548 (Mbl)

Allan, James B. BA	1965	1993	(Motherwell: South Dalziel)	42 Catherine Street, Motherwell ML1 2RN	01698 264756
Anderson, Catherine B. (Mrs) DCS	1944	1984	(Deaconess)	13 Mosshill Road, Bellshill ML4 1NQ	01698 745907
Baird, George W. MA	1951	1986	(Crimond with St Fergus)	42 Neilsland Drive, Motherwell ML1 3EB	01698 262038
Beattie, William G. BD BSc	1963	2002	(Hamilton St-Andrew's)	33 Dungavel Gardens, Hamilton ML3 7PE	01698 423834
Black, John M. MA BD	1995	2003	(Coatbridge: Blairhill Dundyvan)	3 Grantown Avenue, Airdrie ML6 8HH	01236 750638
Brown, Allan B. BD MTh	1974	2001	(Chaplain: Shotts Prison)	18 Don Drive, Livingston EH54 5LN	
Cook, J. Stanley BD Dip PSS			(Hamilton: West)	Mansend, 137A Old Manse Road, Netherton, Wishaw ML2 0EW	01698 299630
				[E-mail: stancook@blueyonder.co.uk]	
Cowper, Macknight C. MA BD STM	1947	1983	(East Kilbride West)	17 Manor Place, Edinburgh EH3 7DH	0131-225 6214
Fraser, James P.	1951	1988	(Strathaven Avendale Old and Drumclog)	26 Hamilton Road, Strathaven ML10 6JA	01357 522758
Gilchrist, Kay (Miss) BD	1996	1999	(Chaplain: Rachel House)	45 Hawthorn Drive, Craigneuk, Airdrie ML6 8AP	
Handley, John	1954	1993	(Motherwell: Clason Memorial)	12 Airbles Crescent, Motherwell ML1 3AR	01698 262733
Hunter, James E. LTh	1974	1997	(Blantyre: Livingstone Memorial)	57 Dalwhinnie Avenue, Blantyre, Glasgow G72 9NQ	01698 826177
King, Crawford S. MA	1958	1984	(Glenboig)	77 Faskine Avenue, Airdrie ML6 9EA	01236 761753
McCabe, George	1963	1996	(Airdrie: High)	Flat 8, Park Court, 2 Craighouse Park, Edinburgh EH10 5LD	0131-447 9522
McDonald, John A. MA BD	1978	1997	(Cumbernauld: Condorrat)	17 Thomson Drive, Bellshill ML4 3ND	
Martin, James MA BD DD	1946	1987	(Glasgow: High Carntyne)	9 Magnolia Street, Wishaw ML2 7EQ	01698 385825
Melrose, J.H. Loudon MA BD MEd	1955	1996	(Gourock: Old Gourock & Ashton [Assoc])	24 Avonbridge Drive, Hamilton ML3 7EJ	01698 891033
Munton, J.H. MA BD	1969	2002	(Coatbridge: Old Monkland)	2 Moorcroft Drive, Airdrie ML6 8ES	01236 754848
				[E-mail: jacjim@supanet.com]	
Nelson, James R. BD	1986	2003	(Chapelhall)	4 Glen Orchy Place, Airdrie ML6 8QT	01236 766685
Niven, William LTCL	1955	1994	(Lesmahagow: Old)	92 Linden Lea, Hamilton ML3 9AG	01698 420653
Price, Peter O. CBE QHC BA FPhS	1960	1996	(Blantyre: Old)	20A Old Bothwell Road, Bothwell, Glasgow G71 8AW	01698 854032
				[E-mail: peteroprice@aol.com]	
Rogerson, Stuart D. BSc BD	1980	2001	(Strathaven: West)	17 Westfield Park, Strathaven ML10 6XH	01357 523221
				[E-mail: srogerson@cnetwork.co.uk]	
Thorne, Leslie W. BA LTh	1987	2001	(Coatbridge: Clifton)	'Hatherleigh', 9 Chatton Walk, Coatbridge ML5 4FH	01236 432241
Wyllie, James H. LTh	1970	1996	(Cleland)	21 Austine Drive, Hamilton ML3 7YE	01698 457642
				[E-mail: wilsonjh@blueyonder.co.uk]	
Wyllie, Hugh R. MA DD FCIBS	1962	2000	(Hamilton: Old)	18 Chantinghall Road, Hamilton ML3 8NP	01698 420002
Zambonini, James LlADip	1997		(Auxiliary Minister)	100 Old Manse Road, Wishaw ML2 0EP	01698 350887

HAMILTON ADDRESSES

Airdrie
Broomknoll — Broomknoll Street
Clarkston — Forrest Street
Flowerhill — 89 Graham Street
High — North Bridge Street
Jackson — Glen Road
New Monkland — Glenmavis
St Columba's — Thrashbush Road
The New Wellwynd — Wellwynd

Coatbridge
Blairhill Dundyvan — Blairhill Street
Calder — Calder Street
Clifton — Muiryhall Street x Jackson Street
Middle — Bank Street
Old Monkland — Woodside Street
St Andrew's — Church Street
Townhead — Crinan Crescent

East Kilbride
Claremont — High Common Road, St Leonard's
Greenhills — Greenhills Centre
Moncreiff — Calderwood Road
Mossneuk — Eden Drive
Old — Montgomery Street
South — Baird Hill, Murray
West — Kittoch Street
Westwood — Belmont Drive, Westwood

Hamilton
Burnbank — High Blantyre Road
Cadzow — Woodside Walk
Gilmour and Whitehill — Glasgow Road, Burnbank
Hillhouse — Abbotsford Road, Whitehill
North — Clerkwell Road
Old — Windmill Road
St Andrew's — Leechlee Road
St John's — Avon Street
South — Duke Street
Trinity — Strathaven Road
West — Neilsland Square off North Road, Burnbank Road

Motherwell
Crosshill — Windmillhill Street x Airbles Street
Dalziel St Andrew's — Merry Street and Muir Street
North — Manse Road
St Margaret's — Gavin Street
St Mary's — Chesters Crescent
South Dalziel — Shields Road
— Avon Street
— 504 Windmillhill Street

Uddingston
Burnhead — Laburnum Road
Old — Old Glasgow Road.
Park — Main Street
Viewpark — Old Edinburgh Road

Wishaw
Cambusnethan North — Kirk Road
Old — Kirk Road
Chalmers — East Academy Street
Craigneuk and Belhaven — Craigneuk Street
— Main Street
St Mark's — Coltness Road
Thornlie — West Thornlie Street

(18) DUMBARTON

Meets at Dumbarton in Riverside Church Halls, on the first Tuesday of February, March, April, May, October, November, December, and on the second Tuesday of June and September (and April when the first Tuesday falls in Holy Week).

Clerk:	REV. DAVID P. MUNRO MA BD STM		14 Birch Road, Killearn, Glasgow G63 9SQ [E-mail: akph43@uk.uumail.com] [E-mail: dmunro@uk.uumail.com]	01360 550098 (Tel) 01360 551198 (Fax)

Alexandria

Elizabeth W. Houston (Miss) MA BD DipEd	1985	1995	32 Ledrish Avenue, Balloch, Alexandria G83 8JB	01389 751933
Archibald M. Ferguson MSc PhD CEng FRINA (Aux)	1989	2001	The Whins, Barrowfield, Cardross, Dumbarton G82 5NL [E-mail: archieferguson@supanet.com]	01389 841517

Arrochar linked with Luss
H. Dane Sherrard BD DMin — 1971 1998
The Manse, Luss, Alexandria G83 8NZ
[E-mail: dane@cadder.demon.co.uk]
01436 860240
07801 939138 (Mbl)

Baldernock (H)
Andrew P. Lees BD — 1984 2002
The Manse, Bardowie, Milngavie, Glasgow G62 6ES
01360 620471

Bearsden: Killermont (H)
Alan S. Hamilton LLB BD — 2003
8 Clathic Avenue, Bearsden, Glasgow G61 2HF
[E-mail: hamiltonalan@hamilton63.freeserve.co.uk]
0141-942 0021

Bearsden: New Kilpatrick (H) (0141-942 8827)
David D. Scott BSc BD — 1981 1999
51 Manse Road, Bearsden, Glasgow G61 3PN
[E-mail: nkbearsden@btopenworld.com]
0141-942 0035

Bearsden: North (H) (0141-942 2818)
Keith T. Blackwood BD Dip Min — 1997
5 Fintry Gardens, Bearsden, Glasgow G61 4RJ
[E-mail: kblackwood@totalise.co.uk]
0141-942 0366
07961 442972 (Mbl)

Bearsden: South (H)
John W.F. Harris MA — 1967 1987
61 Drymen Road, Bearsden, Glasgow G61 2SU
[E-mail: jwfh@globalnet.co.uk]
0141-942 0507
07711 573877 (Mbl)

Bearsden: Westerton Fairlie Memorial (H) (0141-942 6960)
Eric V. Hudson LTh — 1971 1990
3 Canniesburn Road, Bearsden, Glasgow G61 1PW
[E-mail: evhudson@canniesburn.fsnet.co.uk]
0141-942 2672

Alistair E. Ramage BA ADB CertEd (Aux) — 1996
16 Claremont Gardens, Milngavie, Glasgow G62 6PG
[E-mail: a.ramage@gcal.ac.uk]
0141-956 2897

Bonhill (H) (01389 756516)
Ian H. Miller BA BD — 1975
1 Glebe Gardens, Bonhill, Alexandria G83 9NZ
[E-mail: ianmiller@bonhillchurch.freeserve.co.uk]
01389 753039

Cardross (H) (01389 841322)
Andrew J. Scobie MA BD — 1963 1965
Church of Scotland Manse, Main Road, Cardross, Dumbarton G82 5LB
[E-mail: ascobie55@cardross.dunbartonshire.co.uk]
01389 841289
07889 670252 (Mbl)

Clydebank: Abbotsford (E-mail: abbotsford@lineone.net; Website: http://www.abbotsford.org.uk)
Roderick G. Hamilton MA BD — 1992 1996
35 Montrose Street, Clydebank G81 2PA
[E-mail: rghamilton@ntlworld.com]
0141-952 5151

Clydebank: Faifley
Gregor McIntyre BSc BD — 1991 — Kirklea, Cochno Road, Hardgate, Clydebank G81 6PT — 01389 876836
[E-mail: mail@gregormcintyre.com]
Agnes Tait (Mrs) DCS — 2 Lennox Drive, Faifley, Clydebank G81 5JU — 01389 873196

Clydebank: Kilbowie St Andrew's
Peggy Roberts (Mrs) BA BD — 2003 — 5 Melfort Avenue, Clydebank G81 2HX — 0141-951 2455
[E-mail: peggyroberts@btopenworld.com]

Clydebank: Radnor Park
Margaret J.B.Yule (Mrs) BD — 1992 — Church Manse, Spencer Street, Clydebank G81 3AS — 0141-951 1007
[E-mail: mjbyule@tinyworld.co.uk]

Clydebank: St Cuthbert's (T) linked with Duntocher (H)
David Donaldson MA BD — 1969 2002 — The Manse, Roman Road, Duntocher, Clydebank G81 6BT — 01389 878846
[E-mail: david.donaldson3@btopenworld.com]

Craigrownie linked with Rosneath St Modan's (H)
Vacant — Edenkiln, Argyll Road, Kilcreggan, Helensburgh G84 0JW — 01436 842274

Dalmuir Barclay (0141-941 3988)
James F. Gatherer BD — 1984 — Parkhall Road, Dalmuir, Clydebank G81 3RJ — 0141-941 3317

Dumbarton: Riverside (H) (01389 742551)
Robert J. Watt BD — 1994 2002 — 5 Kirkton Road, Dumbarton G82 4AS — 01389 762512
[E-mail: robertjwatt@blueyonder.co.uk]

Dumbarton: St Andrew's (H)
Leslie G. Donaghy — 1990 1998 — 17 Mansewood Drive, Dumbarton G82 3EU — 01389 604259
BD DipMin PGCE FSAScot — 07654 553473 (Pager)
[E-mail: info@bellsmyre.co.uk]

Dumbarton: West Kirk (H)
Christine Liddell (Miss) BD — 1999 — 3 Havoc Road, Dumbarton G82 4JW — 01389 604840
[E-mail: thewestkirk@aol.com]

Duntocher (H) See Clydebank: St Cuthbert's

Garelochhead (01436 810589)
Alastair S. Duncan MA BD — 1989 — Old School Road, Garelochhead, Helensburgh G84 0AT — 01436 810022
[E-mail: gpc@churchuk.fsnet.co.uk]

Helensburgh: Park (H) (01436 671714)
James H. Brown BD — 1977 — 35 East Argyle Street, Helensburgh G84 7EL — 01436 672209
[E-mail: jh@jhbrown.freeserve.co.uk] — 07941 173299 (Mbl)

Helensburgh: St Columba (H)
Frederick M. Booth LTh ... 1970 ... 46 Suffolk Street, Helensburgh G84 9QZ ... 01436 672054

Helensburgh: The West Kirk (H) (01436 676880)
David W. Clark MA BD ... 1975 ... 1986 ... 37 Campbell Street, Helensburgh G84 9NH ... 01436 674063
[E-mail: clarkdw@lineone.net]

Jamestown (H)
Vacant ... Appin House, Drymen Road, Balloch, Alexandria G83 8HT ... 01389 752734

Kilmaronock Gartocharn
Vacant ... Kilmaronock Manse, Alexandria G83 8SB ... 01360 660295

Luss See Arrochar

Milngavie: Cairns (H) (0141-956 4868)
Andrew Frater BA BD ... 1987 ... 1994 ... 4 Cairns Drive, Milngavie, Glasgow G62 8AJ ... 0141-956 1717
[E-mail: office@cairnschurch.org.uk]

Milngavie: St Luke's (0141-956 4226)
Ramsay B. Shields BA BD ... 1990 ... 1997 ... 70 Hunter Road, Milngavie, Glasgow G62 7BY ... 0141-577 9171 (Tel)
[E-mail: rbshields@ntlworld.com] ... 0141-577 9181 (Fax)

Milngavie: St Paul's (H) (0141-956 4405)
Fergus C. Buchanan MA BD ... 1982 ... 1988 ... 8 Buchanan Street, Milngavie, Glasgow G62 8DD ... 0141-956 1043
[E-mail: f.c.buchanan@btinternet.com]

Old Kilpatrick Bowling
Jeanette Whitecross (Mrs) BD ... 2002 ... The Manse, Dumbarton Road, Old Kilpatrick, Glasgow G60 5JQ ... 01389 873130
[E-mail: jeanettewx@yahoo.com]

Renton Trinity (H)
Ian Wilkie BD PGCE ... 2001 ... 38 Main Street, Renton, Dumbarton G82 4PU ... 01389 752017
[E-mail: rtpccofs@aol.com] ... 07751 155552 (Mbl)

Rhu and Shandon (H)
J. Colin Caskie BA BD ... 1977 ... 2002 ... 11 Ardenconnel Way, Rhu, Helensburgh G84 8LX ... 01436 820213
[E-mail: colin@caskie.freeserve.co.uk]

Rosneath St Modan's See Craigrownie

Crombie, W.M.D. MA BD	1947 1987	(Calton New with St Andrew's)	32 Westbourne Drive, Bearsden, Glasgow G61 4BH	0141-943 0235
Dalton, Mark F. BD DipMin	2002	Chaplain: Royal Navy	CIC Britannia Royal Naval College, 35 Regt Royal, Dartmouth, Devon TQ6 0HJ	
Davidson, Professor Robert MA BD DD FRSE	1956 1991	(University of Glasgow)	30 Dumgoyne Drive, Bearsden, Glasgow G61 3AP	0141-942 1810
Easton, I.A.G. MA FIPM	1945 1988	Lecturer	6 Edgehill Road, Bearsden, Glasgow G61 3AD	0141-942 4214
Hamilton, David S.M. MA BD STM	1958 1996	(University of Glasgow)	2 Roselea Drive, Milngavie, Glasgow G62 8HQ	0141-956 1839
Houston, Peter M. FPhS	1952 1997	(Renfrew Old)	25 Honeysuckle Lane, Jamestown, Alexandria G83 8PL	01389 721165 (Mbl) 07770 390936
Jack, Robert MA BD	1950 1996	(Bearsden: Killermont)	142 Turnhill Drive, Erskine PA8 7AH	0141-812 8370
Lawson, Alexander H. ThM ThD FPhS	1950 1988	(Clydebank: Kilbowie)	1 Glebe Park, Mansewood, Dumbarton G82 3HE	01389 742030
McFadzean, Iain MA BD	1989 1999	Chaplain: Royal Navy	Lochhaven, Portincaple, Garelochhead, Helensburgh G84 0EU	01436 810811
McIntyre, J. Ainslie MA BD	1963 1984	(University of Glasgow)	60 Bonnaughton Road, Bearsden, Glasgow G61 4DB [E-mail: jamcintyre@hotmail.com]	0141-942 5143 (Mbl) 07050 295103
Mackenzie, Ian M. MA	1967 1989	(BBC)	1 Glennan Gardens, Helensburgh G84 8XT	01436 673429
Morton, Andrew Q. MA BSc BD FRSE	1949 1987	(Culross and Torryburn)	4 Upper Adelaide Street, Helensburgh G84 7HT	01436 675152
Munro, David P. MA BD STM	1953 1996	(Bearsden: North)	14 Birch Road, Killearn, Glasgow G63 9SQ	01360 550098
Paul, Alison (Miss) MA BD Dip Theol	1986 2001	(Rhu and Shandon)	30 Perrays Drive, Lennox Gardens, Dumbarton G82 5HT	01389 733698
Rae, Scott M. MBE BD CPS	1976 2002	Chaplain: Royal Navy	HMS *Neptune*, Faslane, Helensburgh G84 8HL	
Spence, C.K.O. MC TD MA BD	1949 1983	(Craigrownie)	8B Cairndhu Gardens, Helensburgh G84 8PG	01436 678838
Steven, Harold A.M. LTh FSA Scot	1970 2001	(Baldernock)	9 Cairnhill Road, Bearsden, Glasgow G61 1AT	0141-942 1598
Wilson, Roy DA ARIBA ARIAS	1986 2002	Auxiliary Minister with Presbytery Clerk	20 William Ure Place, Bishopbriggs, Glasgow G64 3BH	0141-563 1829
Wright, Malcolm LTh	1970 2003	(Craigrownie with Rosneath St Modan's)	30 Clairinsh, Drumkinnon Gate, Balloch, Alexandria G83 8SE	01389 754844

DUMBARTON ADDRESSES

Clydebank
Abbotsford	Town Centre
Faifley	Faifley Road
Kilbowie St Andrew's	Kilbowie Road
Radnor Park	Radnor Street
St Cuthbert's	Linnvale

Dumbarton
Riverside	High Street
St Andrew's	off Bonhill Road
West Kirk	West Bridgend

Helensburgh
Park	Charlotte Street
St Columba	Sinclair Street
The West Kirk	Colquhoun Square

(19) SOUTH ARGYLL

Meets on first Wednesday of February (at Clachan), March (at Ardrishaig), June (island), November (at Clachan) and December (at Tarbert) and first Tuesday of May and September (at Tarbert).

Clerk: MR HUGH PATERSON   South Lodge, Whitehouse, Tarbert, Argyll PA29 6XR   01880 730221
[E-mail: akph73@uk.uumail.com]

Ardrishaig (H) linked with South Knapdale David Carruthers BD	1998		The Manse, Park Road, Ardrishaig, Lochgilphead PA30 8HD	01546 603269
Campbeltown: Highland (H) Michael J. Lind LLB BD	1984	1997	Highland Church Manse, Kirk Street, Campbeltown PA28 6BN [E-mail: mijalind@hotmail.com]	01586 551146
Campbeltown: Lorne and Lowland (H) Vacant			Castlehill, Campbeltown PA28 6AN	01586 552468
Craignish linked with Kilninver and Kilmelford Vacant	1985	1992	The Manse, Kilmelford, Oban PA34 4XA	01852 200373
Cumlodden, Lochfyneside and Lochgair Roderick MacLeod MA BD PhD(Edin) PhD(Open)	1966	1985	Cumlodden Manse, Furnace, Inveraray PA32 8XU [E-mail: revroddy@yahoo.co.uk]	01499 500288
Gigha and Cara (H) (GD) Rosemary Legge (Mrs) BSc BD MTh	1992	2002	The Manse, Isle of Gigha PA41 7AA	01583 505245
Glassary and Kilmartin and Ford Vacant			The Manse, Kilmichael Glassary, Lochgilphead PA31 8QA	01546 606926
Glenaray and Inveraray W. Brian Wilkinson MA BD	1968	1993	The Manse, Inveraray PA32 8XT [E-mail: brianwilkinson@freeuk.com]	01499 302060
Jura (GD) [Dwin Capstick]	1999		Church of Scotland Manse, Craighouse, Isle of Jura PA60 7XG	01496 820384
Kilarrow (H) linked with Kilmeny Vacant			The Manse, Bowmore, Isle of Islay PA43 7LH	01496 810271
Kilberry linked with Tarbert (H) William Gray LTh	1971	2003	Glenakil Cottage, Tarbert, Argyll PA29 6XX [E-mail: gray98@hotmail.com]	01880 820156
Kilcalmonell linked with Skipness Vacant			The Manse, Whitehouse, Tarbert, Argyll PA29 6XS	01880 730224
Kilchoman (GD) linked with Portnahaven (GD) Vacant			Main Street, Port Charlotte, Isle of Islay PA48 7TX	01496 850241

Kildalton and Oa (GD) (H)
Norman MacLeod BTh — 1999 — Port Ellen, Isle of Islay PA42 7DB — 01496 302447

Killean and Kilchenzie (H)
John H. Paton JP BSc BD — 1983 1984 — The Manse, Muasdale, Tarbert, Argyll PA29 6XD [E-mail: jonymar@globalnet.co.uk] — 01583 421249

Kilmeny See Kilarrow
Kilninver and Kilmelford See Craignish

Lochgilphead
Alastair H. Gray MA BD — 1978 1996 — Parish Church Manse, Manse Brae, Lochgilphead PA31 8QZ [E-mail: a.gray1@tinyworld.co.uk] — 01546 602238

North Knapdale
Vacant — Church of Scotland Manse, Tayvallich, Lochgilphead PA31 8PN — 01546 870611

Portnahaven See Kilchoman

Saddell and Carradale (H)
Alistair J. Dunlop MA FSAScot — 1965 1979 — The Manse, Carradale, Campbeltown PA28 6QN [E-mail: alistair.dunlop@ntlworld.com] — 01583 431253

Skipness See Kilcalmonell

Southend (H)
Martin R. Forrest BA MA BD — 1988 2001 — St Blaans Manse, Southend, Campbeltown PA28 6RQ — 01586 830274

South Knapdale See Ardrishaig
Tarbert See Kilberry

Bristow, W.H.G. BEd HDipRE DipSpecEd	1951 2002	Part-time Hospital Chaplain: Campbeltown	Laith Cottage, Southend, Campbeltown PA28 6RU	01586 830667
Campbell, Margaret M. (Miss) DCS	1948 1991	(Deaconess)	Tigh-an-Rudha, Pier Road, Port Ellen, Isle of Islay PA42 7DJ	01496 302006
Carmichael, Robert C.M. MA	1987 1998	(Craignish with Kilninver and Kilmelford)	13 The Glebe, Kilmelford, Oban PA34 4AF	01852 200346
Davidson, David W. (Aux)		Moderator's Chaplain	Grainail, Glenegedale, Port Ellen, Isle of Islay PA42 7AS	01496 302194
Forrest, Janice (Mrs) DCS		Part-time Hospital Chaplain: Campbeltown	St Blaans Manse, Southend, Campbeltown PA28 6RQ	01586 830274
Gibson, Frank S. BL BD STM DSWA DD	1963 1995	(Kilarrow with Kilmeny)	163 Gilbertstoun, Edinburgh EH15 2RG	0131-657 5208
Henderson, Charles M.	1952 1989	(Campbeltown Highland)	Springbank House, Askomill Walk, Campbeltown PA28 6EP	01586 552759
Hood, H. Stanley C. MA BD	1966 2000	(London: Crown Court)	10 Dalriada Place, Kilmichael Glassary, Lochgilphead PA31 8QA	01546 606168
Montgomery, David	1961 1996	(North Knapdale)	Flat 1, 99 Quarry Street, Hamilton ML3 7AG	01698 200029
Morrison, Angus W. MA BD	1959 1999	(Kildalton and Oa)	1 Livingstone Way, Port Ellen, Isle of Islay PA42 7EP	01496 300043

Ritchie, Malcolm A.	(Kilbrandon and Kilchattan)	1955 1990	Roadside Cottage, Tayvallich, Lochgilphead PA31 8PN	01546 8706 6
Ritchie, Walter M.	(Uphall: South)	1973 1999	8 The Walled Garden, Achnaba, Lochgilphead PA31 8UG	01546 602941
Stewart, Jean E. (Mrs)	(Kildalton and Oa)	1983 1989	Tigh-na-Truain, Port Ellen, Isle of Islay PA42 7AH	01496 302068

SOUTH ARGYLL Communion Sundays

Ardrishaig	4th Apr, 1st Nov	Invertussa and Bellanoch	2nd May, Nov
Campbeltown		Jura	Passion Sun., 2nd Jul, 3rd Nov
Highland	1st May, Nov	Kilarrow	1st Mar, Jun, Sep, Dec
Lorne and Lowland	1st May, Nov	Kilberry with Tarbert	1st May, Oct
Craignish	1st Jun, Nov	Kilcalmonell	1st Jul, 3rd Nov
Cumlodden, Lochfyneside		Kilchoman	1st Jul, 2nd Dec, Easter
and Lochgair	1st May, 3rd Nov	Kildalton	Last Jan, Jun, Oct, Easter
Gigha and Cara	1st May, Nov	Killean and Kilchenzie	1st Mar, Jul, Oct
Glassary, Kilmartin and Ford	1st Apr, Sep	Kilmeny	2nd May, 3rd Nov
Glenaray and Inveraray	1st Apr, Jul, Oct, Dec	Kilninver and Kilmelford	2nd Jun, Oct

Lochgair	2nd May, Nov
Lochgilphead	2nd Oct (Gaelic)
North Knapdale	1st Apr, Nov
Portnahaven	3rd Oct, 2nd May
Saddell and Carradale	3rd Jul
Skipness	2nd May, 1st Nov
Southend	2nd May, Nov
South Knapdale	1st Jun, Dec
Tayvallich	4th Apr, 1st Nov
	2nd May, Nov

(20) DUNOON

Meets at Dunoon St John's, on the first Tuesday of February, April, June and November; at Rothesay Trinity on the first Tuesday of March, October and December; and at the Moderator's Church on the first Tuesday of September.

Clerk:	**REV. RONALD SAMUEL, TD BSc BD STM**	**9 Bishop Terrace, Rothesay, Isle of Bute PA20 9HF**	**01700 504378 (Tel/Fax)**
		[E-mail: akph48@uk.uumail.com]	

Bute United

Iain M. Goring BSc BD	1976	2003	10 Bishop Terrace, Rothesay, Isle of Bute PA20 9HF	01700 502407
			[E-mail: iain.goring@ukonline.co.uk]	

Dunoon: St John's linked with Sandbank (H)

Joseph Stewart LTh	1979	1989	23 Bullwood Road, Dunoon PA23 7QJ	01369 702128

Dunoon: The High Kirk (H)

I. Pat Lang (Miss) BSc	1996		1 Royal Crescent, Dunoon PA23 7AH	01369 701291
			[E-mail: patlang@tinyworld.co.uk]	

Innellan (H) linked with Toward (H)
David P. Anderson BSc BD — 2002 — 7A Matheson Lane, Innellan, Dunoon PA23 7SH — [E-mail: davidshar.anderson@ntlworld.com] — 01369 830276

Kilfinan linked with Kyles (H)
David J. Kellas MA BD — 1966 1998 — The Manse, Tighnabruaich PA21 2DX — [E-mail: davidkellas@britishlibrary.net] — 01700 811887 (Tel/Fax)

Kilmodan and Colintraive
Robert M. Donald BA — 1969 1998 — Kilmodan Manse, Glendaruel, Colintraive PA22 3AA — [E-mail: robdon@colglen.freeserve.co.uk] — 01369 820232 (Tel/Fax)

Kilmun (St Munn's) (H) linked with Strone (H) and Ardentinny
Evelyn M. Young (Mrs) (H) BSc BD — 1984 1997 — Blairmore, Dunoon PA23 8TE — 01369 840313

Kirn (H)
Vacant — Stewart Street, Kirn, Dunoon PA23 8DS — 01369 702220

Kyles See Kilfinan

Lochgoilhead (H) and Kilmorich
James Macfarlane PhD — 1991 2000 — The Manse, Lochgoilhead, Cairndow PA24 8AA — [E-mail: macfarlane-cofs@beeb.net] — 01301 703059

Rothesay: Trinity (H)
Vacant — 12 Crichton Road, Rothesay, Isle of Bute PA20 9JR — 01700 502797

Sandbank See Dunoon: St John's

Strachur and Strathlachlan
Robert K. Mackenzie MA BD PhD — 1976 1998 — The Manse, Strachur, Cairndow PA27 8DG — [E-mail: rkmackenzie@strachurmanse.fsnet.co.uk] — 01369 860246

Strone and Ardentinny See Kilmun
Toward (H) See Innellan

Cumming, David P.L. MA	1957 1997	(Kilmodan and Colintraive)	Shillong, Tarbat Ness Road, Portmahomack, Tain IV20 1YA	01862 871794
Erskine, Austin U.	1986 2001	(Anwoth and Girthon with Borgue)	99 Sandhaven, Sandbank, Dunoon PA23 8QW [E-mail: austin@erskine81.freeserve.co.uk]	01369 701295
Fenemore, John H.C.	1980 1993	(Edinburgh Colinton Mains)	Seaford Cottage, 74E Shore Road, Innellan, Dunoon PA23 7TR	01369 830678
Forrest, Alan B. MA	1956 1993	(Uphall: South)	126 Shore Road, Innellan, Dunoon PA23 7SX	01369 830424

Gisbey, John E. MA BD MSc	1964 2002 (Thornhill)	Kames Haven, Chapel Lane, Isle of Bute PA20 0LQ	01700 503346
Hamilton, Patrick J.R. MA	1948 1979 (East Kilbride South)	La Madrugada, Tighnabruaich PA21 2BE	01700 811536
Inglis, Donald B.C. MA MEd BD	1975 2000 (Turriff St Andrew's)	'Lindores', 11 Bullwood Road, Dunoon PA23 7QJ [E-mail: dbcinglis@aol.com]	01369 701334
Mackenzie, Iain MA BD	1967 2000 (Tarbat)	3 Southern Beeches, Sandbank, Dunoon PA23 8PD [E-mail: iandg@imackenzie.fsnet.co.uk]	01369 703537
Marshall, James S. BA BD FFA MDiv	1986 1989 (Lochgoilhead and Kilmorich)	12 Manse Gardens, Strachur, Cairndow PA27 8DS	01369 860544
Miller, Harry Galbraith MA BD	1941 1985 (Iona and Ross of Mull)	16 Lobnitz Avenue, Renfrew PA4 0TG	0141-886 2147
Samuel, Ronald TD BSc BD STM	1960 2000 (Rothesay Trinity)	9 Bishop Terrace, Rothesay, Isle of Bute PA20 9HF [E-mail: ronald.samuel@ukgateway.net]	(Tel/Fax) 01700 504378
Stewart, Donald MA	1944 1984 (Fenwick)	Seafield, Toward, Dunoon PA23 7UG	01369 870206
Watson, James LTh	1968 1994 (Bowden with Lilliesleaf)	7 Lochan Avenue, Kirn, Dunoon PA23 8HT	01369 702851

DUNOON Communion Sundays

Bute United	1st Feb, May, Nov	Kilmodan and Colintraive	1st Apr, Sep
Dunoon		Kilmun	Last Jun, Nov
St John's	1st Mar, Jun, Nov	Kirn	Last Feb, Jun, Oct
The High Kirk	1st Feb, Jun, Oct	Kyles	1st May, Nov
Innellan	1st Mar, Jun, Sep, Dec	Lochgoilhead and Kilmorich	Last Apr, Oct
Kilfinan	Last Apr, Oct		2nd Mar, Jun, Sep, Nov
			1st Aug, Easter
Rothesay Trinity	1st Feb, May, Nov		
Sandbank	1st Jan, May, Nov		
Strachur and Strathlachlan	1st Mar, Jun, Nov		
Strone and Ardentinny	Last Feb, Jun, Oct		
Toward	Last Feb, May, Aug, Nov		

(21) LORN AND MULL

Meets at Oban, in the Church of Scotland Centre, Glencruitten Road, on the first Wednesday of February and December, and on the first Tuesday of June and October.

Clerk: REV. JEFFREY A. McCORMICK BD   The Manse, Ardchattan, Oban PA37 1QZ   **01631 710364**
[E-mail: akph64@uk.uumail.com]

Appin linked with Lismore
John A.H. Murdoch BA BD DPSS   1979 2001   The Manse, Appin PA38 4DD   01631 730206

Ardchattan (H)
Jeffrey A. McCormick BD   1984   Ardchattan Manse, Ardchattan, Oban PA37 1RG   01631 710364

Coll linked with Connel				
George G. Cringles BD	1981	2002	St Oran's Manse, Connel, Oban PA37 1PJ	01631 710242
Colonsay and Oronsay linked with Kilbrandon and Kilchattan				
Freda Marshall (Mrs) BD FCII	1993	1997	The Manse, Winterton Road, Balvicar, Oban PA34 4TF [E-mail: f.marshall@ukonline.co.uk]	01852 300240
Connel See Coll				
Glenorchy and Innishael linked with Strathfillan				
John Shedden CBE BD DipPSS	1971	2001	The Manse, Dalmally PA33 1AA [E-mail: john@scottishweddingsonline.com]	01838 200386
Iona linked with Kilfinichen and Kilvickeon and the Ross of Mull				
Vacant			The Manse, Bunessan, Isle of Mull PA67 6DW	01681 700227
Kilbrandon and Kilchattan See Colonsay and Oronsay				
Kilchrenan and Dalavich linked with Muckairn				
Margaret R.M. Millar (Miss) BTh	1977	1996	Muckairn Manse, Taynuilt PA35 1HW [E-mail: macoje@aol.com]	01866 822204
Kilfinichen and Kilvickeon and the Ross of Mull See Iona				
Kilmore (GD) and Oban				
Andrew B. Campbell BD DPS MTh	1979		Kilmore and Oban Manse, Ganavan Road, Oban PA34 5TU [E-mail: revabc@obancofs.freeserve.co.uk]	01631 562322
Lismore See Appin				
Muckairn See Kilchrenan				
Mull, Isle of, Kilninian and Kilmore linked with Salen (H) and Ulva linked with Tobermory (GD) (H) linked with Torosay (H) and Kinlochspelvie				
Alan T. Taylor BD		1980	Erray Road, Tobermory, Isle of Mull PA75 6PS	01688 302226 / 01688 302037 (Fax)
Robert C. Nelson BA BD (Assoc)	1980	2003	Trewince, Western Road, Strongarbh, Tobermory, Isle of Mull PA75 6RA	01688 302356
Salen and Ulva See Mull				
Strathfillan See Glenorchy				
Tiree (GD)				
Vacant			The Manse, Scarinish, Isle of Tiree PA77 6TN	01879 220377

Tobermory See Mull
Torosay and Kinlochspelvie See Mull

Grainger, Ian G.	1985	1991	(Maxton with Newtown)	Seaview, Ardtun, Bunessan, Isle of Mull PA67 6DH	01681 700457
Lamont, Archibald	1952	1994	(Kilcalmonell with Skipness)	8 Achlonan, Taynuilt PA35 1JJ	01866 822385
MacKechnie, J.M. MBE MA	1938	1978	(Kilchrenan and Dalavich)	Eastwing, Manton Grounds, Windermere, Cumbria	
Pollock, William MA BD PhD	1987	2002	(Isle of Mull Parishes)	Correay, Salen, Aros, Isle of Mull PA72 6JF	01680 300507
				[E-mail: wpollock@salen.freeserve.co.uk]	
Spencer, John MA BD	1962	2001	(Dumfries: Lincluden with Holywood)	Rhugarbh Cottage, North Shian, Appin PA38 4BA	01631 730416
Troup, Harold J.G. MA	1951	1980	(Garelochhead)	Tighshee, Isle of Iona PA76 6SP	01681 700309

(22) FALKIRK

Meets at St Andrew's West, Falkirk, on the first Tuesday of September, October, November, December and March, and on the fourth Tuesday of January and June; and in Kildrum Church, Cumbernauld on the first Tuesday in May.

Clerk: REV. IAN W. BLACK MA BD
Zetland Manse, Ronaldshay Crescent, Grangemouth FK3 9JH
[E-mail: akph51@uk.uumail.com]
01324 472868
01324 471656 (Presby)

Depute Clerk: REV. ROBERT S.T. ALLAN LLB DipLP BD
9 Major's Loan, Falkirk FK1 5QF
01324 625124

Treasurer: MR. I. MACDONALD
1 Jones Avenue, Larbert FK5 3ER
01324 553603

Airth (H)
Richard J. Hammond BA BD   1993   2002   The Manse, Airth, Falkirk FK2 8LS   01324 831474

Blackbraes and Shieldhill
James H.D.C. Drysdale LTh   1987   1997   Shieldhill, Falkirk FK1 2EG   01324 621938
[E-mail: jmdrysdl1@aol.com]

Bo'ness: Old (H)
Vacant   10 Dundas Street, Bo'ness EH51 0DG   01506 822206

Bo'ness: St Andrew's
Albert O. Bogle BD MTh   1981   St Andrew's Manse, 11 Erngath Road, Bo'ness EH51 9DP   01506 822195
[E-mail: a.bogle@blueyonder.co.uk]
[Website: http://www.standonline.org.uk]

Bonnybridge: St Helen's (H) (01324 815756)
Alisdair T. MacLeod-Mair MEd DipTheol — 2002 — 133 Falkirk Road, Bonnybridge FK4 1BA — 01324 812621 (Tel/Fax)

Bothkennar and Carronshore
Patricia A. Carruth (Mrs) BD — 1998 — 11 Hunter Place, Greenmount Park, Carronshore, Falkirk FK2 8QS — 01324 570525

Brightons (H)
Scott R.McL. Kirkland BD MAR — 1996 — The Manse, Maddiston Road, Brightons, Falkirk FK2 0JP [E-mail: scott@kirklands.net] — 01324 712062 / 01324 713855 (2nd num)

Carriden (H)
R. Gordon Reid BSc BD AMIEE — 1993 — The Spires, Foredale Terrace, Carriden, Bo'ness EH51 9LW — 01506 822141

Cumbernauld: Abronhill (H)
Vacant
Marilyn Douglas (Miss) DCS — 26 Ash Road, Cumbernauld, Glasgow G67 3ED / 201 Almond Road, Cumbernauld, Glasgow G67 3LS — 01236 723833 / 01236 732136

Cumbernauld: Condorrat (H)
Vacant
Janette McNaughton (Miss) DCS — 11 Rosehill Drive, Cumbernauld, Glasgow G67 4FD / 4 Dunellan Avenue, Moodiesburn, Glasgow G69 0GB — 01236 721464 / 01236 870180

Cumbernauld: Kildrum (H)
Vacant
David Nicholson DCS — Clouden Road, Cumbernauld, Glasgow G67 2JQ / 2D Doon Side, Kildrum, Cumbernauld, Glasgow G67 2HX [E-mail: deacdave@btopenworld.com] — 01236 723204 / 01236 732260

Cumbernauld: Old (H)
Catriona Ogilvie (Mrs) MA BD — 1999 — Baronhill, Cumbernauld, Glasgow G67 2SD — 01236 721912

Cumbernauld: St Mungo's
Neil MacKinnon BD — 1990 1999 — The Manse, Fergusson Road, Cumbernauld, Glasgow G67 1LS [E-mail: neil@box200.fsnet.co.uk] — 01236 721513

Denny: Dunipace (H)
Jean W. Gallacher (Miss) BD CMin CTheol — 1989 — Dunipace Manse, Denny FK6 6QJ — 01324 824540

Denny: Old
John Murning BD — 1988 — 31 Duke Street, Denny FK6 6NR — 01324 824508

Denny: Westpark (H)
Andrew Barrie BSc BD — 1984 — 13 Baxter Crescent, Denny FK6 5EZ [E-mail: andrew.barrie@blueyonder.co.uk] [Website: http://www.westparkchurch.org.uk] — 01324 876224

Falkirk: Bainsford
Michael R. Philip BD — 1978 — 2001 — 1 Valleyview Place, Newcarron Village, Falkirk FK2 7JB [E-mail: mrphilip@btinternet.com] — 01324 621087

Falkirk: Camelon Irving (H)
Vacant — 8 Macintosh Place, Falkirk FK1 5UL — 01324 623035

Falkirk: Camelon St John's
Stuart Sharp MTheol DipPA — 2001 — 24 Rennie Street, Falkirk FK1 5QW — 01324 623631
Margaret Corrie (Miss) DCS — 44 Sunnyside Street, Falkirk FK1 4BH — 01324 670656

Falkirk: Erskine (H)
Glen D. Macaulay BD — 1999 — Burnbrae Road, Falkirk FK1 5SD — 01324 623701

Falkirk: Grahamston United (H)
Neil W. Barclay BSc BEd BD — 1986 — 2001 — 30 Russel Street, Falkirk FK2 7HS — 01324 624461

Falkirk: Laurieston linked with Redding and Westquarter
Geoffrey H. Smart LTh — 1994 — 2002 — 11 Polmont Road, Laurieston, Falkirk FK2 9QQ — 01324 621196

Falkirk: Old and St Modan's (H)
Robert S.T. Allan LLB DipLP BD — 1991 — 9 Major's Loan, Falkirk FK1 5QF — 01324 625124
Ronald W. Smith BA BEd BD (Assoc) — 1979 — 19 Neilson Street, Falkirk FK1 5AQ — 01324 621058

Falkirk: St Andrew's West (H)
Alastair M. Horne BSc BD — 1989 — 1997 — 1 Maggiewood's Loan, Falkirk FK1 5SJ — 01324 623308

Falkirk: St James'
Eric G. McKimmon BA BD MTh — 1983 — 1992 — 13 Wallace Place, Falkirk FK2 7EN — 01324 622757

Grangemouth: Dundas
Douglas B. Blair LTh — 1969 — 5 Abbotsgrange Road, Grangemouth FK3 9JD — 01324 482467

Grangemouth: Kerse (H) (01324 482487)
Andrew C. Donald BD DPS — 1992 — 8 Naismith Court, Grangemouth FK3 9BQ — 01324 482109

Grangemouth: Kirk of the Holy Rood
Vacant — Bowhouse Road, Grangemouth FK3 0EX — 01324 471595
Colin Mailer (Aux) — 1996 — 2003 — Innis Chonain, Back Row, Polmont, Falkirk FK2 0RD — 01324 712401

Grangemouth: Zetland (H)
Ian W. Black MA BD — 1976 — 1991 — Ronaldshay Crescent, Grangemouth FK3 9JH — 01324 472868

Haggs (H)

Helen F. Christie (Mrs) BD	1998	2001	5 Watson Place, Dennyloanhead, Bonnybridge FK4 2BG	01324 813786
David Wandrum (Aux)	1993		5 Cawder View, Carrickstone Meadows, Cumbernauld, Glasgow G68 0BN	01236 723288

Larbert: East

Melville D. Crosthwaite BD DipEd DipMin	1984	1995	1 Cortachy Avenue, Carron, Falkirk FK2 8DH	01324 562402

Larbert: Old (H)

Clifford A.J. Rennie MA BD	1973	1985	The Manse, 38 South Broomage Avenue, Larbert FK5 3ED	01324 562868

Larbert: West (H)

Gavin Boswell BTheol	1993	1999	11 Carronvale Road, Larbert FK5 3LZ	01324 562878

Muiravonside

Joan Ross (Miss) BSc BD PhD	1999		The Manse, South Brae, Main Road, Maddiston, Falkirk FK2 0LX	01324 712876

Polmont: Old

Vacant			The Manse, Main Street, Polmont, Falkirk FK2 0QY	01324 713081

Redding and Westquarter See Falkirk: Laurieston

Slamannan

Raymond Thomson BD DipMin	1992		Slamannan, Falkirk FK1 3EN	01324 851307

Stenhouse and Carron (H)

Robert K. Hardie MA BD	1968	1969	Stenhouse Church Manse, Church Street, Stenhousemuir, Larbert FK5 4BU	01324 562393

Name			(Previous charge)	Address	Tel
Brown, James BA BD DipHSW DipPsychol	1973	2001	(Abercorn with Dalmeny)	Fern Cottage, 3 Philpingstone Lane, Bo'ness EH51 9JP	01506 822454
Chalmers, George A. MA BD MLitt	1962	2002	(Catrine with Sorn)	3 Cricket Place, Brightons, Falkirk FK2 0HZ	01324 712030
Goodman, Richard A.	1976	1986	(Isle of Mull Associate)	13/2 Glenbrae Court, Falkirk FK1 1YT	01324 621315
Heriot, Charles R. JP BA	1962	1996	(Brightons)	20 Eastcroft Drive, Polmont, Falkirk FK2 0SU	01324 711352
Hill, Stanley LTh	1967	1998	(Muiravonside)	28 Creteil Court, Falkirk FK1 1UL	01324 634483
Holland, John C.	1976	1985	(Strone and Ardentinny)	7 Polmont Park, Polmont, Falkirk FK2 0XT	01324 880109
Kellock, Chris N. MA BD	1998		Chaplain: RAF	Chaplaincy Services, HQPTC, RAF Innsworth, Gloucester GL3 1EZ	
McCallum, John	1962	1998	(Falkirk: Irving Camelon)	11 Burnbrae Gardens, Falkirk FK1 5SB	01324 619766
McDonald, William G. MA BD	1959	1975	(Falkirk: Grahamston United)	38 St Mary Street, St Andrews KY16 8AZ	
McDowall, Ronald J. BD	1980	2001	(Falkirk: Laurieston with Redding and Westquarter)	'Kailas', Windsor Road, Falkirk FK1 5EJ	01324 871947
Maclaren, William B. MA JP	1944	1983	(Bothkennar and Carronshore)	7 Malcolm Drive, Stenhousemuir, Larbert FK5 4JP	01324 551274
MacLeod, Ian I.S. MA BD	1954	1991	(Arbroath: St Andrew's)	48 Wellside Court, 6 Wellside Place, Falkirk FK1 6RG	01324 610158
McMullin, Andrew MA	1960	1996	(Blackbraes and Shieldhill)	33 Eastcroft Drive, Polmont, Falkirk FK2 0SU	01324 624938

Martin, Neil DCS	(Deacon)	1982	2001	3 Strathmiglo Place, Stenhousemuir, Larbert FK5 4UQ	01324 551362
Mathers, Daniel L. BD	(Grangemouth: Charing Cross and West)	1955	1995	10 Ercall Road, Brightons, Falkirk FK2 0RS	01324 872253
Maxton, Ronald M. MA	(Dollar: Associate)			5 Rulley View, Denny FK6 6QQ	01324 8254-1
Miller, Elsie M. (Miss) DCS	(Deacon)			30 Swinton Avenue, Rowansbank, Baillieston, Glasgow G69 6JR	0141-771 0857
Munroe, Henry BA LTh LTl	(Denny Dunipace North with Old)	1971	1988	Viewforth, High Road, Maddiston, Falkirk FK2 0BL	01324 712446
Murray, Eric J.	(Larbert: East)	1958	1995	21 Redpath Drive, Greenmount Park, Carron, Falkirk FK5 8QL	01324 563764
Paul, Iain BSc PhD BD PhD	(Wishaw Craigneuk and Belhaven)	1976	1991	116 Tryst Road, Larbert FK5 4QJ	01324 5626-1
Scott, Donald H. BA BD	Prison Chaplain	1987	2002	Polmont Young Offenders' Institution, Newlands Road, Brightons, Falkirk FK2 0DE	01324 711558
Smith, Richard BD	(Denny Old)	1976	2002	Easter Wayside, 46 Kennedy Way, Airth, Falkirk FK2 8GB	01324 831386
Talman, Hugh MA	(Polmont Old)	1943	1987	Niagara, 70 Lawers Crescent, Polmont, Falkirk FK2 0RQ	01324 7112-0
Whiteford, Robert S. MA	(Shapinsay)	1945	1986	3 Wellside Court, Wellside Place, Falkirk FK1 5RG	01324 610562

FALKIRK ADDRESSES

Falkirk

Bainsford	Hendry Street, Bainsford
Camelon	Dorrator Road, Camelon
Irving	Glasgow Road x Stirling Road
Erskine	Cockburn Street x Hodge Street
Grahamston	Bute Street
Laurieston	Main Falkirk Road
Old and St Modan's	Kirk Wynd
St Andrew's West	Newmarket Street
St James'	Thornhill Road x Firs Street

Grangemouth

Charing Cross and West	Charing Cross
Dundas	Bo'ness Road
Kerse	Abbot's Road
Kirk of the Holy Rood	Bowhouse Road
Zetland	Ronaldshay Crescent

(23) STIRLING

Meets at the Moderator's Church on the second Thursday of September; and at Stirling Management Centre, Stirling University on the second Thursday of every other month except January, July and August when there is no meeting.

Clerk:	MOIRA G. MacCORMICK BA LTh	Presbytery Office, St Columba's Church, Park Terrace, Stirling FK8 2NA [E-mail: akph75@uk.uumail.com] [E-mail: stirling-presbytery@uk.uumail.com]	01786 449522 (Tel) 01786 473930 (Fax) (Mon–Fri: 9.30am–12 noon)
Depute Clerk:	MR ALASTAIR ROSS	Presbytery Office (as above)	
Treasurer:	MR GILMOUR CUTHBERTSON	'Denovan', 1 Doune Road, Dunblane FK15 9AR	01786 823487

Aberfoyle (H) linked with Port of Menteith (H)

James Daniel Gibb BA LTh	1994	2000	The Manse, Loch Ard Road, Aberfoyle, Stirling FK8 3SZ [E-mail: rev.danny@gibb.fsworld.co.uk]	01877 382391

Alloa: North (H)
Elizabeth Clelland (Mrs) BD — 2002 — 30 Claremont, Alloa FK10 2DF — 01259 210403

Alloa: St Mungo's (H)
Alan F:M. Downie MA BD — 1977 — 1996 — 37a Claremont, Alloa FK10 2DG
[E-mail: alan@stmungos.freeserve.co.uk] — 01259 213872

Alloa: West
Irene C. Gillespie (Mrs) BD — 1991 — 2001 — 29 Claremont, Alloa FK10 2DF — 01259 214204

Alva
James N.R. McNeil BSc BD — 1990 — 1997 — The Manse, 34 Ochil Road, Alva FK12 5JT — 01259 760262

Balfron linked with Fintry (H)
John Turnbull LTh — 1994 — 7 Station Road, Balfron, Glasgow G63 0SX — 01360 440285

Balquhidder linked with Killin and Ardeonaig (H)
John Lincoln MPhil BD — 1986 — 1997 — The Manse, Killin FK19 8TN
[E-mail: gm0jol@zetnet.co.uk] — 01567 820247

Bannockburn: Allan (H)
Jim Landels BD CertMin — 1990 — The Manse, Bogend Road, Bannockburn, Stirling FK7 8NP
[E-mail: revjimlandels@btinternet.com] — 01786 814692

Marina Brown (Mrs) MA (Aux) — 2000 — 3 Lover's Loan, Dollar FK14 7AB — 01259 742870

Bannockburn: Ladywell (H)
Elizabeth M.D. Robertson (Miss) BD CertMin — 1997 — 57 The Firs, Bannockburn FK7 0EG
[E-mail: lizr@tinyonline.uk] — 01786 812467

Bridge of Allan: Chalmers (H)
Vacant — 34 Kenilworth Road, Bridge of Allan, Stirling FK9 4EH — 01786 832118

Bridge of Allan: Holy Trinity (H) (01786 834155)
Vacant — 29 Keir Street, Bridge of Allan, Stirling FK9 4QJ — 01786 832093

Buchanan linked with Drymen
Alexander J. MacPherson BD — 1986 — 1997 — Buchanan Manse, Drymen, Glasgow G63 0AQ — 01360 870212

Buchlyvie (H) linked with Gartmore (H)
Vacant — 8 Culbowie Crescent, Buchlyvie, Stirling FK8 3NH — 01360 850249

Callander (H) (Tel/Fax: 01877 331409)
Vacant — 3 Aveland Park Road, Callander FK17 8FD — 01877 330097
June Cloggie (Mrs) (Aux) — 1997 — 1998 — 11A Tulipan Crescent, Callander FK17 8AR — 01877 331021

Cambusbarron: The Bruce Memorial (H) Brian G. Webster BSc BD	1998		14 Woodside Court, Cambusbarron, Stirling FK7 9PH [E-mail: revwebby@aol.com]	01786 450579
Clackmannan (H) J. Gordon Mathew MA BD	1973	1999	The Manse, Port Street, Clackmannan FK10 4JH [E-mail: jgmathew@lineone.net]	01259 211255
Cowie (H) linked with Plean Vacant			The Manse, Plean, Stirling FK7 8BX	01786 813287
Dollar (H) linked with Glendevon linked with Muckhart John P.S. Purves BSc BD	1978	1990	2 Manse Road, Dollar FK14 7AJ [E-mail: dollar.parish@btinternet.com]	01259 743432
Jean S. Watson (Miss) MA (Aux)	1993	1998	29 Strachan Crescent, Dollar FK14 7HL	01259 742872
Drymen See Buchanan				
Dunblane: Cathedral (H) Colin G. McIntosh BSc BD	1976	1988	Cathedral Manse, The Cross, Dunblane FK15 0AQ	01786 822205
Dunblane: St Blane's (H) Alexander B. Mitchell	1981	2003	49 Roman Way, Dunblane FK15 9DJ [E-mail: alex.mitchell6@btopenworld.com]	01786 822268
Alistair A.B. Cruickshank MA (Aux)	1991	2000	2A Chapel Place, Dollar FK14 7DW	01259 742549
Fallin Eleanor D. Muir (Miss) MTheol DipPTheol	1986		4 King Street, Fallin, Stirling FK7 7JY	01786 812243
Fintry See Balfron				
Gargunnock linked with Kilmadock linked with Kincardine in Menteith Richard S. Campbell LTh	1993	2001	The Manse, Gargunnock, Stirling FK8 3BQ	01786 860678
Gartmore See Buchlyvie **Glendevon** See Dollar				
Killearn (H) Philip R.M. Malloch LLB BD	1970	1993	2 The Oaks, Killearn, Glasgow G63 9SF [E-mail: pmalloch@killearnkirk.freeserve.co.uk]	01360 550045
Killin and Ardeonaig (H) See Balquhidder **Kilmadock** See Gargunnock				

Kincardine in Menteith See Gargunnock				
Kippen (H) linked with Norrieston Gordon MacRae BA BD	1985	1998	The Manse, Kippen, Stirling FK8 3DN	01786 870229
Lecropt (H) William M. Gilmour MA BD	1969	1983	5 Henderson Street, Bridge of Allan, Stirling FK9 4NA	01786 832382
Logie (H) Regine U. Cheyne (Mrs) MA BSc BD	1988	2000	128 Causewayhead Road, Stirling FK9 5HJ	01786 463060
Menstrie (H) George T. Sherry LTh	1977		The Manse, Menstrie FK11 7EA	01259 761461
Muckhart See Dollar **Norrieston** See Kippen **Plean** See Cowie **Port of Menteith** See Aberfoyle				
Sauchie and Coalsnaughton Alan T. McKean BD	1982	2003	19 Graygoran, Sauchie, Alloa FK10 3ET [E-mail: almack@freeuk.com]	01259 212037
Stirling: Allan Park South (H) linked with Church of the Holy Rude (H) Morris C. Coull BD	1974	1996	22 Laurelhill Place, Stirling FK8 2JH	01786 473999
Stirling: Church of the Holy Rude (H) See Stirling: Allan Park South				
Stirling: North (H) Paul M.N. Sewell MA BD	1970	1978	18 Shirra's Brae Road, Stirling FK7 0BA	01786 475378
Stirling: St Columba's (H) (01786 449516) Kenneth G. Russell BD CCE	1986	2001	5 Clifford Road, Stirling FK8 2AQ [E-mail: kenrussell1000@hotmail.com]	01786 475802
Stirling: St Mark's Rodney P.T. Robb	1995		176 Drip Road, Stirling FK8 1RR	01786 473716
Stirling: St Ninian's Old (H) Gary J. McIntyre BD DipMin	1993	1998	7 Randolph Road, Stirling FK8 2AJ	01786 474421
Stirling: Viewfield (T)(H) Ian Taylor BD ThM	1995		7 Windsor Place, Stirling FK8 2HY [E-mail: taylorian@btinternet.com]	01786 474534

Strathblane (H)

Alex H. Green MA BD	1986	1995	The Manse, Strathblane, Glasgow G63 9AQ	01360 770226

Tillicoultry (H)

James Cochrane LTh	1994	2000	The Manse, Dollar Road, Tillicoultry FK13 6PD [E-mail: jc@cochranemail.co.uk]	01259 750340 / 01259 752951 (Fax)

Tullibody St Serf's (H)

John Brown MA BD	1995	2000	16 Menstrie Road, Tullibody, Alloa FK10 2RG [E-mail: john@browntj.fsnet.co.uk]	01259 213236

Aitken, E. Douglas MA	1961	1998	(Clackmannan)	1 Dolan Grove, Saline, Dunfermline KY12 9UP	01383 852730
Benson, James W. BA BD DipEd	1975	1996	(Balquhidder)	1 Sunnyside, Dunblane FK15 9HA	01786 822624
Blackley, Jean R.M. (Mrs) BD	1989	2001	(Banton with Twechar)	8 Rodders Grove, Alva, Clackmannan FK12 5RR	01259 760198
Burnett, John B.	1964	1985	(Dollar: Associate)	30 Manor House Road, Dollar FK14 7HB	01259 742892
Cheyne, Magnus	1963	1996	(Community Minister: Shetland)	128 Causewayhead Road, Stirling FK9 5HJ	01786 463050
Craig, Maxwell D. BD ThM	1966	2000	(Jerusalem: St Andrew's: Locum)	3 Queen's Road, Stirling FK8 2QY	01786 472319
Doherty, Arthur James DipTh	1957	1993	(Fintry)	1 Murdiston Avenue, Callander FK17 8AY	
Fleming, Alexander F. MA BD	1966	1995	(Strathblane)	4 Horsburgh Avenue, Kilsyth, Glasgow G65 9BZ	01236 821461
Gallan, Alex MA	1955	1989	(Wishaw Cambusnethan North)	16 Dundas Road, Stirling FK9 5QQ	01786 470796
Izett, William A.F.	1968	2000	(Law)	1 Duke Street, Clackmannan FK10 4EF	01259 724203
Jamieson, G.T. BA	1936	1969	(Stirling: Viewfield)	10 Grendon Court, Snowdon Place, Stirling FK8 2JX	01786 461646
Jamieson, John LTh	1967	1993	(Balfron)	Ardnablane, Dunblane FK15 0QR	01786 823610
MacCormick, Moira G. BA LTh	1986	2003	(Buchlyvie with Gartmore)	12 Rankine Wynd, Tullibody, Alloa FK10 2UW	01259 724619
Paterson, John L. MA BD STM	1964	2003	(Linlithgow: St Michael's)	'Kirkmichael', 22 Waterfront Way, Stirling FK9 5GH [E-mail: lomandian.paterson@virgin.net]	
McIntosh, Hamish N.M. MA	1949	1987	(Fintry)	1 Forth Crescent, Stirling FK8 1LE	01786 470-53
MacRae, Elaine H. (Mrs) BD	1985	1998	Prison Chaplain	The Manse, Kippen, Stirling FK8 3DN	01786 870229
McRae, Malcolm H. MA PhD	1986	1994	(Coalsnaughton)	10B Victoria Place, Stirling FK8 2QU	
Nicol, John C. MA BD	1965	2002	(Bridge of Allan: Holy Trinity)	37 King O'Muirs Drive, Tullibody, Alloa FK10 3AY	01259 212505
Orrock, Archibald A. MA BD	1938	1982	(Teacher: Religious Instruction)	3 Kilbryde Court, Dunblane FK15 9AX	01786 822821
Ovens, Samuel B. BD	1982	1993	(Slamannan)	17 Swinburne Drive, Sauchie, Alloa FK10 3EQ	01259 222723
Pryce, Stuart F.A.	1963	1997	(Dumfries: St George's)	36 Forth Park, Bridge of Allan, Stirling FK9 5NT	01786 831026
Reid, Alan A.S. MA BD STM	1962	1995	(Bridge of Allan: Chalmers)	Wayside Cottage, Bridgend, Ceres, Cupar KY15 5LS	01334 828509
Reid, David T. BA BD	1954	1993	(Cleish linked with Fossoway St Serf's and Devonside)		
Rennie, James B. MA	1959	1992	(Leochel Cushnie and Lynturk with Tough)	14 Argyle Park, Dunblane FK15 9DZ	01786 824563
Robertson, Alex	1974	1993	(Baldernock)	4 Moray Park, Moray Street, Doune FK16 6DJ	01786 841894
Sangster, Ernest G. BD ThM	1958	1997	(Alva)	6 Law Hill Road, Dollar FK14 7BG	
Scott, James F.	1957	1997	(Dyce)	5 Gullipen View, Callander FK17 8HN	01877 330565

Scoular, J. Marshall	1954	1996	(Kippen)	2H Buccleuch Court, Dunblane FK15 0AH	01786 825976
Silcox, John R. BD	1976	1984	School Chaplain	Queen Victoria School, Dunblane FK15 0JA	01786 824944
Stewart, Angus T. MA BD PhD	1962	1999	(Glasgow: Greenbank)	Mansefield, Station Road, Buchlyvie, Stirling FK8 3NE	01360 850117
Symington, Robert C. BA	1954	1997	(Community Minister: Lorn and Mull)	3 Belmont, The Crescent, Dunblane FK15 0DW	01786 823902
Todd, A. Stewart MA BD DD	1952	1993	(Aberdeen: St Machar's Cathedral)	Ferntoun House, 11 Bedford Place, Alloa FK10 1LJ	01259 212737
Watt, Robert MA BD	1943	1982	(Aberdeen: Woodside South)	1 Coldstream Avenue, Dunblane FK15 9JN	01786 823632
Wright, John P. BD	1977	2000	(Glasgow: New Govan)	Plane Castle, Airth, Falkirk FK2 8SF	01786 480840

STIRLING ADDRESSES

Allan Park South	Dumbarton Road	St Ninian's	St Ninian's	Kirk Wynd. St Ninians	St Columba's	Park Terrace
Holy Rude	St John Street	Old		Barnton Street	St Mark's	Drip Road
North	Springfield Road	Viewfield				

(24) DUNFERMLINE

Meets at Dunfermline, in the Abbey Church Hall, Abbey Park Place on the first Thursday of each month, except January, July and August when there is no meeting, and June when it meets on the last Thursday.

Clerk: REV. WILLIAM E. FARQUHAR BA BD   161 Main Street, Townhill, Dunfermline KY12 0EZ   **01383 723835**
[E-mail: akph46@uk.uumail.com]

Aberdour St Fillan's (H)
Vacant   36 Bellhouse Road, Aberdour, Fife KY3 0TL   01383 860349

Ballingry and Lochcraig See Lochgelly: Macainsh: Team Ministry

Beath and Cowdenbeath North (H)
David W. Redmayne BSc BD   2001   10 Stuart Place, Cowdenbeath KY4 9BN   01383 511033
[E-mail: david@redmayne.freeserve.co.uk]

Cairneyhill (H) (01383 882352) linked with Limekilns (H) (01383 873337)
Norman M. Grant BD   1990   Limekilns, Dunfermline KY11 3HT   01383 872341
[E-mail: norman.grant@which.net]

Carnock and Oakley (H)
Elizabeth S.S. Kenny (Miss) BD RGN SCM   1989   Carnock, Dunfermline KY12 9JG   01383 850327
[E-mail: esskenny@ecosse.net]

Cowdenbeath: Trinity (H)
David G. Adams BD 1991 1999 66 Barclay Street, Cowdenbeath KY4 9LD 01383 515089
[E-mail: adams@cowden69.freeserve.co.uk]

Culross and Torryburn (H)
Thomas Moffat BSc BD 1976 2000 Culross, Dunfermline KY12 8JD 01383 880231
[E-mail: tsmoffat@fish.co.uk]

Dalgety (H) (01383 824092; E-mail: office@dalgety-church.co.uk)
Donald G.B. McCorkindale BD DipMin 1992 2000 9 St Colme Drive, Dalgety Bay, Dunfermline KY11 9LQ 01383 822316 (Tel/Fax)
[E-mail: donald@dalgety-church.co.uk]
[Website: http://www.dalgety-church.co.uk]

Dunfermline: Abbey (H)
Alistair L. Jessamine MA BD 1979 1991 12 Garvock Hill, Dunfermline KY12 7UU 01383 721022
[Website: http://www.dunfabbey.freeserve.co.uk]

Dunfermline: Gillespie Memorial (H) (01383 621253; E-mail: gillespie.church@btopenworld.com)
A. Gordon Reid BSc BD 1982 1988 4 Killin Court, Dunfermline KY12 7XF 01383 723329
[E-mail: reid501@fsmail.net]

Dunfermline: North
Gordon F.C. Jenkins MA BD PhD 1968 1998 13 Barbour Grove, Dunfermline KY12 9YB 01383 721061

Dunfermline: St Andrew's Erskine
Ann Allison BSc PhD BD 2000 71A Townhill Road, Dunfermline KY12 0BN 01383 734657
[E-mail: ann.allison@lineone.net]

Dunfermline: St Leonard's (01383 620106)
Vacant 12 Torvean Place, Dunfermline KY11 4YY 01383 721054
Andrew E. Paterson (Aux) 1994 6 The Willows, Kelty KY4 0FG 01383 830998
[E-mail: andrew@andrewepaterson.freeserve.co.uk]

Dunfermline: St Margaret's
Fiona Nicolson BA BD 1996 38 Garvock Hill, Dunfermline KY12 7UU 01383 723955

Dunfermline: St Ninian's
Elizabeth A. Fisk (Mrs) BD 1996 51 St John's Drive, Dunfermline KY12 7TL 01383 722256

Dunfermline: Townhill and Kingseat (H)
William E. Farquhar BA BD 1987 161 Main Street, Townhill, Dunfermline KY12 0EZ 01383 723835
[E-mail: akph46@uk.uumail.com]

Inverkeithing: St John's linked with North Queensferry (T)
Vacant · 34 Hill Street, Inverkeithing KY11 1AB · 01383 412422

Inverkeithing: St Peter's (01383 412626)
George G. Nicol BD DPhil · 1982 · 1988 · 20 Struan Drive, Inverkeithing KY11 1AR · 01383 410032
[E-mail: ggnicol@totalise.co.uk]

Kelty (Website: www.keltykirk.org.uk)
Scott Burton BD DipMin · 1999 · 15 Arlick Road, Kelty KY4 0BH · 01383 830291
[E-mail: sburton@supanet.com]

Limekilns See Cairneyhill

Lochgelly: Macainsh: Team Ministry
Irene A. Bristow (Mrs) BD (Team Leader) · 1989 · 2002 · 82 Main Street, Lochgelly KY5 9AA · 01592 780435
[E-mail: ibristow@btinternet.com]
Gareth W. Davies BA BD · 1979 · 2003 · Station Road, Lochgelly KY5 9QX · 01592 780319

Lochgelly: St Andrew's (T) (H) See Lochgelly: Macainsh: Team Ministry

North Queensferry See Inverkeithing: St John's

Rosyth
Violet C.C. McKay (Mrs) BD · 1988 · 2002 · 42 Woodside Avenue, Rosyth KY11 2LA · 01383 412776
[E-mail: v.mckay@btinternet.com]
Morag Crawford (Miss) DCS · 118 Wester Drylaw Place, Edinburgh EH4 2TG · 0131-332 2253
[E-mail: morag.crawford@virgin.net]

Saline and Blairingone
Robert P. Boyle LTh · 1990 · 2003 · 8 Dolan Grove, Saline, Dunfermline KY12 9UP · 01383 853062

Tulliallan and Kincardine
Jock Stein MA BD · 1973 · 2002 · 62 Toll Road, Kincardine, Alloa FK10 4QZ · 01259 730538
[E-mail: handsel@dial.pipex.com]
Margaret E. Stein (Mrs) DA BD DipRE · 1984 · 2002 · 62 Toll Road, Kincardine, Alloa FK10 4QZ · 01259 730538
[E-mail: handsel@dial.pipex.com]

Britchfield, Alison E.P. (Mrs) MA BD	1986	1992	Chaplain RN	13 Tregoning Road, Torpoint, Cornwall PL11 2LX	01752 818430
Brown, Peter MA BD FRAScot	1953	1987	(Holm)	24 Inchmickery Avenue, Dalgety Bay, Dunfermline KY11 5NF	01383 822456
Campbell, John MA	1943	1978	(Urquhart)	15 Foulden Place, Dunfermline KY12 7TQ	01383 738055
Mackenzie, R.P. MA BD	1936	1980	(Dunfermline: St Leonard's)	23 Foulis Crescent, Juniper Green, Edinburgh EH14 5BN	0131-453 3599
Macpherson, Stewart M. MA	1953	1990	(Dunfermline: Abbey)	176 Halbeath Road, Dunfermline KY11 4LB	01383 722851
Munro, Sheila BD	1995	2003	Chaplain: RAF	Chaplaincy Centre, RAF Odiham, Hook RG29 1QT	

Orr, J. McMichael MA BD PhD	1949	1986	(Aberfoyle with Port of Menteith)	9 Overhaven, Limekilns, Dunfermline KY11 3JH	01383 872245
Pogue, Victor C. BA BD	1945	1980	(Baird Research Fellow)	5/2 Plewlands Court, Edinburgh EH10 5JY	0131-445 1628
Reid, David MSc LTh FSAScot	1961	1992	(St Monans with Largoward)	North Lethans, Saline, Dunfermline KY12 9TE	01383 7331e4
Ross, Evan J. LTh	1986	1998	(Cowdenbeath: West with Mossgreen and Crossgates)	43 Auld Mart Road, Milnathort, Kinross KY13 7FR	01577 861484
Scott, John LTh	1969	1996	(Aberdour St Fillan's)	32 White's Quay, St David's Harbour, Dalgety Bay, Dunfermline KY11 5HT	01383 820896
Smith, T. Forrest	1959	1986	(Arbuthnott with Kinneff)	71 Whitehills Gardens, Musselburgh EH21 6PH	
Stuart, Anne (Miss) DCS			(Deaconess)	19 St Colme Crescent, Aberdour, Burntisland KY3 0ST	01383 860049
Whyte, Isabel H. (Mrs) BD	1993		Chaplain: Queen Margaret Hospital, Dunfermline	14 Carlingnose Point, North Queensferry, Inverkeithing KY11 1ER	01383 410732

(25) KIRKCALDY

Meets at Kirkcaldy, in St Brycedale Hall, on the first Tuesday of February, March, April, May, November and December, on the second Tuesday of September, and on the fourth Tuesday of June.

| Clerk: | **MR ANDREW F. MOORE BL** | **Annandale, Linksfield Street, Leven KY8 4HX**
[E-mail: akph59@uk.uumail.com] | **01333 422644** |
| Depute Clerk: | **MR IAN WALKER** | **62 Centenary Court, Leven KY8 4AL**
[E-mail: walkerleven@aol.com] | **01333 301332** |

Auchterderran St Fothad's linked with Kinglassie

| J. Ewen R. Campbell MA BD | 1967 | 1977 | 7 Woodend Road, Cardenden, Lochgelly KY5 0NE | 01592 720213 |

Auchtertool linked with Kirkcaldy Linktown (H) (01592 641080)

| Catríona M. Morrison (Mrs) MA BD | 1995 | 2000 | 16 Raith Crescent, Kirkcaldy KY2 5NN | 01592 265536 |

Buckhaven (01592 715577)

| Vacant | | | 181 Wellesley Road, Buckhaven, Leven KY8 1JA | 01592 712870 |

Burntisland (H)

| Alan Sharp BSc BD | 1980 | 2001 | 21 Ramsay Crescent, Burntisland KY3 9JL
[E-mail: alansharp@compuserve.com] | 01592 874303 |

Denbeath linked with Methilhill

| Elizabeth F. Cranfield (Miss) MA BD | 1988 | | 9 Chemiss Road, Methilhill, Leven KY8 2BS | 01592 713142 |

Dysart (H)

| Tilly Wilson (Miss) MTh | 1990 | 1998 | 1 School Brae, Dysart, Kirkcaldy KY1 2XB | 01592 655887 |

Glenrothes: Christ's Kirk (H)
Vacant — 12 The Limekilns, Glenrothes KY6 3QJ — 01592 620536

Glenrothes: St Columba's (01592 752539)
Alistair G. McLeod — 1988 — 40 Liberton Drive, Glenrothes KY6 3PB — 01592 744558

Glenrothes: St Margaret's (H) (01592 610310)
John P. McLean BSc BPhil BD — 1994 — 8 Alburne Park, Glenrothes KY7 5RB
[E-mail: john@stmargaretschurch.org.uk] — 01592 752241
Sarah Hankey DCS — 116 Scott Road, Glenrothes KY6 1AE

Glenrothes: St Ninian's (H) (01592 610560)
Linda J. Dunbar (Ms) BSc BA BD PhD — 2000 — 1 Cawdor Drive, Glenrothes KY6 2HN
[E-mail: linda.dunbar0@ouvip.com] — 01592 611963 (Tel/Fax)

Innerleven East (H)
James L. Templeton BSc BD — 1975 — 77 McDonald Street, Methil, Leven KY8 3AJ — 01333 426310

Kennoway, Windygates and Balgonie: St Kenneth's (Tel: 01333 351372; E-mail: administration@st-kenneths.freeserve.co.uk)
Richard Baxter MA BD — 1997 — 2 Fernhill Gardens, Windygates, Leven KY8 5DZ
[E-mail: richard-baxter@msn.com] — 01333 352329

Kinghorn
James Reid BD — 1985 — 17 Myre Crescent, Kinghorn, Burntisland KY3 9UB
[E-mail: jim17reid@aol.com] — 01592 890269

Kinglassie See Auchterderran St Fothad's

Kirkcaldy: Abbotshall (H)
Bryan L. Tomlinson TD — 1969 1980 — 83 Milton Road, Kirkcaldy KY1 1TP
[E-mail: abbkirk@blueyonder.co.uk] — 01592 260315

Kirkcaldy: Linktown (01592 641080) See Auchtertool

Kirkcaldy: Pathhead (H) (Tel/Fax: 01592 204635; E-mail: pathhead@btinternet.com)
John D. Thomson BD — 1985 1993 — 73 Loughborough Road, Kirkcaldy KY1 3DD
[Website: www.pathheadparishchurch.co.uk]
[E-mail: john.d.thomson@blueyonder.co.uk] — 01592 652215
Maureen Paterson (Mrs) BSc (Aux) — 1992 1994 — 91 Dalmahoy Crescent, Kirkcaldy KY2 6TA
[E-mail: m.e.paterson@btinternet.com] — 01592 262300

Kirkcaldy: St Andrew's (H)
Donald M. Thomson BD — 1975 2000 — 15 Harcourt Road, Kirkcaldy KY2 5HQ
[E-mail: dmacthomson@aol.com] — 01592 260816

Kirkcaldy: St Bryce Kirk (H) (Tel: 01592 640016; E-mail: office@stbee.freeserve.co.uk)

Ken Froude MA BD	1979	6 East Fergus Place, Kirkcaldy KY1 1XT [E-mail: jkfroude@kfroude.freeserve.co.uk]	01592 264480

Kirkcaldy: St John's

Vacant		25 Bennochy Avenue, Kirkcaldy KY2 5QE	01592 263821

Kirkcaldy: Templehall (H)

Vacant		Appin Crescent, Kirkcaldy KY2 6EJ	01592 260156

Kirkcaldy: Torbain

Ian Elston BD MTh	1999	91 Sauchenbush Road, Kirkcaldy KY2 5RN	01592 263015

Kirkcaldy: Viewforth (H) linked with Thornton

Anne J. Job	2000	66 Viewforth Street, Kirkcaldy KY1 3DJ	01592 652502

Leslie Trinity

David J. Smith BD DipMin	1992	4 Valley Drive, Leslie, Glenrothes KY6 3BQ	01592 741008

Leven

Alan Miller BA MA BD	2000 2001	5 Forman Road, Leven KY8 4HH [E-mail: alan.miller@ukgateway.net]	01333 303339

Markinch

Alexander R. Forsyth TD BA MTh	1973	7 Guthrie Crescent, Markinch, Glenrothes KY7 6AY	01592 758264

Methil (H)

Vacant		Alma House, 2 School Brae, Methilhill, Leven KY8 2BT	01592 713708

Methilhill See Denbeath
Thornton See Kirkcaldy: Viewforth

Wemyss

Kenneth W. Donald BA BD	1982 1999	33 Main Road, East Wemyss, Kirkcaldy KY1 4RE [E-mail: kwdonald@4unet.co.uk]	01592 713260

Connolly, Daniel BD DipTheol DipMin	1983	Army Chaplain	2 CS Reg, RLC, BFPO 47	01577 263204
Cooper, M.W. MA	1944 1979	(Kirkcaldy Abbotshall)	Applegarth, Sunny Park, Kinross KY13 7BX	
Dick, James S. MA BTh	1988 1997	(Glasgow: Ruchazie)	1 Hawkmuir, Kirkcaldy KY1 2AN	01592 260289
Duncan, John C. BD MPhil	1987 2001	Army Chaplain	35 Engr Regt, Barker Barracks, Paderborn, BFPO 22	
Elston, Peter K.	1963 2000	(Dalgety)	6 Cairngorm Crescent, Kirkcaldy KY2 5RF	01592 205622

Ferguson, David J. MA	1966	2001	(Bellie with Speymouth)		
Forrester, Ian L. MA	1964	1996	(Friockheim, Kinnell with Inverkeilor and Luman)	4 Russell Gardens, Ladybank, Cupar KY15 7LT	01337 831406
Gatt, David W.	1981	1995	(Thornton)	8 Bennochy Avenue, Kirkcaldy KY2 5QE	01592 260251
Gibson, Ivor MA	1957	1993	(Abercorn with Dalmeny)	15 Beech Avenue, Thornton, Kirkcaldy KY1 4AT	01592 774328
Gordon, Ian D. LTh	1972	2001	(Markinch)	15 McInnes Road, Glenrothes KY7 6BA	01592 759982
Howden, Margaret (Miss) DCS			(Deaconess)	2 Somerville Way, Glenrothes KY7 5GE	01592 742487
McAlpine, Robin J. BDS BD	1988	1997	Adviser in Mission and Evangelism	38 Munro Street, Kirkcaldy KY1 1PY	01592 205913
				10 Seton Place, Kirkcaldy KY2 6UX	01592 643518
				[E-mail: robin.mcalpine@virgin.net]	
McDonald, Iain J.M. MA BD	1984	1996	Chaplain, Kirkcaldy Acute Hospitals	26 Cairngorm Crescent, Kirkcaldy KY2 5RG	01592 263012
McKenzie, Donald M. TD MA	1947	1986	(Auchtertool with Burntisland)	76 Forth Park Gardens, Kirkcaldy KY2 5TD	01592 610281
MacLeod, Norman	1960	1988	(Orwell with Portmoak)	324 Muirfield Drive, Glenrothes KY6 2PZ	01592 742352
McNaught, Samuel M. MA BD MTh	1968	2002	(Kirkcaldy: St John's)	6 Munro Court, Glenrothes KY7 5GD	01592 566129
Munro, Andrew MA BD PhD	1972	2000	(Glencaple with Lowther)	7 Dunvegan Avenue, Kirkcaldy KY2 5SG	01592 620053
Reid, Martin R.B.C. BD	1960	1990	(Falkirk West)	13 Rothes Park, Leslie, Glenrothes KY6 3LL	01334 473406
Simpson, Gordon M. MA BD	1959	1996	(Leslie Trinity)	37 Spottiswoode Gardens, St Andrews KY16 8SA	01592 205510
Sutherland, William	1964	1993	(Bo'ness Old)	88 Dunrobin Road, Kirkcaldy KY2 5YT	01592 741009
Taylor, John T.H.	1947	1983	(Glenrothes Christ's Kirk on the Green)	9 Douglas Road, Leslie, Glenrothes KY6 3JZ	01337 857431
Thomson, Gilbert L. BA	1965	1996	(Glenrothes Christ's Kirk)	3 Fortharfield, Freuchie, Cupar KY15 7JJ	01592 873616
Webster, Elspeth H. (Miss) DCS			(Deaconess)	82 Broomhill Avenue, Burntisland KY3 0BP	01337 840646
Young, W. Finlayson MA	1943	1979	(Kinglassie)	17 Whitecraig Road, Newburgh, Cupar KY14 6BP	

KIRKCALDY ADDRESSES

Abbotshall	Abbotshall Road	St Andrew's	Victoria Road x Victoria Gdns	Templehall	Beauly Place
Linktown	Nicol Street x High Street	St Bryce Kirk	St Brycedale Avenue x Kirk Wynd	Torbain	Lindores Drive
Old	Kirk Wynd	St John's	Elgin Street	Viewforth	Viewforth Street x Viewforth Terrace
Pathhead	Harriet Street x Church Street				

(26) ST ANDREWS

Meets at Cupar, in St John's Church Hall, on the second Wednesday of February, March, April, May, September, October, November and December, and on the last Wednesday of June.

Clerk:	REV. PETER MEAGER MA BD CertMgmt	7 Lorraine Drive, Cupar KY15 5DY	01334 656991
		[E-mail: akph74@uk.uumail.com]	

Abdie and Dunbog (H) linked with Newburgh (H) 1996
Lynn Brady (Miss) BD DipMin   2002
2 Guthrie Court, Cupar Road, Newburgh, Cupar KY14 6HA   01337 842228
[E-mail: lynn@revbrady.freeserve.co.uk]

Anstruther
Ian A. Cathcart BSc BD   1994
The James Melville Manse, Anstruther KY10 3EX   01333 311808

Auchtermuchty (H)
Ann G. Fraser (Mrs) BD CertMin   1990
2 Burnside, Auchtermuchty, Cupar KY14 7AJ   01337 828519
[E-mail: anngilfraser@bushinternet.com]

Balmerino (H) linked with Wormit (H)
Vacant
5 Westwater Place, Newport-on-Tay DD6 8NS   01382 542626

Boarhills and Dunino linked with St Andrews Martyrs' 1990
J. Mary Henderson (Miss) MA BD DipEd PhD   2000
49 Irvine Crescent, St Andrews KY16 8LG   01334 472948
[E-mail: jmh@smokeypuss.freeserve.co.uk]

Cameron linked with St Andrews: St Leonard's (01334 478702) 1979
Alan D. McDonald LLB BD MTh   1998
1 Cairnhill Gardens, St Andrews KY16 8UR   01334 472793
[E-mail: alan.d.mcdonald@talk21.com]

Carnbee linked with Pittenweem
Vacant
The Manse, 2 Milton Place, Pittenweem, Anstruther KY10 2LR   01333 311255

Cellardyke (H) linked with Kilrenny
David J.H. Laing BD DPS   1976   1999
Toll Road, Cellardyke, Anstruther KY10 3BH   01333 310810
[E-mail: davith@v21mail.co.uk]

Ceres and Springfield
Vacant
The Manse, St Andrews Road, Ceres, Cupar KY15 5NQ   01334 828233

Crail linked with Kingsbarns (H)
Michael J. Erskine MA BD   1985   2002
Church Manse, St Andrews Road, Crail, Anstruther KY10 3UH   01333 450358

Creich, Flisk and Kilmany linked with Monimail 1996
Mitchell Collins BD CPS
Creich Manse, Brunton, Cupar KY15 4PA   01337 870332
[E-mail: chellc@care4free.net]

Cupar: Old (H) and St Michael of Tarvit
Kenneth S. Jeffrey BA BD PhD   2002
76 Hogarth Drive, Cupar KY15 5YH   01334 653196
[E-mail: ksjeffrey@btopenworld.com]

Cupar: St John's
A. Sheila Blount (Mrs) BD BA — 1978 2002 — 23 Hogarth Drive, Cupar KY15 5YH — 01334 655851

Dairsie linked with Kemback linked with Strathkinness (H)
Alexander Strickland JP LTh — 1971 1981 — Dairsie Manse, Dairsie, Cupar KY15 4RS — 01334 653283

Edenshead and Strathmiglo
Thomas G.M. Robertson LTh — 1971 1984 — The Manse, Kirk Wynd, Strathmiglo, Cupar KY14 7QS — 01337 860256

Elie (H) linked with Kilconquhar and Colinsburgh (H)
Iain F. Paton BD FCIS — 1980 1998 — 30 Bank Street, Elie, Leven KY9 1BW
[E-mail: iain.paton@tesco.net] — 01333 330685

Falkland (01337 858442) linked with Freuchie (H)
John W. Jarvie BD CertMin MTh — 1990 — 1 Newton Road, Falkland, Cupar KY15 7AQ
[E-mail: jarvie@cwcom.net] — 01337 857696

Freuchie (H) See Falkland

Howe of Fife
Marion J. Paton (Miss) BMus BD — 1991 1994 — 83 Church Street, Ladybank, Cupar KY15 7ND
[E-mail: marion@marionpaton.f9.co.uk] — 01337 830513

Kemback See Dairsie
Kilconquhar and Colinsburgh See Elie
Kilrenny See Cellardyke
Kingsbarns See Crail

Largo and Newburn (H) linked with Largo St David's
Rosemary Frew (Mrs) MA BD — 1988 — The Manse, Church Place, Upper Largo, Leven KY8 6EH
[E-mail: rosemaryfrew@breathemail.net] — 01333 360286

Largo St David's See Largo and Newburn

Largoward linked with St Monans (H)
Donald G. MacEwan MA BD PhD — 2001 — The Manse, St Monans, Anstruther KY10 2DD
[E-mail: maiadona@fish.co.uk] — 01333 730258

Leuchars: St Athernase
Caroline Taylor (Mrs) MA BD — 1995 2003 — 7 David Wilson Park, Balmullo, St Andrews KY16 0NP
[E-mail: enilorac@fish.com.uk] — 01334 870038

Monimail See Creich, Flisk and Kilmany
Newburgh See Abdie and Dunbog

Newport-on-Tay (H)
W. Kenneth Pryde DA BD   1994   57 Cupar Road, Newport-on-Tay DD6 8DF   01382 543165 (Tel/Fax)
[E-mail: wkpryde@aol.com]

Pittenweem See Carnbee

St Andrews: Holy Trinity
Vacant   17 Queen's Gardens, St Andrews KY16 9TA   01334 474494

St Andrews: Hope Park (H)
A. David K. Arnott MA BD   1971 1996   20 Priory Gardens, St Andrews KY16 8XX   01334 472912 (Tel/Fax)
[E-mail: adka@st-andrews.ac.uk]

St Andrews: Martyrs' (H) See Boarhills and Dunino
St Andrews: St Leonard's (H) See Cameron
St Monans See Largoward
Strathkinness See Dairsie

Tayport
Colin J. Dempster BD   1990   27 Bell Street, Tayport DD6 9AP   01382 552861
[E-mail: demps@tayportc.fsnet.co.uk]

Wormit See Balmerino

Alexander, James S. MA BD BA PhD	1966 1973	University of St Andrews	5 Strathkinness High Road, St Andrews KY16 9RP	01334 472630
Armour, Charles MA	1939 2003	(St Andrews: Holy Trinity)	3 Hay Fleming Avenue, St Andrews KY16 8YH	01334 474434
Bennett, Alestair TD MA	1938 1976	(Strathkinness)	7 Bonfield Park, Strathkinness, St Andrews KY16 9SY	01334 850249
Best, Ernest MA BD PhD DD	1949 1982	(University of Glasgow)	13 Newmill Gardens, St Andrews KY16 8RY	01334 473315
Bews, James MA	1942 1981	(Dundee: Craigiebank)	21 Balrymonth Court, St Andrews KY16 8XT	01334 476037
Blount, Graham K. LLB BD PhD	1976 1998	Parliamentary Officer	23 Hogarth Drive, Cupar KY15 5YH	01334 655851
Bogie, A.P. MA FSAScot	1944 1979	(Forgan)	7 Gourlay Wynd, St Andrews KY16 8HP	
Bradley, Ian MA BD DPhil	1990 1990	Lecturer: University of Aberdeen	4 Donaldson Gardens, St Andrews KY16 9DN	01334 475339
Brown, Lawson R. MA	1960 1997	(Cameron with St Andrew's St Leonard's)	10 Park Street, St Andrews KY16 8AQ	01334 473413
Buchan, Alexander MA BD	1975 1992	(North Ronaldsay with Sanday)	26 Allan Robertson Drive, St Andrews KY16 8EY	01334 473875
Cameron, James K. MA BD PhD FRHistS	1953 1989	(University of St Andrews)	Priorscroft, 71 Hepburn Gardens, St Andrews KY16 9LS	01334 473996
Casebow, Brian C. MA BD	1959 1993	(Edinburgh: Salisbury)	'The Rowans', 67 St Michael's Drive, Cupar KY15 5BP	01334 656335
Craig, Gordon W. MBE MA BD	1972 2000	(Chaplain: RN)	1 Beley Bridge, Dunino, St Andrews KY16 8LT	01334 880235
Douglas, J.D. MA BD PhD	1957		2 Doocot Road, St Andrews KY16 8QP	01334 474876
Douglas, Peter C. JP	1966 1993	(Boarhills linked with Dunino)	The Old Schoolhouse, Flisk, Newburgh, Cupar KY14 6HN	01337 8702 8
Earnshaw, Philip BA BSc BD	1986 1996	(Glasgow: Pollokshields)	22 Castle Street, St Monans, Anstruther KY10 2AP	01333 730640
Edington, George L.	1952 1989	(Tayport)	64B Burghmuir Road, Perth PH1 1LH	

Name	Charge / Appointment	Ordained	Inducted	Address	Tel
Fairlie, George BD BVMS MRCVS	(Crail with Kingsbarns)	1971	2002	41 Warrack Street, St Andrews KY18 8DR	01334 475868
Galloway, Robert W.C. LTh	(Cromarty)	1970	1998	22 Haughgate, Leven KY8 4SG	01382 542199
Gibson, Henry M. MA BD PhD	(Dundee: The High Kirk)	1960	1999	4 Comerton Place, Drumoig, Leuchars, St Andrews KY16 0NQ	01334 652341
Gordon, Peter M. MA BD	(Airdrie West)	1958	1995	3 Cupar Road, Cuparmuir, Cupar KY15 5RH [E-mail: machrie@madasafish.com]	
Henney, William MA DD	(St Andrews Hope Park)	1957	1996	30 Doocot Road, St Andrews KY16 9LP	01334 472560
Hill, Roy MA	(Lisbon)	1962	1997	Forgan Cottage, Kinnessburn Road, St Andrews KY16 8AD	01334 472121
Howieson, R.A. JP MA	(Newport-on-Tay St Thomas's)	1937	1977	3 Baker Lane, St Andrews KY16 9PJ	01334 473711
Kinnis, Robert L. MA BD	(Baillieston Mure Memorial)	1931	1972	Gibson House, St Andrews KY16 9JE	01334 656290
Law, Arthur ACIB	(Kincardine in Menteith with Norrieston)	1968	1988	4 Holmhill Court, Dunblane FK15 0AF	
Learmonth, Walter LTh	(Ceres with Springfield)	1968	1997	14 Marionfield Place, Cupar KY15 5JN	
Lithgow, Thomas MA	(Banchory Devenick with Maryculter)	1945	1982	Pitlair House, Bow of Fife, Cupar KY15 5RF	
McCartney, Alexander C. BTh	(Caputh and Clunie with Kinclaven)	1973	1995	10 The Glebe, Crail, Anstruther KY10 3UT	01333 451194
McFadyen, Gavin J.	(Whiteinch)	1963	1992	62 Toll Court, Lundin Links, Leven KY8 6HH	01333 320434
McGregor, Duncan J. FIMA	(Channelkirk with Lauder Old)	1982	1996	14 Mount Melville, St Andrews KY16 8NG	01334 478314
Macintyre, William J. MA BD DD	(Crail with Kingsbarns)	1951	1989	Tigh a' Ghobhainn, Lochton, Crail, Anstruther KY10 3XE	01333 450327
McKane, William MA PhD DLitt DD FBA	(University of St Andrews)	1949	1990	51 Irvine Crescent, St Andrews KY16 8LG	01334 473797
Mackenzie, A. Cameron MA	(Biggar)	1955	1995	Hedgerow, 5 Shiels Avenue, Freuchie, Cupar KY15 7JD	01337 857763
Mackenzie, J.A.R. MA	(Largo St David's)	1947	1987	West Lodge, Inverness Road, Nairn 1V12 4SD	01667 452827
MacNab, Hamish S.D. MA	(Kilrenny)	1948	1987	Fairhill, Northmuir, Kirriemuir DD8 4PF	01575 572564
McPhail, Peter MA BD	(Creich, Flisk and Kilmany)	1940	1982	44 Doocot Road, St Andrews KY16 8QP	01334 473093
Meager, Peter MA BD CertMgmt(Open)	(Elie with Kilconquhar and Colinsburgh)	1971	1998	7 Lorraine Drive, Cupar KY15 5DY [E-mail: akph74@uk.uumail.com]	01334 656991
Nicol, Robert M.	(Jersey: St Columba's)	1984	1996	35 Upper Greens, Auchtermuchty, Cupar KY14 7BX	01337 828327
Ord, J.K.	(Falkirk Condorrat)	1963		24 Forth Street, St Monance, Anstruther KY10 2AX	01333 730461
Patterson, John W. BA BD	(St Andrews Martyrs)	1948	1989	34 Claybraes, St Andrews KY16 8RS	01334 473606
Porchmouth, Roland John NDD ATD	(Bendochy)	1980	1989	1 West Braes, Pittenweem, Anstruther KY10 2PS	01333 311448
Porteous, James K. DD	(Cupar St John's)	1944	1997	16 Market Street, St Andrews KY16 9NS	
Robb, Nigel J. FCP MA BD ThM MTh	Director of Educational Services, Board of Ministry	1981	1998	c/o 121 George Street, Edinburgh EH2 4YN [E-mail: nrobb@cofscotland.org.uk]	0131-225 5722
Robertson, Norma P. (Miss) BD DMin	(Kincardine O'Neil with Lumphanan)	1993	2002	82 Hogarth Drive, Cupar KY15 5YU [E-mail: normapr@fish.co.uk]	01334 650595
Roy, Alan J. BSc BD	(Aberuthven with Dunning)	1960	1999	14 Comerton Place, Drumoig, Leuchars, St Andrews KY16 0NQ [E-mail: a.r.roy@ondigital.com]	
Salters, Robert B. MA BD PhD	(University of St Andrews)	1966	1971	Vine Cottage, 119 South Street, St Andrews KY16 9UH	01382 542225
Scott, J. Miller MA BD FSAScot DD	(Jerusalem)	1949	1988	St Martins, 6 Trinity Place, St Andrews KY16 8SG	01334 473198
Shaw, Duncan LTh CPS	Chaplain: RAF	1984		Chaplain's Office, RAF Leuchars, St Andrews KY16 0JX	01334 479518
Sinclair, David I. BSc BD PhD DipSW	Secretary: Church and Nation Committee	1990	1998	42 South Road, Cupar KY15 5JF	01334 656957
Stevenson A.L. LLB MLitt DPA FPEA	(Balmerino linked with Wormit)	1984	1993	41 Main Street, Dairsie, Cupar KY15 4SR	01334 870582
Stoddart, David L.	(Lagan with Newtonmore)	1961	1987	3 Castle Street, Anstruther KY10 3DD	01333 310668
Strong, Clifford LTh	(Creich, Flisk and Kilmany with Monimail)	1983	1995	60 Maryknowe, Gauldry, Newport-on-Tay DD6 8SL	01382 330445
Taylor, Ian BSc MA LTh DipEd	(Abdie and Dunbog with Newburgh)	1983	1997	Lundie Cottage, Arncroach, Anstruther KY10 2RN	01333 720222
Thomson, P.G. MA BD MTh ThD	(Irvine Fullarton)	1947	1989	Fullarton, 2 Beech Walk, Crail, Anstruther KY10 3UN	01333 450423

Thrower, Charles G. BSc — 1965 2002 — (Cambee with Pittenweem) — Grange House, Wester Grangemuir, Pittenweem, Anstruther KY10 2RB [E-mail: craigroundh@aol.com] — 01333 312631

Torrance, Alan J. MA BD DrTheol — 1984 1999 — University of St Andrews — Kincaple House, Kincaple, St Andrews KY16 9SH — (Home) 01334 850755 / (Office) 01334 462843

Turnbull, James J. MA — 1940 1981 — (Arbirlot with Colliston) — Woodlands, Beech Avenue, Ladybank, Cupar KY15 7NG — 01337 830279

Walker, James B. MA BD DPhil — 1975 1993 — Chaplain: University of St Andrews — 1 Gillespie Terrace, The Scores, St Andrews KY16 9AT [E-mail: jbw1@st-andrews.ac.uk] — (Tel) 01334 477471 / (Fax) 01334 462697

Whyte, James A. MA LLD DD DUniv — 1945 1987 — (University of St Andrews) — 13 Hope Street, St Andrews KY16 9HJ — 01334 472323

Wilson, Robert McL. MA BD PhD DD FBA

Wright, Lynda (Miss) BEd DCS — 1946 1983 — (University of St Andrews) Deacon: Retreat Leader, Key House — 10 Murrayfield Road, St Andrews KY16 9NB — 01334 474331 ; 6 Key Cottage, High Street, Falkland, Cupar KY15 7BD — 01337 857705

(27) DUNKELD AND MEIGLE

Meets at Pitlochry on the first Tuesday of September and December, on the third Tuesday of February, April and October, and at the Moderator's church on the third Tuesday of June.

Clerk: REV. JOHN RUSSELL MA — Kilblaan, Gladstone Terrace, Birnam, Dunkeld PH8 0DP [E-mail: akph47@uk.uumail.com] — 01350 728896

Aberfeldy (H) linked with Amulree and Strathbraan linked with Dull and Weem
Alexander M. Gunn MA BD — 1967 1986 — Taybridge Terrace, Aberfeldy PH15 2BS [E-mail: sandy@aberfeldypc.co.uk] — 01887 820656 (Tel/Fax)

Alyth (H)
Neil N. Gardner MA BD — 1991 1998 — Cambridge Street, Alyth, Blairgowrie PH11 8AW [E-mail: nng@surfaid.org] — 01828 632104

Amulree and Strathbraan See Aberfeldy

Ardler, Kettins and Meigle
Linda Stewart (Mrs) BD — 2001 — The Manse, Dundee Road, Meigle, Blairgowrie PH12 8SB — 01828 640278

Bendochy linked with Coupar Angus Abbey
Bruce Dempsey BD — 1997 — Caddam Road, Coupar Angus, Blairgowrie PH13 9EF [E-mail: revbruce.dempsey@btopenworld.com] — 01828 627331

Blair Atholl and Struan linked with Tenandry
Brian Ian Murray BD — 2002 — Blair Atholl, Pitlochry PH18 5SX [E-mail: ian.murray@pgen.net] — 01796 481213

Blairgowrie
Donald Macleod BD LRAM DRSAM   1987   2002   The Manse, Upper David Street, Blairgowrie PH10 6HB
[E-mail: donmac@fish.co.uk]   01250 872146

Braes of Rannoch linked with Foss and Rannoch (H)
David G. Hamilton MA BD   1971   1998   Kinloch Rannoch, Pitlochry PH16 5QA
[E-mail: davidhamilton@onetel.net.uk]   01882 632381

Caputh and Clunie (H) linked with Kinclaven (H) (T)
Linda J. Broadley (Mrs) LTh DipEd   1996   Caputh Manse, Caputh, Perth PH1 4JH
[E-mail: linda.broadley@tesco.net]   01738 710520

Coupar Angus Abbey See Bendochy
Dull and Weem See Aberfeldy

Dunkeld (H)
R. Fraser Penny BA BD   1984   2001   Cathedral Manse, Dunkeld PH8 0AW
[E-mail: fraserpenn@aol.com]   01350 727249
01350 727102 (Fax)

Fortingall and Glenlyon linked with Kenmore and Lawers
Anne J. Brennan BSc BD MTh   1999   The Manse, Balnaskeag, Kenmore, Aberfeldy PH15 2HB
[E-mail: annebrennan@yahoo.co.uk]   01887 830218

Foss and Rannoch See Braes of Rannoch

Grantully, Logierait and Strathtay
Christine M. Creegan (Mrs) MTh   1993   2000   The Manse, Strathtay, Pitlochry PH9 0PG
[E-mail: christine@creegans.co.uk]   01887 840251

Kenmore and Lawers (H) See Fortingall and Glenlyon
Kinclaven See Caputh and Clunie

Kirkmichael, Straloch and Glenshee linked with Rattray (H)
Hugh C. Ormiston BSc BD MPhil PhD   1969   1998   The Manse, Alyth Road, Rattray, Blairgowrie PH10 7HF
[E-mail: hugh@ormistonh.fsnet.co.uk]   01250 872462

Pitlochry (H) (01796 472160)
Malcolm Ramsay BA LLB DipMin   1986   1998   Manse Road, Moulin, Pitlochry PH16 5EP
[E-mail: amramsay@aol.com]   01796 472774

Rattray See Kirkmichael Straloch and Glenshee
Tenandry See Blair Atholl and Struan

Name	(Charge)			Address	Tel
Barbour, Robin A.S. KCVO MC BD STM DD	(University of Aberdeen)	1954	1982	Fincastle, Pitlochry PH16 5RJ	01796 473209
Cassells, Alexander K. MA BD	(Leuchars St Athernase and Guardbridge)	1961	1990	Tighaness, Keltney Burn, Aberfeldy PH15 2LS	01887 830758
Dick, Tom MA	(Dunkeld)	1951	1990	Mo Dhachaidh, Callybrae, Dunkeld PH8 0EP	01350 727338
Duncan, James BTh FSAScot	(Blair Atholl and Struan)	1980	1995	25 Knockard Avenue, Pitlochry PH16 5JE	01796 474096
Forsyth, David Stuart MA	(Belhelvie)	1948	1992	Birchlea, 38 Fonab Crescent, Pitlochry PH16 5SR	01796 473708
Fulton, Frederick H. MA	(Clunie, Lethendy and Kinloch)	1942	1983	Grampian Cottage, Chapel Brae, Braemar, Ballater AB35 5YT	01339 741277
Grieve, David S.A. MA BD	(Arbirlot with Carmyllie with Colliston)	1954	1991	Dundarroch, Meigle Road, Alyth, Blairgowrie PH11 8EU	01828 632318
Henderson, John D. MA BD	(Cluny with Monymusk)	1953	1992	Aldersyde, George Street, Blairgowrie PH10 6HP	01250 875181
Knox, John W. MTheol	(Lochgelly: Macainsh)	1992	1997	Heatherlea, Main Street, Ardler, Blairgowrie PH12 8SR	01828 640731
McAlister, D.J.B. MA BD PhD	(North Berwick Blackadder)	1951	1989	2 Duff Avenue, Moulin, Pitlochry PH16 5EN	01796 473591
Macdonald, James F. TD	(Bendochy with Kinclaven)	1930	1984	Stormont Lodge, Kirk Wynd, Blairgowrie PH10 6HN	
Macpherson, Norman J. TD	(Blairgowrie St Mary's South)	1954	1980	31 Glenburn Drive, Inverness IV2 4NE	01463 230536
MacVicar, Kenneth MBE DFC TD MA	(Kenmore with Lawers with Fortingall & Glenlyon)	1950	1990	Illeray, Kenmore, Aberfeldy PH15 2HE	01887 830514
Martin, Francis BL	(Pitlochry East)	1956	1991	58 West Moulin Road, Pitlochry PH16 5EQ	01796 472619
Robertson, Iain M. MA	(Carriden)	1967	1992	St Colme's, Perth Road, Birnam, Dunkeld PH8 0BH	01350 727455
Robertson, Matthew LTh	(Cawdor with Croy and Dalcross)	1968	2002	Inver, Strathtay, Pitlochry PH9 0PG	01887 840780
Russell, John MA	(Tillicoultry)	1959	2000	Kilblaan, Gladstone Terrace, Birnam, Dunkeld PH8 0DP	01350 728896
Shannon, W.G.H. MA BD	(Pitlochry)	1955	1998	19 Knockard Road, Pitlochry PH16 5HJ	01796 473533
Stewart, Walter T.A.	(Barry)	1964	1999	7A Tummel Crescent, Pitlochry PH16 5DF	01796 473422
Tait, Thomas W. BD	(Rattray)	1972	1997	20 Cedar Avenue, Blairgowrie PH10 6TT	01250 874833
White, Brock A. LTh	(Kirkcaldy: Templehall)	1971	2001	1 Littlewood Gardens, Blairgowrie PH10 6XZ	01250 870399
Young, G. Stuart	(Blairgowrie: St Andrew's)	1961	1996	7 James Place, Stanley, Perth PH1 4PD	01738 828473

(28) PERTH

Meets at Scone: Old, at 7:00pm, in the Elizabeth Ashton Hall, on the second Tuesday of every month except January, July and August, when there is no meeting, and on the last Tuesday of June, when it meets in the church of the incoming Moderator.

Clerk:	**Rev. DEREK G. LAWSON LLB BD**	**209 High Street, Perth PH1 5PB**	**01738 451177 (Tel)**
Presbytery Office:		**[E-mail: akph70@uk.uumail.com]**	**01738 638226 (Fax)**

Abernethy and Dron linked with Arngask

Kenneth G. Anderson MA BD	1967	1988	Manse Road, Abernethy, Perth PH2 9JP	01738 850607

Almondbank Tibbermore
Donald Campbell BD — 1998 — The Manse, Pitcairngreen, Perth PH1 3LU [E-mail: revdonaldcampbell@btinternet.com] — 01738 583217

Ardoch (H) linked with Blackford (H)
Hazel Wilson (Ms) MA BD DipEd DMS — 1991 — Manse of Ardoch, Feddal Road, Braco, Dunblane FK15 9RE [E-mail: hazel@feddal.freeserve.co.uk] — 01786 880217

Arngask See Abernethy and Dron

Auchterarder (H)
Michael R.R. Shewan MA BD CPS — 1985 1998 — 24 High Street, Auchterarder, Perth PH3 1DF — 01764 662210

Auchtergaven and Moneydie
Vacant — Bankfoot, Perth PH1 4BS — 01738 787235

Blackford See Ardoch

Cargill Burrelton linked with Collace
Jose R. Carvalho BD — 2002 — Manse Road, Woodside, Blairgowrie PH13 9NQ [E-mail: jrcarvalho@aol.com] — 01828 670352

Cleish (H) linked with Fossoway St Serf's and Devonside
A. David Macleod MA BD — 1993 1994 — The Manse, Cleish, Kinross KY13 7LR [E-mail: cleishrev@hotmail.com] — 01577 850231 (Tel/Fax)

Collace See Cargill and Burrelton

Comrie (H) linked with Dundurn (H)
Peter D. Thomson MA BD — 1968 1978 — The Manse, Comrie, Crieff PH6 2HE [E-mail: revpdt@the-manse.freeserve.co.uk] — 01764 670269

Crieff (H)
James W. MacDonald BD — 1976 2002 — 8 Strathearn Terrace, Crieff PH7 3AQ — 01764 653907

Dunbarney (H) linked with Forgandenny
W. Duncan Stenhouse MA BD — 1989 — Dunbarney Manse, Bridge of Earn, Perth PH2 9DY [E-mail: duncan@stenhouse58.freeserve.co.uk] — 01738 812463

Dundurn See Comrie

Errol (H) linked with Kilspindie and Rait
John M. Pickering BSc BD DipEd — 1997 — South Bank, Errol, Perth PH2 7PZ [E-mail: john.m.pickering@talk21.com] — 01821 642279

Forgandenny See Dunbarney
Fossoway St Serf's and Devonside See Cleish

Fowlis Wester linked with Madderty linked with Monzie
Alexander F. Bonar LTh LRIC   1988   1996   Beechview, Abercairney, Crieff PH7 3NF   01764 652116
                                                                [E-mail: sandy.bonar@btinternet.com]

Gask (H) linked with Methven and Logiealmond (H)
Brian Bain LTh   1980   Sauchob Road, Methven, Perth PH1 3QD   01738 840274 (Tel/Fax)
                                                                [E-mail: brian@methvenmanse.freeserve.co.uk]

Kilspindie and Rait See Errol

Kinross (H)
John P.L. Munro MA BD PhD   1977   1998   15 Station Road, Kinross KY13 8TG   01577 862952
                                                                [E-mail: john@lochleven.freeserve.co.uk]

Madderty See Fowlis Wester
Methven and Logiealmond See Gask
Monzie See Fowlis Wester

Muthill (H) linked with Trinity Gask and Kinkell
John Oswald BSc PhD BD   1997   2002   Muthill, Crieff PH5 2AR   01764 681205
                                                                [E-mail: revdocoz@bigfoot.com]

Orwell (H) linked with Portmoak (H)
Robert Pickles BD MPhil   2003   3 Perth Road, Milnathort, Kinross KY13 9XU   01577 863461

Perth: Craigie (H)
William Thomson   2001   46 Abbot Street, Perth PH2 0EE   01738 623748

Perth: Kinnoull (H)
David I. Souter BD   1996   2001   1 Mount Tabor Avenue, Perth PH2 7BT   01738 626046
                                                                [E-mail: d.souter@virgin.net]

Perth: Letham St Mark's (H)
James C. Stewart BD DipMin   1997   35 Rose Crescent, Perth PH1 1NT   01738 624167
                                                                [E-mail: jimstewartrev@lineone.net]
Kenneth McKay DCS   11F Balgowan Road, Perth PH1 2JG   01738 621169

Perth: Moncreiffe (T)
Isobel Birrell (Mrs) BD   1994   1999   Rhynd Road, Perth PH2 8PT   01738 625694
                                                                [E-mail: isobel.birrell3@ntlworld.com]

Perth: North (01738 622298)

David W. Denniston BD DipMin	1981	1996	127 Glasgow Road, Perth PH2 0LU [E-mail: david.denniston@virgin.net]	01738 625728
Brian R. Hendrie BD (Assoc)	1992	2000	98 Duncansby Way, Perth PH1 5XF [E-mail: brianandyvonne@98duncansby.freeserve.uk]	01738 441029

Perth: Riverside (New Charge Development)

Alfred G. Drummond BD DMin	1991	2000	44 Hay Street, Perth PH1 5HS [E-mail: ncdriverside@uk.uumail.com]	01738 621305
John Buchanan DCS			22 Brora Court, North Muirton, Perth PH1 3DQ [E-mail: liz.brown@blueyonder.co.uk]	01738 631697

Perth: St John the Baptist's (H) (01738 626159)

David D. Ogston MA BD	1970	1980	15 Comely Bank, Perth PH2 7HU [E-mail ogston@cwcom.net]	01738 621755
Elizabeth Brown (Mrs)	1996		25 Highfield Road, Scone, Perth PH2 6RN [E-mail: liz.brown@blueyonder.co.uk]	01738 552391 (Tel/Fax)

Perth: St Leonard's-in-the-Fields and Trinity (H) (01738 632238)

Gilbert C. Nisbet CA BD	1993	2000	5 Strathearn Terrace, Perth PH2 0LS [E-mail: gcnisbet@stleonardsmanse.fsnet.co.uk]	01738 621709

Perth: St Matthew's (Office: 01738 636757; Vestry: 01738 630725)

Ewen J. Gilchrist BD DipMin DipComm	1982	1988	23 Kincarrathie Crescent, Perth PH2 7HH [E-mail: ewen.gilchrist@st-matthews.org.uk]	01738 626828

Portmoak See Orwell

Redgorton linked with Stanley

Derek G. Lawson LLB BD	1998	22 King Street, Stanley, Perth PH1 4ND [E-mail: lawson@stanley9835.freeserve.co.uk]	01738 828247

St Madoes and Kinfauns

Marc F. Bircham BD MTh	2000	Glencarse, Perth PH2 7NF [E-mail: mf.bircham@virgin.net]	01738 860837

St Martin's linked with Scone New (H) (01738 553900)

Robert Sloan BD	1997	2001	24 Victoria Road, Scone, Perth PH2 6JW [E-mail: robertsloan@lineone.net]	01738 551467

Scone: New See St Martin's

Scone: Old (H)

J. Bruce Thomson JP MA BD	1972	1983	Burnside, Scone, Perth PH2 6LP [E-mail: jock.tamson@talk21.com]	01738 552030

Stanley See Redgorton

The Stewartry of Strathearn (H) (Tel: 01738 621674; Fax: 01738 643321; E-mail: stewartry@beeb.net)

Colin R. Williamson LLB BD   1972   2000   Manse of Aberdalgie, Aberdalgie, Perth PH2 0QD   01738 625854
[E-mail: stewartry@beeb.net]

Trinity Gask and Kinkell See Muthill

Barr, George K. ARIBA BD PhD	1967	1993	(Uddingston: Viewpark)	7 Tay Avenue, Comrie, Crieff PH6 2PE [E-mail: gbarr2@compuserve.com]	01764 670454
Barr, T. Leslie LTh	1969	1997	(Kinross)	8 Fairfield Road, Kelty KY4 0BY	01383 839330
Bartholomew, Julia (Mrs) BSc BD	2002		Auchterarder: Associate	Kippenhill, Dunning, Perth PH2 0RA	01764 684929
Bertram, Thomas A.	1972	1995	(Patna Waterside)	3 Scrimgeours Corner, 29 West High Street, Crieff PH7 4AP	01764 652066
Birrell, John M. MA LLB BD	1974	1996	Hospital Chaplain: Perth Royal Infirmary	Rhynd Road, Perth PH2 8QL [E-mail: john.birrell@tuht.scot.nhs.uk]	01738 625694
Bonomy, William MA BD	1946	1987	(Inverkip)	Viewlands House, Viewlands Road, Perth PH1 1BL	01738 632469
Brown, R. Russell MA	1940	1986	(Perth Kinnoull)	Viewlands House, Viewlands Road, Perth PH1 1BL	01764 660306
Buchan, William DipTheol BD	1987	2001	(Kilwinning Abbey)	34 Bridgewater Avenue, Auchterarder PH3 1DQ	01738 627422
Carr, W. Stanley MA	1951	1991	(Largs: St Columba's)	16 Gannochy Walk, Perth PH2 7LW	01738 565072
Coleman, Sidney H. BA BD MTh	1961	2001	(Glasgow: Merrylea)	'Blaven', 11 Clyde Place, Perth PH2 0EZ	01577 864762
Cowie, J.L. MA	1950	1977	(Edinburgh: Richmond Craigmillar)	16 Curate Wynd, Kinross KY13 7DX	01738 565379
Denniston, Jane MA BD	2002		Board of Parish Education	127 Glasgow Road, Perth PH2 0LU	01764 654976
Donaldson, Robert B. BSocSc	1953	1997	(Kilchoman with Portnahaven)	11 Strathearn Court, Crieff PH7 3DS	01738 561945
Ferguson, John F. MA BD	1987	2001	(Perth: Kinnoull)	71 Burghmuir Road, Perth PH1 1LH	01764 679178
Fleming, Hamish M. MA	1966	2001	(Banchory Ternan East)	36 Earnmuir Road, Comrie, Crieff PH6 2EY	01577 863887
Galbraith, W. James L. BSc BD MICE	1973	1996	(Kilchrenan and Dalavich with Muckairn)	19 Mayfield Gardens, Kinross KY13 7GD	01259 743202
Gaston, A. Ray C. MA BD	1969	2002	(Leuchars: St Athernase)	'Hamewith', 13 Manse Road, Dollar FK14 7AL	0131-447 5060
Gordon, Elinor J. (Miss) BD	1988	2001	Board of World Mission	McPhail Flat, 14 Thirlestane Road, Edinburgh EH9 1AN	01764 664594
Gregory, J.C. LTh	1968	1992	(Blantyre St Andrew's)	2 Southlands Road, Auchterarder PH3 1BA	01764 653063
Grimson, John A. MA	1950	1986	(Glasgow Wellington: Associate)	29 Highland Road, Turret Park, Crieff PH7 4LE	01764 681275
Halliday, Archibald R. BD	1964	1999	(Duffus with Forres: St Leonard's with Rafford)	2 Pittenzie Place, Crieff PH7 3JL	
Henry, Malcolm N. MA BD	1951	1987	(Perth Craigie)	Kelton, Castle Douglas DG7 1RU	01556 504144
Houston, Alexander M.	1939	1977	(Tibbermore)	120 Glasgow Road, Perth PH2 0LU	01738 628056
Hughes, Clifford E. MA BD	1993	2001	(Haddington: St Mary's)	Pavilion Cottage, Briglands, Rumbling Bridge, Kinross KY13 0PS	01577 840506
Kelly, T. Clifford	1973	1995	(Ferintosh)	7 Bankfoot Park, Scotlandwell, Kinross KY13 7JP	01592 840387
Lacey, Eric R. BD	1971	1992	(Creich with Rosehall)	The Bungalow, Forteviot, Perth PH2 9BT	01764 684041
Lawson, James B. MA BD	1961	2002	(South Uist)	4 Cowden Way, Comrie, Crieff PH6 2NW	01764 679180
Lawson, Ronald G. MA BD	1964	1999	(Greenock: Wellpark Mid Kirk)	6 East Brougham Street, Stanley, Perth PH1 4NJ	01738 828871
Low, J.E. Stewart MA	1957	1997	(Tarbat)	15 Stormont Place, Scone, Perth PH2 6SR	
McCormick, Alastair F.	1962	1998	(Creich with Rosehall)	14 Balmanno Park, Bridge of Earn, Perth PH2 9RJ	01738 813588
Macdonald, W.U. JP MA	1939	1984	(Aberdalgie and Dupplin with Forteviot)	30 Muircroft West Terrace, Perth PH1 1DY	01738 627948

McGregor, William LTh	1987	2003	(Auchtergaven and Moneydie)	Ard Choille, 7 Taypark Road, Luncarty, Perth PH1 3FE [E-mail: bill.mcgregor@ukonline.co.uk]	01738 827866
MacKenzie, Donald W. MA	1941	1983	(Auchterarder The Barony)	81 Kingswell Terrace, Perth PH1 2DA	01738 633716
MacLean, Nigel R. MA BD	1940	1986	(Perth: St Paul's)	9 Hay Street, Perth PH1 5HS	01738 626728
McLeish, D. Nairn MA	1938	1977	(Fisherton)	Wardside House, Muthill, Crieff PH5 2AS	01764 681275
MacMillan, Riada M. (Mrs) BD	1991	1998	(Perth: Craigend Moncreiffe with Rhynd)	73 Muirend Gardens, Perth PH1 1JR	01738 628867
McNaughton, David J.H. BA CA	1976	1995	(Killin and Ardeonaig)	30 Hollybush Road, Crieff PH7 3HB	01764 653028
MacPhee, Duncan P.	1951	1980	(Braemar with Crathie: Associate)	Braemar Cottage, Ben Alder Place, Kirkcaldy KY2 5RH	01592 201984
McQuilken, John E. MA BD	1969	1992	(Glenaray and Inveraray)	18 Clark Terrace, Crieff PH7 3QE	01764 655764
Millar, Alexander M. MA BD MBA	1980	2001	Secretary Depute: National Mission	17 Mapledene Road, Scone, Perth PH2 6NX [E-mail: millar@millar62.freeserve.co.uk]	01738 550270
Millar, Archibald E. DipTh	1965	1991	(Perth: St Stephen's)	7 Maple Place, Perth PH1 1RT	01738 621813
Munro, Gillian (Miss) BSc BD	1989	2003	Head of Department of Spiritual Care	Royal Dundee Liff Hospital, Liff, Dundee DD2 5ND	
Ritchie, Bruce BSc BD	1977	2001	Board of World Mission	2 Laurel Avenue, Crieff PH7 3EN [E-mail: brucecrieff@compuserve.com]	01764 652531
Shirra, James MA	1945	1987	(St Martin's with Scone New)	17 Dunbarney Avenue, Bridge of Earn, Perth PH2 9BP	01738 812610
Simpson, James A. BSc BD STM DD	1960	2000	(Dornoch Cathedral)	'Dornoch', Perth Road, Bankfoot, Perth PH1 4ED	01738 787710
Stewart, Gordon G. MA	1961	2000	(Perth: St Leonard's-in-the-Fields and Trinity)	'Balnoe', South Street, Rattray, Blairgowrie PH10 7BZ	01250 870626
Stewart, Robin J. MA BD STM	1959	1995	(Orwell with Portmoak)	Oakbrae, Perth Road, Murthly, Perth PH1 4HF	01738 710220
Tait, Henry A.G. MA BD	1966	1997	(Crieff: South and Monzievaird)	14 Shieling Hill Place, Crieff PH7 4ER	01764 652325
Taylor, A.H.S. MA BA BD	1957	1992	(Brydekirk with Hoddam)	41 Anderson Drive, Perth PH1 1LF	01738 626579

PERTH ADDRESSES

Craigie	Abbot Street	North	Mill Street near Kinnoull Street
Kinnoull	Dundee Rd near Queen's Bridge	Riverside	Bute Drive
Letham St Mark's	Rannoch Road	St John's	St John's Street
Moncreiffe	Glenbruar Crescent	St Leonard's-in-the-Fields and Trinity	Marshall Place
		St Matthew's	Tay Street

(29) DUNDEE

Meets at Dundee, Meadowside St Paul's Church Halls, Nethergate, on the second Wednesday of February, March, May, September, October, November and December, and on the fourth Wednesday of June.

Clerk:	**REV. JAMES A. ROY MA BD**	**[E-mail: akph45@uk.uumail.com]**
Presbytery Office:		**Nicoll's Lane, Dundee DD2 3HG**	**01382 611415**

Abernyte linked with Inchture and Kinnaird linked with Longforgan (H)

Diana Hobson (Mrs) BA BD	2002		The Manse, Longforgan, Dundee DD2 5EU	01382 360238
Elizabeth Kay (Miss) DipYCS (Aux)	1993	1999	1 Kintail Walk, Inchture, Perth PH14 9RY [E-mail: lizkay@clara.co.uk]	01828 686029

Auchterhouse (H) linked with Murroes and Tealing (T)
Sydney S. Graham BD DipYL MPhil — 1987 1995 — The Manse, Balgray, Tealing, Dundee DD4 0QZ
[E-mail: graythorn@sol.co.uk] — 01382 380224

Gordon Campbell MA CDipAF DipHSM MCMI MIHM MRIN ARSGS FRGS FSAScot (Aux) — 2 Falkland Place, Kingoodie, Invergowrie, Dundee DD2 5DY — 01382 561383

Dundee: Balgay (H)
George K. Robson LTh DPS BA — 1983 1987 — 150 City Road, Dundee DD2 2PW
[E-mail: gkrobson@rev-balgay.freeserve.co.uk] — 01382 668806

Dundee: Barnhill St Margaret's (H)
Fraser M.C. Stewart BSc BD — 1980 2000 — The Manse, Invermark Terrace, Broughty Ferry, Dundee DD5 2QU — 01382 779278

Dundee: Broughty Ferry East (H) (01382 738264)
Vacant — 8 West Queen Street, Broughty Ferry, Dundee DD5 1AR — 01382 778972

Dundee: Broughty Ferry St Aidan's (T) (H)
Vacant — 63 Collingwood Street, Barnhill, Dundee DD5 2UF — 01382 736828

Dundee: Broughty Ferry St James' (H)
Vacant

Dundee: Broughty Ferry St Luke's and Queen Street
C. Graham Taylor BSc BD FIAB — 2001 — 22 Albert Road, Broughty Ferry, Dundee DD5 1AZ — 01382 779212

Dundee: Broughty Ferry St Stephen's and West (H)
John U. Cameron BA BSc PhD BD ThD — 1974 — 33 Camperdown Street, Broughty Ferry, Dundee DD5 3AA — 01382 477403

Dundee: Camperdown (H) (01382 623958)
Vacant — Camperdown Manse, Myrekirk Road, Dundee DD2 4SF — 01382 621383
James H. Simpson BSc (Aux) — 1996 1999 — 11 Claypotts Place, Broughty Ferry, Dundee DD5 1LG — 01382 776520

Dundee: Chalmers Ardler (H)
Kenneth D. Stott MA BD — 1989 1997 — The Manse, Turnberry Avenue, Dundee DD2 3TP
[E-mail: arkstott@aol.com] — 01382 827439

Jane Martin (Miss) DCS — 12A Carnoustie Court, Ardler, Dundee DD2 3RB — 01382 813786

Dundee: Clepington linked with Dundee: Fairmuir
James G. Redpath BD DipPTh — 1988 2003 — 9 Abercorn Street, Dundee DD4 7HY — 01382 458314

Dundee: Craigiebank (H) (01382 457951) linked with Douglas and Angus (01382 739884)

Michael V.A. Mair MA BD	1967	1998	244 Arbroath Road, Dundee DD4 7SB	01382 452237
Edith F. McMillan (Mrs) MA BD (Assoc)	1981	1999	19 Americanmuir Road, Dundee DD3 9AA	01382 812423
			[E-mail: edith.stewart-macmillan@ukonline.co.uk]	

Dundee: Douglas and Angus (01382 739884) See Dundee: Craigiebank

Dundee: Downfield South (H) (01382 810624)
Lezley J. Kennedy (Mrs) BD ThM MTh	2000		15 Elgin Street, Dundee DD3 8NL	01382 889498

Dundee: Dundee (St Mary's) (H) (01382 226271)
Keith F. Hall MA BD	1980	1994	33 Strathern Road, West Ferry, Dundee DD5 1PP	01382 778808

Dundee: Fairmuir (H) See Dundee: Clepington

Dundee: Lochee Old and St Luke's (T)
Vacant

Dundee: Lochee West (H)
James A. Roy MA BD	1965	1973	Beechwood, 7 Northwood Terrace, Wormit, Newport-on-Tay DD6 8PP	01382 543578
			[E-mail: j.roy@btinternet.com]	

Dundee: Logie and St John's Cross (H)
David S. Scott MA BD	1987	1999	7 Hyndford Street, Dundee DD2 1HQ	01382 641572

Dundee: Mains (H) (01382 812166)
Vacant			9 Elgin Street, Dundee DD3 8NL	01382 825562
Jean Allan (Mrs) DCS			12C Hindmarsh Avenue, Dundee DD3 7LW	01382 827299

Dundee: Mains of Fintry (01382 508191)
Colin M. Brough BSc BD	1998	2002	4 Clive Street, Dundee DD4 7AW	01382 458629
			[E-mail: colin.brough@btinternet.com]	

Dundee: Meadowside St Paul's (H) (01382 225420)
Maudeen I. MacDougall (Miss) BA BD	1978	1984	36 Blackness Avenue, Dundee DD2 1HH	01382 668828

Dundee: Menzieshill
Harry J. Brown LTh	1991	1996	The Manse, Charleston Drive, Dundee DD2 4ED	01382 667446
			[E-mail: harrybrown@aol.com]	
David Sutherland (Aux)			6 Cromarty Drive, Dundee DD2 2UQ	01382 621473

Dundee: Mid Craigie (T) (01382 506147)
Vacant			96 Forfar Road, Dundee DD4 7BG	01382 453926

Dundee: St Andrew's (H) (01382 224860)
Ian D. Petrie MA BD — 1970 1986 — 77 Blackness Avenue, Dundee DD2 1JN — 01382 641695

Dundee: St David's High Kirk (H) (01382 224433)
William B. Ross LTh CPS — 1988 — 6 Adelaide Place, Dundee DD3 6LF — 01382 322955

Dundee: Steeple (H) (01382 223880)
David M. Clark MA BD — 1989 2000 — 128 Arbroath Road, Dundee DD4 7HR — 01382 455411

Dundee: Stobswell (H)
Jane L. Barron (Mrs) BA DipEd BD MTh — 1999 — 23 Shamrock Street, Dundee DD4 7AH
[E-mail: jane.ian@virgin.net] — 01382 459119

Dundee: Strathmartine (H) (01382 825817)
Stewart McMillan BD — 1983 1990 — 19 Americanmuir Road, Dundee DD3 9AA
[E-mail: edith.stewart-macmillan@ukonline.co.uk] — 01382 812423

Dundee: Trinity (H) (01382 459997)
James MacMillan BD — 1997 2003 — 48 Hawthorn Grove, Ballumbie Castle Estate, Dundee DD5 3NA — 01382 350104

Dundee: West
Andrew T. Greaves BD — 1985 2000 — 22 Hyndford Street, Dundee DD2 1HX — 01382 646586

Dundee: Whitfield (E) (H) (01382 503012) (New Charge Development)
James L. Wilson BD CPS — 1986 2001 — 53 Old Craigie Road, Dundee DD4 7JD
[E-mail: r3vjw@aol.com] — 01382 459249

Fowlis and Liff linked with Lundie and Muirhead of Liff (H) (01382 580550)
Vacant — 149 Coupar Angus Road, Muirhead of Liff, Dundee DD2 5QN — 01382 580210

Inchture and Kinnaird See Abernyte

Invergowrie (H)
Robert J. Ramsay LLB NP BD — 1986 1997 — 2 Boniface Place, Invergowrie, Dundee DD2 5DW
[E-mail: robert@r-j-ramsay.fsnet.co.uk] — 01382 561118

Longforgan See Abernyte
Lundie and Muirhead of Liff See Fowlis and Liff

Monifieth: Panmure (H)
David B. Jamieson MA BD STM — 1974 — 8A Albert Street, Monifieth, Dundee DD5 4JS — 01382 532772

Monifieth: St Rule's (H)
Robert W. Massie LTh | 1989 | 1999 | Church Street, Monifieth, Dundee DD5 4JP [E-mail: revrwm@lineone.net] | 01382 532607

Monifieth: South
Donald W. Fraser MA | 1958 | 1959 | Queen Street, Monifieth, Dundee DD5 4HG | 01382 532646

Monikie and Newbigging
Gordon R. Mackenzie BScAgr BD | 1977 | 1985 | 59B Broomwell Gardens, Monikie, Dundee DD5 3QP [E-mail: grmackenzie@talk21.com] | 01382 370200

Murroes and Tealing See Auchterhouse

Barrett, Leslie M. BD FRICS	1991	2001	Chaplain: University of Abertay, Dundee	26 Shoregate, Crail, Anstruther KY10 3SU [E-mail: leslie@abertay.ac.uk]	01333 451599
Clarkson, Robert G.	1950	1989	(Dundee: Strathmartine)	320 Strathmartine Road, Dundee DD3 8QG [E-mail: rob.gov@virgin.net]	01382 825380
Craig, Iain R. MA	1948	1988	(Invergowrie)	Hope View, Burton Row, Brent Knoll, Highbridge, Somerset TA9 4BX	01278 760719
Craik, Sheila (Mrs) BD	1989	2001	(Dundee: Camperdown)	35 Haldane Terrace, Dundee DD3 0HT	01382 802078
Cramb, Erik M. LTh	1973	1989	Industrial Mission Organiser	65 Clepington Road, Dundee DD4 7BQ [E-mail: erikcramb@aol.com]	01382 458764
Douglas, Fiona C. (Miss) MA BD PhD	1989	1997	Chaplain: University of Dundee	10 Springfield, Dundee DD1 4JE	01382 344157
Gammack, George BD	1985	1999	(Dundee: Whitfield)	13A Hill Street, Broughty Ferry, Dundee DD5 2JP	01382 778636
Hamilton, James BA BD	1939	1982	(Auchterhouse)	Telford House, Blairlogie, Stirling FK9 5PX	01259 761721
Hawdon, John E. BA MTh AICS	1961	1995	(Dundee: Clepington)	53 Hillside Road, Dundee DD2 1QT [E-mail: jandjhawdon@btopenworld.com]	01382 646212
Hudson, J. Harrison DipTh MA BD	1961	1999	(Dundee: St Peter's McCheyne)	22 Hamilton Avenue, Tayport DD6 9BW	01382 552052
Ingram, J.R.	1954	1978	(Chaplain: RAF)	48 Marlee Road, Broughty Ferry, Dundee DD5 3EX	01382 736400
Laidlaw, John J. MA	1964	1973	(Adviser in Religious Education)	14 Dalhousie Road, Barnhill, Dundee DD5 2SQ	01382 477458
Mackenzie, George R.R. MA BD	1942	1987	(Dundee: Logie and St John's Cross)	39 Middlebank Crescent, Dundee DD2 1HZ	01382 668491
McLeod, David C. BSc MEng BD	1969	2001	(Dundee: Fairmuir)	6 Carseview Gardens, Dundee DD2 1NE [E-mail: david.mcleod1@tesco.net]	01382 641371
McMillan, Hector G.	1964		(Hamilton North)	6 Kinghorne Terrace, Dundee DD3 6HX	01382 224803
Malvenan, Dorothy DCS	1964	1990	The Deaf Association, Dundee	Flat 19, 6 Craigie Street, Dundee DD4 6PF	01382 462495
Miller, Charles W. MA	1953	1994	(Fowlis and Liff)	'Palm Springs', Parkside, Auchterhouse, Dundee DD3 0RS	01382 320407
Milroy, Tom	1960	1992	(Monifieth: St Rule's)	9 Long Row, Westhaven, Carnoustie DD7 6BE	01241 856654
Mitchell, Jack MA BD CTh	1987	1996	(Dundee: Menzieshill)	10 Invergowrie Drive, Dundee DD2 1RF	01382 642301
Mowat, Gilbert M. MA	1948	1986	(Dundee: Albany-Butterburn)	7 Dunmore Gardens, Dundee DD2 1PP	01382 566013
Powrie, James E. LTh	1969	1995	(Dundee: Chalmers Ardler)	3 Kirktonhill Road, Kirriemuir DD8 4HU	01575 572503
Rae, Robert LTh	1968	1983	Chaplain: Dundee Acute Hospitals	14 Neddertoun View, Liff, Dundee DD3 5RU	01382 581790
Robertson, Thomas P.	1963	2001	(Dundee: Broughty Ferry St James')	20 Kilnburn, Newport-on-Tay DD6 8DE	01382 542422
Rogers, James M. BA DB DCult	1955	1996	(Gibraltar)	24 Mansion Drive, Dunclaverhouse, Dundee DD4 9DD	01382 506162

Scott, Gideon G. MA BD ThM	1963	2003	(Dundee: Albany-Butterburn with St David's North)	150 Kingsway, Dundee DD3 8JR	01382 813728
Scroggie, John C.	1951	1985	(Mains)	4 Bell Tree Gardens, Balmossie, Dundee DD5 2LJ	01382 739354
Scoular, Stanley	1963	2000	(Rosyth)	31 Duns Crescent, Dundee DD4 0RY	01382 501653
Smith, Lilian MA DCS			(Deaconess)	6 Fintry Mains, Dundee DD4 9HF	01382 500052

DUNDEE ADDRESSES

Church	Address	Church	Address	Church	Address
Balgay		Craigiebank	Craigie Avenue at Greendyke Road	Meadowside St Paul's	114 Nethergate
Barnhill St Margaret's	200 Lochee Road	Douglas and Angus	Balbeggie Place	Menzieshill	Charleston Drive, Lochee
Broughty Ferry	10 Invermark Terrace	Downfield South	Haldane Street off Strathmartine Road	Mid Craigie	Longtown Terrace
East		Dundee (St Mary's)	Nethergate	St Andrew's	2 King Street
St Aidan's	370 Queen Street	Fairmuir	329 Clepington Road	St David's High Kirk	119A Kinghorne Road and 273 Strathmore Avenue
St James'	408 Brook Street	Lochee		Steeple	Nethergate
St Luke's and Queen Street	5 Fort Street	Old and St Luke's	Bright Street, Lochee	Stobswell	Top of Albert Street
St Stephen's and West	5 West Queen Street	West	191 High Street, Lochee	Strathmartine	513 Strathmartine Road
Camperdown	96 Dundee Road	Logie and St John's (Cross)		Trinity	73 Crescent Street
Chalmers Ardler	22 Brownhill Road	Mains	Foot of Old Glamis Road	West	130 Perth Road
Clepington	Turnberry Avenue	Mains of Fintry	Fintry Road x Fintry Drive	Whitfield	Haddington Crescent
	Isla Street x Main Street		Shaftsbury Rd x Blackness Ave		

(30) ANGUS

Meets at Forfar in St Margaret's Church Hall, on the first Tuesday of each month, except June when it meets on the last Tuesday, and January, July and August when there is no meeting.

Clerk: **REV. MALCOLM I.G. ROONEY DPE BEd BD**
Depute Clerk: **MRS HELEN McLEOD MA**
Presbytery Office: **St Margaret's Church, West High Street, Forfar DD8 1BJ** **01307 464224** (Tel)
[E-mail: akph36@uk.uumail.com] **01307 465589** (Fax)

Aberlemno linked with Guthrie and Rescobie
Brian Ramsay BD DPS 1980 1984 The Manse, Guthrie, Forfar DD8 2TP 01241 828243

Airlie Ruthven Kingoldrum linked with Glenisla (H) Kilry Lintrathen
Ben Pieterse BA BTh LTh 2001 Balduff House, Kilry, Blairgowrie PH11 8HS 01575 560260
[E-mail: benhp@lineone.net]

Arbirlot linked with Carmyllie linked with Colliston
Vacant — The Manse, Arbirlot, Arbroath DD11 2NX — 01241 875118

Arbroath: Knox's (H) linked with Arbroath: St Vigeans (H)
Ian G. Gough MA BD MTh DMin — 1974 1990 — The Manse, St Vigeans, Arbroath DD11 4RD [E-mail: ianggough@btinternet.com] — 01241 873206

Arbroath: Old and Abbey (H)
Valerie L. Allen (Miss) BMus MDiv — 1990 1996 — 51 Cliffburn Road, Arbroath DD11 5BA [E-mail: vl2allen@aol.com] — 01241 872196 (Tel/Fax)

Arbroath: St Andrew's (H)
W. Martin Fair BA BD — 1992 — Albert Street, Arbroath DD11 1RA [E-mail: martinfair@aol.com] — 01241 873238 (Tel/Fax)

Arbroath: St Vigeans See Arbroath: Knox's

Arbroath: West Kirk (H)
Alasdair G. Graham BD DipMin — 1981 1986 — 1 Charles Avenue, Arbroath DD11 2EY [E-mail: alasdair.graham@lineone.net] — 01241 872244

Barry linked with Carnoustie
Michael S. Goss BD DPS — 1991 2003 — 44 Terrace Road, Carnoustie DD7 7AR — 01241 852289

Brechin: Cathedral (H)
Scott Rennie MA BD STM — 1999 — Chanonry Wynd, Brechin DD9 6JS — 01356 622783

Brechin: Gardner Memorial (H)
Moira Herkes (Mrs) BD — 1985 1999 — 36 Park Road, Brechin DD9 7AP [E-mail: mossherkes@aol.com] — 01356 622789

Carmyllie See Arbirlot
Carnoustie See Barry

Carnoustie Panbride
Matthew S. Bicket BD — 1989 — 8 Arbroath Road, Carnoustie DD7 6BL [E-mail: matthew@bicket.freeserve.co.uk] — 01241 854478 (Tel) / 01241 855088 (Fax)

Colliston See Arbirlot

Dun linked with Hillside
Vacant — 4 Manse Road, Hillside, Montrose DD10 9FB — 01674 830288

Dunnichen, Letham and Kirkden
Allan F. Webster MA BD — 1978 1990 — 7 Braehead Road, Letham, Forfar DD8 2PG [E-mail: allanfwebster@aol.com] — 01307 818916

Eassie and Nevay linked with Newtyle
Carleen Robertson (Miss) BD — 1992 — 2 Kirkton Road, Newtyle, Blairgowrie PH12 8TS — 01828 650461

Edzell Lethnot (H) linked with Fern, Careston and Menmuir linked with Glenesk
Alan G.N. Watt MTh — 1996 2003 — Glenesk Cottage, Dunlappie Road, Edzell, Brechin DD9 7UB — 01356 648455

Farnell linked with Montrose St Andrew's
Vacant — 49 Northesk Road, Montrose DD10 8TQ — 01674 672060

Fern, Careston and Menmuir See Edzell Lethnot

Forfar: East and Old (H)
Graham Norrie MA BD — 1967 1978 — East Manse, Lour Road, Forfar DD8 2BB — 01307 464303

Forfar: Lowson Memorial (H)
Robert McCrum BD — 1982 1992 — 1 Jamieson Street, Forfar DD8 2HY [E-mail: robert.mccrum@virgin.net] — 01307 462248

Forfar: St Margaret's (H)
Jean B. Montgomerie (Miss) MA BD — 1973 1998 — 15 Potters Park Crescent, Forfar DD8 1HH [E-mail: revjeanb@onetel.net.uk] — 01307 466390 (Tel/Fax)

Friockheim Kinnell linked with Inverkeilor and Luman
Vacant — 18 Middlegate, Friockheim, Arbroath DD11 4TS — 01241 828781

Glamis, Inverarity and Kinnettles (T)
John V. Gardner — 1997 2000 — 10 Kirk Wynd, Glamis, Forfar DD8 1RT [E-mail: jvg66@hotmail.com] — 01307 840206 (Tel) / 01307 840724 (Fax)

Glenesk See Edzell Lethnot
Glenisla Kilry Lintrathen See Airlie Ruthven Kingoldrum

Glens, The and Kirriemuir Old
Malcolm I.G. Rooney DPE BEd BD — 1993 1999 — 20 Strathmore Avenue, Kirriemuir DD8 4DJ [E-mail: malcolmrooney@gkopc.freeserve.co.uk] — 01575 573724 (Tel) / 07909 993233 (Mbl)

Guthrie and Rescobie See Aberlemno
Hillside See Dun

Inchbrayock linked with Montrose Melville South
David S. Dixon MA BD — 1976 1994 — The Manse, Ferryden, Montrose DD10 9SD [E-mail: davidsdixon@ukonline.co.uk] — 01674 672108

Inverkeilor and Luman See Friockheim Kinnell

Kirriemuir: St Andrew's linked with Oathlaw Tannadice

David J. Taverner MCIBS ACIS BD   1996   2002   26 Quarry Park, Kirriemuir DD8 4DR   01575 575561
[E-mail: rahereuk@hotmail.com]

Montrose: Melville South See Inchbrayock

Montrose: Old

Laurence A.B. Whitley MA BD PhD   1975   1985   2 Rosehill Road, Montrose DD10 8ST   01674 672447
[E-mail: labwhitley@btinternet.com]

Montrose: St Andrew's See Farnell
Newtyle See Eassie and Nevay
Oathlaw Tannadice See Kirriemuir: St Andrew's

Anderson, James W. BSc MTh	(Kincardine O'Neil with Lumphanan)	1986 1997	47 Glebe Road, Arbroath DD11 4HJ	01241 873298
Brodie, James BEM MA BD STM	(Hurlford)	1955 1974	25A Keptie Road, Arbroath DD11 3ED	01241 873062
Brownlie, Gavin D. MA	(Arbroath: Ladyloan St Columba's)	1955 1990	12 Cliffburn Road, Arbroath DD11 5BB	01241 411078
Bruce, Wallace C. MA BD	(Motherwell: Dalziel)	1961 1995	31 Kirkton Terrace, Carnoustie DD7 7BZ	01241 828030
Butters, David	(Turriff: St Ninian's and Forglen)	1964 1998	68A Millgate, Friockheim, Arbroath DD11 4TN	01241 828717
Douglas, Iain M. MA BD MPhil DipEd	(Farnell with Montrose St Andrew's)	1960 2002	Old School House, Kinnell, Friockheim, Arbroath DD11 4UL	01356 625201
Drysdale James P.R.	(Brechin: Gardner Memorial)	1967 1999	51 Airlie Street, Brechin DD9 6JX	01575 573973
Duncan, Robert F. MTheol	(Lochgelly: St Andrew's)	1986 2001	25 Rowan Avenue, Kirriemuir DD8 4TB	01674 675522
Finlay, Quintin BA BD	(North Bute)	1975 1996	1 Brougham Square, Northesk Road, Montrose DD10 8TD	
Henderson, David C. CBE DD	(Glamis)	1938 1981	c/o Brewster, Easter Denoon, Eassie, Forfar DD8 1SY	
Hodge, William N.T.	(Longside)	1966 1995	'Tullochgorum', 61 South Street, Forfar DD8 2BS	01307 461944
Jones, William	(Kirriemuir: St Andrew's)	1952 1987	14 Muir Street, Forfar DD8 3JY	01307 463193
MacKinnon, A.W.	(Fern, Careston and Menmuir with Oathlaw Tannadice)	1951 1986		
Milton, Eric G.	(Blairdaff)	1963 1994	19 Gallowhill, Brechin DD9 6BL	01356 623812
Perry, Joseph B.	(Farnell)	1955 1989	16 Bruce Court, Links Parade, Carnoustie DD7 7JE	01241 854928
Reid, Albert B. BD BSc	(Ardler, Kettins and Meigle)	1996 2001	19 Guthrie Street, Letham, Forfar DD8 2PS	01307 818741
Russell, A.C. CMG ED MA	(Aberlemno)	1959 1976	1 Dundee Street, Letham, Forfar DD8 2PQ	01307 818416
Searle, David C. MA DipTh	(Warden: Rutherford House)	1965 2003	Balgavies Lodge, Forfar DD8 2TH	01307 818571
Smith, Hamish G.	(Auchterless with Rothienorman)	1965 1993	12 Cairnie Road, Arbroath DD11 3DY	01241 872794
Stevens, David MA	(Glenesk)	1935 1972	11A Guthrie Street, Letham, Forfar DD8 2PS	01307 818973
			c/o Brown, Easter East Coates Cottage, Newburn, Upper Largo, Leven KY8 6JG	
Thomas, Martyn R.H. CEng MIStructE	(Fowlis and Liff with Lundie and Muirhead of Liff)	1987 2002	14 Kirkgait, Letham, Forfar DD8 2XQ	01307 818084
Thomas, Shirley (Mrs)	Auxiliary Minister	2000	14 Kirkgait, Letham, Forfar DD8 2XQ	01307 818084
Tyre, Robert	(Aberdeen: St Ninian's with Stockethill)	1960 1998	8 Borrowfield Crescent, Montrose DD10 9BR	01674 676961
Warnock, Denis MA	(Kirkcaldy: Torbain)	1952 1990	19 Keptie Road, Arbroath DD11 3ED	01241 872740
Weatherhead, James L. CBE MA LLB DD	(Principal Clerk)	1960 1996	59 Brechin Road, Kirriemuir DD8 4DE	01575 572237
Youngson, Peter	(Kirriemuir: St Andrew's)	1961 1996	Coreen, Woodside, Northmuir, Kirriemuir DD8 4PG	01575 572832

ANGUS ADDRESSES

Arbroath
Old and Abbey — West Abbey Street
Knox's — Howard Street
St Andrew's — Hamilton Green
West Kirk — Keptie Street

Brechin
Cathedral — Bishops Close
Gardner Memorial — South Esk Street

Carnoustie
Panbride — Dundee Street / Arbroath Road

Forfar
East: Old — East High Street
Lowson Memorial — Jamieson Street
St Margaret's — West High Street

Kirriemuir
Old — High Street
St Andrew's — Glamis Road

Montrose
Melville South — Castle Street
Old — High Street
St Andrew's — George Street

(31) ABERDEEN

Meets at St Mark's Church, Rosemount Viaduct, Aberdeen, on the first Tuesday of February, March, April, May, September, October, November and December, and on the fourth Tuesday of June.

Clerk:	REV. IAN A. McLEAN BSc BD		
Presbytery Office:	Mastrick Church, Greenfern Road, Aberdeen AB16 6TR		01224 690494 (Tel/Fax)
	[E-mail: akph34@uk.uumail.com]		
Hon. Treasurer:	MR A. SHARP	27 Hutchison Terrace, Aberdeen AB10 7NN	01224 315702

Aberdeen: Beechgrove (H) (01224 632102)
Iain M. Forbes BSc BD   1964   2000   156 Hamilton Place, Aberdeen AB15 5BB   01224 642615
[E-mail: beechgro@fish.co.uk]

Aberdeen: Bridge of Don Oldmachar (E) (01224 709299)
Jim Ritchie BD MTh DipTh   2000   60 Newburgh Circle, Aberdeen AB22 8QZ   01224 708137
[E-mail: revjim@tinyworld.co.uk]

Aberdeen: Cove (E)
Fyfe Blair BA BD DMin   1989   1998   4 Charleston Way, Cove, Aberdeen AB12 3FA   01224 898030
[E-mail: ncdcove@uk.uumail.com]

Aberdeen: Craigiebuckler (H) (01224 315649)
Kenneth L. Petrie MA BD   1984   1999   185 Springfield Road, Aberdeen AB15 8AA   01224 315125
[E-mail: patandkenneth@aol.com]

Aberdeen: Denburn (H)
James Patterson — 2003 — 122 Deswood Place, Aberdeen AB15 4DQ
[E-mail: jimandmegan@btopenworld.com] — 01224 641033

Aberdeen: Ferryhill (H) (01224 213093)
John H.A. Dick MA MSc BD — 1982 — 54 Polmuir Road, Aberdeen AB11 7RT
[E-mail: jhadick@fish.co.uk] — 01224 586933

Aberdeen: Garthdee (H)
Christine Houghton (Mrs) BD — 1997 2002 — 27 Ramsay Gardens, Aberdeen AB10 7AE
[E-mail: christine@houghton1027.fsnet.co.uk] — 01224 317452

Aberdeen: Gilcomston South (H) (01224 647144)
D. Dominic Smart BSc BD MTh — 1988 — 37 Richmondhill Road, Aberdeen AB15 5EQ
[E-mail: smartdd@lineone.net] — 01224 314326

Aberdeen: Greyfriars John Knox (T) (01224 644719)
Vacant — 41 Gray Street, Aberdeen AB10 6JD — 01224 584594

Aberdeen: High Hilton (H) (01224 494717)
A. Peter Dickson BSc BD — 1996 — 24 Rosehill Drive, Aberdeen AB24 4JJ
[E-mail: peter@highhilton.com] — 01224 484155

Aberdeen: Holburn Central (H) (01224 580967)
George S. Cowie BSc BD — 1991 — 6 St Swithin Street, Aberdeen AB10 6XE
[E-mail: gscowie@aol.com] — 01224 593302

Aberdeen: Holburn West (H) (01224 571120)
Duncan C. Eddie MA BD — 1992 — 31 Cranford Road, Aberdeen AB10 7NJ
[E-mail: nacnud@ceddie.freeserve.co.uk] — 01224 325873

Aberdeen: Mannofield (H) (01224 310087)
John F. Anderson MA BD FSAScot — 1966 1975 — 21 Forest Avenue, Aberdeen AB15 4TU
[E-mail: mannofieldchurch@lineone.net] — 01224 315748

Aberdeen: Mastrick (H) (01224 694121)
Vacant — 13 Beechgrove Avenue, Aberdeen AB15 5EZ — 01224 638011

Aberdeen: Middlefield (H)
Vacant — 73 Manor Avenue, Aberdeen AB16 7UT — 01224 685214

Aberdeen: New Stockethill (New Charge Development)
Ian M. Aitken — 1999 — 52 Ashgrove Road West, Aberdeen AB16 5EE
[E-mail: ncdstockethill@uk.uumail.com] — 01224 686929

Aberdeen: North of St Andrew (T) (01224 643567)
Graeme W.M. Muckart MTh MSc FSAScot   1983   1997
51 Osborne Place, Aberdeen   AB25 2BX
[E-mail: gw2m@clara.net]
01224 646429

Aberdeen: Northfield
Scott C. Guy BD   1989   1999
28 Byron Crescent, Aberdeen   AB16 7EX
[E-mail: scguy@xalt.co.uk]
01224 692332

Duncan Ross DCS
64 Stewart Crescent, Aberdeen   AB16 5SR
[E-mail: dross@fish.co.uk]
01224 692519

Aberdeen: Queen's Cross (H) (01224 644742)
Robert F. Brown MA BD ThM   1971   1984
1 St Swithin Street, Aberdeen   AB10 6XH
[E-mail: qxc@globalnet.co.uk]
01224 322549

Aberdeen: Rosemount (H) (01224 620111)
A. David M. Graham BA BD   1971   1983
22 Osborne Place, Aberdeen   AB25 2DA
01224 648041

Aberdeen: Rubislaw (H) (01224 645477)
Andrew G.N. Wilson MA BD DMin   1977   1987
45 Rubislaw Den South, Aberdeen   AB15 4BD
[E-mail: andrewg.wilson@virgin.net]
01224 314878

Aberdeen: Ruthrieston South (H) (01224 211730)
Hugh F. Kerr MA BD   1968   1985
39 Gray Street, Aberdeen   AB10 6JD
01224 586762

Aberdeen: Ruthrieston West (H)
Sean Swindells BD DipMin   1996
451 Great Western Road, Aberdeen   AB10 6NL
[E-mail: seanswinl@aol.com]
01224 313075

Aberdeen: St Columba's Bridge of Don (H) (01224 825653)
Louis Kinsey BD DipMin   1991
151 Jesmond Avenue, Aberdeen   AB22 8UG
[E-mail: revkinsey@aol.com]
01224 705337

Aberdeen: St George's Tillydrone (H) (01224 482204)
James Weir BD   1991   2003
127 Clifton Road, Aberdeen   AB24 3RH
01224 483976

Ann V. Lundie (Miss) DCS
20 Langdykes Drive, Cove, Aberdeen   AB12 3HW
01224 898416

Aberdeen: St John's Church for Deaf People (H) (01224 494566)
John R. Osbeck BD   1979   1991
15 Deeside Crescent, Aberdeen   AB15 7PT
[E-mail: info@aneds.org.uk]
(Voice/Text) 01224 315595

Aberdeen: St Machar's Cathedral (H) (01224 485988)
Vacant
18 The Chanonry, Old Aberdeen   AB24 1RQ
01224 483688

Aberdeen: St Mark's (H) (01224 640672)
John M. Watson LTh — 1989 — 65 Mile-end Avenue, Aberdeen AB15 5PU [E-mail: jomwat@aol.com] — 01224 622470

Aberdeen: St Mary's (H) (01224 487227)
Vacant — 456 King Street, Aberdeen AB24 3DE — 01224 633778

Aberdeen: St Nicholas Uniting, Kirk of (H) (01224 643494)
J. Ross McLaren MBE — 1964 2002 — 8 Hilton Street, Aberdeen AB24 4QX — 01224 491160

Aberdeen: St Nicholas Kincorth, South of
Edward C. McKenna BD DPS — 1989 2002 — The Manse, Kincorth Circle, Aberdeen AB12 5NX — 01224 872820

Aberdeen: St Ninian's (T) (01224 319519)
Alison J. Swindells (Mrs) LLB BD — 1998 2000 — 451 Great Western Road, Aberdeen AB10 6NL [E-mail: alisonswindells@aol.com] — 01224 317667

Aberdeen: St Stephen's (H) (01224 624443)
James M. Davies BSc BD — 1982 1989 — 6 Belvidere Street, Aberdeen AB25 2QS [E-mail: james.davies85@hotmail.com] — 01224 635694

Aberdeen: Summerhill
Ian A. McLean BSc BD — 1981 — 36 Stronsay Drive, Aberdeen AB15 6JL [E-mail: iamclean@lineone.net] — 01224 324669

Aberdeen: Torry St Fittick's (H) (01224 899183)
Iain C. Barclay MBE TD MA BD MTh MPhil PhD — 1976 1999 — 11 Devanha Gardens East, Aberdeen AB11 7UH [E-mail: st.fittick@virgin.net] — 01224 588245 / 07968 131930 (Mbl) / 07625 383830 (Pager)

Aberdeen: Woodside (H) (01224 277249)
Alistair Murray BD — 1984 1990 — 322 Clifton Road, Aberdeen AB24 4HQ [E-mail: ally.murray@btopenworld.com] — 01224 484562
Ann V. Lundie DCS — 20 Langdykes Drive, Cove, Aberdeen AB12 3HW — 01224 898416

Bucksburn Stoneywood (H) (01224 712411)
Nigel Parker BD MTh — 1994 — 25 Gilbert Road, Bucksburn, Aberdeen AB21 9AN [E-mail: nigel@revparker.fsnet.co.uk] — 01224 712635

Cults: East (T) (H) (01224 869028)
Flora J. Munro (Mrs) BD — 1993 — Cults, Aberdeen AB15 9TD [E-mail: cults-east.church@breathemail.net] — 01224 867587

Cults: West (H) (01224 869566)
Thomas C. Richardson LTh ThB — 1971 1978 — 3 Quarry Road, Cults, Aberdeen AB15 9EX [E-mail: tom.richardson2@virgin.net] — 01224 867417

Dyce (H) (01224 771295)
Russel Moffat BD MTh PhD   1986   1998   144 Victoria Street, Dyce, Aberdeen AB21 7BE   01224 722380
[E-mail: russelbrenda@dyce144.freeserve.co.uk]

Kingswells
Harvey L. Grainger LTh   1975   1989   Kingswells Manse, Lang Stracht, Aberdeen AB15 8PL   01224 740229 (Tel)
[E-mail: harvey.grainger@btinternet.com]   07713 855815 (Mbl)

Newhills (H) (Tel/Fax: 01224 716161)
Norman Maciver MA BD DMin   1976   Newhills Manse, Bucksburn, Aberdeen AB21 9SS   01224 712655
[E-mail: newhillsnm@aol.com]

Peterculter (H) (01224 735845)
John A. Ferguson BD DipMin   1988   1999   7 Howie Lane, Peterculter, Aberdeen AB14 0LJ   01224 735041
[E-mail: jc.ferguson@virgin.net]

Aitchison, James W. BD	1993		Chaplain: Army	HQ Briton, UNFICUP, BFPO 567	
Alexander, William M. BD	1971	1998	(Berriedale and Dunbeath with Latheron)	110 Fairview Circle, Danestone, Aberdeen AB22 8YR	01224 703752
Ballantyne, Samuel MA BD	1941	1982	(Rutherford)	26 Cairncry Road, Aberdeen AB16 5DP	01224 483049
Beattie, Walter G. MA BD	1956	1995	(Arbroath Old and Abbey)	126 Seafield Road, Aberdeen AB15 7YQ	01224 329259
Bryden, Agnes Y. (Mrs) DCS			(Deaconess)	9 Rosewell Place, Aberdeen AB15 6HN	01224 315042
Campbell, W.M.M. BD CPS	1970	1986	(Hospital Chaplain)	43 Murray Terrace, Aberdeen AB11 7SA	07761 235815
Coutts, Fred MA BD	1973	1989	Hospital Chaplain	9A Millburn Street, Aberdeen AB11 6SS	01224 583805
Crawford, Michael S.M. LTh	1966	2002	(Aberdeen: St Mary's)	9 Craigton Avenue, Aberdeen AB15 7RR	
Deans, John Bell	1951	1986	(Hospital Chaplain)	14 Balmoral Avenue, Ellon AB41 9EW	01358 721539
Dickson, John C. MA	1950	1987	(Aberdeen St Fittick's)	36 Queen Victoria Park, Inchmarlo, Banchory AB31 4AL	01330 826236
Douglas, Andrew M. MA	1957	1995	(High Hilton)	219 Countesswells Road, Aberdeen AB15 7RD	01224 311932
Falconer, James B. BD	1982	1992	Hospital Chaplain	3 Brimmond Walk, Westhill, Skene AB32 6XH	01224 744621
				[E-mail: james.falconer@virgin.net]	
Finlayson, Ena (Miss) DCS	1953	1995	(Deaconess)	16E Denwood, Aberdeen AB15 6JF	01224 321147
Goldie, George D. ALCM	1960	1995	(Greyfriars)	27 Broomhill Avenue, Aberdeen AB10 6JL	01224 322503
Gordon, Laurie Y.	1937	1986	(John Knox)	1 Alder Drive, Portlethen, Aberdeen AB12 4WA	01224 782703
Grubb, Anthony J. MA BD	1963	1999	(Deer)	Ardier House, Oakdale Terrace, Aberdeen AB15 7PT	01224 352177
Haddow, Angus BSc			(Methlick)	25 Lerwick Road, Aberdeen AB16 6RF	01224 696362
Hamilton, Helen (Miss) BD	1991	2003	(Glasgow: St James' Pollok)	The Cottage, West Tilbouries, Maryculter, Aberdeen AB12 5GD	01224 739632
Hutchison, A. Scott MA BD DD	1957	1991	(Hospital Chaplain)	Ashfield, Drumoak, Banchory AB31 5AG	01330 811309
Hutchison, Alison M. (Mrs) BD DipMin	1988	1988	Hospital Chaplain	Ashfield, Drumoak, Banchory AB31 5AG	01330 811309
				[E-mail: amhutch62@aol.com]	
Hutchison, David S. BSc BD ThM	1991	1999	(Aberdeen: Torry St Fittick's)	51 Don Street, Aberdeen AB24 1UH	01224 276122
Jack, David LTh	1984	1999	(West Mearns)	7 Cromwell Road, Aberdeen AB15 4UH	01224 325355
Johnstone, William MA BD	1963	2001	(University of Aberdeen)	9/5 Mount Alvernia, Edinburgh EH16 6AW	0131-664 3140

Name	Dates	Position	Address	Telephone
McCallum, Moyra (Miss) MA BD DCS	1963 2001	(Deaconess)	176 Hilton Drive, Aberdeen AB24 4LT [E-mail: moymac@aol.com]	01224 486240
Main, Alan TD MA BD STM PhD		(University of Aberdeen)	Kirkfield, Barthol Chapel, Inverurie AB51 8TD [E-mail: amain@fish.co.uk]	01651 806773
Mirrilees, J.B. MA BD	1937 1977	(High Hilton)	22 King's Gate, Aberdeen AB15 4EJ	01224 638351
Russell, Andrew M. MA BD	1940 1976	(Woodside North)	3 Hill Place, Alloa FK10 2LP	01259 213115
Sefton, Henry R. MA BD STM PhD	1957 1992	(University of Aberdeen)	25 Albury Place, Aberdeen AB11 6TQ	01224 572305
Skakle, George S. MA	1945 1987	(Aberdeen Powis)	30 Whitehall Terrace, Aberdeen AB25 2RY	01224 646478
Smith, Angus MA LTh	1965 1991	Industrial Chaplain	1 Fa'burn Terrace, Lumphanan, Banchory AB31 4AG	01339 883395
Stewart, James C. MA BD STM	1960 2000	(Aberdeen: Kirk of St Nicholas)	54 Murray Terrace, Aberdeen AB11 7SB	01224 587071
Strachan, Ian M. MA BD	1959 1994	(Ashkirk with Selkirk)	'Cardenwell', Glen Drive, Dyce, Aberdeen AB21 7EN	01224 772028
Swinton, John BD PhD	1999	University of Aberdeen	51 Newburgh Circle, Bridge of Don, Aberdeen AB22 8XA [E-mail: j.swinton@abdn.ac.uk]	01224 825637
Torrance, Iain R. TD MA BD DPhil	1982 1993	University of Aberdeen (01224 272274)	Concraig Smiddy, Clinterty, Kingswells, Aberdeen AB15 8RN [E-mail: i.r.torrance@abdn.ac.uk]	01224 790902
Walton, Ainslie MA MEd	1954 1995	(University of Aberdeen)	359 Great Western Road, Aberdeen AB10 6NU	01224 318218
Watt, William G.	1970 1977	(South of St Nicholas Kincorth)	50 Rosewell Gardens, Aberdeen AB15 6HZ	01224 321915
Wilkie, William E. LTh	1978 2001	(Aberdeen: St Nicholas Kincorth, South of)	38 St Anne's Crescent, Newtonhill, Stonehaven AB39 3WZ	01569 731630
Wood, James L.K.	1967 1995	(Ruthrieston West)	1 Glen Drive, Dyce, Aberdeen AB21 7EN	01224 722543

ABERDEEN ADDRESSES

Beechgrove	Beechgrove Avenue
Bridge of Don Oldmachar	Ashwood Park
Cove	Loirston Primary School, Loirston Avenue
Craigiebuckler	Springfield Road
Cults East	North Deeside Road, Cults
Cults West	Quarry Road, Cults
Denburn	Summer Street
Dyce	Victoria Street, Dyce
Ferryhill	Fonthill Road x Polmuir Road
Garthdee	Ramsay Gardens
Gilcomston South	Union Street x Summer Street
Greyfriars John Knox	Broad Street
High Hilton	Hilton Drive
Holburn Central	Holburn Street
Holburn West	Great Western Road
Kingswells	Old Skene Road, Kingswells
Mannofield	Great Western Road x Craigton Road
Mastrick	Greenfern Road
Middlefield	Manor Avenue
North Church of St Andrew	Queen Street
Northfield	Byron Crescent
Peterculter	Craigton Crescent
Queen's Cross	Albyn Place
Rosemount	Rosemount Place
Rubislaw	Queen's Gardens
Ruthrieston South	Holburn Street
Ruthrieston West	Broomhill Road
St Columba's	Braehead Way, Bridge of Don
St George's	Hayton Road, Tillydrone
St John's for the Deaf	Smithfield Road
St Machar's	The Chanonry
St Mark's	Rosemount Viaduct
St Mary's	King Street
St Nicholas Kincorth, South of	Kincorth Circle
St Nicholas Uniting, Kirk of	Union Street
St Ninian's	Mid Stocket Road
St Stephen's	Powis Place
New Stockethill	Castleton Crescent
Summerhill	Stronsay Drive
Torry St Fittick's	Walker Road
Woodside	Church Street, Woodside

(32) KINCARDINE AND DEESIDE

Meets at Fetteresso, Stonehaven on the first Tuesday of February, the last Tuesday of March, the first Tuesday of May, the last Tuesday of June, the last Tuesday of September, the first Tuesday of November and the first Tuesday of December at 7pm.

Clerk: **REV. JACK HOLT BSc BD**   **The Manse, Finzean, Banchory AB31 6PB**   **01330 850339**
[E-mail: akph58@uk.uumail.com]
[E-mail: kincardinedeeside.presbytery@uk.uumail.com]

Aberluthnott linked with Laurencekirk (H)
Ronald Gall BSc BD   1985   2001   Aberdeen Road, Laurencekirk AB30 1AJ   01561 378838
[E-mail: ronniegall@aol.com]

Aboyne – Dinnet (H)
Vacant   49 Charlton Crescent, Charlton Park, Aboyne AB34 5GN   01339 886447

Arbuthnott linked with Bervie
Alastair McKillop BD DipMin   1995   10 Kirkburn, Inverbervie, Montrose DD10 0RT   01561 362633
[E-mail: alastairmckillop<revicar@revicar.freeserve.co.uk]

Banchory-Devenick and Maryculter/Cookney
Bruce K. Gardner MA BD PhD   1988   2002   The Manse, Kirkton of Maryculter, Aberdeen AB12 5FS   01224 735776
[E-mail: ministerofbdmc@aol.com]

Banchory Ternan: East (H) (Tel: 01330 820380; E-mail: eastchurch@banchory.fsbusiness.co.uk)
Mary M. Haddow (Mrs) BD   2001   East Manse, Station Road, Banchory AB31 5YP   01330 822481
[E-mail: mary_haddow@ntlworld.com]
Anthony Stephen Haddow MA BD (Assistant Minister   2001   72 Grant Road, Banchory AB31 5UU   01330 825038
and Youth Leader)

Banchory Ternan: West (H)
Donald K. Walker BD   1979   1995   2 Wilson Road, Banchory AB31 5UY   01330 822811
[E-mail: walkerdk.exzam@virgin.net]
Anthony Stephen Haddow MA BD (Assistant Minister   2001   72 Grant Road, Banchory AB31 5UU   01330 825038
and Youth Leader)

Bervie See Arbuthnott

Birse and Feughside
Jack Holt BSc BD   1985   1994   The Manse, Finzean, Banchory AB31 6PB   01330 850237
[E-mail: jack@finzean.freeserve.co.uk]

Braemar linked with Crathie
Robert P. Sloan MA BD — 1968 — 1996 — Manse, Crathie, Ballater AB35 5UL — 01339 742208

Crathie See Braemar

Cromar
Lawrie I. Lennox MA BD DipEd — 1991 — 2001 — Aberdeen Road, Tarland, Aboyne AB34 4UA — 01339 881464

Drumoak (H) and Durris (H)
James Scott MA BD — 1973 — 1992 — Manse, Durris, Banchory AB31 6BU — 01330 844557
[E-mail: jimscott@durrismanse.freeserve.co.uk]

Glenmuick (Ballater) (H)
Anthony Watts BD DipTechEd JP — 1999 — The Manse, Craigendarroch Walk, Ballater AB35 5ZB — 01339 754014

Kinneff linked with Stonehaven South (H)
David J. Stewart BD MTh DipMin — 2000 — South Church Manse, Cameron Street, Stonehaven AB39 2HE — 01569 762576
[E-mail: brigodon@ifb.co.uk]

Laurencekirk See Aberluthnott

Mearns Coastal
George I. Hastie MA BD — 1971 — 1998 — The Manse, Kirkton, St Cyrus, Montrose DD10 0BW — 01674 850880 (Tel/Fax)

Mid Deeside
Norman Nicoll BD — 2003 — The Manse, Torphins, Banchory AB31 4GQ — 01339 882276

Newtonhill
Hugh Conkey BSc BD — 1987 — 2001 — 39 St Ternans Road, Newtonhill, Stonehaven AB39 3PF — 01569 730143
[E-mail: conkey@tesco.net]

Portlethen (H) (01224 782883)
Douglas M. Main BD (Interim Minister) — 1986 — 2002 — 18 Rowanbank Road, Portlethen, Aberdeen AB12 4QY — 01224 780211

Stonehaven: Dunnottar (H)
Gordon Farquharson MA BD DipEd — 1998 — Dunnottar Manse, Stonehaven AB39 3XL — 01569 762874
[E-mail: gfarqu@lineone.net]

Stonehaven: Fetteresso (H) (Tel: 01569 767689; E-mail: office@fetteressokirk.org.uk)
John R. Notman BSc BD — 1990 — 2001 — 11 South Lodge Drive, Stonehaven AB39 2PN — 01569 762876
[E-mail: jr.notman@virgin.net]

Stonehaven: South See Kinneff

West Mearns

Catherine A. Hepburn (Miss) BA BD	1986	2000	West Mearns Parish Church Manse, Fettercairn, Laurencekirk AB30 1YA [E-mail: chepburn@fish.co.uk]	01561 340203

Brown, Alastair BD	1986	1992	(Glenmuick, Ballater)	52 Henderson Drive, Kintore, Inverurie AB51 0FB	01467 632787
Brown, J.W.S. BTh	1960	1995	(Cromar)	10 Forestside Road, Banchory AB31 5ZH	01330 824353
Caie, Albert LTh	1983	1997	(Glenmuick [Ballater])	34 Ringwell Gardens, Stonehouse, Larkhall ML9 3QW	
Christie, Andrew C. LTh	1975	2000	(Banchory-Devenick and Maryculter/Cookney)	17 Broadstraik Close, Elrick, Aberdeen AB32 6JP	01224 746888
Forbes, John W.A. BD	1973	1999	(Edzell Lethnot with Fern, Careston and Menmuir with Glenesk)	Mid Clune, Finzean, Banchory AB31 6PL	01330 850283
Gray, Robert MA BD	1942	1982	(Stonehaven Fetteresso)	4 Park Drive, Stonehaven AB39 2NW	01569 767027
Hood, E.C.P. MA	1946	1989	(Methlick)	1 Silver Gardens, Stonehaven AB39 2LH	
Kimburgh, Elizabeth B.F. (Miss) MA BD	1970	1986	(Birse with Finzean with Strachan)	7 Huntly Cottages, Aboyne AB31 5HD	01339 886757
Lamb, A. Douglas MA	1964	2002	(Dalry: St Margaret's)	130 Denstrath Road, Edzell Woods, Brechin DD9 7XF [E-mail: a.d.lamb@lamb.junglelink.co.uk]	01356 648139
MacLeod, Kenneth	1950	1986	(Bourtreebush with Portlethen)	30 Woodlands Place, Inverbervie, Montrose DD10 0SL	01561 362414
Nicholson, William	1949	1986	(Banchory Ternan East with Durris)	10 Pantoch Gardens, Banchory AB31 5ZD	01330 823875
Rennie, Donald B. MA	1956	1996	(Industrial Chaplain)	Mernis Howe, Inverurie Street, Auchenblae, Laurencekirk AB30 1XS	01561 320622
Skinner, Silvester MA	1941	1979	(Lumphanan)	29 Silverbank Gardens, Banchory AB31 3YZ	01330 823032
Smith, J.A. Wemyss MA	1947	1983	(Garvock St Cyrus)	30 Greenbank Drive, Edinburgh EH10 5RE	0131-447 2205
Taylor, Peter R. JP BD	1977	2001	(Torphins)	42 Beltie Road, Torphins, Banchory AB31 4JT	01339 882780
Tierney, John P. MA	1945	1985	(Peterhead West Associate)	3 Queenshill Drive, Aboyne AB34 5DG	01339 886741
Urie, D.M.L. MA BD PhD	1940	1980	(Kincardine O'Neil)	5 Glebe Park, Kincardine O'Neil, Aboyne AB34 5ED	01339 884204
Watt, William D. LTh	1978	1996	(Aboyne – Dinnet)	2 West Toll Crescent, Aboyne AB34 5GB	01339 886943

(33) GORDON

Meets at various locations on the first Tuesday of February, March, April, May, September, October, November and December; and on the fourth Tuesday of June.

Clerk:	REV. G. EUAN D. GLEN BSc BD	The Manse, 26 St Ninian's, Monymusk, Inverurie AB51 7HF 01467 651470 [E-mail: akph52@uk.uumail.com]

Barthol Chapel linked with Tarves

Vacant	8 Murray Avenue, Tarves, Ellon AB41 7LZ	01651 851250

Belhelvie (H)
Daniel Hawthorn MA BD DMin   1965   Balmedie, Aberdeen AB23 8YR   01358 742227
[E-mail: donhawthorn@compuserve.com]

Blairdaff linked with Chapel of Garioch
Kim Cran (Mrs) MDiv BA   1993   2000   Chapel of Garioch, Inverurie AB51 9HE   01467 681619
[E-mail: blairdaff.chapelofgariochparish@btinternet.com]

Chapel of Garioch See Blairdaff

Cluny linked with Monymusk (H)
G. Euan D. Glen BSc BD   1992   The Manse, 26 St Ninian's, Monymusk, Inverurie AB51 7HF   01467 651470
[E-mail: euanglen@aol.com]

Culsalmond and Rayne linked with Daviot (H)
Mary M. Cranfield (Miss) MA BD DMin   1989   The Manse, Daviot, Inverurie AB51 0HY   01467 671241
[E-mail: marymc@ukgateway.net]

Cushnie and Tough (T) (H)
Margaret J. Garden (Miss) BD   1993   2000   The Manse, Muir of Fowlis, Alford AB33 0HY   01975 581239
[E-mail: m.garden@virgin.net]

Daviot See Culsalmond and Rayne

Drumblade linked with Huntly Strathbogie
Neil I.M. MacGregor BD   1995   Deveron Road, Huntly AB54 5DU   01466 792702

Echt linked with Midmar (T)
Alan Murray BSc BD PhD   2003   The Manse, Echt, Skene AB32 7AB   01330 860004

Ellon
Eleanor E. Macalister (Mrs) BD   1994   1999   The Manse, Ellon AB41 9BA   01358 720476
[E-mail: macal1ster@aol.com]
Pauline Steenbergen (Ms) MA BD (Assoc)   1996   1999   1 Landale Road, Peterhead AB42 1QN   01779 472141
[E-mail: psteenb@fish.co.uk]
Sheila Craggs (Mrs) (Aux)   2001   7 Morar Court, Ellon AB41 9GG   01358 723055

Fintray and Kinellar linked with Keithhall
Vacant   20 Kinmhor Rise, Blackburn, Aberdeen AB21 0LJ   01467 620435

Foveran
Neil Gow BSc MEd BD   1996   2001   The Manse, Foveran, Ellon AB41 6AP   01358 789288
[E-mail: the-gows@lineone.net]

Howe Trinity
John A. Cook MA BD — 1986 — 2000 — The Manse, 110 Main Street, Alford AB33 8AD
[E-mail: j-a-cook@howe-trinity.freeserve.co.uk] — 01975 562282

Huntly Cairnie Glass
Thomas R. Calder LLB BD WS — 1994 — The Manse, Queen Street, Huntly AB54 8EB — 01466 792630

Huntly Strathbogie See Drumblade

Insch-Leslie-Premnay-Oyne (H)
Jane C. Taylor (Miss) BD DipMin — 1990 — 2001 — Western Road, Insch AB52 6JR — 01464 820914

Inverurie: St Andrew's
T. Graeme Longmuir KSJ MA BEd — 1976 — 2001 — St Andrew's Manse, 1 Ury Dale, Inverurie AB51 3XW
[E-mail: standrew@ukonline.co.uk] — 01467 620468
Risby, Lesley P. (Mrs) BD (Assoc) — 1994 — 2002 — Mid Pitmunie, Monymusk, Inverurie AB51 7HX

Inverurie: West
Ian B. Groves BD CPS — 1989 — West Manse, 42 Westfield Road, Inverurie AB51 3YS
[E-mail: igroves@fish.co.uk] — 01467 620285

Keithhall See Fintray and Kinellar

Kemnay
John P. Renton BA LTh — 1976 — 1990 — Kemnay, Inverurie AB51 9ND
[E-mail: johnrenton@btinternet.com] — 01467 642219 (Tel/Fax)

Kintore (H)
Alan Greig BSc BD — 1977 — 1992 — 6 Forest Road, Kintore, Inverurie AB51 0XG
[E-mail: greig@kincarr.free-online.co.uk] — 01467 632219 (Tel/Fax)

Meldrum and Bourtie
Hugh O'Brien CSS MTheol — 2001 — Oldmeldrum, Inverurie AB51 0EQ
[E-mail: minister@meldrum-bourtiechurch.org] — 01651 872250

Methlick
Albert E. Smith BD FSAScot — 1983 — 1999 — Methlick, Ellon AB41 0DS
[E-mail: AESMethlick@aol.com] — 01651 806215

Midmar See Echt
Monymusk See Cluny

New Machar
Manson C. Merchant BD CPS — 1992 — 2001 — The Manse, Disblair Road, Newmachar, Aberdeen AB21 0RD
[E-mail: manson@tinyworld.co.uk] — 01651 862278

Noth
John McCallum BD DipPTh — 1989 — Manse, Kennethmont, Huntly AB54 4NP — [E-mail: rev.john@btopenworld.com] — 01464 831244

Skene (H)
Iain U. Thomson MA BD — 1970 — The Manse, Kirkton of Skene, Skene AB32 6LX — 01224 743277
Marion G. Stewart (Miss) DCS — 1972 — Kirk Cottage, Kirkton of Skene, Skene AB32 6XE — 01224 743407

Tarves See Barthol Chapel

Udny and Pitmedden
George R. Robertson LTh — 1985 — Manse Road, Udny Green, Udny, Ellon AB41 0RS — 01651 842052

Upper Donside (H)
Richard J.G. Darroch BD MTh — 1993 1999 — Lumsden, Huntly AB54 4GQ — [E-mail: richdarr@aol.com] — 01464 861757

Name	Dates	Role	Address	Tel
Andrew, John MA BD DipRE DipEd	1961 1995	(Teacher: Religious Education)	Cartar's Croft, Midmar, Inverurie AB51 7NJ	01330 833208
Bowie, Alfred LTh	1974 1998	(Alford with Keig with Tullynessle Forbes)	17 Stewart Road, Alford AB33 8UD	01975 563824
Collie, Jeannie P. (Miss) DCS		(Deaconess)	3 Formartindale, Udny Station, Ellon AB41 6QJ	01651 842575
Collie, Joyce P. (Miss) MA PhD	1966 1994	(Corgarff Strathdon and Glenbuchat Towie)	35 Foudland Court, Insch AB52 6LG	01464 820945
Dryden, Ian MA DipEd	1988 2001	(New Machar)	16 Glenhome Gardens, Dyce, Aberdeen AB21 0FG	01224 722820
Jones, Robert A. LTh CA	1966 1997	(Marnoch)	13 Gordon Terrace, Inverurie AB51 4GT	01467 622691
Lister, Douglas	1945 1986	(Largo and Newburn)	Gowanbank, Port Elphinstone, Inverurie AB51 3UN	01467 621262
Macallan, Gerald B.	1954 1992	(Kintore)	82 Angusfield Avenue, Aberdeen AB15 6AT	01224 316125
McLeish, Robert S.	1970 2000	(Insch-Leslie-Premnay-Oyne)	19 Western Road, Insch AB52 6JR	01464 820749
Mack, John C. JP (Aux)	1985 2001	Presbytery Auxiliary Minister	The Willows, Auchleven, Insch AB52 6QD	01464 820387
Mellis, Robert J. BTh CA	1982 1998	(Shapinsay)	81 Western Avenue, Ellon AB41 9EX	01358 721929
Milligan, Rodney	1949 1985	(Culsalmond with Rothienorman)	Cameron House, Culduthel Road, Inverness IV2 4YG	01463 243241
Rodger, Matthew A. BD	1978 1999	(Ellon)	57 Eilean Rise, Ellon AB41 9NF	01358 724556
Scott, Allan D. BD	1977 1989	(Culsalmond with Daviot with Rayne)	20 Barclay Road, Inverurie AB51 3QP	01467 625161
Stewart, George C. MA	1952 1995	(Drumblade with Huntly Strathbogie)	104 Scott Drive, Huntly AB54 5PF	
Stoddart, A. Grainger	1975 2001	(Meldrum and Bourtie)	6 Mayfield Gardens, Insch AB52 6XL	01464 821124
Wallace, R.J. Stuart MA	1947 1986	(Foveran)	Manse View, Manse Road, Methlick, Ellon AB41 7DW	01651 806843

(34) BUCHAN

Meets at the places listed on the first Tuesday of the following months: September and October (Peterhead), November and December (Banff), February and March (Fraserburgh), April and June (Turriff).

Clerk: REV. MRS MARGARET McKAY — The Smithy, Knowes of Elrick, Aberchirder, Huntly AB54 7PN — 01466 780208 (Tel)
MA BD MTh — [E-mail: akph41@uk.uumail.com] — 01466 780015 (Fax)
[E-mail: mgt_mckay@yahoo.com.uk]

Aberdour linked with Pitsligo linked with Sandhaven
Vacant — The Manse, 49 Pitsligo Street, Rosehearty, Fraserburgh AB43 7JL — 01346 571237

Auchaber United linked with Auchterless
Alison Jaffrey (Mrs) MA BD — 1990 — 1999 — The Manse, Auchterless, Turriff AB53 8BA — 01888 511217
[E-mail: alison.jaffrey@bigfoot.com]
Margaret McKay MA BD MTh — 1991 — 1999 — The Smithy, Knowes of Elrick, Aberchirder, Huntly AB54 7PP — 01466 780208 (Tel) / 01466 780015 (Fax)
[E-mail: mgt_mckay@yahoo.com.uk]

Auchterless See Auchaber United

Banff linked with King Edward
Alan Macgregor BA BD — 1992 — 1998 — 7 Colleonard Road, Banff AB45 1DZ — 01261 812107 (Tel) / 01261 818526 (Fax
[E-mail: alan.macgregor@banff98.freeserve.co.uk]

Crimond linked with Lonmay linked with St Fergus
Vacant — The Manse, Crimond, Fraserburgh AB43 8QJ — 01346 532431

Cruden
Rodger Neilson JP BSc BD — 1972 — 1974 — Hatton, Peterhead AB42 0QQ — 01779 841229 (Tel) / 01779 841822 (Fax)
[E-mail: r.neilson@tiscali.co.uk]

Deer (H)
James Wishart JP BD — 1986 — Old Deer, Peterhead AB42 5JB — 01771 623582
[E-mail: jimmy_wishart@lineone.net]

Fordyce
Iain A. Sutherland BSc BD — 1996 — 2000 — Seafield Terrace, Portsoy, Banff AB45 2QB — 01261 842272
[E-mail: REVSUTHY@aol.com]

Fraserburgh: Old
Douglas R. Clyne BD — 1973 — The Old Parish Church Manse, 4 Robbies Road, Fraserburgh AB43 7AF — 01346 518536
[E-mail: manse1@supanet.com]

Fraserburgh: South (H) linked with Inverallochy and Rathen East
Ronald F. Yule — 1982 — 15 Victoria Street, Fraserburgh AB43 9PJ — 01346 518244 (Tel) / 0870 055 4665 (Fax)

Fraserburgh: West (H) linked with Rathen West
B. Andrew Lyon LTh — 1971 — 1978 — 23 Strichen Road, Fraserburgh AB43 9SA — 01346 513303 (Tel) / 01346 512398 (Fax)
[E-mail: balyon@tiscali.co.uk]

Fyvie linked with **Rothienorman**
Vacant
The Manse, Fyvie, Turriff AB53 8RD
01651 891230

Gardenstown
Donald N. Martin BD   1996
The Manse, Fernie Brae, Gardenstown, Banff AB45 3YL
[E-mail: d.n.martin@virgin.net]
01261 851256 (Tel)
01261 851022 (Fax)

Inverallochy and Rathen East See Fraserburgh South
King Edward See Banff

Longside
Norman A. Smith MA BD   1997
9 Anderson Drive, Longside, Peterhead AB42 4XG
[E-mail: norm@smith1971.fsnet.co.uk]
01779 821224

Lonmay See Crimond

Macduff
David J. Randall MA BD ThM   1971
Manse of Doune, Banff AB45 3QL
[E-mail: djrandall@macduff.force9.co.uk]
01261 832316 (Tel)
01261 832301 (Fax)

Marnoch
Vacant
Aberchirder, Huntly AB54 7TS
01466 780276

Maud and Savoch linked with **New Deer**
Alistair P. Donald MA PhD BD   1999
Fordyce Terrace, New Deer, Turriff AB53 6TD
[E-mail: alistair@donalds99.freeserve.co.uk]
01771 644216

Monquhitter and New Byth linked with **Turriff: St Andrew's**
James Cook MA MDiv   1999   2002
Balmellie Road, Turriff AB53 4SP
[E-mail: therev@jimmiecook.freeserve.co.uk]
01888 560304

New Deer St Kane's See Maud and Savoch

New Pitsligo linked with **Strichen and Tyrie**
Vacant
Kingsville, Strichen, Fraserburgh AB43 6SQ
01771 637365 (Tel)
01771 637941 (Fax)

Ordiquhill and Cornhill (H) linked with **Whitehills**
Vacant
6 Craigneen Place, Whitehills, Banff AB45 2NE
01261 861671

Peterhead: Old
David S. Ross MSc PhD BD   1978
1 Hawthorn Road, Peterhead AB42 2DW
[E-mail: dsross@btinternet.com]
01779 472618 (Tel/Fax)

Peterhead: St Andrew's (H)
David G. Pitkeathly LLB BD — 1996 — 1 Landale Road, Peterhead AB42 1QN
[E-mail: davidgp@fish.co.uk] — 01779 472141

Peterhead: Trinity
L. Paul McClenaghan BA — 1973 1996 — 18 Landale Road, Peterhead AB42 1QP
[E-mail: paul.mcclenaghan@virgin.net] — 01779 472405 (Tel) / 01779 471174 (Fax)

Pitsligo See Aberdour
Rathen West See Fraserburgh: West
Rothienorman See Fyvie
St Fergus See Crimond
Sandhaven See Aberdour
Strichen and Tyrie See New Pitsligo
Turriff: St Andrew's See Monquhitter and New Byth

Turriff: St Ninian's and Forglen
Murdo C. MacDonald — 2002 — 4 Deveronside Drive, Turriff AB53 4SP — 01888 563850

Whitehills See Ordiquhill and Cornhill

Bell, Douglas W. MA LLB	1975	1993	(Alexandria: North)	76 Burnside Road, Mintlaw, Peterhead AB42 5PE	01771 623299
Birnie, Charles J. MA	1969	1995	(Aberdour and Tyrie)	'The Dookit', 23 Water Street, Strichen, Fraserburgh AB43 6ST	01771 637775
Blaikie, James BD	1972	1997	(Berwick-on-Tweed: St Andrew's Wallace Green and Lowick)	57 Glenugie View, Peterhead AB42 2BW	01779 490625
Douglas, Ian P. LTh	1974	1998	(Aberdeen: Craigiebuckler)	1 Torterston Drive, Blackhills, Peterhead AB42 7LB	01779 474728
Dunlop, M. William B. LLB BD	1981	1995	(Peterhead: St Andrew's)	18 Iona Avenue, Peterhead AB42 1NZ	01779 479189
Fawkes, G.M. Allan BA BSc JP	1979	2000	(Lonmay with Rathen West)	3 Northfield Gardens, Hatton, Peterhead AB42 0SW	01779 841814
Jeffrey, Stewart D. BSc BD	1962	1997	(Banff with King Edward)	8 West End, Whitehills, Banff AB42 2NL	01261 861523
Mackenzie, Seoras L. BD	1996	1998	(Chaplain: Army)	1 RHF, BFPO 38	
Noble, George S. DipTh	1972	2000	(Carfin with Newarthill)	Craigowan, 3 Main Street, Inverallochy, Fraserburgh AB43 8XX	01346 582749
Scott, W.D.	1956	1989	(Maud with Savoch)	2 Thistle Gardens, Mintlaw, Peterhead AB42 5FG	01771 622258
Taylor, William MA MEd	1984	1996	(Buckie North)	23 York Street, Peterhead AB42 6SN	01779 481798
Walker, Colin D.	1977	1982	(Auchindoir and Kildrummy)	The Old Manse, Alvah, Banff AB45 3US	01261 821656

(35) MORAY

Meets at St Andrew's-Lhanbryd and Urquhart on the first Tuesday of February, March, April, May, September, October, November, December, and at the Moderator's Church on the fourth Tuesday of June.

Clerk: REV. G. MELVYN WOOD MA BD   3 Seafield Place, Cullen, Buckie AB56 4UU
[E-mail: akph67@uk.uumail.com]

01542 841851 (Tel)
01542 841991 (Fax)
07974 095840 (Mbl)

Aberlour (H)
Elizabeth M. Curran (Miss) BD   1995 1998   Mary Avenue, Aberlour AB38 9QN
[E-mail: ecurran8@aol.com]
01340 871027

Alves and Burghead linked with Kinloss and Findhorn
John C. Beck BD   1975 1995   Dunbar Street, Burghead, Elgin IV30 5XB
[E-mail: pictkirk@aol.com]
01343 830365

Bellie linked with Speymouth
Vacant   11 The Square, Fochabers IV32 7DG
01343 820256

Birnie linked with Pluscarden
Vacant   The Manse, Birnie, Elgin IV30 8SU
01343 542621

Buckie: North (H)
Vacant   14 St Peter's Road, Buckie AB56 1DL
01542 831328

Buckie: South and West (H) linked with Enzie
John D. Hegarty LTh ABSC   1988 2002   East Church Street, Buckie AB56 1ES
[E-mail: john.hegarty@tesco.net]
01542 832103

Cullen and Deskford
G. Melvyn Wood MA BD   1982 1997   3 Seafield Place, Cullen, Buckie AB56 4UU
[E-mail: melvynwood@cullenmanse.freeserve.co.uk]
01542 841851 (Tel)
01542 841991 (Fax)
07974 095840 (Mbl)

Dallas linked with Forres St Leonard's (H) linked with Rafford
Paul Amed LTh DPS   1992 2000   Nelson Road, Forres IV36 1DR
[E-mail: paulamed@stleonardsmanse.freeserve.co.uk]
01309 672380

Duffus, Spynie and Hopeman (H)
Bruce B. Lawrie BD   1974 2001   The Manse, Duffus, Elgin IV30 5QP
[E-mail: blawrie@zetnet.co.uk]
01343 830276

Andrew F. Graham BTh (Aux)   2001   4 Woodside Park, Forres IV36 2GT
[E-mail: andy@afg1.fsnet.co.uk]
01309 673886

Dyke linked with Edinkillie
Vacant
Manse of Dyke, Brodie, Forres IV36 2TD — 01309 641239

Edinkillie See Dyke

Elgin: High
Charles D. McMillan LTh   1979 1991
5 Forteath Avenue, Elgin IV30 1TQ — 01343 542449 (Tel/Fax)
[E-mail: revchaselginhigh@btinternet.com]

Elgin: St Giles' (H) and St Columba's South (01343 551501)
George B. Rollo BD   1974 1986
(Office and Church Halls: Greyfriars Street, Elgin IV30 1LF)
18 Reidhaven Street, Elgin IV30 1QH — 01343 547208
[E-mail: gbrstgiles@hotmail.com]
Norman R. Whyte BD DipMin (Assoc)   1982 2000
2 Hay Place, Elgin IV30 1LZ — 01343 540143
[E-mail: burraman@msn.com]

Enzie See Buckie South and West

Findochty linked with Portknockie linked with Rathven
Graham Austin BD   1997
20 Netherton Terrace, Findochty, Buckie AB56 4QD — 01542 833484
[E-mail: grahamaustin@ntlworld.com]

Forres: High

Forres: St Laurence (H)
Barry J. Boyd LTh DPS   1993
12 Mackenzie Drive, Forres IV36 2JP — 01309 672260 / 07778 731018 (Mbl)

Forres: St Leonard's See Dallas

Keith: North, Newmill, Boharm and Rothiemay (H) (01542 886390)
T. Douglas McRoberts BD CPS FRSA   1975 2002
North Manse, Church Road, Keith AB55 5BR — 01542 882559
[E-mail: doug.mcroberts@btinternet.com]
Ian Cunningham DCS
The Manse, Rothiemay, Huntly AB54 7NE — 01466 711334
[E-mail: icunninghamdcs@btopenworld.com]

Keith: St Rufus, Botriphnie and Grange (H)
Ranald S.R. Gauld MA LLB BD   1991 1995
Church Road, Keith AB55 5BR — 01542 882799
Kay Gauld (Mrs) BD STM PhD (Assoc)   1999
Church Road, Keith AB55 5BR — 01542 882799
[E-mail: kay_gauld@strufus.fsnet.co.uk]

Kinloss and Findhorn See Alves and Burghead

Knockando, Elchies and Archiestown (H) linked with Rothes
Robert J.M. Anderson BD   1993 2000
Manse Brae, Rothes, Aberlour AB38 7AF — 01340 831381 (Tel/Fax)
[E-mail: robert@carmanse.freeserve.co.uk]

Lossiemouth: St Gerardine's High (H)
Thomas M. Bryson BD — 1997   2002 — The Manse, St Gerardine's Road, Lossiemouth IV31 6RA — 01343 813146
[E-mail: thomas@bryson547.freeserve.co.uk]

Lossiemouth: St James'
Graham W. Crawford BSc BD STM — 1991   2003 — The Manse, Prospect Terrace, Lossiemouth IV31 6JS — 01343 810676
[E-mail: pictishreiver@aol.com]

Mortlach and Cabrach (H)
Hugh M.C. Smith LTh — 1973   1982 — The Manse, Church Street, Dufftown, Keith AB55 4AR — 01340 820380

Pluscarden See Birnie
Portknockie See Findochty
Rafford See Dallas
Rathven See Findochty
Rothes See Knockando, Elchies and Archiestown

St Andrew's-Lhanbryd (H) and Urquhart
Rolf H. Billes BD — 1996   2001 — 39 St Andrews Road, Lhanbryde, Elgin IV30 8PU — 01343 843995
[E-mail: rolf.billes@lineone.net]

Speymouth See Bellie

Name			(Position)	Address	Tel.
Cowie, Gordon S. MA LLB	1986	1992	(Birnie with Pluscarden)	Strathspey, Lower Inchberry, Orton, Fochabers IV32 7QH	01343 880377
Davidson, A.A.B. MA BD	1960	1997	(Grange with Rothiemay)	9 Woodlands Park, Rosemount, Blairgowrie PH10 6UW	01250 875957
Diack, Peter MA	1951	1994	(Elgin South)	3A Gordon Street, Elgin IV30 1JQ	01343 542545
Douglas, Christina A. (Mrs)	1987	1993	(Inveraven and Glenlivet)	White Cottage, St Fillans, Crieff PH6 2ND	01343 543607
Evans, John W. MA BD	1945	1984	(Elgin High)	15 Weaver Place, Elgin IV30 1HB	01309 672558
Henig, Gordon BSc BD	1997	2003	(Bellie with Speymouth)	59 Woodside Drive, Forres IV36 2UF	01343 820937
King, Margaret R. (Miss) MA DCS				56 Murrayfield, Fochabers IV32 7EZ [E-mail: MargaretRKing@aol.com]	
Macaulay, Alick Hugh MA	1943	1981	(Bellie with Speymouth)	5 Duke Street, Fochabers IV32 7DN	01343 820726
Miller, William B.	1950	1987	(Cawdor with Croy and Dalcross)	10 Kirkhill Drive, Lhanbryde, Elgin IV30 8QA	01343 842368
Murray, Duncan BTh	1986	2002	(Lossiemouth: St Gerardine's High)	6 Golf View, Hopeman, Elgin IV30 5PF	01343 830913
Poole, Ann McColl (Mrs) DipEd ACE LTh	1983	2003	(Dyke with Edinkillie)	Kirkside Cottage, Dyke, Forres IV36 0TS	01309 641046
Porter, John C.	1962	1987	(Forres: St Leonard's)	20 Coppice Court, Grantown-on-Spey PH26 3LF	01479 873082
Robertson, John T. FPhS	1961	1993	(Keith: North, Newmill and Boharm)	43 Nelson Terrace, Keith AB55 5EF	01542 886339
Scotland, Ronald J. BD	1993	2003	(Birnie with Pluscarden)	7A Rose Avenue, Elgin IV30 1NX	01343 543086
Spence, Alexander	1944	1989	(Elgin St Giles': Associate)	16 Inglis Court, Edzell, Brechin DD9 7SR	01356 648502
Stuart, John T. MA	1958	1993	(Duffus, Spynie and Hopeman)	1 Seafield Farm Paddock, Cummingston, Burghead, Elgin IV30 2XY	01343 830890
Wright, David L. MA BD	1957	1998	(Stornoway: St Columba)	84 Wyvis Drive, Nairn IV12 4TP	01667 451613
Thomson, James M. BA	1952	2000	(Elgin: St Giles' and St Columba's South: Associate)	48 Mayne Road, Elgin IV30 1PD	01343 547664

(36) ABERNETHY

Meets at Boat of Garten on the first Tuesday of February, March, April, June, September, October, November and December.

Clerk: REV. JAMES A.I. MACEWAN MA BD   The Manse, Nethy Bridge PH25 3DG   **01479 821280**
[E-mail: akph35@uk.uumail.com]

Abernethy (H) linked with Cromdale (H) and Advie
James A.I. MacEwan MA BD   1973   The Manse, Nethy Bridge PH25 3DG   01479 821280
[E-mail: manse@nethybridge.freeserve.co.uk]

Alvie and Insh (T) (H)
Vacant   Kincraig, Kingussie PH21 1NA

Boat of Garten (H) and Kincardine linked with Duthil (H)
David W. Whyte LTh   1993 1999   Deshar Road, Boat of Garten PH24 3BN   01479 831252
[E-mail: djwhyte@fish.co.uk]

Cromdale and Advie See Abernethy

Dulnain Bridge linked with Grantown-on-Spey (H)
Morris Smith BD   1988   Golf Course Road, Grantown-on-Spey PH26 3HY   01479 872084
[E-mail: mosmith.themanse@virgin.net]

Duthil See Boat of Garten and Kincardine
Grantown-on-Spey See Dulnain Bridge

Kingussie (H)
Helen Cook (Mrs) BD   1974 2003   The Manse, West Terrace, Kingussie PH21 1HA   01540 661311
[E-mail: bhja@cookville.freeserve.co.uk]

Laggan linked with Newtonmore (H)
Douglas F. Stevenson BD DipMin   1991 2001   The Manse, Fort William Road, Newtonmore PH20 1DG   01540 673238
[E-mail: dfstevenson@lineone.net]

Newtonmore See Laggan

Rothiemurchus and Aviemore (H)
Ron C. Whyte BD CPS   1990   Dalfaber Park, Aviemore PH22 1QF   01479 810280
[E-mail: ron4xst@aol.com]

Tomintoul (H), Glenlivet and Inveraven
Sven S. Bjarnason CandTheol   1975 1992   The Manse, Tomintoul, Ballindalloch AB37 9HA   01807 580254
[E-mail: sven@bjarnason.org.uk]

Stewart, Matthew S. LTh   1981 1998   (Boat of Garten and Kincardine with Duthil)   2 Ruarden Court, Grantown-on-Spey PH26 3DA   01479 872210
[E-mail: mattstewart1@tinyworld.co.uk]

(37) INVERNESS

Meets at Inverness, in the Dr Black Memorial Hall, on the first Tuesday of February, March, April, May, September, October, November and December, and at the Moderator's church on the fourth Tuesday of June.

Clerk: REV. ALASTAIR S. YOUNGER BScEcon ASCC   3 Elm Park, Inverness IV2 4WN   **01463 232462 (Tel/Fax)**
[E-mail: akph55@uk.uumail.com]
[E-mail: inverness.presbytery@uk.uumail.com]

Ardclach linked with Auldearn and Dalmore
Vacant   Auldearn, Nairn IV12 5SX   01667 453180

Ardersier (H) linked with Petty
Alexander Whiteford LTh   1996   Ardersier, Inverness IV2 7SX   01667 462224
[E-mail: revwhiteford@cs.com]

Auldearn and Dalmore See Ardclach

Cawdor (H) linked with Croy and Dalcross (H)
Vacant   Croy, Inverness IV2 5PH   01667 493217

Croy and Dalcross See Cawdor

Culloden The Barn (H)
James H. Robertson BSc BD   1975   1994   45 Oakdene Court, Culloden IV2 7XL   01463 790504
[E-mail: revjimrobertson@netscape.net]

Daviot and Dunlichity linked with Moy, Dalarossie and Tomatin
Vacant   Daviot, Inverness IV2 5XL   01463 772242

Dores and Boleskine
Vacant   The Manse, Foyers, Inverness IV2 6XU   01456 486206

Inverness: Crown (H) (01463 238929)
Peter H. Donald MA PhD BD   1991   1998   39 Southside Road, Inverness IV2 4XA   01463 231140
[E-mail: crownchurch@tesco.net]
Willis A. Jones BA MDiv DMin (Assoc)   1964   2003   4 Beechwood, Wellington Road, Nairn IV12 4RE

Inverness: Dalneigh and Bona (GD) (H)
Fergus A. Robertson MA BD   1971   1999   9 St Mungo Road, Inverness IV3 5AS   01463 232339

Inverness: East (H)
Aonghas I. MacDonald MA BD   1967   1981   2 Victoria Drive, Inverness IV2 3QD   01463 231269
[E-mail: aonghas@online.co.uk]

Inverness: Hilton
Duncan MacPherson LLB BD   1994   4 Tomatin Road, Inverness IV2 4UA   01463 231417
[E-mail: duncan@hiltonchurch.freeserve.uk]

Inverness: Inshes (H)
Alistair Malcolm BD DPS   1976   1992   48 Redwood Crescent, Milton of Leys, Inverness IV2 6HB   01463 772402
[E-mail: alimalcolm@7inverness.freeserve.co.uk]

Inverness: Kinmylies (E) (H)
Peter M. Humphris BSc BD   1976   2001   2 Balnafettack Place, Inverness IV3 8TQ   01463 709893
[E-mail: peter@humphris.co.uk]

Inverness: Ness Bank (T) (H)
S. John Chambers OBE BSc   1972   1998   15 Ballifeary Road, Inverness IV3 5PJ   01463 234653
[E-mail: chambers@ballifeary.freeserve.co.uk]

Inverness: St Columba High (H)
Alastair S. Younger BScEcon ASCC   1969   1976   3 Elm Park, Inverness IV2 4WN   01463 232462 (Tel/Fax)
[E-mail: asyounger@aol.com]

Inverness: St Stephen's linked with The Old High (1st Charge) (T) (H)
Vacant   24 Damfield Road, Inverness IV2 3HU   01463 237129

Inverness: The Old High See Inverness: St Stephen's

Inverness: Trinity (H)
Vacant   60 Kenneth Street, Inverness IV3 5PZ   01463 234756

Kilmorack and Erchless
George Duthie BSc MSc PhD BD   1998   'Roselynn', Croyard Road, Beauly IV4 7DJ   01463 782260
[E-mail: gduthie@tinyworld.co.uk]

Kiltarlity linked with Kirkhill
Fraser K. Turner LTh   1994   2002   Wardlaw Manse, Wardlaw Road, Kirkhill, Inverness IV5 7NZ   01463 831662
[E-mail: fraseratq@yahoo.co.uk]

Kirkhill See Kiltarlity
Moy, Dalarossie and Tomatin See Daviot and Dunlichity

Nairn: Old (H)

Ian W.F. Hamilton BD LTh ALCM AVCM	1978	1986	3 Manse Road, Nairn IV12 4RN [E-mail: reviwfh@btinternet.com]	01667 452203

Nairn: St Ninian's (H)

Vacant	7 Queen Street, Nairn IV12 4AA	01667 452202

Petty See Ardersier

Urquhart and Glenmoriston (H)

Hugh F. Watt BD DPS	1986	1996	Blairbeg, Drumnadrochit, Inverness IV3 6UG [E-mail: hw@tinyworld.co.uk]	01456 450231

Anderson, Colin M. BA BD STM MPhil	1968	2003	(Inverness: St Stephen's with The Old High)	83 Marlborough Avenue, Glasgow G11 7BT	0141-357 2838
Black, Archibald T. BSc	1964	1997	(Inverness: Ness Bank)	16 Elm Park, Inverness IV2 4WN	01463 230588
Brown, Derek G. BD DipMin DMin	1989	1994	Chaplain: Raigmore Hospital and Highland Hospice	Cathedral Manse, Cnoc-an-Lobht, Dornoch IV25 3HN [E-mail: revsbrown@aol.com]	01862 810296
Buell, F. Bart BA MDiv	1980	1995	(Urquhart and Glenmoriston)	6 Towerhill Place, Cradlehall, Inverness IV1 2FN [E-mail: bart@tower22.freeserve.co.uk]	01463 794634
Charlton, George W.	1952	1992	(Fort Augustus with Glengarry)	61 Drumfield Road, Inverness IV2 4XL	01463 242802
Chisholm, Archibald F. MA	1957	1997	(Braes of Rannoch with Foss and Rannoch)	32 Seabank Road, Nairn IV12 4EU	01667 452001
Christie, James LTh	1993	2003	(Dores and Boleskine)	20 Wester Inshes Crescent, Inverness IV2 5HL	01463 710534
Donaldson, Moses	1972	2000	(Fort Augustus with Glengarry)	'Tabgha', 10 Garden Place, Beauly IV4 7AW	(Tel/Fax) 01463 783701
Donn, Thomas M. MA	1932	1969	(Duthil)	6 Cawdor Road, Inverness IV2 3NR	01463 236410
Frizzell, R. Stewart BD	1961	2000	(Wick Old)	98 Boswell Road, Inverness IV2 3EW	01463 231907
Gibbons, Richard BD	1997		Adviser in Mission and Evangelism	3 Holm Burn Place, Inverness IV2 6WT [E-mail: nmadvisernorth@uk.uumail.com]	01463 226889
Gibson, A. Cameron MRCVS	1962	1990	(Eskdalemuir with Hutton and Corrie with Tundergarth)	Langleigh, 10 Rowan Place, Nairn IV12 4TL	01667 455413
Henderson, Roderick B.	1973	1982	(Kingswells)	5 Holm Park, Inverness IV2 4XT	01463 224022
Livesley, Anthony LTh	1979	1997	(Kiltearn)	87 Beech Avenue, Nairn IV12 5SX	01667 455126
Logan, Robert J.V. MA BD	1962	2001	(Abdie and Dunbog with Newburgh)	Lindores, 1 Murray Place, Smithton, Inverness IV2 7PX [E-mail: rjvlogan@aol.com]	01463 790226
Macaskill, Duncan	1952	1974	(Lochs-in-Bernera)	71 Smithton Park, Inverness IV2 7PD	01463 791376
MacRae, Norman I. LTh	1966	2003	(Inverness: Trinity)	144 Hope Park Gardens, Bathgate EH48 2QX	01506 635254
Macritchie, Iain A.M. BSc BD STM PhD	1987	1998	Chaplain: Inverness Hospitals	7 Merlin Crescent, Inverness IV2 3TE	01463 235204
Morrison, Hector BSc BD MTh	1981	1994	Lecturer: Highland Theological College	24 Oak Avenue, Inverness IV2 4NX	01463 238561
Prentice, Donald K. BSc BD	1989	1992	Army Chaplain	Fort George, Inverness IV1 2TD	
Rettie, James A. BTh	1981	1999	(Melness and Eriboll with Tongue)	2 Trantham Drive, Westhill, Inverness IV2 5QT	01463 798896
Stirling, G. Alan S. MA	1960	1999	(Leochel Cushnie and Lynturk linked with Tough)		
Waugh, John L. LTh	1973	2002		97 Lochlaan Road, Culloden, Inverness IV2 7HS 58 Wyvis Drive, Nairn IV12 4TP [E-mail: jswaugh@care4free.net]	(Tel/Fax) 01463 798313 01667 456397
Whyte, William B. BD	1973	2003	(Nairn: St Ninian's)	The Old Inn, Park Hill Road, Rattray, Blairgowrie PH10 7DS	
Wilson, Ian M.	1988	1993	(Cawdor with Croy and Dalcross)	3 Kilravock Crescent, Nairn IV12 4QZ	01667 452977

INVERNESS ADDRESSES

Inverness
Crown — Kingsmills Road x Midmills Road
Dalneigh and Bona — St Mary's Avenue
East — Academy Street x Margaret Street
Hilton — Druid Road x Tomatin Road
Inshes — Huntly Street x Greig Street

Kinmylies — Kinmylies Way
Ness Bank — Ness Bank x Castle Road
St Columba High — Bank Street x Fraser Street
St Stephen's — Old Edinburgh Road x Southside Road

The Old High — Church Street x Church Lane
Trinity — Huntly Place x Upper Kessock Street

Nairn
Old — Academy Street x Seabank Road
St Ninian's — High Street x Queen Street

(38) LOCHABER

Meets at Caol, Fort William, in Kilmallie Church Hall, on the first Tuesday of each month, except January, May, July and August, when there is no meeting.

Clerk: REV. DAVID M. ANDERSON   'Mirlos', 1 Dumfries Place, Fort William PH33 6UQ   01397 703203
MSc FCOptom   [E-mail: akph62@uk.uumail.com]

Acharacle (H) linked with Ardnamurchan
Ian R. Pittendreigh BA BD   2002   The Manse, Acharacle, Argyll PH36 4JU   01967 431665
[E-mail: ian@biglight.co.uk]

Ardgour linked with Strontian
James A. Carmichael LTh   1976   The Manse, Ardgour, Fort William PH33 7AH   01855 841230

Ardnamurchan See Acharacle

Arisaig and the Small Isles
Alan H.W. Lamb BA MTh (Locum)   1959 1992   The Manse, Mid Road, Arisaig PH39 4NJ   01687 450227
[E-mail: a.lamb@tinyonline.co.uk]

Duror (H) linked with Glencoe St Munda's (H) (T)
Alison H. Burnside (Mrs) MA BD   1991 2002   The Manse, Ballachulish PH49 4JG   01855 811998

Fort Augustus linked with Glengarry
Adrian P.J. Varwell BA BD PhD   1983 2001   The Manse, Fort Augustus PH32 4BH   01320 366210
[E-mail: a-varwell@ecosse.net]

Fort William: Duncansburgh (H) linked with Kilmonivaig
Donald A. MacQuarrie BSc BD   1979 1990   The Manse of Duncansburgh, The Parade, Fort William   01397 702297
PH33 6BA
[E-mail: pdmacq@ukgateway.net]

Fort William: MacIntosh Memorial (H)

Alan Ramsay MA   1967   The Manse, 26 Riverside Park, Lochyside, Fort William PH33 7RB   01397 702054
[E-mail: linandalan@btopenworld.com]

David M. Anderson MSc FCOptom (Aux)   1984   2001   'Mirlos', 1 Dumfries Place, Fort William PH33 6UQ   01397 703203
[E-mail: david@mirlos.co.uk]

Glencoe St Munda's   See Duror
Glengarry   See Fort Augustus

Kilmallie

Vacant   Kilmallie Manse, Corpach, Fort William PH33 7JS   01397 772210

Kilmonivaig   See Fort William: Duncansburgh

Kinlochleven (H) linked with Nether Lochaber (H)

Archibald Speirs BD   1995   2002   Lochaber Road, Kinlochleven, Argyll PA40 4QW   01855 831227
[E-mail: archiespeirs1@aol.com]

Mallaig St Columba and Knoydart

Vacant   The Manse, Mallaig PH41 4RG   01687 462256

Morvern

Alicia Ann Winning MA BD   1984   The Manse, Lochaline, Morvern, Oban PA34 5UU   01967 421267
[E-mail: annw@morvern12.fslife.co.uk]

Nether Lochaber   See Kinlochleven
Strontian   See Ardgour

Beaton, Jamesina (Miss) DCS   (Deaconess)   Farhills, Fort Augustus PH32 4DS   01320 366252
Burnside, William A.M. MA BD PGCE   1990   Teacher: Religious Education   The Manse, Ballachulish PH49 4JG   01855 811998
MacLean, Hector A.M. MA   1937   1978   (Duror with Glencoe)   Gearra Beag, Duror, Argyll PA38 4BW   01631 74215
Millar, John L. MA BD   1981   1990   (Fort William: Duncansburgh with Kilmonivaig)   17 Whittingehame Court, 1350 Great Western Road, Glasgow G12 0BH   0141-339 4098
Rae, Peter C. BSc BD   1968   2000   (Beath and Cowdenbeath North)   Rodane, Badabrie, Banavie, Fort William PH33 7LX   01397 772603

LOCHABER Communion Sundays

Parish	Date	Parish	Date	Parish	Date
Acharacle	1st Mar, Jun, Sep, Dec	Fort William		Kilmonivaig	1st May, Nov
Ardgour	1st Jun, Sep, Dec, Easter	Duncansburgh	1st Apr, Jun, Oct	Kinlochleven	1st Feb, Apr, Jun, Oct, Dec
Ardnamurchan	1st Apr, Aug, Dec	M'Intosh Memorial	1st Mar, Jun, Sep, Dec	Mallaig	4th May, 3rd Nov
Arisaig and Moidart	1st May, Nov	Glencoe	1st Apr, Oct	Morvern	Easter, 1st Jul, 4th Sep, 1st Dec
Duror	2nd Jun, 3rd Nov	Glengarry	1st Jan, Apr, Jul, Oct	Nether Lochaber	1st Apr, Oct
Fort Augustus	1st Jan, Apr, Jul, Oct	Kilmallie	3rd Mar, May, Sep, 1st Dec	Strontian	1st Jun, Sep, Dec

(39) ROSS

Meets in Dingwall on the first Tuesday of each month, except January, May, July and August.

Clerk: REV. THOMAS M. McWILLIAM MA BD   The Manse, Contin, Strathpeffer IV14 9ES   01997 421380
[E-mail: akph71@uk.uumail.com]   *01349- 877014*

Alness
Ronald Morrison BD   1996   27 Darroch Brae, Alness IV17 0SD   01349 882238

Avoch linked with Fortrose and Rosemarkie
Samuel Torrens BD   1995   5 Nessway, Fortrose IV10 8SS   01381 620068
[E-mail: sam@nessway5.fsnet.co.uk]

Contin
Thomas M. McWilliam MA BD   1964   1997   The Manse, Contin, Strathpeffer IV14 9ES   01997 421380

Cromarty
John Tallach MA MLitt   1970   1999   Denny Road, Cromarty IV11 8YT   01381 600802
[E-mail: john.tallach@cali.co.uk]

Dingwall: Castle Street (H)
Grahame M. Henderson BD   1974   1987   16 Achany Road, Dingwall IV15 9JB   01349 863167
[E-mail: GHende5884@aol.com]

Dingwall: St Clement's (H)
Russel Smith BD   1994   8 Castlehill Road, Dingwall IV15 9PB   01349 861011

Fearn Abbey and Nigg linked with Tarbat
John Macgregor BD   2001   The Manse, Fearn, Tain IV20 1TN   01862 832626

Ferintosh
Daniel J.M. Carmichael MA BD   1994   Ferintosh Manse, Leanaig Road, Conon Bridge, Dingwall IV7 8BE   01349 861275
[E-mail: djm@carmichael39.fsnet.co.uk]

Fodderty and Strathpeffer
Ivan C. Warwick MA BD   1980   1999   The Manse, Strathpeffer IV14 9DL   01997 421398

Fortrose and Rosemarkie See Avoch

Invergordon

Minister	Year(s)	Address	Tel
Kenneth Donald Macleod BD CPS	1989	The Manse, Cromlet Drive, Invergordon IV18 0BA	01349 852273

Killearnan linked with Knockbain

Minister	Year(s)	Address	Tel
Iain Ramsden BTh	1999	The Church of Scotland Manse, Coldwell Road, Artafallie, North Kessock, Inverness IV1 3ZE [E-mail: s4rev@cqm.co.uk]	01463 731333

Kilmuir and Logie Easter

Minister	Year(s)	Address	Tel
Kenneth J. Pattison MA BD STM	1967 1996	Delny, Invergordon IV18 0NW [E-mail: ken@thepattisons.fsnet.co.uk]	01862 842280

Kiltearn (H)

Minister	Year(s)	Address	Tel
Donald A. MacSween BD	1991 1998	Kiltearn, Evanton, Dingwall IV16 9UY	01349 830472

Knockbain See Killearnan

Lochbroom and Ullapool (GD)

Minister	Year(s)	Address	Tel
James Gemmell BD MTh	1999	The Manse, Garve Road, Ullapool IV26 2SX [E-mail: JasGemmell@aol.com]	01854 612050

Resolis and Urquhart (T)

Minister	Year(s)	Address	Tel
C.J. Grant Bell	1983	The Manse, Culbokie, Conon Bridge, Dingwall IV7 8JN	01349 877452

Rosskeen

Minister	Year(s)	Address	Tel
Robert Jones BSc BD	1990	Rosskeen Manse, Perrins Road, Alness IV17 0SX [E-mail: rob-jones@freeuk.com]	01349 882265

Tain

Minister	Year(s)	Address	Tel
Douglas A. Horne BD	1977	14 Kingsway Avenue, Tain IV19 1BN [E-mail: douglas@kingswayavenue.freeserve.co.uk]	01862 894140

Tarbat (T) See Fearn Abbey and Nigg

Urray and Kilchrist

Minister	Year(s)	Address	Tel
J. Alastair Gordon BSc BD	2000	The Manse, Corrie Road, Muir of Ord IV6 7TL [E-mail: jagordon.pci@virgin.net]	01463 870259

Name	Year(s)	Charge/Note	Address	Tel
Buchan, John BD MTh	1968 1993	(Fodderty and Strathpeffer)	'Faithlie', 45 Swanston Avenue, Inverness IV3 6QW	01463 713114
Dupar, Kenneth W. BA BD PhD	1965 1993	(Christ's College, Aberdeen)	The Old Manse, The Causeway, Cromarty IV11 8XJ	01381 600428
Forsyth, James LTh	1970 2000	(Fearn Abbey with Nigg Chapelhill)	Rhivs Lodge, Golspie, Sutherland KW10 6DD	
Glass, Alexander OBE MA	1998	Auxiliary Minister: Attached to Presbytery Clerk	Craigton, Tulloch Avenue, Dingwall IV15 9TU	01349 863258

Harries, David A.	1950 1990	(British Sailors Society)	Odessey, 5 Farm Lane, Englands Road, Acle, Norfolk	
Holroyd, Gordon BTh FPhS FSAScot	1959 1993	(Dingwall: St Clement's)	22 Stuarthill Drive, Maryburgh, Dingwall IV15 9HU	01349 863379
Howe, Andrew Y. BTh	1957 1989	(Rosskeen)	2 Springfield Terrace, Alness IV17 0SP	01349 882302
Liddell, Margaret (Miss) BD DipTh	1987 1997	(Contin)	20 Wyvis Crescent, Conon Bridge, Dingwall IV7 8BZ	01349 865997
McGowan, Prof. Andrew T.B. BD STM PhD	1979 1994	Highland Theological College	6 Kintail Place, Dingwall IV15 9RL	
Mackenzie, A. Ian	1945 1986	(Glenelg with Glenshiel with Kintail)	4 St Mary's Well, Tain IV19 1LS	01862 893305
Mackinnon, R.M. LTh	1968 1995	(Kilmuir and Logie Easter)	27 Riverford Crescent, Conon Bridge, Dingwall IV7 8HL	01349 866293
MacLeman, Alasdair J. BD DCE	1978 2001	(Resolis and Urquhart)	Airdale, Seaforth Road, Muir of Ord IV6 7TA	01463 870704
Macleod, John MA	1959 1993	(Resolis and Urquhart)	'Benview', 19 Balvaird, Muir of Ord IV6 7RG	01463 871286
Niven, William W. BTh	1982 1995	(Alness)	4 Obsdale Park, Alness IV17 0TP	01349 882427
Rutherford, Eilon B. (Miss) MBE DCS		(Deaconess)	41 Duncanston, Conon Bridge, Dingwall IV7 8JB	01349 877439

(40) SUTHERLAND

Meets at Lairg on the first Tuesday of March, May, September, November and December, and on the first Tuesday of June at the Moderator's church.

Clerk:	REV. J.L. GOSKIRK LTh		The Manse, Lairg, Sutherland IV27 4EH [E-mail: akph76@uk.uumail.com]	01549 402373

Altnaharra and Farr
John M. Wilson MA BD	1965	1998	The Manse, Bettyhill, Thurso KW14 7SZ	01641 521208

Assynt and Stoer
Vacant			Canisp Road, Lochinver, Lairg IV27 4LH	01571 844342

Clyne (H)
Ian W. McCree BD	1971	1987	Golf Road, Brora KW9 6QS [E-mail: ian.mccree@lineone.net]	01408 621239

Creich linked with Rosehall
Olsen, Heather C. (Miss) BD	1978	1999	Church of Scotland Manse, Dornoch Road, Bonar Bridge, Ardgay IV24 3EB	01863 766256

Dornoch Cathedral (H)
Susan M. Brown (Mrs) BD DipMin	1985	1998	Croc-an-Lobht, Dornoch IV25 3HN [E-mail: revsbrown@aol.com]	01862 810296

Durness and Kinlochbervie
John T. Mann BSc BD	1990	1998	Manse Road, Kinlochbervie, Lairg IV27 4RG [E-mail: jtmklb@aol.com]	01971 521287

Eddrachillis
John MacPherson BSc BD   1993   Church of Scotland Manse, Scourie, Lairg IV27 4TQ   01971 502431

Golspie
William D. Irving LTh   1985 2003 The Manse, Fountain Road, Golspie KW10 6TH   01408 633295

Kildonan and Loth Helmsdale (H)
Vacant   Church of Scotland Manse, Helmsdale KW8 6HT   01431 821674

Kincardine Croick and Edderton
Vacant   The Manse, Ardgay IV24 3BG   01863 766285

Lairg (H) linked with Rogart (H)
J.L. Goskirk LTh   1968   Church of Scotland Manse, Lairg IV27 4EH   01549 402373

Melness and Tongue (H)
John F. Mackie BD   1979 2000   New Manse, Glebelands, Tongue, Lairg IV27 4XL   01847 611230
                                                                      [E-mail: john.mackie1@virgin.net]

Rogart See Lairg
Rosehall See Creich

Hurst, Frederick R. MA   1965 2002   Apartment 10, 20 Abbey Drive, Glasgow G14 9JX
Wilson, Mary D. (Mrs) RGN SCM DTM   1990 1998   The Manse, Bettyhill, Thurso KW14 7SZ   01641 521208
                                         (Assynt and Stoer)
                                         Auxiliary Minister

(41) CAITHNESS

Meets alternately at Wick and Thurso on the first Tuesday of February, March, May, September, November and December; and the third Tuesday of June.

Clerk: MRS MYRTLE A. GILLIES MBE   Ardachadh, Halladale, Forsinard, Sutherland KW13 6YT   **01641 571241**
                                               [E-mail: akph42@uk.uumail.com]   **01641 571288 (Fax)**

Berriedale and Dunbeath linked with Latheron
Vacant   Ross Manse, Dunbeath KW6 6EA   01593 731228

Bower linked with Watten
Vacant   Station Road, Watten, Wick KW1 5YN   01955 621220

Canisbay linked with Keiss Iain Macnee LTh BD MA PhD	1975	1998	The Manse, Canisbay, Wick KW1 4YH [E-mail: i.macnee@amserve.com]	01955 611309
Dunnet linked with Olrig James F. Todd BD CPS	1984	1999	Olrig, Castletown, Thurso KW14 8TP	01847 821221
Halkirk and Westerdale Kenneth Warner BD DA DipTD	1981		Abbey Manse, Halkirk KW12 6UU [E-mail: WrnrKen@aol.com]	01847 831227
Keiss See Canisbay				
Latheron See Berriedale and Dunbeath				
Lybster and Bruan (T) Vacant			Central Manse, Lybster KW3 6BN	01593 721231
Olrig See Dunnet				
Reay linked with Strathy and Halladale (H) Vacant			Church of Scotland Manse, Reay, Thurso KW14 7RE	01847 811272
Strathy and Halladale See Reay				
Thurso: St Peter's and St Andrew's (H) Kenneth S. Borthwick MA BD	1983	1989	46 Rose Street, Thurso KW14 7HN [E-mail: kennysamuel@aol.com]	01847 895186
Thurso: West (H) Ronald Johnstone BD	1977	1984	Thorkel Road, Thurso KW14 7LW [E-mail: ronaldjohnstone@onetel.net.uk]	01847 892663
Watten See Bower				
Wick: Bridge Street A.A. Roy MA BD	1955		Mansefield, Miller Avenue, Wick KW1 4DF	01955 602822
Wick: Old (H) (L) Steven Thomson	2001		The Old Manse, Miller Avenue, Wick KW1 4DF [E-mail: stevie.thomson@btinternet.com]	01955 604252
Wick: Pulteneytown (H) and Thrumster William F. Wallace BDS BD	1968	1974	The Manse, Coronation Street, Wick KW1 5LS [E-mail: williamwallace39@btopenworld.com]	01955 603166

Craw, John DCS		'Craiglockhart', Latheronwheel, Latheron KW5 6DW	01593 741779
Mappin, Michael G. BA	1961 1998 (Bower with Watten)	Mundays, Banks Road, Watten, Wick KW1 5YL	01955 621720

CAITHNESS Communion Sundays

Berriedale and Dunbeath	2nd Mar, Jun, Sep, Dec	Lybster and Bruan	3rd Jun, Nov, Easter
Bower	1st Jul, Dec	Olrig	last May, Nov
Canisbay	1st Jun, Nov	Reay	last Apr, Sep
Dunnet	last May, Nov	Strathy and Halladale	1st Jun, last Nov, Easter
Halkirk	Oct, Apr, Jul	Thurso	
Keiss	1st May, 3rd Nov	St Peter's and	1st Feb, Apr, Jun, Sep, Nov
Latheron	1st Jul, 2nd Sep, 1st Dec, 2nd Mar	West	4th Mar, Jun, Nov

Watten	1st Jul, Dec
Westerdale	Apr, Oct, 4th Dec
Wick	
Bridge Street	1st Apr, Oct
Old	4th Apr, Sep
Pulteneytown and	1st Mar, Jun, Sep, Dec
Thrumster	

(42) LOCHCARRON – SKYE

Meets in Kyle on the first Tuesday of each month, except January, May, July and August.

Clerk:	REV. ALLAN J. MACARTHUR BD		High Barn, Croft Road, Lochcarron, Strathcarron IV54 8YA	**01520 722278 (Tel)**
			[E-mail: akph63@uk.uumail.com]	**01520 722674 (Fax)**
			[E-mail: a.macarthur@btinternet.com]	

Applecross, Lochcarron and Torridon (GD)

George M. Martin MA BD	1987		The Manse, Lochcarron, Strathcarron IV54 8YD	01520 722829
David V. Scott BTh (Assoc)	1994		Camusterrach, Applecross, Strathcarron IV54 8LU	01520 744263

Bracadale and Duirinish (GD)

Gary Wilson BD	1996	2000	Kinloch Manse, Dunvegan, Isle of Skye IV55 8WQ	01470 521457
			[E-mail: gary@shalom55.fsnet.co.uk]	

Gairloch and Dundonnell

Derek Morrison	1995	2000	Church of Scotland Manse, The Glebe, Gairloch IV21 2BT	01445 712053 (Tel/Fax)
			[E-mail: derekmorrison@tinyworld.co.uk]	

Glenelg and Kintail

Vacant			Church of Scotland Manse, Inverinate, Kyle IV40 8HE	01599 511245

Kilmuir and Stenscholl (GD)

Ivor MacDonald BSc MSc BD	1993	2000	Staffin, Portree, Isle of Skye IV51 9JX	01470 562759 (Tel/Fax)
			[E-mail: ivormacd@aol.com]	

Lochalsh
John M. Macdonald — 2002 — The Church of Scotland Manse, Main Street, Kyle IV40 8DA — 01599 534294

Portree (GD)
Vacant — Viewfield Road, Portree, Isle of Skye IV51 9ES — 01478 612019

Snizort (H) (GD)
Iain M. Greenshields BD DipRS ACMA MSc MTh — 1985 2002 — The Manse, Kensaleyre, Snizort, Portree, Isle of Skye IV51 9XE [E-mail: rev_imaclg@hotmail.com] — 01470 532260

Strath and Sleat (GD)
Ben Johnstone MA BD DMin — 1973 2003 — The Shiants, 5 Upper Breakish, Breakish, Isle of Skye IV42 8PY [E-mail: benonskye@onetel.com] — 01471 820063

John M. Nicolson BD DipMin (Assoc) — 1997 — The Manse, The Glebe, Kilmore, Teangue, Isle of Skye IV44 8RG [E-mail: jnico84967@aol.com] — 01471 844469

Beaton, Donald MA BD MTh	1961	2002	(Glenelg and Kintail)	Kilmaluag Croft, North Duntulm, Isle of Skye IV51 9UF	01470 552296
Ferguson, John LTh BD DD	1973	2002	(Portree)	9 Braeview Park, Beauly, Inverness IV4 7ED	01463 783900
Macarthur, Allan J. BD	1973	1998	(Applecross, Lochcarron and Torridon)	High Barn, Croft Road, Lochcarron, Strathcarron IV54 8YA	(Tel) 01520 722278 (Fax) 01520 722674
McCulloch, Alen J.R. MA BD	1990	1995	Chaplain: Army	Vimy Barracks, Catterick Garrison, North Yorkshire DL9 3PS	
MacDonald, Kenneth	1965	1992	(Associate: Applecross l/w Lochcarron)	Tigharry, Main Street, Lochcarron, Strathcarron IV54 8YB	01520 722433
MacDougall, Angus	1940	1982	(Sleat)	Tigh Ard, Earlish, Portree, Isle of Skye IV51 9XL	01470 542466
Mackinnon, Duncan	1956	1989	(Plockton and Kyle)	7 Garth Road, Inverness IV2 4DA	01463 230971
Macleod, Donald LTh	1988	2000	(Snizort)	20 Caulfield Avenue, Cradlehall, Inverness IV1 2GA	01463 798093
Matheson, James G. MA BD DD	1936	1979	(Portree)	The Elms, 148 Whitehouse Loan, Edinburgh EH9 2EZ	0131-446 6211
Murray, John W.	2003		Auxiliary Minister	Totescore, Kilmuir, Portree, Isle of Skye IV51 9YN	01470 542297
Williamson, Tom MA BD	1941	1982	(Dyke with Edinkillie)	16 Cove, Inverasdale, Poolewe, Achnasheen IV22 2LT	01445 781423

LOCHCARRON – SKYE   Communion Sundays

Applecross	4th Jun	
Arnisort	1st Sep	
Bracadale	3rd Mar, Sep	
Duirinish	3rd Jan, Easter, 2nd Jun, 3rd Sep	
Dundonnell	4th Jun	
Gairloch	3rd Jun, Nov	
Glenelg	2nd Jun, Nov	
Glenshiel	1st Jul	
Kilmuir	1st Mar, Sep	
Kintail	3rd Apr, Jul	
Kyleakin	Easter, 1st Nov	
Lochalsh and Stromeferry	4th Jun, Sep, Christmas, Easter	
Lochcarron and Shieldaig	Easter, 3rd Jun, 1st Oct	
Plockton and Kyle	2nd May, 1st Oct	
Portree	Easter, Pentecost, Christmas, 2nd Mar, Aug, 1st Nov	
Sleat	2nd Jun, Dec	
Snizort	1st Jan, 4th Mar	
Stenscholl	1st Jun, Dec	
Strath	2nd Mar, Sep	
Torridon and Kinlochewe	2nd May	

(43) UIST

Meets on the fourth Wednesday of January, March, September and November in Berneray, and the fourth Wednesday of June in Leverburgh.

Clerk: REV. MURDO SMITH MA BD — Scarista, Isle of Harris HS3 3HX [E-mail: akph77@uk.uumail.com] — **01859 550200**

Barra (GD) John D. Urquhart BA BD	1998	2000	Cuithir, Castlebay, Isle of Barra HS9 5XD [E-mail: jurquh8218@aol.com]	01871 810230
Benbecula (GD) (H) Vacant			Griminish, Isle of Benbecula HS7 5QA	01870 602180
Berneray and Lochmaddy (GD) (H) Vacant			Lochmaddy, Isle of North Uist HS6 5BD	01876 500414
Carinish (GD) (H) Thomas J.R. Mackinnon LTh DipMin	1996	1998	Clachan, Isle of North Uist HS6 5HD [E-mail: tmackinnon@aol.com]	01876 580219
Kilmuir and Paible (GE) Vacant			Paible, Isle of North Uist HS6 5ED	01876 510310
Manish-Scarista (GD) (H) Murdo Smith MA BD	1988		Scarista, Isle of Harris HS3 3HX [E-mail: akph77@uk.uumail.com]	01859 550200
South Uist (GD) Vacant			Daliburgh, Isle of South Uist HS8 5SS	01878 700265
Tarbert (GE) (H) Norman MacIver BD	1976	1988	The Manse, Manse Road, Tarbert, Isle of Harris HS3 3DF [E-mail: norman@n-cmaciver.freeserve.co.uk]	01859 502231

MacDonald, Angus J. BSc BD	(Lochmaddy and Trumisgarry)	1995 2001	7 Memorial Avenue, Stornoway, Isle of Lewis HS1 2QR	01851 706634
MacInnes, David MA BD	(Kilmuir and Paible)	1966 1999	9 Golf View Road, Kinmylies, Inverness IV3 8SZ	01463 717377
Macpherson, Kenneth J. BD	(Benbecula)	1988 2002	70 Baile na Cille, Balivanich, Isle of Benbecula HS7 5ND	01870 602751
Macrae, D.A. JP MA	(Tarbert)	1942 1988	5 Leverhulme Road, Tarbert, Isle of Harris HS3 3DD	01859 502310
Macrae, William DCS	(Deacon)		6 Park View Terrace, Isle of Scalpay, Tarbert, Isle of Harris HS4 3XX	01859 540288
Morrison, Donald John	Auxiliary Minister	2001	Lagnam, Brisgean 22, Kyles, Isle of Harris HS3 3BS	01859 502341
Muir, Alexander MA BD	(Carinish)	1982 1996	14 West Mackenzie Park, Inverness IV2 3ST	01463 712096
Smith, John M.	(Lochmaddy)	1956 1992	Hamersay, Clachan, Isle of North Uist HS6 5HD	01876 580332

UIST Communion Sundays

Barra	Easter, Pentecost, Christmas	
Benbecula	2nd Mar, Sep	
Berneray and Lochmaddy	4th Jun, 1st Nov	
Carinish	4th Mar, Aug	
Kilmuir and Paible	1st Jun, 3rd Nov	
Manish-Scarista	3rd Apr, 1st Oct	
South Uist – Iochdar		1st Mar
Hownore		1st Jun
Daliburgh		1st Sep
Tarbert		2nd Mar, 3rd Sep

(44) LEWIS

Meets at Stornoway, in St Columba's Church Hall, on the first Tuesday of February, March, April, September and November. It also meets in June and December on dates to be decided.

Clerk: REV. THOMAS S. SINCLAIR MA LTh BD
Martin's Memorial Manse,
Matheson Road, Stornoway, Isle of Lewis HS1 2LR
[E-mail: akphf1@uk.uumail.com]
[E-mail: thomas@sinclair0438.freeserve.co.uk]
01851 702206
07766 700110 (Mbl)

Barvas (GD) (H)
Thomas MacNeil MA BD — 2002 — Barvas, Isle of Lewis HS2 0QY [E-mail: tommymacneil@hotmail.com] — 01851 840218

Carloway (GD) (H)
Murdo M. Campbell BD DipMin — 1997 — Carloway, Isle of Lewis HS2 9AU [E-mail: primera@madasafish.com] — 01851 643255

Cross Ness (GE) (H)
Ian Murdo M. Macdonald DPA BD — 2001 — Cross Manse, Swainbost, Ness, Isle of Lewis HS2 0TB [E-mail: ianmurdo@crosschurch.fsnet.co.uk] — 01851 810375

Kinloch (GE) (H)
Donald Angus MacLennan — 1975 1989 — Laxay, Lochs, Isle of Lewis HS2 9LA [E-mail: donaldkinloch@tiscali.co.uk] — 01851 830218 / 07799 668270 (Mbl)

Knock (GE) (H)
Fergus J. MacBain BD DipMin — Knock Manse, Garrabost, Point, Isle of Lewis HS2 0PW — 1999 2002 — 01851 870362

Lochs-Crossbost (GD) (H)
Andrew W.F. Coghill BD DPS — Leurbost, Lochs, Isle of Lewis HS2 9NS [E-mail: andcoghill@aol.com] — 1993 — 01851 860243 (Tel/Fax) / 07776 480748 (Mbl)

Lochs-in-Bernera (GD) (H)
Vacant — Bernera, Isle of Lewis HS2 9LU — 01851 612371

Stornoway: High (GD) (H)
William B. Black MA BD — 1 Goathill Road, Stornoway, Isle of Lewis HS1 2NJ [E-mail: willieblack@lineone.net] — 1972 1998 — 01851 703106

Stornoway: Martin's Memorial (H)
Thomas Suter Sinclair MA LTh BD — Matheson Road, Stornoway, Isle of Lewis HS1 2LR [E-mail: thomas@sinclair0438.freeserve.co.uk] [E-mail: akph61@uk.uumail.com] — 1966 1976 — 01851 702206 / 07766 700110 (Mbl)

Stornoway: St Columba (GD) (H)
Angus Morrison MA BD PhD — Lewis Street, Stornoway, Isle of Lewis HS1 2JF [E-mail: angusmorrison@lineone.net] — 1979 2000 — 01851 703350

Uig (GE) (H)
William Macleod — Miavaig, Uig, Isle of Lewis HS2 9HW — 1957 1964 — 01851 672216 (Tel/Fax)

Name	(Charge)	Years	Address	Telephone
Macaulay, Donald OBE JP	(Park)	1968 1992	6 Kirkibost, Bernera, Isle of Lewis HS2 9RD [E-mail: garymiiis@talk21.com]	01851 612341
Macdonald, Alexander	(Cross Ness)	1957 1991	5 Urquhart Gardens, Stornoway, Isle of Lewis HS1 2TX	01851 702825
Macdonald, James LTh CPS	(Knock)	1984 2001	Elim, 8A Lower Bayble, Point, Isle of Lewis HS2 0QA	01851 870173
Maclean, Donald A. DCS	(Deacon)		8 Upper Barvas, Barvas, Isle of Lewis HS2 0QX	01851 840454
MacRitchie, Murdanie	(Acharacle)	1958 1969	15A New Garrabost, Isle of Lewis HS2 0PR	01851 870763
MacSween, Norman	(Kinloch)	1952 1986	7 Balmerino Drive, Stornoway, Isle of Lewis HS1 2TD	01851 703369
Montgomery, Donald J. DCS	(Deacon)		17 Murray Place, Stornoway, Isle of Lewis HS1 2JB	01851 704346
Morrison, Alexander	(Barvas)	1952 1973	Ceol Mara, Marig, Isle of Harris HS3 3AG	01859 502267

LEWIS Communion Sundays

Barvas	3rd Mar, Sep
Carloway	1st Mar, last Sep
Cross, Ness	2nd Mar, Oct
Kinloch	3rd Mar, 2nd Jun, 2nd Sep
Knock	1st Apr, Nov
Lochs-Crossbost	4th Mar, Sep
Lochs-in-Bernera	1st Apr, 2nd Sep
Stornoway High	3rd Feb, last Aug
Martin's Memorial	3rd Feb, last Aug, 1st Dec, Easter
Stornoway St Columba	3rd Feb, last Aug
Uig	3rd Jun, 1st Sep

(45) ORKNEY

Normally meets at Kirkwall, in the East Church King's Street Halls, on the second Tuesday of September, February and May, and on the last Tuesday of November. Once a year, the Presbytery meets elsewhere.

Clerk: **REV. TREVOR G. HUNT BA BD** **The Manse, Finstown, Orkney KW17 2EG**
[E-mail: akph68@uk.uumail.com]
[E-mail (personal): trevorghunt@yahoo.co.uk] **01856 761328 (Tel/Fax)**
07753 423333 (Mbl)

Birsay, Harray and Sandwick
Andrea E. Price (Mrs) 1997 2001 The Manse, North Biggings Road, Dounby, Orkney KW17 2HZ. 01856 771803
[E-mail: andrea-neil@ukonline.co.uk]

Deerness linked with Holm linked with St Andrews
Joan H. Craig (Miss) MTheol 1986 Holm, Orkney KW17 2SB 01856 781422 (Tel/Fax)
[E-mail: joanhcraig@bigfoot.com]

Eday linked with Stronsay Moncur Memorial (H)
Joyce A. Keyes (Mrs) BD 1996 Stronsay, Orkney KW17 2AF 01857 616311

Evie linked with Firth linked with Rendall
Trevor G. Hunt BA BD 1986 Finstown, Orkney KW17 2EG 01856 761328 (Tel/Fax)
[E-mail: trevorghunt@yahoo.co.uk] 07753 423333 (Mbl)

Firth (01856 761117) See Evie

Flotta linked with Hoy and Walls (T)
Vacant South Isles Manse, Longhope, Stromness, Orkney KW16 3PG 01856 701325

Holm See Deerness
Hoy and Walls See Flotta

Kirkwall: East
Allan McCafferty BSc BD 1993 Thom Street, Kirkwall, Orkney KW15 1PF 01856 875469
[E-mail: amccafferty@beeb.net]

Kirkwall: St Magnus Cathedral (H)
G. Fraser H. Macnaughton MA BD 1982 2002 Berstane Road, Kirkwall, Orkney KW15 1NA 01856 873312
[E-mail: fmacnaug@fish.co.uk]

North Ronaldsay linked with Sanday (H)
John L. McNab MA BD — 1997 — Sanday, Orkney KW17 2BW — 01857 600429

Orphir (H) linked with Stenness (H)
Thomas L. Clark BD — 1985 — Stenness, Stromness, Orkney KW16 3HH — 01856 761331

Papa Westray linked with Westray
Iain D. MacDonald BD — 1993 — The Manse, Hilldavale, Westray, Orkney KW17 2DW
[E-mail: macdonald@rapnessmanse.freeserve.co.uk] — 01857 677357 (Tel/Fax) 07710 443780 (Mbl)

Rendall See Evie

Rousay
Vacant

St Andrew's See Deerness
Sanday See North Ronaldsay

Shapinsay
Vacant — Shapinsay, Balfour, Orkney KW17 2EA — 01856 711332

South Ronaldsay and Burray
Graham D.S. Deans MA BD MTh — 1978 2002 — St Margaret's Manse, Church Road, St Margaret's Hope, Orkney KW17 2SR
[E-mail: graham.deans@btopenworld.com] — 01856 831288

Stenness See Orphir

Stromness (H)
Fiona L. Lillie (Mrs) BA BD MLitt — 1995 1999 — 5 Manse Lane, Stromness, Orkney KW16 3AP
[E-mail: fiona@lilliput23.freeserve.co.uk] — 01856 850203

Stronsay See Eday
Westray See Papa Westray

Brown, R. Graeme BA BD — 1961 1998 — (Birsay with Rousay) — Bring Deeps, Orphir, Orkney KW17 2LX
[E-mail: grasibrown@bringdeeps.fsnet.co.uk] — (Tel/Fax) 01856 811707

Cant, H.W.M. MA BD STM — 1951 1990 — (Kirkwall: St Magnus Cathedral) — Quoylobs, Holm, Orkney KW17 2RY — 01856 781300
Ward, Michael J. BSc BD PhD — 1983 1999 — Community Minister — Ploverhall, Deerness, Orkney KW17 2QJ
[E-mail: revmw@lineone.net] — 01856 741349   (Mbl) 07770 895543

(46) SHETLAND

Meets at Lerwick on the first Tuesday of March, April, June, September, October, November and December.

Clerk: REV. CHARLES H.M. GREIG MA BD   The Manse, Sandwick, Shetland ZE2 9HW   **01950 431244**
[E-mail: akph72@uk.uumail.com]

Burra Isle linked with Tingwall
Edgar J. Ogston BSc BD   1976   2001   Park Neuk, Meadowfield Place, Scalloway, Shetland ZE1 0UE   01595 880865
[E-mail: ogston@ntlworld.com]

Delting linked with Northmavine
Winnie Munson (Ms) BD   1996   2001   The Manse, Grindwell, Brae, Shetland ZE2 9QJ   01806 522219

Dunrossness and St Ninian's inc. Fair Isle linked with Sandwick Cunningsburgh and Quarff
Charles H.M. Greig MA BD   1976   1997   The Manse, Sandwick, Shetland ZE2 9HW   01950 431244
[E-mail: chm.greig@btopenworld.com]

Fetlar linked with Unst linked with Yell
R. Alan Knox MA LTh Alnst AM   1965   2000   The Manse, Mid Yell, Shetland ZE2 9BN   01957 702283

Lerwick and Bressay
Gordon Oliver BD   1979   2002   The Manse, 82 St Olaf Street, Lerwick, Shetland ZE1 0ES   01595 692125
[E-mail: gordon@cofslerwick.freeserve.co.uk]

Nesting and Lunnasting linked with Whalsay and Skerries
Irene A. Charlton (Mrs) BTh   1994   1997   The Manse, Marrister, Symbister, Whalsay, Shetland ZE2 9AE   01806 566767
[E-mail: irene.charlton@virgin.net]
Richard M. Charlton (Aux)   2001   The Manse, Marrister, Symbister, Whalsay, Shetland ZE2 9AE   01806 566767
[E-mail: malcolm.charlton@virgin.net]

Northmavine See Delting

Sandsting and Aithsting linked with Walls and Sandness
William J. McMillan CA LTh BD   1969   1997   Westside Manse, Effirth, Bixter, Shetland ZE2 9LY   01595 810386 (Tel/Fax)
[E-mail: rev-w-mcmillan@btinternet.com]

Sandwick, Cunningsburgh and Quarff See Dunrossness and St Ninian's
Tingwall See Burra Isle
Unst See Fetlar
Walls and Sandness See Sandsting and Aithsting
Whalsay and Skerries See Nesting and Lunnasting
Yell See Fetlar

Blair, James N.	1962 1986	(Sandsting and Aithsting with Walls)	2 Swinister, Sandwick, Shetland ZE2 9HH	01950 431472
Kirkpatrick, Alice H. (Miss) MA BD FSAScot	1987 2000	(Northmavine)	6 Valladale, Urafirth, Shetland ZE2 9RW	
Smith, Catherine (Mrs) DCS	1964 2003	(Presbytery Assistant)	21 Lingaro, Bixter, Shetland ZE2 9NN	01595 810207
Williamson, Magnus J.C.	1982 1999	(Fetlar with Yell)	Creekhaven, Houll Road, Scalloway, Shetland ZE1 0XA	01595 880023
Wilson, W. Stewart DA	1980 1997	(Kirkcudbright)	Aesterhoull, Fair Isle, Shetland ZE2 9JU	01595 760273

(47) ENGLAND

Meets at London, in Crown Court Church, on the second Tuesday of March and December, and at St Columba's, Pont Street, on the second Tuesday of June and October.

Clerk:	REV. W.A. CAIRNS BD	6 Honiton Gardens, Corby, Northants NN18 8BW	01536 203175
		[E-mail: akph14@uk.uumail.com]	
		[E-mail: englandpresbytery@uk.uumail.com]	

Corby: St Andrew's (H)

W. Alexander Cairns BD	1978	2001	6 Honiton Gardens, Corby, Northants NN18 8BW	01536 203175
			[E-mail: englandpresbytery@uk.uumail.com]	
Marjory Burns (Mrs) DCS			25 Barnsley Square, Corby, Northants NN18 0PQ	01536 264819
			[E-mail: mburns8069@aol.com]	

Corby: St Ninian's (H) (01536 265245)

Melvyn J. Griffiths BTh DipTheol	1978	2002	46 Glyndebourne Gardens, Corby, Northants NN18 0PZ	01536 747378
			[E-mail: thehavyn@tiscali.co.uk]	
Marjory Burns (Mrs) DCS			25 Barnsley Square, Corby, Northants NN18 0PQ	01536 264819
			[E-mail: mburns8069@aol.com]	

Guernsey: St Andrew's in the Grange (H)

Graeme W. Beebee BD	1993	2003	The Manse, Le Villocq, Castel, Guernsey GY5 7SB	01481 257345

Jersey: St Columba's (H)

James G. Mackenzie BA BD	1980	1997	18 Claremont Avenue, St Saviour, Jersey JE2 7SF	01534 730659
			[E-mail: jgmackenzie@jerseymail.com]	

Liverpool: St Andrew's
Continued Vacancy

Session Clerk: Mr Robert Cottle	0151-524 1915

London: Crown Court (H) (020 7836 5643)

Sigrid Marten	1997	2001	53 Sidmouth Street, London WC1H 8JX [E-mail: minister@crowncourtchurch.org.uk]	020 7278 5022
Timothy Fletcher BA FCMA (Aux)	1998		37 Hareston Valley Road, Caterham, Surrey CR3 6HN	01883 340826

London: St Columba's (H) (020 7584 2321) linked with Newcastle St Andrew's (H)

Barry W. Dunsmore MA BD	1982	2000	29 Hollywood Road, Chelsea, London SW10 9HT [E-mail: office@stcolumbas.org.uk]	020 7376 5230
Alexander G. Horsburgh MA BD (Assoc)	1996	2001	2 Tedworth Court, 15 Tedworth Square, London SW3 4DR [E-mail: office@stcolumbas.org.uk]	020 7376 3386
Dorothy Lunn (Aux)	2001		14 Bellerby Drive, Ouston, Co. Durham DH2 1TW	0191-492 0647
Patricia Munro (Miss) BSc DCS	2002		11 Hurlingham Square, Peterborough Road, London SW6 3DZ [E-mail: patm@totalise.co.uk]	020 7610 6994

Bowie, A. Glen CBE BA BSc	1954	1984	(Principal Chaplain: RAF)	16 Weir Road, Hemingford Grey, Huntingdon PE18 9EH	01480 381425
Brown, Scott J. BD	1993		Chaplain: RN	4 Darwin Close, Lee-on-Solent, Hants PO13 8LS [E-mail: leeonsolent@hotmail.com]	02392 554116
Cameron, R. Neil	1975	1981	Chaplain: Community	The Church Centre, Rhine Area Support Unit, BFPO 40	0049 2161 472770
Coulter, David G. BA BD PhD	1989	1994	Chaplain: Army	14 Fairfield, Lisburn, Co. Antrim BT27 4EE [E-mail: padrecoulter@aol.com]	02890 427540
Davison, Charles F. MA	1947	1987	(Guernsey: St Andrew's in the Grange)	Maryfield, Green Lanes, St Peter Port, Guernsey GY1 1TN	01481 727446
Deverney, David J. BD	1997	2003	Chaplain: RN	8 Hunton Close, Lympstone, Exmouth, Devon EX8 5JG [E-mail: davidjdevenney@freeuk.com]	01395 266570
Dowswell, James A.M.	1991	2001	(Lerwick and Bressay)	Mill House, High Street, Staplehurst, Tonbridge, Kent TN12 0AV	01580 891271
Drummond, J.S. MA	1946	1978	(Corby: St Ninian's)	77 Low Road, Hellesdon, Norwich NR6 5AG	01603 417736
Duncan, Denis M. BD PhD	1944	1986	(Editor: *The British Weekly*)	80A Woodland Rise, London N10 3UJ	020 8883 1831
Fields, James MA BD STM	1988	1997	School Chaplain	The Bungalow, The Ridgeway, Mill Hill, London NW7 1QX	(Tel) 020 8374 4708
Fyall, Robert S. MA BD	1986	1989	Tutor: St John's College, Durham	7 Briardene, Durham DH1 4QU	(Fax) 020 8201 1397
Hood, Adam J.J. MA BD DPhil	1989		Lecturer	67A Farquhar Road, Edgbaston, Birmingham B15 2QP [E-mail: adamhood1@hotmail.com]	0121-452 2606
Hughes, O. Tudor MBE BA	1934	1976	(Guernsey: St Andrew's in the Grange)	4 Belcher Court, Dorchester on Thames, Oxon	01865 340779
Jolly, Andrew J. BD	1989	1996	Chaplain: RAF	Chaplaincy Services, RAF Uxbridge, Middlesex UB10 0RX [E-mail: andrewchrissiejolly@btopenworld.com]	01895 815387
Lugton, George L. MA BD	1955	1997	(Guernsey: St Andrew's in the Grange)	6 Clos de Beauvoir, Rue Cohu, Guernsey GY5 7TE	01481 254285
McEnhill, Peter BD PhD	1992	1996	Lecturer	Westminster College, Madingley Road, Cambridge CB3 0AA	01223 353997
Macfarlane, Peter T. BA LTh	1970	1994	(Chaplain: Army)	2 Grosvenor House, Warwick Square, Carlisle CA1 1LB	01228 521519
McIndoe, John H. MA BD STM DD	1966	2000	(London: St Columba's with Newcastle St Andrew's)	5 Dunlin, Westerlands Park, Glasgow G12 0FE	0141-579 1366
MacLeod, Angus BD	1996		Chaplain: Army	RMA Sandhurst, Camberley, Surrey GU15 4PQ [E-mail: padrermas@btconnect.com]	01276 691498
MacLeod, Rory BA MBA BD	1994	1998	Chaplain: Royal Navy	Royal Marines, Hamworthy Barracks, Poole, Dorset BH15 4NQ [E-mail: annice@eurobell.co.uk]	

MacLeod, R.N. MA BD	1986	1992	Chaplain: Army	St Andrew's Garrison Church, Queen's Avenue, Aldershot, Hants GU11 2BY	01252 331123
Majcher, Philip L. BD	1982	1987	Chaplain: Army	18 Britannia Drive, Cempshot Park, Basingstoke RE22 4FN	01256 398868
Martin, Anthony M. BA BD	1989	1989	Chaplain: Army	Army Technical Foundation College, Rowcroft Barracks, Arborfield, Reading, Berks RG2 9NJ [E-mail: am_km_martin@hotmail.com]	01189 763409
Milloy, A. Miller DPE LTh DipTrMan	1979	1998	Regional Secretary: United Bible Societies	United Bible Societies, Allied Dunbar House, East Park, Crawley, West Sussex RH10 6AS	
Mills, Peter W. BD CPS	1984		Principal Chaplain: RAF	Chaplaincy Services RAF, HQ PTC Innsworth, Gloucs GL3 1EZ	01452 510828
Milton, A. Leslie MA BD PhD	1996	2001	Lecturer	Ripon College, Cuddesdon, Oxford OX4 9HP	01865 877408
Norwood, David W. BA	1948	1980	(Lisbon)	6 Kempton Close, Thundersley, Benfleet, Essex SS7 3SG	01268 747219
Rennie, Alistair M. MA BD	1939	1986	(Kincardine Croick and Edderton)	Noble's Yard, St Mary's Gate, Wirksworth, Derbyshire DE4 4DQ	
Richmond, James MA BD PhD	1956	1994	(Lancaster University)	10 Wallace Lane, Forton, Preston, Lancs PR3 0BA	01524 791705
Shackleton, Scott S.S. BA BD PhD	1993		Chaplain: Royal Navy	RM Stonehouse, Plymouth, Devon	01752 836397
Stewart, Charles E. BSc BD PhD	1976	2000	(Chaplain of the Fleet)	The Royal Hospital School, Holbrook, Ipswich IP9 2RX	01473 326200
Trevorrow, James A. LTh	1971	2003	(Glasgow: Cranhill)	12 Test Green, Corby, Northants NN17 2HA [E-mail: jimtrevorrow@compuserve.com]	01536 264018
Walker, R. Forbes BSc BD ThM	1987	2000	School Chaplain	2 Holmleigh, Priory Road, Ascot, Berks SL5 8EA	01344 883272
Wallace, Donald S.	1950	1980	(Chaplain: RAF)	7 Dellfield Close, Watford, Herts WD1 3BL	01923 223289
White, Earlsley M. BA	1957	1998	(Uddingston: Park)	13 Isis Lakes, Spine Road, South Cerney, Gloucs GL7 5TL	01285 862898
Whiton, John P.	1977	1999	Assistant Chaplain General	115 Sycamore Road, Farnborough, Hants GU14 6RE	01262 674488

ENGLAND – Church Addresses

Corby		
St Andrew's	Occupation Road	
St Ninian's	Beanfield Avenue	
Liverpool	The Western Rooms, Anglican Cathedral	
London		Crown Court WC2
Crown Court		Pont Street SW1
St Columba's		Sandyford Road
Newcastle		

(48) EUROPE

Clerk: REV. JOHN A. COWIE BSc BD   Jan Willem Brouwersstraat 9, NL-1071 LH Amsterdam [E-mail: j.cowie@chello.nl]   **Tel: 0031 20 672 2288** **Fax: 0031 842 221513**

Amsterdam

John A. Cowie BSc BD	1983	1989	Jan Willem Brouwersstraat 9, NL-1071 LH Amsterdam, The Netherlands [E-mail: j.cowie@chello.nl]	0031 20 672 2288 Fax: 0031 842 221513

Brussels
Thomas C. Pitkeathly MA CA BD | 1984 | 1991 | 23 Square des Nations, B-1000 Brussels, Belgium [E-mail: pitkeathly@tiscali.be] | 0032 2 672 40 56

Budapest
Kenneth I. Mackenzie BD CPS | 1990 | 1999 | St Columba's Scottish Mission, Vorosmarty utca 51, H-1064 Budapest, Hungary; Oltvany Arok 25, H-1112 Budapest, Hungary (Manse) [E-mail: mackenzie@mail.datanet.hu] | 0036 1 343 8479 / 0036 1 246 2258

Costa del Sol linked with Gibraltar
Vacant | 11 Calle Margarita Blanca, E-29640 Fuengirola, Malaga, Spain; c/o Lux Mundi Ecumenical Centre, Calle Nueva 7, Fuengirola, Malaga, Spain | 0034 5 258 8394

Geneva
Ian A. Manson BA BD | 1989 | 2001 | 6 Chemin Taverney, CH-1218 Grand Saconnex, Geneva, Switzerland [E-mail: cofsg@pingnet.ch] | 0041 22 798 29 09 / 0041 22 788 08 31 (Office)

Gibraltar linked with Costa del Sol
Vacant | 1988 | 1996 | St Andrew's Manse, 29 Scud Hill, Gibraltar [E-mail: billsmith@gibnet.gi] | 00350 77040

Lausanne
Douglas R. Murray MA BD | 1965 | 1994 | 26 Avenue de Rumine, CH-1005 Lausanne, Switzerland [E-mail: scotskirklausanne@bluewin.ch] | (Tel/Fax) 0041 21 323 98 28

Lisbon
Vacant | The Manse, Rua da Arriaga 11, 1200-608 Lisbon, Portugal [E-mail: st.andrewschurch@clix.pt] | (Tel/Fax) 00351 21 395 7677

Malta
David Morris | 2002 | La Romagnola, 13 Triq is-Seiqja, Mosra Kola, Attard BZN 05, Malta [E-mail: djlmorris@onvol.net]; Church address: 210 Old Baker Street, Valletta, Malta | (Tel/Fax) 00356 214 15465

Paris
William M. Reid MA BD | 1966 | 1993 | 10 Rue Thimmonier, F-75009 Paris, France [E-mail: scotskirk@wanadoo.fr] | 0033 1 48 78 47 94

Rome St Andrew's
William B. McCulloch BD | 1997 | 2002 | Via XX Settembre 7, 00187 Rome, Italy [E-mail: revwbmcculloch@hotmail.com] | (Tel) 0039 06 482 7627 / (Fax) 0039 06 487 4370

Rotterdam				
Robert A. Calvert BSc BD DMin	1983	1995	Gelebrem 59, NL-3068 TJ Rotterdam, The Netherlands [E-mail: scotsintchurch@cs.com]	0031 10 220 4199
Joost Pot BSc (Aux)		1992	[E-mail: j.pot@wanadoo.nl]	
Turin				
Robert A. Mackenzie LLB BD	1993	2001	Via Sant Anselmo 6, 10125 Turin, Italy [E-mail: valdese.english@arpnet.it]	0039 011 650 9467
Conference of European Churches				
Matthew Z. Ross LLB BD FSAScot	1998	2003	Church and Society Commission, Ecumenical Centre, Rue Joseph II 174, B-1000 Brussels, Belgium [E-mail: matthewross@beeb.net]	(Tel) 0032 2 230 1732 (Fax) 0032 2 231 1413 (Mbl) 07711 706950
World Alliance of Reformed Churches				
Paraic Raemonn BA BD	1982	1993	WARC, 150 Route de Ferney, CH-1211 Geneva 2, Switzerland [E-mail: par@warc.ch]	0041 22 791 62 43
World Council Secretariat				
Alan D. Falconer MA BD DLitt	1972	1995	WCC, 150 Route de Ferney, CH-1211 Geneva 2, Switzerland [E-mail: af@wcc-coe.org]	0041 22 791 63 37
CORRESPONDING MEMBERS				
James M. Brown MA BD	1982		Neustrasse 15, D-4630 Bochum, Germany [E-mail: j.brown@web.de]	0049 234 133 65
Dr Virgil Cruz	1956	1996	(Senior Professor of New Testament: Louisville Presbyterian Theological Seminary)	
Nii Teiko Dagadu			Geelvinckstraat 21, NL-1901 AE Castricum, The Netherlands Startenweg 130A, NL-3039 JM Rotterdam, The Netherlands [E-mail: niiteiko.dagadu@12move.nl]	0031 10 244 0898
R. Graeme Dunphy	1988	1993	Institut für Anglistik, Universitätsstrasse 31, D-93053 Regensburg, Germany	
Rhona Dunphy (Mrs)				
Professor A.I.C. Heron BD DTheol	1975	1987	University of Erlangen, Kochstrasse 6, D-91054 Erlangen, Germany [E-mail: arheron@theologie.uni-erlangen.de]	0049 9131 852202
Jane M. Howitt (Miss) MA BD	1996		Scripture Union, PO Box 476, LV-1050 Riga, Latvia [E-mail: janesu@com.latnet.lv]	00371 7 220877
Stewart J. Lamont BSc BD	1972		La Poujade, F-82160 Caylus, France [E-mail: lamonts@wanadoo.fr]	0033 5 63 67 03 77
Bertalan Tamas	2002		St Columba's Scottish Mission, Vorosmarty utca 51, H-1064 Budapest, Hungary [E-mail: rch@mail.elender.hu]	0036 1 343 8479
Derek Yarwood			Chaplain's Department, Garrison HQ, Princess Royal Barracks, BFPO 47, Germany	0044 5241 77924

(Rome)	David F. Huie MA BD	1962	(2001)	9 Kennedy Crescent, Alverstoke, Gosport, Hants PO12 2NL	02392 529310
	David V.F. Kingston BD	1993		Army Chaplain: 20 Armoured Brigade, Paderborn, Germany [E-mail: d.v.f.k@btinternet.com]	
(Brussels)	A.J. Macleod MA BD	1943	(1974)	72A Cathcart Road, London SW10 9DJ	
(Brussels)	Charles C. McNeill OBE BD	1962	(1991)	17 All Saints Way, Beachamwell, Swaffham, Norfolk PE37 8BU	
(Gibraltar)	John R. Page BD DipMin	1988	2003	Astighi 2, Fifth Floor, Number 4, E-29640 Fuengirola, Malaga, Spain	0034 952 582836
(Gibraltar)	D. Stuart Philip MA	1952	(1990)	6 St Bernard's Crescent, Edinburgh EH4 1NP	0131-332 7499
(Malta)	Colin A. Westmarland MBE BD	1971	(2001)	PO Box 5, Cospicua CSP 01, Malta	00356 216 923552

(49) JERUSALEM

Jerusalem: St Andrew's

| Clarence W. Musgrave BA BD ThM | 1966 | 2000 | PO Box 8619, 91086 Jerusalem, Israel [E-mail: standjer@netvision.net.il] | (Tel) 00972 2 673 2401 (Fax) 00972 2 673 1711 |

Tiberias: St Andrew's

| Frederick W. Hibbert BD | 1986 | 1995 | St Andrew's, Galilee, PO Box 104, 14100 Tiberias, Israel [E-mail: scottie@netvision.net.il] | (Tel) 00972 4 672 1165 (Fax) 00972 4 679 0145 |

SECTION 6

Additional Lists
of Personnel

LIST A – AUXILIARY MINISTERS

NAME	ORD	ADDRESS	TEL	PR
Anderson, David M. MSc FCOptom	1984	1 Dumfries Place, Fort William PH33 6UQ	01397 703203	38
Birch, Jim PGDip FRSA FIOC	2001	1 Kirkhill Grove, Cambuslang, Glasgow G72 8EH	0141-583 1722	16
Brown, Elizabeth (Mrs) JP RGN	1996	25 Highfield Road, Scone, Perth PH2 6RN	01738 552391	28
Brown, Marina D. (Mrs) MA	2000	Elmbank, 3 Lovers Loan, Dollar FK14 7AB	01259 742870	23
Campbell, Gordon MA CDipAF DipHSM MCMI MIHM MRIN ARSGS FRGS FSAScot	2001	2 Falkland Place, Kingoodie, Invergowrie, Dundee DD2 5DY	01382 561383	29
Charlton, Richard	2001	The Manse, Symbister, Whalsay, Shetland ZE2 9AE	01806 566767	46
Cloggie, June (Mrs)	1997	11A Tulipan Crescent, Callander FK17 8AR	01877 331021	23
Craggs, Sheila (Mrs)	2001	7 Morar Court, Ellon AB41 9GG	01358 723055	33
Cruikshank, Alistair A.B. MA	1991	Thistle Cottage, 2A Chapel Place, Dollar FK14 7DW	01259 742549	23
Davidson, David W.	1987	Grianail, Glenegedale, Port Ellen, Isle of Islay PA42 7AS	01496 302194	19
Durno, Richard C. DSW CQSW	1989	Durnada House, 31 Springfield Road, Bishopbriggs, Glasgow G64 1PJ	0141-772 1052	16
Ferguson, Archibald M. MSc PhD CEng FRINA	1989	The Whins, Barrowfield, Station Road, Cardross, Dumbarton G82 5NL	01389 841517	18
Fletcher, Timothy E.G. BA FCMA	1998	37 Hareston Valley Road, Caterham, Surrey CR3 6HN	01883 340826	47
Glass, Alexander OBE MA	1998	Craigton, Tulloch Avenue, Dingwall IV15 9TU	01349 863258	39
Graham, Andrew	2001	4 Woodside Park, Forres IV36 2GJ	01309 673886	35
Howie, Marion L.K. (Mrs) MA ARCS	1992	51 High Road, Stevenston KA20 3DY	01294 466571	12
Jenkinson, John J. JP LTCL ALCM DipEd DipSen	1991	8 Rosehall Terrace, Falkirk FK1 1PY	01324 625498	22
Kay, Elizabeth (Miss) Dip YCS	1993	1 Kintail Walk, Inchture, Perth PH14 9RY	01828 686029	29
Lunn, Dorothy	2002	14 Bellerby Drive, Ouston, Co. Durham DH2 1TN	0191-492 0647	47
McAlpine, John BSc	1988	Braeside, 201 Bonkle Road, Newmains, Wishaw ML2 9AA	01698 384610	17
McCann, George McD. BSc ATI	1994	Rosbeg, Parsonage Road, Galashiels TD1 3HS	01896 752055	4
MacDonald, Kenneth MA BA	2001	5 Henderland Road, Bearsden, Glasgow G61 1AH	0141-943 1103	16
Mack, Elizabeth (Miss) Dip PEd	1994	24 Roberts Crescent, Dumfries DG2 7RS	01387 264847	8
Mack, John C. JP	1985	The Willows, Auchleven, Insch AB52 6QD	01464 820393	33
Mailer, Colin	2000	Innis Chonain, Back Row, Polmont, Falkirk FK2 0RD	01324 712401	22
Manson, Eileen (Mrs) DCE	1994	1 Cambridge Avenue, Gourock PA19 1XT	01475 632401	15
Morrison, Donald John	2001	22 Kyles Harris, Isle of Harris HS3 3BS	01859 502341	43
Munro, Mary (Mrs) BA	1993	High Barbeth, Leswalt, Stranraer DG9 0QS	01776 870250	9
Paterson, Andrew E. JP	1994	6 The Willows, Kelty KY4 0FQ	01383 830998	24
Paterson, Maureen (Mrs) BSc	1992	91 Dalmahoy Crescent, Kirkcaldy KY2 6TA	01592 262300	25
Pot, Joost BSc	1992	Rijksstraatweg 12, NL-2988 BJ Ridderkerk, The Netherlands	0031 18 042 0894	48
Ramage, Alistair E. BA	1996	16 Claremont Gardens, Milngavie, Glasgow G62 6PG	0141-956 2897	18
Riddell, Thomas S. BSc CEng FIChemE	1993	4 The Maltings, Linlithgow EH49 6DS	01506 843251	2
Ritchie, Christine (Mrs)	2002	Throughgate, 78 High Street, Dunbar EH42 1JH	01368 863141	3
Shaw, Catherine A.M. MA	1998	40 Merrygreen Place, Stewarton, Kilmarnock KA3 5EP	01560 483352	11

Simpson, James H. BSc	11 Claypotts Place, Broughty Ferry, Dundee DD5 1LG	1996	01382 776520	29
Sutherland, David	6 Cromarty Drive, Dundee DD2 2UQ	2001	01382 621473	29
Thomas, Shirley A. (Mrs) Dip Soc Sci AMIA	14 Kirkgait, Letham, Forfar DD8 2XQ	1988	01307 818084	30
Wandrum, David	5 Cawder View, Carrickstone Meadows, Cumbernauld, Glasgow G68 0BN	1993	01236 723288	22
Watson, Jean S. (Miss) MA	29 Strachan Crescent, Dollar FK14 7HL	1993	01259 742872	23
Wilson, Mary D. (Mrs) RGN SCM DTM	The Manse, Bettyhill, Thurso KW14 7SS	1990	01641 521208	40
Wilson, Roy DA ARIBA ARIAS	20 William Ure Place, Bishopbriggs, Glasgow G64 3BH	1986	141-563 1829	18
Zamboni, James LIADip	100 Old Manse Road, Netherton, Wishaw ML2 0EP	1997	01698 350889	17

LIST B – CHAPLAINS TO HM FORCES

NAME	ORD	COM	BCH	ADDRESS
Abeledo, Benjamin J.A. BTh DipTh PTh	1991	1999	A	1 Highlanders, Redford Barracks, Edinburgh EH13 0PP
Aitchison, James W. BD	1993	1993	A	7th Armoured Brigade HQ, BFPO 30
Britchfield, Alison E.P. (Mrs) MA BD	1987	1992	RN	Britannia Royal Naval College, Dartmouth, Devon
Brown, Scott J. BD	1993	1993	RN	HMS *Sultan*, Military Road, Gosport, Hants PO12 3BY
Cameron, Robert N.	1975	1981	A	Church Centre, Rhine Garrison, BFPO 40
Cobain, Alan R. BD	2000		A	1 Cheshire, Kiwi Barracks, Bulford Camp, Salisbury, Wilts SP4 9HZ
Connolly, Daniel BD DipTheol DipMin	1983		A	2CS Regt Royal Logistics Corps, BFPO 47
Coulter, David G. BA BD PhD	1989	1994	RAF	Senior Chaplain, HQ Northern Ireland, BFPO 825
Craig, Gordon T. BD DipMin	1988	1988	A	College Staff Chaplain, Church Centre, RAF Cosford, Wolverhampton NG34 8HB
Dailly, J.R. BD DipPS	1979	1979	A	DACC, HQ15(NW) Bde, Imphal Barracks, Fuller Road, York YO10 4AU
Dalton, Mark BD DipMin	2002	2002	RN	CIC Britannia Royal Naval College, 35 Regt Royal, Dartmouth, Devon TQ6 0HJ
Deveney, David BD	1997	2002	RN	CIC Britannia Royal Naval College, 35 Regt Royal, Dartmouth, Devon TQ6 0HJ
Duncan, John C. BD MPhil	1987	2001	A	35 Regt Royal Engineers, Paderborn, BFPO 31
Jolly, Andrew J. BD CertMin	1983	1996	RAF	Chaplaincy Centre, RAF Uxbridge UB10 0RX
Kellock, Chris N. MA BD	1998		RAF	Force Chaplains, RAF Mount Pleasant, BFPO 655
Kennon, Stan MA BD			RN	1 Anson Way, Helston, Cornwall TR13 8BS
Kingston, David V.F. BD	1992	2000	A	Senior Chaplain, HQ20, Armoured Brigade, BFPO 31
McCulloch, Alen J.R. MA BD	1993	1993	A	Senior Chaplain, 2nd BN ITC, Helles Barracks, Catterick Garrison, North Yorks DL9 4HH
McFadzean, Iain MA BD	1990	1995	RN	Bedevere, BFPO 42
Mackenzie, Seoras L. BD	1989	1999	A	1 KOSB, Somme Barracks, Catterick Garrison, North Yorks DL9 4LD
MacLeod, Charles A. MA BD	1996	1998	A	Royal Military Academy, Camberley, Surrey GU15 4PQ
MacLeod, Roderick N. MA BD	1986	1996	A	101 Logistic Brigade, Buller Barracks, Aldershot, Hants GU11 2BX
MacLeod, Rory A.R. BA BD MBA	1994	1992	RN	Hamworthy Barracks, Royal Marines, Poole, Dorset BH15 4NQ
MacPherson Duncan J. BSc BD	1993	1998	A	IBW, Fallingbostel, St Barbara's Barracks, Fallingbostel, BFPO 38
Majcher, Philip L. BD	1982	2002	A	HQ ARRC, Joint Headquarters, BFPO 40
Martin, Anthony M. BA BD	1989	1987	A	AFT College, Rowcroft Barracks, Arobfield, Reading, Berks RG2 9NJ
Mills, Peter W. BD CPS	1984	1989	RAF	Principal Chaplain, RAF Room F89, HQ PTC, RAF Innsworth, Gloucester GL3 1EZ

NAME	ORD	COM		ADDRESS	TEL
Munro, Sheila BD	1995	2003	RAF	Chaplaincy Centre, RAF Odiham, Hook RG29 1QT	
Prentice, Donald K. BSc BD	1987	1992	A	F1 BN Royal Highland Fusiliers, Fort George, Ardersier, Inverness IV1 2TD	
Rae, Scott M. MBE BD CPS	1976	1981	RN	HMS *Neptune*, Faslane, Helensburgh G84 8HL	
Shackleton, Scott J.S. BA BD	1993	1993	RN	Staff Chaplain Commandant General Royal Navy Marines, RM Barracks, Stonehouse, Plymouth PL1 3QS	
Shaw, Duncan LTh CPS	1984	1984	RAF	Chaplains Office, RAF Leuchars, St Andrews KY16 0XJ	
Whitton, John P. MA BD	1977	1977	A	Assistant Chaplain General, Headquarters 4th Division, Steele's Road, Aldershot GU11 2DP	

CHAPLAINS TO HM FORCES (Territorial Army)

NAME	ORD	COM	ADDRESS	TEL
Barclay, Iain C. MBE TD	1976	1982	HQ 2 Division, South Queensferry EH30 9TN	0131-310 2124
Blakey, Stephen A.	1977	1996	32 (Scottish) Signal Regiment (Volunteers), Glasgow G20 6JU	0141-224 5025
Forsyth, Alex R. TD	1973	1983	71 Engineer Regiment (Volunteers), RAF Leuchars KY16	01334 839471
Gibson, James M.	1978	1986	205 (Scottish) Field Hospital (Volunteers), Glasgow G51 6JU	0141-224 5172
Kinsey, Louis	1991	1992	205 (Scottish) Field Hospital (Volunteers), Glasgow G51 6JU	0141-224 5172
Swindells, Sean	1996	2001	225 Field Ambulance (Volunteers), Dundee DD4 7DL	0131-310 4760
Thomson, John M.A.	1978	1992	105 Regiment RA (Volunteers), Glasgow G20 8LQ	0141-224 5025
Warwick, Ivan C.	1980	1990	51 Highland Regiment (Volunteers), Perth PH1 5BT	0131-310 8547

CHAPLAINS TO HM FORCES (Army Cadet Force)

NAME	ORD	COM	ADDRESS	TEL
Almond, David M.	1996	1998	West Lowland Bn ACF, Ayr KA8 9HX	01292 264612
Andrews, J. Edward	1985	1998	Glasgow & Lanarkshire Bn ACF, Glasgow G72 8YP	0141-641 0858
Barclay, Iain C. MBE TD	1976	1996	Black Watch Bn ACF, Perth PH1 5BT	01738 626571
Campbell, Roderick D.M. TD	1975	1998	Argyll & Sutherland Highlands Bn ACF, Dumbarton G82 2DG	01389 763451
Charlton, Irene A.	1994	2000	Shetland (Independent) Bty ACF, Lerwick ZE1 0JN	01595 692043
Fisk, Elizabeth A.	1996	1999	Black Watch Bn ACF, Perth PH1 5BT	01738 626571
Goskirk, J. Leslie	1968	1985	1 Bn Highlands, ACF, Inverness IV2 4SU	01463 231829
Homewood, I. Max	1997	1998	Argyll & Sutherland Highlands Bn ACF, Dumbarton G82 2DG	01389 763451
Keyes, Joyce	1996	2000	Orkney (Independent) Bty ACF, Kirkwall KW1 5LP	01856 872661
Sherratt, Arthur	1994	1999	West Lowland Bn ACF, Ayr KA8 9HX	01292 264612

Sutherland, Iain A.   1996   1999   2 Bn Highlands ACF, Aberdeen AB24 8DV   01224 826239
Thomson, Stephen   2001   2003   1 Bn Highlands, ACF, Inverness IV2 4SU   01463 231829

LIST C – HOSPITAL CHAPLAINS ('Full-time' Chaplains are listed first in each area)

LOTHIAN

EDINBURGH – LOTHIAN UNIVERSITY HOSPITALS NHS TRUST
ROYAL INFIRMARY
Rev. Alexander Young   19B Craigour Drive, Edinburgh EH17 7NY   0131-242 1997
Rev. Iain Telfer   32 Alnwickhill Park, Edinburgh EH16 6UH   0131-242 1991
Ms Anne Mulligan   27A Craigour Avenue, Edinburgh EH17 1NH   0131-242 1996
WESTERN GENERAL HOSPITAL [0131-537 1000]
Rev. Alistair K. Ridland   13 Stewart Place, Kirkliston EH29 2BQ   0131-537 1401
LOTHIAN PRIMARY CARE NHS TRUST
ROYAL EDINBURGH HOSPITAL [0131-537 6734]
Rev. Murray Chalmers   25 Greenbank Road, Edinburgh EH10 5RX
Rev. Lynne MacMurchie
Rev. Patricia Allen   1 Westgate, Dunbar EH42 1JL
   Chaplain's Assistant
ROYAL HOSPITAL FOR SICK CHILDREN/LIBERTON [0131-536 0000]
Rev. Caroline Upton   10 (3FL) Montagu Terrace, Edinburgh EH3 5QX   0131-536 0144
EDINBURGH COMMUNITY MENTAL HEALTH
Rev. Lynne MacMurchie   41 George IV Bridge, Edinburgh EH1 1EL   0131-220 5150
Rev. Iain Whyte   41 George IV Bridge, Edinburgh EH1 1EL   0131-220 5150
LIVINGSTON – WEST LOTHIAN HEALTHCARE NHS TRUST [01506 419666]
Rev. Thomas Crichton   18 Carlton Terrace, Edinburgh EH7 5DD
Rev. Dr Georgina Nelson   6 Pentland Park, Craigshill, Livingston EH54 5NR

HOSPICES

MARIE CURIE CENTRE   Rev. Tom Gordon   Frogston Road West, Edinburgh EH10 7DR   (Tel) 0131-445 2141
                                                                                (Fax) 0131-445 5845
ST COLUMBA'S HOSPICE   Rev. Alison Wagstaff   Challenger Lodge, 15 Boswall Road, Edinburgh EH5 3RW   0131-551 1381

HOSPITALS

WESTERN GENERAL   Rev. Joanne Finlay   6 Herd Green, Livingston EH54 8PU   0131-537 1400
                  Rev. Harry Telfer   32 Mayfield Road, Edinburgh EH9 2NJ   0131-537 1400
CORSTORPHINE   Rev. J. William Hill   23 Belgrave Road, Edinburgh EH12 6NG   0131-334 3188

Hospital	Chaplain	Address	Telephone
EASTERN GENERAL	Rev. John Tait	52 Pilrig Street, Edinburgh EH6 5AS	0131-554 1842
ROYAL EDINBURGH HOSPITAL	Rev. John Whitley	114 Viewforth, Edinburgh EH10 4LN	0131-229 0133
LINLITHGOW ST MICHAEL'S	Rev. James Francis	Cross House, Kirkgate, Linlithgow EH49 7AL	01506 842665
BELHAVEN	Rev. Laurence H. Twaddle	The Manse, Belhaven Road, Dunbar EH42 1NH	01368 863098
EDENHALL	Rev. Anne M. Jones	7 North Elphinstone Farm, Tranent EH33 2ND	01875 614442
HERDMANFLAT	Rev. Anne M. Jones	7 North Elphinstone Farm, Tranent EH33 2ND	01875 614442
LOANHEAD	Mrs Susan Duncan	35 Kilmaurs Road, Edinburgh EH16 5DB	0131-667 2995
ROODLANDS	Rev. Kenneth D.F. Walker	The Manse, Athelstaneford, North Berwick EH39 5BE	01620 880378
ROSSLYNLEE	Rev. John W. Fraser	North Manse, Penicuik EH26 8AG	01968 672213
	Mrs Diane Kettles	10 Millway, Pencaitland, Tranent EH34 5HQ	07812 032226

BORDERS

Hospital	Chaplain	Address	Telephone
MELROSE – BORDERS GENERAL HOSPITAL NHS TRUST [01896 754333]	Rev. J. Ronald Dick	Chaplaincy Centre, Borders General Hospital, Melrose TD6 9BS	
DINGLETON	Rev. John Riddell	42 High Street, Jedburgh TD8 6NQ	01835 863223
HAY LODGE, PEEBLES	Rev. James H. Wallace	Innerleithen Road, Peebles EH45 8BD	01721 721749
KNOLL	Rev. Andrew Morrice	The Manse, Castle Street, Duns TD11 3DG	01361 883755
INCH	Rev. Robin McHaffie	Kirk Yetholm, Kelso TD5 8RD	01573 420308

DUMFRIES AND GALLOWAY

Hospital	Chaplain	Address	Telephone
DUMFRIES HOSPITALS [01387 246246]	Rev. Alexander E. Strachan	2 Leafield Road, Dumfries DG1 2DS	01387 279460
THOMAS HOPE, LANGHOLM	Rev. Robert Milne	The Manse, Langholm DG13 0BL	01896 668577
LOCHMABEN	Rev. Alexander Stoddart	The Manse, Hightae, Lockerbie DG11 1JL	01387 811499
MOFFAT	Rev. David McKay	The Manse, Moffat DG10 9LR	01683 220128
NEW ANNAN	Rev. Mairi Byers	Meadowbank, Plumdon Road, Annan DG12 6SJ	01461 206512
CASTLE DOUGLAS	Rev. Robert Malloch	1 Castle View, Castle Douglas DG7 1BG	01556 502171
DUMFRIES AND GALLOWAY ROYAL INFIRMARY	Mrs Morven Archer	1 Gilloch Drive, Dumfries DG1 4DP	01387 263946
KIRKCUDBRIGHT	Rev. Douglas R. Irving	6 Bourtree Avenue, Kirkcudbright DG6 4AU	01557 330489
THORNHILL			
DALRYMPLE			
GARRICK			
NEWTON STEWART	Rev. Samuel McC. Harris	Linden, Leswalt Road, Stranraer DG9 0AA	01776 706387

AYRSHIRE AND ARRAN

AYRSHIRE AND ARRAN PRIMARY CARE NHS TRUST [01292 513023]

AILSA HOSPITAL, AYR	Rev. Sheila Mitchell	Chaplaincy Centre, Dalmellington Road, Ayr KA6 6AB	

AYRSHIRE AND ARRAN ACUTE HOSPITALS NHS TRUST [01563 521133]

CROSSHOUSE HOSPITAL KILMARNOCK	Rev. Judith Huggett	4 Westmoor Crescent, Kilmarnock KA1 1TX	
AYR/BIGGART HOSPITALS [01292 610555]	Rev. Roderick H. McNidder	6 Hollow Park, Alloway, Ayr KA7 4SR	01292 442554
ARROL PARK	Mrs Norma Livingstone	31 Victoria Drive, Troon KA10 6JF	01292 269161
BALLOCHMYLE	Rev. A.M. McPhail	87 Forehill Road, Ayr KA7 3JR	01465 831282
DAVIDSON	Rev. Robert Bell	The Manse, Ballantrae, Girvan KA26 0UH	01290 420769
HOLMHEAD	Rev. John Paterson	33 Barrhill Road, Cumnock KA18 1PJ	01863 538289
CROSSHOUSE	Rev. John Urquhart	9 Standalane, Kilmaurs, Kilmarnock KA3 2NB	
	Mrs Norma Livingstone	31 Victoria Drive, Troon KA10 6JF	
KIRKLANDSIDE	Rev. James McNaughtan	35 South Gargieston Drive, Kilmarnock KA1 1TB	01563 521665
STRATHLEA	Mrs Barbara Urquhart	9 Standalane, Kilmaurs, Kilmarnock KA3 2NB	01863 538289
AYRSHIRE CENTRAL	Mrs Barbara Urquhart	9 Standalane, Kilmaurs, Kilmarnock KA3 2NB	01863 538289
	Rev. Hugh M. Adamson	Mure Church Manse, West Road, Irvine KA12 8RE	01294 279916
BROOKSBY HOUSE, LARGS	Mrs Norma Livingstone	31 Victoria Drive, Troon KA10 6JF	01475 672370
WAR MEMORIAL, ARRAN	Rev. Stephen J. Smith	31 Douglas Street, Largs KA30 8PT	01770 700289
LADY MARGARET, MILLPORT	Rev. Elizabeth Watson	The Manse, Whiting Bay, Isle of Arran KA27 8RE	01475 530460
	Rev. Marjory MacKay	The Manse, Millport, Isle of Cumbrae KA28 0EE	

LANARKSHIRE

LOCKHART	Rev. Catherine Collins	2 Friarsdene, Lanark ML11 9EJ	01555 663363
	Rev. Bruce Gordon	The Rectory, Cleghorn Road, Lanark ML11 7QT	
CLELAND	Rev. John Jackson	The Manse, Bellside Road, Cleland, Motherwell ML1 5NP	01698 860260
KELLO	Rev. Gavin Elliott	61 High Street, Biggar ML12 6DA	01899 220227
LADY HOME	Rev. Bryan Kerr	The Manse, Douglas, Lanark ML11 0RB	01555 851213
ROADMEETINGS	Rev. Geoff McKee	Kirkstyle Manse, Church Street, Carluke ML8 4BA	
WISHAW GENERAL	Rev. James S.G. Hastie	Chalmers Manse, Quarry Road, Larkhall ML9 1HH	01698 882238
	Rev. Klaus Buwert	The Manse, West Thornlie Street, Wishaw ML2 7AR	01698 372356
	Rev. J. Allardyce	6 Ryde Road, Wishaw ML2 7DU	01698 372657
	Rev. David Collins	Greyfriars Manse, Friarsdene, Lanark ML11 9EJ	01355 663363
STRATHCLYDE	Rev. Sharon Colvin	48 Dunrobin Road, Airdrie ML6 8LR	01236 763154
BIRKWOOD	Rev. David W. Doyle	19 Orchard Street, Motherwell ML1 3JE	01698 263472

HAIRMYRES	Rev. John Brewster	21 Turnberry Place, East Kilbride, Glasgow G75 8TB	01355 242564
	Rev. Dr John McPake	30 Eden Grove, East Kilbride, Glasgow G75 8XY	01355 234196
	Rev. Marjorie Taylor	1 Kirkhill Road, Strathaven ML10 6HN	01357 520643
	Rev. James S.G. Hastie	Chalmers Manse, Quarry Road, Larkhall ML9 1HH	01698 882238
KIRKLANDS	Rev. Rosemary Smith	Blantyre Old Manse, High Blantyre, Glasgow G72 9UA	01698 823130
STONEHOUSE	Rev. James P. Fraser	26 Hamilton Road, Strathaven ML10 6JA	01357 522758
UDSTON	Rev. J. Stanley Cook	137A Old Manse Road, Netherton, Wishaw ML2 0EW	01698 299600
	Rev. William Beattie	33 Dungavel Gardens, Hamilton ML3 7PE	01698 423804
COATHILL	Rev. James Munton	2 Moorcroft Drive, Airdrie ML6 8ES	01236 754848
MONKLANDS GENERAL	Rev. James Munton	2 Moorcroft Drive, Airdrie ML6 8ES	01236 754848
	Rev. Andrew Thomson	38 Commonhead Street, Airdrie ML6 6NS	01236 602538
	Rev. James Grier	47 Blair Road, Coatbridge ML5 1JQ	01236 432427
	Rev. James Munton	2 Moorcroft Drive, Airdrie ML6 8ES	01263 754848
WESTER MOFFAT			
HARTWOODHILL	Rev. Henry J.W. Findlay	St Mark's Manse, Coltness Road, Wishaw ML2 7EX	01698 384596
HATTONLEA	Rev. Colin Cuthbert	Yieldshields Farm, Carluke ML8 4QB	
	Rev. Agnes Moore	16 Croftpark Street, Bellshill ML4 1EY	01698 842877
MOTHERWELL PSYCHIATRIC	Rev. John Handley	12 Airbles Crescent Motherwell ML1 3AR	01698 262733
COMMUNITY MENTAL HEALTH CARE	Rev. J. Stanley Cook	137A Old Manse Road, Netherton, Wishaw ML2 0EW	01698 299600
	Rev. Sharon Colvin	48 Dunrobin Road, Airdrie ML6 8LR	01236 763154
	Rev. Rosemary Smith	Blantyre Old Manse, High Blantyre, Glasgow G72 9UA	01698 823130

GREATER GLASGOW

NORTH GLASGOW UNIVERSITY HOSPITALS NHS TRUST			
GLASGOW ROYAL INFIRMARY [0141-211 4000/4661]	Rev. Patricia McDonald	4 Whithope Terrace, Glasgow G53 7LT	
	Rev. Anne J.M. Harper	122 Greenock Road, Bishopton, PA7 5AS	
WESTERN INFIRMARY [0141-211 2000]	Rev. Keith Saunders	1 Beckfield Drive, Robroyston, Glasgow G33 1SR	0141-211 2000/2812
GARTNAVEL GENERAL [0141-211 3000]	Rev. Keith Saunders	1 Beckfield Drive, Robroyston, Glasgow G33 1SR	0141-211 3000/3026
GLASGOW HOMEOPATHIC [0141-211 1600]	Rev. Keith Saunders	1 Beckfield Drive, Robroyston, Glasgow G33 1SR	0141-211 1600
GREATER GLASGOW PRIMARY CARE NHS TRUST	Rev. Cameron H. Langlands: Co-ordinator		
GARTNAVEL ROYAL HOSPITAL [0141-211 3686]	Rev. Gordon B. Armstrong: North/East Sector	Chaplain's Office, Old College of Nursing, Stobhill Hospital, 133 Balornock Road, Glasgow G21 3UW	0141-232 0609
	Ms Anne MacDonald: South Sector	Chaplain's Office, Leverndale Hospital, 510 Crookston Road, Glasgow G53 7TU	0141-211 6695

SOUTH GLASGOW UNIVERSITY HOSPITALS NHS TRUST

SOUTHERN GENERAL HOSPITAL [0141-201 2156]	Rev. Ann Purdie	14 Crosbie Street, Glasgow G20 0BD	
	Rev. Blair Robertson: Co-ordinator		
VICTORIA INFIRMARY	Rev. Iain Reid	Chaplain's Office, Langside Road, Glasgow G42 9TT	0141-201 5164
YORKHILL NHS TRUST [0141-201 0595]	Rev. Alistair Bull	Royal Hospital for Sick Children, Glasgow G3 8SG	
	Rev. Hilda Smith	Royal Hospital for Sick Children, Glasgow G3 8SG	
GREATER GLASGOW PRIMARY CARE	Rev. David Torrance	19 Redhills View, Lennoxtown, Glasgow G65 7BL	01360 312527
	Rev. Alastair MacDonald	42 Roman Way, Dunblane FK15 9DJ	
LIGHTBURN GERIATRIC	Rev. Patricia McDonald	4 Whithope Terrace, Glasgow G53 7LT	0141-876 1408
ROYAL INFIRMARY	Mrs Sandra Bell	62 Loganswell Road, Thornliebank, Glasgow G46 8AX	
	Rev. Norma Stewart	127 Nether Auldhouse Road, Glasgow G43 2YS	0141-637 6956
STOBHILL	Rev. Elizabeth W. Sutherland	54 Etive Crescent, Bishopbriggs, Glasgow G54 1ES	0141-772 1453
	Rev. John Beaton	33 North Birbiston Road, Lennoxtown, Glasgow G65 7LZ	
LEVERNDALE	Rev. Kenneth Coulter	8 Abbotsford Avenue, Rutherglen, Glasgow G73 3NX	0141-647 6250
DARNLEY COURT	Miss Anne MacDonald	62 Berwick Drive, Glasgow G52 3JA	0141-883 5618
VICTORIA INFIRMARY/MEARNSKIRK	Rev. Alan Raeburn	110 Mount Annan Drive, Glasgow G44 4RZ	0141-632 1514
GARTNAVEL GENERAL/WESTERN	Rev. Stuart Macdonald	20 Hillfoot Avenue, Bearsden, Glasgow G61 3QB	0141-942 1313
BLAWARTHILL	Mrs Deirdre Lyon	14 Melfort Avenue, Clydebank, Glasgow G81 2HX	
COWGLEN	Mrs Deirdre Lyon	14 Melfort Avenue, Clydebank, Glasgow G81 2HX	
GREENFIELD PARK	Rev. Patricia McDonald	4 Whithope Terrace, Glasgow G53 7LT	0141-876 1408
KNIGHTSWOOD/DRUMCHAPEL	Rev. Andrew McMillan	1 Swallow Gardens, Glasgow G13 4QD	0141-959 7158
LENZIE	Rev. James Ferguson	The Manse, Larch Avenue, Lenzie, Glasgow G66 4HX	0141-776 3831
RUTHERGLEN TAKARE	Rev. J.W. Drummond	21 Albert Drive, Rutherglen, Glasgow G73 3RT	0141-643 0234
	Rev. Alexander Thomson	31 Highburgh Drive, Rutherglen, Glasgow G73 3RR	0141-647 6178
PRINCE AND PRINCESS OF WALES HOSPICE	Rev. Alan Donald	71 Carlton Place, Glasgow G5 9TD	0141-429 5599
FOURHILLS NURSING HOME	Rev. W.G. Ramsay	3 Tofthill Avenue, Bishopbriggs, Glasgow G64 3PN	0141-762 1844
HUNTERS HILL MARIE CURIE CENTRE	Rev. David Mitchell	1 Belmont Road, Glasgow G21 3AY	0141-558 2555

ARGYLL AND CLYDE

INVERCLYDE ROYAL HOSPITAL (Whole-time) GREENOCK [01475 633777]	Rev. Fergus McLachlan	Chaplain's Office, Inverclyde Royal Hospital, Larkfield Road, Greenock PA16 0XN	
(Part-time)	Mrs Joyce Nicol	93 Brisbane Street, Greenock PA16 8NY	01475 723235
DYKEBAR	Rev. Alistair Morrison	36 Newtyle Road, Paisley PA1 3JX	0141-889 4279
	Rev. Alexander MacDonald	The Manse, Neilston, Glasgow G78 3NP	0141-881 1958
	Rev. George Mackay	10 Hawick Avenue, Paisley PA2 9LD	0141-884 8903
	Miss Margaret McBain	33 Quarry Road, Paisley PA2 7RD	0141-854 2920
HAWKHEAD	Rev. Georgina Baxendale	The Manse, Main Street, Houston, Johnstone PA6 7EL	01505 612569
MERCHISTON HOUSE	Rev. Thomas Cant	18 Oldhall Road, Paisley PA1 3HL	0141-882 2277

Hospital	Chaplain	Address	Tel.
JOHNSTONE	Rev. Thomas Cant	18 Oldhall Road, Paisley PA1 3HL	0141-882 2277
ROYAL ALEXANDRA	Rev. Arthur Sherratt	West Manse, Kilbarchan, Johnstone PA10 2JR	01505 702669
	Rev. Douglas Ralph	24 Kinpurnie Road, Paisley PA1 3HH	0141-883 3505
	Rev. Ian S. Currie	9 Hawkhead Road, Paisley PA1 3ND	0141-887 0884
	Rev. Alexander Wark	31 Gibson Road, Renfrew PA4 0RH	0141-886 2005
	Rev. Ritchie Gillon	31 Southfield Avenue, Paisley PA2 8BX	0141-884 6215
	Rev. E. Lorna Hood (Mrs)	North Manse, 1 Alexandra Drive, Renfrew PA4 8UB	0141-886 2074
	Rev Owain Jones		
RAVENSCRAIG	Rev. James H. Simpson	76 Finnart Street, Greenock PA16 8HJ	01475 722338
DUMBARTON JOINT	Rev. Douglas Cranston	6 Churchill Road, Kilmacolm PA13 4LH	01505 873271
VALE OF LEVEN GENERAL	Rev. Christine Liddell	3 Havoc Road, Dumbarton G82 4JW	01389 604840
VALE OF LEVEN GERIATRIC	Rev. Ian Miller	1 Glebe Gardens, Bonhill, Alexandria G83 9HB	01389 753039
CAMPBELTOWN	Rev. Ian Wilkie	38 Main Street, Renton, Dumbarton G82 4PU	01389 752017
LOCHGILPHEAD	Mrs Janice Forrest	The Manse, Southend, Campbeltown PA28 6RQ	01586 830274
ISLAY	Rev. Norman Macleod	The Manse, Port Ellen, Isle of Islay PA42 7DB	01496 302447
DUNOON	Rev. Patricia Lang	1 Royal Crescent, Dunoon PA23 7AH	01369 701291
DUNOON ARGYLL UNIT	Rev. Austin Erskine	99 Sandhaven, Sandbank, Dunoon PA23 8QW	01369 701295
ROTHESAY	Rev. Ronald Samuel	9 Bishop Terrace, Rothesay PA20 9HF	01700 504378
LORN AND THE ISLANDS DISTRICT GENERAL	Rev. Elizabeth Gibson		

FORTH VALLEY

Hospital	Chaplain	Address	Tel.
BELLSDYKE	Rev. Ann Smith	16 Mannerston Holdings, Linlithgow EH49 7ND	01506 834350
	Rev. Henry Munroe	Viewforth, High Road, Maddiston, Falkirk FK2 0BL	01324 712446
	Rev. Robert MacLeod	13 Cannons Way, Falkirk FK2 7QG	01324 631008
BO'NESS	Rev. Stuart Webster	36 Blair Avenue, Bo'ness EH51 0QT	01506 204485
BONNYBRIDGE	Rev. Alisdair MacLeod-Mair	133 Falkirk Road, Bonnybridge FK4 1BA	01324 812621
FALKIRK ROYAL INFIRMARY	Rev. Joanne Finlay	6 Herd Green, Livingston EH54 8PU	
	Rev. Helen Christie	5 Watson Place, Dennyloanhead, Bonnybridge FK4 2BG	01324 813786
	Rev. Margery Collin	2 Saughtonhall Crescent, Edinburgh EH12 5RF	0131-337 7153
RSNH LARBERT	Rev. Robert Philip	Congregational Church Manse, Avonbridge, Falkirk FK1 2LU	01324 861252
BANNOCKBURN	Rev. James Landels	Allan Manse, Bogend Road, Bannockburn, Stirling FK7 8NP	01324 814692
CLACKMANNAN COUNTY	Rev. Eleanor Forgan	18 Alexandra Drive, Alloa FK10 2DQ	01259 212836
KILDEAN	Rev. Robert Symington	3 Belmont House, The Crescent, Dunblane FK15 0DW	01786 823902
SAUCHIE	Rev. Malcolm MacRae	10b Victoria Place, Stirling FK8 2QU	01786 465547
STIRLING ROYAL INFIRMARY	Rev. Stuart Pryce	36 Forth Park, Bridge of Allan FK9 5NT	01786 831026
	Rev. Gary McIntyre	7 Randolph Road, Stirling FK8 2AJ	01786 474421
	Rev. Kenneth Russell	5 Clifford Road, Stirling FK8 2QU	01786 475802

FIFE

FIFE ACUTE HOSPITALS NHS TRUST
QUEEN MARGARET HOSPITAL, DUNFERMLINE [01383 674136]
VICTORIA HOSPITAL, KIRKCALDY [01592 643355]

Institution	Chaplain	Address	Tel
VICTORIA HOSPITAL, KIRKCALDY	Rev. Isabel Whyte	11 James Grove, Kirkcaldy KY1 1TN	01592 253775
LYNEBANK	Rev. Iain J.M. McDonald	51 St John's Drive, Dunfermline FK12 7TL	01383 720256
MILESMARK	Rev. Elizabeth Fisk		01383 674136
CAMERON	Rev. Isabel Whyte		01333 426310
	Rev. James L. Templeton	Innerleven Manse, McDonald Street, Methil, Leven KY8 3AJ	01592 713260
GLENROTHES	Rev. Kenneth Donald	33 Main Road, East Wemyss, Kirkcaldy KY1 4RE	01592 758264
RANDOLPH WEMYSS	Rev. Ian D. Gordon	7 Guthrie Crescent, Markinch, Glenrothes KY7 6AY	01592 713142
ADAMSON, CUPAR	Rev. Elizabeth Cranfield	9 Chemiss Road, Methilhill, Leven KY8 2BS	01337 842228
NETHERLEA, NEWPORT	Rev. Lynn Brady	2 Guthrie Court, Cupar Road, Newburgh, Cupar KY14 6HA	01382 552861
STRATHEDEN, CUPAR	Rev. Colin Dempster	27 Bell Street, Tayport DD6 9AP	01382 542199
	Rev. Dr Henry Gibson	4 Comerton Place, Drumoig, St Andrews KY16 0NQ	01382 542225
	Rev. Alan Roy	14 Comerton Place, Drumoig, St Andrews KY16 0NQ	01382 542140
	Miss Margaret Browning	4 Wellpark Terrace, Newport-on-Tay DD6 8HT	
ST ANDREWS MEMORIAL	Rev. David Arnott	20 Priory Gardens, St Andrews KY16 8XX	01334 472912

TAYSIDE

TAYSIDE UNIVERSITY HOSPITALS NHS TRUST
DUNDEE NINEWELLS HOSPITAL [01382 660111]

Institution	Chaplain	Address	Tel
DUNDEE NINEWELLS HOSPITAL	Rev. David J. Gordon		
PERTH ROYAL INFIRMARY [01738 473896]	Rev. John M. Birrell	Rhynd Road, Perth PH2 8TP	01738 552237
	Rev. Anne Findlay	Balcraig House, Scone, Perth PH2 7PG	01887 820656
ABERFELDY	Rev. Alexander M. Gunn	The Manse, Taybridge Terrace, Aberfeldy PH15 2BS	01828 640731
BLAIRGOWRIE RATTRAY	Rev. Ian Knox	Heatherlea, Main Street, Ardler, Blairgowrie PH12 8SR	01796 472719
IRVINE MEMORIAL	Rev. Christopher Brown	8 Tom-na-Moan Road, Pitlochry PH16 5HN	01764 652325
CRIEFF COTTAGE	Rev. Henry A.G. Tait	14 Shieling Hill Place, Crieff PH7 4ER	01738 552237
MACMILLAN HOSPICE	Rev. Anne Findlay	Balcraig House, Scone, Perth PH2 7PG	01738 552237
MURRAY ROYAL	Rev. Peter Meager	7 Lorraine Drive, Cupar KY15 5DY	01334 656991
	Rev. Isobel Birrell	Rhynd Road, Perth PH2 8TP	01738 625694
ST MARGARET'S COTTAGE	Rev. Randal MacAlister	St Kessog's Rectory, High Street, Auchterarder PH3 1AD	01764 662525
ASHLUDIE	Rev. Roy Massie	St Rule's Manse, 8 Church Street, Monifieth, Dundee DD5 4JP	01382 532607
	Rev. David Jamieson	Panmure Manse, 8A Albert Street, Monifieth, Dundee DD5 4JS	01382 532772
TAYSIDE ORTHOPAEDIC AND REHAB. CENTRE DUNDEE, ROYAL LIFF ROYAL VICTORIA	Rev. Thomas P. Robertson	20 Kilnburn, Newport-on-Tay DD6 8DE	01382 542422

NINEWELLS	Rev. Tom Milroy	9 Long Row, Westhaven, Carnoustie DD7 6BE	01241 856654
STRATHMARTINE			
ARBROATH INFIRMARY	Rev. Alasdair G. Graham	1 Charles Avenue, Arbroath DD11 2EZ	01241 872244
BRECHIN INFIRMARY	Rev. James P.R. Drysdale	36 Park Road, Brechin DD9 7AP	01356 622789
FORFAR INFIRMARY	Rev. Graham Norrie	East Manse, Lour Road, Forfar DD8 2BB	01307 464303
LITTLE CAIRNIE	Rev. Ian G. Gough	St Vigeans Manse, Arbroath DD11 4RD	01241 873206
MONTROSE ROYAL	Rev. Iain M. Douglas	49 North Esk Road, Montrose DD10 8TQ	01674 672060
STRACATHRO	Rev. James Drysdale	51 Airlie Street, Brechin DD9 6JX	01356 625201
SUNNYSIDE ROYAL	Mr Gordon Anderson	33 Grampian View, Montrose DD10 9SU	01674 674915

GRAMPIAN

GRAMPIAN UNIVERSITY HOSPITALS NHS TRUST			
ABERDEEN ROYAL INFIRMARY			
[01224 681818]	Rev. Fred Coutts	9a Millburn Street, Aberdeen AB11 6SS	01224 553166
	Rev. James Falconer	3 Brimmond Walk, Westhill, Skene AB32 6XH	01224 554905
	Rev. Muriel Knox	35 Valentine Drive, Aberdeen AB22 8YF	01224 553316
	(Chaplain's Assistant)		
	Miss Monica Stewart	9 Craigton Avenue, Aberdeen AB15 7RD	01224 554907
	(Chaplain's Assistant)		
	Rev. Alison Hutchison	'Ashfield', Drumoak, Banchory AB31 3AA	01224 556788

WOODEND HOSPITAL [01224 557293]

GRAMPIAN PRIMARY CARE NHS TRUST			
ROYAL CORNHILL and WOODLANDS HOSPITAL			
[01224 557293]	Mr Donald Meston	20 Rosehill Place, Aberdeen AB2 2LE	01224 557484
	(Chaplain's Assistant)		
	Miss Pamela Adam	409 Holburn Street, Aberdeen AB10 7GS	
	(Chaplain's Assistant)		

ABERDEEN CITY	Rev. Marian Cowie	6 St Swithin Street, Aberdeen AB10 6XE	01224 593302
KINCARDINE COMMUNITY	Rev. Gordon Farquharson	Dunnottar Manse, Stonehaven AB39 3XL	01569 762874
	Rev. David Stewart	South Church Manse, Cameron Street, Stonehaven AB39 2HE	01569 762576
GLEN O' DEE	Rev. Donald Walker	2 Wilson Road, Banchory AB31 3UY	01330 822811
KINCARDINE O'NEIL	Rev. Peter R. Taylor	The Manse, Torphins, Banchory AB31 4JS	01339 882276
INVERURIE	Rev. Ian B. Groves	West Manse, Inverurie AB51 9YS	01467 620285
JUBILEE	Rev. Thomas Calder	The Manse, Queen Street, Huntly AB54 5EB	01466 792630
CAMPBELL	Rev. Iain Sutherland	The Manse, Portsoy, Banff AB45 2QB	01261 842272
CHALMERS	Rev. David Randall	Manse of Doune, Banff AB45 3QL	01261 832316

FRASERBURGH	Rev. Andrew Lyon	23 Strichen Road, Fraserburgh AB43 9SA	01346 513303
LADYSBRIDGE	Rev. Stewart Jeffrey	8 West End, Whitehills, Banff AB42 2NL	01261 861523
MAUD	Rev. Alastair Donald	New Deer Manse, Turriff AB53 6TG	01771 644216
PETERHEAD COTTAGE	Rev. David S. Ross	1 Hawthorn Road, Peterhead AB42 6DW	01779 472618
TURRIFF	Rev. Sylvia Dyer	The Shieling, Westfield Road, Turriff AB53 4AF	01888 562530
UGIE	Rev. David Pitkeathly	1 Landale Road, Peterhead AB42 1QN	01779 472141
DR GRAY'S	Rev. George B. Rollo	18 Reidhaven Street, Elgin IV30 1QH	01343 547208
FLEMING COTTAGE	Rev. Ruth Tait	30 Mayne Road, Elgin IV30 1PB	
LEANCHOIL	Rev. John Beck	The Manse, Dunbar Street, Burghead, Elgin IV30 2XB	01343 830365
SPYNIE	Rev. Ray Hall	21 St Peter's Road, Duffus, Elgin IV30 5QL	01343 830985
SEAFIELD	Rev. John Hegarty	The Manse, East Church Street, Buckie AB56 1ES	01542 832103
STEPHEN AND COUNTY HOSPITALS	Rev. Hugh M.C. Smith	The Manse, Church Street, Dufftown, Keith AB55 4AR	01340 820380
TURNER MEMORIAL	Rev. Dr Kay Gauld	The Manse, Church Road, Keith AB55 5BR	01542 882799

HIGHLAND

HIGHLAND ACUTE HOSPITALS NHS TRUST
THE RAIGMORE HOSPITAL [01463 704000]

	Rev. Iain MacRitchie	7 Merlin Crescent, Inverness IV2 3TE	
	Rev. Derek Brown	Cathedral Manse, Dornoch IV25 3HV	
IAN CHARLES	Rev. Morris Smith	Golfcourse Road, Grantown-on-Spey PH26 3HY	01479 872084
ST VINCENT	Rev. Helen Cook	The Manse, West Terrace, Kingussie PH21 1HA	01340 661311
CRAIG DUNAIN	Rev. William J. Campbell	20 Birchview Court, Inverness IV22 5WA	01463 791690
NAIRN TOWN AND COUNTY	Rev. William B. Whyte	St Ninian's Manse, Queen Street, Nairn IV12 4AA	01667 452202
BELFORD AND BELHAVEN	Rev. Donald A. MacQuarrie	Manse of Duncansburgh, Fort William PH33 6BA	01397 702297
GLENCOE	Rev. Alison Burnside	The Manse, Ballachulish PH49 4JG	01855 811998
ROSS MEMORIAL, DINGWALL	Rev. Russel Smith	8 Castlehill Road, Dingwall IV15 9PB	01349 861011
	Rev. Grahame M. Henderson	16 Achany Road, Dingwall IV15 9JB	01349 863167
INVERGORDON COUNTY	Rev. Kenneth D. Macleod	The Manse, Cromlet Drive, Invergordon IV18 0BA	01349 852273
LAWSON MEMORIAL	Rev. Iain McCree	The Manse, Golf Road, Brora KW9 6QS	01408 766256
MIGDALE	Rev. Heather Olsen	The Manse, Bonar Bridge, Ardgay IV24 3EB	01863 602822
CAITHNESS GENERAL	Rev. A.A. Roy	Mansefield, Miller Avenue, Wick KW1 4DF	01955 602822
	Rev. Steven Thomson	The Manse, Miller Avenue, Wick KW1 4DF	01955 604252
DUNBAR	Rev. Kenneth Borthwick	46 Rose Street, Thurso KW14 7HN	01847 895186
	Rev. Ronald Johnstone	West Church Manse, Thorkel Road, Thurso KW14 7LW	01847 892663
BROADFORD MACKINNON MEMORIAL	Rev. Dr Ben Johnstone	The Shiants, 5 Upper Breakish, Breakish, Isle of Skye IV42 8PY	01471 822538
GESTO	Rev. Iain Greenshields	The Manse, Kensaleyre, Snizort, Portree, Isle of Skye IV51 9XE	01470 532260

WESTERN ISLES HEALTH BOARD

UIST AND BARRA HOSPITAL	Rev. Thomas MacKinnon	The Manse, Clachan, Isle of North Uist HS6 5HD	01876 580219
WESTERN ISLES, STORNOWAY	Rev. Alexander MacDonald	5 Urquhart Gardens, Stornoway HS1 2TX	01851 702825

ORKNEY HEALTH BOARD

| BALFOUR AND EASTBANK | Rev. Michael J. Ward | Ploverhall, Deerness, Orkney KW17 2QJ | 01856 741349 |

LIST D – FULL-TIME INDUSTRIAL CHAPLAINS

EDINBURGH (Edinburgh City Mission Appointment)	Mr John Hopper	26 Mulberry Drive, Dunfermline KY11 5BZ	01383 737189
EDINBURGH (Methodist Appointment)			
EDINBURGH (part-time)	Mrs Dorothy Robertson	15/1 Meadowhouse Road, Edinburgh EH12 7HW	0131-334 5440
GLASGOW	Rev. Elisabeth Spence	45 Selvieland Road, Glasgow G52 4ES	0141-883 8973 / 0141-883 1714
(part-time)	Mr William Shirlaw	194 Redpath Drive, Glasgow G52 2ER	(Office) 0141-332 4458
WEST OF SCOTLAND	Rev. Alister Goss	79 Weymouth Crescent, Gourock PA19 1HR	01475 638944 / (Office) 01475 629383
OFFSHORE OIL INDUSTRY	Rev. Angus Smith	1 Fa'burn Terrace, Lumphanan, Banchory AB31 4AG	01339 883395 / (Office) 01224 297532
NORTH OF SCOTLAND	Mr Lewis Rose DCS	16 Gean Drive, Blackburn, Aberdeen AB21 0YN	01224 790145
TAYSIDE and NATIONAL CO-ORDINATOR	Rev. Erik M. Cramb	65 Clepington Road, Dundee DD4 7BQ	01382 458764

LIST E – PRISON CHAPLAINS

CO-ORDINATOR (NATIONAL)

ABERDEEN CRAIGINCHES

CASTLE HUNTLY	Rev. David MacLeod	6 Carseview Gardens, Dundee DD2 1NE	01382 641371
CORNTON VALE	Rev. Elaine MacRae	The Manse, Kippen, Stirling FK8 3DN	01786 870229
DUMFRIES	Rev. Dennis S. Rose	The Manse, Kirkmahoe, Dumfries DG1 1ST	01387 710572
EDINBURGH: SAUGHTON	Rev. Colin Reed	Chaplaincy Centre, HMP Edinburgh EH11 3LN	0131-444 3115
	Rev. Jennifer Booth	39 Lilyhill Terrace, Edinburgh EH8 7DR	0131-661 3813
	Miss Norma Ronald	43/26 Gillespie Crescent, Edinburgh EH10 4HY	0131-228 1008
GLASGOW: BARLINNIE	Rev. Edward V. Simpson	5 Langtree Avenue, Glasgow G46 7LN	0141-638 8767
	Rev. C. Blair Gillon	3 Dargarvel Avenue, Glasgow G41 5LD	0141-427 1282
	Rev. Ian McInnes	46 Earlbank Avenue, Glasgow G14 9HL	0141-954 0328
	Rev. Douglas Clark	41 Kirkintilloch Road, Lenzie, Glasgow G66 4LB	0141-770 2184
LOW MOSS	Rev. William B. Moore	Chaplaincy Centre, HMP Low Moss, Glasgow G64 2QB	0141-762 4848
GLENOCHIL	Rev. Malcolm MacRae	10B Victoria Place, Stirling FK8 2QU	01786 465547
	Rev. Alan F.M. Downie	37A Claremont, Alloa FK10 2DG	01259 213872
GREENOCK			
INVERNESS	Rev. George Charlton	61 Drumfield Road, Inverness IV2 4XL	01463 242802
KILMARNOCK	Rev. Andrew A. Downie	HMP Bowhouse, Mauchline Road, Kilmarnock KA1 5AA	01563 548928
	Rev. Morag Dawson	206 Bank Street, Irvine KA12 0YB	01294 211403
NORANSIDE			
PERTH INCLUDING FRIARTON	Rev. Graham Matthews	Chaplaincy Centre, HMP Perth PH2 8AT	01738 622293
	Mrs Deirdre Yellowlees	Ringmill House, Gannochy Farm, Perth PH2 7JH	01738 633773
	Rev. Isobel Birrell	Wester Tarsappie, Rhynd, Perth PH2 8QL	01738 625694
PETERHEAD	Rev. G.M. Allan Fawkes	3 Northfield Gardens, Hatton, Peterhead AB42 0SW	01779 841814
POLMONT	Rev. Donald H. Scott	Chaplaincy Centre, HMYOI Polmont, Falkirk FK2 0AB	01324 711558
	Rev. Daniel L. Mathers	36 Thistle Avenue, Grangemouth FK3 8YQ	01324 474511
SHOTTS	Rev. Andrew Campbell	70 Baron's Road, Motherwell ML1 2NB	01698 263803
	Rev. Allan Brown	Chaplaincy Centre, HMP Shotts ML7 4LE	01501 824071

LIST F – UNIVERSITY CHAPLAINS

ABERDEEN	Easter Smart MDiv	01224 484271
ABERTAY, DUNDEE	Leslie M. Barrett BD FRICS	01382 308447
CALEDONIAN	Rev. J. Owain Jones MA BD FSAScot (Visiting)	0141-637 0797
CAMBRIDGE	Keith Rislin (U.R.C. and C. of S.)	01223 503726
DUNDEE	Fiona C. Douglas BD PhD	01382 344157
EDINBURGH	Diane Williams	0131-650 2596
GLASGOW	Stuart D. MacQuarrie JP BD BSc	0141-330 5419
HERIOT-WATT	Howard G. Taylor BSc BD	0131-449 5111 (ext 4508)
NAPIER	Deryck Collingwood	0131-455 4694
OXFORD	Susan Durber (U.R.C. and C. of S.)	01865 554358
PAISLEY		
ROBERT GORDON	James B. Walker MA BD DPhil	01224 262000
ST ANDREWS	Regine U. Cheyne MA BSc BD (Honorary)	01334 462866
STIRLING	Marjory Macaskill LLB BD	01786 463060 (ext 3506)
STRATHCLYDE		0141-553 4144

LIST G – THE DIACONATE

NAME	COM	APP	ADDRESS	TEL	PRES
Allan, Jean (Mrs) DCS	1989	1988	12C Hindmarsh Avenue, Dundee DD3 7LW	01382 827299	29
Anderson, Janet (Miss) DCS	1979	1982	1/1, 338 Gartcraig Road, Glasgow G33 2TE	0141-774 5329	16
Beaton, Margaret (Miss) DCS	1989	1988	64 Gardenside Grove, Carmyle, Glasgow G32 8EZ	0141-646 2297	16
Bell, Sandra (Mrs)	2001		62 Loganswell Road, Thornliebank, Glasgow G46 8AX	0141-638 5884	16
Black, Linda (Miss) BSc DCS	1993	2001	378 Alwyn Green, Glenrothes KY7 6TS	01592 742346	1
Buchanan, Linda (Mr) DCS	1988	1994	22 Brora Court, North Muirton, Perth PH1 3DQ	01738 631697	28
Buchanan, Marion (Mrs) DCS	1983	1997	6 Hamilton Terrace, Edinburgh EH15 1NB	0131-669 5312	1
Burns, Marjorie (Mrs) DCS	1997	1998	25 Barnsley Square, Corby, Northants NN18 0PQ [E-mail: mburns8069@aol.com]	01536 264819 (Mbl) 07989 148464	47
Carson, Christine (Miss) MA DCS	1992	2000	1FR, 7 Kirkwood Street, Cessnock, Glasgow G51 1QQ	0141-427 2349	16
Cathcart, John Paul (Mr) DCS	1998		5A Atholl Gardens, Springhall, Rutherglen, Glasgow G73 5HF	0141-569 6865	17
Corrie, Margaret (Miss) DCS	1989	1988	44 Sunnyside Street, Camelon, Falkirk FK1 4BH	01324 670656	22
Craw, John DCS	1998		'Craiglockhart', Latheronwheel, Latheron KW5 6DW	01593 741779	41

Crawford, Morag (Miss) DCS	1977	1998	118 Wester Drylaw Place, Edinburgh EH4 2TG [E-mail: morag.crawford@virgin.net]	(Tel/Fax) 0131-332 2253; (Mbl) 07970 982563	24
Crocker, Elizabeth (Mrs) DCS	1985	1992	77C Craigcrook Road, Edinburgh EH4 3PH [E-mail: crock@crook77c.freeserve.co.uk]	0131-332 0227	1
Cunningham, Ian (Mr) DCS	1994	1997	The Manse, Rothiemay, Huntly AB54 7NE	01466 711334	35
Deans, Raymond (Mr) DCS	1994	1998	22 Garrowhill Drive, Garrowhill, Glasgow G69 6HL [E-mail: deans@fish.co.uk]	0141-771 6847	17
Dickson, Carol (Miss) DCS	1991	1996	South Lodge, Walkerton Drive, Leslie, Glenrothes KY6 3BT	01592 743272	26
Douglas, Marilyn (Miss) DCS	1988	1987	201 Almond Road, Abronhill, Cumbernauld, Glasgow G67 3LS	01236 732136	22
Dunnett, Linda (Mrs)	1976	2000	17 Munro Road, Glasgow G13 1SQ	0141-959 3732	[16]
Erskine, Morag (Miss) DCS	1979	1986	111 Mains Drive, Park Mains, Erskine PA8 7JJ	(Office) 0141-552 4040; 0141-812 6096	14
Evans, Mark (Mr) RGN DCS	1988	2000	13 Easter Drylaw Drive, Edinburgh EH4 2QA [E-mail: mevansdcs@aol.com]	0131-343 3089	1
Gargrave, Mary (Mrs) DCS	1989	1998	229/2 Calder Road, Edinburgh EH11 4RG	0131-476 3493	1
Gordon, Margaret (Mrs)	1998	2001	92 Lanark Road West, Currie EH14 5LA	0131-443 9452; (Office) 0131-449 2554	1
Gray, Christine (Mrs) DCS	1969	1987	11 Woodside Avenue, Thornliebank, Glasgow G46 7HR	0141-571 1008	16
Gray, Greta (Miss) DCS	1992	1998	67 Crags Avenue, Paisley PA2 6SG	0141-884 6178	14
Hamilton, James (Mr) DCS	1997	2000	6 Beckfield Gate, Glasgow G33 1SW [E-mail: kg@hamilton692.freeserve.co.uk]	0141-558 3195	16
Hamilton, Karen (Mrs) DCS	1995	1998	6 Beckfield Gate, Glasgow G33 1SW	0141-558 3195	16
Hankey, Sarah (Miss) DCS	1991	1990	9 Earn Crescent, Menzieshill, Dundee DD2 4BS	01382 641549	29
Hughes, Helen (Miss) DCS	1977	1980	3/2, 31 Bank Street, Glasgow G12 8NE	0141-357 1552	16
Johnston, Mary (Miss)	1988	1987	19 Lounsdale Drive, Paisley PA2 9ED	0141-849 1615	14
King, Chris (Mrs)	2002		28 Kilnford, Dundonald, Kilmarnock KA2 9ET	01563 851197	10
King, Margaret (Miss) DCS	2002		56 Murrayfield, Fochabers, Moray IV32 7EZ	01343 820937	35
Love, Joanna (Ms) BSc DCS	1992	2000	92 Everard Drive, Glasgow G21 1XQ [E-mail: jolove14@hotmail.com]	0141-563 5859	16
Lundie, Ann V. (Miss) DCS	1972	1992	20 Langdykes Drive, Cove, Aberdeen AB12 3HW	01224 898416	31
Lyall, Ann (Miss) DCS	1980	1979	117 Barfia Drive, Glasgow G45 0AY	0141-631 3643	16
MacDonald, Anne (Miss) BA	1980	1998	62 Berwick Drive, Glasgow G52 3JA	0141-883 5618; (Mbl) 07976 786174	16
McIntosh, Kay (Mrs)	1990		4 Jacklin Green, Livingston EH54 8PZ	(Mbl) 01506 495472	3
McKay, Kenneth (Mr) DCS	1996	1995	11F Balgowan Road, Letham, Perth PH1 2JG [E-mail: ken@deaken.fsnet.co.uk]	01738 621169	28
MacKinnon, Ronald (Mr) DCS	1996	1995	70 Eildon Road, Hawick TD9 8ES	01450 374816	6
McLellan, Margaret (Mrs)	1986	1997	18 Broom Road East, Newton Mearns, Glasgow G77 5SD	0141-639 6853	16
McNaughton, Janette (Miss) DCS	1982	1997	4 Dunellan Avenue, Moodiesburn, Glasgow G69 0GB	01236 870180	22
McPheat, Elspeth (Miss)	1985-	1997	11/5 New Orchardfield, Edinburgh EH6 5ET	0131-554 4143/01224 486240	1
Martin, Jane (Miss) DCS	1979	1979	12A Carnoustie Court, Ardler, Dundee DD2 3RB [E-mail: janemar@aol.com]	01382 813786	29
Merrilees, Ann (Miss) DCS	1994	2000	0/1, 15 Crookston Grove, Glasgow G52 3PN [E-mail: ann@merrilees.freeserve.co.uk]	0141-883 2488	16

NAME			ADDRESS	TEL	PRES
Mitchell, Joyce (Mrs) DCS	1994	1993	16/4 Murrayburn Place, Edinburgh EH14 2RR [E-mail: joyce@mitchell71.freeserve.co.uk]	0131-453 6548	1
Morrison, Jean (Mrs)	1964	1994	45 Corslet Road, Currie EH14 5LZ	0131-449 6859	1
Mulligan, Anne (Miss)	1974	1986	27A Craigour Avenue, Edinburgh EH17 7NH [E-mail: mulliganne@aol.com]	0131-664 3426	
Munro, Patricia (Miss) BSc DCS	1986	2002	11 Hurlingham Square, Peterborough Road, London SW6 3DZ [E-mail: patm@totalise.co.uk]	(Office) 0131-242 1996 / 020 7610 6994	47
Nicholson, David (Mr) DCS	1994	1993	2D Doonside, Kildrum, Cumbernauld, Glasgow G67 2HX	01236 732260 / (Mbl) 07703 332270	22
Nicol, Joyce (Mrs)	1974	1998	93 Brisbane Street, Greenock PA16 8NY	01475 723235 / (Mbl) 07957 642709	15
Nicol, Senga (Miss) DCS	1993	2000	0/2, 367 Wellshot Road, Glasgow G32 9QP	0141-778 2667	16
Ogilvie, Colin (Mr) DCS	1998	1998	6 Ranfurly Drive, Carrickstone, Cumbernauld, Glasgow G68 0DS	01236 728301	22
Rennie, Agnes M. (Miss) DCS	1974	1979	3/1 Craigmillar Court, Edinburgh EH16 4AD	0131-661 8475	1
Rose, Lewis (Mr)	1993	1998	16 Gean Drive, Blackburn, Aberdeen AB21 0YN [E-mail: scimnorth@dial.pipex.com]	01224 790145 / (Mbl) 07901 607331	31
Ross, Duncan (Mr) DCS	1996	1996	64 Stewart Crescent, Aberdeen AB16 5SR	01224 692519	31
Rycroft, Pauline (Miss) DCS			5 Thornville Terrace, Edinburgh EH6 8DB	0131-554 6564	1
Steele, Marilynn J. (Mrs) BD DCS			2 Northfield Gardens, Prestonpans EH32 9LQ	01875 811497	1
Steven, Gordon BD DCS	1997		51 Nantwich Drive, Edinburgh EH7 6RB	0131-669 2054 / (Mbl) 07094 385256	3
Stewart, Marion (Miss) DCS	1991	1994	Kirk Cottage, Kirkton of Skene, Westhill, Skene AB32 6XE	01224 743407	33
Tait, Agnes (Mrs) DCS	1995	1994	2 Lennox Drive, Faifley, Clydebank G81 5JU	01389 873196	18
Urquhart, Barbara (Mrs)	1986	1994	9 Standalane, Kilmaurs, Kilmarnock KA3 2NB	01563 538289	11
Wilson, Glenda (Mrs) DCS	1990	2000	118 Old Rows, Seafield, Bathgate EH47 7AW	01506 655298	2
Wilson, Muriel (Miss) MA BD DCS	1997	2001	23 Jellieston Terrace, Patna, Ayr KA6 7JZ	01292 532492	10
Wishart, William (Mr) DCS	1994	1993	17 Swift Bank, Earnock, Hamilton ML3 8PX	01698 429371 / (Mbl) 07971 422201	17
Wright, Lynda (Miss) BEd	1979	1992	6 Key Cottage, High Street, Falkland, Cupar KY15 7BD	01337 857705	26

THE DIACONATE (Retired List)

NAME	COM	ADDRESS	TEL	PRES
Anderson, Catherine B. (Mrs) DCS	1975	13 Mosshill Road, Bellshill, Motherwell ML4 1NQ	01698 745907	17
Anderson, Mary (Miss) DCS	1955	33 Ryehill Terrace, Edinburgh EH6 8EN	0131-553 2818	1

Name	Year	Address	Tel	No.
Bayes, Muriel C. (Mrs) DCS	1963	Flat 6, Carleton Court, 10 Fenwick Road, Glasgow G46 4AN	0141-633 0865	16
Beaton, Jamesina (Miss) DCS	1953	Fairhills, Fort Augustus PH32 4DS	01320 366252	38
Bryden, Agnes Y. (Mrs) DCS	1963	9 Rosewell Place, Aberdeen AB15 6HN	01224 315042	31
Cameron, Margaret (Miss) DCS	1961	2 Rowans Gate, Paisley PA2 6RD	0141-840 2479	14
Campbell, Margaret M.M. (Miss) DCS	1958	Kirkcare, 11 Leodamus Place, Port Ellen, Isle of Islay PA42 7EL		19
Collie, Jeannie P. (Miss) DCS	1950	Maud Hospital, Bank Road, Peterhead AB42 5NR	01475 631870	33
Copland, Agnes M. (Mrs) MBE DCS	1950	3 Craigmuschat Road, Gourock PA19 1SE		15
Cunningham, Alison G. (Miss) DCS	1961	23 Strathblane Road, Milngavie, Glasgow G62 8DL	0141-563 9232	18
Drummond, Rhoda (Miss) DCS	1960	23 Grange Loan, Edinburgh EH9 2ER	0131-668 3631	1
Finlayson, Ellena B. (Miss) DCS	1963	16E Denwood, Summerhill, Aberdeen AB15 6JF	01224 321147	31
Flockhart, Andrew (Mr) DCS	1988	31 Castle Street, Rutherglen, Glasgow G73 1DY	0141-569 0716	16
Gillespie, Ann M. (Miss) DCS	1969	Barlochan House, Palnackie, Castle Douglas DG7 1PF	01556 600378	8
Gillon, Phyllis (Miss) DCS	1957	The Hermitage Home, 15 Hermitage Drive, Edinburgh EH10 6BX	0131-447 0664	1
Glass, Irene (Miss) DCS	1976	3E Falcon Road West, Edinburgh EH10 4AA	0131-447 6554	1
Gordon, Fiona S. (Mrs) MA DCS	1958	Machrie, 3 Cupar Road, Cuparmuir, Cupar KY15 5RH [E-mail: machrie@madasafish.com]	01334 652341	26
Gray, Catherine (Miss) DCS	1969	10C Eastern View, Gourock PA19 1RJ	01475 637479	15
Howden, Margaret (Miss) DCS	1954	38 Munro Street, Kirkcaldy KY1 1PY	01592 205913	25
Hutchison, Alan E.W. (Mr) DCS	1988	132 Lochbridge Road, North Berwick EH39 4DR	01620 894077	3
Hutchison, Maureen (Mrs) DCS	1961	23 Drylaw Crescent, Edinburgh EH4 2AU	0131-332 8020	1
McBain, Margaret (Miss) DCS	1974	33 Quarry Road, Paisley PA2 7RD	0141-884 2920	14
McCallum, Moyra (Miss) MA BD DCS	1965	176 Hilton Drive, Aberdeen AB24 4LT [E-mail: moymac@aol.com]	01224 486240	31
McCully, M. Isobel (Miss) DCS	1974	10 Broadstone Avenue, Port Glasgow PA14 5BB	01475 742240	15
McGarva, Sadie (Miss) DCS	1954	87 Hunter Drive, Irvine KA12 9BS	01294 271257	11
MacLean, Donald A. (Mr) DCS	1988	8 Upper Barvas, Isle of Lewis HS2 0QX	01851 840454	44
MacPherson, James B. (Mr) DCS	1988	104 Cartside Street, Glasgow G42 9TQ	0141-616 6468	16
MacQuien, Duncan (Mr) DCS	1988	2 Manor Crescent, Gourock PA19 1VY	01475 633407	15
Macrae, William (Mr) DCS	1988	6 Park View Terrace, Isle of Scalpay, Isle of Harris HS4 3XX	01859 540288	43
MacSween, Helen (Miss) DCS	1960	4 Craig Aonaich, Isle of Scalpay, Isle of Harris PA85 3DH	01859 540346	43
Malvenan, Dorothy (Miss) DCS	1955	Flat 19, 6 Craigie Street, Dundee DD4 6PF	01382 462495	29
Martin, Neil (Mr) DCS	1988	3 Strathmiglo Place, Stenhousemuir, Larbert FK5 4UQ	01324 551362	22
Miller, Elsie M. (Miss) DCS	1974	30 Swinton Avenue, Rowanbank, Baillieston, Glasgow G69 6JR	0141-771 0857	22
Montgomery, Donald (Mr) DCS	1992	17 Murray Place, Stornoway, Isle of Lewis HS1 2JB	01851 704346	22
Mortimer, Aileen (Miss) DCS	1976	38 Sinclair Way, Knightsridge, Livingston EH54 8HW	01506 430504	44
Moyes, Sheila (Miss) DCS	1957	158 Pilton Avenue, Edinburgh EH5 2JZ	0131-551 1731	2
Nicoll, Janet M. (Miss) DCS	1968	74 Brucefield Avenue, Dunfermline KY11 4SY	01383 725734	1
Potts, Jean M. (Miss) DCS	1973	28B East Claremont Street, Edinburgh EH7 4JP	0131-557 2144	24
Ramsay, Katherine (Miss) MA DCS	1958	25 Homeroyal House, 2 Chalmers Crescent, Edinburgh EH9 1TP	0131-667 4791	1

Name	Year	Address	Phone	No.
Ronald, Norma A. (Miss) MBE DCS	1961	43/26 Gillespie Crescent, Edinburgh EH10 4HY	0131-228 1008	1
Rutherford, Ellen B. (Miss) MBE DCS	1962	41 Duncanston, Conon Bridge, Dingwall IV7 8JB	01349 877439	39
Scrimgeour, Alice M. (Miss) DCS	1950	265 Golfhill Drive, Glasgow G31 2PB	0141-564 9602	16
Sloan, Elma C. (Miss) DCS	1957	Ferryfield House, Willowsuite, Pilton Drive, Edinburgh EH5 2HX	0131-537 6246	1
Smith, Catherine (Mrs) DCS	1964	21 Lingaro, Bixter, Shetland ZE2 9NN	01595 810207	46
Smith, Lillian (Miss) MA DCS	1977	6 Fintry Mains, Dundee DD4 9HF	01382 500052	29
Steele, Jean (Miss) DCS	1952	93 George Street, Paisley PA1 2JX	0141-889 9512	14
Stuart, Anne (Miss) DCS	1966	19 St Colme Crescent, Aberdour, Burntisland KY3 0ST	01383 860049	24
Teague, Yvonne (Mrs) DCS	1965	46 Craigcrook Avenue, Edinburgh EH4 3PX	0131-336 3113	1
Thom, Helen (Miss) BA DipEd MA DCS	1959	84 Great King Street, Edinburgh EH3 6QU	0131-556 5687	1
Trimble, Robert DCS	1988	5 Templar Rise, Livingston EH54 6PJ	01506 412504	2
Webster, Elspeth H. (Miss) DCS	1950	82 Broomhill Avenue, Burntisland KY3 0BP	01592 873616	25
Weir, Minnie Mullo (Miss) MA DCS	1934	37 Strathearn Court, Strathearn Terrace, Crieff PH7 3DS	01764 654189	
White, Elizabeth (Miss) DCS	1950	Rodger Park Nursing Home, Rutherglen, Glasgow G73 3QZ		16

SUPPLEMENTARY LIST

Name	Year	Address	Phone
Forrest, Janice (Mrs)	1990	The Manse, Southend, Campbeltown, Argyll PA28 6RQ	
Gilroy, Lorraine (Mrs)	1988	5 Bluebell Drive, Cheverel Court, Bedward CV12 0GE	
Guthrie, Jennifer (Miss)	1993	35 William Rodgers Drive, Montrose DD10 8TX	01674 674413
Harris, Judith (Mrs)	1988	243 Western Avenue, Sandfields, Port Talbot, West Glamorgan SA12 7NF	
Hood, Katrina (Mrs)	1982	67C Farquhar Road, Edgbaston, Birmingham B18 2QP	
Hudson, Sandra (Mrs)	1969	10 Albany Drive, Rutherglen, Glasgow G73 3QN	
Muir, Alison M. (Mrs)	1978	77 Arthur Street, Dunfermline KY12 0JJ	
Ramsden, Christine (Miss)	1970	52 Noel Street, Nottingham NG7 6AW	
Walker, Wikje (Mrs)		24 Brodie's Yard, Queen Street, Coupar Angus PH13 9RA	
Wallace, Catherine (Mrs)		4 Thornwood Court, Setauket, NY 11733, USA	

LIST H – MINISTERS HAVING RESIGNED MEMBERSHIP OF PRESBYTERY
(in Terms of Act III 1992)

NAME	ORD	ADDRESS	TEL	PRES
Bailey, W. Grahame MA BD	1939	148 Craiglea Drive, Edinburgh EH10 5PU	0131-447 1663	1
Balfour, Thomas MA BD	1945	1 Dean Court, Longniddry EH32 0QT	01875 852694	3
Bogle, Michael M. MA	1936	30 Woodburn Terrace, Edinburgh EH10 4SS	0131-447 3231	1
Chirnside, Charles	1950	11 Stevenson Grove, Edinburgh EH11 2SE	0131-337 2957	23
Cooper, George MA BD	1943	69 Montpelier Park, Edinburgh EH10 4ND	0131-228 2435	1
Craig, Eric MA BD	1959	5 West Relugas Road, Edinburgh EH9 2PW	0131-667 8210	1
Craig, John W. MA BD	1951	83 Milton Road East, Edinburgh EH15 2NL	0131-657 2309	1
Crawford, S.G. Victor	1980	Crofton, 65 Main Road, East Wemyss, Kirkcaldy KY1 4RL	01592 712325	25
Ferguson, Ronald MA BD ThM	1972	Vinbreck, Orphir, Orkney KW17 2RE	01856 811378	45
		[E-mail: ronblueyonder@aol.com]		
Finlayson, Duncan	1943	Flat 3, Nicholson Court, Kinnettas Road, Strathpeffer IV14 9BG	01997 420014	39
Forrester-Paton, Colin MA BD	1944	Acharn, Glen Road, Peebles EH45 9AY	01721 720136	4
Gordon, Alasdair B. BD LLB	1970	31 Binghill Park, Milltimber, Aberdeen AB13 0EE	01224 571633	31
Greig, James C.G. MA BD STM	1955	44 Rockmount Avenue, Glasgow G46 7DW	0141-621 1302	16
		[E-mail: jcggreig@netcomuk.co.uk]		
Grubb, George D.W.	1962	10 Wellhead Close, South Queensferry EH30 9WA	0131-331 2072	1
BA BD BPhil DMin				
Hosie, James MA BD MTh	1959	Hilbre, Strachur, Cairndow, Dunoon, Argyll PA27 8BY	01369 860634	20
Howie, William MA BD STM	1964	26 Morgan Road, Aberdeen AB2 5JY	01224 483669	31
Lambie, Andrew BD	1957	1 Mercat Loan, Biggar ML12 6DG	01899 221352	13
Levison, Mary I. (Mrs) BA BD DD	1978	2 Gillsland Road, Edinburgh EH10 5BW	0131-228 3118	1
Lynn, Joyce (Mrs) MIPM BD	1995	Grunavi, Sanday, Orkney KW17 2BA	01857 600349	45
McCaskill, George I.L. MA BD	1953	3/5 Dun-ard Garden, Edinburgh EH9 2HZ	0131-668 2721	1
Macfarlane, Alwyn J.C. MA	1957	Flat 12, Homeburn House, 177 Fenwick Road, Giffnock, Glasgow G46 6JD	0141-620 3235	1
Macfarlane, Donald MA	1940	8 Muirfield Gardens, Inverness IV2 4HF	01463 231977	37
Macfarlane, Kenneth	1963	9 Bonnington Road, Peebles EH45 9HF	01721 723609	4
Mackie, Steven G. MA BD	1956	38 Grange Loan, Edinburgh EH9 2NR	0131-667 9532	1
McCluskey, J. Fraser MC DD	1938	54/5 Eildon Terrace, Edinburgh EH3 5LU	0131-652 3950	47
Mair, John BSc	1965	21 Kenilworth Avenue, Helensburgh G84 7JR	01436 671744	18
Malcolm, John W. MA BD PhD	1939	16 Abbotsford Court, Edinburgh EH10 5EH	0131-447 0326	1
Marshall, James S. MA PhD	1939	25 St Mary's Street, St Andrews KY16 8AZ	01334 476136	26
Millar, Jennifer M. (Mrs)	1986	17 Mapledene Road, Scone, Perth PH2 6NX	01738 550270	28
BD DipMin				
Miller, Irene B. (Mrs) MA BD	1984	5 Braeside Park, Aberfeldy PH15 2DT	01887 829396	27
Monro, George D. TD MA	1935	Flat 79, 303 Colinton Road, Edinburgh EH13 0HS	0131-441 7303	1
Morris, Gordon C. MA BD	1941	Belleville Lodge, 5 Blacket Avenue, Edinburgh EH9 1RR		1

	ORD		TEL	PRES
Nelson, John MA BD	1941	7 Manse Road, Roslin EH25 9LF	0131-440 3321	3
Ogilvie, Kenneth G. MA	1953	124 Comiston Drive, Edinburgh EH10 5QU	0131-447 8909	1
Petty, P.W.P.	1962	7 Marchbank Place, Balerno EH14 7EU	0131-449 2123	26
Robertson, Crichton MA	1938	Robin Hill, Ludlow Road, Church Stretton SY6 6AD	01694 722046	3
Ross, John H.G. OBE MA BD	1940	43 Arden Street, Edinburgh EH9 1BS	0131-447 2027	1
Shaw of Chapelverna, Duncan	1951	4 Sydney Terrace, Edinburgh EH7 6SL	0131-669 1089	20
Bundesverdienstkreuz PhD ThDr				
Drhc JP				
Shaw, D.W.D. BA BD LLB WS DD	1960	4/13 Succoth Court, Edinburgh EH12 6BZ	0131-337 2130	26
Smith, Ralph C.P. MA STM	1960	2A Waverley Road, Eskbank, Dalkeith EH22 3DJ	0131-663 1234	2
Spowart, Mary G. (Mrs)	1978	Aldersyde, St Abbs Road, Coldingham, Eyemouth TD14 5NR	01890 771697	26
Stobie, Charles I.G.	1942	18 Market Street, St Andrews KY16 9NS	01334 476806	26
Swan, Andrew MA	1941	11 The Terrace, Ardbeg, Rothesay, Isle of Bute PA20 0NP	01700 502138	14
Taylor, Alexander T.H. MA BD	1938	4 The Pleasance, Strathkinness, St Andrews KY16 9SD	01334 850585	26
Webster, John G. BSc	1964	Plane Tree, King's Cross, Brodick, Isle of Arran KA27 8RG	01770 700747	1
Wilkie, George D. OBE BL	1948	2/37 Barnton Avenue West, Edinburgh EH4 6EB	0131-339 3973	
Wylie, W. Andrew	1953	Well Rose Cottage, Peat Inn, Cupar KY15 5LH	01334 840600	26

LIST I – MINISTERS HOLDING PRACTISING CERTIFICATES (under Act II, as amended by Act VIII 2000)

NAME	ORD	ADDRESS	TEL	PRES
Aitken, Ewan R. BA BD	1992	159 Restalrig Avenue, Edinburgh EH7 6PJ	0131-346 0685	1
Alexander, Helen J.R. (Miss) BD	1981	7 Polwarth Place, Edinburgh EH11 1LG		1
Anderson, David MA BD	1975	1A Sanquhar Road, Forres IV36 1DG	01309 672426	35
Arbuthnott, Joan (Mrs) MA BD	1993	139/1 New Street, Musselburgh EH21 6DH	0131-665 6736	3
Archer, Nicholas D.C. BA BD	1971	Hillview, Edderton, Tain IV19 4AJ	01862 821494	47
Atkins, Yvonne E.S. (Mrs) BD	1997	13 Grange Crescent East, Prestonpans EH32 9LS	01875 815137	3
Bardgett, Frank D. MA BD PhD	1987	6 Inchcolm Drive, North Queensferry, Inverkeithing KY11 1LD	01383 416863	36
Beattie, Warren R. BSc BD	1991	33A Chancery Lane, Singapore 908554	0065 256 3208	1
Black, James S. BD DPS	1976	7 Breck Terrace, Penicuik EH26 0RJ	01968 677559	3
Black, W. Graham MA BD	1983	c/o 60 Newburgh Circle, Bridge of Don, Aberdeen AB22 8QZ	07866 819899	31
Blakey, Stephen A. BSc BD	1977	Abercrombie House, Abercrombie, Anstruther KY10 2DE	01333 730334	26
Blane, Quintin A. BSc BD MSc	1979	18D Kirkhill Road, Penicuik EH26 8HZ	01968 670017	3
Bowman, Norman M. MA BD	1940	18 Eglinton Court, Eglinton Street, Saltcoats KA21 5DN	01294 463453	12
Boyd, Ian R. MA BD PhD	1989	33 Castleton Drive, Newton Mearns, Glasgow G77 3LE		16

Name	Year	Address	Phone	No.
Boyd, Kenneth M. MA BD PhD	1970	1 Doune Terrace, Edinburgh EH3 6DY	0131-225 6485	1
Buchan, Isabel C. (Mrs) BSc BD	1975	26 Allan Robertson Drive, St Andrews KY16 8EY	01334 473875	26
Buchanan-Smith, Robin D. BA ThM	1962	Isle of Eriska, Ledaig, Oban, Argyll PA37 1SD		
Cairns, Wilma (Miss) BD	1999	161 Eagle Road, Buckhaven, Leven KY8 1HD	01592 712717	25
Campbell, Reginald F. BD DipChEd	1979	145 Lime Crescent, Cumbernauld, Glasgow G67 3PG	01236 611983	22
Campbell, Thomas R. MA BD	1986	Craigleith, Bowfield Road, Howwood, Johnstone PA9 1BS	0141-884 8291	14
Chilton, R. Michael L. BD BA(Open) BA(Hull) MA DipEurHum	1972	Flat 31, All Saints Court, Churchside, Market Weighton, York YO43 3NT	01430 873046	47
Cowie, Marion (Mrs) MA BD	1990	6 St Swithin Street, Aberdeen AB10 6XE	01224 593302	31
Currie, Gordon C.M. MA BD	1975	43 Deanburn Park, Linlithgow EH49 6HA	01506 842722	2
Davidson, John F. BSc	1970	49 Craigmill Gardens, Carnoustie DD7 6HX	01241 855412	30
Drummond, Norman W. MA BD	1976	c/o Columba 1400 Ltd, Staffin, Isle of Skye IV51 9JY	01478 611400	42
Ellis, David W. GIMechE GIProdE	1962	4 Wester Tarsappie, Rhynd Road, Perth PH2 8PT	01738 449618	16
Ferguson, Sinclair B. MA BD PhD	1971	Westminster Seminary, 3878 Oak Lawn Avenue, Dallas, TX 75219, USA [E-mail: jfdavid@breathemail.net]		
Finlay, Joanne G. (Mrs) DipMusEd	1996	6 Herd Green, Livingston EH54 8PU	01324 552004	22
Fleming, Thomas G.	1961	5 Glenbervie Drive, Larbert FK5 4NP	01875 833208	22
Flockhart, D. Ross OBE MA BD DUniv	1955	Longwood, Humbie EH36 5PN		3
Fowler, Richard C.A. BSc MSc BD	1978	4 Gardentown, Whalsay, Shetland ZE2 9AB	01806 566538	46
Fraser, Ian M. MA BD PhD	1946	Ferndale, Gargunnock, Stirling FK8 3BW	01786 860612	23
Frew, John M. MA BD	1946	17 The Furrows, Walton-on-Thames KT12 3JQ		16
Gilmour, Robert M. MA BD	1942	'Bellevue', Station Road, Watten, Wick KW1 5YN	01955 621317	37
Gunn, F. Derek BD	1986	6 Yardley Place, Falkirk FK2 7FH	01324 624938	22
Hendrie, Yvonne (Mrs)	1995	98 Duncansby Way, Perth PH1 5XF	01738 441029	28
Higgins, G.K.	1957	150 Broughty Ferry Road, Dundee DD4 6JJ	01382 461288	29
Howitt, Jane M. (Miss) MA BD	1996	PO Box 476, LV-1050 Riga 50, Latvia		16
Ireland, Andrew BA BTh DipRD	1963	48 Jubilee Court, St Margaret's Street, Dunfermline KY12 7PE	01383 732223	24
Jack, Alison M. (Mrs) MA BD PhD	1998	Glenallan, Doune Road, Dunblane FK15 9AT	01786 823241	23
Jamieson, Esther M.M. (Mrs) BD	1984	1 Renburn, Bayview, Stornoway HS1 2UV	01851 704789	44
Johnstone, Donald B.	1969	22 Glenhove Road, Cumbernauld, Glasgow G67 2IZ	01236 612479	22
Johnstone, Robert MTheol	1973	59 Cliffburn Road, Arbroath DD11 5BA	01241 439292	32
Kirby, Paul S. BD	1976	Flat 2, 1 Trafalgar Terrace, New St John's Road, St Helier, Jersey JE2 3LE	01534 625825	47
Lawrie, Robert M. BD MSc DipMin LLCM(TD)	1994	West Benview, Main Road, Langbank, Port Glasgow PA14 6XP	01475 540240	14
Liddiard, F.G.B. MA	1957	34 Trinity Fields Crescent, Brechin DD9 6YF	01356 622966	30
Logan, Thomas M. LTh	1971	3 Duncan Court, Kilmarnock KA3 7TF	01563 524398	11
MacArthur, Alexander MA	1946	Luath, St Barchan's Road, Kilbarchan, Johnstone PA10 2AR	01505 702598	14
Macaskill, Donald MA BD PhD	1994	44 Forfar Avenue, Glasgow G52 3JQ	0141-883 5956	16
McDonald, Ross J. BA BD ThM	1998	14 Crosbie Street, Glasgow G20 0BD		16
McKean, Martin J. BD DipMin	1984	14 Morriston Drive, Murieston, Livingston EH54 9HT	01506 418150	2

Name	Year	Address	Tel	No.
McKillop, Keith MB ChB BD	1999	8 Wallace Gate, Bishopbriggs, Glasgow G64 1GB	0141-558 2180	16
McKinnon, Lily F. (Mrs) MA BD	1993	12 Carleton Gate, Giffnock, Glasgow G46 6NU	0141-637 8399	16
McLellan, Andrew R.C. MA BD STM DD	1970	4 Liggars Place, Dunfermline KY12 7XZ		1
MacPherson, Gordon C.	1963	203 Capelrig Road, Patterton, Newton Mearns, Glasgow G77 6ND	0141-616 2107	16
McPherson, William BD DipEd	1993	83 Laburnum Avenue, Port Seton, Prestonpans EH32 0UD	01875 812252	22
Main, Arthur W.A. BD	1954	13/3 Eildon Terrace, Edinburgh EH3 5NL	0131-556 1344	16
Marr, Ian MA BD	1984	116 Jeanfield Road, Perth PH1 1LP	01738 632530	28
Masson, John D.	1984	5 Wheatlands, Wigton Road, Carlisle CA2 7ER	ex-directory	7
Matheson, Iain G. BD BMus	1985	16 New Street, Musselburgh EH21 6JP	0131-665 2128	3
Mill, John Stuart MA BD MBA DipEd	1974	13 Succoth Park, Edinburgh EH12 6BX	0131-346 4124	1
Millar, Peter W. MA BD PhD	1971	Iona Cottage, Laggan, Newtonmore PH20 1AN [E-mail: ionacottage@hotmail.com]	01528 544337	36
Mills, Archibald MA PhD	1953	32 High Street, South Queensferry EH30 9PP	0131-331 3906	1
Moodie, Alastair R. MA BD	1978	5 Buckingham Terrace, Glasgow G12 8EB		16
Morrice, Alastair M. MA BD	1968	5 Brechin Road, Kirriemuir DD8 4BX		16
Munro, Alexander W. MA BD	1978	Gilldrive, Gill Bank Road, Ilkley, West Yorks LS29 0AV		47
Newell, Alison M. (Mrs) BD	1986	1A Inverleith Terrace, Edinburgh EH3 5NS		1
Newell, J. Philip	1982	1A Inverleith Terrace, Edinburgh EH3 5NS		1
Noble, Alexander B. MA BD ThM	1982	23 Huntly Avenue, Giffnock, Glasgow G46 6LW	0141-571 7675	34
Ostler, John H. MA LTh	1975	52E Middleshot Square, Prestonpans EH32 9RJ	01875 814358	3
Peat, S. William BSc BD PhD	1977	27/320 West Savile Terrace, Edinburgh EH9 3DS	0131-662 9319	1
Picken, Stuart D.B. MA BD PhD	1967	8 Barnwell Road, Stirling FK9 5SD	01786 462625	23
Provan, Iain W. MA BA PhD	1991	Regent College, 5800 University Boulevard, Vancouver BC V6T 2E4, Canada	001 604 224 3245	1
Quigley, Barbara D. (Mrs) MTheol ThM DPS	1979	7 Albany Terrace, Dundee DD3 6HQ	01382 223059	29
Ross, Alison J. (Mrs) BD	1995	Blendowan, Glenmanna, Penpont, Thornhill DG3 4NJ		19
Sawers, Hugh BA	1968	2 Rosemount Meadows, Castlepark, Bothwell, Glasgow G71 8EL	01698 853960	17
Scouller, Hugh BSc BD	1985	39 Melbourne Place, North Berwick EH39 4JS	01620 893021	3
Squires, J. Finlay R. MA BD	1964	16 Bath Street, Stonehaven AB39 2DH	01569 762458	32
Stewart, Anne S. (Mrs) BD	1998	35 Rose Crescent, Perth PH1 1NT	01738 624167	28
Stewart, Margaret L. (Mrs) BSc MB ChB BD	1985	28 Inch Crescent, Bathgate EH48 1EU	01506 653428	2
Strachan, David G. BD DPS	1978	1 Deeside Park, Aberdeen AB15 7PQ	01224 324101	31
Strachan, Gordon MA BD PhD	1963	59 Merchiston Crescent, Edinburgh EH10 5AH	0131-229 3654	1
Thomas, W. Colville BTh BPhil DPS DSc	1964	11 Muirfield Crescent, Gullane EH31 2HN	01620 842415	3
Tollick, Frank BSc DipEd	1958	3 Bellhouse Road, Aberdour, Burntisland KY3 0TL	01383 860559	24
Turnbull, Julian S. BSc BD MSc CEng MBCS	1980	25 Hamilton Road, Gullane EH31 2HP [E-mail: jules-turnbull@zetnet.co.uk]	01620 842958	3
Watt, John H.I. MA BD	1960	Lyndale, 24 Bank Street, Wigtown DG8 9HP	01546 602143	20
Weir, Mary K. (Mrs) BD PhD	1968	1249 Millar Road RR1, SITEH-46, BC V0N 1G0, Canada	001 604 947 0636	1

Williams, Linda J. (Mrs) BD	1993	The Manse, Kirtlebridge, Lockerbie DG11 3LY	01461 500378	7
Wilson, Thomas F. BD	1984	55 Allison Close, Cove, Aberdeen AB12 3WG	01224 873501	31
Winn, Fiona M.M. MA BD RGN	1994	35 Ashwood Avenue, Melbourne 3190, Australia	0061 3 9555 2038	1
Wood, Peter J. MA BD	1993	97 Broad Street, Cambourne, Cambridgeshire CB3 6DH	01954 715558	47

LIST J – MISSION AND EVANGELISM ADVISERS

SENIOR ADVISER with South Region	Rev. David E.P. Currie BSc BD	21 Rosa Burn Avenue, Lindsayfield, East Kilbride, Glasgow G75 9DE [E-mail: nmsenioradviser@uk.uumail.com] Office: contact via the Church of Scotland Offices	01355 248510 (Tel) 07775 515594 (Mbl)
CONGREGATIONAL DEVELOPMENT ADVISER	Mr Brian Burden	'Edinbane', Mid Road, Northmuir, Kirriemuir DD8 4QX [E-mail: nmadvisercd@uk.uumail.com]	01575 575280 (Tel/Fax) 07899 790466 (Mbl)
MISSIONS CO-ORDINATOR	Mr Philip Wray BSc Msc	59 Elmbank Street, Glasgow G2 4PQ (Office) [E-mail: missionco-ordinator@uk.uumail.com]	0141-352 6946 (Tel) 07900 900776 (Mbl)
REGIONAL ADVISER (EAST)	Rev. Robin J. McAlpine BDS BD	10 Seton Place, Kirkcaldy KY2 6UX [E-mail: nmadvisereast@uk.uumail.com] St Bryce Kirk Centre, St Brycedale Avenue, Kirkcaldy KY1 1ET (Office) [E-mail: nmkirkcaldy@uk.uumail.com]	01592 643518 (Tel) 01592 646406 (Tel/Fax)
REGIONAL ADVISER (NORTH)	Rev. Richard Gibbons	3 Holm Burn Place, Inverness IV2 6WT [E-mail: nmadvisernorth@uk.uumail.com] National Mission Highland Office, Main Street, North Kessock, Inverness IV1 3XN [E-mail: nminverness@uk.uumail.com]	01463 226889 01463 731712
PRIORITY AREAS ADVISER	Rev. Martin J. Johnstone MA BD	3 Herries Road, Glasgow G41 4DE [E-mail: upaadviser@uk.uumail.com] 59 Elmbank Street, Glasgow G2 4PQ (Office) [E-mail: nmglasgow@uk.uumail.com]	0141-423 3760 (Tel) 0141-333 1948 (Tel/Fax)
ANGUS PRESBYTERY CONGREGATIONAL DEVELOPMENT ADVISER	Mr Gordon Anderson	33 Grampian View, Ferryden, Montrose DD10 9SU	01674 674915

| GLASGOW PRESBYTERY CONGREGATIONAL FACILITATOR | Rev. John K. Collard MA BD | 1 Nelson Terrace, East Kilbride, Glasgow G74 2EY | 01355 520093 |
| HAMILTON PRESBYTERY CONGREGATIONAL DEVELOPMENT OFFICER | Mr David Geddes | 108 Maxwelton Avenue, East Kilbride, Glasgow G74 3DU | 01355 235998 |

LIST K – OVERSEAS LOCATIONS

EUROPE

AMSTERDAM
Rev. John A. Cowie and Mrs Gillian Cowie
Jan Willem Brouwersstraat 9, NL-1071 LH Amsterdam, The Netherlands   (Tel) 0031 20 672 2288
                                                                                 (Fax) 0031 20 676 4895
[E-mail: j.cowie2@chello.nl; Website: http://www.ercadam.nl]
The English Reformed Church, The Begijnhof (off the Spui).   Service each Sunday at 10:30am.

BRUSSELS
Rev. Thomas C. Pitkeathly   (Tel/Fax) 0032 2 672 40 56
23 Square des Nations, B-1000 Brussels, Belgium
[E-mail: pitkeathly@tiscali.be; Website: http://www.welcome.to/st-andrews]
St Andrew's Church, Chaussée de Vleurgat 181 (off Ave. Louise).   Service each Sunday at 11:00am.
[E-mail: st-andrews@welcome.to]

BUDAPEST
Rev. Kenneth I. Mackenzie and Mrs Jayne Mackenzie, Oltvany Arok 25, XI Budapest   (Tel/Fax) 0036 1 246 2258
St Columba's Scottish Mission, Vorosmarty utca 51, H-1064 Budapest, Hungary   (Church Tel) 0036 1 343 8479
[E-mail: mackenzie@mail.datanet.hu]
Service in English and Sunday School each Sunday at 11:00am.
Rev. Bertalan Tamas (1976, held previous appointment) and Mrs Elizabeth Tamas   (Tel/Fax) 0036 1 460 0708
[E-mail: zsinatko@axelero.hu]

COSTA DEL SOL
Vacant   (Tel) 0034 95 247 8077
Astighi 2, 5th Floor, No. 4, E-29640 Malaga, Spain
Services at Lux Mundi Ecumenical Centre, Calle Nueva 7, Fuengirola.   Service each Sunday at 10:30am.

GENEVA
Rev. Ian A. Manson and Mrs Roberta Manson   (Tel/Fax) 0041 22 798 29 09
[E-mail: cofsg@pingnet.ch; Website: http://www.welcome.to/cofsgeneva]
6 Chemin Tavernay, CH-1218 Grand Saconnex, Geneva, Switzerland
The Calvin Auditoire, Place de la Taconnerie (beside Cathedral of St Pierre).   Service each Sunday at 11:00am.

GIBRALTAR
Vacant
St Andrew's Manse, 29 Scud Hill, Gibraltar
St Andrew's Church, Governor's Parade. Service each Sunday at 10:30am.
[E-mail: billsmth@gibnet.gi]
(Tel) 00350 77040
(Fax) 00350 40852

LAUSANNE
Rev. Douglas R. Murray and Mrs Sheila Murray
26 Avenue de Rumine, CH-1005 Lausanne, Switzerland
[E-mail: scotskirklausanne@bluewin.ch]
Service each Sunday at 10:30am.
(Tel/Fax) 0041 21 323 98 28

LISBON
Vacant
The Manse, Rua da Arriaga 11, 1200-608, Lisbon, Portugal
[E-mail: st.andrewschurch@clix.pt]
St Andrew's Church, Rua da Arriaga 13–15, Lisbon. Service each Sunday at 11:00am.
(Tel/Fax) 00351 21 395 7677

MALTA
Rev. David Morris
[E-mail: davidmorris486@hotmail.com]
La Romagnola, 13 Triq is-Siegiamisrah Eola, Attard BZN 05
St Andrew's Church, 210 Old Bakery Street, Valletta. Service each Sunday at 10:30am.
(Tel/Fax) 00356 222 643

PARIS
Rev. William M. Reid and Mrs Esther Reid
10 Rue Thimonnier, F-75009 Paris, France
[E-mail: scotskirk@wanadoo.fr; Website: http://www.scotskirkparis.com]
The Scots Kirk, 17 Rue Bayard, F-75008 Paris (Metro: Roosvelt)
Service each Sunday at 10:30am.
(Tel/Fax) 0033 1 48 78 47 94

ROME
Rev. William B. McCulloch and Mrs Jean McCulloch
[E-mail: revwbmcculloch@hotmail.com]
Via XX Settembre 7, 00187 Rome, Italy. Service each Sunday at 11:00am.
(Tel) 0039 06 482 7627
(Fax) 0039 06 487 4370

ROTTERDAM
Rev. Robert A. Calvert and Mrs Lesley-Ann Calvert
Gelebrem 59, NL-3068 TJ Rotterdam, The Netherlands
[E-mail: scotsintchurch@cs.com; Website: http://www.scotsintchurch.com]
The Scots Kirk, Schiedamsevest 121, Rotterdam. Service each Sunday at 10:30am.
Informal service at 9:15am.
(Tel/Fax) 0031 10 220 4199
(Tel) 0031 10 412 4779

TURIN
Rev. Robert A. Mackenzie and Mrs Anne Mackenzie
Via Sante Anselmo 6, 10125 Turin, Italy
[E-mail: valdese.english@arpnet.it; Website: http://www.englishspeakingchurchturin.com]
The English-Speaking Church in Turin: service each Sunday at 10:30am.
Casa Valdese, Corbo Vittoro Emanuele 25, 10125 Turin, Italy
(Church office Tel) 0039 11 650 9467

AFRICA

KENYA

Presbyterian Church of East Africa
Dr Elizabeth Borlase (1992) and Kevin Borlase
Rev. Elaine W. McKinnon (1992)

PCEA Kikuyu Hospital, PO Box 45, Kikuyu, Kenya (Fax) 00254 665 01626
Presbyterian College, PO Box 387, Kikuyu, Kenya
[E-mail: ewrnck@wananchi.com]

Dr Alison Wilkinson (1992)

PCEA Chogoria Hospital, PO Box 35, Chogoria, Kenya (Fax) 00254 166 22122
[E-mail: alisonjwilkinson@swiftkenya.com]

MALAWI

Church of Central Africa Presbyterian
Synod of Blantyre
Rev. Bruce Ritchie (2001)
Mr Tom Gilling (2003)

Zomba Theological College, PO Box 130, Zomba, Malawi
CCAP Blantyre Synod, PO Box 413, Blantyre, Malawi

Synod of Livingstonia
Dr Andrew and Mrs Felicity Gaston (1997)
(on study leave in UK until October 2003)

CCAP Ekwendeni Hospital, PO Box 19, Ekwendeni, Malawi

Miss Helen Scott (2000, held previous appointment)
Dr Alex Maclean (2001) and Mrs Carolyn Maclean

CCAP Girls' Secondary School, PO Box 2, Ekwendeni, Malawi
Embangweni Hospital, PO Box 7, Embangweni, Mzimba District, Malawi

Mrs Dorothy Halliday (2003)

David Gordon Memorial Hospital, PO Box 5, Livingstonia, Rumpi, Malawi

SOUTH AFRICA

Rev. Graham Duncan (1998, held previous appointment) and Mrs Sandra Duncan (1998)

56 Daphne Road, Maroelana 00081, Pretoria, South Africa

ZAMBIA

United Church of Zambia
Rev. Colin D. Johnston (1994)

Trinity UCZ, PO Box 30079, Lusaka, Zambia
[E-mail: trinity@zamnet.zm]

Ms Jane Petty (2000)
Mr Brian Payne (2002) and Mrs Georgina Payne (2002)

Mwandi Mission Hospital, PO Box 60693, Livingstone, Zambia (Tel) 00260 1 250 641
United Church of Zambia Synod Office, Lusaka, Zambia (Fax) 00260 1 252 198
[E-mail: uczsynod@zamnet.zm]

THE CARIBBEAN, CENTRAL AND SOUTH AMERICA

BAHAMAS

Rev. John Fraser (2002) and Mrs Jillian Fraser

St Andrew's Manse, PO Box N1099, Nassau (Tel) 001 242 322 5475 (Fax) 001 242 323 1960
Lucaya Presbyterian Kirk, PO Box F-40777, Freeport (Tel) 001 242 373 2568 (Fax) 001 242 373 4961

BERMUDA

Rev. T. Alan W. Garrity (1999) and Mrs Elizabeth Garrity

The Manse, PO Box PG88, Paget PGBX, Bermuda (Tel) 001 441 236 0400 and (Tel) 001 441 236 1882
[E-mail: revtawg@ibl.bm and christchurch@ibl.bm] (Fax) 001 441 232 0552

JAMAICA

United Church of Jamaica and Grand Cayman
Rev. Roy A. Dodman and Mrs Jane Dodman (1983)

8 Wishaw Drive, Kingston 8, Jamaica
[E-mail: rdodman@cwjamaica.com]
(Tel) 001 876 925 8491
(Fax) 001 876 931 5004

Rev. Margaret Fowler (1988)

PO Box 3097, Negril,
Westmoreland, Jamaica
[E-mail: revm@cwjamaica.com]
(Tel) 001 876 640 0846

Ms Maureen Burke (1998)

1B Woodley Drive, Meadowbrook, Kingston 19,
Jamaica
[E-mail: moburke@cwjamaica.com]
(Tel/Fax) 001 876 905 3206

TRINIDAD

Rev. Harold Sitahal (2000) and Mrs Ruth Sitahal

Church of Scotland Greyfriars St Ann's,
50 Frederick Street, Port of Spain, Trinidad
(Tel/Fax) 001 868 622 1757

ASIA

Ecumenical Appointments

BANGLADESH

Church of Bangladesh
Ms Gillian Rose (1996)
Mr Andrew and Mrs Rosemary Symonds (1999)

Bollobhpur Hospital, PC Kedargonj, DR Meherpur, Bangladesh
St Andrew's College, Dhaka, Bangladesh
[E-mail: ajsymond@bd.drik.net]

Ms Ann Tuesley (2000)

Rajshahi Hospital, Kushtia, Bangladesh

CHINA

Together with Scottish Churches China Group
Mr Ian Groves (1996)
Mr Mick and Mrs Anne Kavanagh (1997)
Mr Richard Brunt (1998)
Michelle and Jody Marshall (2002)

Amity Foundation, Overseas Office, 4 Jordan Road, Kowloon, Hong Kong
Nanping Teachers' College, 45 Guanshatian, Nanping, Fujian 353000, China
Tai'an Teachers' College, 56 Wenhua Road, Tai'an, Shandong 271000, China
Yichun Teachers' College, Jiangxi Province, China

Janet Dickinson, Joanna White, Matthew Syddall and Alan Moss (all 2003) have no placements at present because of the SARS situation.

INDIA

Church of South India
Rev. Eileen Thompson

c/o CSI Diocesan Office, Melukavumattom PO, Kerala 686 652

NEPAL

United Mission to Nepal
Mr John Ross (1995)

PO Box 126, Kathmandu, Nepal
[E-mail: jross@wlink.com.np]
(Fax) 00977 1 225 559

Mrs Moira and Alasdair Murray (1999)

Kathmandu International Study Centre, Kathmandu,
Nepal
[E-mail: amurray@wlink.com.np]
(Fax) 00977 1 225 559

	Mrs Marianne Karsgaard (2001)	PO Box 126, Kathmandu, Nepal [E-mail: marianne@wlink.com.np]	(Fax) 00977 1 225 559
KOREA	Rev. Elinor Gordon (2002)	Flat 202, Ichon Apartments, Ichon, I-Dong, Yongsan-gu, Seoul, Korea [E-mail: elinorgordon@aol.com]	

SRI LANKA

Presbytery of Lanka

Rev. Anthony McLean-Foreman (1995) — Theological College of Lanka, Nandana Uyana, Pilimatalawa, Sri Lanka
[E-mail: tony@slt.lk]   (Fax) 00948 232 343

THAILAND

Church of Christ in Thailand

Mr Michael D. Fucella and Mrs E. Jane Fucella (1990) — 2, MU3, Tambon Nongloo, Sangklaburi, Kanchanaburi 71240, Thailand
[E-mail: jfucella@loxinfo.co.th]

MIDDLE EAST AND NORTH AFRICA

EGYPT   Dr Keith Russell (2000) and Mrs Lai Fun Russell — The Joint Relief Ministry of All Saints' Anglican Cathedral, Michel Lutfallah Street, Zamalek 11211, Cairo, Egypt
[E-mail: russell@link.net]   (Tel) 00202 738 0821   (Fax) 00202 735 8941

ISRAEL   [NOTE: Church Services are held in St Andrew's Scots Memorial Church, Jerusalem, Jerusalem, each Sunday at 10.00am, and at St Andrew's, Galilee (contact minister for worship time)]

Jerusalem

Rev. Clarence W. Musgrave (2000) and Mrs Joan Musgrave — St Andrew's, Jerusalem, PO Box 8619, Jerusalem 91086, Israel
(Tel: 00972 2 6732401; Fax: 00972 2 673 1711)
[E-mail: standjer@netvision.net.il] [Private E-mail: stachjer@netvision.net.il;
Website: http://www.scothotels.co.il]

Tiberias

Rev. Fred Hibbert (1996) and Mrs Diane Hibbert — St Andrew's, Galilee, PO Box 104, Tiberias, Israel
[E-mail: scottie@netvision.net.il] (Tel: 00972 4 6721165; Fax: 00972 4 6790145)
[Private e-mail: scotdir@netvision.net.il]
[Website: http://www.scothotels.co.il]

Jaffa

Mr Christopher Mottershead (2000) and Mrs Sue Mottershead — Tabeetha School, PO Box 8170, 21 Yefet Street, Jaffa, Israel
(Tel: 00972 3 6821581; Fax: 00972 3 6819357)
[E-mail: costab@netvision.net.il;
Website: http://www.tabeetha.htmlplant.com]
Tabeetha School

Mrs Karen Anderson (1992) — Tabeetha School
Ms Irene Wilson (1993)

Ibillin

Rev. Dr Bryson Arthur and Mrs May Arthur (2001)	Mar Elias University College, Mar Elias Educational Institutions, PO Box 102, Ibillin 30012, Galilee, Israel (Tel: 00972 4 986 6848; Fax: 00972 4 986 9573; Website: http://www.m-e-c.org) [E-mail: arthurz@netvision.net.il]

(Tel) 00961 1346 708
(Fax) 00961 1347 129

LEBANON	Mr David Kerry (1999)	Near East School of Theology, Sourati Street, PO Box 13-5780, Chouran, Beirut, Lebanon [E-mail: nest.lib@inco.com.lb]

LIST L – OVERSEAS RESIGNED AND RETIRED MISSION PARTNERS (ten or more years' service)

NAME	APP	RET	AREA	ADDRESS
Archibald, Mary L. (Miss)	1964	1982	Nigeria/Ghana	490 Low Main Street, Wishaw ML2 7PL
Bailey, Winifred (Miss)	1949	1979	Kolhapur	Marian House, Room 10, 7/10 Oswald Road, Edinburgh EH9 2HE
Barbour, Edith R. (Miss)	1952	1983	North India	13/11 Pratik Nagar, Yerwada, Pune 411006, Maharashta, India
Bogle, Rev. Michael M.	1936	1961	Lovedale	30 Woodburn Terrace, Edinburgh EH10 4SS
Boyle, Lexa (Miss)	1959	1992	Aden/Yemen/Sudan	7 Maxwell Grove, Glasgow G41 5JP
Burnett, Dr Fiona	1988	1998	Zambia	The Glenholm Centre, Broughton, Biggar ML12 6JF
Burt, M.R.C. (Miss)	1940	1975	Kenya	22 The Loaning, Chirnside, Duns TD11 3YE
Campbell, George H.	1957	1971	Livingstonia	27 Avenue Street, Stewarton, Kilmarnock KA3 5AP
Coltart, Rev. Ian O.	1967	1985	North India	161 Kirk Road, Wishaw ML2 7BZ
Conacher, Marion (Miss)	1963	1993	India	41 Magdalene Drive, Edinburgh EH15 3BG
Conn, A. (Mr)	1937	1960	Blantyre	90 Endbutt Lane, Great Crosby, Liverpool L23
Cooper, Rev. George	1966	1986	Kenya	69 Montpelier Park, Edinburgh EH10 4WD
Cowan, Dr Betty	1969	1988	North India	2 Sunningdale Square, Kilwinning KA13 6PH
Dabb, Dr R. Gwen	1943	1971	Blantyre	14/44 Ethel Terrace, Edinburgh EH10 5NA
Dawson, Miss Anne	1976	2000	Malawi	5 Cattle Market, Clackmannan FK10 4EH
Dougall, Ian C.	1960	1990	Kenya	60B Craigmillar Park, Edinburgh EH16 5PU
Drever, Dr Bryan	1962	1982	Aden/Yemen/Pakistan	188 Addison Road, King's Head, Birmingham
Dunlop, Walter T. (Mr)	1979	1994	Malawi/Israel	50 Oxgangs Road, Edinburgh EH13 9DR
Fauchelle, Rev. Don and Mrs Margaret	1971 1991	1979 1999	Zambia, Malawi, Zimbabwe	Flat 3, 22 North Avenue, Devonport, Auckland 1309, New Zealand
Ferguson, John K.P. (Mr) and Mrs Margaret	1977	1989	Pakistan	12 Bencleuch Place, Bourtreehill South, Irvine KA11 1EL
Finlay, Carol (Ms)	1990	2001	Malawi	96 Broomfield Crescent, Edinburgh EH12 7LX
Fischbacher, Dr Colin M. and Mrs Sally	1984	1998	Malawi	11 Barclay Square, Gosforth, Newcastle-upon-Tyne NE3 2JB

Forrester-Paton, Rev. Colin	Ghana	1946	1972	Acharn, Glen Road, Peebles EH45 9AY
Gall, E.G. (Miss)	Blantyre	1940	1962	151 Raeburn Heights, Glenrothes KY16 1BW
Glass, Irene (Miss)	Delhi	1945	1976	3E Falcon Road West, Edinburgh EH10 4AA
Hutchison, C.M. (Mr)	Calabar	1951	1972	75 Grampian Road, Torry, Aberdeen AB11 8ED
Irvine, Mr Clive and Mrs Su	Nepal	1984	1999	McGregor Flat, 92 Blackford Avenue, Edinburgh EH9 3ES
Irvine, Dr Geoffrey C. and Mrs Dorothy				
Lamont, Rev. A. Donald	Kenya	1952	1989	Lakeside, PO Box 1356 Naivasha, Kenya
Liddell, Margaret (Miss)	Kenya	1941	1975	36 St Clair Terrace, Edinburgh EH10 5PS
Lyon, Rev. D.H.S.	Zambia	1964	1980	20 Wyvis Crescent, Conon Bridge, Dingwall IV7 8BZ
McArthur, G. (Mr)	Nagpur	1952	1972	30 Mansfield Road, Balerno EH14 7JZ
McCulloch, Lesley (Mrs)	South Africa	1956	1972	3 Craigcrook Road, Edinburgh EH4 3NQ
McCutcheon, Agnes W.F. (Miss)	Malawi/Pakistan	1982	1992	c/o 19 North Approach Road, Kincardine, Alloa FK10 4NW
Macdonald, Rev. R.M.	India	1957	1989	10A Hugh Murray Grove, Cambuslang, Glasgow G72 7NG
McDougall, Rev. John N.	Calabar	1929	1968	Pinewood Nursing Home, Leny Road, Callander FK17 8AP
McGoff, A.W. (Miss)	West Pakistan	1935	1960	2/58 Allendale Road, Mount Albert, Auckland 3, New Zealand
MacGregor, Rev. Margaret	Kolhapur	1954	1974	6 Mossvale Walk, Craigend, Glasgow G33 5PF
McKenzie, Rev. Robert	India	1959	1994	Gordon Flat, 16 Learmonth Court, Edinburgh EH4 1PB
McKenzie, Rev. W.M.	India	1938	1951	23 Foulis Crescent, Edinburgh EH14 5BN
MacKinnon, E.L. (Miss)	Zambia	1958	1974	Troqueer Road, Dumfries DG2 7DF
Malley, Beryl Stevenson (Miss)	Nigeria	1952	1972	142 Glencairn Street, Stevenston KA20 3BU
Marshall, Rev. Fred J.	Bermuda	1982	1992	272/2 Craigcrook Road, Edinburgh EH4 7TF
Millar, Rev. Margaret R.M.	Malawi/Zambia	1946	1992	Flat 3, 31 Oswald Road, Edinburgh EH9 2HT
Millar, Rev. Peter	South India	1967	1996	The Manse, Taynuilt, Argyll PA35 1HW
Morrice, Rev. Dr Charles and Mrs Margaret	Buenos Aires/Kenya	1976	1989	104 Baron's Hill Avenue, Linlithgow EH49 7JG
Morris, Rev. Gordon C.	Zambia, Argentina	1971	1998	42 Regent Street, Edinburgh EH5 2AY
Morton, Rev. Alasdair J.	Zambia	1948	1983	8 Ormiston Grove, Melrose TD6 9SR
Morton, Rev. Colin	Israel	1960	1973	313 Lanark Road West, Currie EH14 5RS
Murison, Rev. W.G.	Santalia	1988	1998	21 Hailes Gardens, Edinburgh EH13 0JL
Murray, Mr Ian and Mrs Isabel	Pakistan	1951	1971	17 Piershill Terrace, Edinburgh EH8 7EY
Nicholson, Rev. Thomas S.	Taiwan	1962	2000	Todholes, Greenlaw, Duns TD10 6XD
Nicol, Catherine (Miss)	Pakistan	1981	1995	St Columba Christian Girls' RTC, Barah Patthar, Sialkot 2, Pakistan
Nicol, J.M. (Miss)	Rajasthan	1960	2000	74 Brucefield Avenue, Dunfermline KY11 4SY
Pacitti, Rev. Stephen A.	Taiwan	1950	1967	157 Nithsdale Road, Pollokshields, Glasgow G41 5RD
Pattison, Rev. Kenneth and Mrs Susan	Malawi	1977	1996	The Manse, Delny, Invergordon IV18 0NW
Philip, Rev. David Stuart	Gibraltar	1966	1977	6 St Bernard's Crescent, Edinburgh EH4 1NP
Philpot, Rev. David	WCC Geneva	1978	1991	2/27 Pentland Drive, Edinburgh EH10 6PX
Rae, Rev. David	India	1981	1995	29 Falcon Avenue, Edinburgh EH10 4AL
Reid, Margaret I. (Miss)	Malawi	1953	1989	26A Angle Park Terrace, Edinburgh EH11 2JT

Name	App	Country	Address
Rennie, Rev. Alistair M.	1939	Malawi	13 Tullich Terrace, Tillicoultry FK13 6RD
Rhodes, Rev. William S.	1954	North India	22 Hamilton Place, Edinburgh EH3 5AU
Ritchie, Ishbel M. (Miss)	1955	Eastern Himalaya	8 Ross Street, Dunfermline KY12 0AN
Ritchie, Rev. J.M.	1974	Yemen	46 St James' Gardens, Penicuik EH26 9DU
Ritchie, Mary Scott (Miss)	1968	Malawi/Israel	Afton Villa, 1 Afton Bridgend, New Cumnock KA18 4AX
Ross, Rev. Prof. Kenneth and Mrs Hester	1988	Malawi	35 Madeira Street, Edinburgh EH6 4AJ
Rough, Mary E. (Miss)	1987	Blantyre	6 Glebe Street, Dumfries DG1 2LF
Roy, Rev. Alan J.	1972	Zambia	14 Comerton Place, Drumoig, St Andrews KY16 0NQ
Russell, M.M. (Miss)	1969	Nigeria	14 Hozier Street, Carluke ML8 5DW
Samuel, Lynda (Mrs)	1990	Madras	c/o Balgownie, 1 Argyll Street, Brechin DD9 6JL
Smith, M.L. (Miss)	1973	Madras	6 Fintry Mains, Dundee DD4 9HF
Smith, Dr R.B.	1958	Yemen	Flat G4, 21 Queen's Bay Crescent, Edinburgh EH15 2NA
Smith, Rev. W. Ewing	1978	Delhi	8 Hardy Gardens, Bathgate EH48 1NH
Sneddon, Mr Sandy and Mrs Marie	2003	Pakistan	9 Blackford Glen Road, Edinburgh EH16 6AD
Stewart, Marion G. (Miss)	1976	Malawi/Israel	Kirk Cottage, Kirkton of Skene, Westhill, Skene AB32 6XX
Stone, Christine (Miss)	1981	Nepal	UMN, PO Box 126, Kathmandu, Nepal
Stone, W. Vernon MA BD	1949	Zambia	36 Woodrow Court, Port Glasgow Road, Kilmacolm PA13 4QA
Taylor, Rev. A.T.H.	1938	Nigeria/Jamaica	4 The Pleasance, Strathkinness, St Andrews KY16 9SD
Wallace, A. Dorothy (Miss)	1953	North India	7 Bynack Place, Nethy Bridge PH25 3DU
Westmarland, Rev. Colin	1975	Malta	PO Box 5, Cospicua, CSPO1, Malta
Wilkie, Rev. James L.	1959	Zambia	7 Comely Bank Avenue, Edinburgh EH4 1EW
Wilkinson, Rev. John	1946	Kenya	70 Craigleith Hill Gardens, Edinburgh EH4 2JH
Wilson, M.H. (Miss)	1977	Nasik	7 Lady's Well, Moat Road, Annan DG12 5AD
Wilson, Rev. Mark	1953	Nagpur	37 Kings Avenue, Longniddry EH32 0QN

LIST M – PARISH ASSISTANTS and PROJECT WORKERS

NAME	APP	ADDRESS	APPOINTMENT	TEL	PRES
Adam, Dougie	2001	175 Fairview Drive, Danestone, Aberdeen AB22 8ZZ	Aberdeen: Bridge of Don	07729 781634	31
Bauer, Alex (Mrs)	2001	26 Netherhouse Avenue, Lenzie, Glasgow G66 5NG	Linwood	07900 531196	14
Black, Colm	2001	2B Mason Road, Inverness IV2 3SZ	Inverness: Hilton	01463 717208	37
Campbell, Alasdair	2000	3 Gellatly Road, Dunfermline KY11 4BH	Dunfermline: St Ninian's	01383 726238	24
Close, David	2001	5 Shortroods Road, Paisley PA3 2NT	The Star Project: Paisley North	0141-889 5850	14
Conlin, Melodie	2000	427 Carmunnock Road, Glasgow G45 9DG	Glasgow East End	0141-583 0790	16
Cowie, Marjorie	2002	35 Balbirnie Avenue, Markinch, Glenrothes KY7 6BS	Glenrothes: St Margaret's	01592 758402	25

Name	Year	Address	Congregation	Phone	No.
Douglas, Jessie (Mrs)	1999	24 Niddrie Marischal Crescent, Edinburgh EH16 4LA	Edinburgh: Richmond Craigmillar	0131-669 6848	1
Falconer, Alexander J.	1996	59 Waldegrave Road, Carlisle CA2 6EW	Carlisle Chapel Street/Longtown	01228 544757	7
Finch, John	2002	6 Balmuildy Road, Glasgow G64 3BS	Glasgow: St Francis in the East	0141-772 1363	16
Fraser, Lesley (Ms)	2001	40 Muir Wood Road, Currie EH14 5JN	Edinburgh: North Leith	0131-451 5628	1
Govan, Alec	1999	Braeside Cottage, 1 School Road, Sandford, Strathaven ML10 6BF	Hamilton: Trinity	01357 523815	17
Hutchison, John BA	2001	30/4 West Pilton Gardens, Edinburgh EH4 4EG	Edinburgh: The Old Kirk	0131-538 1622	1
McBean, Archie	1999	28 Taransay Crescent, Aberdeen AB16 6UG	Aberdeen: Mastrick	01224 789784	31
McCorkindale, Yvonne (Mrs)	1997	118 Ardfin Road, Prestwick KA9 2LE	Kilmarnock: Shortlees	01292 678874	11
McLaren, Kirsty Ann (Miss)	2002	37 West Main Street, Blackburn, Bathgate EH47 7LU	Edinburgh: Kaimes Lockhart Meml	01506 626904	1
McLauchlan, Dorothy Jean	2001	114 Brownside Road, Glasgow G72 8AF	Glasgow: Cranhill	0141-641 3171	16
Morrison, Rosie (Ms)	2000	12 Hailes Place, Dunfermline KY12 7XJ	Cowdenbeath: Trinity	01383 626904	24
Muir, Graeme	2001	2 Nithsdale Place, Noblehill, Dumfries DG1 3HT	Dumfries: St George's	01387 267470	8
Philip, Elizabeth MA BA	2001	43 Smithycroft Road, Glasgow G33 2RH [E-mail: elizabethphilip@cheerful.com]	Glasgow: Garthamlock/Craigend East	0141-770 7593	16
Reford, Susan	2001	32 Jedburgh Street, Blantyre, Glasgow G72 0SU	East Kilbride: Moncreiff	01698 820122	17
White, Ken	2002	28 Victoria Street, Perth PH2 8LY	Perth: North	01738 627549	31
Young, Neil James	2001	1/2, 33 Alexandra Park Street, Glasgow G31 2UB	Glasgow: St Paul's	07748 808488	16

LIST N – READERS

1. EDINBURGH

Beasley, Ronald E.	37 Warrender Park Terrace, Edinburgh EH9 1EB	0131-229 8383
Davies, Ruth (Mrs) (attached to Liberton)	4 Hawkhead Grove, Edinburgh EH16 6LS	0131-664 3608
Farrant, Yvonne (Mrs)	Flat 7, 14 Duddingston Mills, Edinburgh EH8 7NF	
Farrell, William J.	50 Ulster Crescent, Edinburgh EH8 7JS	0131-661 1026
Farrow, Edmund	14 Brunswick Terrace, Edinburgh EH7 5PG	0131-558 8210
Kerrigan, Herbert A. MA LLB QC	Airdene, 20 Edinburgh Road, Dalkeith EH22 1JY	0131-660 3007
Kinnear, M.A.	25 Thorburn Road, Edinburgh EH13 0BH	0131-441 3150
Morrison, Peter K.	65 Balgreen Road, Edinburgh EH12 5UA	0131-337 7711
Wyllie, Anne (Miss)	46 Jordan Lane, Edinburgh EH10 4QX	0131-447 9035

2. WEST LOTHIAN

Blackwood, Michael	Inshaig Cottage, Hatton, Kirknewton EH27 8DZ	0131-333 1448
Coyle, Charlotte (Mrs)	28 The Avenue, Whitburn EH47 0DA	01501 740687
Davidson, Sheila (Mrs)	12 Slamannan Road, Avonbridge, Falkirk FK1 2LW	01324 861554
Elliott, Sarah (Miss)	105 Seafield, Bathgate EH47 7AW	01506 654950

Notman, Jean G.S. (Miss) — 31 South Loch Park, Bathgate EH48 2QZ — 01506 633820

3. LOTHIAN
Booth, Sidney J. IEng CCME — 6 Winton Court, Cockenzie, Prestonpans EH32 0JW — 01875 813978
Cannon, S. Christopher MA — Briarwood, Winterfield Place, Belhaven, Dunbar EH42 1QQ — 01368 864991
Evans, W. John IEng MIIE(Elec) — Edenwood, 29 Smileyknowes Court, North Berwick EH39 4RG — 01620 894309
[E-mail: jevans7@compuserve.com]
Gibson, C.B. Stewart — 27 King's Avenue, Longniddry EH32 0QN — 01875 853464
Hogg, David MA — 82 Eskhill, Penicuik EH26 8DQ — 01968 676350
Lyall, George JP — Mossgiel, 13 Park Road, Bonnyrigg EH19 2AW — 0131-663 9343
[E-mail: george.lyall@bigfoot.com]
Trevor, A. Hugh MA — 29A Fidra Road, North Berwick EH39 4NE — 01620 894924
[E-mail: hughtrevor@compuserve.com]
Yeoman, Edward T.N. FSA(Scot) — 75 Newhailes Crescent, Musselburgh EH21 6ES — 0131-653 2291

4. MELROSE AND PEEBLES
Butcher, John W. — 'Sandal', 13 Ormiston Grove, Melrose TD6 9SR — 01896 822339
Cashman, Margaret D. (Mrs) — 38 Abbotsford Road, Galashiels TD1 3HR — 01896 752711

5. DUNS
Deans, M. (Mrs) BA — The Lodge, Edrington House, Mordington, Berwick-on-Tweed TD15 1UF — 01289 386222
Elphinston, Enid (Mrs) — Edrington House, Berwick-on-Tweed TD15 1UF — 01289 386359
Landale, William — Cranshaws House, Cranshaws, Duns TD11 3SJ — 01361 890242

6. JEDBURGH
Finlay, Elizabeth (Mrs) — 10 Inch Park, Kelso TD5 7EQ — 01573 226641
Knox, Dagmar (Mrs) — 3 Stichill Road, Ednam, Kelso TD5 7QQ — 01573 224883
Thomson, Robert R. — 34/36 Fisher Avenue, Hawick TD9 9NB — 01450 373851

7. ANNANDALE AND ESKDALE
Boncey, David — Redbrae, Beattock, Moffat DG10 9RF — 01683 300613
[E-mail: bonceyofredbrae@yahoo.co.uk]
Brown, S. Jeffrey BA — Skara Brae, 8 Ballplay Road, Moffat DG10 9AR — 01683 220475
Chisholm, Dennis A.G. MA BSc — Moss-side, Hightae, Lockerbie DG11 1JR — 01387 811803
Dodds, Alan — Trinco, Battlehill, Annan DG12 6SN — 01461 201235
Jackson, Sue (Mrs) — 48 Springbells Road, Annan DG12 6LQ — 01461 204159
[E-mail: sue.jackson@highstream.com]
Morton, Andrew A. BSc — 19 Sherwood Park, Lockerbie DG11 2DX — 01576 203164
[E-mail: thecroft@macunlimited.net]

8. DUMFRIES AND KIRKCUDBRIGHT
Archer, Morven (Mrs) — 1 Grilloch Drive, Dumfries DG1 4DP — 01387 263946
Carroll, J. Scott — 17 Downs Place, Heathhall, Dumfries DG1 3RF — 01387 265350
Greer, Kathleen (Mrs) — 10 Watling Street, Dumfries DG1 1HF — 01387 256113
Marsh, Sally (Mrs) BTh — 32 Queen Street, Castle Douglas DG7 1HS — 01556 503706
Ogilvie, D.W. MA FSAScot — Lingerwood, 2 Nelson Street, Dumfries DG2 9AY — 01387 264267

Paterson, Ronald M. (Dr) — Mirkwood, Ringford, Castle Douglas DG7 2AL — 01557 820202
Piggins, Janette (Mrs) — Cleugh Wood, Dalbeattie DG5 4PF — 01387 780655

9. WIGTOWN AND STRANRAER
Clough, Alan — Dowiesbank, Whauphill, Newton Stewart DG8 9PN — 01988 700824
Connery, Graham — Skellies Knowe, West Ervie, Stranraer DG9 — 01776 854277
Robinson, J.J. — Kirwaugh, Wigtown, Newton Stewart DG8 9AY — 01988 403244
Williams, Roy — 120 Belmont Road, Stranraer DG9 7BG

10. AYR
Coghlan, Tony — 'Hawthorns', Auchendoon, Hollybush, Ayr KA6 6HA — 01242 560307
Fleming, William H. — 35 Briar Grove, Ayr KA7 3PD — 01292 268599
Jamieson, I. — 2 Whinfield Avenue, Prestwick KA9 2BH — 01242 476898
McNally, David BEd MEd PhD ACP — 50 Kenmore, Troon KA10 6PF — 01292 312015
Murphy, I. — 56 Lamont Crescent, Cumnock KA18 3DU — 01290 423675
Riome, Elizabeth (Mrs) — Monkwood Mains, Minishant, Maybole KA19 8EY — 01292 443440
Todd, Joy M. (Mrs) BD — 15 Firth Road, Troon KA10 6TF — 01292 312995
Wallace, D. — 4 Holmston Crescent, Ayr KA7 3JJ — 01292 261620

11. IRVINE AND KILMARNOCK
Bircham, James — 8 Holmlea Place, Kilmarnock KA1 1UU — 01563 532287
Cuthbert, Helen (Miss) MA MSc — 63 Haining Avenue, Kilmarnock KA1 3QN — 01563 550403
Crosbie, Shona (Mrs) — 4 Campbell Street, Darvel KA17 0PA — 01560 322229
Findlay, Elizabeth (Mrs) — 19 Keith Place, Kilmarnock KA3 7NS — 01563 528084
Hamilton, Margaret A. (Mrs) — 59 South Hamilton Street, Kilmarnock KA1 2DT — 01563 534431
Jamieson, John BSc(Hons) DEP AFBPSS — 22 Moorfield Avenue, Kilmarnock KA1 1TS — 01563 534065
Lightbody, Hunter B. — 36 Rannoch Place, Irvine KA12 9NQ — 01294 273955
McAllister, Anne C. (Mrs) — 39 Bowes Rigg, Stewarton KA3 5EN — 01560 483191
McLean, Donald — 1 Four Acres Drive, Kilmaurs, Kilmarnock KA3 2ND — 01563 381475
MacTaggart, Elspeth (Miss) — 21 Scargie Road, Kilmarnock KA3 1QR — 01563 527713
Mills, Catherine (Mrs) — 59 Crossdene Road, Crosshouse, Kilmarnock KA2 0JU — 01563 535305
Scott, William BA DipEd — 6 Elgin Avenue, Stewarton, Kilmarnock KA3 3HJ — 01560 484273
Storm, Iain — 17 Kilwinning Road, Irvine KA12 8RR — 01294 277647
Wilson, Robert L.S. MA BD — 57 Woodstock Street, Kilmarnock KA1 2JH — 01563 526658

12. ARDROSSAN
Allan, J.H. — Creag Dhubh, Golf Course Road, Whiting Bay, Brodick, Isle of Arran KA27 8RE — 01770 700462
Barclay, Elizabeth (Mrs) — 2 Jacks Road, Saltcoats KA21 5NT — 01294 471855
Hunter, Jean C.Q. (Mrs) — The Manse, Shiskine, Isle of Arran KA27 8EP — 01770 860380
Mackay, Brenda H. (Mrs) — 19 Eglinton Square, Ardrossan KA22 8LN — 01294 464491
Mills, Colin J. — Roadend Christian Guesthouse, Shiskine, Brodick, Isle of Arran KA27 8EW — 01770 860448
Price, James — Dunjara, The Orchard, West Kilbride KA23 9AE — 01294 822247

13. LANARK

Allan, Robert	59 Jennie Lee Drive, Overtown, Wishaw ML2 0EE	01698 376738
Grant, Alan	25 Moss-side Avenue, Carluke ML8 5UG	01555 771419
Kerr, Sheilagh I. (Mrs)	Dunvegan, 29 Wilsontown Road, Forth, Lanark ML11 8ER	01555 812214

14. GREENOCK AND PAISLEY

Campbell, Tom BA FRICS DipCPC	100 Craigielea Road, Renfrew PA4 8NJ	0141-886 2503
Davey, Charles L.	16 Divert Road, Gourock PA19 1DT [E-mail: charles@davey2.freeserve.co.uk]	01475 631544
Glenny, John C.	49 Cloch Road, Gourock PA19 1AT	01475 636415
Jamieson, J.A.	148 Finnart Street, Greenock PA16 8HY	01475 729531
McHugh, Jack	'Earlshaugh', Earl Place, Bridge of Weir PA11 3HA	01505 612789
Marshall, Leon M.	Glenisla, Gryffe Road, Kilmacolm PA13 4BA	01505 872417
Maxwell, Margaret (Mrs) BD	2 Grants Avenue, Paisley PA2 6AZ	0141-884 3710

16. GLASGOW

Armstrong, J.	44 Eckford Street, Glasgow G32 7AJ	0141-778 4745
Birchall, Edwin R.	11 Sunnybank Grove, Clarkston, Glasgow G76 7SU	0141-638 4332
Calder, William	111 Muirside Avenue, Kirkintilloch, Glasgow G66 3PP	0141-776 5495
Callander, Thomas M.S.	31 Dalkeith Avenue, Bishopbriggs, Glasgow G64 2HQ	0141-563 6955
Campbell, Jack T. BD BEd	27 Springfield Road, Bishopbriggs, Glasgow G64 1PJ	0141-563 5837
Clarke, Samuel	'Gola', 142 Shelley Road, Glasgow G12 0XN	0141-337 2238
Dickson, Hector	'Guito', 61 Whitton Drive, Giffnock, Glasgow G46 6EF	0141-637 0080
Findlay, William	36 Firpark Road, Bishopbriggs, Glasgow G64 1SP	0141-772 7253
Gibson, James N.	153 Peveril Avenue, Glasgow G41 3SF	0141-632 4162
Horner, David J.	32 Burnside Road, Rutherglen, Glasgow G73 4RS	0141-634 2178
Lennie, Henry	14 Clyde Place, Cambuslang, Glasgow G72 7QT	0141-641 1410
Lockhart, James C.	56 Springfield Road, Bishopbriggs, Glasgow G64 1PN	0141-772 1852
MacColl, Duncan N.	14 Mosspark Avenue, Glasgow G52 1JX	0141-427 2395
McFarlane, Robert	25 Avenel Road, Glasgow G13 2PB	0141-954 5540
McLaughlin, C.	8 Lamlash Place, Glasgow G33 3XH	0141-774 2483
McLellan, Duncan	138 King's Park Avenue, Glasgow G44 4HS	0141-632 8433
Middleton, W.G.	20 Rannoch Avenue, Bishopbriggs, Glasgow G64 1BU	0141-772 6240
Montgomery, Hamish	13 Avon Avenue, Kessington, Bearsden, Glasgow G61 2PS	0141-942 3640
Nairne, Elizabeth (Mrs)	229 Southbrae Drive, Glasgow G13 1TT	0141-959 5066
Philips, John B.	2/3, 30 Handel Place, Glasgow G5 0TP	0141-429 7716
Robertson, Adam	423 Amulree Street, Glasgow G32 7SS	0141-573 6662
Shirlaw, William	77 Southpark Avenue, Glasgow G12 8LE	0141-339 0454
Stuart, Alex	107 Baldorran Crescent, Cumbernauld, Glasgow G68 9EX	01236 727710
Tindall, Margaret (Mrs)	23 Ashcroft Avenue, Lennoxtown, Glasgow G65 7EN	01360 310911
Williamson, John G.	34 King Edward Road, Glasgow G13 1QW	0141-959 1300
Wilson, George A.	46 Maxwell Drive, Garrowhill, Baillieston, Glasgow G69 6LS	0141-771 3862

17. HAMILTON

Bell, Sheena	2 Langdale, East Kilbride, Glasgow G74 4RP	01355 248217

Black, Gavin	11 Torrance Road, West Mains, East Kilbride, Glasgow G74 1AR	01355 224600
Clemenson, Anne	25 Dempsey Road, Lochview, Bellshill ML4 2UF	01698 747032
Cruickshanks, William	63 Progress Drive, Caldercruix, Airdrie ML6 7PU	01236 843352
Falconer, Leslie D.	48 Fraser River Tower, East Kilbride, Glasgow G75 8AD	01355 230133
Haggarty, Frank	46 Glen Road, Caldercruix, Airdrie ML6 7PZ	01236 842182
Hawthorne, William	172 Main Street, Plains, Airdrie ML6 7JH	01236 842230
Hewitt, Samuel	3 Corrie Court, Earnock, Hamilton ML3 9XE	01698 457403
Hislop, Eric	3 Kellie Grove, East Kilbride, Glasgow G74 4DN	01355 231600
Leckie, Elizabeth	41 Church Street, Larkhall ML9 1EZ	01698 308933
McCleary, Isaac	719 Coatbridge Road, Bargeddie, Glasgow G69 7PH	0141-236 0158
McRae, James	36 Crosshill Road, Strathaven ML10 6DS	01357 520053
Queen, Leslie	60 Loch Assynt, East Kilbride, Glasgow G74 2DW	01355 233932
Robertson, Rowan	68 Townhead Road, Coatbridge ML5 2HU	01236 425703
Smith, Alexander	6 Coronation Street, Wishaw ML2 8LF	01698 385797
White, Ian	21 Muirhead, Stonehouse, Larkhall ML9 3HG	01698 792772
Wilson, William	115 Chatelherault Crescent, Low Waters Estate, Hamilton ML3 9PL	01698 421856

18. DUMBARTON

Galbraith, Iain B.	Beechwood, Overton Road, Alexandria G83 0LJ	01389 753563
Hart, R.J.M. BSc	7 Kidston Drive, Helensburgh G84 8QA	01436 672039
Neville, Robert	4 Glen Drive, Helensburgh G84 9BJ	01436 671481

19. SOUTH ARGYLL

Holden, Robert	Orsay, West Bank Road, Ardrishaig, Lochgilphead PA30 8HG	01546 603211
Logue, David	3 Braeface, Tayvallich, Lochgilphead PA31 8PN	01546 870647
Mitchell, James S.	4 Main Street, Port Charlotte, Isle of Islay PA48 7TX	01496 850650
Morrison, John	Tigh na Barnashaig, Tayvallich, Lochgilphead PA31 8PN	01546 870637
Ramsay, Matthew M.	Portnastorm, Carradale, Campbeltown PA28 6SB	01583 431381
Sinclair, Margaret (Mrs)	2 Quarry Place, Furnace, Inveraray PA32 8XW	01499 500633
Stewart, Agnes	Creagdhu Mansions, New Quay Street, Campbeltown PA28 6BB	01586 552805
Stewart, John Y.S.	9 Foulis Road, Inveraray PA32 8UW	01499 302077

20. DUNOON

Challis, John O.	Bay Villa, Strachur, Cairndow PA27 8DE	01369 860436

21. LORN AND MULL

Binner, Aileen	'Ailand', Connel, Oban PA37 1QX	01631 710264
Elwis, Michael	Erray Farm Cottage, Tobermory, Mull PA75 6PS	01688 302331
Roberts, John V.	20 Toberonochy, Isle of Luing, Oban PA34 4UE	01852 314301
	(Prefix 18001 Text, prefix 18002 Voice)	
Simpson, J.	Ardmhullean, Longsdale Road, Oban PA34 5JW	01631 562022

22. FALKIRK

Duncan, Lorna (Mrs) BA	Richmond, 28 Solway Drive, Head of Muir, Denny FK5 5NS	01324 813020
O'Rourke, Edith (Mrs)	16 Achray Road, Cumbernauld, Glasgow G67 4JH	01236 732813
Stewart, Arthur MA	34 Raith Drive, Blackwood, Cumbernauld, Glasgow G68 9PF	01236 732532
Struthers, I.	169 The Auld Road, Cumbernauld, Glasgow G67 2RQ	01236 733879

23. STIRLING

Brown, Kathryn (Mrs)	The Manse, Tullibody, Alloa FK10 2RG	01259 213236
Durie, Alastair	25 Forth Place, Stirling FK8 1UD	01786 451029
Kimmitt, Alan	111 Glasgow Road, Bannockburn, Stirling FK7 0PF	01360 850313
Lamont, John	'Serendipity', Wardpark, Gartmore, Stirling FK8 3RN	01259 742094
Tilly, Patricia	4 Innerdownie Place, Dollar FK14 7BY	

24. DUNFERMLINE

Arnott, Robert G.K.	25 Sealstrand, Dalgety Bay, Dunfermline KY11 5GH	01383 822293
Conway, Bernard	4 Centre Street, Kelty KY4 0DU	01383 830442
McCaffery, Joyce (Mrs)	79 Union Street, Cowdenbeath KY4 9SA	ex-directory

25. KIRKCALDY

Biernat, Ian	13 Westpark Avenue, Leslie, Glenrothes KY6 3BX	01592 741487
Mackay, William H.	7 Gifford Court, Glenrothes KY6 1NF	01592 751234
Weatherston, Catriona M.A. (Miss) BSc	'Cruachan', Church Road, Leven KY8 4JB	01333 424636

26. ST ANDREWS

Allan, Angus J.	Craigmore, The Barony, Cupar KY15 5ER	01334 653369
Browning, Margaret (Miss)	4 Wellpark Terrace, Newport-on-Tay DD6 8HT	01382 542140
Elder, Morag (Mrs)	5 Provost Road, Tayport DD6 9JE	01382 552218
King, C.M. (Mrs)	8 Bankwell Road, Anstruther KY10 3DA	01333 310017
Kinnis, W.K.B. (Dr)	4 Dempster Court, St Andrews KY16 9EU	01334 476959
Smith, Elspeth (Mrs)	Whinstead, Dalgairn, Cupar KY15 4PH	01334 653269

27. DUNKELD AND MEIGLE

Carr, Graham	St Helen's, Meigle Road, Alyth PH11 8EU	01828 632474
Davidson, Margaret (Mrs)	9 Woodlands Park, Blairgowrie PH10 6UW	01250 875957
Howat, David	Lilybank Cottage, Newton Street, Blairgowrie PH10 6MZ	01250 874715
Macmartin, Duncan M.	Teallach, Old Crieff Road, Aberfeldy PH15 2DG	01887 820693
Saunders, Grace (Ms)	40 Perth Street, Blairgowrie PH10 6DQ	01250 873981
Templeton, Elizabeth (Mrs)	Tenandry Manse, Killiecrankie, Pitlochry PH16 5LH	01796 472360

28. PERTH

Begg, James	Benholm, 12 Commissioner Street, Crieff PH7 3AY [E-mail: begg1@supanet.com]	01764 655907
Brown, Stanley	14 Buchan Drive, Perth PH1 1NQ	01738 628818
Buchan, James S.	47 Dunkeld Road, Perth PH1 5RP	01738 621814
Chappell, E. (Mrs)	Strathdon, 2 Acharn, Perth PH1 2SR	01738 634640
Coulter, Hamish	95 Cedar Drive, Perth PH1 1RW [E-mail: hamish@coulter9530.freeserve.co.uk]	01738 636761
Hastings, W.P.	5 Craigroyston Road, Scone, Perth PH2 6NB	01738 560498

Johnstone, David	92 Duncansby Way, Perth PH1 5XF	01738 442051
Laing, John	Flat 1, Middle Church, 6 Tay Street, Perth PH1 5LQ	01738 623888
Michie, Margaret (Mrs)	3 Loch Leven Court, Wester Balgedie, Kinross KY13 7NE [E-mail: margaretmichie@balgedie.freeserve.co.uk]	01592 840602
Ogilvie, Brian	67 Whitecraigs, Kinnesswood, Kinross KY13 9TN [E-mail: brianj.ogilvie1@btopenworld.com]	01592 840823
Packer, Joan (Miss)	11 Moredun Terrace, Perth PH2 0DA	01738 623873
Thorburn, Susan (Mrs)	3 Daleally Cottages, St Madoes Road, Errol, Perth PH2 7TJ	01821 642681
Wilkie, Robert	24 Huntingtower Road, Perth PH1 2JS	01738 628301
Yellowlees, Deirdre (Mrs)	Ringmill House, Gannochy Farm, Perth PH2 7JH	01738 633773

29. DUNDEE

Baxter, John T.G.	2 Garten Street, Broughty Ferry, Dundee DD5 3HH	01382 739997
Bell, S. (Dr)	10 Victoria Street, Newport-on-Tay DD6 8DJ	01382 542315
Doig, Andrew	6 Lyndhurst Terrace, Dundee DD2 3HP	01382 610596
Johnston, William (Emeritus)	62 Forthill Road, Broughty Ferry, Dundee DD5 3TJ	01382 739704
Owler, Harry G. (Emeritus)	43 Brownhill Road, Dundee DD2 4LH	01382 622902
Ramsay, Thomas A.	Inchcape Place, Broughty Ferry, Dundee DD5 2LP	01382 778915
Rodgers, Mary (Mrs)	12 Balmerino Road, Dundee DD4 8RN	01382 500291
Shepherd, E.	34 Dalmahoy Drive, Dundee DD2 3UT	01382 815825
Simpson, Webster	51 Wemyss Crescent, Monifieth, Dundee DD5 4RA	01382 535218
Webster, Charles A.	16 Bath Street, Broughty Ferry, Dundee DD5 2BY	01382 739520
Woodley, A.G. (Dr)	67 Marlee Road, Broughty Ferry, Dundee DD5 3EU	01382 739820

30. ANGUS

Anderson, Gordon	33 Grampian View, Ferryden, Montrose DD10 9SU	01674 674915
Beedie, A.W.	62 Newton Crescent, Arbroath DD11 3JZ	01241 875001
Davidson, P.I.	27 Dorward Road, Montrose DD10 8SB	01674 674098
Edwards, Dougal	25 Mackenzie Street, Carnoustie DD7 6HD	01241 852666
Gray, Ian	15 Rossie Island Road, Montrose DD10 9NH	01674 677126
Gray, Linda (Mrs)	8 Inchgarth Street, Forfar DD8 3LY	01307 464039
Ironside, C.T. PhD	21 Tailyour Crescent, Montrose DD10 9BL	01674 673959
Leslie Melville, Ruth (Hon. Mrs)	Little Deuchar, Fern, Forfar DD8 3RA	01356 650279
Nicol, Douglas C.	Edenbank, 16 New Road, Forfar DD8 2AE	01307 463264
Stevens, Peter J. BSc BA	7 Union Street, Montrose DD10 8PZ	01674 673710
Thompson, Anne	22 Braehead Drive, Carnoustie DD7 7SX	01241 852084
Wade, Nan (Mrs)	Lea-Rig, Charleston, Forfar DD8 1UF	01307 840204
Wheat, M.	16A South Esk Street, Montrose DD10 8BJ	01674 676083

31. ABERDEEN

Forrester, Arthur A.	158 Lee Crescent North, Bridge of Don AB22 8FR	01224 822783
Gray, Peter PhD	165 Countesswells Road, Aberdeen AB15 7RA	01224 318172
Sinton, George P. FIMLS	12 North Donside Road, Bridge of Don, Aberdeen AB23 8PA	01224 702273

32. KINCARDINE AND DEESIDE

Bell, Peter D. BA	63 St Nicholas Drive, Banchory AB31 5YE	01330 823661
Cameron, Ann (Mrs)	30 Wilson Road, Banchory AB31 5UY	01330 825953
Grant, Prof. Raymond MA PhD	Ballochbrock, Braemar, Ballater AB35 5YQ	01339 741340
Haddow, Steven	East Manse, Station Road, Banchory AB31 5YP	01330 822481
Harris, Michael	The Gables, Netherley Park, Netherley, Stonehaven AB39 3QM	01569 731091
McCafferty, W. John	East Crossley, Netherley, Stonehaven AB39 3QY	01569 730281
Middleton, Robbie (Capt.)	7 St Ternan's Road, Newtonhill, Stonehaven AB39 2PF	01569 730852
Sedgwick, Sheila (Dr) BA BD MEd PhD	Girnock Shiel, Glengirnock, Ballater AB35 5SS	01339 755292
Woods, Julie (Mrs)	23 St Aidan Crescent, Banchory AB31 5YX	01330 824184

33. GORDON

Findlay, Patricia (Mrs)	Douglas View, Tullynessle, Alford AB33 8QR	01975 562379
Hart, Elsie (Mrs)	The Knoll, Craigearn, Kemnay AB51 9LN	01467 642105
Rennie, Lyall	2 West Balhalgardy Cottages, Inverurie AB51 0HR	01467 624636
Robb, Margaret (Mrs)	Chrislouan, Keithhall, Inverurie AB51 0LN	01651 882310
Robertson, James Y.	1 Nicol Road, Kintore, Inverurie AB51 0QA	01467 633001

34. BUCHAN

Brown, Lillian (Mrs)	Bank House, 45 Main Street, Aberchirder, Huntly AB54 7ST	01466 780330
Davidson, James	19 Great Stuart Street, Peterhead AB42 1JX	01779 470242
Lumsden, Vera (Mrs)	8 Queen's Crescent, Portsoy, Banff AB45 2PX	01261 842712
McColl, John	East Cairnchina, Lonmay, Fraserburgh AB43 8RH	01346 532558
Mair, Dorothy (Miss)	53 Dennyduff Road, Fraserburgh AB43 9LY	01346 513879
Michie, William	34 Seafield Street, Whitehills, Banff AB45 2NR	01261 861439
Noble, John	44 Henderson Park, Peterhead AB42 2WR	01779 472522
Ogston, Norman	Rowandale, 6 Rectory Road, Turriff AB53 4SU	01888 560342
Simpson, Andrew C.	10 Wood Street, Banff AB45 1JX	01261 812538
Smith, Ian M.G. MA	Chomriach, 2 Hill Street, Cruden Bay, Peterhead AB42 0HF	01779 812698
Smith, Jenny (Mrs)	5 Seatown Place, Cairnbulg, Fraserburgh AB43 8WP	01346 582980
Sneddon, Richard	8 School Road, Peterhead AB42 2BE	01779 474492

35. MORAY

Benson, F. Stuart	8 Springfield Court, Forres IV36 3WY	01309 671525
Carson, John	2 Woodside Drive, Forres IV36 2UF	01309 674541
Forbes, Jean (Mrs)	Greenmoss, Drybridge, Buckie AB56 5JB	01542 831646
MacKenzie, Stuart G. MA	Woodend Cottage, Blackburn, Fochabers IV32 7LN	01343 843248
Middleton, Alex	Coral Cottage, Pilmuir Road, Forres IV36 2HU	01309 676912

36. ABERNETHY

Berkeley, John S. (Dr)	Drumbeg, Coylumbridge, Aviemore PH22 1QU	01479 811055

37. INVERNESS

Cook, Arnett D.	128 Laurel Avenue, Inverness IV3 5RS	01463 242586

Maclean, Hamish	63 Ashton Road, Inverness IV2 3UY	01463 239030
Robertson, Hendry	'Park House', 51 Glenurquhart Road, Inverness IV3 5PB	01463 231858

38. LOCHABER

Chalkley, Andrew	2 Telford Place, Claggan, Fort William PH33 6QG [E-mail: andrew.chalkley@btinternet.com]	01397 700271
Dick, Robert	8 Lanark Place, Fort William PH33 6UD	01397 704833
Fraser, John A.	26 Clunes Avenue, Caol, Fort William PH33 7BJ	01397 703467
Maitland, John	St Monance, Ardgour, Fort William PH33 7AA	01855 841267
Thomas, Geoff	Drumcanmach, Station Road, Arisaig PH39 4NJ	01687 450230

39. ROSS

Finlayson, Michael R.	Amberlea, Evanton IV16 9UY	01349 830598
Gilbertson, Ian	Firth View, Craigrory, North Kessock, Inverness IV1 1XH	01463 73538
Galbraith, Hamish	Kinnettas House, Strathpeffer IV14 9AJ	01997 421832
McCredie, Frederick	Highfield Park, Conon Bridge, Inverness IV7 8AP	01349 862171
Robertson, John (Dr)	East Wing, Kincurdie House, Rosemarkie IV10 8SJ	01381 621388
Woodham, Maisey F. (Mrs)	Scardroy, Greenhill, Dingwall IV15 9JQ	01349 862116

40. SUTHERLAND

Betts-Brown, Andrew	54 Muirfield Road, Brora KW9 6QY	01408 621610
Mackay, Donald F.	The Retreat, Lillieshall Street, Helmsdale KW8 6JF	01431 821469
Stobo, Mary (Mrs)	Druim-an-Sgairnich, Lower Gledfield, Ardgay IV24 3BG	01863 766529

41. CAITHNESS

Clarkson, David	22 Ola Drive, Scrabster, Thurso KW14 7VE	01955 611455
Duncan, Esme (Miss)	Avalon, Upper Warse, Canisbay, Wick KW1 4YD	01955 611309
Macnee, Anthea (Mrs)	The Manse, Canisbay, Wick KW1 4YH	

42. LOCHCARRON – SKYE

Mackenzie, Hector	53 Strath, Gairloch IV21 2DB	01445 712433
Macrae, D.E.	Nethania, 52 Strath, Gairloch IV21 2DB	01445 712235
Murray, John W.	Totescore, Kilmuir, Portree, Skye IV51 9YW	01470 522297
Ross, R. Ian	St Conal's, Inverinate, Kyle of Lochalsh IV40 8HB	01599 511371

43. UIST

Lines, Charles	240 Ullswater Road, Southmead, Bristol BS10 6EQ	01779 508978
MacAulay, John	Fernhaven, Flodabay, Isle of Harris HS3 3HA	01859 530340
MacNab, Ann (Mrs)	Druim Skillivat, Scolpaig, Lochmaddy, Isle of North Uist HS6 5DH	01876 510701
MacSween, John	5 Scott Road, Tarbert, Isle of Harris HS3 3DL	01859 502338
Taylor, Hamish	Tigh na Tobair, Flodabay, Isle of Harris HS3 3HA	01859 530310

44. LEWIS

Forsyth, William	1 Berisay Place, Stornoway, Isle of Lewis HS1 2TF	01851 702332

McAlpin, Robert J.G. MA FEIS — 42A Upper Coll, Back, Isle of Lewis HS2 0LS — 01851 820288
Murray, Angus — 4 Ceann Chilleagraidh, Stornoway, Isle of Lewis HS1 2UJ — 01851 703550

45. ORKNEY
Alexander, Malcolm — Copwillo', Button Road, Stenness, Stromness, Orkney KW16 3HA — 01856 850444
Kent, Reginald F. — Greenfield, Stronsay, Orkney KW17 2AG — 01857 616351
Steer, John — Beckington, Hillside Road, Stromness, Orkney KW16 3AH — 01856 850815

46. SHETLAND
Christie, William C. — 11 Fullaburn, Bressay, Shetland ZE2 9ET — 01595 820244
Greig, Diane (Mrs) MA — The Manse, Sandwick, Shetland ZE2 9HW — 01950 431244
Jamieson, Ian MA — Linksview, Ringesta, Quendale, Shetland ZE2 9JD — 01950 460477
Laidlay, Una (Mrs) — 5 Bells Road, Lerwick, Shetland ZE1 0QB — 01595 695147
Macdonald, Michael — 8 Roebrek, Brae, Shetland ZE2 9QY — 01806 522318
MacGregor, Robert — Olna Cottage, Brae, Shetland ZE2 9QS — 01806 522773

47. ENGLAND
Green, Peter (Dr) — Samburu Cottage, Russells Green Road, Ninfield, East Sussex — 01424 892033
Mackay, Donald (Reader Emeritus) — 90 Hallgarth Street, Elvet, Durham DH1 3AS — 0191-383 2110
Munro, William H. — 4 Bryn-Teg, Llanberis, Caernarfon, Gwynedd LL55 4HF
Goodbourne, David (Dr) — 145 Westcombe Hill, Blackheath, London SE3 7DP — 020 8305 0126

48. EUROPE
Ross, David — 9 Cormorant Wharf, Gibraltar — (Tel/Fax) 00350 46780
[E-mail: macross@gibnynex.gi]
Sharp, James — 102 Rue des Eaux-Vives, CH-1207 Geneva, Switzerland — 0041 22 786 48 47
[E-mail: jsharp@world.scout.org]

LIST O – REPRESENTATIVES ON COUNCIL EDUCATION COMMITTEES

COUNCIL	NAME	ADDRESS
ABERDEEN CITY	Mr Ronald Riddell	66 Hammersmith Road, Aberdeen AB10 6ND
ABERDEENSHIRE	Mr William Michie	34 Seafield Street, Whitehills, Banff AB45 2NR
ANGUS	Rev. Allan Webster	7 Braehead Road, Letham, Forfar DD8 2PG
ARGYLL and BUTE	Miss Fiona Fisher	2 Nursery Cottages, Kilmun, Dunoon PA23 8SE
BORDERS	Professor George O.B. Thomson	Rathmore, Springhill Road, Peebles EH45 9ER
CLACKMANNAN	Rev. T. John Brown	The Manse, Tullibody, Alloa FK10 2RG
DUMFRIES and GALLOWAY	Mr Robert McQuistan	Kirkdale Schoolhouse, Carsluith, Newton Stewart DG8 7DT
DUNDEE	Rev. James L. Wilson	53 Old Craigie Road, Dundee DD4 7JD
EAST AYRSHIRE	Rev. John Taylor	62 Woodlands Grove, Kilmarnock KA3 1TZ

EAST DUNBARTONSHIRE	Mrs Barbara Jarvie	18 Cannerton Crescent, Milton of Campsie, Glasgow G66 8DR
EAST LOTHIAN	Rev. Cameron Mackenzie	15 West Road, Haddington EH41 3RD
EAST RENFREWSHIRE	Rev. Maureen Leitch	6 Maxton Avenue, Barrhead, Glasgow G78 1DY
EDINBURGH CITY	Mr A. Craig Duncan	2 East Barnton Gardens, Edinburgh EH4 6AR
EDINBURGH CITY	Rev. W. Armitage	26 Inchview Terrace, Edinburgh EH7 6TQ
FALKIRK	Mrs Margaret Coutts	34 Pirleyhill Gardens, Falkirk FK1 5NB
FIFE	Rev. Alistair McLeod	40 Liberton Drive, Glenrothes KY6 3PB
GLASGOW CITY	Rev. Andrew J. Philip	The Manse, 43 Smithycroft Road, Riddrie, Glasgow G33 2RH
HIGHLAND	Rev. Alexander Glass	Craigton, Tulloch Avenue, Dingwall IV15 9LH
INVERCLYDE	Rev. John Miller	Clunebraehead, Clune Brae, Port Glasgow PA14 5SL
MIDLOTHIAN	Rev. Mrs Jan Gillies	The Manse, Newton Church Road, Danderhall, Dalkeith EH22 1SR
MORAY	Mrs Mary Nelson	Skeoberry, Mosstowie, Elgin IV30 8TX
NORTH AYRSHIRE	Miss Elspeth McTaggart	21 Scargie Road, Kilmarnock KA1 4UR
NORTH LANARKSHIRE	Rev. James Munton	Mamre, 2 Moorcroft Drive, Airdrie ML6 8ES
ORKNEY	Mrs Jenny Deans	Kenmore, Tankerness, Orkney KW17 2QT
PERTH and KINROSS	Mr Alex Dunlop	3 Auchmore Drive, Rosemount, Blairgowrie PH10 6LZ
RENFREWSHIRE	Mr Edward Smith	82 Main Street, Elderslie, Johnstone PA5 9AX
SHETLAND	Rev. Winnie Munson	The Manse, Grindwell, Brae, Shetland ZE2 9QJ
SOUTH AYRSHIRE	Rev. Dr John Lochrie	Manse Road, Colmonell, Girvan KA26 0SA
SOUTH LANARKSHIRE	Mrs Marion Dickie	2 Murchison Drive, East Kilbride, Glasgow G75 8HF
STIRLING	Mr George Bennie	3 Baron Court, Buchlyvie, Stirling FK8 3NJ
WEST DUNBARTONSHIRE	Miss Sheila Rennie	128 Dumbuie Avenue, Dumbarton G82 2JW
WEST LOTHIAN	Rev. John Povey	The Manse, 19 Maryfield Park, Mid Calder, Livingston EH53 0SB
WESTERN ISLES	Rev. Andrew W.F. Coghill	Leurbost, Lochs, Isle of Lewis HS2 9NS

LIST P – RETIRED LAY AGENTS

Forrester, Arthur A.	158 Lee Crescent North, Bridge of Don, Aberdeen AB22 8FR
Lamont, Donald	Staffin House Nursing Home, Portree, Isle of Skye IV51 9JS
Scott, John W.	15 Manor Court, Forfar DD8 1BR
Shepherd, Dennis	Mission House, Norby, Sandness, Shetland ZE2 9PL

LIST Q – MINISTERS ORDAINED FOR SIXTY YEARS AND UPWARDS

Until 1992, the *Year Book* contained each year a list of those ministers who had been ordained 'for fifty years and upwards'. For a number of reasons, that list was thereafter discontinued. In response to a number of requests, last year's volume included a list of those ordained for sixty years and upwards. With ministers, no less than the rest of society, living longer, it was felt reasonable to proceed on that basis. Correspondence has made it clear that this list has been welcomed, and it is continued in an appropriately updated form this year. It has been compiled following the best enquiries that could be made. The date of ordination is given in full where this is known.

1929	26 June	Norman Walker Porteous (Professor of Hebrew and Semitic Languages: Edinburgh University)
1930	4 June	James Clarence Finlayson (Edinburgh: Grange)
		James Ferguson Macdonald (Bendochy with Kinclaven)
1931	18 December	Robert Law Kinnis (Baillieston: Mure Memorial)
1932	14 August	Thomas Mackenzie Donn (Duthil)
1933	1 January	Robert Crawford (Annan: Erskine)
	20 October	The Very Rev. William Roy Sanderson (Stenton with Whittingehame)
	16 November	Edward Rankine Marr (Buittle)
1934	10 July	Walter Macfarlane Calderwood (Leven: Forman)
	31 July	Thomas Roberts Robertson (Broughton, Glenholm and Kilbucho with Skirling)
	3 November	Owain Tudor Hughes (Guernsey: St Andrew's in the Grange)
1935	10 April	George Douglas Monro (Yester)
	30 October	David Stevens (Glenesk)
	6 November	Joseph Blair Gillon (Borthwick with Heriot)
1936	5 April	George Thomas Jamieson (Stirling: Viewfield)
	29 April	Robert Paterson Mackenzie (Dunfermline: St Leonard's)
	13 May	Norman Birnie (Monquhitter)
	12 July	Michael McCulloch Bogle (Banton)
	25 August	Ronald Stewart Wallace (Edinburgh: Lothian Road)
	September	The Very Rev. James Gunn Matheson (Portree)
1937	14 February	Robert Allan Howieson (Newport-on-Tay: St Thomas's)
	31 March	James Brown Mirrilees (Aberdeen: High Hilton)

	14 April	Anthony James Grubb (Deer)
	19 August	Hector Angus Macintosh MacLean (Duror with Glencoe)
	15 October	Robert Anderson Philp (Stepps: St Andrew's)
1938	26 February	John Macgregor MacKechnie (Kilchrenan and Dalavich)
	31 March	David Cecil Henderson (Glamis)
	8 June	Crichton Robertson (Cockpen and Carrington with Lasswade)
	29 June	George Alestair Alison Bennett (Strathkinness)
	1 July	Alexander Thomas Hain Taylor (Dunoon Old and St Cuthbert's)
	28 September	David Nairn McLeish (Fisherton)
	13 October	Robert Hamilton (Kelso Old)
	8 November	Archibald Alexander Orrock (Teacher: Religious Instruction)
	15 November	The Very Rev. James Fraser McLuskey (London St Columba's with Newcastle)
1939	23 February	William Uist Macdonald (Aberdalgie and Dupplin with Forteviot)
	6 April	Charles Armour (St Andrews: Holy Trinity)
	2 June	David Noel Fisher (Glasgow: Sherbrooke St Gilbert's)
	7 June	Murdo Ewen Macdonald (Professor of Practical Theology: Glasgow University)
	28 June	James Hamilton (Auchterhouse)
	7 July	John Welsh Malcolm (Uddingston: Park)
	27 October	James Scott Marshall (Associate Minister: Leith South)
	12 November	David Sloan Walker (Makerstoun with Smailholm with Stichill, Hume and Nenthorn)
	18 November	Wellesley Grahame Bailey (Ladykirk with Whitsome)
	10 December	Alastair McRae Rennie (Kincardine Croick and Edderton)
	22 December	
1940	24 February	James Johnstone Turnbull (Arbirlot with Colliston)
	20 March	The Very Rev. Thomas Forsyth Torrance (Professor of Christian Dogmatics: Edinburgh University)
	22 March	Donald MacKellar Leitch Urie (Kincardine O'Neil)
	24 April	Robert Russell Brown (Perth: Kinnoull)
	25 April	Angus MacDougall (Sleat)
	29 May	Norman McGathan Bowman (Edinburgh: St Mary's)
	23 June	Andrew Montgomery Russell (Aberdeen: Woodside North)
	14 July	Nigel Ross MacLean (Perth: St Paul's)
	21 August	Donald MacFarlane (Inverness: East)
	3 September	Arthur Thomas Hill (Ormiston with Prestonpans: Grange)
	6 September	Peter McPhail (Creich, Flisk and Kilmany)
	29 September	John Hugh Gunn Ross (Dundurn)

1941	
18 December	Colin Campbell (Glasgow: Williamwood)
26 January	Samuel Ballantyne (Aberdeen: Rutherford)
29 May	Harry Galbraith Miller (Iona and Ross of Mull)
1 June	The Very Rev. John McIntyre (Professor of Divinity: Edinburgh University)
1 June	Robert Bernard William Walker (Lesmahagow: Abbeygreen)
6 June	Thomas Williamson (Dyke with Edinkillie)
3 July	Donald William MacKenzie (Auchterarder: The Barony)
20 July	Allan Donald Lamont (Nakuru)
21 September	Silvester Skinner (Lumphanan)
21 September	Andrew Swan (Greenock: St Margaret's)
31 October	Gordon Cumming Morris (Buenos Aires)
9 December	John Nelson (Crawford and Elvanfoot with Leadhills and Wanlockhead)
1942	
2 January	James Gilbert Morrison (Rotterdam)
4 February	Robert Macbean Gilmour (Kiltarlity)
15 April	Frank Haughton (Kirkintilloch: St Mary's)
5 July	Norman Christopher MacRae (Loanhead)
26 August	Arthur William Bruce (Fortingall and Glenlyon)
3 September	James Robert Moffett (Paisley: St Matthew's)
27 October	George Ramsay Rattray MacKenzie (Dundee: Logie and St John's Cross)
19 November	Donald Angus MacRae (Tarbert)
22 November	Robert Gray (Stonehaven: Fetteresso)
23 November	Frederick Haslehurst Fulton (Clunie, Lethendy and Kinloch)
25 November	Charles Ian Graham Stobie (Fyvie)
24 December	James Bews (Dundee: Craigiebank)

LIST R – DECEASED MINISTERS

The Editor has been made aware of the following ministers who have died since the publication of the previous volume of the *Year Book*.

Adamson, Tom Sidney Senior	(Musselburgh: St Michael's Inveresk)
Anderson, Duncan Wilson McIntosh	(Glasgow: New Cathcart)
Anderson, Hugh	(University of Edinburgh)
Anderson, Kenneth Mackenzie	(Glasgow: Hillington Park)
Archibald, David Yule	(Cairneyhill with Torryburn and Newmills)
Boath, Gibson Kennedy	(Kilmarnock: Howard St Andrew's)

Brown, William Hay (Peterhead: St Andrew's)
Campbell, Patrick Douglas Gordon (Geneva)
Chapman, Ernest Aberdeen: Middlefield
Chisholm, William Douglas (Monifieth North and Newbigging with Monikie)
Day, Colin Traquain (Warden: Carberry Tower)
Elliot, George Lamb (Board of Stewardship and Finance)
Fairweather, Ian Coutts Macintyre (Jordanhill College of Education)
Fenton, Robert James (Glasgow: St Kiaran's Dean Park)
Hardy, Basil Gathorne (Dundee: Meadowside St Paul's)
Herron, Andrew (Glasgow Presbytery Clerk)
Hollins, Roger Mansel (Lecturer in Religious Education)
Hunter, George (Glasgow: Scotstoun West)
Hunter, George Lindsay (Teacher: Religious Education)
Kirkwood, Hugh (Saltcoats Erskine)
Lane, Christina Macfarlan (Ms) (Irvine: Girdle Toll)
Learmonth, Adam James (Airdrie: Wellwynd)
Macarthur, John Murdo Macleod (Glasgow: St Columba)
Macfarlane, William James Edwin (Alexandria: St Andrew's)
McIntosh, Hamish (Auchterarder: St Andrew's and West)
Mackay, Murdoch Macbeth (Hospital Chaplain)
McKenzie, Morris Glyndwr (South Ronaldsay and Burray)
McLean, John (Glasgow: St Andrew's Plantation)
MacLennan, William (Lochbroom and Ullapool)
Macmillan, William Boyd Robertson (Dundee: St Mary's)
O'Neill, John Cochrane (University of Edinburgh)
Porteous, Alexander (Greenock: Mid Kirk)
Robertson, Bruce (Paris)
Robertson, George Booth (Irvine: Mure)
Rutherford, Brian Craig Aberdeen: Mastrick
Scott, John Leonard (Inverurie West)
Steel, David (Linlithgow: St Michael's)
Stirling, James (Stirling: St Ninian's Old)
Sutherland, Ian Douglas Grant (Aberdeen: Causewayend)
Thomson, John Steven (Covington and Thankerton with Libberton and Quothquan)
Wood, Charles Richard (Kilcalmonell with Skipness)

SECTION 7

Congregational
Statistics
2002

CHURCH OF SCOTLAND STATISTICS
FOR 2002

Congregations 1,546
Communicants 571,698
Elders 42,992
Charges 1,237
Ministers serving charges 1,061
Chaplains to HM Forces 33
Students completing their courses 17

NOTES ON CONGREGATIONAL STATISTICS

Com   Number of communicants at 31 December 2002.

Eld   Number of elders at 31 December 2002.

G   Membership of the Guild including Young Woman's Group. The letter 'j' beside a figure indicates that the figure is a joint figure for all the congregations making up the charge.

In 02   Ordinary General Income for 2002. Ordinary General Income consists of members' offerings, contributions from congregational organisations, regular fund-raising events, income from investments, deposits and so on. This figure does not include extraordinary or special income, or income from special collections and fund-raising for other charities.

Ass   Amount allocated to congregations for the Mission and Aid Fund in 2002.

Gvn   Amount contributed by congregations to the Mission and Aid Fund in 2002. The amount shown includes contributions to allocation and voluntary extra contributions. The figures do not take into account late payments made in 2003 for 2002 but may contain late payments made in 2002 for 2001 and prior years.

–18   This new figure shows 'the number of children and young people aged 17 years and under who are involved in the life of the congregation'.

(NB Figures may not be available for new charges created or for congregations which have entered into readjustment late in 2002 or during 2003.)

Congregation	Com	Eld	G	In 02	Ass	Gvn	–18
1. Edinburgh							
Dalmeny	139	9	10	12150	600	600	–
Albany Deaf Church of Edinburgh	136	12	–	866	–	–	–
Balerno	849	66	53	110573	26000	28409	60
Barclay	366	43	–	97512	17580	18118	61
Blackhall St Columba	1131	91	50	147238	45790	45790	94
Bristo Memorial Craigmillar	194	7	25	22555	–	–	43
Broughton St Mary's	315	34	35	46495	8180	8180	104
Canongate	458	43	–	51692	13370	13370	20
Carrick Knowe	662	43	92	60907	11550	11739	40
Cluny	573	68	23	101289	23500	23500	55
Colinton	1142	87	–	180195	38860	39722	236
Colinton Mains	249	17	24	40147	3280	3508	33
Corstorphine Craigsbank	685	30	–	98015	21820	24036	94
Corstorphine Old	684	59	58	78113	16990	16990	45
Corstorphine St Anne's	510	49	48	71145	15780	16780	50
Corstorphine St Ninian's	1111	86	65	156509	37990	37990	100
Craigentinny St Christopher's	182	16	–	32360	–	–	80
Craiglockhart	601	58	45	116710	28110	28110	80
Craigmillar Park	322	26	36	83158	18490	18490	46
Cramond	1352	111	24	186743	47000	47000	50
Currie	1366	66	94	145176	39460	39460	185
Davidson's Mains	848	69	62	139954	38910	38910	150
Dean	249	26	21	57888	11540	11540	20
Drylaw	240	17	–	20678	–	–	–
Duddingston	860	61	46	82877	16170	16170	167
Fairmilehead	1046	77	35	96712	22310	22610	129
Gilmerton	–	–	–	–	–	–	–
Gorgie	359	42	–	73826	12890	13090	60
Granton	381	35	–	40010	4560	4560	30
Greenbank	1002	95	95	178027	53300	63300	153
Greenside	260	21	–	36054	8880	8880	10
Greyfriars Tolbooth and Highland	409	45	19	84133	20400	20400	7
High (St Giles')	696	48	–	158395	37610	36061	–
Holyrood Abbey	276	34	25	150529	35640	35640	178
Holy Trinity	172	24	–	63841	6000	7000	58
Inverleith	396	44	–	69740	16240	16699	21
Juniper Green	443	32	–	80350	17960	17960	32
Kaimes Lockhart Memorial	100	9	10	14887	–	–	20
Kirkliston	374	41	47	48930	5990	5990	–
Kirk o' Field	243	30	–	35355	7190	7190	7
Leith North	508	50	–	68966	13950	13950	50
Leith St Andrew's	329	33	–	52967	7610	7610	174
Leith St Serf's	325	33	24	44292	7240	7240	185
Leith St Thomas' Junction Road	311	26	–	46907	6860	7050	7
Leith South	660	84	–	97399	26680	26680	32
Leith Wardie	616	76	71	107048	25750	25750	150

Congregation. . . . . Com	Eld	G	In 02	Ass	Gvn	–18
Liberton 920	77	87	125267	24000	24000	91
Liberton Northfield. 294	10	30	46588	–	1247	35
London Road 417	34	29	52682	7750	7750	82
Marchmont St Giles' 349	41	36	66768	15000	15000	46
Mayfield Salisbury 808	74	35	182494	53930	54930	45
Morningside Braid 301	49	23	42183	7210	8006	6
Morningside United 221	28	–	56866	6305	6305	31
Muirhouse St Andrew's 129	9	–	7552	–	–	49
Murrayfield 603	61	9	119392	32670	32670	60
Newhaven. 280	18	49	63777	11390	11390	79
New Restalrig. 371	14	30	105496	16480	16480	41
Old Kirk. 201	14	–	18248	–	233	–
Palmerston Place 528	75	–	136878	38910	38910	65
Pilrig St Paul's 390	32	37	51781	1250	1250	14
Polwarth. 370	38	20	64070	12812	12812	60
Portobello Old 424	62	39	59988	7520	7520	100
Portobello St James'. 422	40	–	51153	8000	8086	37
Portobello St Philip's Joppa 734	64	99	126411	26770	38370	82
Priestfield. 255	25	31	58651	7870	8382	30
Queensferry 838	58	81	71199	11480	11480	150
Ratho 253	23	21	34210	–	180	28
Reid Memorial 457	25	–	78601	19750	20120	30
Richmond Craigmillar 124	8	7	14666	–	–	5
St Andrew's and St George's. 400	50	25	142784	36140	36140	40
St Andrew's Clermiston 354	25	–	37183	–	235	32
St Catherine's Argyle 315	28	27	116634	27990	27990	59
St Colm's 199	22	32	32327	3030	3030	25
St Cuthbert's. 555	66	–	157653	43100	43100	37
St David's Broomhouse 201	17	–	45299	5250	5250	27
St George's West 201	43	–	82757	24660	24660	26
St John's Oxgangs 337	25	34	25819	–	744	15
St Margaret's 466	45	27	48017	7790	7790	25
St Martin's 265	14	–	15971	–	–	25
St Michael's 526	33	–	64489	12180	12180	35
St Nicholas' Sighthill 589	37	21	52240	7570	7773	40
St Stephen's Comely Bank 528	25	44	106654	23920	23920	150
Slateford Longstone 337	27	52	48220	8560	15960	32
Stenhouse St Aidan's 259	20	–	27066	–	154	30
Stockbridge 389	42	35	42209	7660	7660	8
Tron Moredun 158	15	–	–	–	–	12
Viewforth. 252	31	17	50565	11870	11870	28

2. West Lothian

Abercorn 88	9	12	10072	650	650	–
Pardovan, Kingscavil and Winchburgh . . . 316	24	21			–	21
Armadale 708	45	32	59937	10410	10410	184
Avonbridge. 89	10	10	11333	400	–	10
Torphichen 292	21	–	36599	3090	–	56

Congregation.	Com	Eld	G	In 02	Ass	Gvn	–18
Bathgate Boghall	303	39	25	59951	10000	10000	108
Bathgate High.	646	41	42	60762	12260	12260	100
Bathgate St David's	307	15	17	53081	6980	11970	18
Bathgate St John's	400	25	35	54546	6760	6760	122
Blackburn and Seafield.	560	34	–	52421	5670	5670	110
Blackridge	119	6	12	14059	1790	1790	16
Harthill – St Andrew's	269	21	38	51436	6570	6851	115
Breich Valley	237	11	18	27407	–	–	6
Broxburn	551	29	44	58367	7340	7340	120
Fauldhouse St Andrew's	297	20	20	37522	4270	4270	–
Kirknewton and East Calder	555	36	27	82568	11650	12150	106
Kirk of Calder	747	44	32	62625	12910	9037	95
Linlithgow St Michael's	1566	110	64	222655	51625	53743	344
Linlithgow St Ninian's Craigmailen	637	64	79	62230	10470	10745	136
Livingston Ecumenical.	–	–	–	–	–	–	489
Livingston Old	506	36	30	62768	9690	9690	116
Polbeth Harwood	287	36	–	31402	–	809	5
West Kirk of Calder	357	30	42	38454	6460	7060	31
Strathbrock.	381	42	25	69719	16930	16930	93
Uphall South	238	18	–	39430	–	–	4
Whitburn – Brucefield	471	23	28	57816	9690	9690	192
Whitburn – South	401	32	38	54026	11280	11280	37

3. Lothian

Aberlady.	322	33	–	24774	6150	6150	15
Gullane.	491	36	50	49963	9270	9270	54
Athelstaneford	218	18	15	18934	2600	1600	18
Whitekirk and Tyninghame.	169	18	–	20678	5780	5780	20
Belhaven.	783	32	66	54521	10070	10120	125
Spott.	107	7	–	10810	1110	1110	12
Bolton and Saltoun	218	16	18	23335	3830	3830	17
Humbie	95	7	12	12319	3190	3190	14
Yester.	324	25	26	24202	3040	3040	15
Bonnyrigg.	883	73	74	77106	15900	16376	59
Borthwick.	90	5	13	10505	–	1800	10
Newtongrange	266	9	19	25066	–	–	10
Cockenzie & Port Seton Chalmers M'rl	313	31	60	60098	8350	8350	40
Cockenzie and Port Seton Old	441	12	21	23493	–	2000	14
Cockpen and Carrington.	362	25	37	20219	2440	2520	15
Lasswade	361	24	22	20191	3430	3430	18
Rosewell.	212	11	–	11408	1720	1500	10
Cranstoun, Crichton and Ford	285	16	–	37963	4410	7528	34
Fala and Soutra.	82	6	12	7114	1406	1406	4
Dalkeith St John's and King's Park	588	47	26	69996	13220	13220	50
Dalkeith St Nicholas Buccleuch	586	20	27	43116	8130	8130	9
Dirleton	273	20	19	28379	5090	5090	15
North Berwick Abbey.	339	29	54	80824	12080	12093	39
Dunbar.	879	33	51	64113	9230	9230	50

Congregation. . . . . Com	Eld	G	In 02	Ass	Gvn	–18
Dunglass. 366	22	20	30182	–	300	3
Garvald and Morham 49	9	–	9079	1710	1710	30
Haddington West 509	36	54	60018	9430	9430	80
Gladsmuir. 238	12	15	20190	2730	2730	–
Longniddry. 466	38	61	67334	16300	17523	64
Glencorse 368	11	–	29699	4300	4300	25
Roslin. 405	15	–	27396	2860	2860	1
Gorebridge 499	21	48	51331	3990	3990	40
Haddington St Mary's. 808	64	–	90008	23000	23000	35
Howgate. 44	5	8	13473	2000	2000	2
Penicuik South 283	23	–	92240	18980	24830	75
Loanhead 452	27	45	47809	3710	3828	40
Musselburgh Northesk 488	38	15	58771	9590	9590	90
Musselburgh St Andrew's High. 480	41	32	52888	5790	6561	14
Musselburgh St Clement's & St Ninian's . 393	45	9	28021	–	–	30
Musselburgh St Michael's Inveresk. 550	32	32	60084	9030	9030	47
Newbattle. 560	40	26	45330	4950	4950	37
Newton. 309	12	19	15114	–	–	–
North Berwick St Andrew Blackadder . . . 785	62	31	85390	16890	16890	103
Ormiston 188	14	31	24953	3560	3891	–
Pencaitland. 271	15	13	42924	8530	8530	45
Penicuik North 648	41	–	73157	12460	13260	48
Penicuik St Mungo's. 528	25	27	39121	8360	203	25
Prestonpans: Prestongrange 421	60	28	37896	4840	4840	24
Tranent. 402	18	36	46621	5290	5290	14
Traprain 576	37	35	49020	10620	10620	5

4. Melrose and Peebles

Ashkirk 78	4	11	5999	1440	1440	8
Selkirk 641	29	37	55775	9500	9755	25
Bowden 103	14	9	18283	2530	2530	–
Newtown 214	14	–	14791	3170	3170	–
Broughton, Glenholm and Kilbucho 171	15	29j	11173	–	960	–
Skirling 89	8	j	7941	–	360	9
Stobo and Drumelzier. 112	6	j	9672	–	720	–
Tweedsmuir 47	7	j	3895	–	360	11
Caddonfoot. 216	16	–	11368	1470	1530	18
Galashiels St Ninian's. 586	47	46	47564	9450	8692	16
Carlops. 73	12	–	11819	1470	1470	10
Kirkurd and Newlands 115	8	10	12836	1920	1920	31
West Linton St Andrew's 262	17	36	28609	5018	5150	35
Channelkirk 85	6	7	6678	810	810	12
Lauder Old. 352	17	20	32496	2490	2490	21
Earlston 588	18	19	34221	3680	3680	20
Eddleston 120	7	12	8248	660	760	23
Peebles Old 716	45	–	71287	12960	12960	163
Ettrick and Yarrow 213	16	8	21946	–	200	–
Galashiels Old and St Paul's. 437	27	36	51765	7350	7600	44

Congregation. . . . . Com	Eld	G	In 02	Ass	Gvn	–18
Galashiels St Aidan's 499	25	25	38518	4700	4700	70
Galashiels St John's 274	18	–	32901	–	–	15
Innerleithen, Traquair and Walkerburn . . . 649	40	67	58171	9900	9900	20
Lyne and Manor 111	9	–	17166	160	160	56
Maxton and Mertoun 156	16	15	16100	3060	3060	10
St Boswells. 347	24	25	33870	4570	4570	45
Melrose 907	56	45	90722	15480	16039	50
Peebles: St Andrew's Leckie 730	40	–	72562	14010	14943	51
Stow St Mary of Wedale and Heriot 205	16	–	26910	–	800	35

5. Duns

Ayton and Burnmouth. 217	13	–	13950	–	–	4
Grantshouse and Houndwood and Reston . 144	5	14	9655	–	–	–
Berwick on Tweed: St Andrew's Wallace Green & Lowick 521	28	40	49964	2918	2239	15
Bonkyl and Preston 92	7	–	4289	980	1041	–
Chirnside 428	22	–	19072	2200	2200	25
Edrom Allanton 87	9	–	4932	640	640	–
Coldingham and St Abb's 117	6	15	13712	1527	1527	16
Eyemouth 289	25	61	33059	4770	4930	50
Coldstream 442	27	24	35147	3770	3831	70
Eccles. 111	10	19	3768	870	921	5
Duns. 576	26	52	41903	2862	2862	35
Fogo and Swinton. 143	5	–	9850	1110	1110	–
Ladykirk. 38	7	12	6686	1120	1120	–
Leitholm. 111	9	–	10461	1440	1440	1
Whitsome. 50	4	11	3498	465	465	–
Foulden and Mordington 95	11	12	7848	–	–	–
Hutton and Fishwick and Paxton. 110	10	13	10797	–	–	–
Gordon St Michael's. 77	6	13j	7209	790	1840	9
Greenlaw 162	12	20	17662	2790	2790	13
Legerwood 69	8	–	6009	537	537	3
Westruther 59	6	j	5830	650	650	6
Kirk of Lammermuir 67	9	–	13401	–	–	6
Langton and Polwarth. 92	8	21	13551	–	–	7

6. Jedburgh

Ancrum 221	16	17	16807	350	905	16
Crailing and Eckford 113	11	–	5520	300	300	–
Lilliesleaf 164	10	11	12592	350	350	10
Bedrule. 38	4	28j	4955	350	350	6
Denholm. 206	14	j	16610	350	350	–
Minto 93	7	j	8047	350	350	5
Cavers and Kirkton. 158	11	–	9930	976	976	20
Hawick St Mary's and Old 674	33	50	45345	7230	7230	131
Hawick Burnfoot 226	15	12	26290	–	–	79
Hawick Teviot and Roberton. 395	13	9	44587	5740	6005	24
Hawick Trinity 924	32	57	50433	8420	9176	103

Congregation. . . . . Com	Eld	G	In 02	Ass	Gvn	–18
Hawick Wilton 453	26	36	35219	2133	2276	85
Teviothead 82	4	8	5480	1270	1270	–
Hobkirk and Southdean 187	13	10	8034	840	756	20
Jedburgh Old and Edgerston 788	25	20	45422	8700	7250	30
Jedburgh Trinity 267	12	32	38821	4410	4832	23
Kelso North and Ednam 1544	75	69	103517	20390	20390	40
Kelso Old and Sprouston 680	42	41	48747	6840	7463	13
Linton. 88	5	–	6579	860	860	6
Morebattle and Hownam. 215	12	34	19184	2140	2140	22
Yetholm 215	11	16	19652	2630	2899	10
Makerstoun and Smailholm 77	5	–	6627	–	–	10
Roxburgh 67	6	–	6214	–	–	2
Stichill, Hume and Nenthorn 86	7	13	8683	–	–	4
Oxnam 101	6	–	6333	583	583	–

7. Annandale and Eskdale

Annan Old 460	40	51	57155	11270	12170	65
Annan St Andrew's. 828	36	88	58774	7310	9053	119
Applegarth and Sibbaldbie 184	8	19	9884	940	940	–
Lochmaben. 565	23	48	38272	4460	5610	12
Brydekirk. 71	7	–	5876	–	–	–
Hoddam 162	8	–	10605	–	–	–
Canonbie 188	13	–	17996	160	160	11
Liddesdale 167	8	16	36762	350	560	39
Carlisle. 392	38	49	54164	9990	9990	28
Longtown. 47	8	18	4104	540	540	–
Dalton 128	8	8	16473	1450	1450	12
Hightae. 103	6	18	11103	878	878	25
St Mungo 146	8	13	12470	945	945	10
Dornock 201	13	–	12478	–	–	29
Eskdalemuir 36	2	–	3132	–	65	–
Hutton and Corrie. 83	6	–	9333	–	70	–
Tundergarth 78	8	8	6134	–	95	–
Gretna Old, St Andrew's & Half Morton						
& Kirkpatrick Fleming 427	32	26	30944	1260	1420	84
Johnstone 131	7	–	5326	160	160	–
Kirkpatrick Juxta 157	8	–	8365	300	200	10
Kirtle – Eaglesfield. 130	10	21	15627	663	–	–
Middlebie. 108	9	17	4648	160	–	6
Waterbeck 74	6	–	6212	160	336	–
Langholm, Ewes and Westerkirk. 584	33	65	35778	5230	7263	41
Lockerbie Dryfesdale 941	45	54	46784	4570	4570	41
Moffat St Andrew's. 530	42	39	64767	8520	8520	49
Wamphray 60	7	–	6692	1110	1110	–

8. Dumfries and Kirkcudbright

Anwoth and Girthon 418	24	25	40730	10210	10210	10
Borgue 64	6	9	3774	200	200	–

Congregation	Com	Eld	G	In 02	Ass	Gvn	−18
Auchencairn and Rerrick	148	12	20	10192	1390	1668	6
Buittle and Kelton	239	21	24	22643	1880	1880	7
Balmaclellan and Kells	161	13	17	13323	–	–	9
Carsphairn	112	9	10	7533	–	600	14
Dalry	193	12	26	10441	–	–	12
Balmaghie	163	6	12	11407	1240	1116	6
Tarff and Twynholm	209	17	39	26095	3670	3670	14
Caerlaverock	177	8	–	7146	–	200	14
Castle Douglas	609	32	65	57439	3650	3650	40
Closeburn	275	12	–	18506	1658	1658	–
Durisdeer	180	7	28	24624	1650	1650	–
Colvend, Southwick and Kirkbean	392	28	40	45753	10738	10738	12
Corsock and Kirkpatrick Durham	220	18	27	18698	1560	1560	39
Crossmichael and Parton	202	14	15	21003	2790	2790	22
Cummertrees	64	5	8	4393	500	416	–
Mouswald	94	7	18	8861	420	560	–
Ruthwell	108	9	17	10246	1040	1040	16
Dalbeattie	701	44	54j	40936	8060	9513	70
Urr	236	15	j	14568	1990	2299	30
Dumfries Greyfriars	438	22	26	51846	11450	11450	5
Dumfries Lincluden	145	12	–	11944	650	1715	35
Holywood	189	12	–	19319	500	500	10
Dumfries Lochside	412	16	30	26343	–	–	16
Dumfries Maxwelltown West	765	49	55	57764	10820	10820	129
Dumfries St George's	550	49	49	70624	11240	11240	120
Dumfries St Mary's	798	49	43	49082	8480	8480	11
Dumfries St Michael's and South	968	52	40	69609	8060	8060	60
Dumfries Troqueer	471	31	25	66475	9230	9230	60
Dunscore	259	18	10	27452	2990	2990	15
Glencairn and Moniaive	227	13	–	22432	2450	2543	6
Irongray, Lochrutton and Terregles	540	34	21	28591	2870	2870	–
Kirkconnel	386	11	17	47252	5260	5260	8
Kirkcudbright	772	49	–	64980	12090	12090	10
Kirkgunzeon	63	11	–	6974	–	–	–
Kirkmahoe	420	19	34	28506	890	890	35
Kirkmichael and Tinwald and Torthorwald	608	37	35	45238	6620	6620	43
Lochend	58	4	8	3112	–	–	–
New Abbey	231	13	10	23225	–	–	8
Penpont Keir and Tynron	199	12	–	17119	200	200	11
Sanquhar St Bride's	541	25	46	39339	5270	5270	55
Thornhill	324	13	23	22725	900	900	–

9. Wigtown and Stranraer

Congregation	Com	Eld	G	In 02	Ass	Gvn	−18
Ervie Kirkcolm	263	22	–	16965	1538	1538	30
Leswalt	315	13	23	20606	2630	1500	15
Glasserton and Isle of Whithorn	141	9	–	11799	1710	1761	4
Whithorn St Ninian's Priory	328	11	20	22630	2500	2753	52

Congregation	Com	Eld	G	In 02	Ass	Gvn	–18
Inch	275	22	13	9795	1920	1152	9
Stranraer St Andrew's	503	30	–	37058	6130	6130	92
Kirkcowan	216	11	14	24075	2380	2380	16
Wigtown	281	14	17	31302	4440	4440	25
Kirkinner	177	7	14	13552	–	–	18
Sorbie	180	9	11	15632	–	–	–
Kirkmabreck	198	12	23	15110	2200	2355	9
Monigaff	460	30	19	32190	5190	5401	42
Kirkmaiden	246	19	24	21066	3550	3663	45
Stoneykirk	410	25	15	27376	3210	3210	44
Mochrum	311	22	48	27255	–	–	34
New Luce	115	10	44j	9362	1840	1840	16
Old Luce	335	23	j	35828	4920	4920	33
Penninghame	653	49	29	62050	13690	13690	20
Portpatrick	271	12	30	16627	2440	2561	16
Stranraer St Ninian's	520	26	27	40425	7530	7530	51
Stranraer High Kirk	644	33	25	50077	6930	6930	90
Stranraer Old	364	24	35	39662	6630	6630	6

10. Ayr

Congregation	Com	Eld	G	In 02	Ass	Gvn	–18
Alloway	1432	97	46	160714	46300	47500	–
Annbank	312	16	23	26203	3000	3222	19
Arnsheen Barrhill	110	4	14	8098	–	–	1
Colmonell	219	15	–	16665	–	300	3
Auchinleck	411	26	39	36220	5745	5745	–
Ayr Auld Kirk of Ayr (St John the Baptist)	726	61	56	77834	22910	22910	32
Ayr Castlehill	871	53	80	74912	16320	16320	105
Ayr Newton on Ayr	468	45	48	81978	16490	17082	98
Ayr St Andrew's	627	67	28	77032	15880	16910	140
Ayr St Columba	1807	122	66	163690	40740	40740	155
Ayr St James'	553	36	48	54781	8190	8190	146
Ayr St Leonard's	660	57	43	73209	14900	14900	37
Ayr St Quivox	415	30	21	41025	6000	6000	–
Ayr Wallacetown	416	25	42	43555	7380	7853	17
Ballantrae	299	21	37	35757	2830	2830	32
Barr	79	6	13	5416	225	225	–
Dailly	193	15	19	13228	225	225	24
Girvan South	350	22	37	33349	1600	3762	21
Catrine	186	20	32	24079	2538	2538	–
Sorn	191	15	23	22982	2640	2790	26
Coylton	370	20	–	21274	–	–	126
Drongan The Schaw Kirk	297	21	17	17423	–	–	110
Craigie	126	6	–	9134	1718	1718	23
Symington	400	22	26	46855	11171	11171	30
Crosshill	194	12	28	15160	840	840	11
Dalrymple	367	17	–	21967	2140	2140	–
Dalmellington	363	25	88	44909	2830	2830	107

Congregation. Com	Eld	G	In 02	Ass	Gvn	–18
Dundonald 607	53	65	60358	8610	10122	38
Fisherton 167	12	13	11071	–	–	–
Maybole West. 284	14	22	21396	–	–	–
Girvan North (Old and St Andrew's). . . . 1116	74	48	67688	13990	14294	–
Kirkmichael 241	17	20	20538	–	2000	9
Straiton St Cuthbert's 170	11	14	11998	–	100	16
Kirkoswald. 282	20	14	39431	2370	2370	7
Lugar 184	7	19	13215	2100	2100	8
Old Cumnock Old 434	19	50	45180	9390	9390	84
Mauchline 610	25	75	63249	12480	12480	85
Maybole Old 426	23	28	39185	5260	5405	12
Monkton and Prestwick North 586	49	61	80531	11450	11450	129
Muirkirk. 261	19	27	19273	–	–	6
New Cumnock 622	43	54	48344	5700	5855	62
Ochiltree. 290	20	21	20906	3270	3270	18
Stair 225	14	27	22807	4420	4670	51
Old Cumnock Crichton West						
and St Ninian's 449	33	59	36544	4930	4930	42
Patna Waterside 159	12	18	15511	–	–	15
Prestwick Kingcase. 1151	104	57	95642	18060	18060	320
Prestwick St Nicholas' 868	72	60	92869	19140	19340	–
Prestwick South 432	39	73	66101	14200	14200	100
Tarbolton 579	36	31	36355	6760	6997	20
Troon Old. 1285	82	–	132588	32050	32181	80
Troon Portland 798	52	51	99120	21000	21000	57
Troon St Meddan's 1190	129	87	148147	30540	30539	85

11. Irvine and Kilmarnock

Congregation	Eld	G	In 02	Ass	Gvn	–18
Crosshouse. 380	31	31	48727	1421	1421	45
Darvel 643	33	49	39196	5170	5170	22
Dreghorn and Springside 692	60	37	63590	16420	16420	60
Dunlop. 444	40	40	51221	9090	9390	38
Fenwick 447	28	44	49704	8100	8100	30
Galston. 826	62	88	104066	15820	16120	160
Hurlford 618	27	40	62459	4160	4160	25
Irvine Fullarton. 535	37	40	91615	17620	18020	150
Irvine Girdle Toll 223	21	30	34663	–	–	190
Irvine Mure 468	28	34	69860	12590	12590	30
Irvine Old. 596	41	32	84685	20410	20410	26
Irvine Relief 416	36	34	42604	2031	2031	110
Irvine St Andrew's 496	26	57	56549	4730	4577	224
Kilmarnock Grange 478	32	50	61441	10360	10360	42
Kilmarnock Henderson. 819	78	65	111479	19060	19180	50
Kilmarnock Howard St Andrew's 477	44	45	64942	13210	13210	5
Kilmarnock Laigh West High 974	62	60	–	33250	33250	213
Kilmarnock Old High Kirk 327	18	20	44213	4570	4570	28
Kilmarnock Riccarton. 392	35	30	65727	8560	8560	161
Kilmarnock St Andrew's Glencairn. 190	–	14	–	–	–	–

Congregation. . . . . Com	Eld	G	In 02	Ass	Gvn	–18
Kilmarnock St John's Onthank 310	24	30	37419	3950	3950	120
Kilmarnock St Kentigern's 291	29	–	50221	4930	4930	160
Kilmarnock St Marnock's. 755	77	–	103405	14820	14820	31
Kilmarnock St Ninian's Bellfield 236	21	20	28033	1452	1452	12
Kilmarnock Shortlees 136	14	25	28170	1970	1970	50
Kilmaurs St Maur's Glencairn 384	23	25	50401	7530	7530	30
Newmilns Loudoun 432	14	–	75090	9760	9760	25
Stewarton John Knox 407	38	25	66454	12840	12840	125
Stewarton St Columba's 568	42	75	65381	11200	12067	48

12. Ardrossan

Ardrossan Barony St John's 368	20	42	43234	6130	6130	25
Ardrossan Park 509	37	45	56902	6560	6910	65
Beith High 989	87	46	60101	13750	14198	71
Beith Trinity 259	36	57	43593	7420	7420	–
Brodick. 219	21	–	34882	–	1095	15
Corrie. 64	8	–	13347	–	207	–
Cumbrae. 355	25	53	35341	–	400	16
Dalry St Margaret's. 1101	60	50	94937	21150	22077	110
Dalry Trinity. 341	21	37	72219	14950	14950	18
Fairlie. 285	29	48	53630	6730	6961	23
Fergushill 52	5	–	6135	–	–	10
Kilwinning Erskine. 130	14	19	29664	–	2100	10
Kilbirnie Auld Kirk. 547	38	30	42601	3660	3660	25
Kilbirnie St Columba's 637	37	32	43957	6650	8350	26
Kilmory 41	4	–	6731	–	100	7
Lamlash 152	13	40	20368	–	–	14
Kilwinning Abbey. 922	62	55	75130	16640	16640	25
Kilwinning Mansefield Trinity 235	16	33	32756	–	300	–
Largs Clark Memorial. 1027	94	65	94027	22620	22620	80
Largs St Columba's 651	55	65	62348	13160	13160	61
Largs St John's 910	51	72	111475	23440	28240	79
Lochranza and Pirnmill. 75	7	30	11882	–	–	8
Shiskine 67	4	12	17926	–	–	8
Saltcoats New Trinity 398	49	35	54070	7670	7670	25
Saltcoats North 417	23	25	39441	5410	5410	42
Saltcoats St Cuthbert's 549	55	41	78452	17410	17811	95
Stevenston Ardeer. 368	24	35	39747	5780	3600	102
Stevenston High 275	31	52	54669	11060	11060	25
Stevenston Livingstone 405	34	35	39281	6480	7266	22
West Kilbride Overton 380	33	28	49371	7430	7431	25
West Kilbride St Andrew's 735	51	42	85106	16100	16100	80
Whiting Bay and Kildonan 134	12	–	35287	–	1334	15

13. Lanark

Biggar 731	46	77	59398	14830	14830	28
Black Mount. 111	7	14	10103	–	29	2
Culter 99	7	–	12397	–	–	–

Congregation. . . . . Com	Eld	G	In 02	Ass	Gvn	–18
Libberton and Quothquan 90	9	–	8483	–	300	6
Cairngryffe 292	20	22	22033	3660	3660	16
Symington 268	18	23	23950	4860	4860	23
Carluke Kirkton 846	52	28	85766	18960	18960	387
Carluke St Andrew's 417	20	27	47907	4420	5618	29
Carluke St John's 878	67	51	69852	16360	16960	67
Carnwath 419	18	30	36682	2250	–	56
Carstairs 238	13	31	22161	2110	2399	–
Carstairs Junction 140	6	23	18133	2410	2292	–
Coalburn 185	6	17	11569	400	500	3
Lesmahagow Old 716	36	30	40956	7312	7512	24
Crossford 209	7	16	33948	3340	3340	21
Kirkfieldbank 137	6	17	14954	1020	1020	23
Douglas St Bride's 355	26	22	35894	3350	3350	20
Douglas Water and Rigside 94	10	13	14287	1900	1978	11
Forth St Paul's 437	28	56	39387	2400	6390	49
Glencaple 274	22	15	20563	1006	1006	17
Lowther 48	5	–	6071	516	516	13
Kirkmuirhill 301	19	57	83018	17980	17980	80
Lanark Greyfriars 937	58	42	67710	12420	13235	91
Lanark St Nicholas' 650	40	46	73106	13620	13620	36
Law 167	22	33	34428	–	400	–
Lesmahagow Abbeygreen 236	18	20	68148	10550	10550	30

14. Greenock and Paisley

Barrhead Arthurlie 390	29	24	74443	14020	14088	143
Barrhead Bourock 569	57	74	69828	11930	11930	250
Barrhead South and Levern 500	42	33	66956	12200	12700	28
Bishopton 906	55	–	76499	14180	14180	181
Bridge of Weir Freeland 452	53	–	97742	18570	18570	84
Bridge of Weir St Machar's Ranfurly 539	46	59	68581	16400	17773	45
Caldwell 280	19	–	54479	7570	7570	90
Elderslie Kirk 657	64	69	91884	21350	21970	118
Erskine 456	33	60	91577	14531	14531	231
Gourock Old Gourock and Ashton . . . . –	–	83	109825	26741	30741	–
Gourock St John's 733	64	30	83799	21550	21550	80
Greenock Ardgowan 492	51	38	75489	10521	10521	38
Greenock Cartsdyke 237	28	–	18405	800	800	7
Greenock Finnart St Paul's 388	36	–	73478	14954	14953	30
Greenock Mount Kirk 381	45	25	58266	10180	10180	94
Greenock Old West Kirk 376	34	40	73105	14443	14443	28
Greenock St George's North 477	37	–	46334	12282	11054	31
Greenock St Luke's 779	73	54	111501	27660	27660	210
Greenock St Margaret's 251	25	37	29021	–	–	35
Greenock St Ninian's 278	21	18	24208	–	37	12
Greenock Wellpark Mid Kirk 718	55	30	77767	11200	11200	157
Houston and Killellan 756	54	48	102397	21670	21670	–
Howwood 230	19	30	48500	7130	7130	25

Congregation.................... Com	Eld	G	In 02	Ass	Gvn	–18
Inchinnan......................... 465	41	27	64269	5940	10100	180
Inverkip 447	25	43	47019	8118	6089	40
Johnstone High..................... 399	55	57	77280	9520	9520	47
Johnstone St Andrew's Trinity 253	26	42	38794	5830	5830	138
Johnstone St Paul's.................. 694	82	31	66516	12530	12828	–
Kilbarchan East 410	35	44	53295	8670	8670	51
Kilbarchan West.................... 512	47	40	84945	18830	18830	83
Kilmacolm Old..................... 883	67	–	114748	36223	36986	100
Kilmacolm St Columba 586	41	22	91788	16700	16700	50
Langbank.......................... 165	12	–	31393	1331	1331	35
Linwood........................... 517	43	38	56493	9380	9380	–
Lochwinnoch 165	12	–	33886	–	–	160
Neilston 791	45	38	83138	13900	13900	–
Paisley Abbey...................... 823	57	–	123746	23020	23020	110
Paisley Castlehead 313	33	17	57833	7500	7500	33
Paisley Glenburn.................... 334	26	18	44345	4320	4320	56
Paisley Laigh Kirk 604	81	66	68643	12520	12520	68
Paisley Lylesland 508	55	59	69834	13920	13920	55
Paisley Martyrs' 586	65	20	73745	12080	12080	94
Paisley Oakshaw Trinity.............. 880	106	60	112815	27846	27846	174
Paisley Sandyford (Thread Street)....... 345	24	26	50380	8120	8120	144
Paisley Sherwood Greenlaw .... –	–	70	–	–	–	100
Paisley St Columba's Foxbar 309	32	33	43467	3820	5610	15
Paisley St James' 396	36	25	49581	6120	6120	24
Paisley St Luke's 312	36	30	49670	8850	8850	22
Paisley St Mark's Oldhall............. 661	68	116	104195	20840	20840	100
Paisley St Ninian's Ferguslie 65	–	6	9322	–	–	52
Paisley Wallneuk North.............. 576	64	–	91160	12930	17750	65
Port Glasgow Hamilton Bardrainney..... 478	22	14	44027	4570	4827	41
Port Glasgow St Andrew's 741	65	62	74598	13545	13545	277
Port Glasgow St Martin's 193	17	–	20309	–	–	30
Renfrew North 722	70	31	85120	15130	15130	139
Renfrew Old....................... 738	39	69	71747	16650	16650	–
Renfrew Trinity 427	44	77	64048	9820	9820	48
Skelmorlie and Wemyss Bay........... 420	29	–	58869	8340	8925	30
15. Glasgow						
Banton............................ 83	11	–	9773	–	–	35
Twechar 79	12	–	9252	–	–	–
Bishopbriggs Kenmure............... 372	26	53	68560	13070	13759	140
Bishopbriggs Springfield 1004	55	78	92299	20850	20906	104
Broom 976	72	69	134980	49600	25000	88
Burnside – Blairbeth................. 766	51	81	–	46600	46626	159
Busby............................. 434	45	40	61381	12000	12000	30
Cadder 982	86	70	137312	37280	37280	–
Cambuslang Flemington Hallside 209	15	21	30840	–	–	50
Cambuslang Old.................... 445	64	32	70116	16000	16500	23
Cambuslang St Andrew's 465	40	21	87741	16260	21603	50

Congregation. . . . . Com	Eld	G	In 02	Ass	Gvn	–18
Cambuslang Trinity St Paul's 343	20	–	70727	13770	15570	70
Campsie 338	25	18	49688	3250	4117	30
Chryston. 841	45	33	138647	32650	32650	105
Eaglesham 740	57	68	106267	27690	27690	270
Fernhill and Cathkin. 342	23	43	35382	2500	6484	116
Gartcosh. 160	9	14	21323	–	–	60
Glenboig. 166	9	14	11655	–	–	11
Giffnock Orchardhill. 589	62	29	151545	45650	45650	120
Giffnock South 1015	95	59	166046	47760	49760	176
Giffnock The Park 338	37	–	49348	5900	5900	281
Greenbank 1181	84	63	192757	60780	60880	350
Kilsyth Anderson 467	24	50	70872	10060	11060	55
Kilsyth Burns and Old 630	40	45	66905	6520	6520	56
Kirkintilloch Hillhead. 174	14	19	17592	–	–	13
Kirkintilloch St Columba's 636	53	46	87045	17670	18070	120
Kirkintilloch St David's Memorial Park . . 823	69	50	96319	24080	24080	151
Kirkintilloch St Mary's. 798	60	73	114521	21660	21660	270
Lenzie Old 511	48	–	71156	13870	14970	82
Lenzie Union 906	93	102	145715	35600	35996	305
Maxwell Mearns Castle 355	36	–	129218	25290	25290	162
Mearns 813	49	–	129443	32290	32290	75
Milton of Campsie 386	40	36	44838	3280	3280	105
Netherlee 907	73	71	168117	49700	52038	200
Newton Mearns 808	60	27	108351	30000	30000	224
Rutherglen Old. 446	37	–	43790	7000	2100	47
Rutherglen Stonelaw. 485	48	65	103949	27430	27585	48
Rutherglen Wardlawhill 413	39	61	45790	9300	9385	135
Rutherglen West 516	29	27	58901	10210	10210	125
Stamperland 477	41	33	80172	17750	17750	176
Stepps. 414	27	27	50273	5840	5840	125
Thornliebank 270	21	54	46759	3125	3125	40
Torrance 286	15	–	49690	3000	3000	129
Williamwood 585	71	44	114575	30310	28310	277
Glasgow Anderston Kelvingrove. 144	22	18	17003	–	–	12
Glasgow Baillieston Mure Memorial 609	44	133	81868	17170	17170	350
Glasgow Baillieston St Andrew's 438	31	60	59708	9720	9720	–
Glasgow Balshagray Victoria Park 317	33	24	71051	16750	16750	40
Glasgow Barlanark Greyfriars. 159	17	30	30633	–	100	114
Glasgow Battlefield East. 191	14	36	41488	3630	3630	6
Glasgow Blawarthill 245	29	57	23662	–	–	60
Glasgow Bridgeton St Francis in the East . 116	18	11	29098	–	–	26
Glasgow Broomhill. 687	64	90	120152	31020	31430	60
Glasgow Calton Parkhead. 186	16	14	20572	–	–	20
Glasgow Cardonald 553	65	113	110571	28320	31015	42
Glasgow Carmunnock. 395	29	39	55972	11620	11920	40
Glasgow Carmyle. 133	7	30	21964	1725	1725	41
Glasgow Kenmuir Mount Vernon 160	9	41	43127	4330	4338	89
Glasgow Carntyne Old 169	17	19	35431	5650	5650	19

Congregation. Com	Eld	G	In 02	Ass	Gvn	–18
Glasgow Eastbank 177	19	26	32903	4560	4560	20
Glasgow Carnwadric. 166	19	28	23684	–	200	24
Glasgow Castlemilk East 174	13	22	26165	–	–	20
Glasgow Castlemilk West 156	23	33	22693	–	–	31
Glasgow Cathcart Old. 387	45	56	63042	12060	13285	300
Glasgow Cathcart Trinity 685	72	94	–	32610	33560	54
Glasgow Cathedral (St Mungo's or High) . 441	50	–	79094	14900	14900	9
Glasgow Colston Milton. 148	16	–	27869	–	–	109
Glasgow Colston Wellpark 219	19	–	28465	–	–	72
Glasgow Cranhill 68	11	–	9781	–	–	7
Glasgow Croftfoot 398	46	34	81976	12790	12916	60
Glasgow Dennistoun Blackfriars. 162	28	24	37545	2720	2720	15
Glasgow Dennistoun Central 283	27	23	48683	5000	6000	198
Glasgow Drumchapel Drumry St Mary's . 148	13	–	10345	–	–	12
Glasgow Drumchapel St Andrew's 489	40	–	53601	7430	15430	30
Glasgow Drumchapel St Mark's 82	12	16	9211	–	–	12
Glasgow Easterhouse St George's						
and St Peter's 49	8	–	4753	–	–	–
Glasgow Eastwood 421	56	65	80033	13270	13270	100
Glasgow Gairbraid 250	22	22	37430	–	–	24
Glasgow Gardner Street 47	9	–	43526	5000	2000	21
Glasgow Garthamlock and Craigend East . . 87	11	–	9915	–	–	100
Glasgow Gorbals 128	12	12	27624	–	–	16
Glasgow Govan Old 233	34	20	32672	6060	6060	10
Glasgow Govanhill Trinity 151	20	44	30907	–	536	1
Glasgow High Carntyne 531	33	85	73575	14130	14130	168
Glasgow Hillington Park. 461	31	73	79789	12370	12485	150
Glasgow Househillwood St Christopher's . 123	10	24	16655	–	573	93
Glasgow Hyndland 295	47	39	83647	17430	17430	43
Glasgow Ibrox 246	21	33	45507	5500	3500	140
Glasgow John Ross Memorial						
(For the Deaf) 74	7	–	–	–	–	–
Glasgow Jordanhill 697	83	37	141045	38560	40560	384
Glasgow Kelvin Stevenson Memorial 196	35	20	36165	3550	3550	111
Glasgow Kelvinside Hillhead 198	30	–	71627	12690	12790	110
Glasgow King's Park 896	76	81	130148	34400	35400	118
Glasgow Kinning Park 197	14	16	31860	3500	3500	31
Glasgow Knightswood St Margaret's 683	33	52	53621	10230	10580	90
Glasgow Langside 278	40	34	60004	2500	2833	114
Glasgow Lansdowne. 156	16	–	18327	–	–	4
Glasgow Linthouse St Kenneth's 164	16	22	25766	–	–	60
Glasgow Lochwood 78	6	12	11804	–	–	114
Glasgow Martyrs', The 128	7	–	13884	–	–	5
Glasgow Maryhill. 232	20	17	–	–	–	57
Glasgow Merrylea 541	64	48	82963	19170	19170	75
Glasgow Mosspark 249	35	50	58505	11720	13873	–
Glasgow Mount Florida 319	34	64	83087	19300	19300	36
Glasgow New Govan 143	19	18	25561	5440	5440	67

Congregation. . . . . Com	Eld	G	In 02	Ass	Gvn	–18
Glasgow Newlands South 721	79	40	144994	48210	53710	60
Glasgow North Kelvinside 78	3	29	36797	2625	2625	20
Glasgow Partick South 259	39	35	52712	4610	4610	163
Glasgow Partick Trinity 220	28	–	59319	7120	7248	32
Glasgow Penilee St Andrew's 174	26	–	34153	3100	3250	45
Glasgow Pollokshaws 191	28	28	38262	1800	1800	70
Glasgow Pollokshields 373	45	85	105101	24970	26927	25
Glasgow Possilpark 195	21	30	27957	1300	1320	2
Glasgow Priesthill and Nitshill 191	19	18	30014	–	50	29
Glasgow Queen's Park 328	33	42	76714	11250	11250	83
Glasgow Renfield St Stephen's 198	27	36	69135	9700	10500	15
Glasgow Robroyston 23	–	–	1090	–	–	13
Glasgow Ruchazie 80	9	–	15685	–	–	40
Glasgow Ruchill 128	24	–	38760	2730	2730	70
Glasgow St Andrew's East 151	24	31	33203	–	100	12
Glasgow St Columba 139	15	20	29019	–	–	36
Glasgow St David's Knightswood. 688	31	61	78873	16000	16350	45
Glasgow St Enoch's Hogganfield 230	11	57	40659	3500	–	86
Glasgow St George's Tron 463	43	–	211556	55090	55090	70
Glasgow St James' (Pollok) 269	28	25	42646	2340	865	60
Glasgow St John's Renfield 477	58	–	131047	26400	26400	75
Glasgow St Luke's and St Andrew's 85	9	12	17319	–	–	9
Glasgow St Margaret's Tollcross 158	5	–	30106	–	100	27
Glasgow St Nicholas' Cardonald 423	40	21	47697	7220	10197	54
Glasgow St Paul's 76	7	–	9893	–	–	32
Glasgow St Rollox 113	15	–	25064	–	125	–
Glasgow St Thomas' Gallowgate 74	7	–	5635	–	100	10
Glasgow Sandyford Henderson						
Memorial 198	27	18	100491	18460	18460	15
Glasgow Sandyhills 379	33	56	70098	11670	11670	66
Glasgow Scotstoun 301	23	–	59515	10450	21450	55
Glasgow Shawlands . . . . –	–	62	–	–	–	50
Glasgow Sherbrooke St Gilbert's 433	56	43	100689	28650	28650	61
Glasgow Shettleston Old 302	29	34	51948	3910	3910	90
Glasgow South Carntyne 155	12	–	24234	–	50	64
Glasgow South Shawlands 241	24	–	53158	9360	9360	110
Glasgow Springburn 346	37	28	42498	12320	12320	–
Glasgow Temple Anniesland 511	42	50	71872	16420	16671	30
Glasgow Toryglen 130	12	33	19939	–	–	60
Glasgow Trinity Possil						
and Henry Drummond 137	10	–	42941	1760	1760	24
Glasgow Tron St Mary's 143	16	–	24923	–	–	60
Glasgow Victoria Tollcross 157	12	32	32209	–	–	112
Glasgow Wallacewell 197	19	22	–	–	–	20
Glasgow Wellington 308	40	–	74863	18540	21138	25
Glasgow Whiteinch 30	–	–	31380	–	–	8
Glasgow Yoker 135	11	11	20047	–	–	4

Congregation. . . . . Com	Eld	G	In 02	Ass	Gvn	–18
17. Hamilton						
Airdrie Broomknoll 424	42	54	54254	10620	10621	40
Calderbank 145	13	25	19906	2290	2290	–
Airdrie Clarkston 484	42	27	61079	12680	7813	15
Airdrie Flowerhill 826	69	34	89500	16840	16840	148
Airdrie High 436	31	–	46755	4640	4640	46
Airdrie Jackson 358	44	29	56011	9300	9300	127
Airdrie New Monkland 461	35	48	39170	7530	20515	–
Greengairs 203	8	–	17476	1920	1920	–
Airdrie St Columba's 252	14	10	21261	–	–	81
Airdrie The New Wellwynd 762	80	32	88435	17770	17770	–
Bargeddie 171	15	–	47724	9090	10183	20
Bellshill Macdonald Memorial 324	25	28	41386	6010	6010	20
Bellshill Orbiston 270	20	18	18131	2110	2110	14
Bellshill West 844	65	44	63313	12640	12640	155
Blantyre Livingstone Memorial 291	17	31	36545	4750	4750	60
Blantyre Old 407	27	49	48527	11350	11350	72
Blantyre St Andrew's 302	22	25	59004	10600	10600	58
Bothwell 579	54	47	103792	23530	23530	103
Caldercruix and Longriggend 245	13	21	47595	6820	6820	60
Carfin 64	5	–	9363	1220	1220	–
Newarthill 606	26	20	49738	7350	7350	–
Chapelhall 306	24	42	33374	2410	2410	75
Chapelton 207	15	39	22024	3520	3520	48
Strathaven Rankin 607	55	34	70751	15500	15500	205
Cleland 242	15	19	27666	–	–	68
Coatbridge Blairhill-Dundyvan 451	31	31	57385	6860	6860	12
Coatbridge Calder 481	34	58	45984	9220	9466	87
Coatbridge Clifton 272	24	33	31861	6190	6190	6
Coatbridge Middle 416	37	49	46654	5730	6265	164
Coatbridge Old Monkland . . . . –	–	45	29276	2870	5870	–
Coatbridge St Andrew's 730	68	52	81312	17910	17910	202
Coatbridge Townhead 365	30	39	45933	5560	5097	130
Dalserf 271	24	23	51086	9130	9130	79
East Kilbride Claremont 820	91	44	103300	17840	10190	220
East Kilbride Greenhills 255	16	25	28246	–	–	–
East Kilbride Moncrieff 984	74	58	102152	24990	24990	300
East Kilbride Mossneuk 282	23	–	29050	–	–	300
East Kilbride Old 688	62	96	69064	15230	15689	101
East Kilbride South 421	46	53	79680	17170	17170	50
East Kilbride Stewartfield . . . . –	–	–	–	–	40	–
East Kilbride West 712	32	81	72479	10770	10770	87
East Kilbride Westwood 813	51	159	78112	13810	13810	45
Glasford 199	12	22	16117	2650	2650	20
Strathaven East 319	32	35	44200	7220	7220	31
Hamilton Burnbank 148	18	–	24475	4810	4810	3
Hamilton North 174	30	31	30458	5520	5520	19
Hamilton Cadzow 816	65	73	86228	18300	18300	175

Congregation................Com	Eld	G	In 02	Ass	Gvn	–18
Hamilton Gilmour and Whitehill........221	26	–	34768	3220	3220	60
Hamilton Hillhouse.................481	44	33	83854	14370	15231	34
Hamilton Old......................740	71	40	111408	28230	28230	117
Hamilton St Andrew's...............377	33	33	57086	10750	10850	36
Hamilton St John's.................637	64	51	94706	21220	21220	98
Hamilton South 324	33	28	46464	6730	6922	142
Quarter...........................85	11	19	15426	2430	2430	14
Hamilton Trinity...................329	29	–	40094	3960	3960	133
Hamilton West 402	33	–	58740	12790	12790	200
Holytown 351	23	28	46590	4480	4480	22
Kirk o' Shotts.....................231	10	12	22050	–	–	20
Larkhall Chalmers 239	18	30	35296	3400	3400	68
Larkhall St Machan's 620	60	55	76636	20210	20210	112
Larkhall Trinity 352	25	47	42967	5740	6140	128
Motherwell Crosshill 552	59	55	70755	13530	13530	139
Motherwell Dalziel St Andrew's........662	71	61	97911	26780	8482	200
Motherwell Manse Road.............272	33	23	41757	8670	8670	30
Motherwell North..................226	33	45	43298	4730	4730	150
Motherwell St Margaret's............397	15	31	37715	3520	–	177
Motherwell St Mary's...............1027	109	104	93940	21080	21080	240
Motherwell South Dalziel............457	64	64	80216	15030	16230	116
Newmains Bonkle..................198	17	24	29736	6210	6260	20
Newmains Coltness Memorial 241	31	31	38838	8760	8760	20
New Stevenston: Wrangholm Kirk 200	14	29	37399	3860	3913	63
Overtown.........................296	26	41	37496	3450	4943	53
Shotts Calderhead Erskine 635	43	49	64528	7520	7520	75
Stonehouse St Ninian's..............433	40	50	54421	10070	10070	60
Strathaven Avendale Old and Drumclog ..823	70	75	117638	27360	27360	130
Strathaven West 269	19	41	44327	4800	4800	–
Uddingston Burnhead...............294	24	15	38598	4550	2280	70
Uddingston Old 709	65	88	89669	17660	19160	70
Uddingston Park...................243	24	31	63077	8860	9000	53
Uddingston Viewpark...............486	36	38	61374	11540	12276	300
Wishaw Cambusnethan North.........569	41	52	70739	14060	14060	160
Wishaw Cambusnethan Old and						
Morningside 602	51	21	72222	13120	13120	200
Wishaw Chalmers..................520	29	42	54823	9570	1945	43
Wishaw Craigneuk and Belhaven 239	29	30	49538	7800	7800	25
Wishaw Old 400	39	–	40565	5620	5628	75
Wishaw St Mark's 526	38	56	63323	10090	10090	255
Wishaw Thornlie 280	26	49	42641	3818	3902	28
18. Dumbarton						
Alexandria 486	36	27	54997	12000	12000	69
Arrochar..........................58	–	15	18074	–	400	–
Luss..............................82	9	15	15802	–	–	42
Baldernock........................235	21	16	39174	5780	5780	14
Bearsden Killermont................659	56	72	125317	30260	29600	85

Congregation. . . . . Com	Eld	G	In 02	Ass	Gvn	–18
Bearsden New Kilpatrick 1818	133	134	254434	94020	94020	170
Bearsden North. 719	78	77	99847	26370	26670	70
Bearsden South. 991	85	49	140877	40250	40250	113
Bearsden Westerton Fairlie Memorial 512	47	56	81883	18820	18820	92
Bonhill 935	65	–	71805	14980	14980	170
Cardross 498	36	34	87734	22210	22221	70
Clydebank Abbotsford 377	25	39	55002	7680	7680	31
Clydebank Faifley. 242	21	52	34909	–	–	19
Clydebank Kilbowie St Andrew's 334	24	45	41569	6190	6190	7
Clydebank Radnor Park 277	35	37	44427	5910	5910	10
Clydebank St Cuthbert's 145	17	30	21256	500	1000	5
Craigrownie 246	24	19	30183	5520	5520	26
Rosneath St Modan's 200	14	28	23735	2700	2700	13
Dalmuir Barclay 373	22	61	40315	6940	6940	–
Dumbarton Riverside 820	86	86	89402	20810	15164	61
Dumbarton St Andrew's 166	28	19	32136	–	–	14
Dumbarton West Kirk. 381	44	26	37731	8430	11447	15
Duntocher. 342	35	24	38781	1062	1062	45
Garelochhead 166	17	–	54960	5010	5010	129
Helensburgh Park 509	57	38	79759	19790	20110	39
Helensburgh St Columba 649	51	40	87442	18030	18030	76
Helensburgh: The West Kirk. 674	54	63	111880	28350	28350	36
Jamestown 456	23	29	48402	9490	9490	12
Kilmaronock Gartocharn 276	12	–	31048	–	–	12
Milngavie Cairns 773	50	–	96165	25890	25890	80
Milngavie St Luke's 443	35	51	66918	12910	12910	39
Milngavie St Paul's. 1187	95	117	204608	48200	49218	278
Old Kilpatrick Bowling 300	20	34	48420	7570	5000	143
Renton Trinity 349	30	–	32346	1780	1780	15
Rhu and Shandon 333	24	53	67391	14000	14473	27
19. South Argyll						
Ardrishaig 194	28	35	35121	3670	3670	57
South Knapdale 37	6	–	5149	510	510	10
Campbeltown Highland 495	34	32	47273	6171	6171	52
Campbeltown Lorne and Lowland 976	45	68	75537	13890	13890	115
Craignish 40	5	–	12819	–	–	–
Kilninver and Kilmelford 57	7	–	8705	–	–	–
Cumlodden, Lochfyneside and Lochgair. . 112	11	14	19716	–	60	20
Gigha and Cara. 44	7	–	10277	–	–	7
Glassary and Kilmartin and Ford 133	12	12	23004	–	–	12
Glenaray and Inveraray. 144	13	12	18252	–	–	13
Jura 40	6	–	10576	–	–	21
Kilarrow. 104	12	19	20716	–	–	22
Kilmeny 49	6	–	11138	–	–	19
Kilberry 14	5	–	1372	–	–	2
Tarbert 172	16	30	25077	–	–	–
Kilcalmonell. 69	10	19	9369	–	–	8

Congregation. . . . . Com	Eld	G	In 02	Ass	Gvn	–18
Skipness. 31	2	–	6453	–	–	5
Kilchoman 84	5	–	8553	760	760	15
Portnahaven 17	3	10	4013	422	422	–
Kildalton and Oa 128	16	17	24769	–	500	40
Killean and Kilchenzie 197	14	25	30998	–	–	44
Lochgilphead 232	20	16	31644	–	75	14
North Knapdale 72	11	–	28618	–	170	–
Saddell and Carradale. 242	12	31	25194	–	–	15
Southend 251	14	30	28840	–	75	30
20. Dunoon						
Bute United 757	40	74	76681	16250	16250	29
Dunoon St John's 260	30	35	34801	5260	5260	25
Sandbank 162	12	–	12310	2040	2115	14
Dunoon The High Kirk. 452	37	36	45144	8163	8163	30
Innellan 152	–	24	19389	–	–	–
Toward. 113	10	–	14098	–	–	8
Kilfinan 29	5	8	4445	–	472	–
Kyles 194	16	28	25693	–	180	15
Kilmodan and Colintraive. 128	11	15	20185	–	–	–
Kilmun (St Munn's) 119	11	22	15280	–	702	4
Strone and Ardentinny 136	12	14	16178	–	350	14
Kirn. 366	30	32	70619	8470	9152	67
Lochgoilhead and Kilmorich. 117	15	18	24264	–	100	8
Rothesay Trinity. 512	45	46	58475	6580	6580	103
Strachur and Strachlachlan 168	18	17	25519	–	–	17
21. Lorn and Mull						
Appin. 96	13	21	16589	–	–	16
Lismore 57	6	13	7331	–	–	12
Ardchattan 174	13	10	19090	–	438	29
Coll 13	3	–	2504	–	–	–
Colonsay and Oronsay 15	2	–	3500	–	–	–
Kilbrandon and Kilchattan 106	11	–	24215	–	273	28
Connel 161	17	29	33928	–	–	27
Glenorchy and Innishael. 88	8	–	10004	–	–	–
Strathfillan. 55	5	–	6460	–	100	–
Iona 26	4	–	4273	–	–	7
Kilfinichen and Kilvickeon						
and the Ross of Mull 32	8	–	10602	–	95	9
Kilchrenan and Dalavich 34	5	9	9073	–	–	6
Muckairn 147	17	15	19290	–	500	5
Kilmore and Oban 757	69	58	92005	17140	17775	42
Mull (Isle of), Kilninian and Kilmore 43	5	9	12773	–	–	–
Salen and Ulva. 33	6	–	9755	–	–	12
Tobermory 89	17	13	17350	–	100	–
Torosay and Kinlochspelvie 31	5	–	5041	–	–	5
Tiree. 123	10	20	18456	–	–	–

Congregation. . . . . Com	Eld	G	In 02	Ass	Gvn	–18
22. Falkirk						
Airth. 190	7	28	35693	2680	2680	38
Blackbraes and Shieldhill 203	16	18	23960	–	–	22
Bo'ness Old. 554	49	39	60592	6660	6660	52
Bo'ness St Andrew's. 581	29	–	62380	9610	9610	51
Bonnybridge St Helen's 649	27	38	45930	5860	5860	25
Bothkennar and Carronshore. 325	29	10	31312	–	–	20
Brightons 771	42	68	98263	19220	20280	250
Carriden 696	54	22	47043	7740	7740	30
Cumbernauld Abronhill 314	35	35	36909	–	330	35
Cumbernauld Condorrat 499	38	33	58398	8470	8470	190
Cumbernauld Kildrum 470	40	–	34756	4950	4950	209
Cumbernauld Old 504	34	–	53751	7790	7868	167
Cumbernauld St Mungo's 366	34	–	45936	3430	3430	50
Denny Dunipace. 459	34	26	51609	6320	6320	33
Denny Old 499	50	22	56969	10720	10720	80
Denny Westpark 777	67	40	74862	15190	15190	55
Falkirk Bainsford 369	16	–	43433	4570	4570	106
Falkirk Camelon: Irving 320	18	16	34848	–	–	37
Falkirk Camelon St John's 377	23	28	56775	6370	6370	15
Falkirk Erskine. 599	69	35	66696	15140	15140	–
Falkirk Grahamston United. 545	56	42	75069	15300	15309	58
Falkirk Laurieston 279	20	33	31569	5710	5710	35
Redding and Westquarter 147	13	38	18332	2240	2240	24
Falkirk Old and St Modan's 1073	75	37	107567	17300	17300	60
Falkirk St Andrew's West 631	48	34	93313	23380	23380	23
Falkirk St James' 345	29	15	42921	4200	4402	–
Grangemouth Dundas. 371	26	–	33578	2500	2500	6
Grangemouth Kerse 620	58	27	51122	6070	6070	158
Grangemouth Kirk of the Holy Rood 701	48	–	50737	9770	10785	50
Grangemouth Zetland. 971	69	73	89637	18470	18470	86
Haggs. 334	31	13	43291	4660	3495	78
Larbert East 662	42	41	75662	11820	11820	55
Larbert Old. 733	46	22	84987	17580	17580	130
Larbert West. 579	49	32	63482	12740	12956	191
Muiravonside 265	23	17	33374	–	–	–
Polmont Old. 587	32	56	67807	12710	12924	24
Slamannan 255	9	11	23606	–	–	9
Stenhouse and Carron. 654	44	34	67780	9310	9310	35
23. Stirling						
Aberfoyle 134	10	17	18620	–	200	62
Port of Menteith 71	6	8	13701	–	–	16
Alloa North 298	22	25	45478	5510	5510	30
Alloa St Mungo's 739	56	50	59965	14830	14830	35
Alloa West 239	16	32	44465	5600	5600	11
Alva. 624	51	33	60312	8950	9519	106
Balfron. 214	22	20	60310	9520	9520	30

Congregation. Com	Eld	G	In 02	Ass	Gvn	–18
Limekilns 371	46	–	54590	13075	13550	40
Carnock and Oakley 239	17	21	51730	4062	4062	37
Cowdenbeath Trinity 434	25	30	43223	1562	1562	56
Culross and Torryburn 314	21	32	40287	3910	8320	12
Dalgety. 682	42	39	90505	16650	18000	80
Dunfermline Abbey 806	65	–	113535	19820	19820	200
Dunfermline Gillespie Memorial 412	71	26	97459	17730	17730	93
Dunfermline North 233	17	–	31368	–	–	15
Dunfermline St Andrew's Erskine. 298	29	14	34203	1730	1730	1
Dunfermline St Leonard's. 561	46	51	67820	10970	10970	123
Dunfermline St Margaret's 447	54	35	55467	7420	7420	30
Dunfermline St Ninian's. 382	37	52	38946	–	2000	35
Dunfermline Townhill and Kingseat 442	33	43	55052	7040	7040	40
Inverkeithing St John's 200	21	20	30896	3390	3833	93
North Queensferry 87	8	–	17790	1820	2294	–
Inverkeithing St Peter's. 337	12	–	16136	2183	2183	18
Kelty 395	27	55	48144	5590	5590	71
Lochgelly Macainsh 402	30	–	29508	3530	3530	5
Lochgelly St Andrew's 347	24	–	30192	3810	3810	10
Rosyth 353	28	–	35650	–	–	16
Saline and Blairingone 253	12	17	40700	6450	6650	–
Tulliallan and Kincardine 610	53	80	42364	7060	7454	45

25. Kirkcaldy

Auchterderran St Fothad's 429	28	19	32488	5625	5625	16
Kinglassie. 197	13	–	13223	2420	2585	16
Auchtertool 86	6	–	7307	1577	1577	6
Kirkcaldy Linktown 442	35	38	48601	7920	8898	32
Buckhaven 262	32	16	30335	3210	8267	15
Burntisland. 696	45	56	49733	9620	9832	40
Denbeath 96	–	21	6824	–	–	5
Methilhill 178	16	36	19119	–	200	20
Dysart. 406	35	18	50779	6800	6800	62
Glenrothes Christ's Kirk 380	28	69	36646	–	900	29
Glenrothes St Columba's 666	36	26	70444	9400	9400	54
Glenrothes St Margaret's 467	34	43	53953	8790	8790	85
Glenrothes St Ninian's 328	41	14	54521	6320	6320	23
Innerleven East. 305	7	20	20586	–	–	40
Kennoway, Windygates and						
Balgonie St Kenneth's 795	52	74	–	–	–	103
Kinghorn 461	32	37	50467	9120	9120	40
Kirkcaldy Abbotshall 781	55	–	68057	14590	14590	27
Kirkcaldy Pathhead. 600	52	66	70254	12570	12770	136
Kirkcaldy St Andrew's 317	26	39	42229	6370	6370	21
Kirkcaldy St Bryce Kirk 875	69	49	80896	19000	19000	44
Kirkcaldy St John's. 430	52	66	61961	11000	11000	20
Kirkcaldy Templehall 377	22	20	42720	6230	17082	–
Kirkcaldy Torbain. 289	37	27	36220	–	–	29

Congregation. Com	Eld	G	In 02	Ass	Gvn	–18
Kirkcaldy Viewforth 398	15	–	32024	4910	4910	–
Thornton. 253	9	–	18409	1950	2017	40
Leslie Trinity 397	27	41	26521	799	–	17
Leven 942	63	17	80334	12808	7808	40
Markinch 661	38	47	56306	8240	8240	40
Methil. 419	25	34	34771	1840	1840	6
Wemyss 291	16	35	25391	653	653	18

26. St Andrews

Congregation.	Eld	G	In 02	Ass	Gvn	–18
Abdie and Dunbog 181	18	–	11711	1600	1600	–
Newburgh. 354	15	–	16941	2930	2930	21
Anstruther 382	26	–	45232	3870	4192	10
Auchtermuchty. 339	21	20	34533	1350	1350	–
Balmerino. 200	19	14	24778	3280	3280	18
Wormit 311	24	54	30365	5700	5700	40
Boarhills and Dunino 184	9	j	13860	2910	2910	–
St Andrews Martyrs'. 411	31	38j	40566	6660	6660	–
Cameron. 103	12	13	13143	2390	2390	26
St Andrews St Leonard's. 670	54	41	92107	20470	20820	44
Carnbee 104	12	18	11985	1780	1780	–
Pittenweem. 321	20	39	25524	3940	3940	17
Cellardyke 336	23	45	33555	4800	4800	13
Kilrenny 134	11	17	18954	3110	3110	27
Ceres and Springfield 559	28	39	27782	10624	10624	25
Crail 483	34	39	37578	7600	7760	15
Kingsbarns 109	11	–	12079	2100	2238	–
Creich, Flisk and Kilmany 114	9	17	21912	2840	2840	12
Monimail 133	15	–	22647	3580	3580	15
Cupar Old and St Michael of Tarvit 651	47	23	74232	18000	18000	67
Cupar St John's 841	40	62	56348	11390	11390	53
Dairsie 144	9	22	14647	1900	1900	6
Kemback 116	8	19	13985	2440	2440	–
Strathkinness 153	14	15	18814	2760	2760	9
Edenshead and Strathmiglo. 244	13	22	25270	1050	1050	16
Elie. 391	30	66	65809	13740	13755	25
Kilconquhar and Colinsburgh 211	17	–	26566	4420	4420	24
Falkland 352	24	9	27470	6050	6050	8
Freuchie 255	17	24	27189	5210	5210	8
Howe of Fife 834	46	–	57534	9150	9150	59
Largo and Newburn 291	16	–	32936	7200	7200	18
Largo St David's. 205	13	53	19252	5070	5070	18
Largoward 80	5	12	7409	520	520	15
St Monans 263	15	58	38197	6150	6150	45
Leuchars St Athernase 530	32	36	51018	4430	4430	–
Newport-on-Tay 443	38	–	59545	12790	12790	95
St Andrews Holy Trinity. 707	28	56	38514	10770	10770	9
St Andrews Hope Park 864	96	63	120555	33630	33630	45
Tayport. 472	29	24	37423	6000	6000	46

Congregation. Com	Eld	G	In 02	Ass	Gvn	–18
27. Dunkeld and Meigle						
Aberfeldy 280	21	25	42579	4680	4832	130
Amulree and Strathbraan 22	3	–	1400	750	750	2
Dull and Weem. 93	8	18	12432	1696	1696	20
Alyth 823	37	40	55421	10760	11260	55
Ardler Kettins and Meigle 499	26	50	34684	5980	6385	28
Bendochy 87	6	–	11921	1610	1610	9
Coupar Angus Abbey 412	34	33	49224	3410	3410	66
Blair Atholl and Struan. 183	17	20	16973	160	160	17
Tenandry 71	8	10	13368	160	160	5
Blairgowrie. 1022	50	55	75987	13230	13230	24
Braes of Rannoch 31	5	j	11490	–	1013	–
Foss and Rannoch. 139	16	24	23164	–	300	26
Caputh and Clunie 222	28	15	17010	2843	2843	10
Kinclaven 175	19	9	15408	2681	2681	2
Dunkeld 468	37	35	61123	15300	15300	20
Fortingall and Glenlyon 54	6	–	10673	1000	1000	–
Kenmore and Lawers 106	7	17	23848	1090	1090	12
Grantully, Logierait and Strathtay 172	15	16	30089	1090	1090	28
Kirkmichael, Straloch and Glenshee 152	16	13	13948	812	406	22
Rattray 565	24	32	37803	5510	5750	–
Pitlochry. 536	51	30	76365	12670	12670	35
28. Perth						
Abernethy and Dron 262	16	15	20481	2040	2040	–
Arngask 151	13	23	16601	2360	2360	–
Almondbank Tibbermore 350	21	42	30225	–	–	42
Ardoch 164	10	26	25573	–	2500	20
Blackford 84	11	–	15337	–	–	12
Auchterarder. 708	44	63	75214	15940	14346	–
Auchtergaven and Moneydie. 548	23	45	35640	4120	4120	118
Cargill Burrelton. 355	20	43	43274	3000	3000	12
Collace. 140	10	18	21220	3670	3670	–
Cleish 252	20	19	47429	9210	9210	–
Fossoway St Serf's and Devonside 228	20	–	32615	6850	6850	–
Comrie 519	32	48j	52793	11170	12667	14
Dundurn. 62	7	j	10707	1540	1856	6
Crieff 1065	60	54	97729	15840	15840	72
Dunbarney 572	30	61	49731	8930	8930	56
Forgandenny. 88	7	10	10939	1710	1710	15
Errol. 320	14	17	36028	5430	5517	26
Kilspindie and Rait. 73	5	–	9745	970	970	5
Fowlis Wester. 128	13	–	14616	1116	1116	–
Madderty 106	9	11	13945	912	1212	12
Monzie. 109	11	–	11608	912	912	–
Gask. 126	12	12	9238	–	500	–
Methven and Logiealmond 381	32	26	24606	–	1000	2
Kinross. 701	34	27	67693	11880	11880	65

Congregation.................... Com	Eld	G	In 02	Ass	Gvn	–18
Muthill............................ 351	21	13j	24125	3030	6230	40
Trinity Gask and Kinkell 62	5	j	6948	730	907	6
Orwell 360	24	24	31092	4030	5079	–
Portmoak 158	13	–	18503	3770	3964	17
Perth Craigie 761	35	30	58758	11450	11450	45
Perth Kinnoull 435	29	36	55233	11060	11760	30
Perth Letham St Mark's 710	46	36	74314	11410	11410	90
Perth Moncrieffe................... 204	–	–	–	–	500	181
Perth North...................... 1473	113	23	191818	52830	53875	–
Perth Riverside..................... 52	–	–	23223	–	–	120
Perth St John the Baptist's 799	44	–	69463	16180	16886	–
Perth St Leonard's-in-the-Fields and Trinity...................... 645	75	39	88493	20600	20600	45
Perth St Matthew's 982	61	44	81395	17820	17820	41
Redgorton........................ 157	11	18	16691	1150	1150	40
Stanley........................... 296	18	26	26564	5050	5050	28
St Madoes and Kinfauns.............. 333	19	27	26712	–	1000	27
St Martin's 212	10	17	12003	1460	1460	16
Scone New........................ 627	55	68	46272	11400	11400	47
Scone Old......................... 753	51	39	54389	9310	10310	45
The Stewartry of Strathearn 554	41	32	52309	2500	400	24
29. Dundee						
Abernyte......................... 100	9	–	10899	1700	1700	–
Inchture and Kinnaird................ 252	24	–	22650	3730	3730	38
Longforgan....................... 248	24	22	25882	6510	6510	–
Auchterhouse 160	17	21	21518	3920	4020	21
Murroes and Tealing................ 365	17	30	25969	2171	2300	19
Dundee Albany – Butterburn .... –	–	9	5327	–	–	–
Dundee St David's North 112	7	19	11318	–	–	–
Dundee Balgay..................... 564	50	31	58397	9590	9590	30
Dundee Barnhill St Margaret's 877	72	53	103094	23540	23540	54
Dundee Broughty Ferry East........... 623	51	37	69776	14950	14950	54
Dundee Broughty Ferry St Aidan's...... 667	53	63	69670	11660	11660	32
Dundee Broughty Ferry St James' 256	14	35	41645	6250	7600	40
Dundee Broughty Ferry St Luke's .... – and Queen Street................. 539	55	53	71674	14190	14432	35
Dundee Broughty Ferry St Stephen's ...... – and West....................... 384	23	–	37627	4223	4223	10
Dundee Camperdown 216	21	23	27118	–	400	13
Dundee Chalmers Ardler............. 251	22	23	62275	8290	8290	–
Dundee Clepington.................. 476	24	–	29449	4440	4440	–
Dundee Fairmuir.................... 252	17	14	24181	2490	2490	97
Dundee Craigiebank................. 390	12	31	44325	8690	4559	191
Dundee Douglas and Angus 362	19	21	23919	3125	1563	60
Dundee Downfield South 459	31	27	58360	8890	9028	215
Dundee – Dundee (St Mary's) 708	74	37	90591	23180	28760	19
Dundee Lochee Old and St Luke's 275	26	28	31755	2990	2990	4

Congregation. . . . . Com	Eld	G	In 02	Ass	Gvn	–18
Dundee Lochee West 574	38	21	33549	4680	4680	30
Dundee Logie and St John's Cross 471	23	32	81728	17470	17470	53
Dundee Mains 248	12	–	23907	–	–	25
Dundee Mains of Fintry 164	10	–	60814	6160	6160	43
Dundee Meadowside St Paul's 567	51	32	61173	14550	15485	79
Dundee Menzieshill 474	30	–	44092	625	900	2
Dundee Mid Craigie 54	3	–	7684	–	–	3
Dundee St Andrew's 847	78	44	69097	12650	12750	62
Dundee Steeple. 349	36	–	82401	15940	15940	40
Dundee Stobswell. 629	43	–	61194	11920	11920	28
Dundee Strathmartine. . . . . –	–	40	53110	8320	8395	–
Dundee The High Kirk 520	55	55	47061	7270	7270	90
Dundee Trinity 710	43	42	38563	5640	5640	30
Dundee West 523	45	26	–	12580	12580	–
Dundee Whitfield . . . . –	–	–	9334	–	–	–
Fowlis and Liff. 167	10	8	13331	2230	2230	20
Lundie and Muirhead of Liff 359	28	–	33084	4810	4888	–
Invergowrie. 480	45	60	53036	6730	6984	126
Monifieth Panmure 471	38	34	54891	6640	7015	88
Monifieth St Rule's. 770	33	64	54014	7630	7790	38
Monifieth South 430	21	37	42393	3870	4157	8
Monikie and Newbigging 283	15	11	24875	500	500	–

30. Angus

Aberlemno 205	11	–	11888	1500	1700	12
Guthrie and Rescobie 221	8	17	20400	1800	3450	12
Airlie Ruthven Kingoldrum 169	14	x	10665	790	1780	–
Glenisla Kilry Lintrathen 169	17	12	22634	3540	2950	–
Arbirlot. 297	14	–	25618	4120	4120	18
Carmyllie 143	8	5	17364	3180	3180	12
Colliston. 228	11	12	17310	3000	3000	24
Arbroath Knox's 440	28	41	29188	5670	5720	12
Arbroath St Vigeans 665	49	32	47363	10590	10590	40
Arbroath Old and Abbey. 880	48	49	64968	10060	10360	60
Arbroath St Andrew's 777	55	27	74856	13940	13940	120
Arbroath West Kirk. 1142	96	51	71900	13880	13880	40
Barry 317	19	13	28946	2123	1623	18
Brechin Cathedral. 1081	42	17	60572	6460	6460	100
Brechin Gardner Memorial. 705	44	21	47401	7740	7740	6
Carnoustie 600	49	41	61043	11560	11560	–
Carnoustie Panbride 781	38	–	54388	9340	9340	–
Dun 90	7	j	7423	1087	1087	–
Hillside. 440	28	44	38295	3358	3358	30
Dunnichen, Letham and Kirkden 474	21	40	40801	–	289	20
Eassie and Nevay 66	9	9	8376	900	720	–
Newtyle 310	15	23	23802	2600	–	10
Edzell Lethnot 430	27	51	27154	8410	8410	–
Fern, Careston and Menmuir 141	10	–	12703	1901	1901	4

Congregation. Com	Eld	G	In 02	Ass	Gvn	–18
Glenesk 60	4	–	3693	1220	976	12
Farnell 110	9	–	6185	1120	1120	–
Montrose St Andrew's 558	24	29	35766	5390	5590	19
Forfar East and Old. 1559	53	61	79822	17280	17280	111
Forfar Lowson Memorial 1100	45	34	58588	10670	10670	144
Forfar St Margaret's 1073	42	34	75871	15340	15340	30
Friockheim and Kinnell 241	17	24	18889	1228	1228	4
Inverkeillor and Lunan 208	12	16	18752	2510	2510	7
Glamis, Inverarity and Kinettles 523	28	23	38821	4940	4940	30
Glens, The and Kirriemuir Old 1247	102	41	–	24380	24380	60
Inchbrayock 233	11	–	29035	5560	6360	3
Montrose Melville South 386	20	–	29563	8230	8230	–
Kirriemuir St Andrew's. 474	27	47j	38196	6650	6650	23
Oathlaw Tannadice 177	8	j	11387	1450	1550	12
Montrose Old 648	49	47	77330	16334	16334	75

31. Aberdeen

Congregation	Eld	G	In 02	Ass	Gvn	–18
Aberdeen Beechgrove. 637	78	52	101585	25720	26840	29
Aberdeen Bridge of Don Oldmachar. 236	9	–	47529	–	–	60
Aberdeen Cove. 83	–	–	–	–	–	23
Aberdeen Craigiebuckler 898	66	54	75508	17340	17340	41
Aberdeen Denburn 414	41	22	31549	4500	4500	21
Aberdeen Ferryhill 553	57	34	60623	11260	11260	45
Aberdeen Garthdee. 311	16	20	28862	–	1000	28
Aberdeen Gilcomston South 269	28	–	110169	21437	21437	66
Aberdeen Greyfriars John Knox 597	43	38	46290	7580	8191	18
Aberdeen High Hilton. 629	54	42	102628	15290	16590	40
Aberdeen Holburn Central 535	51	20	60223	10940	10940	8
Aberdeen Holburn West 601	50	31	97021	26330	26330	49
Aberdeen Mannofield 1782	121	93	162515	44670	45639	223
Aberdeen Mastrick 642	24	24	43971	6050	4387	85
Aberdeen Middlefield. 195	11	–	12532	–	–	12
Aberdeen New Stockethill 61	–	–	6672	–	–	2
Aberdeen North of St Andrew. 527	55	32	61116	15770	15770	15
Aberdeen Northfield 368	18	27	33673	3710	1930	18
Aberdeen Queen's Cross. 698	57	40	129663	33520	36520	133
Aberdeen Rosemount 175	20	13	23931	300	300	–
Aberdeen Rubislaw. 698	88	52	125742	33940	33940	161
Aberdeen Ruthrieston South 702	45	64	59584	9860	10980	128
Aberdeen Ruthrieston West. 436	41	28	57280	6680	6680	15
Aberdeen St Columba's Bridge of Don . . . 472	32	–	76141	13890	13890	210
Aberdeen St George's Tillydrone 183	10	20	15216	–	–	10
Aberdeen St John's Church for Deaf People 105	7	–	–	–	–	2
Aberdeen St Machar's Cathedral. 652	53	–	101987	20220	20220	35
Aberdeen St Mark's 574	71	33	69980	13070	13099	47
Aberdeen St Mary's 544	47	25	40854	8995	13303	25
Aberdeen St Nicholas Uniting, Kirk of . . . 677	65	24	46752	9970	10370	10

Congregation. . . . . Com	Eld	G	In 02	Ass	Gvn	–18
Aberdeen St Nicholas Kincorth, South of . 513	36	38	39877	7500	7500	25
Aberdeen St Ninian's 354	22	22	49733	4430	4672	30
Aberdeen St Stephen's 297	28	19	50977	7890	7890	–
Aberdeen Summerhill. 221	21	–	29874	–	201	30
Aberdeen Torry St Fittick's. 590	29	30	45203	4770	4995	10
Aberdeen Woodside 421	35	38	44041	4240	4738	30
Bucksburn Stoneywood 618	26	23	43253	5880	5880	38
Cults East. 367	35	22	49836	7230	7830	40
Cults West 634	44	29	94678	24740	24740	60
Dyce. 1397	76	56	71812	12360	12416	294
Kingswells 502	39	24	40838	3530	3530	44
Newhills. 1012	43	81	88320	17000	17000	249
Peterculter 854	53	36	75555	12820	12820	43

32. Kincardine and Deeside

Aberluthnott. 238	8	16	14285	2920	2992	12
Laurencekirk 550	13	52	25039	4350	4350	16
Aboyne – Dinnet 484	18	28	39997	7800	7800	30
Arbuthnott 125	7	8	9010	1460	1460	–
Bervie. 573	25	30	44292	5800	5800	50
Banchory-Devenick and						
Maryculter/Cookney 416	18	10	27358	3250	3250	18
Banchory-Ternan East. 1217	62	44	75664	14608	14608	93
Banchory-Ternan West 679	53	40	92396	12920	17092	65
Birse and Feughside 311	30	–	35479	5200	8228	35
Braemar 113	10	24j	20992	2320	2320	10
Crathie 176	17	j	30119	5800	5800	5
Cromar. 264	11	–	23492	–	–	20
Drumoak and Durris. 489	23	48	44216	1250	1250	28
Glenmuick (Ballater) 382	23	32	35838	4200	4200	25
Kinneff. 186	8	5	7895	1050	1050	2
Stonehaven South 334	27	18	39180	4730	4730	20
Mearns Coastal. 412	18	39	–	–	–	2
Mid Deeside. 864	50	53	57672	–	–	40
Newtonhill 414	19	25	30951	2450	1960	133
Portlethen. 535	18	–	38880	10810	11794	66
Stonehaven Dunnottar. 907	46	38	67660	11270	11270	32
Stonehaven Fetteresso. 947	47	50	85549	18160	18160	32
West Mearns. 628	25	70	41986	7371	7588	25

33. Gordon

Barthol Chapel 104	9	10	8209	1030	1030	21
Tarves. 521	35	34	32540	6020	8020	13
Belhelvie 590	37	17	44298	4630	4630	48
Blairdaff. 110	12	–	11937	1320	1320	–
Chapel of Garioch 314	22	18	29254	2520	2520	54
Cluny 219	13	13	19442	1930	1930	15
Monymusk. 143	4	9	16078	1390	1390	25

Congregation. Com	Eld	G	In 02	Ass	Gvn	-18
Culsalmond and Rayne. 255	8	–	9818	747	379	10
Daviot 176	9	10	18917	1710	1710	12
Cushnie and Tough. 300	19	10	28419	–	1000	23
Drumblade 133	9	10	6842	1673	1673	8
Huntly Strathbogie 834	51	30	61175	9870	9870	94
Echt 306	16	14	19719	2300	2108	–
Midmar. 176	12	–	14177	2020	2020	–
Ellon. 2113	98	42	118792	23940	23940	192
Fintray and Kinellar 196	12	14j	13325	692	692	–
Keithhall. 82	8	j	4534	1100	1100	–
Foveran 395	20	–	35613	2080	2080	44
Howe Trinity 732	33	46	46497	7115	7115	39
Huntly Cairnie Glass 869	31	38	39020	5722	5722	23
Insch-Leslie-Premnay-Oyne 604	46	48	38575	7730	8295	50
Inverurie St Andrew's 1852	42	73	100616	18250	18250	28
Inverurie West. 768	48	42	59574	10250	14350	60
Kemnay 672	37	–	41542	7180	7180	127
Kintore. 866	52	41	62860	18150	22150	54
Meldrum and Bourtie 559	34	48	44961	4073	4073	50
Methlick. 393	24	30	43375	3278	3278	24
New Machar. 586	29	29	31742	6930	11260	75
Noth. 384	15	–	16094	–	–	17
Skene 1619	100	53	105048	19490	19490	203
Udny and Pitmedden 549	33	14	40397	7350	4410	80
Upper Donside 490	21	–	31962	550	579	20

34. Buchan

Aberdour 145	8	10	10149	780	780	23
New Pitsligo. 360	11	–	21955	1012	1012	18
Auchaber United. 191	15	11	14312	810	833	25
Auchterless. 251	21	20	19232	2273	2570	13
Banff 909	49	38	76552	17010	17666	60
King Edward 182	15	13	11311	3450	3450	10
Crimond. 304	9	10	19030	–	–	12
St Fergus 218	9	15	11632	–	–	16
Cruden 514	35	27	42519	5950	5950	46
Deer. 960	34	27	44147	5410	5410	55
Fordyce 542	30	29	41619	6500	6955	23
Fraserburgh Old 933	59	89	121436	28680	28680	321
Fraserburgh South. 352	21	28	41115	3530	3530	75
Inverallochy and Rathen East 95	9	–	16623	2370	2370	30
Fraserburgh West 723	43	–	53195	8720	8720	49
Fyvie 428	25	46	44149	5513	5513	24
Rothienorman. 202	10	15	12536	860	860	–
Gardenstown 71	11	30	44444	2520	3420	45
Longside. 595	31	–	45540	4700	4925	180
Lonmay 184	14	11	11034	998	998	–
Rathen: West 115	8	–	9490	820	820	–

Congregation. . . . . Com	Eld	G	In 02	Ass	Gvn	–18
Macduff 920	44	58	69828	15550	18796	76
Marnoch. 414	19	15	30065	2987	2985	5
Maud and Savoch 312	16	20	18213	700	700	–
New Deer St Kane's 493	21	19	34434	6430	6430	138
Monquhitter and New Byth. 408	21	26	21909	–	–	17
Ordiquhill and Cornhill. 173	11	13	13312	362	652	16
Whitehills. 324	18	39	25587	3050	3258	21
Peterhead Old. 555	42	38	53345	8400	8400	15
Peterhead St Andrew's 625	38	36	50345	7170	7170	54
Peterhead Trinity 395	30	27	23967	18990	18990	20
Pitsligo. 161	13	–	15465	1763	1763	38
Sandhaven 95	8	–	11036	750	750	31
Strichen and Tyrie. 659	24	45	32917	3815	3815	18
Turriff St Andrew's. 576	27	12	36854	5030	5030	15
Turriff St Ninian's and Forglen 1056	51	56	50993	13341	13341	70

35. Moray

Aberlour. 384	21	34	36757	3262	3323	30
Alves and Burghead 176	17	48	20822	–	–	20
Kinloss and Findhorn 98	14	11	11939	–	300	21
Bellie 405	17	38	33370	8350	8350	37
Speymouth 238	13	25	15626	2150	2150	–
Birnie. 233	18	26	19122	1340	1340	12
Pluscarden 131	10	17	16073	2250	2250	22
Buckie North 626	43	76	53308	8690	8940	43
Buckie South and West. 357	23	32	31741	6640	6914	224
Enzie 121	9	17	12152	670	670	10
Cullen and Deskford. 430	35	53	34967	6410	6571	30
Dallas. 58	6	11	7714	1910	1910	–
Forres St Leonard's. 358	29	46	51244	8160	8160	40
Rafford. 85	6	16	10772	1640	1951	–
Duffus, Spynie and Hopeman 417	43	36	46529	5890	5890	23
Dyke. 180	16	17	22436	3200	3200	42
Edinkillie 93	13	–	18154	2760	2760	12
Elgin High 790	59	46	75048	14850	14850	12
Elgin St Giles' and St Columba's						
South. 1634	104	60	–	25430	25430	34
Findochty. 68	10	19	20484	500	1765	22
Portknockie 106	8	34	18769	688	688	35
Rathven 113	14	29	15180	976	976	–
Forres St Laurence 663	43	44	62009	12240	12240	20
Keith North, Newmill, Boharm and						
Rothiemay. 703	53	45	45320	12540	12615	40
Keith St Rufus, Botriphnie and Grange. . 1102	64	37	55693	7823	7823	84
Knockando, Elchies and Archiestown 278	16	13	18361	1050	1400	10
Rothes 320	14	23	24821	3450	3450	37
Lossiemouth St Gerardine's High 405	27	40	39614	8900	8900	22
Lossiemouth St James' 349	22	32	41915	5810	5810	20

Congregation. Com	Eld	G	In 02	Ass	Gvn	–18
Mortlach and Cabrach. 468	23	44	22271	–	–	5
St Andrew's-Lhanbryd and Urquhart. 518	35	26	49875	7650	7650	45

36. Abernethy

Abernethy. 167	16	–	34959	2620	2620	62
Cromdale and Advie. 106	3	–	8927	830	55	21
Alvie and Insh 77	7	–	21875	2430	2430	16
Kingussie 126	12	–	18879	1600	1600	24
Boat of Garten and Kincardine 102	10	13	22380	–	–	10
Duthil. 70	10	14	8205	–	–	15
Dulnain Bridge. 43	6	–	8963	803	803	8
Grantown-on-Spey 300	21	31	35465	5570	5570	8
Laggan 38	6	–	10435	–	–	–
Newtonmore. 96	12	–	22466	–	–	–
Rothiemurchus and Aviemore. 97	5	–	21614	–	–	12
Tomintoul, Glenlivet and Inveraven 178	15	7	–	–	–	–

37. Inverness

Ardclach. 41	3	–	3009	–	–	6
Auldearn and Dalmore 80	8	17	11974	–	–	–
Ardersier 77	14	13	16526	–	50	16
Petty. 71	11	12	16028	–	200	–
Cawdor. 174	15	21	23945	–	2000	10
Croy and Dalcross . . . . –	–	15	9191	–	50	–
Culloden The Barn 371	31	35	66285	9765	9765	125
Daviot and Dunlichity 63	8	–	10437	–	–	1
Moy, Dalarossie and Tomatin 38	4	10	8925	–	–	14
Dores and Boleskine. 110	8	–	20456	–	–	–
Inverness Crown. 809	89	81	105674	20910	20910	215
Inverness Dalneigh and Bona 295	21	29	73048	10960	10960	102
Inverness East. 326	44	21	107873	26230	26230	157
Inverness Hilton 271	12	31	62803	–	–	109
Inverness Kinmylies 194	12	–	34980	–	–	70
Inverness Ness Bank. 605	61	32	88880	15130	15130	136
Inverness St Columba High 261	33	20	52238	10040	10190	12
Inverness St Stephen's 408	43	–	62051	12690	12730	–
Inverness The Old High 186	30	–	29464	9260	9261	–
Inverness Trinity. 392	36	32	61648	12580	12580	94
Inverness West 174	18	–	66285	13730	13730	4
Kilmorack and Erchless 147	16	21	35609	–	250	30
Kiltarlity. 53	7	–	17674	–	103	20
Kirkhill. 77	8	13	13135	–	–	22
Nairn Old 927	68	37	92023	17950	17950	128
Nairn St Ninian's 297	17	35	37202	2860	2860	30
Urquhart and Glenmoriston 140	8	4	45357	5160	5160	–

38. Lochaber

Acharacle. 34	1	–	10936	–	–	4

Congregation. . . . . Com	Eld	G	In 02	Ass	Gvn	–18
Ardnamurchan 19	4	–	5808	–	–	14
Ardgour 52	8	15	12767	–	166	–
Strontian. 23	3	10	8600	–	159	8
Arisaig and The Small Isles 60	8	20	14378	–	235	15
Duror 50	10	14	11378	–	–	–
Glencoe St Munda's 75	9	16	15902	–	–	12
Fort Augustus 80	7	16	19830	–	–	25
Glengarry 41	8	14	9979	–	–	12
Fort William Duncansburgh 315	24	22	60955	7430	7932	25
Kilmonivaig 81	8	8	18421	4450	7934	12
Fort William MacIntosh Memorial 215	27	20	43788	5290	5290	32
Kilmallie 165	22	25	32417	6830	13129	18
Kinlochleven 78	5	18	18233	–	–	12
Nether Lochaber. 66	7	–	11981	–	–	28
Mallaig St Columba and Knoydart 98	6	–	29828	–	–	–
Morvern 54	5	10	13360	–	–	6

39. Ross

Congregation	Eld	G	In 02	Ass	Gvn	–18
Alness 118	13	–	35550	–	–	25
Avoch. 27	4	12	13429	1920	1540	7
Fortrose and Rosemarkie 143	11	–	31074	5250	5250	11
Contin 58	12	–	17572	–	–	12
Cromarty 74	6	15	19612	–	600	40
Dingwall Castle Street 145	18	25	45595	4910	4910	14
Dingwall St Clement's 255	25	22	46059	5140	11100	44
Fearn Abbey and Nigg 116	13	33	22805	200	200	18
Tarbat. 70	11	–	17919	200	400	–
Ferintosh 202	25	39	48698	2295	3693	35
Fodderty and Strathpeffer 155	19	27	29872	–	612	20
Invergordon 241	13	33	46237	6270	6270	38
Killearnan. 146	20	–	26607	1300	1300	22
Knockbain 78	11	13	17652	650	650	10
Kilmuir and Logie Easter 73	12	16	23154	–	–	10
Kiltearn 81	5	5	26067	–	–	42
Lochbroom and Ullapool 55	5	12	19412	–	–	25
Resolis and Urquhart 101	10	–	21671	–	–	–
Rosskeen 143	12	25	39905	–	900	41
Tain 179	13	27	45570	6710	7291	25
Urray and Kilchrist. 123	17	21	38432	–	163	25

40. Sutherland

Congregation	Eld	G	In 02	Ass	Gvn	–18
Altnaharra and Farr. 35	–	–	12526	–	–	18
Assynt and Stoer 26	2	–	15800	–	–	20
Clyne 102	14	–	20276	–	–	25
Creich. 46	4	–	9935	–	–	10
Rosehall 26	1	–	8058	–	–	6
Dornoch Cathedral 401	33	54	80447	13100	13100	46
Durness and Kinlochbervie. 40	4	13	27564	–	231	10

Congregation. . . . . Com	Eld	G	In 02	Ass	Gvn	–18
Eddrachillis 19	2	–	13661	–	–	6
Golspie. 101	22	12	24959	–	–	10
Kildonan and Loth Helmsdale 49	4	20	15532	–	–	–
Kincardine Croick and Edderton. 86	11	15	22114	–	125	37
Lairg. 53	8	25	18297	–	459	37
Rogart 28	3	13	10474	–	–	7
Melness and Tongue. . . . . –	–	8	–	–	–	9

41. Caithness

Berriedale and Dunbeath 17	3	–	7108	–	–	–
Latheron. 20	1	–	6411	–	–	7
Bower. 28	4	10	10003	–	–	12
Watten 46	5	–	9756	–	–	15
Canisbay. 44	4	21	11861	–	–	15
Keiss 29	3	11	9591	–	–	1
Dunnet 23	2	9	6252	–	–	5
Olrig. 61	5	10	9160	–	–	12
Halkirk and Westerdale. 89	6	19	17870	–	–	45
Lybster and Bruan 43	8	29	15380	–	–	10
Reay. 37	5	10	11363	–	–	–
Strathy and Halladale 26	5	17	10047	–	–	–
Thurso St Peter's and St Andrew's 246	24	50	69541	6250	6250	55
Thurso West 290	28	42	45766	4650	4650	–
Wick Bridge Street 184	12	15	36579	3827	4592	–
Wick Old 246	38	33	49318	5900	5900	29
Wick Pulteneytown and Thrumster 242	14	31	52378	8500	14327	241

42. Lochcarron – Skye

Applecross, Lochcarron and Torridon 87	6	19	–	–	–	30
Bracadale and Duirinish 94	7	7	–	–	–	40
Gairloch and Dundonnell 96	5	–	59758	4720	4720	50
Glenelg and Kintail 56	11	–	21936	–	39	20
Kilmuir and Stenscholl 83	10	–	32155	–	750	45
Lochalsh. 91	5	30	35982	–	2866	40
Portree 159	8	–	55252	3260	7213	61
Snizort 85	10	–	43619	2030	2330	49
Strath and Sleat 187	14	26	55439	7860	7860	72

43. Uist

Barra 34	5	–	9248	–	–	11
Benbecula. 66	12	17	27943	–	180	23
Berneray and Lochmaddy. 62	4	13	24958	–	–	15
Carinish 79	8	21	41482	–	–	32
Kilmuir and Paible 23	5	–	29119	–	–	12
Manish-Scarista 46	4	–	29650	–	–	14
South Uist 61	12	12	17149	–	–	12
Tarbert 164	16	–	70626	11150	11150	45

Congregation.....................Com	Eld	G	In 02	Ass	Gvn	–18
44. Lewis						
Barvas 93	13	–	46103	3020	3020	–
Carloway 38	1	–	25831	–	700	–
Cross Ness 57	8	–	34448	–	–	21
Kinloch 44	9	–	26590	–	–	21
Knock........................... 82	5	–	44151	–	–	25
Lochs-in-Bernera 33	6	–	16148	–	–	18
Lochs – Crossbost 22	2	–	18905	–	–	25
Stornoway High 261	16	–	119341	20170	20170	–
Stornoway Martin's Memorial 116	9	20	46205	5590	5590	73
Stornoway St Columba.............. 131	13	39	62485	10840	10840	94
Uig.............................. 45	6	–	20767	–	–	20
45. Orkney						
Birsay, Harray and Sandwick 390	32	57	26759	2353	2353	37
Deerness........................ 100	9	–	7363	518	575	14
Holm 135	8	14	11811	1050	263	16
St Andrew's 85	9	8	7154	590	28	6
Eday............................. 7	2	5	1798	–	–	–
Stronsay Moncur Memorial 74	10	22	10705	–	300	–
Evie 47	3	–	5905	950	950	–
Firth............................ 126	7	23	20355	3230	3230	25
Rendall.......................... 56	4	15	7485	510	510	1
Flotta 27	4	–	2883	–	–	2
Hoy and Walls 71	11	13	6388	–	–	9
Kirkwall East 514	47	43	55079	10440	10440	75
Kirkwall St Magnus Cathedral 840	70	34	66252	15990	15990	40
North Ronaldsay.................. 17	2	–	1253	–	–	–
Sanday.......................... 104	10	18	8631	–	–	14
Orphir.......................... 135	13	19	18854	–	77	10
Stenness........................ 91	9	11	14871	–	25	6
Papa Westray 12	3	–	3390	–	20	13
Westray 71	14	24	18142	–	250	34
Rousay.......................... 29	4	10	1922	–	–	–
Shapinsay........................ 69	8	–	5742	–	–	5
South Ronaldsay and Burray.......... 196	11	14	18645	–	–	16
Stromness........................ –	–	32	51073	4800	4800	–
46. Shetland						
Burra Isle 46	7	29	8730	–	–	14
Tingwall........................ 172	17	32	20967	–	–	45
Delting.......................... –	–	–	20831	–	112	–
Nesting and Lunnasting 44	5	20	6550	–	–	–
Dunrossness and St Ninian's........... 71	17	–	20735	–	–	22
Sandwick, Cunningsburgh and Quarff.... 150	11	33	24358	–	500	52
Fetlar........................... –	–	–	1560	–	–	–
Yell............................ 143	11	34	13264	–	–	–
Lerwick and Bressay 546	40	–	56441	10210	10210	37

Congregation. . . . . Com	Eld	G	In 02	Ass	Gvn	–18
Northmavine. 87	9	–	7695	–	–	11
Sandsting and Aithsting 55	10	–	9612	–	50	44
Walls and Sandness 50	11	13	8145	–	50	12
Unst 134	11	26	14856	–	–	18
Whalsay and Skerries 249	18	20	23530	–	–	–
47. England						
Corby St Andrew's 339	24	29	51315	1620	1620	15
Corby St Ninian's. 360	24	11	41110	5060	5060	15
Guernsey St Andrew's in the Grange 247	25	–	47551	5170	5170	22
Jersey St Columba's 145	24	–	48843	4325	4325	41
Liverpool St Andrew's 52	7	7	15472	1990	1990	6
London Crown Court 296	47	10	82565	17050	17050	27
London St Columba's. 1469	66	–	204903	63000	63000	59
Newcastle St Andrew's 134	21	7	–	2770	2770	19

Congregation.................... Com	Eld	G	In 02	Ass	Gvn	–18
Fintry 171	10	19	11518	2690	2690	9
Balquhidder 100	5	–	17006	1620	1620	6
Killin and Ardeonaig 177	10	16	14793	1550	1540	36
Bannockburn Allan.................. 531	37	25	47089	5840	5840	92
Bannockburn Ladywell.............. 704	47	35	34452	4260	3031	14
Bridge of Allan Chalmers............ 292	24	20	37739	5200	5658	40
Bridge of Allan Holy Trinity........... 620	39	54	86196	17500	18000	116
Buchanan 110	10	29j	22376	2963	2963	17
Drymen 306	22	j	48231	6340	6340	30
Buchlyvie........................ 248	16	22	25014	3020	3020	16
Gartmore 72	12	–	15534	2230	2230	26
Callander 707	43	49	98329	20860	20860	100
Cambusbarron The Bruce Memorial..... 425	23	–	42569	2700	2700	60
Clackmannan 598	42	35	70212	16630	16880	40
Cowie........................... 156	12	12	12658	540	584	–
Plean 298	8	–	17762	530	530	–
Dollar........................... 712	49	52	96959	17350	17350	120
Glendevon 54	4	–	5307	480	480	1
Muckhart 155	12	–	21598	4090	4090	23
Dunblane Cathedral 1104	94	93	170729	51160	51511	325
Dunblane St Blane's................ 441	46	32	78745	17760	17888	41
Fallin 271	9	–	38585	–	–	120
Gargunnock 218	18	–	19970	2320	2320	23
Kincardine-in-Menteith.............. 122	9	–	8832	570	570	8
Killearn 611	46	68	60568	15310	15310	54
Kilmadock 247	12	–	16798	300	–	–
Kippen.......................... 318	24	23	27120	4580	4580	24
Norrieston 159	11	16	17257	1385	1385	22
Lecropt.......................... 278	13	29	43586	3260	3260	11
Logie 684	57	65	80628	19070	19165	39
Menstrie......................... 443	32	30	57758	9510	9510	70
Sauchie and Coalsnaughton 910	35	32	53908	11200	11200	18
Stirling Allan Park South 282	46	50	38725	6470	6470	30
Stirling Church of The Holy Rude 274	43	–	48536	4490	4490	22
Stirling North 572	44	23	57836	9020	9020	215
Stirling St Columba's 587	66	–	81023	17820	17820	95
Stirling St Mark's.................. 346	14	–	32717	2230	2230	4
Stirling St Ninian's Old 822	48	–	78307	12450	12450	45
Stirling Viewfield 536	34	35	68813	12690	12690	40
Strathblane....................... 378	25	46	48321	7360	7360	–
Tillicoultry....................... 922	63	45	78197	16760	17366	113
Tullibody St Serf's 638	26	18	66858	6880	7209	28
24. Dunfermline						
Aberdour St Fillan's................ 416	31	–	58423	11250	11250	42
Ballingry and Lochcraig 126	17	–	13211	–	–	14
Beath and Cowdenbeath North 212	15	17	–	–	–	48
Cairneyhill 228	27	–	25895	3610	3610	50

INDEX OF MINISTERS

NOTE: Ministers who are members of a Presbytery are designated 'A' if holding a parochial appointment in that Presbytery, or 'B' if otherwise qualifying for membership.

'A-1, A-2' etc. indicate the numerical order of congregations in the Presbyteries of Edinburgh, Glasgow and Hamilton.

Also included are:

(1) Ministers who have resigned their seat in Presbytery (List 6-H)
(2) Ministers who hold a Practising Certificate (List 6-I)
(3) Ministers serving overseas (List 6-K)
(4) Auxiliary Ministers (List 6-A)
(5) Ministers ordained for sixty years and upwards (List 6-Q)
(6) Ministers who have died since the publication of the last *Year Book* (List 6-R)

NB *For a list of the Diaconate, see List 6-G.*

INDEX OF PARISHES AND PLACES

NOTE: Numbers on the right of the column refer to the Presbytery in which the district lies. Names in brackets are given for ease of identification. They may refer to the name of the Parish, which may be different from that of the district, or they distinguish places with the same name, or they indicate the first named charge in a union.

INDEX OF FORMER PARISHES AND CONGREGATIONS

The following index updates and corrects the 'Index of Former Parishes and Congregations' printed in the previous edition of the *Year Book*. As before, it contains the names of parishes of the Church of Scotland and of congregations of the Free Church, the United Free Church and the United Presbyterian Church (and its constituent denominations) which no longer have a separate existence, largely as a consequence of union.

It should be stressed that this index is not intended to be a comprehensive guide to readjustment in the Church of Scotland and does not therefore include the names of *all* parishes and congregations which no longer exist as independent entities. Its purpose is rather to assist those who are trying to identify the present successor of some former parish or congregation whose name may no longer be recognisable. Where a connection between the former name and the present name may easily be established, the former name has not been included, as the following examples will illustrate.

- Where all the former congregations in a town have been united into one, as in the case of Melrose or Selkirk, the names of these former congregations have not been included; but in the case of towns with more than one congregation, such as Galashiels or Hawick, the names of the various constituent congregations are listed.
- Where a prefix such as North, Old, Little, Mid or the like has been lost but the substantive part of the name has been retained, the former name has not been included: it is assumed that someone searching for Little Dalton or Mid Yell will have no difficulty in connecting these with Dalton or Yell.
- Where the present name of a united congregation includes the names of some or all of its constituent parts, these former names do not appear in the index: thus, neither Glasgow: Anderston nor Glasgow: Kelvingrove appears, since both names are easily traceable to Glasgow: Anderston Kelvingrove.
- Some parishes and congregations have disappeared, and their names have been lost, as a consequence of suppression, dissolution or secession. The names of rural parishes in this category have been included, together with the names of their Presbyteries to assist with identification, but those in towns and cities have not been included, as there will clearly be no difficulty in establishing the general location of the parish or congregation in question.

Since 1929, a small number of rural parishes have adopted a new name (for example Whitehills, formerly Boyndie). The former names of these parishes have been included, but it would have been too unwieldy to include either the vast numbers of such changes of name in towns and cities, especially those which occurred at the time of the 1900 and 1929 unions, or the very many older names of pre-Reformation parishes which were abandoned in earlier centuries (however fascinating a list of such long-vanished names as Fothmuref, Kinbathock and Toskertoun might have been).

In this index, the following abbreviations have been used:

C of S	Church of Scotland
FC	Free Church
R	Relief Church
RP	Reformed Presbyterian Church
UF	United Free Church
UP	United Presbyterian Church
US	United Secession Church

Name no longer used	Present name of parish
Abbey St Bathan's	Kirk of Lammermuir
Abbotrule	charge suppressed: Presbytery of Jedburgh
Aberargie	charge dissolved: Presbytery of Perth
Aberchirder	Marnoch
Aberdalgie	The Stewartry of Strathearn
Aberdeen: Belmont Street	Aberdeen: St Mark's
Aberdeen: Bon Accord	Aberdeen: Denburn
Aberdeen: Carden Place	Aberdeen: Queen's Cross
Aberdeen: Causewayend	Aberdeen: St Stephen's
Aberdeen: East	Aberdeen: St Mark's
Aberdeen: Gallowgate	Aberdeen: St Mary's
Aberdeen: Gilcomston St Colm's	Aberdeen: Denburn
Aberdeen: Hilton	Aberdeen: Woodside
Aberdeen: King Street	Aberdeen: North of St Andrew
Aberdeen: Melville	Aberdeen: Queen's Cross
Aberdeen: Nelson Street	Aberdeen: North of St Andrew
Aberdeen: North	Aberdeen: North of St Andrew
Aberdeen: Pittodrie	Aberdeen: St Mary's
Aberdeen: Powis	Aberdeen: St Stephen's
Aberdeen: Rutherford	Aberdeen: Rosemount
Aberdeen: South (C of S)	Aberdeen: St Nicholas South of Kincorth
Aberdeen: South (FC)	Aberdeen: St Mark's
Aberdeen: St Columba's	Aberdeen: High Hilton
Aberdeen: St Mary's	Aberdeen: St Machar's Cathedral
Aberdeen: St Paul's	Aberdeen: Denburn
Aberdeen: Trinity (C of S)	Aberdeen: Kirk of St Nicholas Uniting
Aberdeen: Trinity (FC)	Aberdeen: St Mark's
Aberdeen: Union	Aberdeen: Denburn
Aberuthven	The Stewartry of Strathearn
Abington	Glencaple
Addiewell	Breich Valley
Afton	New Cumnock
Airdrie: West	Airdrie: New Wellwynd
Aldbar	Aberlemno
Aldcambus	Dunglass
Alford	Howe Trinity
Alloa: Chalmers	Alloa: North
Alloa: Melville	Alloa: North
Alloa: St Andrew's	Alloa: North
Altries	charge dissolved: Presbytery of Kincardine and Deeside
Altyre	Rafford
Alvah	Banff
Annan: Erskine	Annan: St Andrew's
Annan: Greenknowe	Annan: St Andrew's
Arbroath: East	Arbroath: St Andrew's
Arbroath: Erskine	Arbroath: West Kirk
Arbroath: High Street	Arbroath: St Andrew's
Arbroath: Hopemount	Arbroath: St Andrew's
Arbroath: Ladyloan	Arbroath: West Kirk
Arbroath: Princes Street	Arbroath: West Kirk
Arbroath: St Columba's	Arbroath: West Kirk
Arbroath: St Margaret's	Arbroath: West Kirk
Arbroath: St Ninian's	Arbroath: St Andrew's
Arbroath: St Paul's	Arbroath: St Andrew's
Ardallie	Deer
Ardwell	Stoneykirk
Ascog	Bute United
Auchindoir	Upper Donside

Name no longer used	Present name of parish
Auchmithie	Arbroath: St Vigean's
Auldcathie	Dalmeny
Aultbea	Gairloch and Dundonnell
Ayr: Cathcart	Ayr: St Columba
Ayr: Darlington New	Ayr: Auld Kirk of Ayr
Ayr: Darlington Place	Ayr: Auld Kirk of Ayr
Ayr: Lochside	Ayr: St Quivox
Ayr: Martyrs'	Ayr: Auld Kirk of Ayr
Ayr: Sandgate	Ayr: St Columba
Ayr: St John's	Ayr: Auld Kirk of Ayr
Ayr: Trinity	Ayr: St Columba
Ayr: Wallacetown South	Ayr: Auld Kirk of Ayr
Back	charge dissolved: Presbytery of Lewis
Badcall	Eddrachillis
Balbeggie	Collace
Balfour	charge dissolved: Presbytery of Dundee
Balgedie	Portmoak
Baliasta	Unst
Ballachulish	Nether Lochaber
Ballater	Glenmuick
Balmacolm	Howe of Fife
Balmullo	charge dissolved: Presbytery of St Andrews
Balnacross	Tarff and Twynholm
Baltasound	Unst
Banchory-Ternan: North	Banchory-Ternan: West
Banchory-Ternan: South	Banchory-Ternan: West
Bandry	Luss
Bara	Garvald and Morham
Bargrennan	Penninghame
Barnweil	Tarbolton
Barrhead: Westbourne	Barrhead: Arthurlie
Barrock	Dunnet
Bedrule	Ruberslaw
Beith: Hamilfield	Beith: Trinity
Beith: Head Street	Beith: Trinity
Beith: Mitchell Street	Beith: Trinity
Belkirk	Liddesdale
Benholm	Mearns Coastal
Benvie	Fowlis and Liff
Binny	Linlithgow: St Michael's
Blackburn	Fintray and Kinellar
Blackhill	Longside
Blairlogie	congregation seceded: Presbytery of Stirling
Blanefield	Strathblane
Blantyre: Anderson	Blantyre: St Andrew's
Blantyre: Burleigh Memorial	Blantyre: St Andrew's
Blantyre: Stonefield	Blantyre: St Andrew's
Blyth Bridge	Kirkurd and Newlands
Boddam	Peterhead: Trinity
Bonhill: North	Alexandria
Bothwell: Park	Uddingston: Viewpark
Bourtreebush	Newtonhill
Bow of Fife	Monimail
Bowmore	Kilarrow
Boyndie	Whitehills
Brachollie	Petty
Braco	Ardoch
Braehead	Forth

Name no longer used	Present name of parish
Brechin: East	Brechin: Gardner Memorial
Brechin: Maison Dieu	Brechin: Cathedral
Brechin: St Columba's	Brechin: Gardner Memorial
Brechin: West	Brechin: Gardner Memorial
Breich	Breich Valley
Bridge of Allan: St Andrew's	Bridge of Allan: Holy Trinity
Bridge of Allan: Trinity	Bridge of Allan: Holy Trinity
Bridge of Teith	Kilmadock
Brora	Clyne
Buccleuch	Ettrick and Yarrow
Burnhead	Penpont, Keir and Tynron
Cairnryan	charge dissolved: Presbytery of Wigtown and Stranraer
Cambuslang: Rosebank	Cambuslang: St Andrew's
Cambuslang: West	Cambuslang: St Andrew's
Cambusmichael	St Martin's
Campbeltown: Longrow	Campbeltown: Lorne and Lowland
Campsail	Rosneath St Modan's
Canna	Mallaig St Columba and Knoydart
Carbuddo	Guthrie and Rescobie
Cardenden	Auchterderran St Fothad's
Carmichael	Cairngryffe
Carnoch	Contin
Carnousie	Turriff: St Ninian's and Forglen
Carnoustie: St Stephen's	Carnoustie
Carrbridge	Duthil
Carruthers	Middlebie
Castle Kennedy	Inch
Castleton	Liddesdale
Caterline	Kinneff
Chapelknowe	congregation seceded: Presbytery of Annandale and Eskdale
Clatt	Noth
Clayshant	Stoneykirk
Climpy	charge dissolved: Presbytery of Lanark
Clola	Deer
Clousta	Sandsting and Aithsting
Clova	The Glens and Kirriemuir: Old
Clydebank: Bank Street	Clydebank: St Cuthbert's
Clydebank: Boquhanran	Clydebank: Kilbowie St Andrew's
Clydebank: Hamilton Memorial	Clydebank: St Cuthbert's
Clydebank: Linnvale	Clydebank: St Cuthbert's
Clydebank: St James'	Clydebank: Abbotsford
Clydebank: Union	Clydebank: Kilbowie St Andrew's
Clydebank: West	Clydebank: Abbotsford
Coatbridge: Cliftonhill	Coatbridge: Clifton
Coatbridge: Coatdyke	Coatbridge: Clifton
Coatbridge: Coats	Coatbridge: Clifton
Coatbridge: Dunbeth	Coatbridge: St Andrew's
Coatbridge: Gartsherrie	Coatbridge: St Andrew's
Coatbridge: Garturk	Coatbridge: Calder
Coatbridge: Maxwell	Coatbridge: St Andrew's
Coatbridge: Trinity	Coatbridge: Clifton
Coatbridge: Whifflet	Coatbridge: Calder
Cobbinshaw	charge dissolved: Presbytery of West Lothian
Cockburnspath	Dunglass
Coigach	charge dissolved: Presbytery of Lochcarron-Skye
Coldstone	Cromar
Collessie	Howe of Fife
Corgarff	Upper Donside

Name no longer used	Present name of parish
Cortachy	The Glens and Kirriemuir: Old
Coull	Cromar
Covington	Cairngryffe
Cowdenbeath: Cairns	Cowdenbeath: Trinity
Cowdenbeath: Guthrie Memorial	Beath and Cowdenbeath: North
Cowdenbeath: West	Cowdenbeath: Trinity
Craggan	Tomintoul, Glenlivet and Inveraven
Craig	Inchbrayock
Craigdam	Tarves
Craigend	Perth: Moncreiffe
Cranshaws	Kirk of Lammermuir
Crawford	Glencaple
Crawfordjohn	Glencaple
Cray	Kirkmichael, Straloch and Glenshee
Creetown	Kirkmabreck
Crofthead	Fauldhouse St Andrew's
Crombie	Culross and Torryburn
Crossgates	Cowdenbeath: Trinity
Cruggleton	Sorbie
Cuikston	Farnell
Culbin	Dyke
Cullicudden	Resolis and Urquhart
Cults	Howe of Fife
Cumbernauld: Baird	Cumbernauld: Old
Cumbernauld: Bridgend	Cumbernauld: Old
Cumbernauld: St Andrew's	Cumbernauld: Old
Dalgarno	Closeburn
Dalguise	Dunkeld
Daliburgh	South Uist
Dalkeith: Buccleuch Street	Dalkeith: St Nicholas Buccleuch
Dalkeith: West (C of S)	Dalkeith: St Nicholas Buccleuch
Dalkeith: West (UP)	Dalkeith: St John's and King's Park
Dalmeath	Huntly Cairnie Glass
Dalreoch	charge dissolved: Presbytery of Perth
Dalry: Courthill	Dalry: Trinity
Dalry: St Andrew's	Dalry: Trinity
Dalry: West	Dalry: Trinity
Denholm	Ruberslaw
Denny: Broompark	Denny: Westpark
Denny: West	Denny: Westpark
Dennyloanhead	charge dissolved: Presbytery of Falkirk
Dolphinton	Black Mount
Dowally	Dunkeld
Drainie	Lossiemouth St Gerardine's High
Drumdelgie	Huntly Cairnie Glass
Dumbarrow	charge dissolved: Presbytery of Angus
Dumbarton: Bridgend	Dumbarton: West
Dumbarton: Dalreoch	Dumbarton: West
Dumbarton: High	Dumbarton: Riverside
Dumbarton: Knoxland	Dumbarton: Riverside
Dumbarton: North	Dumbarton: Riverside
Dumbarton: Old	Dumbarton: Riverside
Dumfries: Maxwelltown Laurieknowe	Dumfries: Troqueer
Dumfries: Townhead	Dumfries: St Michael's and South
Dunblane: East	Dunblane: St Blane's
Dunblane: Leighton	Dunblane: St Blane's
Dundee: Albert Square	Dundee: Meadowside St Paul's
Dundee: Baxter Park	Dundee: Trinity

Name no longer used	Present name of parish
Dundee: Broughty Ferry Union	Dundee: Broughty Ferry St Stephen's and West
Dundee: Chapelshade (FC)	Dundee: Meadowside St Paul's
Dundee: Downfield North	Dundee: Strathmartine
Dundee: Hawkhill	Dundee: Meadowside St Paul's
Dundee: Lochee East	Dundee: Lochee Old and St Luke's
Dundee: Lochee St Ninian's	Dundee: Lochee Old and St Luke's
Dundee: Martyrs'	Dundee: Balgay
Dundee: Maryfield	Dundee: Stobswell
Dundee: McCheyne Memorial	Dundee: West
Dundee: Ogilvie	Dundee: Stobswell
Dundee: Park	Dundee: Stobswell
Dundee: Roseangle	Dundee: West
Dundee: Ryehill	Dundee: West
Dundee: St Andrew's (FC)	Dundee: Meadowside St Paul's
Dundee: St Clement's Steeple	Dundee: Steeple
Dundee: St David's (C of S)	Dundee: Steeple
Dundee: St Enoch's	Dundee: Steeple
Dundee: St George's	Dundee: Meadowside St Paul's
Dundee: St John's	Dundee: West
Dundee: St Mark's	Dundee: West
Dundee: St Matthew's	Dundee: Trinity
Dundee: St Paul's	Dundee: Steeple
Dundee: St Peter's	Dundee: West
Dundee: Tay Square	Dundee: Meadowside St Paul's
Dundee: Victoria Street	Dundee: Stobswell
Dundee: Wallacetown	Dundee: Trinity
Dundee: Wishart Memorial	Dundee: Steeple
Dundurcas	Keith: North, Newmill, Boharm and Rothiemay
Duneaton	Glencaple
Dunfermline: Chalmers Street	Dunfermline: St Andrew's Erskine
Dunfermline: Maygate	Dunfermline: Gillespie Memorial
Dunfermline: Queen Anne Street	Dunfermline: St Andrew's Erskine
Dungree	Kirkpatrick Juxta
Duninald	Inchbrayock
Dunlappie	Brechin: Cathedral
Dunning	The Stewartry of Strathearn
Dunoon: Gaelic	Dunoon: St John's
Dunrod	Kirkcudbright
Dunsyre	Black Mount
Dupplin	The Stewartry of Strathearn
Ecclefechan	Hoddam
Ecclesjohn	Dun
Ecclesmachan	Strathbrock
Ecclesmoghriodan	Abernethy and Dron
Edinburgh: Abbey	Edinburgh: Greenside
Edinburgh: Abbeyhill	Edinburgh: Holyrood Abbey
Edinburgh: Arthur Street	Edinburgh: Kirk o' Field
Edinburgh: Barony	Edinburgh: Greenside
Edinburgh: Belford	Edinburgh: Palmerston Place
Edinburgh: Braid	Edinburgh: Morningside
Edinburgh: Bruntsfield	Edinburgh: Barclay
Edinburgh: Buccleuch	Edinburgh: Kirk o' Field
Edinburgh: Cairns Memorial	Edinburgh: Gorgie
Edinburgh: Candlish	Edinburgh: Polwarth
Edinburgh: Canongate (FC,UP)	Edinburgh: Holy Trinity
Edinburgh: Chalmers	Edinburgh: Barclay
Edinburgh: Charteris Memorial	Edinburgh: Kirk o' Field
Edinburgh: Cluny	Edinburgh: Morningside

Name no longer used	Present name of parish
Edinburgh: St James' (FC)	Edinburgh: Inverleith
Edinburgh: St James' Place	Edinburgh: Greenside
Edinburgh: St John's	Edinburgh: Greyfriars Tolbooth and Highland
Edinburgh: St Luke's	Edinburgh: St Andrew's and St George's
Edinburgh: St Matthew's	Edinburgh: Morningside
Edinburgh: St Oran's	Edinburgh: Greyfriars Tolbooth and Highland
Edinburgh: St Oswald's	Edinburgh: Viewforth
Edinburgh: St Paul's	Edinburgh: Kirk o' Field
Edinburgh: St Stephen's (C of S)	Edinburgh: Stockbridge
Edinburgh: St Stephen's (FC)	Edinburgh: St Stephen's Comely Bank
Edinburgh: Tolbooth (C of S)	Edinburgh: Greyfriars Tolbooth and Highland
Edinburgh: Tolbooth (FC)	Edinburgh: St Andrew's and St George's
Edinburgh: Trinity College	Edinburgh: Holy Trinity
Edinburgh: Tynecastle	Edinburgh: Gorgie
Edinburgh: Warrender	Edinburgh: Marchmont St Giles
Edinburgh: West St Giles	Edinburgh: Marchmont St Giles
Eigg	Arisaig and the Small Isles
Eilean Finain	Ardnamurchan
Elgin: Moss Street	Elgin: St Giles and St Columba's South
Elgin: South Street	Elgin: St Giles and St Columba's South
Ellem	Kirk of Lammermuir
Elsrickle	Black Mount
Eshaness	Northmavine
Essie	Noth
Essil	Speymouth
Ethie	Inverkeilor and Lunan
Ettiltoun	Liddesdale
Ewes Durris	Langholm, Ewes and Westerkirk
Falkirk: Graham's Road	Falkirk: Grahamston United
Farnua	Kirkhill
Ferryden	Inchbrayock
Fetterangus	Deer
Fettercairn	West Mearns
Fetternear	Chapel of Garioch
Finzean	Birse and Feughside
Fochabers	Bellie
Forbes	Howe Trinity
Fordoun	West Mearns
Forfar: South	Forfar: St Margaret's
Forfar: St James'	Forfar: St Margaret's
Forfar: West	Forfar: St Margaret's
Forgan	Newport-on-Tay
Forgue	Auchaber United
Forres: Castlehill	Forres: St Leonard's
Forres: High	Forres: St Leonard's
Forteviot	The Stewartry of Strathearn
Forvie	Ellon
Foula	Walls and Sandness
Galashiels: East	Galashiels: St Ninian's
Galashiels: Ladhope	Galashiels: St Aidan's
Galashiels: South	Galashiels: St Aidan's
Galashiels: St Andrew's	Galashiels: St Ninian's
Galashiels: St Columba's	Galashiels: St Ninian's
Galashiels: St Cuthbert's	Galashiels: St Aidan's
Galashiels: St Mark's	Galashiels: St Ninian's
Galashiels: Trinity	Galashiels: St Aidan's
Galtway	Kirkcudbright
Gamrie	charge dissolved: Presbytery of Buchan

Name no longer used	Present name of parish
Garmouth	Speymouth
Gartly	Noth
Garvell	Kirkmichael, Tinwald and Torthorwald
Garvock	Mearns Coastal
Gatehouse	Anwoth and Girthon
Gauldry	Balmerino
Gelston	Buittle and Kelton
Giffnock: Orchard Park	Giffnock: The Park
Girvan: Chalmers	Girvan: North (Old and St Andrew's)
Girvan: Trinity	Girvan: North (Old and St Andrew's)
Glasgow: Abbotsford	Glasgow: Gorbals
Glasgow: Auldfield	Glasgow: Pollokshaws
Glasgow: Baillieston Old	Glasgow: Baillieston St Andrew's
Glasgow: Baillieston Rhinsdale	Glasgow: Baillieston St Andrew's
Glasgow: Balornock North	Glasgow: Wallacewell
Glasgow: Barmulloch	Glasgow: Wallacewell
Glasgow: Barrowfield (C of S)	Glasgow: Bridgeton St Francis in the East
Glasgow: Barrowfield (RP)	Glasgow: St Luke's and St Andrew's
Glasgow: Bath Street	Glasgow: Renfield St Stephen's
Glasgow: Battlefield West	Glasgow: Langside
Glasgow: Bellahouston	Glasgow: Ibrox
Glasgow: Bellgrove	Glasgow: Dennistoun Blackfriars
Glasgow: Belmont	Glasgow: Kelvinside Hillhead
Glasgow: Berkeley Street	Glasgow: Renfield St Stephen's
Glasgow: Bluevale	Glasgow: Dennistoun Central
Glasgow: Blythswood	Glasgow: Renfield St Stephen's
Glasgow: Bridgeton East	Glasgow: Bridgeton St Francis in the East
Glasgow: Bridgeton West	Glasgow: St Luke's and St Andrew's
Glasgow: Buccleuch	Glasgow: Renfield St Stephen's
Glasgow: Burnbank	Glasgow: Lansdowne
Glasgow: Calton New	Glasgow: St Luke's and St Andrew's
Glasgow: Calton Old	Glasgow: Calton Parkhead
Glasgow: Calton Relief	Glasgow: St Luke's and St Andrew's
Glasgow: Cambridge Street	Bishopbriggs: Springfield Cambridge
Glasgow: Candlish Memorial	Glasgow: Govanhill Trinity
Glasgow: Cathcart South	Glasgow: Cathcart Trinity
Glasgow: Central	Glasgow: St Luke's and St Andrew's
Glasgow: Cessnock	Glasgow: Kinning Park
Glasgow: Chalmers (C of S)	Glasgow: St Luke's and St Andrew's
Glasgow: Chalmers (FC)	Glasgow: Gorbals
Glasgow: Claremont	Glasgow: Anderston Kelvingrove
Glasgow: College	Glasgow: Anderston Kelvingrove
Glasgow: Cowcaddens	Glasgow: Renfield St Stephen's
Glasgow: Cowlairs	Glasgow: Springburn
Glasgow: Crosshill	Glasgow: Queen's Park
Glasgow: Dalmarnock (C of S)	Glasgow: Calton Parkhead
Glasgow: Dalmarnock (UF)	Rutherglen: Old
Glasgow: Dean Park	Glasgow: New Govan
Glasgow: Dennistoun South	Glasgow: Dennistoun Blackfriars
Glasgow: Dowanhill	Glasgow: Partick Trinity
Glasgow: Dowanvale	Glasgow: Partick South
Glasgow: Drumchapel Old	Glasgow: Drumchapel St Andrew's
Glasgow: East Campbell Street	Glasgow: Dennistoun Central
Glasgow: East Park	Glasgow: Kelvin Stevenson Memorial
Glasgow: Edgar Memorial	Glasgow: St Luke's and St Andrew's
Glasgow: Eglinton Street	Glasgow: Govanhill Trinity
Glasgow: Elder Park	Glasgow: Govan Old
Glasgow: Elgin Street	Glasgow: Govanhill Trinity

Name no longer used	Present name of parish
Glasgow: Erskine	Glasgow: Langside
Glasgow: Fairbairn	Rutherglen: Old
Glasgow: Fairfield	Glasgow: New Govan
Glasgow: Finnieston	Glasgow: Anderston Kelvingrove
Glasgow: Garnethill	Glasgow: Renfield St Stephen's
Glasgow: Garscube Netherton	Glasgow: Knightswood St Margaret's
Glasgow: Gillespie	Glasgow: St Luke's and St Andrew's
Glasgow: Gordon Park	Glasgow: Whiteinch
Glasgow: Govan Copland Road	Glasgow: New Govan
Glasgow: Govan Trinity	Glasgow: New Govan
Glasgow: Grant Street	Glasgow: Renfield St Stephen's
Glasgow: Greenhead	Glasgow: St Luke's and St Andrew's
Glasgow: Hall Memorial	Rutherglen: Old
Glasgow: Hamilton Crescent	Glasgow: Partick South
Glasgow: Highlanders' Memorial	Glasgow: Knightswood St Margaret's
Glasgow: Hyndland (UF)	Glasgow: St John's Renfield
Glasgow: John Knox's	Glasgow: Gorbals
Glasgow: Johnston	Glasgow: Springburn
Glasgow: Jordanvale	Glasgow: Whiteinch
Glasgow: Kelvinhaugh	Glasgow: Anderston Kelvingrove
Glasgow: Kelvinside Botanic Gardens	Glasgow: Kelvinside Hillhead
Glasgow: Kelvinside Old	Glasgow: Kelvin Stevenson Memorial
Glasgow: Kingston	Glasgow: Carnwadric
Glasgow: Lancefield	Glasgow: Anderston Kelvingrove
Glasgow: Langside Avenue	Glasgow: Shawlands
Glasgow: Langside Hill	Glasgow: Battlefield East
Glasgow: Langside Old	Glasgow: Langside
Glasgow: Laurieston (C of S)	Glasgow: Gorbals
Glasgow: Laurieston (FC)	Glasgow: Carnwadric
Glasgow: London Road	Glasgow: Bridgeton St Francis in the East
Glasgow: Lyon Street	Glasgow: Renfield St Stephen's
Glasgow: Macgregor Memorial	Glasgow: Govan Old
Glasgow: Macmillan	Glasgow: St Luke's and St Andrew's
Glasgow: Milton	Glasgow: Renfield St Stephen's
Glasgow: Netherton St Matthew's	Glasgow: Knightswood St Margaret's
Glasgow: New Cathcart	Glasgow: Cathcart Trinity
Glasgow: Newhall	Glasgow: Bridgeton St Francis in the East
Glasgow: Newton Place	Glasgow: Partick South
Glasgow: Nithsdale	Glasgow: Queen's Park
Glasgow: Old Partick	Glasgow: Partick Trinity
Glasgow: Paisley Road	Glasgow: Kinning Park
Glasgow: Partick Anderson	Glasgow: Partick South
Glasgow: Partick East	Glasgow: Partick Trinity
Glasgow: Partick High	Glasgow: Partick South
Glasgow: Phoenix Park	Glasgow: Springburn
Glasgow: Plantation	Glasgow: Kinning Park
Glasgow: Pollok St Aidan's	Glasgow: St James' Pollok
Glasgow: Pollok Street	Glasgow: Kinning Park
Glasgow: Polmadie	Glasgow: Govanhill Trinity
Glasgow: Queen's Cross	Glasgow: Ruchill
Glasgow: Renfield (C of S)	Glasgow: Renfield St Stephen's
Glasgow: Renfield (FC)	Glasgow: St John's Renfield
Glasgow: Renfield Street	Glasgow: Renfield St Stephen's
Glasgow: Renwick	Glasgow: Gorbals
Glasgow: Robertson Memorial	Glasgow: The Martyrs'
Glasgow: Rockcliffe	Rutherglen: Old
Glasgow: Rockvilla	Glasgow: Possilpark
Glasgow: Rose Street	Glasgow: Langside

Name no longer used	Present name of parish
Glasgow: Rutherford	Glasgow: Dennistoun Central
Glasgow: Shamrock Street	Glasgow: Renfield St Stephen's
Glasgow: Shawholm	Glasgow: Pollokshaws
Glasgow: Shawlands Cross	Glasgow: Shawlands
Glasgow: Shawlands Old	Glasgow: Shawlands
Glasgow: Sighthill	Glasgow: Springburn
Glasgow: Somerville	Glasgow: Springburn
Glasgow: Springbank	Glasgow: Lansdowne
Glasgow: St Clement's	Glasgow: Bridgeton St Francis in the East
Glasgow: St Columba Gaelic	Glasgow: New Govan
Glasgow: St Cuthbert's	Glasgow: Ruchill
Glasgow: St Enoch's (C of S)	Glasgow: St Enoch's Hogganfield
Glasgow: St Enoch's (FC)	Glasgow: Anderston Kelvingrove
Glasgow: St George's (C of S)	Glasgow: St George's Tron
Glasgow: St George's (FC)	Glasgow: Anderston Kelvingrove
Glasgow: St George's Road	Glasgow: Renfield St Stephen's
Glasgow: St James' (C of S)	Glasgow: St James' Pollok
Glasgow: St James' (FC)	Glasgow: St Luke's and St Andrew's
Glasgow: St John's (C of S)	Glasgow: St Luke's and St Andrew's
Glasgow: St John's (FC)	Glasgow: St John's Renfield
Glasgow: St Kiaran's	Glasgow: New Govan
Glasgow: St Mark's	Glasgow: Anderston Kelvingrove
Glasgow: St Mary's Govan	Glasgow: New Govan
Glasgow: St Mary's Partick	Glasgow: Partick South
Glasgow: St Matthew's (C of S)	Glasgow: Renfield St Stephen's
Glasgow: St Matthew's (FC)	Glasgow: Knightswood St Margaret's
Glasgow: St Ninian's	Glasgow: Gorbals
Glasgow: St Peter's	Glasgow: Anderston Kelvingrove
Glasgow: Steven Memorial	Glasgow: Ibrox
Glasgow: Strathbungo	Glasgow: Queen's Park
Glasgow: Summerfield	Rutherglen: Old
Glasgow: Summertown	Glasgow: New Govan
Glasgow: Sydney Place	Glasgow: Dennistoun Cental
Glasgow: The Park	Giffnock: The Park
Glasgow: Titwood	Glasgow: Pollokshields
Glasgow: Tradeston	Glasgow: Gorbals
Glasgow: Trinity	Glasgow: St Luke's and St Andrew's
Glasgow: Trinity Duke Street	Glasgow: Dennistoun Central
Glasgow: Tron St Anne's	Glasgow: St George's Tron
Glasgow: Union	Glasgow: Carnwadric
Glasgow: Victoria	Glasgow: Queen's Park
Glasgow: Wellfield	Glasgow: Springburn
Glasgow: Wellpark	Glasgow: Dennistoun Cental
Glasgow: West Scotland Street	Glasgow: Kinning Park
Glasgow: White Memorial	Glasgow: Kinning Park
Glasgow: Whitehill	Glasgow: Dennistoun Blackfriars
Glasgow: Whitevale (FC)	Glasgow: St Thomas' Gallowgate
Glasgow: Whitevale (UP)	Glasgow: Dennistoun Central
Glasgow: Wilton	Glasgow: Kelvin Stevenson Memorial
Glasgow: Woodlands	Glasgow: Wellington
Glasgow: Woodlands Road	Glasgow: Wellington
Glasgow: Woodside	Glasgow: Lansdowne
Glasgow: Wynd (C of S)	Glasgow: St Luke's and St Andrew's
Glasgow: Wynd (FC)	Glasgow: Gorbals
Glasgow: Young Street	Glasgow: Dennistoun Blackfriars
Glen Convinth	Kiltarlity
Glen Ussie	Fodderty and Strathpeffer
Glenapp	Ballantrae

Name no longer used	Present name of parish
Glenbervie	West Mearns
Glenbuchat	Upper Donside
Glenbuck	Muirkirk
Glencaple	Caerlaverock
Glendoick	St Madoes and Kinfauns
Glenfarg	Arngask
Glengairn	Glenmuick
Glengarnock	Kilbirnie: Auld Kirk
Glenluce	Old Luce
Glenmoriston	Fort Augustus
Glenprosen	The Glens and Kirriemuir Old
Glenrinnes	Mortlach and Cabrach
Glenshiel	Glenelg and Kintail
Glentanar	Aboyne – Dinnet
Gogar	Edinburgh: Corstorphine Old
Gordon	Monquhitter and New Byth
Graemsay	Stromness
Grangemouth: Grange	Grangemouth: Zetland
Grangemouth: Old	Grangemouth: Zetland
Greenloaning	Ardoch
Greenock: Augustine	Greenock: Cartsdyke
Greenock: Cartsburn	Greenock: Cartsdyke
Greenock: Crawfordsburn	Greenock: Cartsdyke
Greenock: Gaelic	Greenock: St Luke's
Greenock: Greenbank	Greenock: St Luke's
Greenock: Martyrs'	Greenock: St George's North
Greenock: Middle	Greenock: St George's North
Greenock: Mount Park	Greenock: Mount Kirk
Greenock: Mount Pleasant	Greenock: Mount Kirk
Greenock: North (C of S)	Greenock: Old West Kirk
Greenock: North (FC)	Greenock: St George's North
Greenock: Sir Michael Street	Greenock: Ardgowan
Greenock: South	Greenock: Mount Kirk
Greenock: South Park	Greenock: Mount Kirk
Greenock: St Andrew's	Greenock: Ardgowan
Greenock: St Columba's Gaelic	Greenock: Old West Kirk
Greenock: St Mark's	Greenock: St Luke's
Greenock: St Thomas'	Greenock: St George's North
Greenock: The Old Kirk	Greenock: St Luke's
Greenock: The Union Church	Greenock: Ardgowan
Greenock: Trinity	Greenock: Ardgowan
Greenock: Union Street	Greenock: Ardgowan
Greenock: West	Greenock: St Luke's
Gress	Stornoway: St Columba
Guardbridge	Leuchars St Athernase
Haddington: St John's	Haddington: West
Hamilton: Auchingramont North	Hamilton: North
Hamilton: Avon Street	Hamilton: St Andrew's
Hamilton: Brandon	Hamilton: St Andrew's
Hamilton: Saffronhall Assoc. Anti-B.	Hamilton: North
Hardgate	Urr
Hassendean	Ruberslaw
Hawick: East Bank	Hawick: Trinity
Hawick: Orrock	Hawick: St Mary's and Old
Hawick: St Andrew's	Hawick: Trinity
Hawick: St George's	Hawick: Teviot
Hawick: St George's West	Hawick: Teviot
Hawick: St John's	Hawick: Trinity

Name no longer used	Present name of parish
Hawick: St Margaret's	Hawick: Teviot
Hawick: West Port	Hawick: Teviot
Hawick: Wilton South	Hawick: Teviot
Haywood	Forth
Helensburgh: Old	Helensburgh: The West Kirk
Helensburgh: St Andrew's	Helensburgh: The West Kirk
Helensburgh: St Bride's	Helensburgh: The West Kirk
Heylipol	Tiree
Hillside	Unst
Hillswick	Northmavine
Hilton	Whitsome
Holywell	Longtown
Hope Kailzie	charge suppressed: Presbytery of Melrose and Peebles
Horndean	Ladykirk
Howford	charge dissolved: Presbytery of Inverness
Howmore	South Uist
Huntly: Princes Street	Huntly: Strathbogie
Inchkenneth	Kilfinichen and Kilvickeon and the Ross of Mull
Inchmartin	Errol
Innerwick	Dunglass
Inverallan	Grantown-on-Spey
Inverchaolain	Toward
Inverkeithny	Auchaber United
Inverness: Merkinch St Mark's	Inverness: Trinity
Inverness: Queen Street	Inverness: Trinity
Inverness: St Mary's	Inverness: Dalneigh and Bona
Inverness: West	Inverness: Inshes
Irving	Gretna, Half Morton and Kirkpatrick Fleming
Jedburgh: Abbey	Jedburgh: Trinity
Jedburgh: Blackfriars	Jedburgh: Trinity
Jedburgh: Boston	Jedburgh: Trinity
Johnshaven	Mearns Coastal
Johnstone: East	Johnstone: St Paul's
Johnstone: West	Johnstone: St Paul's
Kames	Kyles
Kearn	Upper Donside
Keig	Howe Trinity
Keith Marischal	Humbie
Keith: South	Keith: North, Newmill, Boharm and Rothiemay
Kelso: East	Kelso: North and Ednam
Kelso: Edenside	Kelso: North and Ednam
Kelso: St John's	Kelso: North and Ednam
Kelso: Trinity	Kelso: North and Ednam
Kennethmont	Noth
Kettle	Howe of Fife
Kilbirnie: Barony	Kilbirnie: Auld Kirk
Kilbirnie: East	Kilbirnie: St Columba's
Kilbirnie: West	Kilbirnie: St Columba's
Kilblaan	Southend
Kilblane	Kirkmahoe
Kilbride (Dumfries and Kirkcudbright)	Sanquhar
Kilbride (Dunoon)	Kyles
Kilbride (Lorn and Mull)	Kilmore and Oban
Kilbride (Stirling)	Dunblane: Cathedral
Kilchattan Bay	Bute United
Kilchousland	Campbeltown: Highland
Kilcolmkill (Lochaber)	Morvern
Kilcolmkill (South Argyll)	Southend

Name no longer used	Present name of parish
Kildrummy	Upper Donside
Kilkerran	Campbeltown: Highland
Kilkivan	Campbeltown: Highland
Killintag	Morvern
Kilmacolm: St James'	Kilmacolm: St Columba
Kilmahew	Cardross
Kilmahog	Callander
Kilmarnock: King Street	Kilmarnock: Howard St Andrew's
Kilmarnock: Portland Road	Kilmarnock: Howard St Andrew's
Kilmarrow	Killean and Kilchenzie
Kilmichael (Inverness)	Urquhart and Glenmoriston
Kilmichael (South Argyll)	Campbeltown: Highland
Kilmoir	Brechin: Cathedral
Kilmore	Urquhart and Glenmoriston
Kilmoveonaig	Blair Atholl and Struan
Kilmun: St Andrew's	Strone and Ardentinny
Kilpheder	South Uist
Kinairney	Midmar
Kincardine O'Neil	Mid Deeside
Kincraig	Alvie and Insh
Kingarth	Bute United
Kininmonth	charge dissolved: Presbytery of Buchan
Kinkell	Keithhall
Kinloch	Caputh and Clunie
Kinlochewe	Applecross, Lochcarron and Torridon
Kinlochluichart	Contin
Kinlochrannoch	Foss and Rannoch
Kinneil	Bo'ness: Old
Kinnettas	Fodderty and Strathpeffer
Kinnoir	Huntly Cairnie Glass
Kinrossie	Collace
Kirkandrews	Borgue
Kirkapol	Tiree
Kirkcaldy: Abbotsrood	Kirkcaldy: St Andrew's
Kirkcaldy: Bethelfield	Kirkcaldy: Linktown
Kirkcaldy: Dunnikeir	Kirkcaldy: St Andrew's
Kirkcaldy: Gallatown	Kirkcaldy: Viewforth
Kirkcaldy: Invertiel	Kirkcaldy: Linktown
Kirkcaldy: Old	Kirkcaldy: St Bryce Kirk
Kirkcaldy: Raith	Kirkcaldy: Abbotshall
Kirkcaldy: Sinclairtown	Kirkcaldy: Viewforth
Kirkcaldy: St Brycedale	Kirkcaldy: St Bryce Kirk
Kirkcaldy: Victoria Road	Kirkcaldy: St Andrew's
Kirkchrist	Tarff and Twynholm
Kirkconnel	Gretna, Half Morton and Kirkpatrick Fleming
Kirkcormick	Buittle and Kelton
Kirkdale	Kirkmabreck
Kirkforthar	Markinch
Kirkhope	Ettrick and Yarrow
Kirkintilloch: St Andrew's	Kirkintilloch: St Columba's
Kirkintilloch: St David's	Kirkintilloch: St Columba's
Kirkmadrine (Machars)	Sorbie
Kirkmadrine (Rhinns)	Stoneykirk
Kirkmaiden	Glasserton and Isle of Whithorn
Kirkmichael	Tomintoul, Glenlivet and Inveraven
Kirkpottie	Abernethy and Dron
Kirkwall: King Street	Kirkwall: East
Kirkwall: Paterson	Kirkwall: East

Name no longer used	Present name of parish
Kirriemuir: Bank Street	The Glens and Kirriemuir Old
Kirriemuir: Barony	The Glens and Kirriemuir Old
Kirriemuir: Livingstone	Kirriemuir: St Andrew's
Kirriemuir: South	Kirriemuir: St Andrew's
Kirriemuir: St Ninian's	The Glens and Kirriemuir Old
Kirriemuir: West	The Glens and Kirriemuir Old
Ladybank	Howe of Fife
Lagganallochie	Dunkeld
Lamberton	Foulden and Mordington
Lamington	Glencaple
Lanark: Broomgate	Lanark: Greyfriars
Lanark: Cairns	Lanark: Greyfriars
Lanark: St Kentigern's	Lanark: Greyfriars
Lanark: St Leonard's	Lanark: St Nicholas'
Largieside	Killean and Kilchenzie
Lassodie	Dunfermline: Townhill and Kingseat
Lathones	Largoward
Laurieston	Balmaghie
Laxavoe	Delting
Leadhills	Lowther
Leith: Bonnington	Edinburgh: Leith North
Leith: Claremont	Edinburgh: Leith St Andrew's
Leith: Dalmeny Street	Edinburgh: Pilrig St Paul's
Leith: Elder Memorial	Edinburgh: St John's Oxgangs
Leith: Harper Memorial	Edinburgh: Leith North
Leith: Kirkgate	Edinburgh: Leith South
Leith: South (FC)	Edinburgh: Leith St Andrew's
Leith: St Andrew's Place	Edinburgh: Leith St Andrew's
Leith: St John's	Edinburgh: St John's Oxgangs
Leith: St Nicholas	Edinburgh: Leith North
Leith: St Ninian's	Edinburgh: Leith North
Lemlair	Kiltearn
Lempitlaw	Kelso: Old and Sprouston
Leny	Callander
Leochel	Cushnie and Tough
Lesmahagow: Cordiner	Lesmahagow: Abbey Green
Lethendy	Caputh and Clunie
Lindowan	Craigrownie
Linlithgow: East	Linlithgow: St Ninian's Craigmailen
Linlithgow: Trinity	Linlithgow: St Ninian's Craigmailen
Livingston: Tulloch	Livingston: Old
Livingston: West	Livingston: Old
Lochaline	Morvern
Lochdonhead	Torosay and Kinlochspelvie
Lochearnhead	Balquhidder
Lochlee	Glenesk
Lochryan	Inch
Logie (Dundee)	Fowlis and Liff
Logie (St Andrews)	charge dissolved: Presbytery of St Andrews
Logie Buchan	Ellon
Logie Mar	Cromar
Logie Pert	charge dissolved: Presbytery of Angus
Logie Wester	Ferintosh
Logiebride	Auchtergaven and Moneydie
Longcastle	Kirkinner
Longformacus	Kirk of Lammermuir
Longnewton	Ancrum
Longridge	Breich Valley

Name no longer used	Present name of parish
Luce	Hoddam
Lude	Blair Atholl and Struan
Lumphanan	Mid Deeside
Lumphinnans	Beath and Cowdenbeath: North
Lumsden	Upper Donside
Luncarty	Redgorton
Lund	Unst
Lynturk	Cushnie and Tough
Mailor	The Stewartry of Strathearn
Mainsriddle	Colvend, Southwick and Kirkbean
Maryburgh	Ferintosh
Marykirk	Aberluthnott
Maryton	Inchbrayock
Meadowfield	Caldercruix and Longriggend
Meathie	Glamis, Inverarity and Kinnettles
Megget	Lyne and Manor
Melville	charge suppressed: Presbytery of Lothian
Memus	The Glens and Kirriemuir: Old
Methil: East	Innerleven: East
Mid Calder: Bridgend	Kirk of Calder
Mid Calder: St John's	Kirk of Calder
Midholm	congregation seceded: Presbytery of Jedburgh
Migvie	Cromar
Millbrex	Fyvie
Millerston	charge dissolved: Presbytery of Glasgow
Millport	Cumbrae
Milnathort	Orwell
Minto	Ruberslaw
Monecht	charge dissolved: Presbytery of Gordon
Monifieth: North	Monikie and Newbigging
Montrose: Knox's	Montrose: Melville South
Montrose: St George's	Montrose: St Andrew's
Montrose: St John's	Montrose: St Andrew's
Montrose: St Luke's	Montrose: St Andrew's
Montrose: St Paul's	Montrose: Melville South
Montrose: Trinity	Montrose: St Andrew's
Monzievaird	Crieff
Moonzie	charge dissolved: Presbytery of St Andrews
Morton	Thornhill
Mossbank	Delting
Mossgreen	Cowdenbeath: Trinity
Motherwell: Brandon	Motherwell: Crosshill
Motherwell: Cairns	Motherwell: Crosshill
Moulin	Pitlochry
Mount Kedar	Ruthwell
Mow	Morebattle and Hownam
Moy	Dyke
Moyness	charge dissolved: Presbytery of Moray
Muckersie	The Stewartry of Strathearn
Muirton	Aberluthnott
Murthly	Caputh and Clunie
Musselburgh: Bridge Street	Musselburgh: St Andrew's High
Musselburgh: Millhill	Musselburgh: St Andrew's High
Nairn: High	Nairn: St Ninian's
Nairn: Rosebank	Nairn: St Ninian's
Navar	Edzell Lethnott
New Leeds	charge dissolved: Presbytery of Buchan
New Liston	Edinburgh: Kirkliston

Name no longer used	Present name of parish
Newcastleton	Liddesdale
Newdosk	Edzell Lethnott
Newmills	Culross and Torryburn
Newseat	Rothienorman
Newton Stewart	Penninghame
Newtongrange	Newbattle
Nigg	charge dissolved: Presbytery of Aberdeen
Nisbet	Crailing and Eckford
North Bute	Bute United
Norwick	Unst
Ogston	Lossiemouth: St Gerardine's High
Old Kilpatrick: Barclay	Dalmuir Barclay
Oldhamstocks	Dunglass
Ollaberry	Northmavine
Olnafirth	Delting
Ord	Ordiquhill and Cornhill
Paisley: Canal Street	Paisley: Castlehead
Paisley: George Street	Paisley: Glenburn
Paisley: High	Paisley: Oakshaw Trinity
Paisley: Merksworth	Paisley: Wallneuk North
Paisley: Middle	Paisley: Castlehead
Paisley: Mossvale	Paisley: Wallneuk North
Paisley: New Street	Paisley: Glenburn
Paisley: North	Paisley: Wallneuk North
Paisley: Oakshaw West	Paisley: St Luke's
Paisley: Orr Square	Paisley: Oakshaw Trinity
Paisley: South	Paisley: St Luke's
Paisley: St Andrew's	Paisley: Laigh
Paisley: St George's	Paisley: Laigh
Paisley: St John's	Paisley: Oakshaw Trinity
Papa Stour	Walls and Sandness
Park	Kinloch
Pathhead	Ormiston
Pathstruie	The Stewartry of Strathearn
Pearston	Dreghorn and Springside
Peebles: West	Peebles: St Andrew's Leckie
Pennersaughs	Middlebie
Pentland	Lasswade
Persie	Kirkmichael, Straloch and Glenshee
Perth: Bridgend	Perth: St Matthew's
Perth: East	Perth: St Leonard's-in-the-Fields and Trinity
Perth: Knox's	Perth: St Leonard's-in-the-Fields and Trinity
Perth: Middle	Perth: St Matthew's
Perth: St Andrew's	Perth: Riverside
Perth: St Columba's	Perth: North
Perth: St Leonard's	Perth: North
Perth: St Stephen's	Perth: Riverside
Perth: West	Perth: St Matthew's
Perth: Wilson	Perth: St Matthew's
Perth: York Place	Perth: St Leonard's-in-the-Fields and Trinity
Peterhead: Charlotte Street	Peterhead: Trinity
Peterhead: East	Peterhead: St Andrew's
Peterhead: South	Peterhead: St Andrew's
Peterhead: St Peter's	Peterhead: Trinity
Peterhead: West Associate	Peterhead: Trinity
Pettinain	Cairngryffe
Pitcairn (C of S)	Redgorton
Pitcairn (UF)	Almondbank Tibbermore

Name no longer used	Present name of parish
Pitlessie	Howe of Fife
Pitroddie	St Madoes and Kinfauns
Plockton	Lochalsh
Polmont South	Brightons
Poolewe	Gairloch and Dundonnell
Port Bannatyne	Bute United
Port Ellen	Kildalton and Oa
Port Glasgow: Clune Park	Port Glasgow: St Andrew's
Port Glasgow: Newark	Port Glasgow: St Andrew's
Port Glasgow: Old	Port Glasgow: St Andrew's
Port Glasgow: Princes Street	Port Glasgow: St Andrew's
Port Glasgow: West	Port Glasgow: St Andrew's
Port Sonachan	Glenorchy and Inishail
Port William	Mochrum
Portobello: Regent Street	Edinburgh: Portobello Old
Portobello: Windsor Place	Edinburgh: Portobello Old
Portsoy	Fordyce
Prestonkirk	Traprain
Prinlaws	Leslie Trinity
Quarrier's Mount Zion	Kilmacolm: St Columba
Raasay	Portree
Rathillet	Creich, Flisk and Kilmany
Rathmuriel	Noth
Redcastle	Killearnan
Restenneth	Forfar: East and Old
Rhynd	Perth: Moncreiffe
Rhynie	Noth
Rickarton	charge dissolved: Presbytery of Kincardine and Deeside
Rigg	Gretna, Half Morton and Kirkpatrick Fleming
Rinpatrick	Gretna, Half Morton and Kirkpatrick Fleming
Roberton	Glencaple
Rosehearty	Pitsligo
Rossie	Inchture and Kinnaird
Rothesay: Bridgend	Bute United
Rothesay: Craigmore High	Rothesay: Trinity
Rothesay: Craigmore St Brendan's	Bute United
Rothesay: High	Bute United
Rothesay: New	Bute United
Rothesay: St James'	Rothesay: Trinity
Rothesay: St John's	Bute United
Rothesay: West	Rothesay: Trinity
Rutherglen: East	Rutherglen: Old
Rutherglen: Greenhill	Rutherglen: Old
Rutherglen: Munro	Ritherglen: West
Ruthven	Huntly Cairnie Glass
Saltcoats: Erskine	Saltcoats: New Trinity
Saltcoats: Landsborough	Saltcoats: New Trinity
Saltcoats: Middle	Saltcoats: New Trinity
Saltcoats: Trinity	Saltcoats: New Trinity
Saltcoats: West	Saltcoats: New Trinity
Sandhead	Stoneykirk
Saughtree	Liddesdale
Saulseat	Inch
Scalloway	Tingwall
Scatsta	Delting
Sclattie	Blairdaff
Scone: Abbey	Scone: New
Scone: West	Scone: New

Name no longer used	Present name of parish
Torrance	East Kilbride: Old
Towie	Upper Donside
Trailflat	Kirkmichael, Tinwald and Torthorwald
Trailtrow	Cummertrees
Trefontaine	Kirk of Lammermuir
Trossachs	Callander
Trumisgarry	Berneray and Lochmaddy
Tullibole	Fossoway St Serf's and Devonside
Tullich	Glenmuick
Tullichetil	Comrie
Tullynessle	Howe Trinity
Tummel	Foss and Rannoch
Tushielaw	Ettrick and Yarrow
Uddingston: Aitkenhead	Uddingston: Viewpark
Uddingston: Chalmers	Uddingston: Old
Uddingston: Trinity	Uddingston: Old
Uig	Snizort
Uphall: North	Strathbrock
Uyeasound	Unst
Walston	Black Mount
Wandel	Glencaple
Wanlockhead	Lowther
Waternish	Bracadale and Duirinish
Wauchope	Langholm, Ewes and Westerkirk
Waulkmill	Insch-Leslie-Premnay-Oyne
Weisdale	Tingwall
West Kilbride: Barony	West Kilbride: St Andrew's
West Kilbride: St Bride's	West Kilbride: St Andrew's
Wheelkirk	Liddesdale
Whitehill	New Pitsligo
Whiteness	Tingwall
Whittingehame	Traprain
Wick: Central	Wick: Pulteneytown and Thrumster
Wick: Martyrs'	Wick: Pulteneytown and Thrumster
Wick: St Andrew's	Wick: Pulteneytown and Thrumster
Wilkieston	Edinburgh: Ratho
Wilsontown	Forth
Wiston	Glencaple
Wolfhill	Cargill Burrelton
Wolflee	Hobkirk and Southdean
Woomet	Newton
Ythan Wells	Auchaber United

INDEX OF SUBJECTS

INDEX OF ADVERTISERS

Avon
SILVERSMITHS

Celtic Chalices
Sick Call Sets
Repairs

Brochure Free 0800 092 0760
Works: 39 Augusta Street
Hockley, Birmingham B18 6JA
Email: mike@church-silver.com
www. church-silver.com

Iona Chalice

REGULAR GIVING ENVELOPES
•GIFT AID ENVELOPES (Inland Revenue approved)

- • Choice of Weekly and Monthly styles in cartons or booklets
- • Various colours and designs
- • Special occasion envelopes
- • Childrens envelopes
- • Supporting supplies

Thousands of Churches benefit from using our envelopes. Can WE help YOU.

Contact us by:
Phone 01235 524488   **Fax** 01235 534760
E-mail churchfinsup@btconnect.com

or write to:
CHURCH FINANCE SUPPLIES LTD.
FREEPOST
ABINGDON, OXON OX14 3BR
(No stamp required - UK only)